APOLLOS OLD TESTAMENT
COMMENTARY
6

JOSHUA

TITLES IN THIS SERIES

APOLLOS OLD TESTAMENT
COMMENTARY
6

JOSHUA

Series Editors
David W. Baker and Gordon J. Wenham

PEKKA M. A. PITKÄNEN

Apollos
Nottingham, England

InterVarsity Press
Downers Grove, Illinois 60515

InterVarsity Press, USA
P.O. Box 1400
Downers Grove, IL 60515-1426, USA
World Wide Web: www.ivpress.com
Email: email@ivpress.com

APOLLOS (an imprint of Inter-Varsity Press, England)
Norton Street
Nottingham NG7 3HR, England
Website: www.ivpbooks.com
Email: ivp@ivpbooks.com

Inter-Varsity Press, England, is closely linked with the Universities and Colleges Christian Fellowship, a student movement connecting Christian Unions throughout Great Britain, and a member movement of the International Fellowship of Evangelical Students. Website: www.uccf.org.uk

InterVarsity Press®, USA, is the book-publishing division of InterVarsity Christian Fellowship/USA® <www.intervarsity.org> and a member movement of the International Fellowship of Evangelical Students.

Figures 2 and 3 on pp. 91, 92 have been reproduced with the kind permission of PASSIA.

Figure 4 on p. 165 is from K. M. Kenyon and T. A. Holland, Excavations at Jericho, *vol. 3 (London: British School of Archaeology, 1981), Plate 236. Copyright © The Council for British Research in the Levant, reproduced by permission.*

Figures 5 and 6 on pp. 194, 196 are from A. Zertal, 'An Early Iron Age Cultic Site on Mount Ebal: Excavation Seasons 1982–1987: Preliminary Report', Tel Aviv: *Journal of the Institute of Archaeology of Tel Aviv University, 13/14.2 (1986–1987):105–165. Copyright © Maney Publishing, www.maney.co.uk/journals/tav and www.ingentaconnect.com/content/maney/tav, reproduced with the kind permission of the copyright holder.*

Figure 7 on p. 214 is from J. B. Pritchard, Winery, Defences and Soundings at Gibeon *(Philadelphia: University Museum, 1964). Copyright © University of Pennsylvania, reproduced with the kind permission of the copyright holder.*

Material from the author's Central Sanctuary and Centralization of Worship in Ancient Israel: From the Settlement to the Building of Solomon's Temple, *2nd edn (Piscataway, NJ: Gorgias Press, 2004), has been reproduced by kind permission of Gorgias Press.*

Material from the author's 'Memory, Witnesses and Genocide in the Book of Joshua', in J. G. McConville and K. Möller (eds), Reading the Law: Studies in Honour of Gordon J. Wenham *(New York: T. & T. Clark, 2007), pp. 267–282, has been reproduced by kind permission of Continuum International Publishing Group.*

Material from the author's 'Dr Jekyll and Mr Hyde? Deuteronomy and the Rights of Indigenous Peoples', Political Theology *11.3 (2010):399–409 Copyright © Equinox Publishing Ltd 2010, reproduced by permission.*

The translation of the treaty between Hattusili III of Hatti and the Ulmi-Teshshup of Tarhuntassa is quoted from Gary Beckman, Hittite Diplomatic Texts, *SBT Writings from the Ancient World 7 (Atlanta: Scholars Press, 1996), pp. 109–111. Copyright © Society of Biblical Literature. Used by permission.*

UK ISBN 978-1-84474-477-0
USA ISBN 978-0-8308-2506-6

Set in Sabon 10/12 pt
Typeset in Great Britain by CRB Associates, Potterhanworth, Lincolnshire
Printed and bound in Great Britain by MPG Books Group

British Library Cataloguing in Publication Data

A catalogue record for this book is available from the British Library.

Library of Congress Cataloging-in-Publication Data

Pitkänen, Pekka.
  Joshua / Pekka M. A. Pitkänen.
    p. cm.
  Includes bibliographical references and index.
  ISBN 978-0-8308-2506-6 (cloth : alk. paper)
  1. Bible. O.T. Joshua—Commentaries. I. Title.
BS1295.53.P58 2010
222'.207—dc22

                           2010021448

P   20   19   18   17   16   15   14   13   12   11   10   9   8   7   6   5   4   3   2   1

Y   27   26   25   24   23   22   21   20   19   18   17   16   15   14   13   12   11   10

CONTENTS

To my teachers

EDITORS' PREFACE

The Apollos Old Testament Commentary takes its name from the Alexandrian Jewish Christian who was able to impart his great learning fervently and powerfully through his teaching (Acts 18:24–25). He ably applied his understanding of past events to his contemporary society. This series seeks to do the same, keeping one foot firmly planted in the universe of the original text and the other in that of the target audience, which is preachers, teachers and students of the Bible. The series editors have selected scholars who are adept in both areas, exhibiting scholarly excellence along with practical insight for application.

Translators need to be at home with the linguistic practices and semantic nuances of both the original and the target languages in order to be able to transfer the full impact of the one into the other. Commentators, however, serve as interpreters of the text rather than simply its translators. They also need to adopt a dual stance, though theirs needs to be even more solid and diversely anchored than that of translators. While they also must have the linguistic competence to produce their own excellent translations, they must moreover be fully conversant with the literary conventions, sociological and cultural practices, historical background and understanding, and theological perspectives of those who produced the text as well as those whom it concerned. On the other side, they must also understand their own times and culture, able to see where relevance for the original audience is transferable to that of current readers. For this to be accomplished it is not only necessary to interpret the text; one must also interpret the audience.

Traditionally, commentators have been content to highlight and expound the ancient text. More recently, the need for an anchor in the present day has also become more evident, and this series self-consciously adopts this approach, combining both. Each author analyses the original text through a new translation, textual notes, and a discussion of the literary form, structure and background of the passage, as well as commenting on elements of its exegesis. A study of the passage's interpretational development in Scripture and the church concludes each section, serving to bring the passage home to the modern reader. What we intend, therefore, is to provide not only tools of excellence for the academy, but also tools of function for the pulpit.

David W. Baker
Gordon J. Wenham

AUTHOR'S PREFACE

It has been a privilege to be able to work on the book of Joshua. I would like to express my heartfelt thanks to Professor Gordon Wenham, for inviting me to write on this topic and for his helpful editorial comments in the later stages of the project. To work on the book of Joshua is a complicated task if one wants to take seriously the challenges that surround this at first sight innocuous text. At the same time, a lot of ink has been spilled on the topic and many commentaries have been written on the book. What then justifies my writing another commentary on Joshua? I thought about this extensively even after I had accepted the task. And yet I feel that there are grounds for another commentary. In addition to those reasons stated in the editors' preface, and especially in today's often sceptical climate in biblical studies, I feel that it is appropriate to aim to write a commentary on Joshua that takes the text seriously and yet is fully conversant with recent scholarship and the issues that it raises. Another area that I have found particularly interesting is the question of how the book of Joshua should be applied in today's post/neocolonial world, and I have tried to make some relevant comments as the need arises, based on a reading of the book of Joshua. The reader will notice that, as well as a synthesis of the scholarship that precedes me, I have added my own input to this fascinating topic in a number of places. Just as any book has an author, a commentary has an author, and just as any book will give the author's point of view, so will this commentary. The reader is immediately encouraged also to seek other views and to look at works by other authors, as they may and will include a number of insights not brought forward here. Those who have seen my *Central Sanctuary* (Pitkänen 2004a) or some of my articles relating to Joshua may notice that certain parts of the discussion have been adapted from these (I would particularly like to express my thanks to Dr George Kiraz and Gorgias Press for giving me permission to reproduce material from *Central Sanctuary*), but I trust that they will also find that much if not most of the material presented here is new. I have intentionally left some repetition in the commentary, including in the Introduction, in view of those readers who will work through the volume as if they were reading an encyclopedia.

While I have tried to be as accurate as possible in relation to the factual data presented, and the editing process has helped to weed out errors, any that remain are my responsibility alone. Any possible significant omissions are also my responsibility. I would also like to emphasize that the views expressed in this book are my own and do not necessarily represent those of the editors or of the publisher.

It is absolutely impossible to work on a project like this without a lot of support. I am most grateful to my wife, Sowon, who has always supported me with my work in theology. That I was able to visit and use the fantastic library in Oxford when necessary should also be mentioned.

While I am indebted to the many authors whose works I have perused, of those people with whom I was able to discuss matters in person, I would most like to express my thanks to Dr Heath Thomas for some pointers in relation to relevant American history and to Ms Alissa Jones Nelson for hints on reading Joshua in the context of today's post/neocolonial world. Thanks are also due to Ralph Hawkins for sending me a copy of his dissertation on Mount Ebal, and to Piotr Bienkowski and Manfred Weippert for their help with aspects of reading their extremely well-crafted works on Jericho.

Regarding the editing process, I would like to thank the copy editors Helen Birkbeck and Eldo Barkhuizen, and Dr Philip Duce, Senior Commissioning Editor at IVP, for making the process run smoothly and effectively. I would also like to thank Carl Sweatman for preparing the indexes. Sadly, my father, Matti Pitkänen, was diagnosed with cancer and passed away while the book was being copy-edited, but I hope its publication can serve as a testament to his memory.

Finally, a comment should be made for those who wish to preach on Joshua. In my view, before trying to do so, it is important to have a good understanding of the work as a whole and of the main issues that it raises, in so far as it is possible. After that, I believe that the book can serve as a good resource for preaching for those who work in Christian ministry.

Pekka M. A. Pitkänen
Cheltenham, 2010

ABBREVIATIONS

TEXTUAL

Engl.	English
Gm.	German
Gr.	Greek
Hebr.	Hebrew
LXX	Septuagint (The Greek Old Testament)
LXX^A	Septuagint as found in Codex Alexandrinus
LXX^B	Septuagint as found in Codex Vaticanus
LXX^S	Septuagint as found in Codex Sinaiticus
MT	The Masoretic Text

HEBREW GRAMMAR

hiph.	hiphil
hish.	hishtaphel
hith.	hithpael
impf.	imperfect
impt.	imperative
lit.	literally
masc.	masculine
ni.	niphal
part.	participle
pf.	perfect
pil.	pilpel

MISCELLANEOUS

AD	*anno Domini*
BC	Before Christ
BCE	Before Common Era
c.	circa
CE	Common Era
ESV	English Standard Version
FS	Festschrift
HB	Hebrew Bible

lit.	literally
NASB	New American Standard Bible
NIV	New International Version
NRSV	New Revised Standard Version
OT	Old Testament
RS	Ras Shamra
transl.	translator, translated (by)

JOURNALS, REFERENCE WORKS, SERIES

AASF	Annales Academiae scientiarum fennicae
AASOR	Annual of the American Schools of Oriental Research
AB	Anchor Bible
ABD	*Anchor Bible Dictionary*
AfO	*Archiv für Orientforschung*
AHw	W. von Soden, *Akkadisches Handwörterbuch*, Wiesbaden, 1965–1981
ANEP	J. B. Pritchard (ed.), *The Ancient Near East in Pictures*, 2nd edn with supplement, Princeton, NJ: Princeton University Press, 1969
ANET	J. B. Pritchard (ed.), *Ancient Near Eastern Texts Relating to the Old Testament*, 3rd edn with supplement, Princeton, NJ: Princeton University Press, 1969
AnOr	Analecta orientalia
AO	*Archiv Orientalni*
AOAT	Alter Orient und Altes Testament
ARE	J. H. Breasted, *Ancient Records of Egypt*, 5 vols, Chicago: University of Chicago Press, 1906–1907
ASOR	American Schools of Oriental Research
ATD	Das Alte Testament Deutsch
ATANT	Abhandlungen zur Theologie des Alten und Neuen Testaments
BA	*Biblical Archaeologist*
BAR	*Biblical Archaeology Review*
BASOR	*Bulletin of the American Schools of Oriental Research*
BBB	Bonner biblische Beiträge
BBR	*Bulletin for Biblical Research*
BECKMAN	G. Beckman, *Hittite Diplomatic Texts*, SBL Writings from the Ancient World 7, ed. Harry A. Hoffner, Jr, Atlanta: Scholars Press 1996, 2nd edn, 1999
BHS	*Biblia Hebraica Stuttgartensia*
Bib	*Biblica*
BKAT	Biblischer Kommentar, Altes Testament
BM	*Baghdader Mitteilungen*

BWANT	Beiträge zur Wissenschaft vom Alten und Neuen Testament
BZ	*Biblische Zeitschrift*
BZAW	Beihefte zur Zeitschrift für die Alttestamentliche Wissenschaft
BZEATAJ	Beiträge zur Erforschung des Alten Testaments und des Antiken Judentums
CAD	*Chicago Assyrian Dictionary*
CahRB	Cahiers de la Revue biblique
CANE	J. M. Sasson (ed. in chief), *Civilizations of the Ancient Near East*, New York: Simon & Schuster Macmillan, 1996
CAT	Commentaire de l'Ancien Testament
CBET	Contributions to Biblical Exegesis and Theology
CBOTS	Coniectanea biblica Old Testament Series
CBQ	*Catholic Biblical Quarterly*
CH	Code of Hammurabi
COS	W. W. Hallo and K. L. Younger (eds), *The Context of Scripture*, Leiden: Brill, 1997–2002
DLU	G. Del Olmo Lete and J. Sanmartín, *Diccionario de la Lengua Ugarítica*, 2 vols, Sabadell: AUSA, 1996–2000
EA	El Amarna (letter[s])
EAEHL	M. Avi-Yonah and E. Stern (eds), *The Encyclopedia of Archaeological Excavations in the Holy Land*, English edn, London: Oxford University Press, 1975–1978
EBC	*The Expositor's Bible Commentary*
EJ	*Encyclopedia Judaica*
EJT	*Evangelical Journal of Theology*
EQ	*Evangelical Quarterly*
EVEN-SHOSHAN	Abraham Even-Shoshan, *A New Concordance of the Bible: Thesaurus of the Language of the Bible, Hebrew and Aramaic Roots, Words, Proper Names, Phrases and Synonyms*, Jerusalem: Kiryat Sefer Publishing House, 1993
ExpTim	*Expository Times*
FB	Forschung zur Bibel
GAG	W. von Soden, *Grundriss der Akkadischen Grammatik*, 3 Auflage, AnOr 33, Rome: Editrice Pontificio Istituto Biblico, 1995
GHAT	Göttinger Handkommentar zum Alten Testament
HAL	L. Koehler and W. Baumgartner, *Hebräisches und Aramäisches Lexikon zum Alten Testament*, Leiden: Brill
HAR	*Hebrew Annual Review*
HAT	Handbuch zum Alten Testament
HTS	Harvard Theological Studies

HUCA	*Hebrew Union College Annual*
IB	*Interpreter's Bible*
ICC	International Critical Commentary
IDB	*Interpreter's Dictionary of the Bible*
IEJ	*Israel Exploration Journal*
IJIR	*International Journal of Intercultural Relations*
IM	*Istanbuler Mitteilungen*
ISBE	G. W. Bromiley (ed.), *International Standard Bible Encyclopedia*, Grand Rapids, MI: Eerdmans, 1995
JBL	*Journal of Biblical Literature*
JBQ	*Jewish Biblical Quarterly*
JCS	*Journal of Cuneiform Studies*
JETS	*Journal of the Evangelical Theological Society*
JJS	*Journal of Jewish Studies*
JNES	*Journal of Near Eastern Studies*
JNSL	*Journal of Northwest Semitic Languages*
JSOT	*Journal for the Study of the Old Testament*
JSOTSup	Journal for the Study of the Old Testament, Supplement Series
JSS	*Journal of Semitic Studies*
KAI	H. Donner and W. Röllig (eds), *Kanaanäische und Aramäische Inschriften*, 3 vols, Wiesbaden: Otto Harrassowitz, 1964
KAT	Kommentar zum Alten Testament
KHAT	Kurzer Hand-Kommentar zum Alten Testament
KHW	J. Friedrich, *Kurzgefaßtes Hethitisches Wörterbuch*, Heidelberg: Carl Winter Universitätsverlag, 1990, Unveränderter Nachdruck der Ausgabe, 1952–1966
KNUDTZON	J. A. Knudtzon, *Die El-Amarna Tafeln, mit Einleitung und Erläuterungen*, repr. of the 1915 edn, Aalen: Otto Zeller Verlagsbuchhandlung, 1964
KS	Kleine Schriften
KTU	M. Dietrich, O. Loretz and J. Sanmartín, *The Cuneiform Alphabetic Texts from Ugarit, Ras Ibn Hani and Other Places [Keilschrifttexte aus Ugarit]*, 2nd edn, Münster: Ugarit Verlag, 1995
KZ	*Kirchliche Zeitschrift*
LÄ	W. Helck and E. Otto (eds), *Lexikon der Ägyptologie*, Wiesbaden: Otto Harrassowitz, 1972–
Labat	R. Labat and F. Malbran-Labat, *Manuel d'Épigraphie Akkadienne*, 6th edn, Paris: Paul Geuthner, 1994
MDOG	Mitteilungen der Deutschen Orient-Gesellschaft
NAC	New American Commentary
NBD	J. D. Douglas (organizing ed.), *New Bible Dictionary*, London: Inter-Varsity Press, 1962–1965

NCBC	New Century Biblical Commentary
NEAEHL	E. Stern (ed.), *The New Encyclopedia of Archaeological Excavations in the Holy Land*, Jerusalem: Israel Exploration Society & Carta (and Simon & Schuster: New York), 1993; vol. 5, Jerusalem: Israel Exploration Society, 2008
NIB	*The New Interpreter's Bible*
NIBC	New International Biblical Commentary
NICOT	New International Commentary on the Old Testament
NIDOTTE	W. VanGemeren (gen. ed.), *New International Dictionary of Old Testament Theology and Exegesis*, Carlisle: Paternoster Press, 1997
NIGTC	New International Greek Testament Commentary
Nissinen	Martti Nissinen, *Prophets and Prophecy in the Ancient Near East*, with contributions by C. L. Seow and Robert K. Ritner, ed. Peter Machinist, SBL Writings from the Ancient World 12, Atlanta: Society of Biblical Literature, 2003
OEANE	E. M. Meyers (ed. in chief), *Oxford Encyclopedia of Archaeology in the Near East*, Oxford: Oxford University Press, 1997
OLA	Orientalia lovaniensia analecta
OLZ	*Orientalistische Literaturzeitung*
OTG	Old Testament Guides
OTL	Old Testament Library
Parpola	S. Parpola and K. Watanabe, *Neo-Assyrian Treaties and Loyalty Oaths*, SAA 2, Helsinki: Helsinki University Press, 1988
PEFQS	Palestine Exploration Fund Quarterly Statement
PEQ	*Palestine Exploration Quarterly*
PJB	*Palästinajahrbuch*
Porten-Yardeni	B. Porten and A. Yardeni, *Textbook of Aramaic Documents from Ancient Egypt: Newly Copied, Edited and Translated into Hebrew and English*, Winona Lake, IN: Eisenbrauns and the Hebrew University, 1986
RA	*Revue d'assyriologie et d'archéologie orientale*
Rahlfs	A. Rahlfs (ed.), *Septuaginta*, Stuttgart: Deutsche Bibelgesellschaft, 1935
RB	*Revue biblique*
RLA	E. Ebeling et al. (eds), *Reallexikon der Assyriologie*, Berlin: Walter de Gruyter, 1932–
SAA	State Archives of Assyria
SBL	Society of Biblical Literature
SBLDS	SBL Dissertation Series
SBLSP	*SBL Seminar Papers*

SBLWAW	SBL Writings from the Ancient World
SBT	Studies in Biblical Theology
SOTSMS	Society for Old Testament Studies Monograph Series
SPCK	Society for Promoting Christian Knowledge
StBoT	Studien zu den Bogazköy-Texten
Sturtevant-Bechtel	E. H. Sturtevant and G. Bechtel, *A Hittite Chrestomathy*, Philadelphia: University of Pennsylvania, 1935
TA	*Tel Aviv*
TDOT	G. J. Botterweck and H. Ringgren (eds), J. T. Willis, G. W. Bromiley and D. E. Green (transl.), *Theological Dictionary of the Old Testament*, Grand Rapids, MI: Eerdmans, 1977–
Them	*Themelios*
TOTC	Tyndale Old Testament Commentaries
TToday	*Theology Today*
TynB	*Tyndale Bulletin*
TZ	*Theologische Zeitschrift*
UF	*Ugarit-Forschungen*
UG	Josef Tropper, *Ugaritische Grammatik*, AOAT 273, Münster: Ugarit Verlag, 2000
UT	C. H. Gordon, *Ugaritic Textbook*, AnOr 38, Rome: Editrice Pontificio Istituto Biblico, 1998 (rev.) repr. of the 1965–1967 edn
VT	*Vetus Testamentum*
VTSup	Supplements to Vetus Testamentum
WBC	Word Biblical Commentary
WTJ	*Westminster Theological Journal*
ZA	*Zeitschrift für Assyriologie*
ZAW	*Zeitschrift für die Alttestamentliche Wissenschaft*
ZDPV	*Zeitschrift des deutschen Palästina-Vereins*

LIST OF ARCHAEOLOGICAL PERIODS

(Adapted from Mazar 1992: 30 for pre-586 BC, and from *NEAEHL* 1529 for post-586 BC; note that, by convention, the abbreviation BC [and AD] is used throughout this book; however, BCE [and CE] could just as well be used.)

Pre-Pottery Neolithic A	c. 8500–7500 BC
Pre-Pottery Neolithic B	7500–6000 BC
Pottery Neolithic A	6000–5000 BC
Pottery Neolithic A	5000–4300 BC
Chalcolithic	4300–3300 BC
Early Bronze I	3300–3050 BC
Early Bronze II–III	3050–2300 BC
Early Bronze IV/Middle Bronze I	2300–2000 BC
Middle Bronze IIA	2000–1800/1750 BC
Middle Bronze IIB–C	1800/1750–1550 BC
Late Bronze I	1550–1400 BC
Late Bronze IIA–B	1400–1200 BC
Iron IA	1200–1150 BC
Iron IB	1150–1000 BC
Iron IIA	1000–925 BC
Iron IIB	925–720 BC
Iron IIC	720–586 BC
Babylonian and Persian periods	586–332 BC
Early Hellenistic period	332–167 BC
Late Hellenistic period	167–37 BC
Early Roman period	37 BC – AD 132

INTRODUCTION

> That too was considered a land of the Rephaites, who used to live there; but the Ammonites called them Zamzummites. They were a people strong and numerous, and as tall as the Anakites. The LORD destroyed them from before the Ammonites, who drove them out and settled in their place. The LORD had done the same for the descendants of Esau, who lived in Seir, when he destroyed the Horites from before them. They drove them out and have lived in their place to this day. And as for the Avvites who lived in villages as far as Gaza, the Caphtorites coming out from Caphtor destroyed them and settled in their place. (Deut. 2:20–23 [NIV])

Great movements and conquests of peoples have taken place throughout history. An average Westerner is taught about the glory of the Greek and Roman civilizations as foundations of Western civilization. Greek philosophy and the Roman legal system are cited as fundamental models on which Western civilization was built. And yet these countries were not influential only because of their intellectual power; Alexander the Great was a mighty conqueror and the Greeks and Macedonians had an empire in the third and second centuries before the Common Era as a direct result of his conquests. The Romans did not get their empire by politely asking neighbouring countries to submit to their rule; the Roman war machine was legendary and, when at its best, literally crushed everything under it.

As time moved on, the Roman empire was eventually destroyed by the so-called barbarian conquests, accompanied by a series of great people movements from the north and north-east of the Roman empire. Islam was also expanding in the Middle East, and rapidly took over the area in the centuries following Mohammed. After the Middle Ages, Spain and Portugal and other Western powers started to move on a significant scale for world history. With Columbus, South America came under attack from the Spanish and Portuguese, and was conquered in an astonishing manner, considering the sheer size of the continent. New Spanish and Portuguese people moved in eventually to form what is, due to this conquest and the accompanying people movements, properly speaking, Latin America today. Meanwhile, the British formed a bridgehead in North America and started to move westwards. Eventually, the whole of North America was taken over and its native populations largely destroyed, and the countries of the United States and Canada resulted. Elsewhere, the British and the French in particular conquered and colonialized most of the countries in Africa and Asia, with the indigenous inhabitants of Australia in particular suffering largely similar consequences to their North American counterparts. Even the great power China was effectively subdued by the end of the nineteenth century.

And yet it was not only the Greeks and the Romans and the keepers of their legacy who were conquerors. In Asia, in China, various dynasties and factions of the country stood in opposition to each other and tried to subdue each other, until one dynasty rose and conquered all to unify the country in the third century BC. Genghis Khan conquered westwards from Mongolia, reaching the gates of Europe in a quick swoop in the early thirteenth century. The Japanese had a famous warring culture and were renowned for attacking China and Korea throughout centuries, and conquering them at the turn of the twentieth century. In Africa and pre-Columbian America, various tribes and states warred against each other, and empires and civilizations rose and fell.

Before the Greeks and Romans came on the scene, the Ancient Near East had its own share of turmoil. The empire of the Akkads in the third millennium BC was an example of a great power of the ancient world. The Akkads were followed by the Babylonians and Kassites in the second millennium, and the Assyrians and Neo-Babylonians in the first. The Egyptians pushed north-east in the second millennium, subduing countries and establishing garrisons in areas they controlled, and met the Hittite empire in the north at the beginning of the thirteenth century BC.

In this broad context, we come to ancient Israel and the situation there in the latter part of the second millennium BC, the focus of this book. According to the Israelite sources handed down to us in the Hebrew sacred scriptures, Israel was born through a great people movement and a conquest. The Israelite story properly begins with Abraham, the great patriarch and founding father in the Israelite consciousness. According to the Israelite story, Abraham himself migrates from Mesopotamia, from the great city of Ur, and settles in the land of Canaan. There he produces descendants who themselves end up migrating to Egypt through chance events and because of famine. However, as a foreign resident population they are soon seen as a problem by the main population, and are subsequently deprived of any power within society and used for forced labour. But, miraculously, the group escape and return to Canaan, the land of their fathers. In order to do this, they must conquer the land and settle in it. The book of Joshua describes this process of the conquest of the land of Canaan. The story then continues with the book of Judges, which starts by relating more of the Israelite settlement and what happened afterwards. The books of Samuel and Kings describe the subsequent flow of history during the next 500 years or so, all the way to the cataclysmic event of the Babylonian conquest and exile at the beginning of the sixth century BC.

In this commentary, we will concentrate on the book of Joshua and will read and interpret it in its ancient context, interacting with previous scholarship on the book as appropriate. We will also read the book as Christians, recognizing the importance for Christian communities of the continuation of the story of Israel in the events that took place there in the life and ministry of Jesus of Nazareth and the birth of a new movement within Judaism, which subsequently transformed into the new religion of Christianity, with its accompanying sacred Scriptures and history based on the story of Israel. In so doing, we will be looking at how the book can be applied by the present-day Christian community in its devotion, worship and teaching.

In order to read and interpret the book of Joshua, it is the conviction of this author that we must start by looking at questions of how the book was written by its ancient author or authors, and how it was read and understood by its ancient audience. From there, we can then try to see how we as modern readers might be able to read the book and apply it to our own situation or situations. These are all very difficult problems, on which few people agree entirely. Therefore, the best the writer can do is to take the reader on a journey with him and hope that the reader will find it at least in some ways a worthwhile one. It is the hope of the author of this book that the reader will be stimulated to learn more about the book of Joshua in its ancient context and about how to read the book profitably in our modern (or, perhaps, postmodern) context. It is the author's conviction that academic scholarship can contribute immensely to the understanding of the book and can serve as a foundation for interpreting it to modern audiences. With this in mind, let us without further ado delve into the world of ancient Israel and the book of Joshua, which describes a great people movement and conquest and the founding of a great nation in history and in the self-understanding of those people who look back into that history as a sacred history.

We will start with an introduction to various issues surrounding the book and its contemporary interpretation, and will then proceed to the commentary proper.

1. GENERAL

1.1. The story and place of Joshua in the canon, and its overall relationship with the Pentateuch and Judges–Kings

As stated above, the book of Joshua describes the conquest of the land of Canaan by the Israelite tribes. Its place in both Christian and Jewish canons is after the Pentateuch, the five books of Moses, and before the book of Judges, which is followed by the books of Samuel and Kings. The person known as Joshua (Hebr. *yĕhôšuʿa*, 'Yahweh is salvation' [*yāh yišûʿāh*; root *yāšaʿ*]; according to the Old Testament, previously Hoshea ['to save', hiph. from *yāšaʿ*; Num. 13:16] is the central character of the book. He first appears in Exodus 17 (vv. 9ff.), where he fights for Moses against the Amalekites. Joshua is described as 'servant' (*mĕšārēt*) of Moses in Exodus 24:13 in a narrative that tells of Moses' ascent up Mount Sinai to meet God for instructions about the Israelite wilderness cult (Exod. 25ff.), and is also mentioned in the golden calf narrative of Exodus 32 (v. 17). Joshua is further mentioned in passing in Numbers 11, where he speaks against two men prophesying in the camp and is rebuked by Moses. After these occasional mentions, as the storyline of the Pentateuch moves towards the conquest, Joshua really starts to come to the fore. He is one of the twelve men who are sent to survey and spy out the land of Canaan (Num. 13). He and Caleb are the only ones who do not bring back a pessimistic report of the Israelites' ability to conquer the land, and are thus allowed to enter the land instead of dying in the wilderness (Num. 14:28–30, 36–38; 26:65). In Numbers 27:18–23 Moses starts to transfer some of his authority to Joshua, and Joshua is one of the leaders dealing with the Transjordanian issue of settlement on the east side of the river Jordan in Numbers 32 (v. 28) and with the allotment of the land of Canaan in Numbers 34 (v. 17). In the book of Deuteronomy, Moses transfers his authority to Joshua before his death (Deut. 31). Joshua then becomes the leader of the Israelites (Deut. 34) for the imminent conquest of Canaan. After the conquest and at the end of the book of Joshua, Joshua dies (Josh. 24), and the book of Judges starts off with a short statement relating to his death (Judg. 1:1). Judges 2:6–10, 21–23 further refers back to Joshua in helping to introduce the post-Joshua era.

Such is the setting of the book and person of Joshua in the exodus, wilderness and conquest traditions. There appears never to have been any doubt about Joshua's inclusion in the canon, which is natural, as its contents are so fundamental to Israelite history and self-awareness. Joshua is part of the *nevi'im*, the second division of the Hebrew Bible (i.e. *torah* [law], *nevi'im* [prophets] and *ketuvim* [writings]). I will normally be using the term 'Old Testament' throughout this commentary, but the labelling is ultimately a matter of personal preference. Generally, Jews like to use the term 'Hebrew Bible', and Christians the term 'Old Testament', to reflect on the Christian use of the Bible.

1.2. Structure and plotline of the book and chronology of events

The structure of the book of Joshua is fairly straightforward. First of all, chapters 1 – 5 describe the crossing of the river Jordan. Chapters 6 – 12 portray the Israelite conquest. Chapters 13 – 21 then describe the allotment of the land, with some short conquest-related interludes or comments. Finally, chapters 22 – 24 relate a number of events after Israel has settled, with the primary concern of ensuring and exhorting the Israelites to follow Yahweh. Koorevaar (1990) succinctly describes this quadripartite division as follows: 1:1 – 5:12 *'ābar* (cross), 5:13 – 12:24 *lāqaḥ* (take), 13:1 – 21:45 *ḥalaq* (divide), and 22:1 – 24:33 *'ābad* (serve). If one looks at matters from a chronological point of view, it is noteworthy that the beginning of the book is shown as taking place within a short time span at the beginning of the conquest. Yet the events of chapters 13 – 24 are described as taking place when Joshua is 'old and advanced in years' (*zāqēn bā' bayyāmîm*). I will have more to say about this topic later in this Introduction, but it seems that, chronologically, with chapters 1 – 5 describing the crossing of the Jordan, chapters 6 – 10 apparently taking place soon after the crossing, and chapter 11:1–15 rather sooner than later thereafter, these units all pertain to an early time, at least relatively so. Also, while 11:15 – 12:24 belong chronologically between chapters 1 – 11 and 13 – 24, 11:15–23 is a summary and chapter 12 is a list. Therefore, bearing in mind that chapter 13 ostensibly depicts a much later time, it is not straightforward to say exactly when each conquest described within this material should be understood to have taken place according to the text (cf. 11:18, which states that 'Joshua made war a long time [*yāmîm rabîm*] with all those kings'). Such comments as 'Joshua and the Israelites' in 12:7 may actually imply the telescoping of a long chain of events through attribution to Joshua as the leader of the Israelites at the time of an initial conquest and settlement. Finally, there are a number of comments interspersed in the book that immediately imply a later date of writing; see for example 6:25; 7:26; 13:13; 15:63. Thus there is an overall chronological progression in the book, but this consists mainly of two temporally distinct series of events (1 – 11 [or so] and 13 – 24), with material added which can immediately be seen to reflect later concerns. Also, when we keep in mind that, even though textually prominent, 1 – 9 and 13 – 24 describe just a few events, we can think that the book of Joshua is really about the allotment and settlement of the land in a larger context and over a longer period of time, mostly by some type of war, according to the narrative, but also relatively peacefully in parts (e.g. 17:12–13). All this said, as a whole the book contains only a very partial picture of what was happening in the Syro-Palestinian area at the time it portrays, interpreted from a strong and exclusivist Yahwistic perspective. For more information, we must turn to archaeology and other biblical texts (mainly Judges, even though the same reservations apply) and to extrabiblical sources that can be brought forward.

Having made these preliminary comments, the structure of the book can be described as follows:

1. Crossing of the Jordan and preparation for conquest (1 – 5)
    Commissioning of Joshua and by Joshua (1)
    Spying out Jericho (2)
    Crossing the Jordan (3 – 4)
    Circumcision at Gilgal (5:1–12)
    Theophany in preparation for conquest (5:13–15)

2. Conquest (6 – 12)
    Conquest of Jericho (6)
    Conquest of Ai (7 – 8)
      Initial failure due to cultic transgression (7)
      Purging of guilt and subsequent victory (8:1–29)
    Building of altar at Mount Ebal (8:30–35)
    Treaty with the Gibeonites (9)
    Victory over the coalition of five Canaanite kings
        and the southern part of Canaan (10)
    Victory over Hazor (11:1–15)
    Summary of the conquest of the land (11:16–23)
    List of kings defeated (12)

3. Allotment (13 – 21)
    Summary of the situation before allotment proper (13)
      Cisjordan (13:1–7)
    Allotments for Transjordanian tribes (Reuben, Gad and
        eastern Manasseh) (13:8–33)
    Quick summary of allotment (14:1–5)
    Allotment for Caleb (14:6–15)
    Allotment for Judah, Ephraim and Manasseh
      Judah's allotment (15)
      Allotment for Ephraim and Manasseh (16 – 17)
    Setting of Tent of Meeting at Shiloh (18:1)

Allotment for remaining seven and a half tribes
    (18:2 – 19:51)
  Charting of remaining land (18:2–10)
  Allotment for Benjamin (18:11–28)
  Allotment for Simeon (19:1–9)
  Allotment for Zebulun (19:10–16)
  Allotment for Issachar (19:17–23)
  Allotment for Asher (19:24–31)
  Allotment for Naphtali (19:32–39)
  Allotment for Dan (19:40–48)
  Allotment for Joshua (19:49–50)
  Concluding comments to tribal allotments (19:51)
Cities of refuge and Levitical towns (20:1 – 21:42)
  Cities of refuge (20)
  Levitical towns (21:1–42)
Concluding comments (21:43–45)

4. Closing events (22 – 24)
  Transjordanians (22)
    Transjordanians return home (22:1–9)
    Transjordanian altar incident (22:10–34)
  Exhortations by Joshua to serve Yahweh (23)
  Assembly at Shechem (24:1–28)
  Concluding matters, including Joshua's death (24:29–33)

1.3. Textual issues (incl. MT vs LXX)

The text of Joshua as such is in the main very readable. However, there are some difficult parts, and it is also well known that the text diverges quite a bit from that of the LXX. That there are divergences in the text of Joshua suggests that the book was malleable over at least part of the period of its transmission. At the same time, based on what we know from existing versions, the textual differences are not really radical, and this suggests that the essentials of the tradition were transmitted reliably (cf. the comments in Junkkaala 2006: 309–311, making similar conclusions based on slightly differing considerations). On the whole, although one could try to make text-critical conclusions about the priority of either the MT or the Greek text (or any of its possible reconstructed antecedents), I will not attempt that, but will mostly follow the MT in this commentary, noting the main divergences and any possible implications in the translation and the 'Form and structure' and 'Comment' sections. For more on textual issues and proposed solutions to a number of problems, the reader should consult other commentaries, including Butler 1983 and Nelson 1997a. In addition, one should bear in mind comments made in general terms in Van Seters 2006 about the likelihood of the existence of various versions of the biblical texts (especially in the Persian and Greek periods), and one should also, for example, consult Millard 1982 for more details on scribal practices in the Ancient Near East.

We note however that there are main important divergences in connection with 5:2–9 (the circumcision at Gilgal), 6:1–15 (the encircling of Jericho), the placement of 8:30–35 (the Ebal incident) and in 20:1–6 (the setting-up of the cities of refuge), and that there are a few extra verses at the end of the book in Greek. There is also variation between the MT and the Greek in connection with the town and boundary lists of Joshua 13 – 21. Comments are normally made only on MT place names because it is very difficult to be precise about the places, since the identification of many of the places in the MT is already a challenge in itself (cf. my comments about site identifications below, p. 55).

1.4. Sources and composition of Joshua

The book of Joshua itself makes direct reference to a source, or at least implies it. According to Joshua 10:13, the poem in verses 12–13 is (was) also written in the book of Yashar. However, there are other parts in the book that one could easily imagine being based on a source or sources. In particular, the city and territorial lists in chapters 11 – 21 might easily be attributed to external sources. Other than that, one may perhaps ask the question about the provenance of 8:30–35, the narrative that describes the building of an altar at Mount Ebal, as the passage comes after 9:2 in Greek manuscripts (for more details, see commentary on 8:30–35). Similarly, for example, some might at least try to suggest that chapters 23 and 24 may have been appended to the end of the book somewhat loosely (but see my comments on them). Also, other chapters and passages might incorporate some older material. Thus, and even if one denies this last point, one may assume that the author or authors of the book of Joshua did utilize various sources in the composition of the book in order to create the finished product. One might also ask when such sources were composed. However, I will defer such considerations to when I discuss the date and provenance of the book later in this Introduction.

On another level, as far as academic scholarship is concerned, since the birth of source criticism and the Wellhausenian consensus (cf. Wellhausen 1905, 1963/1876), the book of Joshua has generally been considered together with the Pentateuch for source analysis. The entity Genesis–Joshua was conveniently labelled a 'Hexateuch'. Except for the J and E sources and an acknowledged deuteronomic influence, the Joshua town lists in particular were seen to be part of a P source. This said, since the publication of Martin Noth's *Deuteronomistic History* (Noth 1991/1943), Joshua has been seen as part of a Deuteronomistic History rather than as part of a Hexateuch. In relation to this, Noth denied the continuation of the J and E sources and the existence of priestly material in the book of Joshua. Subsequently, most scholars have followed Noth's views. What is important here is that Noth saw a continuous story from Deuteronomy onwards, in contrast to the previous scholarship based on the concept of a Hexateuch. A casual reader might simply skip over this shift in perception as an intellectual and academic curiosity. However, as we will see later in this Introduction, the question of Joshua's relationship to the preceding and following canonical books and the so-called Deuteronomistic History is crucial when determining the date and provenance of the book. Suffice it to say here that the two previous approaches are quite different from each other, and if one were to cast doubt on the validity of Noth's view of Deuteronomistic History and 'resurrect' at least some of the concerns of the Hexateuch view, one might think it conceivable that a quite different approach to the composition of the book could result.

Thus, having laid out some preliminary concerns, I defer my considerations of the composition of Joshua to later in the Introduction, when I discuss the date and provenance of the book. A number of issues are also covered in Excursus 1.

1.5. An overview of the history of interpretation of Joshua and the Israelite conquest and settlement

The most comprehensive work on the history of interpretation is Noort 1998. Of the other commentaries on Joshua that address this topic, Butler 1983 is worth mentioning. As the topic has been well covered before, this section mainly suffices to give a brief summary of the matter in preparation for the discussion that follows, plus some comments on the most recent developments.

The interpretation of the book can perhaps first be divided into pre-critical or pre-modern and critical or modern eras. There is not much that stands out on the pre-modern side, in particular as the commentators of the time did not have much in the way of modern historical tools available to them. However, Calvin's commentary on Joshua (Calvin 1847–1850/1565) and Matthew Henry's section on Joshua in his commentary (Henry 2008/1706) are perhaps worth mentioning for their theological content and overall historical interest.

As far as the modern period is concerned, in a broad sweep, it can be divided into pre- and post-Noth periods. Once historical criticism and the Wellhausenian paradigm took hold of Old Testament studies, as mentioned above, Joshua was first seen as part of a Hexateuch. With Martin Noth's *Überlieferungsgeschichtliche Studien* (Noth 1991/1943), Joshua was rather seen as part of a Deuteronomistic History. Recently, there have been some modifications and challenges to Noth's view (e.g.

multiple redactions etc.), but essentially it still holds sway in mainstream scholarly consciousness. This commentary will be critical of Noth's stance and will take the view that Joshua is essentially a separate book rather than part of an overarching history, for reasons that will be elaborated on in the Introduction below and throughout the commentary. Or, if it *is* part of an overarching history, it should rather be seen as part of a 'Hexateuch', even if not in the classical sense of that hypothesis.

Another important development relating to the modern period is the rise of the discipline of archaeology since the latter part of the nineteenth century (see e.g. Moorey 1991). At first, archaeology in the 'Holy Land' was very much used for trying to understand the biblical text and was in many ways driven by the concerns of those interested in the Bible. However, as time went on, archaeology became very much its own discipline, and, at present, what might previously have been called biblical archaeology is now usually labelled Syro-Palestinian archaeology, a separate discipline largely independent from biblical studies. And yet there is still a good deal of interaction between archaeology and biblical studies. Many biblical scholars wish to understand the Bible based on relevant archaeological discoveries, and a number of archaeologists also attempt to bring out how their discipline can contribute to biblical understanding (see e.g. Mazar 1992 etc.). Later in this Introduction and throughout the commentary we will look into issues relating to how the two disciplines interact.

However, at this stage we should note that archaeology has had a special relationship to the book of Joshua and early Israelite history in general. While the early biblical archaeologists of the nineteenth century were interested in illuminating the Bible based on archaeological discoveries, once actual data from ancient Palestine started to accumulate in any sub-stantial amounts, problems began to arise over how they might relate to the Bible. While events from the period of the judges onwards were generally seen as reflecting actual history, events earlier than that became suspect from the beginning of the twentieth century. Thus the book of Joshua stood on the borderline of where going back in time would rather make fact become fiction in the biblical storyline.

In addition, very recently, some of the more radical scholars have questioned the veracity of the biblical accounts even from Judges on. The most radical of these argue that the biblical Israel is a scholarly construct from the Persian period (see e.g. Lemche 1998; T. L. Thompson 1992). In other words, according to this view, nothing can really be known about pre-exilic Israel based on biblical documents. However, these radical views have not gone unchallenged, and rightly so in the opinion of this writer (see below in more detail). Thus I will be concentrating mainly on inter-acting with more 'traditional' views, where the watershed of historicity lies with Joshua and the time of the conquest and settlement, even though I may interact with the more radical views here and there as well. As part of my interaction, I will look at the relevant archaeological data in detail.

In order to understand the mainstream approach, we will need to have a quick look at how it developed through three main modes that arose as the twentieth century progressed (see e.g. Dever 2003 for a very good summary of this). The first of them, the conquest model whose most notable proponents were William Albright and his disciple John Bright, argued for a general veracity of the biblical record, even though it lowered the date of the conquest to the thirteenth century instead of the fifteenth century implied by the biblical chronology. Secondly, the peaceful infiltration model, with Albrecht Alt and Martin Noth as its most notable proponents, suggested that the Israelites were nomads who immigrated to the land from outside. In this view, importantly, the immigration was peaceful and did not involve a conquest. Finally, the peasants' revolt model advocated by George Mendenhall and Norman Gottwald suggested that the Israelites were Canaanites who revolted against the existing socio-economic structure and withdrew to the highlands to form a new society. Later scholarship has shown problems with all these models. However, while the peasants' revolt model was rejected, the idea of the indigenous origin of the early Israelites was retained. In other words, contemporary scholarship tends to think that Israel was a development indigenous to Canaan (see e.g. Dever 2003). That said, for example, a carefully worked out recent archaeological study by Faust (2006, incl. pp. 170–187) argues that at least a significant number of the early Israelites originated from outside the area, allowing even for the inclusion of a group that escaped Egypt, even if Faust does not subscribe to the idea of a conquest.

I will be interacting with most of the issues relating to the history of interpretation later in this Introduction and throughout the commentary, as most of them still have direct relevance for today, but the position taken here will be to consider seriously the indigenous nature of early Israel while at the same time acknowledging the possibility of an influx of outsiders. More specifically, this commentary suggests that an external group, which had escaped from slavery in Egypt (see esp. Hoffmeier 1997 [also 2005] for evidence of the plausibility of the Egyptian sojourn and the exodus) and brought with it memories of its founding fathers the patriarchs and a belief in Yahweh, somehow gained a foothold in and overall control of the Canaanite highlands, and subsequently assimilated indigenous elements to form Israel, with the process of assimilation continuing well into the period of the monarchy (see Pitkänen 2004b). In fact, the archaeological evidence broadly supports the possibility of such an idea. As Junkkaala summarizes, the change from the Late Bronze Age culture to the Iron Age hill-country culture happened first in the central highlands and expanded from there over the next 200–300 years (see Junkkaala 2006, esp. pp. 308–309 for further details). I am also in many ways following the lines of Faust's recent book (Faust 2006), except that, for example, in particular, I allow for the possibility of a conquest as part of the settlement process (for the conquest aspects, see below and in the commentary proper).

2. UNDERSTANDING JOSHUA TODAY IN ITS ANCIENT CONTEXT

2.1. The role of history and theology in the interpretation of the book

The book of Joshua is one of the historical books of the Old Testament. It portrays events that took place in the past; in other words, it is a piece of historical writing of the ancient world. However, intertwined with the historical events is their interpretation from a theological perspective. This may sound somewhat surprising to a twenty-first-century reader. Modern Western culture in particular has often relegated any belief in the divine to the background, away from the public sphere into the private sphere. In other words, people may privately hold religious beliefs but are not to bring them out in public discussion, where everything must be explicable without recourse to possible divine influence. Of course this is a generalization, but it nevertheless holds true at least in its broad contours. Postmodernity has somewhat alleviated the situation, but the public–private distinction still holds. However, although modern Western culture may operate according to this premise, the situation was completely different in the Ancient Near East of which ancient Israel was a part. In the Ancient Near East, belief in gods and their influence on human affairs was the norm rather than an exception, and all Ancient Near Eastern documents more or less attest this fact. The question in the Ancient Near East was not whether one believed in a god or in the divine generally, as may be asked in the modern world, but, rather, *which* god or gods one believed in. Moreover, in the Ancient Near East, religion was usually national. A particular country and region had its own god or gods that it followed, and the people of that country were assumed to be under the aegis of that particular god or gods. When wars were fought, they were seen as a battle of the gods of the warring factions on a cosmic scale, and the victory of one side was interpreted by that side as a manifestation of the power of their god or gods. A loss, on the other hand, was often interpreted by the losing side as a sign of the displeasure of their own god or gods.

In this context, when we interpret the book of Joshua, an Ancient Near Eastern document, we must ask a different set of questions from those we are used to asking. However, this is of course a matter of the culture of the reader, as some cultures of today around the world are more like the Ancient Near Eastern cultures in their approach to the divine. However, as the main readership for this commentary lies in the Western world and its author is a Westerner, in most cases I will interpret the book in dialogue with Western culture. It is nevertheless hoped that any readers outside the West will find the contents at least somewhat relevant.

Thus we have come to the issue of cultural differences between the ancient world and the modern world when reading the book. If ancient concerns were different from modern ones, we must ask the question of how we 'translate' the concerns of the book from the ancient to the modern. To answer this question, first of all, we must obviously know what the ancient concerns were. Essentially, this is the task of academic scholarship, as we need to look into the text in its original language or languages, and must understand about the life and concerns of ancient Israel as part of the ancient world. In other words, academic scholarship, while seeming dry and uninteresting to many people, is vital for attempting to understand the book. A lot of the commentary will thus be devoted to working on this 'back end' of interpretation, and I will be discussing many of the relevant points further below as part of the Introduction and throughout the commentary.

Secondly, we must know about our world and the concerns of the people living in it. This is an easier task, as we are part of the modern world and live in it. However, our modern world, and, for that matter, the ancient world itself, is diverse in a number of ways, and therefore not all its members have the same concerns. For example, a Christian will have different concerns from a Jew, a Muslim or an atheist. Women think differently from men, and age and cultural backgrounds also come into play. Some may not even be sure what their concerns are. Accordingly, we can only make an approximation of what might be useful for modern readers and what can speak to them.

Finally, we must ask the question of how we are to translate the concerns of the ancient world for the modern world, assuming we are well versed in both. What is important and can be translated? How does it translate? What is not relevant any more? These are not straightforward questions, and this is attested for example by the fact that many of those who preach from the Old Testament find the historical books difficult. Or, even if they simply speak confidently about being strong and courageous, when it comes to the conquest itself and to killing the inhabitants of Canaan, many see a quite perplexing problem coming to the fore. We will be looking at these and other issues and problems below in the Introduction and throughout the commentary. Here again, it should be clear from the above that solutions to these questions can be offered in a number of different ways. Thus it must be emphasized that any possible solutions cannot but be considered as ultimately subjective. However, seeking new solutions by interacting with past approaches and adding new insights seems to be the best possible approach one can take to making sense of this ancient document. And there are a number of human universals – such as power, love, livelihood and justice, to name but a few – that are true throughout history and across cultures and civilizations, and identifying these will provide some anchor points in the quest.

Therefore, with Joshua, we are dealing with both history and theology. But the meaning of these terms themselves is open to debate, and it will serve the reader well to keep this in mind. While the next two sections are labelled 'Understanding history in Joshua' and 'Understanding theology in Joshua' respectively, the two are really intertwined in the book and should not (and cannot) be separated in the grand scheme of things.

3. UNDERSTANDING HISTORY IN JOSHUA

3.1. Approaching history

I have already hinted at some issues relating to the historicity of the book of Joshua. By this, I mean the question of how much and in which ways the book can be seen to reflect real historical events that took place in time and space. To answer this, we must first note that all history writing is selective. Any author always selects a subset of events from all that happened. For example, if we were to write our autobiography, surely we would not include everything that has happened to us. We would select only the most important events (in our opinion; cf. John 21:25 in the New Testament). In addition, in selecting the events and in presenting them, we would probably want to create a particular view of ourselves. To give a trivial example, if we were unreasonably nasty to someone, we might not want to mention that. We might even try to imply that we were nice to them to make ourselves look good. In other words, all history writing reflects the viewpoint of the writer. Moreover, we would write our biography differently if it were for our mother from how we would write it for a national audience. In other words, the intended audience influences the way that a writer shapes his or her material. And we might not even remember everything correctly if writing about events that we experienced, say, some thirty years ago. Finally, it might of course be possible that we would modify and improve on our biography later in our life. Or, for example, if we became famous, someone might want to edit our biography after we have died in order to bring it up to date and also to make it more relevant for the next generation whose concerns might be different from ours, for example owing to changing historical and political circumstances. A writer of the next generation might also see our life differently with hindsight and would want to reflect this in the new biography.

Thus we have selectivity, bias, accuracy and the concerns of the writer and the writer's audience to consider when dealing with historical material. I will be interacting with these below as appropriate when dealing with the book of Joshua. For the moment, suffice it to say that the author or authors described what he or they wanted to present about the early history of Israel to the relevant ancient audience or audiences.

If we then come back to the question of how far the book portrays real history, we need to be aware that there have been various views on the matter. As mentioned above, until the Enlightenment the book was evidently considered to describe actual historical events. However, with the rise of historical criticism and the Wellhausenian consensus (cf. Wellhausen 1905/1878), the outlook of the book was increasingly doubted. The most serious challenges to it came after archaeological excavations in the land of Israel from the late nineteenth century started to show discrepancies between the text and the perceived facts on the ground, resulting in models where many differed considerably from what the biblical text claimed to have happened. Discrepancies between archaeological evidence and the biblical text have continued to the present day. As already mentioned, I will be dealing with issues relating to archaeology later in the Introduction and throughout the commentary.

That there is relevant archaeological evidence in addition to the biblical text brings us further to the question of how we can know about history in Joshua. In particular, if the biblical text and archaeological evidence seem to contradict each other, how can one decide between the two? This problem is exacerbated by the fact, already mentioned, that biblical studies and archaeology have evolved into separate disciplines. Each discipline has its own methods of working, and a resulting body of scholarship has been produced by the respective academic communities. In addition, it is relatively rare that an expert in biblical studies is also an expert in archaeology, and vice versa. Consequently, it is often very difficult for a biblical scholar to evaluate the results of archaeology as a non-specialist. And an archaeologist may often not be aware of the various readings that biblical studies can provide. As a result, the two fields may choose to ignore each other. Or one field or its most vocal representation may dominate the other, at least in effect forcing the other to base its interpretations on the stronger side's premises and results. In fact, at present, it is sometimes at least proposed that archaeology should be completely independent from biblical studies. However, most Syro-Palestinian archaeologists still make at least some kind of reference to the biblical material. MacDonald 2000 is a good example of an archaeological study in which biblical site identifications in Transjordan are proposed based on a particular (albeit mainstream) interpretation of the biblical texts as per when one would expect the sites to have been occupied (see below for further details on this). In other words, it is often not easy to determine how the two disciplines should relate to each other. For this commentary, I am more at home with biblical studies. However, I will also attempt to incorporate archaeological insights as far as possible, while recognizing that I am not a professional archaeologist.

There are still further problems with interpreting the evidence. As was hinted above, it is extremely helpful if one can read the texts from the standpoint of the ancient author and the relevant audience. However, how can we know about the ancient author and audience? We cannot go back to the past to see what happened and how people thought and what their culture was. The only way we can understand the past is to examine remnants or, to use a more conventional term, sources that have survived from the past. However, in order to interpret such sources, essentially a modern brain will be at work. The modern brain, together with the results provided by other brains, will look at the sources and start making sense of them. The relevant person will then start building intellectual models of how the past should be understood. Typically, the person, and for that matter a whole scholarly community, then tests whether these models are logically consistent and cover all available data, refining the models if there are discrepancies. And, even when a perfect model is built, can one prove that it might not be possible to build another perfect model or theory which explains all the data, but in a different way? In fact, it is not all that easy to show that multiple models, or reconstructions, are impossible (see e.g. Pitkänen 2004a: Appendix for one possible way to demonstrate this from a theoretical standpoint). At face value, it may thus even be possible to think that a whole scholarly community could be at least partly wrong when presenting a particular way of understanding the past, since a scholarly community typically builds one particular model through a collective effort.

In addition, there are problems with accounting for all relevant evidence. As was mentioned above, one scholar can rarely be a master of both biblical studies and archaeology. But these are not the only sources relevant to ancient Israel. Ancient Israel did not exist in a vacuum, but was part of the Ancient Near East. And, in fact, various different Ancient Near Eastern peoples are also mentioned in the Old Testament. Moreover, these and other peoples left traces of themselves, and these can be looked into, and have been looked into during the past 150 years or so. There are masses of both textual and archaeological records from the Ancient Near East, so many in fact that not all the written records that have been found have been read and analysed, owing to sheer lack of available resources. In addition, there were different languages, such as Akkadian, Ugaritic, Sumerian, Hittite and Egyptian, in which these records were written. Speaking of the many records that have been analysed, they provide evidence of ways of thinking that are in many ways similar to those of the ancient Israelites, even though there are some differences too. Also, for example, some cuneiform documents have been found in Israel itself (see below, and here and there in the commentary for more details). Therefore, from the standpoint of a person studying ancient Israel, one could legitimately think that a look at the Israelite documents in the light of the other documents of the Ancient Near East might help in understanding the Israelite documents better. And, in fact, such comparisons have been made, and the writer of this commentary agrees that the comparisons have been extremely helpful in shedding light on the thinking of the biblical authors.

This being the case, and realizing that the study of the ancient world cannot but be a field of its own, if only owing to the sheer magnitude of the task, we now have three fields in which we would need to be experts in order to try to understand ancient Israel's past. But there are actually more than three fields, as the study of each of the Ancient Near Eastern countries is a field of its own, such as with Egypt and Assyria. And the results or even methods of investigation of any of them might in reality be in contradiction, or at least in tension, with those of biblical studies. We would then again have to ask the question of how to fit the two together, just as with biblical studies and archaeology, and with similar problems. With all the above issues in mind, this commentary realizes the importance of the study of the Ancient Near East and attempts to draw insights from the relevant fields as best it can, even if it cannot cover them comprehensively.

Furthermore, as the ancient Israelites were people, one could ask whether any insights gained from a general understanding of people could be transported back to the ancient world. For example, if there are any sociological models of human behaviour, these might be transferable. And such work has been done recently (see e.g. McNutt 1999). Another area where some recent work has been done is ethnic studies. For example, the author of this commentary has written on how studies of ethnicity might help with understanding early Israel (see Pitkänen 2004b), and other studies also exist, some of which are quite detailed (e.g. Faust 2006). Other anthropological approaches are also possible. Or any current under-standing of power, economics, politics and ideology may be drawn on, to name but a few prominent possibilities. Approaches involving comparative religion, within the context of the Ancient Near East and of religion in general, may further be utilized from such perspectives. In other words, a whole understanding of humanities and human life is relevant to the biblical world. Such approaches will be drawn on for this commentary, even if, again, it is impossible to be comprehensive.

One may also include insights from some of the 'harder' sciences. For example, studies of climate can be made in the Israelite context to see how it affects (and has affected) the human environment. This might include any possible climate changes during the period of study: for example, climate may have affected the particular environment of the Late Bronze Age Levant, which in turn might have affected the situation of the area one way or another (see e.g. Coote and Whitelam 1987 for one theory). Or one could see how the geology and geography of the area would affect life and customs there as part of an understanding of the life of the ancient Israelites. One could also study art and architecture and compare these with the art and architecture of the biblical world. Such studies would interact with any material remains discoverable from ancient Israel, and could thus easily be part of the archaeological work relating to the area. In fact, besides including these approaches, archae-ology may also encroach on the field of humanities if any conclusions about human beliefs and behaviour can be made on the basis of material remains.

We should also mention that not all biblical scholars are in agreement on how the biblical texts themselves should be read, speaking in terms of no apparent recourse to any external factors, as discussed above. Various methods have been utilized. Traditionally, since Wellhausen, it has been customary to see biblical documents as being composed of various specific sources. Thus, identifying the sources and their provenance and theology was seen to be important. In fact, Wellhausen's *Prolegomena* (Wellhausen 1905/1878) with its dating and analysis of the J, E, D and P sources is a prime example of the source-critical approach. Considerations of the form of different units pertaining to the sources were also seen as important, even if such analysis was often rather centred on the poetic sections of the Bible, most notably the Psalms. To source criticism were added considerations of redaction; i.e. how the final editor had shaped the sources. Unfortunately, especially with the passing of time, there was hardly any consensus about the sources and redactions, and as the biblical text gives no direct clues save for on a few rare occasions (see Whybray 1987 for a number of these problems and other problems with the JEDP hypothesis), the source- and redaction-critical approaches have recently suffered a lack of confidence in many circles. A number of such critics in particular would rather seek to read the biblical documents in their final form. Considerations of plot, characterization and other artistic devices derived from general literary theory have been raised. In addition, the results of some of these literary approaches could be almost diametrically opposed to the conclusions provided by the source and redaction critics. There would then also be those who would seek the middle ground by trying to incorporate insights from both approaches and somehow to negotiate between any differences or conflicts. (Any issues relating to textual criticism would of course also need to be considered, where applicable.)

Finally, it is worth looking in more detail at the challenge of the so-called minimalists to biblical history (e.g. Lemche 1998; T. L. Thompson 1992), even though the following remarks refer to them rather implicitly, as most academics are sceptical about the historical value of the book of Joshua anyway. As was already mentioned, the so-called minimalist scholars take the view that the pre-exilic Israel is a literary creation from Persian times, and does not correspond to historical reality. These views have aroused much discussion during the last ten years or so. One may add to this the fact that some Israeli archaeologists have suggested that the date of a number of Iron Age II archaeological layers should be later than previously thought (see e.g. Finkelstein and Silberman 2001). If so, some of the remains that have been traditionally assumed to relate to Solomonic times and attest to large-scale building works etc., should now be dated to a later time. This would also mean that nothing much would be attested from Solomonic times, and thus the biblical text would become more suspect, playing into the hands of the so-called minimalists. In response, there has been a vigorous defence by those who advocate the traditional dating (see e.g.

Mazar 1997) and the battle lines have pretty well been drawn. And it remains to be seen which camp will increase its influence to the exclusion of the other, but at the time of writing it seems that the traditional archaeo-logical view still has more proponents. As for the so-called minimalists themselves, as already mentioned above, their views have been responded to by a number of scholars (see e.g. Dever 2001, 2003; Long, Baker and Wenham 2002; Hoffmeier and Millard 2004; Kofoed 2005). At the risk of oversimplifying matters, the methodology of the minimalists can be summarized as follows: (1) suggest via literary means that the biblical texts come from the Persian period; (2) assume that texts can be considered correct only if there is direct proof from documents contemporary to the events (e.g. monuments, such as the Mesha stele from the ninth century BC which describes the experiences of Mesha, the then king of Moab, with Israel, or Akkadian inscriptions), otherwise they cannot be assumed to contain historical information. As there are very few contemporary data that directly corroborate the biblical text, the text can then be viewed as unreliable. There are then two avenues of countering the claims: (1) suggest via literary means that the texts come or can come from an earlier time; (2) (a) suggest further parallels with the Bible, at least indirectly, as done for example by Dever (2001, 2003); Kofoed (2005); Hoffmeier and Millard (2004); (b) point out that a requirement of direct external proof is a sceptical but not by any means necessary requirement (see e.g. aspects of Long, Baker and Wenham 2002). One could further point out, as Pitkänen (2004a) has done, that scholarly theories cannot be verified empirically by going back to the past to see what happened; the only way to judge their validity is to see whether they appear 'logical' and 'well constructed'. However, such judgments are often very subjective, and are tied to cultural entities called scholarly communities, in reference to the insights given by Thomas Kuhn (Kuhn 1962; cf. Feyerabend 1993). These judgments also often assume, at least in practice, that there is a single answer which can be obtained by the best possible application of the criteria of investigation. However, this may not necessarily be the case when dealing with history. There can be many different ways of looking at the material and all of these may well be justified, and it may thus be difficult to distinguish objectively between models. As a result, the quest for truth may not necessarily lead to it, or at least to the complete truth, even if done with the best possible intentions and efforts (see Pitkänen 2004a). Interestingly, and also as just indicated above, it can be stressed that there is today quite a lively discussion about which approach or set of approaches is most appropriate in the context of Old Testament scholarship. On the whole, to admit that there are problems would reduce the authority of the academic community. Accordingly, academics seldom acknowledge the full implications of the matter. Perhaps there is also a fear that this would reduce the standing of the field as a whole and thus for example reduce possible funding from whatever sources may be currently available (cf. Lamont 2009: 53–106 for related points).

Thus, as a conclusion to this section dealing with how one can find out about ancient Israel, there are many different ways of doing so, and each may involve a complex field of its own. Even allowing for the complexity of each field, if arriving at a full picture could be a cumulative process, matters would be easy, but we have seen that this is not necessarily the case. Thus we can only say that any possible interpretation is essentially subjective, even if it may be firmly anchored in factual data and in an academic, even (at least at times) scientific method, and even if it has the backing of the scholarly community at large.

In this context, and as already indicated above, this commentary will seek to offer one particular interpretation of the book of Joshua in inter-action with relevant available data, whether biblical or extrabiblical. It is hoped that the reader will find it worthwhile to trawl through the book, or at least to dip in and out here and there. Rather than offering definite authoritative conclusions, the author wishes the reader to be stimulated into thinking further about Joshua and the world in which it came about, and then about how the book of Joshua speaks to us as twenty-first-century human beings, and to do this from the perspective of the first-century Christ event and its influence in particular. By and large, the author does think that it is entirely plausible that, if read in an appro-priate way, the book reflects actual historical events, even though one certainly cannot prove the matter. Readers are welcome to check through other commentaries and works that take different views on a variety of matters. For example, while the writer in many ways disagrees with the views of minimalist scholars, he thinks that they contain valuable insights and are worth consulting. Ultimately, we are all working on the same data and are often using similar methods, albeit coming to differing con-clusions based on different choices we make in the process of interpretation and historical reconstruction. It is this author's view that diversity in interpretation is richness, as long as we acknowledge our differences and the reasons for them, and allow others to follow their own convictions – even if it might perhaps be a bit too much to follow a completely 'anarchic' approach to the subject (cf. Feyerabend 1993 in this respect, who in fact speaks for 'anarchy', and with some very good reasons). However, this author also thinks that it is imperative to try to take into account all possible relevant data, and that there is no excuse for not doing so.

3.2. The historical background of Joshua

In the preceding sections, I have mainly concentrated on giving an over-view of methodological issues relating to the interpretation of Joshua. In the following sections, we will proceed to look at some more detailed relevant evidence while at the same time drawing in any methodological considerations where appropriate for the interpretation of this evidence.

3.2.1. *Canaan in the Late Bronze and Early Iron Ages*

To start with the archaeological evidence, we will first look at the Late Bronze Age in contrast to the Middle Bronze period. Mazar 1992 offers an excellent overview of the archaeology of the land of the Bible, to which I will refer below. (It should also be noted that not very much archaeological fieldwork has been possible in Palestinian areas of Israel since the early 1990s/2000s, owing to the Palestinian Intifada. Jewish religious extremism trying to protect Jewish burial sites has also sometimes hampered progress in areas directly administered by the state of Israel.) During the Middle Bronze period which preceded the Late Bronze Age, Canaan was character- ized by urban culture. As Mazar (1992: 197) describes, the latter part of the Middle Bronze period saw increases in settlement and urban growth throughout the area. There were great fortification systems, which imply sophisticated social organization, centralized authority in the towns surrounded by these fortifications, and rivalry between city-states. In other words, the extant material remains from the time imply a complex social set-up and a high level of culture.

The end of the Middle Bronze Age was marked by turmoil and destruc- tion. As Mazar (1992: 226) notes, a significant number of towns were destroyed around the middle of the sixteenth century BC. Entire urban clusters around the country collapsed as a result. However, there was also continuity. Some cities such as Hazor and Megiddo in the north suffered lesser disturbances and were rebuilt based on their earlier style (Mazar 1992: 227). Temples in these cities also continued into the Late Bronze period. However, there was a decline in population in Palestine as a whole during the period. Part of the reason appears to have been Egypt, which had gained overall control of Palestine by the end of the fifteenth century BC (see e.g. Mazar 1992: 232). At the very least, any Egyptian campaigns in Canaan would have caused destruction, but it is quite possible that Egyptian rule itself had a restricting influence on Palestine owing to accom- panying economic exploitation (see Mazar 1992: 237). There were also other problems. These, together with clear textual evidence for Egyptian dominance, which is also attested in monuments and inscriptions in Egypt and Syria–Palestine, come out very well in a set of diplomatic correspond- ence between Egypt and its Asiatic neighbours. This correspondence consists of some 350 cuneiform letters inscribed on clay tablets found at Tel el-Amarna in Egypt, dated to about 1380–1340 BC. Most of the letters were written in Akkadian, the lingua franca ('English') of the time, with a small number in Assyrian, Hurrian and Hittite (see *ABD* 1: 174–175; for the letters in transliteration, see KNUDTZON; see also Moran 1992). A number of the letters describe how different Canaanite city-states, including Jerusalem (see esp. EA 287), asked for help from Egypt against rival city-states. They also had to provide tribute to Egypt. One could concur with Mazar (1992: 237) that it is likely that the Egyptians would have exploited the principle of 'divide and rule' in their dealings with the city-states. In addition, the city-states faced a problem from a people called *habiru*. When the Amarna letters were first published, it was thought that the *habiru* might be Israelites. However, it soon became clear that the concept must be wider and simply reflect a social class without a permanent attachment (*habiru* are also attested outside the Palestinian context, e.g. in Mari tablets before the Late Bronze Age). As for its implications for biblical studies, it is very possible that the name *habiru* served as a label that was to be attached to the Israelites (even though the derivation is not straightforward; see e.g. *ISBE* under *hapiru*; cf. *UG*: 136–137; *DLU*: 85).

Besides the Amarna letters, another important set of documents relating to the area was found in the ruins of the ancient city of Ugarit from about 1400 to 1200 BC. (The literature on Ugarit is immense. A good place to start one's study is *ABD* 6: 695–706, and *ABD* 6: 706–721.) For the language, albeit now somewhat dated, *UT* is a fair starting point; later and more comprehensive grammars are also available (cf. *DLU*, which is also available in an English translation). While Ugarit is strictly outside Canaan, the documents are important because Ugaritic, the language in which most of them were written, is in many ways very similar to biblical Hebrew. In addition, a number of the poetic and mythological texts are closely related to Hebrew poetry, in particular as relates to the Psalms. Also, such gods as El and Baal are mentioned in Ugaritic texts. In other words, there are clear similarities in the language and world view of the fourteenth-century Ugaritic and biblical Israelite documents. The Ugaritic documents, together with the Amarna letters and other archaeological evidence, also clearly indicate that, at least broadly speaking, there was a common culture throughout the area and that normal life went on in ancient Canaan in the Late Bronze Age (see also below for further comments relating to the international character of the era).

The Late Bronze Age had its share of turmoil. As Mazar (1992: 287) conveniently describes, the Hittite empire, which was prominent in Anatolia during the preceding centuries, collapsed around 1200 BC. At the same time, there was turmoil in the Mycenaean world, and there was also a population movement from the area. The so-called sea peoples arrived in Cyprus and in the Levant (Mazar 1992: 287; 300–328). The famous reliefs at Medinet Habu in Egypt describe how the Egyptians fought against these peoples (see *ANET*: 262–263; *ANEP* 4, 19, 114, 350). The best-known of the sea peoples, the Philistines (also called Caphtorim in Deut. 2:23; cf. above, Introduction), settled on the Levantine sea coast (cf. Mazar 1992: 302), and the archaeological remains they left behind show how their sites were much larger than sites in the Israelite highlands during Iron Age I (see Faust 2006: 139–146). A number of sites in Canaan, such as Megiddo, Beth Shan, Hazor and Aphek, were also destroyed in the thirteenth century (see Mazar 1992: 290 for a fuller list). Egyptian power itself was on the decline at this time, and Egypt lost control of Canaan in the middle of the twelfth century BC.

While the Late Bronze Age was a period of decline in Canaan in comparison to the preceding Middle Bronze Age, the succeeding Iron Age I was marked by an increase in settlements, especially in the northern highlands (see Finkelstein 1988; Dever 2003; note also that a comparable process can be detected in the highlands of Transjordan, with similarities in material culture [see Faust 2006: 221–226]). The increase was so big that it has been called a 'population explosion' (see Dever 2003: 98). The settlements were usually founded at new sites, lacked walled defences, were rural, and consisted of clusters of houses that were similar in structure and size throughout. The settlements in the highlands were different from the sites in the lowlands, which essentially continued in the style of the Late Bronze Age (see Dever 2003: 169, 193 for good summaries of contrasts between the highlands and the lowlands and between the Late Bronze Age and the early Iron Age, also in the light of the Old Testament). In other words, something new was happening in the highlands in the early Iron Age. In addition, as is well known, an Egyptian pharaoh (Merneptah) mentions Israel around 1200 BC on a victory stele found at Thebes in 1896. Most of the text simply consists of propagandistic exaltation of the pharaoh and his prowess. The reference to Israel occurs in the context of references to claimed conquests in the Levant and vicinity, as follows (from B. Davies 1997; for the Egyptian text, see Kitchen 1982: 12–19; note also that a determinative for 'people' is used for Israel in the Egyptian language rather than the usual determinative for a 'region'):

> . . . Tjehenu is plundered whilst Hatti is peaceful, Canaan is seized by every evil, Askalon is carried off and Gezer is seized, Yenoam is made as (though it) never existed, Israel is wasted without seed (*Ysrir fkt bn prt.f*), Khor is made a widow of Egypt . . .

Based on the Merneptah stele, there is good reason to think that Israel did exist in the highlands of Canaan at the time, even if the stele does not give an indication of its exact location (or constitution). I will be drawing on the implications of all these matters and expanding on the details below in the Introduction and throughout the commentary.

3.2.2. *The overall historicity of the events depicted in Joshua*

It seems clear from the preceding section that the birth of Israel should most naturally be associated with the increase in settlements in the highlands during the early Iron Age. Such an increase in settlements of a new kind at least strongly implies the possibility of the birth of a new identity. The even nature of the settlements is very much in line with the overall biblical ideology, which is egalitarian and non-elitist. Their location overall is in line with the portrayal of events in the early part of the book of Judges (1 – 2), and with some of the notes in the book of Joshua (e.g. 17:16–18).

However, the problems start when one tries to find evidence of destruction at sites that were destroyed according to Joshua. These are however alleviated by the fact that the Bible does not necessarily indicate that all the sites that some have thought should be yielding evidence of destruction must have been destroyed. For example, according to Joshua 11:13, Joshua burned only Hazor during his northern campaign, and Joshua 12 only lists kings defeated but does not say anything about destroying any of the relevant towns. Also, comparing biblical accounts in Joshua with the conquest lists of Thutmose (Late Bronze Age) and Shishak (around 900 BC), Junkkaala (2006: 314 and *passim*) notes that archaeological evidence of destruction does not exist in most of the identifiable sites given in the campaign lists. Nevertheless, there are also a number of sites that the Bible indicates were destroyed completely. The most obvious of these are Jericho (Josh. 6, esp. 20–21), Ai (Josh. 8, esp. 28) and, as was mentioned above, Hazor (Josh. 11:13). Of these, Hazor has evidence of a destruction that could have been caused by the Israelites, even though, as with most destructions generally, there is no evidence of who caused it. This leaves us with Jericho and Ai. With Jericho, while the original excavations by Garstang affirmed the biblical story about the conquest, Kenyon's new excavations in the 1950s gave a different story. According to Kenyon (1983: 679–680), the town was destroyed at the end of the Middle Bronze Age (c. 1550) – much too early for the Israelite conquest. What is more, the site was largely abandoned during the Late Bronze Age, and was occupied only late in the Iron Age (NEAEHL 680). While Kenyon suggested that erosion might have erased most of the traces of the Late Bronze Age town, Bienkowski (1986) argued that some traces of erosion would have been expected if this was the case, but none can be seen. Therefore, on this interpretation, and even when tombs from the Late Bronze Age have been found at Jericho, it appears that there was not really any substantial town for the Israelites to conquer, contrary to the biblical account in Joshua.

As for Ai, it has normally been identified with et-Tell, just east of Bethel. This site was occupied during the Early Bronze Age in the third millennium, and there is also evidence of a couple of violent destructions from the time. The site was then abandoned for more than a thousand years and occupied again from about 1200 BC. In other words, archaeological evidence from the site does not support the idea of a conquest.

Another problem is that there does not seem to be evidence of occupation during the Late Bronze Age at a number of sites that feature in the narrative. Prime examples are Arad and Gibeon. We will look at each of these sites in the commentary proper. In addition, I will devote a separate excursus to each of Jericho, Ai, Gibeon and Arad. Overall, as will be seen, negative evidence that is often quoted against these sites is not by any means as conclusive as is often thought. While the saying 'absence of evidence is not evidence of absence' will be taken into account, there is also some positive evidence in relation to Jericho and Gibeon, and possibly Arad.

In addition to the evidence that supports a settlement process that started in the thirteenth century and the perceived lack of archaeological evidence in support of a conquest, when we bear in mind that there are aspects of continuity between the new highland settlements and the Late Bronze Age culture, in recent years scholars have increasingly sought to understand the birth of Israel in terms of indigenous origins and processes. However, the argument from material culture is not by any means conclusive, as the Bible itself indicates that the Israelites adopted Canaanite material culture (see e.g. Deut. 6:10–11). In this regard, we may keep in mind that the Hurrians, who (at least seemingly) migrated to Canaan in the Middle and Late Bronze Ages, left only very limited evidence of their origins, if any, in the material culture that has been unearthed (see Na'aman 1994a, incl. p. 179; see also below for further comments on the Hurrian migration). Similarly, there does not seem to be material evidence for the existence of the 'seven nations' in Deuteronomy and Joshua (see Deut. 7:1; Josh. 9:1; also see comments on 3:9–13 and 9:1–2 for more on this). At the same time, it must be stressed that there *are* clear differences in material culture with the transition from the Late Bronze to the Early Iron Age in the hill country (see esp. Faust 2006). Also, Junkkaala (2006) has collated archaeological information about sites listed as not conquered by the Israelites in Joshua, and noted that there is a significant change in material culture, into the so-called hill-country culture, at around the time when the sites are described as conquered in later Israelite literature (see Junkkaala 2006: 269–297, site by site; summary on p. 300). That the Philistine material culture in Iron Age I was well attested should also be kept in mind here (see e.g. Faust 2006). All this reinforces the idea that some issues relating to early Israel may be archaeologically detectable; others less so. Overall, the main problem in accepting the possibility of the conquest and the historicity of the Joshua narrative relates to evidence about either destruction or occupation of sites in the book, depending on how the narrative describes events relating to the sites. For this reason, bearing in mind their narrative setting, I examine archaeological evidence from all sites mentioned in Joshua and devote separate excurses to the main sites of importance that are either problematic or otherwise worth looking at in detail. I will concentrate on the Late Bronze and Iron Age I periods in my discussions, making reference to other periods as well where relevant.

In addition to the settlement patterns just mentioned, there are other positive indications for an overall historicity of the book. Hess lists the following features in Joshua that are best explained by a second-millennium provenance (see Hess 1996: 26–31): (1) The description of the borders of Canaan in Joshua 1:4 (and in the Pentateuch) 'matches the Egyptian understanding of Canaan in the second-millennium BC sources, where the cities of Byblos, Tyre, Sidon, Acco and Hazor form part of the land'. In relation to this, 'The northern boundary never was clear because the Egyptians, who saw Canaan as part of their empire, were in conflict with the Hittites on the northern border of the land. The Mediterranean Sea formed the western border of Canaan and the Jordan River formed the eastern border (though north of the Sea of Galilee the region included areas farther east).' (2) The plot of Joshua 2 accords with second-millennium Ancient Near Eastern culture. (3) The Hivites, Perizzites and Girgashites (Josh. 3:10) have a distinctive association with the second millennium BC. (4) The act of God bringing down the walls of Jericho (Josh. 6:20) has a parallel in a Hittite text (Hess 1996: 28 includes the Hittite text in English translation). (5) The list of items that Achan stole fits best in the latter half of the second millennium BC. (6) The role of the Gibeonites in Joshua 9 seems to fit well with the archaeology of their region. (7) The names of a number of the original inhabitants of Canaan fit the context expressed by the fourteenth-century Amarna letters and second-millennium Egyptian sources. (8) The names of the three Anakites in Joshua 15:14 indicate a mixed population in the region around Hebron, which is compatible with what is known from extrabiblical evidence. (9) The covenant in Joshua 24:2–27 in its form and content most closely resembles the Hittite vassal-treaty structure which is unique to the second millennium BC.

As indicated above, we will look individually at each site mentioned in the book of Joshua in the chapter-by-chapter and verse-by-verse commentary proper. In fact, except for possible problems with some of the main sites, as mentioned above and to which we devote separate excurses, it will turn out that the picture given by surveys and excavations is that just about all identifiable sites in both Transjordan and Cisjordan that relate to the book of Joshua can be seen to bear witness to occupation during the Late Bronze–Early Iron Age era (see commentary section for details). This applies even to many sites in the territory of Judah, the lists for which I will argue were shaped into their present form during the time of the monarchy (see below for details). As for the date of the conquest, in the light of the problems outlined above, I will leave it ultimately open, recognizing however that if a conquest happened, based on our present knowledge and the state of the evidence it is most natural to envisage that it happened in the thirteenth century BC. On the whole, the message of the book would not be greatly changed even if one were to seek to argue for an earlier date of the conquest (if it took place). Perhaps surprisingly, on many occasions, whether the text reflects real history or not does not affect its message, even though there are also aspects where it clearly does. I will refer to these issues below in the Introduction and throughout the commentary proper, as appropriate.

3.2.3. *Joshua as an Ancient Near Eastern literary document*

When one draws any conclusions about a text, whether related to its historicity or to its overall message, it is first important to know how to read it. As was mentioned above, we as twenty-first-century people, be it in the West or anywhere else, will read the text based on our present cultural understanding and world view. In addition, every person is different and will thus read any text in a different way, at least to some extent. As has already been implied, in order to understand what the text says, we should approach it first as a form of communication from the original author to its original audience and try to understand it from this perspective before attempting to see its meaning for the present audience.

In order to see the text in its original context, we must understand it as an ancient text that utilizes conventions current in the ancient world. As suggested above, Israel was culturally part of the ancient world, and its world view and expressions were similar to those of other cultures of that world. Therefore, we can suppose that seeing Israelite texts in the context of other ancient texts might enlighten us in viewing these texts. Indeed, a groundbreaking study on this has been conducted by Younger (1990). Younger compared Joshua, and chapters 9 – 12 in particular, with other Ancient Near Eastern conquest accounts, in particular those from Assyria, the Hittite empire and Egypt. Younger's study reveals that Ancient Near Eastern conquest accounts share a number of features. And some of these are in fact characteristic of any portrayals of war and of any history writing.

Above all, Younger's study demonstrates that the Ancient Near Eastern accounts have 'figurative and ideological superstructures' (Younger 1990: 265). Typical issues are: selectivity of accounts, presenting one's own cause as just and right, presenting the enemy as despicable and morally decadent, exaggerating victories and the number of enemies killed, and minimizing losses and related numbers. Embellishments and hyperbole are normal, and accuracy of facts has a different meaning from what it would have in modern Western historical writing. Divine presence is considered necessary for victory, and there are specific references to divine intervention in war. Heroic deeds of the leader, with the help of his god or gods, are emphasized. Consider the following extract from the Apology of Hattusili, lines 22–58, as an illustration (quoting from STURTEVANT-BECHTEL, which also contains the Hittite; see also COS 1: 199–200 for a newer translation). The events date to about 1250 BC in Hittite Anatolia.

But when my father Mursilis became a god [i.e. died; cf. COS 1: 199], and my brother Muwattallis sat upon the throne of his father, I became a general in the presence of my brother, and then my brother appointed me to the office of chief of the *Mešedi*, and gave me the Upper Country to rule. Then I governed the Upper Country. Before me, however, Armadattas, son of Zidas, had been ruling it. Now because My Lady Ishtar had favoured me and my brother Muwattallis was well disposed towards me, when my people saw My Lady Ishtar's favour towards me and my brother's kindness, they envied me. And Armadattas, son of Zidas, and other men too began to stir up ill will against me. They brought malice against me, and I had bad luck; and my brother Muwattallis named me for the wheel [possibly a judicial procedure; see COS 1: 200]. My Lady Ishtar, however, appeared to me in a dream, and by means of the dream said this to me: 'Shall I abandon you to a (hostile) deity? Fear not.' And I was cleared from the (hostile) deity. And since the goddess, My Lady, held me by the hand, she did not ever abandon me to the hostile deity, the hostile court; and the weapon of (my) enemy never overthrew me. My Lady Ishtar always rescued me. If ever ill-health befell me, even (while) ill I observed the goddess's divine power. The goddess, My Lady, always held me by the hand. Because, I for my part, was an obedient man, (and) because I walked before the gods in obedience, I never pursued the evil course of mankind. Thou goddess, My Lady, dost always rescue me. Has it not been (so)? In fact, the goddess, My Lady, did not ever in time of danger (?) pass me by; to an enemy she did not ever abandon me, and no more to my opponents in court, my enviers, did she abandon me. If it was a plot of the enemy, if it was a plot of an opponent at law, if it was a plot of the palace, My Lady Ishtar always held over me protection. She always rescued me. Envious enemies My Lady Ishtar put into my hand; and I destroyed them utterly.

Or consider the following example of Egyptian war propaganda, lines 1–8 from the Merneptah stele, c. 1200 BC (from B. Davies 1997: 174–176, which also contains transliteration; for the Egyptian text, see Kitchen 1982: 12–19; for Kitchen's translation, see Kitchen 2003a: 10–15; cf. also my comments on the stele above):

Year 5, 3rd month of Shomu, day 3, Under the Majesty of Horus, Strong Bull, Rejoicing in Truth; King of Upper and Lower Egypt, Baienre Meramun, Son of Re, Merenptah, Contented with Truth, who makes strength greater, And who exalts the power of Horus; Strong Bull, who smites Nine Bows, Whose name is given to eternity forever. His victories in all lands are related to allow every land together to see and to let the goodness of his valour be seen. King of Upper and Lower Egypt, Baienre Meriamun, Son of Re, Merenptah, Contented with Truth. Bull, Lord of strength, who kills his enemies, Beautiful one upon the battlefield of valour when his attack has succeeded. Shu who clears away the storm cloud that was over Egypt; Who allows Egypt to see the rays of the sun-disk; Who removed the mountain of copper from the neck of mankind so that he may give breath to the common-folk who were imprisoned; Who satisfies Memphis over its enemies, allowing Tatanen to rejoice over his rebels; Who opens the doors of Memphis that had been blocked up; Who allowed the temples to receive their food offerings. King of Upper and Lower Egypt, Baienre Meriamun, Son of Re, Merenptah, Contented with Truth, Sole one who fortifies the hearts of hundreds of thousands. Breath entered their nostrils at the sight of him who destroys the land of Tjemehu in his lifetime, who puts eternal fear in the heart(s) of the Meshwesh. He caused the Libyans who entered Egypt to retreat, great in their hearts is the fear of Egypt. Their front troops abandoned their rear(guard), their legs were not (able to) make a stand, except to run away. Their archers threw down their bows, the hearts of their runners became weak (even) as they marched. They undid their water-skins, throwing (them) to the ground, they untied their sacks, throwing (them) away. The vile chief of the Libyan enemy fled into the dark of night, alone, no plume on his head, and his feet were bare. His wives were carried off before him, the loaves of food offerings were taken away. He had no drinking water to nourish him, the faces of his brethren were savage (enough) to kill him. They fought one another amongst his chiefs, their camps were burned into ashes, all his possessions were food for the troops.

Finally, let us take an example from the annals of the Assyrian king Tiglath-Pileser I (from Younger 1990: 83), who lived in the twelfth–eleventh centuries BC:

At that time: I marched to the insubmissive land of Kadmuhu which had withheld tribute and impost from Aššur, my lord. I conquered the land of Kadmuhu in its entirety. Their booty, property, (and) possessions I brought out. Their cities I burned, razed (and) destroyed. The remainder of the land of Kadmuhu, who had fled from my weapons (and) had crossed over to the city of Šerešše which is on the opposite bank of the Tigris, made that city their stronghold. I took my chariots and warriors (and) I hacked through the rough mountain range and difficult paths

with copper picks (and) I made a good way for the passage of
my chariots and troops. I crossed the Tigris (and) I conquered
Šerešše, their stronghold. I laid out in the midst of the battle (the
corpses of) their men-at-arms like grain heaps. I made their blood
flow in the watercourses and the plains of the mountains.

Anyone who has read the book of Joshua, or for that matter almost any
other biblical book, will quickly note a number of similarities between
these three quoted texts and the biblical accounts. Also, just by looking
at the examples above one can quickly see that the ancient world had its
own style of reporting things. And these examples should make the reader
sensitive to the fact that the theology of Joshua is closely tied to its ancient
context. Consequently, it will serve us well if we take the ancient context
into account when reading the book of Joshua, and this is what I will do
throughout the commentary.

In relation to how Joshua portrays its subject matter, we can also
cautiously draw on some insights made by New Testament scholarship
that has included considerations about ancient Greco-Roman biographies,
e.g. those by Herodotus, even when these belong to a slightly different era
and cultural sphere. Such biographies did not generally regard historical
accuracy in the same way that moderns would. By and large, something
that was plausible would also be narrated, even if it were not a verbatim
report or might not correspond exactly to what had happened. Such considerations have been drawn on for example for the study of the Gospel
of John. Many scholars think that there are problems with the historical
accuracy of this Gospel, and yet it has also been suggested that, even if
that is so, it is not necessary to ditch the book completely but rather to
think of it as a portrait of Jesus that is true to his significance and person,
even if matters are already being seen through later interpretation. Andrew
Lincoln notes (unpublished lecture notes, 2007):

> But even historians, such as Thucydides and Tacitus, who claimed
> to have investigated their subject matter closely and to have
> sought out oral or, where available, written sources, would
> compose the discourses that take up a large amount of space in
> their histories in accord with what they thought would fit the
> character of the speaker and the occasion. Similarly, in relating
> events such historians would mix more factual reporting with
> accounts of incidents that might or could have happened. What
> was important to them was that this elaborated material be
> plausible and illustrate the general truths they wanted to draw
> out about their subject.

While the above comments are more at home in ancient Greek historiography and specifically pertain to the study of the New Testament and

the Fourth Gospel, perhaps we could also in a number of ways view the book of Joshua in this manner. Maybe it is not necessary to try to see it as a verbatim report, but as a portrait that remains true to a Yahwistic narration of what in all plausibility happened and what a/the true Yahwistic leader would have been like. In any case, any biography, or, for that matter, any historical piece of writing, is always a representative portrait (as pointed out e.g. by Long 1994), and it is probably impossible to separate the portrait completely from what 'actually' happened. In this respect, to continue our analogy with the Gospel of John, just as the Gospel was (as many think) written some sixty years or so after the events it narrates and already speaks from the perspective of hindsight, even if the book of Joshua was written as early as in the pre-monarchic period, say, in the eleventh century BC, this would already be some 150 years after the events it narrates, and the account would thus already be a narrative that speaks through the voice of a representative of a later generation that is clearly removed from the events related. In this way we arrive at the possibility of a particular selective portrait using both hindsight and plausibility and based on the ideology of the writer, an ardent Yahwist. It would undoubtedly also be natural to think that the writer would be likely to have relied on any sources available to him in crafting his narrative, whatever the balance between utilized sources and any creative retelling might have been.

3.2.4. *The date and provenance of the book of Joshua*

It is relevant for us to know the date and provenance of the book of Joshua as this can help us determine the message that the original writer intended to convey to his readers. This then would naturally help us in determining the message of the book for today's readers, as already discussed above. Another issue of course is the question of to what extent the date of the book has a bearing on its historical reliability. In this regard, most would instinctively think that an earlier date among various possible options would be more likely to imply that the events recounted in the book are true. However, the question of date as an indicator of reliability is not actually as crucial as it might sound to an average modern reader. This is because, first of all, it seems clear that the book was written, or at least compiled, after the death of Joshua, as it for example speaks about his death. In other words, in its present form, the book is in any case already distanced from the events it relates. Secondly, it is well known that in the Ancient Near East literary productions could be transmitted very reliably through centuries (see e.g. Hallo 1996a: 225–226; 1996b: 1872–1873; cf. Kitchen 2003b: 362–363). Therefore, even if the material was put in its final form only quite late, there is still the possibility that it could originate at least partially from an earlier period, and, at the same time, it is possible that any earlier material would have come through to the author or compiler reliably. One should also note, however, that there are cases in which early material can be suspect in itself! Thus, while an important and relevant question in a number of ways, we do not necessarily need to be too worried about the date of the book as an indication of its historical reliability. Also, in any case, as we have already discussed, Joshua is a piece of Ancient Near Eastern history writing, and issues pertaining to Ancient Near Eastern history writing pertain also to the book of Joshua, with their own implications for historical reliability.

Nevertheless, the date of the book remains a pertinent question, and one possible way to make conclusions about it is to try to date it relative to other biblical documents. In particular, as was mentioned above, recent scholarly opinion stemming from Martin Noth has been that the book is part of a Deuteronomistic History spanning from Deuteronomy to 2 Kings, written in the exile or later, even if utilizing some earlier sources too. Or, in a variation of this theme, parts of the history, including Joshua, may have been written slightly earlier, most likely in the time of Josiah, with a final redaction during the exile. Deuteronomy itself (or the bulk of it) has generally been seen in academic circles as having been written in association with Josiah's reforms, even though at least some of the later mainstream scholarship may also have viewed parts of the book as originating from a somewhat earlier time, in some cases even from a time before the Neo-Assyrian period (see e.g. Weinfeld 1991; Tigay 1996).

If Joshua is part of a single Deuteronomistic History, it would follow that it is unlikely that it was written early, even if it is fair to say that a number of the sources for the Deuteronomistic History were seen by Noth as originating from an earlier time. However, if there are grounds for seeing Joshua as a separate book, then its dating is much more open. Recently, there have been challenges to the concept of a Deuteronomistic History (see e.g. Westermann 1994; Pitkänen 2004a), and the view taken here is that the book can be considered as a separate entity rather than as part of a single history. The arguments for this view can be somewhat complex, and we will look at some of them in this commentary. The reader is also advised to refer to the books listed above for a full exposition. However, one example of the problems with the Deuteronomistic History hypothesis worth mentioning here is that the crossing of the Jordan narrative in Joshua 3 – 4 resembles and points back to the crossing of the Sea of Reeds in Exodus 14 – 15. There are other similar examples of narrative connections between Joshua–Kings and Exodus–Numbers. Another issue is that the existence of priestly material in Joshua rather implies a connection with Exodus–Numbers, as these contain a significant amount of priestly material, but there is very little priestly material in Judges – 2 Kings. Noth explained away the existence of any significant priestly features in Joshua precisely for this reason of relationship to the surrounding materials, but it is the position of this writer that Noth's reasoning is not convincing (see 'Form and structure' on Josh. 22 and Excursus 12 on Josh. 22:9–34 for details). In other words, with examples like this, it is difficult to think of a self-standing Deuteronomistic History. And yet these considerations do not preclude the possibility of editing of some kind when the books of Genesis – 2 Kings were put together in their present arrangement in the canon.

On the whole, if the book of Joshua originated from the time of the monarchy (or thereafter), we might expect that it would be likely to reflect the concerns and pre-eminence of the Judean monarchy. However, there are several indications that this is not the case. The indisputable leader of Israel is Joshua *ben* Nun the Ephraimite (cf. Num. 13:8). Also, the Tent of Meeting, the centre of Israel's religious life and the place where Yahweh dwelt among Israel, was set up at Shiloh. These indicate that ultimately both political and religious leadership of the nation was in the north. The situation in the book of Joshua is in fact essentially the same as in Genesis, where Judah together with his brothers is subordinate to Joseph at the conclusion of the book (Gen. 37 – 50; see esp. 37:5–11; 50:18 where Joseph's brothers bow down before him; cf. also 49:22–26), even though Judah and the south at least in places feature prominently in the Genesis narratives. That Joshua is an Ephraimite also casts at least some doubt on the idea that he is construed as an ideal for Judahite kingship during the time of the monarchy (contra Ottosson 1991: 23–24 and *passim*), including that the name is a veiled reference to the Judean king Josiah (*pace* Nelson 1981). Moreover, if one excludes the towns of Judah in Joshua 15, all that really remains of the activities of the Judahites in the book of Joshua is the description of Caleb and his conquest of Hebron, an account of his family giving an allotment of land to Achsah and Othniel (vv. 13–19), and the mention of Jerusalem in verse 63. (One should note here that Hebron is also shown as important at around the time of the beginning of the Davidic monarchy [2 Sam. 2:1; 5:1–5] and that Jerusalem was a significant city in the second millennium BC; cf. comments on 10:1 on Jerusalem.) In fact, that Judah fails to conquer Jerusalem in Joshua 15:63 and that the allotment of Judah is deemed too big for them (Josh. 19:9; cf. Hawk 1991: 156n12) imply that, except for Caleb, the Judahites may not have been very adept at settling their allotment. Mention should also be made that, according to Joshua 7, Achan the covenant-breaker is a Judahite (vv. 16–18), even though admittedly this could also mean that even a Judahite will not be spared in the event of a transgression.

The Transjordanians are strongly emphasized in the book of Joshua, and their unity with Israel is highlighted in Joshua 22:9–34 in particular. The Transjordanian issue is also strongly emphasized in the overall conquest tradition of Numbers–Joshua as a whole. In the book of Joshua itself, the Transjordanians come first in the tribal allotments of Joshua 13 – 21, and this is consistent with Numbers 32 – 35, in which the Transjordanians have already received their share. The emphasis on the Transjordanians is heightened by the statement that they cross over the Jordan in front of the

Israelites, armed and ready to take part in the conquest of Cisjordan (Josh. 4:12; cf. Josh. 1:14).

This strong emphasis on the Transjordanians in the book of Joshua fits best with the time before the eighth century when the Transjordanians and the people of the northern kingdom were deported by the Assyrians (see 1 Chr. 5:26. In fact, that Transjordan features prominently in the Judges narratives (e.g. Judg. 5:14–17; 8:4–17; 11:1 – 12:7) and is still relevant at the time of David according to the lists of the Chronicles (see esp. 1 Chr. 12), but does not feature much afterwards (cf. 2 Kgs 10:33), supports the idea that the book of Joshua is early rather than late. Specifically, it is hardly likely that the Transjordanian issue would have been current between the time of the Assyrian deportation and the exile. Another factor that supports an early rather than a late date is that whereas the Transjordanian issue is strongly emphasized, there is little if any hint of the north–south divide in the book of Joshua (cf. McConville 1993: 100–101; cf. my comments below, p. 61). In fact, the more one goes back in time, the easier it is to think how the emphasis on the Transjordanians would speak to the audience of the book of Joshua, including during the time of the united monarchy and the pre-monarchic period.

Of course, all this possibly takes place only in the narrative world, but if it has any basis in reality, the pointers are towards an early time as opposed to a later time. Those arguing for a Josianic setting of the book (such suggestions generally tie together with modified Deuteronomistic History hypotheses of multiple redaction of Deuteronomistic History) would probably argue that this is part of the vision of the greater Israel in the spirit of the greatness of Josiah. And yet the description of Josiah is itself a narrative construction, apparently during the exile or thereafter (in any case after his death), and the time in question may actually not have been as glorious as is depicted in the narratives. Also, suggestions of a Josianic date for Joshua are tied in with the consensus based on the ideas of de Wette and Wellhausen that Deuteronomy originates from Josiah's time (see Pitkänen 2004a for details; of course, the de Wettian and Wellhausenian premise has been modified, but the essence of what they suggested still holds sway in scholarly discussion). Once this premise about the date of Deuteronomy is no longer assumed (see Pitkänen 2004a for a number of detailed reasons), there are no particular reasons to try to limit the options for the date of the book of Joshua to Josiah's time or later. In such a case, any suggested link between Joshua and Josiah would also seem to weaken (cf. above).

A further issue in dating are the town and boundary lists (chapters 13 – 21). In past scholarship, Albrecht Alt and Martin Noth in the 1930s thought that the boundary lists originated in the pre-monarchical period and the town lists in the time of the monarchy. A lot of ink has been spilled on the topic and the exact dating of the lists during the periods concerned, but any conclusions must remain tentative. However, it does seem possible that the boundary lists stem from the time before the monarchy. In particular, it is not unusual to think of lists delimiting territory in the second millennium. One example is the treaty between Suppiluliuma I of Hatti and Niqmaddu II of Ugarit (see BECKMAN: 31), which delimits the boundaries of Ugarit (the text is partly broken, but, from the context with list of locations, it is hard to think of anything other than a boundary description). This said, it seems more likely that the town lists originate in the period of the monarchy, even though parts of them may be earlier. In particular, a number of locations in Judah (Josh. 15) seem not to have been occupied during the pre-monarchical period. Whatever the case, it is entirely possible that the lists were updated as the book was transmitted through time. I will discuss the lists in fuller detail in the 'Form and structure' section for Joshua 13 – 21.

In relation to interpreting archaeological data, we should also note that there are real problems with identifying the related site for each locality in Joshua. In particular, the work of MacDonald (2000) illustrates the difficulties that relate to Transjordan in this respect. When reading MacDonald's work, one cannot but notice that he suggests a number of identifications based on occupation during the seventh century BC (or so), on the premise that the biblical text should be dated at (about) that time! Then, as the usual argument goes, as sites were occupied only in the late Iron II period, the biblical text should be dated late! In other words, we can easily enter the realm of circular argumentation when dealing with site identifications based on occupation. And, in fact, except for possible problems with some of the main sites, i.e. Jericho, Gibeon, Ai and Arad, which themselves are not necessarily insurmountable (see above, and excurses on Jericho and Gibeon in chapters 6 and 9, plus comments about Arad in Josh. 12:14), the picture from surveys and excavations is that just about all identifiable sites in both Transjordan and Cisjordan that relate to the book of Joshua can be seen to attest occupation during the Late Bronze–Early Iron Age era (for special considerations that pertain to Josh. 15, see below). In other words, ultimately, archaeology does not need to be seen as the determining factor in the dating and provenance of Joshua. I will devote a discussion to each place mentioned in Joshua in the commentary proper, which includes questions about its identification and the occupational history of any possible candidates.

As far as the events in the book are concerned, they take place all around the country, from south (Josh. 10:29–43) to north (Josh. 11:1–15). This emphasizes the focus on all the land of Canaan (plus Transjordan) in the book. Some important places in the book of Genesis, such as Hebron (Gen. 13:18) and Shechem (Gen. 12:6–7; 35:1–4; Josh. 8:30–35; 24) feature in Joshua. On the other hand, Jerusalem, which was conquered by David according to the books of Samuel and Chronicles (2 Sam. 5:6–9; 1 Chr. 11:4–8) is glossed over in Joshua with only a short mention regarding the failure to conquer the city (Josh. 15:63). The focus on all the land is particularly well illustrated by the boundary and city lists. All tribes, including the Transjordanians, are listed. If we look at the order in which the tribes have been listed in the allotments, this may give us some clue about their importance, as those coming first may be seen as more important than others (even when this may not be the case with all passages in the Old Testament, e.g. Gen. 10). If we do so, we can see that the Transjordanians are listed first, followed by Judah, then Ephraim and Manasseh, and after that by Benjamin and Simeon, and then other more northern tribes. Comparing this with other Old Testament books, whereas Judah is first in most lists from Judges on, it is preceded by the Transjordanian tribes in Joshua. Also, the Josephite tribes follow immediately after Judah in Joshua, with Ephraim first and Manasseh second, whereas they are rather further down the lists in later books. In addition, and as was already mentioned above, if one does not count the extensive town lists for Judah (Josh. 15), there is not that much information left in the chapter, except for the boundary list (vv. 1–12), the stories about Caleb and his family (vv. 13–19), and the account of the failure to conquer Jerusalem (v. 63). In relation to this, one might suppose that it is possible that if the book that deals with the whole of Israel was written early and was then transmitted in the southern kingdom, the boundary and town lists of Judah (and Benjamin) were transmitted better and were also revised when the book was kept and passed on. In other words, the all-Israelite perspective may be original and much of the emphasis on Judah through the presentation of the town and boundary lists secondary.

An interesting point that relates to the dating of the book is the prominence of Shiloh as the place where the Tent of Meeting was set up (Josh. 18:1), in contrast to related biblical and archaeological material. According to the priestly material of the Pentateuch in particular, the Tent of Meeting itself normally housed the ark (see Exod. 25 – 40, incl. e.g. Exod. 26:34) at which Yahweh's presence was manifested, in an analogy to Ancient Near Eastern divine images and symbols (see Pitkänen 2004a; see also the commentary proper, including Excursus 3). In relation to this, the loss of such an image or symbol signalled the displeasure of the god in question in Ancient Near Eastern thinking. Thus the loss of the ark at the battle of Aphek (1 Sam. 4) was interpreted as Yahweh's rejection of Shiloh. Conversely, the entering of the ark into Jerusalem signalled the election of the town by Yahweh. From here we may conclude that the emphasis on Shiloh in the book (Josh. 18:1; 22:9–34) would thus rather imply that the book was written before the loss of the ark and the accompanying leadership and the transfer of the leadership to the south. Also, the fact that no books among Genesis – 2 Kings after Joshua include priestly material, which is best at home in Shiloh, would also suggest a composition of Joshua during the time when Shiloh was still prominent (see Excursus 12 for details). At the same time, aspects of Judah's relative prominence in the book (cf. below) might well reflect a time when Judah is rising in the balance of power but has not yet obtained a kingship, which comes to it by the time of David, and this could be the case towards the end of the pre-monarchic period, conceivably even before the loss of the ark at the battle of Aphek (1 Sam. 4).

We should also note that, while deuteronomic overall (cf. Wenham 1971b: 141–148, which lists the theological concepts of holy war, the land and its distribution, the unity of Israel, the role of Joshua and the covenant and the law of Moses as the main conceptual links between Joshua and Deuteronomy), Joshua includes many priestly features and concerns, and it is natural to see these as integral and fundamental to the book (for details of the priestly features, see below and in the commentary proper). This then suggests the possibility of priestly involvement in the composition of the book. If one were to think in terms of an early date for Joshua, a representative of the Shiloh priesthood might be one possibility for a hypothesis about the author. Or, if at least some of the Aaronites were located in the south (Josh. 21), one of them could have been involved (see below for some apparent southern features in the book).

As for the reasons for writing the book of Joshua, much of Faust's (2006) book on Israel's ethnogenesis argues that Israelite ethnicity started to crystallize because of the threat posed by the Philistines during Iron Age I (as already mentioned, the Philistine sites in Iron Age I were much larger than the [Israelite] highland sites [see Faust 2006: 139–146]). If so, a basic collection and writing of ancestral traditions might be in order as well. In this regard, in particular, the traditions about the patriarchs and the exodus from Egypt as constitutive elements of shared history that shape ethnicity would fit the bill perfectly, helping to distinguish the Israelites from the Philistines (see below for further comments on ethnicity). The cultic laws in the priestly material and the laws of Deuteronomy as foundational for the nation could also serve to further shape such an identity. The writing-down and promulgation of the stories of Joshua would then further define Israel's self-understanding of its status and purpose in the area.

And we should further remember that the book of Joshua presents itself as an ancient book. As Kaufmann points out, 'A straightforward examination of Joshua reveals that the latest event explicitly mentioned in it is the conquest of Leshem (Laish) by the Danites (Josh. 19:47)' (Kaufmann 1985/1955: 21). A number of towns include their archaic names, such as Jebus/Jerusalem (Josh. 15:63; 18:28), Kiriath-arbah/Hebron (15:54) and Kiriath Baal/Kiriath Jearim (Josh. 15:60; see Kaufmann 1985/1955: 44). Both Jerusalem and Gezer (Josh. 16:10; cf. 1 Kgs 9:16) are presented as not yet conquered (Kaufmann 1985/1955: 44–45). The Danites are assigned land from the south, not from the north, where they are described as migrating later (Josh. 19:40–48; see Kaufmann 1985/1955: 33–35). The Anakim, rather than the Philistines, are living in Gaza, Ashdod and Ashkelon (Josh. 11:22; see Kaufmann 1985/1955: 76).

In addition, as Hess notes, 'There are difficulties with assumptions that Deuteronomistic theology must be confined to the period of Josiah and with the analysis of the Joshua narratives divorced from their Ancient Near Eastern context' (Hess 1996: 33). Hess summarizes: 'Block has argued that many of the theological ideas traditionally associated with Deuteronomistic themes are not distinctive to Israel or confined to the seventh century, but are common in countries throughout the Ancient Near East' (Hess 1996: 33, referring to Block 1988, which see for details). Moreover, the attitude to the divine in the book of Joshua is compatible with what is known from Israel's surrounding cultures. In this connection, keeping in mind our discussions in the preceding section, we may note the following helpful summary by Hess:

> Younger has demonstrated that the relationship of the central historical section of Joshua 9 – 12 is too close to that of con-temporary (1300–600 BC) conquest accounts (which themselves are normally used as historical sources – though biased – by historians of the Ancient Near East) to allow certainty of identification of later insertions. Thus statements about the work and words of God are not later insertions into a battle chronicle, but are an essential feature of all Ancient Near Eastern battle accounts. The theology and the narrative should not be separated. (Hess 1996: 33, referring to Younger 1990)

In dating the book of Joshua one also needs to take account of the currently prevailing philosophical presuppositions regarding Israelite historiography. As Van Seters (1983: 209–210) points out, 'The issues involved in the current discussion of history writing in ancient Israel arise primarily out of the views developed by H. Gunkel and H. Gressmann.' According to Gunkel and Gressmann, 'history writing arises only under certain social and political conditions at the height of a culture' (Van Seters 1983: 210). In relation to this, according to Gunkel and Gressmann, Israelite his-toriography 'evolved from early preliterate forms of the tradition to a sophisticated way of thinking and writing about the past, whether recent or more distant, by the time of the United Monarchy' (Van Seters 1983: 246). However, as Younger's comparative study of the Ancient Near Eastern evidence indicates, this need not be the case. The work by Younger, which I have already referred to, has shown that the genre of Joshua 9 – 12 is perfectly compatible with other Ancient Near Eastern conquest accounts that demonstrably do not in any way result from a long oral tradition (see Younger 1990). As one particular example of how this might affect our interpretation of the biblical evidence, we may note Younger's (1990: 200–204) treatment of the account of the Gibeonites (Josh. 9). This has generally been seen as a relatively late aetiology which explains the presence of the Gibeonites (see Younger 1990: 201). In response, Younger gives examples from Assyrian, Hittite and Egyptian sources of attempts to gain favour without fight from conquerors. In particular, the account from the Ten Year Annals of Muršili indicates how Manapa-Datta, the ruler of the Seha River land, sent forth his mother, old men and old women to meet Muršili in order to gain his favour. Muršili indicates that when the women bowed down at his feet, he treated them as they wished (ibid.: 202; incidentally, cf. also Gen. 32 – 33). These Ancient Near Eastern sources were generally pretty much contemporaneous with the events they describe, and thus there is no need to assume a long prehistory for a biblical text that depicts similar events.

Moreover, as Younger (1990) points out, many of the ancient conquest accounts date from the second millennium BC. Keeping in mind that these are comparable at least with Joshua 9 – 12, one may ask if the rest of the book of Joshua should be all that different and thus question the validity of a 'traditio-historical' interpretation for the book of Joshua as a whole. Equally, there does not seem to be a prima facie reason for postulating a late dating for the Joshua narratives. And, in fact, Whybray has already pointed out the following problems that are involved with the traditio-historical approach (see Whybray 1987: 133–219 for details):

1. 'According to the traditio-historical approach, writing was not used in the ancient Near East for producing such material as exists in the Pentateuch until a late period' (Whybray 1987: 215–216).
2. 'Attempts to establish the originally oral nature of the Penta-teuchal material and its oral transmission over a long period of time on the basis of analogies drawn from the practice of oral tradition among other peoples and in different periods have, despite their acceptance by a large number of Old Testament scholars, been shown to lack cogency in several respects' (Whybray 1987: 216).
3. 'There is no evidence of a class of professional storytellers in ancient Israel' (Whybray 1987: 218).
4. 'It has been shown that no satisfactory techniques have yet been developed for detecting the origins of written narratives from evidence provided by the texts themselves' (Whybray 1987: 218).

Furthermore, as Westermann has pointed out, the period of the exile was hardly a moment of high culture in Israel, and yet scholarship has generally thought that the Deuteronomistic History was written during that time (see Westermann 1994: 19), and thus it is possible to imagine that significant writing could have been done in Israel in the time before the monarchy. In this respect, one also needs to remember that the alphabet was known in the Levantine area at least from the middle of the second millennium BC (for examples, see Albright 1966, esp. pp. 10–15, incl. figs 1–11), and that we possess a reasonably extensive corpus of (cuneiform) alphabetic texts from Ugarit from c. 1400–1200 BC, including literary compositions (see e.g. *UT*; *ABD* 6: 695–721, and the plethora of specialized works on Ugarit and Ugaritic; note also the three alphabetic cuneiform tablets from around the end of the Late Bronze Age found at Beth Shemesh, Taanach and Tabor, presented in Horowitz, Oshima and Sanders 2006: 157–166). And the recently discovered Tel Zayit inscription directly demonstrates that writing was in use in the Israelite highlands in the tenth century (the Gezer calendar, which states the agricultural seasons, is also from the tenth century, and we also have the 'Izbet Sartah inscription from about the eleventh century; note also the Jehoash inscription from the ninth century, if the inscription can be seen as authentic, and, at the time of writing this commentary, the very recently found Qeiyafa inscription which has [at least initially] been dated to the tenth century), and what I am inferring here as a possible time of composition for the book of Joshua is not that much earlier. Such passages as Judges 8:14, where a young man writes down the names of the seventy-seven officials of Succoth, suggest similarly, even if we cannot be certain about the actual date of the narrative there. The Pentateuch of course suggests that Moses wrote down certain materials, and the book of Joshua notes how the law was written down on stones at Mount Ebal (Josh. 8:32) and how the land allotments were based on a written description of Canaan (Josh. 18:9). Even if only a small percentage of the ancient Israelite population was literate (note that Dever 2005: 28 estimates less than 5% even in the much later Roman period), this would still leave at least a fair number of people who could have known how to read and write. Finally, we must note that scholars have often arguably interpreted the view of the book of Judges on the pre-monarchical period quite uncritically and thus assumed that it was in actuality so confused that nothing organized, including serious writing, could have been done during the period and that no serious institutions could have existed at the time.

The genocide ideology (see below for details) that the book of Joshua (and the books of Numbers and Deuteronomy) attests, suggests an early rather than a late date for the book. This is because later canonical books do not attest such an ideology. Moberly for example has pointed out that the focus of Josiah's reform is on the destruction of non-Yahwistic religious objects and any killing is marginal (Moberly 1999: 137). At the same time, for example, 1 Kings 9:20–21 suggests that the destruction of non-Israelites should have taken place during the time of the conquest, even though such an attitude no longer prevailed during the time of Solomon. In other words, the deuteronomic injunctions were seen to apply fairly literally during the time of the conquest but not any more in such a manner subsequent to the conquest.

All this said, there are also features that might suggest a Judahite emphasis in the book of Joshua, and point towards a later time of composition. First of all, the representatives of both Judah and Ephraim were the only faithful men who spied out the land of Canaan (Num. 13:26–33; 14:6–7, 30), and Caleb is arguably a prominent character in the book of Joshua. Also, even though Judah is listed after the Transjordanians in Joshua 13 – 19, it is nevertheless listed first among the Cisjordanian tribes. Moreover, Judah clearly has the biggest number of towns, which have even been divided into 'districts', and its border is described most comprehensively. Another tribe whose allotment is described comprehensively is Benjamin (with a detailed boundary description and a town list divided into two 'districts'), whereas one sees less detail in the description of the allotments the further one goes from Judah and Benjamin (cf. Hawk 1991: 111–113). In particular, there are practically no towns listed for Ephraim and Manasseh and their borders are described less carefully, even though there is every reason to think that they were the most dominant political force in the period of the judges. Moreover, some tribes lack a boundary description (e.g. Simeon and Dan), and the boundary and town lists are seemingly garbled for the Galilean tribes (Josh. 19:10–39). And the fact that a large number of towns are listed for Judah contrasts with the present state of archaeological knowledge from the hill country of Judea, according to which there was much less settlement there than in the northern hill country during Iron Age I, and, on the other hand, settlement in the south increased strongly from about the time of the beginning of kingship. And yet what makes the matter even more intriguing is that the large number of towns in Judah even contrasts with Joshua 15 itself, which records only Caleb's success at Hebron (Josh. 15:13–15), the giving of land by Caleb to his daughter (Josh. 15:16–19), and the failure of the Judahites to conquer Jerusalem (Josh. 15:63). This gives an impression that only a fairly small number of people were involved in the Judahite conquest, even though it is of course also possible that others that the author understood to be involved were simply not mentioned.

In this connection, it should also be kept in mind that there was a clear division between north and south after the time of Solomon (i.e. according to the canonical documents), and one might think that the book attests such a division (so e.g. Ottosson 1991: 27). However, the separation of Judah from the north is also attested geographically and climatically (see Finkelstein and Silberman 2001: 131–132, 153–158; Finkelstein 1988, incl. p. 326), so such a basic division may simply always have been the case in the land, at least during the Israelite period. It is not at all unusual that political divisions follow geographical and climatic considerations (cf. e.g. England vs Wales at present, where the Welsh territory pretty much starts where the hills/mountains start, and similarly also with England and Scotland). Therefore, while indicative, a possible north–south division in the book does not as such necessitate a late date of composition.

The book of Yashar which is mentioned in Joshua 10:12–14 is also mentioned in 2 Samuel 1:18, and possibly in 1 Kings 8:53 LXX (for further details, see 'Form and structure' for chapter 10). This might suggest that the book of Joshua was written at the same time as or later than the books of Samuel, even Kings. However, the book of Yashar could also have been a continuously updated collection of notable poetry, in a way resembling annals, or it could simply be that the mention of the book was added to the book of Joshua later on.

As I have already mentioned, literary material could be transmitted reliably over centuries in the Ancient Near East. At the same time, such material could also be updated and edited at least to some extent during its transmission (see also comments on the form and structure of Joshua 5 [vv. 2–9 in particular] where the Hebrew and Greek texts differ slightly, albeit not substantially; cf. also Millard 1982 for more details on scribal practices in the Ancient Near East). With this in mind, we can suggest here that the book may have been written in its basic form as early as in the pre-monarchical period before the fall of Shiloh in the eleventh century BC. The city lists and some of the boundary lists are likely to have been edited during the Judean monarchy. Some other redaction may also have taken place after the book was written in its basic form, even though it may be difficult to pinpoint anything specifically in many if not most cases, at least in the context and scope of this study, and even when the process as a whole might have been a fairly dynamic one. At the same time, we bear in mind that mainstream scholarship dates the book in essence to the Josianic period, and readers may consult works that interpret the book from that standpoint, in addition to considerations in academic scholarship in general that are set forth in the Form and structure sections of this commentary.

Having made these comments about the date of Joshua, as the book is heavily deuteronomic, an early date for Joshua would imply an early date for Deuteronomy. In other words, say, if we can date Joshua to the eleventh century BC, this will imply that Deuteronomy also originates from about that time, at the very least. This then would have important implications for Old Testament scholarship in general. Equally, as already implied, the converse would also be the case; that is, a late date for Deuteronomy would imply a late date for Joshua. Overall, as one might expect for a book on Joshua, we cannot devote much direct attention to the date of Deuteronomy in this commentary, except when some of the features in Deuteronomy are repeated in Joshua (e.g. the altar on Mount Ebal: Deut. 27; Josh. 8:30–35), in which case they are commented on as applicable from the perspective of Joshua in the commentary proper. However, I will also make some short comments here about one specific issue, the comparison of Deuteronomy with Hittite and Neo-Assyrian treaties (cf. also 'Form and structure' of chapter 24), as it for example impinges on the nature of Canaan and its vicinity at around the time the events in Joshua are said to have taken place and also to some extent on the validity of comparing Joshua with other contemporary Ancient Near Eastern literary compositions.

The main concern in comparing Deuteronomy with Ancient Near Eastern treaties is that known Hittite treaties date from the second millennium BC and the Neo-Assyrian ones from the first millennium. In relation to this, as one might even guess, there has been a fair bit of dispute about which the book of Deuteronomy resembles more closely, with those preferring an earlier date for Deuteronomy opting for the Hittite treaties, and those preferring a first-millennium date focusing on the Assyrian ones. In order to respond to this question, overall, one needs to keep in mind that there clearly already were links between peoples in the Ancient Near East in the second millennium. Such links are confirmed for example by the Amarna letters, and by cuneiform documents found in Israel from the second millennium BC (see Horowitz, Oshima and Sanders 2006), which indicate links with the Assyro-Babylonian realm. And Faust (2006: 63–64) mentions the international character of Late Bronze pottery in Israel (see also Faust 2006: 49–62 on the lack of imported pottery during the subsequent Iron Age and reasons for this state of affairs, much of which does not seem to be due to lack of trade as such). As already mentioned above, there is also evidence of considerable Hurrian migration towards the south, including Ugarit and Canaan, around the end of the Middle Bronze Age and during the Late Bronze Age (see van Soldt 2003 and Na'aman 1994a, 1994b; cf. a possible mention of them in Gen. 14:6; 36:20–21, 29–30; Deut. 2:12, 22 in the biblical tradition, but note the cautions/objections against such identification expressed in Wenham 1987: 311), and one may keep in mind here that the Hurrians bordered the Hittites (one may also note that the Hittite language includes a good number of Hurrian words). In addition, it is very possible that a number of the features of the Neo-Assyrian treaties may go back in time quite a bit, bearing in mind that Assyria itself already (clearly) existed in the second millennium BC and that we know from other contexts that Assyrian phraseology could be employed across centuries there (see Niehaus 1985, and 'Form and structure' for Josh. 1 below). Thus it should also be noted that the Hurrians who migrated towards the south in the second millennium also bordered the Assyrians (and the kingdom of Mitanni seems to have controlled Assyria during parts of the Late Bronze Age; see Kuhrt 1995: 293), and this would imply that if the Assyrian treaty form and/or language dates back to the second millennium, it could also, or might even be likely to, have been known in Canaan at that time (we should also note here the likely existence of Assyrians in Ugarit; see *UT*, text 1089:3, p. 232, which mentions a 'pitcher to the Assyrians' [*kd l aṯr{y}m*; Gordon, *UT*: 369 suggests that they were 'commercial colonists, as earlier in Cappadocia'; and note that the same text 1089 also seems to mention Egyptians among the various people listed, and, of course, we know that Egypt was strongly involved in Canaan during the Late Bronze Age]).

Even if one does not assume the possibility of Neo-Assyrian treaty forms and language being based on second-millennium Assyrian treaties, as Kitchen has pointed out, for example, similarities of phraseology with Neo-Assyrian treaties are not ubiquitous in Deuteronomy, including Deuteronomy 28 in particular, which is often quoted by supporters of the later dating of Deuteronomy (see Kitchen 2003b: 292–293 for a table, and 283–294 for a wider discussion). Moreover, according to Kitchen, some of the concepts in Deuteronomy 28 are already demonstrably attested in second-millennium material. And one might also ask where the Assyrian treaties got their phraseology from, as Kitchen points out (in terms of a wider Near Eastern setting). All things considered, it does not seem at all impossible that pretty much all the relevant material and concepts attested in Deuteronomy with regard to its treaty form might already have been available in the second millennium. Some updating of phraseology in the first millennium might also be a conceivable possibility, even if it seems that one does not necessarily need to think that this *must* have been the case as such. Also, of course, and coming back to Joshua, the international character of the Late Bronze Age with considerable people migrations from the north and overall Egyptian control of the area in particular then re-inforces the idea that Joshua too could easily have used conventions attested elsewhere in the Ancient Near East during the second millennium BC.

Having made comments on the date of Deuteronomy, with which Joshua is closely linked, we should keep in mind that Joshua also links back to Exodus–Numbers (also in essence to Genesis especially by way of tribal division, see also Josh. 24). Consequently, the date and historicity of Joshua are linked with the date and historicity of (Genesis–)Exodus–Numbers. That is, again, if Joshua is early and can be seen to be historically true at least to some extent, one may think that this might be the case for these earlier books as well, at least at first thought. Or, if Genesis–Exodus–Numbers is late, this would make it likely that the same pertains to Joshua, too. As should be obvious, I cannot cover most of the pertinent issues in the scope of this book. However, where material in Joshua is directly related to material in these earlier books, I will make comments as appropriate.

4. UNDERSTANDING THEOLOGY IN JOSHUA

4.1. Main outlines of the theology of Joshua in its ancient context

I have already alluded to some of the theological issues that relate to Joshua. In particular, I have suggested that the theology should be read from the perspective of the ancient world. Many of the accounts are formulated along the same lines as other ancient conquest accounts. Such accounts reflect the world view of the ancients, according to which the existence and intervention of the divine was a normal part of life. Thus, if for no other reason than this, focus on the divine in the book is natural. In this context, the Israelites believed that Yahweh had given them the land. They also believed that success in the conquest was directly related to Yahweh's intervention. In typical Ancient Near Eastern manner, Yahweh's favour is needed to achieve success (e.g. conquest of Ai, Josh. 7 – 8). Transgressing against Yahweh leads to failure (Josh. 7), and obedience to success (Josh. 8). Yahweh sometimes also intervenes directly, leading to success (e.g. Josh. 3 – 4; 10:10–11, 12–14).

The role of the ark is also important. The ark is the symbol and locus of God's presence and goes in front of the people (see Pitkänen 2004a: 38–52). This reflects the Ancient Near Eastern custom of carrying god images or standards as symbols and vehicles of divine presence before the troops (cf. Pitkänen 2004a: 35–36). Thus Israelite theology is here again strongly linked to the surrounding ancient world.

Another matter pointed out above is that the book has a strong all-Israelite perspective. All the tribes are considered, and it is felt to be important that they are all part of Israel, including the Transjordanians (Josh. 22:9–34). As indicated above, the Transjordanians go to war first (Josh. 4:11–13) and are even listed first in the tribal allotments (Josh. 14). All Israel is summoned twice at the end of the book to hear the words of Yahweh and Joshua (Josh. 23 – 24). Cities of refuge (Josh. 20) and Levitical towns (Josh. 21) are allotted throughout all the tribes.

In this connection, if one considers that neither the Transjordanians (Reuben, Gad and eastern Manasseh) nor the Levites received an inheritance in the land of Canaan (i.e. west of the Jordan), one might think that the Transjordanian allotments in Joshua 13 and the Levitical towns in Joshua 21 frame the allotments in the book of Joshua, and this may emphasize the fact that provisions were made for those who were not part of the tribal inheritance of the land of Canaan (as suggested by Koorevaar 1990: 289; cf. the emphasis in Polzin 1980 on the issue of 'insiders' and 'outsiders' in Israel in the book of Joshua as a whole). If so, this arrangement of the Transjordanians and the Levites then further stresses the all-Israelite character of the book of Joshua. And again, the involvement of the Transjordanians in the conquest (Josh. 1:12–18; 4:12; 22:1–6) and in the worship of Yahweh (Josh. 22:9–34) places still more importance on the all-Israelite nature of the book and on the unity of Israel.

Another important observation that was hinted at above is that the theology of Joshua is clearly deuteronomic. Besides similarities in expression and style, as I have already mentioned, Wenham (1971b) lists the following main features: holy war, the land and its distribution, the unity of Israel, the role of Joshua and the covenant and the law of Moses. I have already indicated that holy war is very much an Ancient Near Eastern concept. While Deuteronomy certainly looks at the land and its distribution, from a narrative standpoint the idea has its roots as far back as Exodus (e.g. Exod. 3:8) and even Genesis (e.g. Gen. 12:7), and in Numbers in particular (e.g. Num. 34 – 35). The unity of Israel is very pronounced in Deuteronomy, and yet it also clearly features as an important overall concept in Exodus–Numbers. The covenant and the law of Moses also have an Ancient Near Eastern foundation (cf. other known Ancient Near Eastern law codes, including the code of Hammurabi), plus their unique expression in Deuteronomy builds on what is there in Exodus–Numbers from a narrative point of view (of course, if the narrative order is not the same as the historical order of composition of the documents, the considerations will have a different slant). Thus, while Joshua is clearly deuteronomic in theology, these comments reinforce the fact that the theology of Deuteronomy itself is founded on the concepts of the ancient world and help us to bear in mind that the theology is also a continuation of what precedes, at least from a narrative standpoint.

Joshua also has a number of priestly features. The following could be mentioned here, even though it is also true that many of them in any case again have their foundations in the thinking of the ancient world: cultic purity (e.g. Josh. 7); the ark as the seat of Yahweh; the role of priests in crossing the Jordan (Josh. 3 – 4), in the ritual during the conquest of Jericho (Josh. 6), in the blessing at Ebal (Josh. 8:30–35), in the allotment of the land (Josh. 14:1–5), and in the Transjordanian incident (Josh. 22:9–34); the importance of the Tent of Meeting (Josh. 18:1); and the allotment of Levitical towns (Josh. 21). We should also note that the system of *herem* would have been advantageous for priests, as they would in many cases be recipients of items under it (see e.g. Num. 18:14; Josh. 6:19; see also Excursus 4 on *herem*). In general, it has of course been a human propensity to give to the divine, and the priesthood may profit at least to some extent if and when they are keepers of treasures, even when this in no way denies the fact of their devotion to the divine per se. From this perspective, the importance of *herem* in Joshua 6 – 7 and the spoils that would transfer to Yahweh and the priesthood can be well accounted for by a priestly view on matters. (One fairly recent parallel from European history would be Spanish churches receiving conquistador gold.) In a related manner, one may surmise that the emphasis on Jericho and Ai (see 'Form and structure' section of chapters 2, 6, 7 and 8) emphasizes the devotion of firstfruits to Yahweh. These then would honour Yahweh on the one hand, and go towards the upkeep of the priests on the other, making the narrative of chapters 2 and 6 – 8 further support the priestly application of Joshua.

In contrast to the comments made above, those following the Deuteronomistic History hypothesis would want to limit priestly features in Joshua to isolated and fragmentary instances. However, in the view of this author, this is rather unlikely in the light of the above. Priestly ideology permeates the book. And, to put it simply, even if any priestly features could be seen as isolated additions, from the perspective of the Deuter-onomistic History hypothesis, which thinks of Deuteronomy–Kings as a unified work, one could ask why such additions were made to Joshua, but not, or at least only to a much lesser degree, to Judges–Kings. It is better to consider that the priestly features in Joshua are specific for the book and are part of its distinctive theology and provenance.

In sum, the overall theology of Joshua in its ancient context centres on the land and its conquest and possession by Israel. This state of affairs is natural, as this is what the book is all about. However, cultic issues are also an important part of what is being depicted.

4.2. The role of historical references in Joshua and the purpose of the book

Historical references in the book of Joshua relate closely to the so-called aetiologies in the book. This term was used in particular by Martin Noth (see Noth 1953a). For Noth, aetiologies in the book of Joshua were basically stories about some state of affairs that explained how it came about. Such stories were later shaped into a form that related to Israel as a whole and to the conquest in Joshua (see Noth 1953a: 11–13, 26 for details, although Noth is not entirely clear here about his position). It is of relevance to note here that, overall, Noth thought that aetiologies were largely fictional. However, one can also think differently about the characteristics of aetiologies. For example, a later treatment of the subject can be found in Childs 1963a. Childs examines a number of occurrences of the formula *ad hayyom hazzeh* (until this day) across the Old Testament as a whole and notes that the formula is normally tied rather to the writer's personal witness than to explaining a phenomenon (see Childs 1963, esp. p. 292). Childs argues in particular that a literary examination of the cases where the formula is used reveals that it has usually been added to the story as a secondary element (Childs 1963: 289–290; for full details, see the whole article). In other words, as the formula 'until this day', which is supposed to be the distinguishing feature of an aetiology, is not part of the original tradition or story, it is not all that likely that the story arose as an aetiology (similarly, Westermann 1994: 51).

There is more to say on the topic of historical referents, many of which are distinguished by the expression *ad hayyom hazzeh*. It appears that the possible role of these referents suggested by the author of Joshua in the context of the book as a whole has not been brought out in full, even if Childs (1963) and van Dyk (1990) come close to a number of aspects of what I will indicate below in this respect. Let us then consider how certain features of the book of Joshua remind its readers about the past. On a related note, I first point out that memorials are used in most if not all countries today to commemorate past events (e.g. Trafalgar Square and the statue of Nelson in the UK, and the Lincoln Memorial and many others in the USA). Looking at Joshua, chapters 3 and 4 describe how twelve stones are lifted from the river and set up in Gilgal, with the intention that they are to remain there as a witness (de facto a memorial) for the coming generations (4:20–24, regardless of what one thinks about the somewhat confusing information in 4:9, which suggests that stones, or *the* stones, were set up in the river itself). In fact, the narrative states that the stones remain there 'to this day' (4:9). The rhetorical device of future children's questions also plays a part (see esp. Soggin 1960: 341–347; Pitkänen 2004a: 207–208). Next, we note that the Israelites are circumcised at Gibeath-haaraloth, translated as the 'hill of foreskins' (5:2–3). This suggests that the place name reminds its later hearers of this event, even if the story was created, or at least embellished, for the place name, as Alt and Noth suggested (see Childs 1963; Noort 1998: 94–95; Noth 1953a, *passim*), or vice versa. Similarly, Gilgal's name is said to have been based on the event of the circumcision and the accompanying removal of the shame (*ḥerpāh*) of Egypt from upon the Israelites (on the derivation of the name 'Gilgal', see comments on 5:9). Thus the name is intended to evoke memories of the conquest in the minds of its later hearers, according to the book of Joshua.

Another possible case is Joshua's curse on Jericho, recorded in Joshua 6:26. Usually what is noted in connection with this is that the curse is said to come true in 1 Kings 16:34 in the context of the Deuteronomistic History (see e.g. Noth 1953a: 41). However, one may also think here that the writer of Joshua might imagine that his readers, upon seeing or hearing about the state of Jericho (cf. Excursus 5 on issues relating to the archaeology of Jericho), will think about the events of the conquest.

In relation to Ai, the writer states that there is a heap of stones over the bodies of Achan and his family, and that it is there to this day (7:25). The heap of stones reminds those who see it of the story of Achan, which itself refers back to the conquest. The place name 'Valley of Achor' (7:26) is a further reminder of the events. Anyone hearing the story needs to be aware that there is a valley somewhere in the area and a heap of stones that confirms the story. Also, when Ai itself is destroyed, it is made a heap of ruins, 'until this day' from the perspective of the author (8:28). The smaller heap in front of the bigger one recalls the fate of the king of Ai (8:29).

In 8:30–35 an altar is built on Mount Ebal. The author does not indicate whether the altar still exists, but if some remains were left intact this would also serve as a reminder of the ceremony that took place there (cf. Excursus 7 on issues relating to the archaeology of Mount Ebal).

In Joshua 9, the Gibeonites are said to have been designated as water-drawers and woodcutters for the altar of Yahweh 'until this day'. Joshua 9 is often taken to be an aetiological story explaining the existence of Gibeonites, a different ethnic group, in the midst of the Israelites (see Noth 1953a: 53). Whether or not this is correct, we note for our present purposes that the existence of the Gibeonites is clearly tied to the time of the conquest (cf. 2 Sam. 21:2). From here, it is not difficult to think that the Gibeonites also serve as a reminder of the conquest, and, in fact, partially as a reminder that the Israelites failed to consult Yahweh at the time (9:14).

The 'scholarly' reference to another source, the 'Book of Yashar' (10:12–13), presumably seeks to lend credibility to the story of Joshua at Gibeon and the accompanying miracle (10:10–11). It is as if the writer is saying, 'I did not make this up; read the poem in the book of Yashar!' In the same narrative, the stones in front of the cave at Makkedah where the bodies of the kings lay are said to remain 'to this day' (10:27).

The tribal allotments (Josh. 13 – 19) do not at first seem relevant to our discussion. However, if they are in any way based on real borders of the tribes, which is at least by and large entirely possible (see the section of the commentary that deals with Josh. 13 – 21), it is unmistakable that the tribal borders are shown to have their basis in the conquest. In other words, any Israelite thinking about the tribal borders should, according to the book, realize that they were decreed by Yahweh through Joshua at the time of the conquest. The same goes for the cities of refuge (Josh. 20) and the Levitical towns (Josh. 21). We should also note a couple of smaller points here. The existence of the Jebusites in Jerusalem (15:63), the Canaanites in Gezer (16:10) and the Geshurites and Maacathites in Transjordan (13:13) 'until this day' is according to the author an unfortunate situation not originally intended, and thus these situations too are tied to the conquest. Even the story of the Danites and the existence of the city of Dan outside the intended area of the Danites serve as a reminder of the conquest (19:47; cf. Judg. 18:1, 27–30). Caleb's ownership of Hebron is also linked to the same event (14:13–14; cf. Childs 1963: 287).

The case of the Transjordanians in chapter 22 follows the tribal allotments. The book of Joshua (cf. Num. 32 and Deut. 3:12–20) emphasizes the importance of the Transjordanians and stresses that they are part of Israel. They are said to have received their land east of the Jordan on the basis of a command from Moses (Josh. 13:8), are portrayed as having taken part in the conquest (Josh. 1:12–18; 4:12; 13:8–32) and are then allowed to go back by Joshua in 22:1–9. The altar incident, which starts with a possible conflict, ends with a twist confirming the unity of Cisjordan and Transjordan. The altar is to serve as a reminder of this unity throughout the generations (22:21–29). Again, the unity here is tied to the events of the conquest, and in this case even to events before the conquest.

Finally, in chapter 24, the stone (and perhaps the accompanying book) in the sanctuary at Shechem (24:26–27) serves as a witness to the last words of Joshua to Israel, where he exhorts them to keep the covenant of Yahweh (24:2–24). Even if the formula 'until this day' or the like is not used, the text may well imply that the sanctuary or holy place is still in existence (cf. Gen. 35:4; Judg. 9:6). The graves of Joshua (24:30), Eleazar (24:33) and Joseph (24:32) may also serve as reminders of the conquest. One might compare these with the supposed tomb of Abraham in Hebron today, and other places attesting to biblical events, even though one inevitably encounters such issues as modern tourism when considering them.

Thus, at least based on a text-centred reading, even if the book of Joshua were a collection of aetiological stories, in their present arrangement they can be seen to serve as a powerful testimony about the Israelite conquest for its readers. It is tempting to suppose that the writer did this intentionally at a time when there were no footnotes and cross-references in the literature that was produced. The writer tied events to localities, not haphazardly but as a powerful testimony about the saving acts of Yahweh for the Israelites, and some of the features of the localities were to serve directly as memorials, in a manner similar to modern memorials. For the writer, reading and hearing about the events narrated was to remind the Israelites of who Yahweh was and what he had done for them, so that they would keep his laws and statutes. This is history writing with a purpose. It is ancient Israelite history writing intended to persuade its readers to follow the god Yahweh and to keep away from those who might compromise such loyalty. As Joshua 24:31 states, 'Israel served Yahweh during the time of Joshua and the time of the elders who lived after Joshua and who knew all the deeds that Yahweh had done for Israel.' The book of Joshua refers to living memory and implies that it itself is a substitute for this living memory for the ancient Israelites of a later generation. The book also refers to such witnesses as the stones at Gilgal, the hill of foreskins and the book of Yashar, which remain after living memory has been extinguished. In fact, the author arguably states, or at least tries to create an impression, that there is evidence available at the time of writing to support his claims (similarly van Dyk 1990: 22–23). The later generation is to know the great and veritable deeds of Yahweh so that they can follow his laws and statutes. Of course, the laws proper are mainly promulgated in the last four books of the entity we call the Pentateuch, that is, in the books of Exodus, Leviticus, Numbers and Deuteronomy. But they are alluded and referred to here with great rhetoric and persuasion. They are connected with the great injunction to Joshua at the beginning of the book, 'Do not let this Book of the Law depart from your mouth: meditate on it day and night, so that you may be careful to do everything written in it. Then you will be prosperous and successful' (Josh. 1:8). This means reading the law, meditating on it, and following it completely. Even negative lessons from failure on the part of the Israelites serve to reinforce this message (for 'subversion' in the narrative of Joshua to show that things were not as ideal as first might appear, see Hawk 1991).

Here it must be emphasized that the book of Joshua is history as written by a Yahwistic author (or authors), and it would seem logical that he did not act alone but was part of a group (or community) of Yahwists. The Yahwistic author of the book of Joshua argues strongly for an exclusive devotion to his god, including a threat and a mandate to kill anyone within Israelite society who does not subscribe to such a way of life and devotion.

However, we may ask the question of how much the ordinary Israelites actually did act in the ways the book wanted them to. In seeking an answer to this question, we may note here that recent studies have demonstrated that there is a gulf between the ideal promulgated by the canonical documents and actual Israelite practice (see e.g. Dever 2005 and the selection of works cited there, and the Bible itself of course gives many hints about a number of people worshipping other gods than Yahweh; but cf. also e.g. Faust 2006 for some common customs that seem to accord with canonical Yahwism). Also, in general, legal material in the Ancient Near East was often seen rather as theoretical and ideal than as something that would be put into practice in detail (see e.g. F. R. Kraus 1984, esp. pp. 111–123; cf. below). With this in mind, one could perhaps think that the rhetorical message of the book is somewhat exaggerated. However, for example, chapters 20 – 21 actually claim an implementation of injunctions about cities of refuge and Levitical towns, in response to their promulgation in books that precede Joshua in the canonical order (Num. 35; Deut. 19; cf. Lev. 25; Deut. 4:41–43), and, as another example, the existence of the ark and the Tent of Meeting in the book at least to some extent imply that they have been made and are being utilized in response to instructions in Exodus 25 – 40.

Also, we may think of Joshua as a product of a pro-Yahwistic party that wished to mould Israelite society in its preferred form, contrary to some other common religious practices prevalent in their day. In relation to this, recent anthropological studies have pointed out that heightened rhetoric often occurs precisely when a segment of society wants the whole of society to 'internalize' its views (cf. Taylor 2006). Thus the Yahwists, in an Ancient Near Eastern setting where the concept of a secular state would have been (at least practically) unthinkable, wanted to employ the strongest possible rhetoric, accompanied by a programme of very forceful measures, in order to get others to follow their vision of a perfect society based on a Yahwistic theocracy. Comparable examples can be seen in recent modern history (cf. e.g. the argumentation and polemics of the feminist movement in the latter part of the twentieth century and the so-called minimalists-versus-maximalists debate in biblical interpretation since the 1990s as examples of strong rhetoric; the Communist revolution in Russia in the early twentieth century and the subsequent moulding of Soviet society especially under Stalin might serve as one example where violence was also actually used). In this way, there is a tension between the rhetoric of the canonical documents and actual practice, with the rhetoric hoping to guide Israelite society towards a particular constitution. The ideals expressed in the documents thus need not necessarily be seen as true reflections of subsequent actual practice in Israel. As for the time depicted in Joshua, one cannot be sure how much rank and file Israelites really had internalized the (new) Yahwistic ideals. Certainly, the canonical documents make one doubt that the people had yet internalized them during the time of Moses (cf. e.g. Exod. 32 – 34 and the murmuring tradition of Numbers). In this respect, according to these documents, Israel was a small cohesive unit during the time of the exodus and wilderness wanderings, and at the time of the initial conquest. At such a time it would have been easier to hold the group together to maintain certain behavioural standards, especially under a charismatic leader such as Moses or Joshua. However, once the Israelites had dispersed to their various allocated areas, as the canonical documents indicate soon happened, the cohesiveness of the group and the ability of a charismatic leader to influence its thinking would diminish. Considering the difficulties described even during the time of Moses when the people were together, it would then be natural that any impulses from their surroundings might start to play an increasingly significant part in forming behavioural patterns and customs after the people had dispersed. As already hinted at, the book of Judges indeed states that as long as Joshua and the elders who had accompanied him were alive (one might imagine that the canonical documents imply that these elders relocated to various places in the land when the people dispersed), the Israelites followed Yahwistic patterns (Judg. 2:6–7; cf. Josh. 24:31). But then, according to Judges, the Israelites started to follow non-Yahwistic practices after the death of the representatives of the wilderness generation and a consequent dying-out of first-hand memories of Yahwism (Judg. 2:10–13). While the contrast between Joshua and Judges sounds stark, it could at the very least indicate the direction in which Israel was moving.

However, with the writing of Joshua, the Yahwists preserved those memories for a later generation (those who speak against the historicity of Joshua might argue that the Yahwists created those memories). These memories were in many ways garbed in an idealized and didactic version of history from their standpoint. Here it must be specifically noted that any possible exaggerations in the text, besides belonging to a common Ancient Near Eastern literary tradition, can also be seen as part of the rhetoric of the authors who wished to emphasize the power and might of Yahweh so that the Israelites would follow him. One should also understand that, whatever the case, the book contains only selected snapshots of any events at the time in the area, and should be looked at together with any other relevant sources that may be available, including archaeological evidence.

And, whenever it might have been that the Yahwists began their programme (see e.g. M. S. Smith 2002; Dever 2005 for some of the issues involved in academic discussion; cf. also Pitkänen 2004b, 2007), history has shown that their view eventually prevailed. In particular, their writings survived and took a pre-eminent position in Israelite society, going on to form a canonical collection that became a foundation for the identity of the Israelite community. And, with the birth of Christianity, these stories were then incorporated into the Christian canon, a set of foundational documents for Christian believers.

In this connection, the state of affairs in Joshua – that an exclusively Yahwistic society was only an ideal, which was never really attained – may at first seem disturbing to those hearing about the matter for the first time. However, it actually shows that even some three thousand years ago ideals were already ideals and reality might not have completely reflected them. For Christians, it reminds us that, except for the period of Christendom in the Middle Ages (which itself is seen as in many ways corrupted from its ideals by most of those who examine church history) and possibly, say, the present-day United States in some respects, they have mostly been a minority in a society whose values by and large lie elsewhere. Christians can also see the matter from the standpoint of Pauline concepts of flesh and spirit, that is, ideals versus reality, even as regards Christian life itself. Such a realization in fact makes one feel much freer, as one may think that ideals, even if desirable, are difficult if not impossible to achieve, and, broadly speaking, the human situation now is similar to the time of Joshua. There never really was a 'golden time'. And yet, just as the book of Joshua exhorted the Israelites to follow Yahweh wholeheartedly, in the same way Christians today are exhorted to follow God wholeheartedly in the context of the new covenant in Christ, even when perfection can never in reality be attained this side of heaven.

From the standpoint of this commentary, as most of Joshua deals with the ideals presented by the Yahwists, our comments will naturally mostly revolve around them. However, we will also make comments on actual realities where relevant and appropriate, and where possible.

4.3. Joshua and the New Testament

There are a few direct references to Joshua in the New Testament. According to the letter to the Hebrews, the walls of Jericho came down by faith, and Rahab was spared by faith (Heb. 11:30–31). Also, according to Hebrews, Joshua did not really bring Israel rest (Heb. 4:8). As part of Stephen's recapitulation of salvation history, Acts 7:45 mentions that the ark was brought to Canaan with Joshua when the Israelites dispossessed the local nations. Another mention of the conquest of the land in the context of salvation history takes place in Acts 13:19 as part of Paul's speech in Antioch in Pisidia.

The name 'Jesus' is the same as 'Joshua' in the Septuagint, the Greek translation of the Old Testament, and an apparent link is also made in Matthew 1:21. In this respect, it seems that the writer of Matthew, apparently reflecting the Jewish tradition of the first century, saw the Joshua of the Old Testament as a kind of saviour figure of the physical nation of

Israel during the time of the conquest (but note also that 'Jesus' was a common name around the time of the New Testament). The issue of naming serves to illustrate how the concepts of salvation, as with many other Old Testament concepts such as land and nationhood (these go wider than Joshua), were transformed from physical into spiritual in the New Testament. We could also perhaps say that as Joshua succeeded Moses, the comparison of Jesus with Moses could be brought in (e.g. Acts 3:22) for comparison.

Apart from this, the New Testament draws little from Joshua directly. However, and as the above examples demonstrate, the stories of Joshua were underlying knowledge for the authors of the New Testament. All things considered, the book of Joshua should be seen as foundational for the New Testament as part of the Old Testament canon as a whole. I have also already commented on the 'ideal' versus 'real' distinction in Joshua and its relevance for the New Testament. In the next section, we will concentrate on the topic of war and violence, an important issue in Joshua that has bearing on the interpretation of the New Testament, but is also tremendously relevant to the modern world at large.

5. MODERN APPROPRIATION OF THE BOOK OF JOSHUA

In this section, I will concentrate on issues that relate to how a book that describes a conquest can be applied to the modern world. We will first look at the problem of war, conquest and genocide in Joshua. We will then consider the use of Joshua for conquest and genocide. Finally, we will look at how the book of Joshua and themes that emerge from it relate to the current struggle between the Israelites and the Palestinians that is taking place on the same piece of land as that portrayed in Joshua. Much of the discussion consists of drawing parallels with the modern world based on looking at the book of Joshua as a conquest document in general terms. The reader is advised to keep in mind that the topics covered can be highly emotive to some, as they impinge on contemporary politics and on sensitive aspects of human self-understanding. However, equally, the following discussion shows that theology *is* political, and shirking from thorny, and even painful, considerations when they arise would mean leaving the theological (and, in general, academic) enterprise incomplete.

Certainly, there are some aspects of Joshua that can be applied to the modern world. I have already made some reference to these, especially in the preceding section on Joshua and the New Testament, and will be referring to them in various places in the commentary. However, the problem of war, conquest and genocide is so central to Joshua and so overarching in its scope in relation to the book that I will devote some considerable space to it below as part of this Introduction. Naturally, especially as the issues raised also impinge on contemporary politics, people will have differing views on them, but, in the view of this author, such issues need to be raised in thinking about the role of Christianity in the contemporary post or neocolonial globalized world at the beginning of the third millennium AD. The comments made below are ultimately intended as pointers for further thinking, and readers wishing to analyse today's global political and economic situation in depth are recommended to delve into the specialist literature of postcolonial studies in particular.

5.1. The problem of war, conquest and genocide in Joshua

I have already covered certain aspects of Joshua's treatment of war, conquest and genocide in this Introduction. In the following, I will also incorporate insights that can be drawn from anthropological and sociological characteristics of conquests and genocides, and from the recent history of the modern world. I will then compare these with Joshua and draw out relevant implications. I will dwell less on theories of just war and pacifism per se: any interested reader is advised to look at the extensive literature on these separately and compare them with Joshua and the presentation here (see e.g. http://www.justwartheory.com on the Internet for a number of excellent links, accessed 28 December 2009).

Let us start by looking at issues that relate to genocide. This topic can be a difficult one for many readers, and some may feel that the issues covered in the following may at least appear to provide a strong criticism of reading the biblical text from a canonical faith-based perspective. However, the comments made below are also intended as pointers for further thinking, and do not necessarily imply the rejection of a Christian view of the Bible, in the opinion of the present author, even if they can be profoundly challenging to such a view. In fact, it is precisely theologians who come from indigenous people groups that have had to endure conquest, dispossession and genocide who have in particular grappled with these questions and have already established a good body of very helpful thinking on the related matters, even if through much pain and agonizing (see e.g. Tinker 1993, 2004, 2008; Ateek 1989; Warrior 2000). Interestingly, for them, it seems that the issue for consideration is not so much a question of the existence of God, but about his 'nature and character' (Ateek 1989: 78; cf. Tinker 1993, 2004, 2008), a view with which this author concurs.

Moving past these preliminary remarks, let us start our treatment of genocide and its relevance to Joshua by defining what genocide is. As noted in Levene 2005a, it is not entirely easy to do this. However, we may note here that the United Nations defines genocide as follows (Article 2, from http://www.hrweb.org/legal/genocide.html, accessed 24 September 2007; note also that Levene comments interestingly that the UN definition of genocide was drafted so that its drafters themselves would not need to be called into account about their own wrongdoings [Levene 2005a: 36–42]; in other words, it should in the view of this writer be considered as an *indicative* but not a completely *definitive* document):

> In the present Convention, genocide means any of the following acts committed with intent to destroy, in whole or in part, a national, ethnic, racial or religious group, as such:
>
> (a) Killing members of the group;
> (b) Causing serious bodily or mental harm to members of the group;
> (c) Deliberately inflicting on the group conditions of life calculated to bring about its physical destruction in whole or in part;
> (d) Imposing measures intended to prevent births within the group;
> (e) Forcibly transferring children of the group to another group.

An important part of the definition, and in general of discussions that relate to genocide, is the concept of an ethnic group (the term 'race' has been much more contested recently, including whether such a designation is appropriate at all, and I will devote only minimal attention to racial issues here; as for issues of religious groups, at least a cursory definition of them would seem self-evident for most). As might again be anticipated, while the terms 'ethnicity', 'ethnic identity' and 'ethnic group or community' can be somewhat slippery and lack any agreed definition, we may note here the well-formulated, comprehensive and helpful definition given by John Hutchinson and Anthony Smith, in Hutchinson and Smith 1996: 5–6. According to Hutchinson and Smith, ethnic communities or ethnies habitually exhibit, albeit in varying degrees, the following six main features:

> 1. a common *proper name*, to identify and express the 'essence' of the community;
> 2. a myth of *common ancestry*, a myth rather than a fact, a myth that includes the idea of a common origin in time and place, and that gives an ethnie a sense of fictive kinship – what Horowitz terms a 'super-family';
> 3. shared *historical memories*, or, better, shared memories of a common past or pasts, including heroes, events and their commemoration;
> 4. one or more *elements of common culture*, which need not be specified but normally include religion, customs and language;

5. a *link* with a *homeland*, not necessarily its physical occupation by the *ethnie*, only its symbolic attachment to the ancestral land, as with diaspora peoples;

6. a *sense of solidarity* on the part of at least some sections of the ethnie's population.

It is of interest to note here that the ancient Israelites had a name, Israel, attached to themselves, believed that they were the descendants of a man called Abraham who lived hundreds of years earlier, most likely (or at the very least possibly) had recollections of the beginning of the world, of the patriarchs and of the exodus from Egypt, shared a common culture (e.g. avoidance of pigs [Lev. 11:7; Deut. 14:8], circumcision [Gen. 17; Josh. 5 etc.]; see Faust 2006 in particular on what can be detected archaeologically about Israelite ethnic markers), had a homeland of Canaan, at least ideologically defined, and attested a form of solidarity towards each other (cf. also the book of Judges and the portrayed getting-together of the tribes there). In other words, ancient Israel as it relates to the book of Joshua and the Israelite conquest tradition can be considered to have been an ethnic group. Finally, we note that ethnicity can be construed as either *primordial* or *instrumental*. The former basically refers to a static view of it (e.g. ethnicity by birth), and the latter sees ethnicity as always redefinable and changeable; for example through changing customs (see Hutchinson and Smith 1996: 8–10; this includes some other possible approaches). In reality, as with the case of Israel and its developing history (e.g. the changes that the Babylonian exile brought about), a mixture of primordialism and instrumentalism seems to be a useful approach.

Having defined what genocide is and having looked at some basic points that relate to ethnicity, let us next look in more detail at the ideology that drives the conquest in the book of Joshua. As we have noted, Joshua is heavily influenced by Deuteronomy, and it will therefore help to look at what Deuteronomy thinks about the land of Canaan and the conquest. According to Deuteronomy and Joshua, Canaan, the territory to be conquered, is seen as a land promised and allocated to the conquerors by their God, Yahweh. The land is to be cleared of its original inhabitants, and then an ideal Yahwistic society, as promulgated by Deuteronomy (and, where applicable, the rest of the Pentateuch) is to be established in the land. This thinking of course amounts to genocide in modern terms, as it involves a systematic destruction of indigenous peoples and people groups (cf. esp. items a–c on p. 76 above). Bearing in mind that Joshua is strongly deuteronomic, in the thinking of Deuteronomy it is true that justice is to be established in the land, including to the widow, orphan and alien, and much of the reasoning for this is that the Israelites have now been liberated from Egyptian (oppressive) slavery (see e.g. Deut. 24:21–22). Israel is also to be a positive example to the nations (see Deut. 4:6; 10:15; 15:6; 26:19; 28:1, 12). However, the justice prescribed assumes a Yahwistic framework; no existence is to be granted outside such a framework in the land of Canaan (cf. Deut. 13:12ff., which commands the killing of anyone who follows other gods, and in fact Israel itself is to be driven out from the land if it does not follow Yahweh). In this context, being an example to the nations also refers to the nations outside the land; the indigenous ones are to be destroyed. In other words, and as already said above, in the thinking of Deuteronomy, an ideal and pure society will be established in Canaan, to which others will look up. On the way to such a pure society, the land is to be emptied and cleared of anything that existed before. Manohar argues that, in anthropological terms, the Canaanites are so-called 'threatening Significant Others'. In this sense, the negative identity of the Canaanites also helps clarify the identity of the Israelites themselves (D. Manohar, personal communication, March 2008). Anything outside the land of Canaan is not the territory or possession of Israel, and Israel is ideally to deal with such peoples as a superior, but not necessarily to destroy them (see e.g. Deut. 20:10–15; 28:12). The following diagram illustrates the relationship of Israel to other nations both within and without the so-called promised land (see elsewhere in this commentary for variation in the portrayal of the borders of the promised land. Any such variation is not a main issue in the present context).

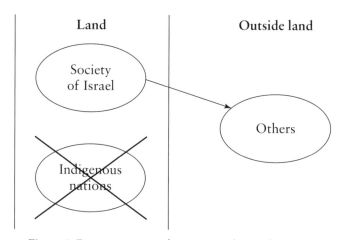

Figure 1: Deuteronomy and nations within and without

This then provides a framework for understanding why genocide is happening in Joshua. When we compare this with some modern examples, we see a number of similarities. For example, in Nazi thinking, there was to be a pure Aryan race, and this warranted destroying the Jews. However, economic arguments could also be advanced. For example, the Jews owned a lot of property, and this was eventually apportioned to the 'Aryans' as the 'final solution' progressed. This can be compared with the idea of the land of Canaan, certainly a big natural resource, being the sole possession and right of the Israelites. This then can be further compared, for example, with the conquest of North America and the doctrine of the white settlers (of European origin) owning the land from the east coast to the west (even if this doctrine of 'manifest destiny' was more a product of the nineteenth century, when the conquest was well under way). In the US, the natives were to be destroyed in this process, and a society of 'freedom and democracy' founded, again with a number of similarities to the thinking of the biblical conquest material (note that the taking of land alone cannot but constitute a systematic action of diminishing and destroying the livelihood and well-being of the natives, even if its full implications may not always have been understood by everyone – for example, the present author is not aware that taking land from the natives was ever discouraged or punished, if it actually ever was). We should also add that, if one compares the ideology of Joshua with modern genocide studies, seeing the Canaanites as a threat and the appeal to their sinfulness can be seen as part of a standard strategy of demonization and dehumanization of the opposition in comparable situations in order to rationalize acts of violence (see e.g. Levene 2005a and Stannard 1992 for more details on these issues and on the examples given. Levene 2005a also includes a systematic treatment of the characteristics of genocide). According to the biblical narrative, the Canaanites were already cursed at the time of Noah (Gen. 9:20–27), and if this tradition reaches back to a time before the conquest and settlement, as the text itself of course suggests, this would have given further legitimation for the ideology of the destruction of the Canaanites.

From a theological perspective, it is difficult to provide an answer to the problem of genocide in Joshua, in particular in the context of the New Testament. In relation to this, it is often said that the God of Joshua is in contradiction with the loving God of the New Testament. However, we may note that even in the New Testament there is judgment for those who do not believe. Therefore, we might say that there is less difference theologically between Joshua and the New Testament than there would at first seem. An interesting point is also that it is only mainly Joshua and Deuteronomy (also Exodus–Numbers) that advocate a genocide ideology. In contrast, most other books of the Old Testament, including the prophetic and wisdom books, the books of Kings and Chronicles and the Psalms, do not pick up on this theme, even if some of them have deuteronomic features. It is really only those books that tell of the conquest and settlement that appear to speak about the extermination of the Canaanites. This would be better accounted for if one thought that Deuteronomy and Joshua dated from an earlier time than late pre-exilic literature and the exilic and post-exilic literature, which rather pick on social justice and the like. For example, the focus of Josiah's reform is on the destruction of non-Yahwistic religious objects and any killing is marginal (as pointed out by Moberly 1999), and the book of Ezra advocates only separation from the peoples of the land (Ezra 9 – 10), not the extermination of those peoples. Also, in accordance with the conquest ideology of Numbers–Joshua, according to 1 Kings 9:20–21, a passage in a book that stems from the time of the exile (or even later in its final form), the destruction of non-Israelites should have taken place during the time of the conquest, but such an attitude no longer prevailed during the time of Solomon.

In further possible mitigation we may also add that, despite the strong rhetoric in the conquest tradition, not all Canaanites were actually killed. Even the book of Joshua hints that not everything was wiped out, as already inferred above, and Judges suggests considerable coexistence. It is also well known in particular that many even suggest that no actual conquest took place, and that Israel's origins were indigenous. The view taken here is that there may have been a partial conquest, and subsequently many Canaanites assimilated to Israel in a process that lasted for centuries (see Pitkänen 2004b). Thus Canaanites could and actually did become part of the Israelite community.

Yet another mitigating factor is that one might argue that the Israelites were simply following ancient thinking in their conquest of the land. In this respect, it was normal for ancient cultures to believe that a god could increase his or her territory, and such territory would obviously normally need to be taken by means of a conquest.

Nevertheless, problems remain. Above all, the rhetoric of Joshua suggests that any inhabitant of Canaan was to be killed, save for Rahab and her family owing to special circumstances. In other words, except for Rahab (and the Gibeonites, albeit through a ruse on their part), the book of Joshua does not seem to allow any chance of survival for the Canaanites. Therefore, it is completely understandable for one to question the justness and fairness of such a rhetoric and approach. In doing this, for example, one could easily suggest that the description of the Canaanites as wicked and degraded is part of the often-used tactic in war of demonizing and dehumanizing the opponent as a way of removing guilt and any other problems relating to the moral justification of the acts of violence. But, even if one were to plead the ignorance and lack of sophistication of the ancients, one might nevertheless ask what this tells about the ancient societies and how it may relate to any positive modern application of the book, including by faith communities, especially if one wishes to take a high view of Scripture. How is it possible for such communities and their individual members to fully admit that 'their own side' has engaged in gross violence and in genocidal activities (if only rhetorical) when they would really like to see their faith and its heritage from a positive, even reverential perspective as a foundational part of their identity?

One possible solution could be to say that this was part of the unique, non-repeatable, salvation-historical plan of God. In relation to this, we can think of the event of Noah's flood (Gen. 6 – 8), in which God destroyed the whole earth because of human wickedness but had grace on Noah and his family and saved them from the destruction to continue the human race. Subsequently, God promised never again to destroy every living creature (Gen. 8:21–22). Looking at it from a Christian canonical standpoint, the destruction of the Canaanites can then be seen as a localized judgment on mankind in order to further God's plan of salvation, culminating in Christ. On this basis, the judgment on the Canaanites takes place not because they are more wicked than others, or because the Israelites were better than they were (cf. Deut. 9, including v. 6), but because the Canaanites happen to be the ones who have to give way in order to further God's plan (this is however itself a 'divine genocide' by virtue of the previous discussion). In fact, in the New Testament, the apostle Paul also seems to confirm that the destruction of the Canaanites was part of God's plan. This comes out as a by-product of Romans 9, where Paul speaks about the role of Israel from the perspective of the Christ event. I quote verses 6–24 in full here (cf. also God's answer to Job in Job 38 – 41 that emphasizes his sovereignty):

(6) It is not as though God's word had failed. For not all who are descended from Israel are Israel. (7) Nor because they are his descendants are they all Abraham's children. On the contrary, 'It is through Isaac that your offspring will be reckoned.' (8) In other words, it is not the natural children who are God's children, but it is the children of the promise who are regarded as Abraham's offspring. (9) For this was how the promise was stated: 'At the appointed time I will return, and Sarah will have a son.' (10) Not only that, but Rebekah's children had one and the same father, our father Isaac. (11) Yet, before the twins were born or had done anything good or bad – in order that God's purpose in election might stand: (12) not by works but by him who calls – she was told, 'The older will serve the younger.' (13) Just as it is written: 'Jacob I loved, but Esau I hated.' (14) What then shall we say? Is God unjust? Not at all! (15) For he says to Moses,

'I will have mercy on whom I have mercy,
and I will have compassion on whom I have compassion.'

It does not, therefore, depend on man's desire or effort, but on God's mercy. (17) For the Scripture says to Pharaoh: 'I raised you up for this very purpose, that I might display my power in you and that my name might be proclaimed in all the earth.' (18) Therefore God has mercy on whom he wants to have mercy, and he hardens whom he wants to harden. (19) One of you will say to me: 'Then why does God still blame us? For who resists his will?' (20) But who are you, O man, to talk back to God? 'Shall what is formed say to him who formed it, "Why did you

> make me like this?"' (21) Does not the potter have the right
> to make out of the same lump of clay some pottery for noble
> purposes and some for common use? (22) What if God, choosing
> to show his wrath and make his power known, bore with great
> patience the objects of his wrath – prepared for destruction? (23)
> What if he did this to make the riches of his glory known to the
> objects of his mercy, whom he prepared in advance for glory –
> (24) even us, whom he also called, not only from the Jews but
> also from the Gentiles? (Rom. 9:6–24 [NIV])

Also, in general, it is easy to see the New Testament concept of salvation
of some and so-called damnation of others as a sort of continuation of
this theme. In this light, if one thinks of matters from the standpoint
of systematic theology, a Reformed theology based on double predestin-
ation fits matters perfectly. And yet, at least arguably, such Reformed
theology, while perfectly logical as such, does not fully answer the problem
of theodicy, or justification of God's actions, for many modern reflective
human beings. In particular, one may ask why an omnipotent and omnis-
cient God should create in the first place and then have a fall, and then
redemption, with all the accompanying human suffering in the process.
In other words, there is a tension in Joshua which cannot but remain
unresolved for many if we want to believe in the goodness of God based
on a human understanding of the matter (cf. Pitkänen 2007). Perhaps this
is part of the 'mystery' of faith that the apostle Paul (or a Pauline author,
depending on one's views about the authorship of the Pauline letters)
refers to (e.g. Eph. 6:19).

Having looked at genocide and Joshua, let me next make some quick
comments on the related problem of the just war. I start by noting that,
by and large, all societal actions take place within a societal framework
with certain rules set up by a society, and are arbitrated and enforced by
that society using the means of power available to it. The power held
by the society keeps the society together; if not, it will disintegrate or
change, as might for example happen in cases of revolution. However,
when dealing with inter-societal actions, two societies with differing
cultures and rules may face each other with a dispute. In such cases there
is often no-one to arbitrate between the two societies, and neither are
there usually agreed rules (the United Nations exists for modern times but
its arbitration is often not heeded; e.g. in the recent war in Iraq). If no
agreement can be reached, the two parties may fight to decide the matter.
This may be a war of words, in economic terms, or, ultimately, by military
means. The end result may be one party subjugating the other, or the two
coming to an agreement after some fighting, even if there has been no
subjugation (or at least no full subjugation). The question then is, who is
right and how can that be decided? Can common rules be devised that are
agreeable to all? In response, for example, some people may believe that

a religion can provide the rules, but, even if that is the case, people may disagree with the interpretation of the religion in question. In relation to religion, some may appeal to divine revelation in starting a war, but others may disagree and doubt the existence of such revelation, or its interpretation in that particular case. Sadly, it is often power that is the final arbiter, and we may say that only power can ultimately carry out justice, but not all exercise of power is exercise of justice.

In the case of ancient Israel, the Israelites would view war in the light of Yahweh's promise to give them the land of Canaan and their existence in that land. The rules given by Yahweh would ideally guide their actions. Yahweh would also provide rules for conducting the war, for example in the case of *herem* in destroying the natives or in offering peace to distant towns (Deut. 20). Yahweh's revelation would also ideally be listened to when thinking about going to war (e.g. Josh. 8:1). For the Christian, the New Testament has brought forward a new set of rules. Much more peaceful action is involved. However, while there are pacifists who believe that war is never justified, most people, including Christians, would agree that war is sometimes necessary to defend what is right and just. The whole revelation of the Bible has to be taken into account in such cases as part of the relevant decision-making process. Of course, there are and will be disagreements about interpretation. There are also those who may not consider a Christian framework as the basis for interpretation. Such people may proceed on the basis of the ethical framework of some other religion or of a completely secular outlook. And still others, as so often in history, either ignore any ethical framework that is generally maintained, or follow one that, for example, allows appropriation to themselves and to their society, either in full or in part, of something that others have previously kept, such as land adjacent to their country, or even further afield.

5.2. Joshua and the justification for conquest and genocide

As was pointed out in the previous section, the biblical tradition itself indicates that the injunction to destroy the original inhabitants applied only to the original Israelite conquest. However, it nevertheless appears that Joshua and the Israelite conquest tradition have sometimes been involved in justifying war and genocide later on. A seemingly clear example of this is the New England Puritans, who believed that North America constituted a promised land for them and that they could use similar methods to those described in Joshua and the Israelite conquest tradition to take hold of it. One particularly interesting belief of some of the Puritans was that they interpreted the lack of resistance of Native Americans to European diseases as an act of God in favour of the settlers (see Stannard 1992: 238). It is also true that there were missionary efforts towards the Native Americans, but ultimately hostility prevailed (see Tichi

1971: 143–155 and Jalalzai 2004; see also the criticisms of the missionary efforts by Tinker 1993). And one might ask whether the Bible was ultimately the cause of or one excuse for genocidal thinking by the settlers. Whatever one may think of all this, most readers in the twenty-first century would be against the application of Joshua to promote genocide.

However, there are some less obvious overtones that one would do well to look into in this context. As I have already intimated in this Introduction, conquests (and, as it seems, genocides) are a universal part of human history from early on. While it has not hitherto been possible to predict genocides so as to prevent them (see e.g. Levene 2005a), one can argue that much of the human problem as regards violence, conquest and genocide results from egocentrism and ethnocentrism. Without denying the importance of the former, certainly, we know from studies of ethnicity that ethnic groups often consider themselves better than others (by implication at the very least; cf. e.g. A. D. Smith 2003; Levene 2005b: 15–16; see also Poo 2005 in relation to the ancient context). When ethnocentrism leads to placing one's own group in a normative position and at the same time denying value to others, we are arguably on a dangerous path that may lead to violence, even to conquest and genocide. As we see in Deuteronomy and Joshua, this is precisely what is happening in the portrayed Israelite conquest, any Christian salvation-historical considerations notwithstanding. A Yahwistic vision of a beautifully arranged and just society is to be achieved through violence and extermination of anything that does not fit in its purview (and through expropriating the lands and property of the other). As I have noted above, interestingly, a rhetoric of justice and righteousness, and acting as an example to other nations not directly within the reach of the new society, is included as part of the self-understanding of the documents.

If we think of modern societies, we may first note that the West has held superior military and economic power in the world for the past 500 years: without a doubt, other localized empires existed before the West, and it may be that the West will be succeeded by another dominant force at some point in the future, maybe China, and the following comments should be taken in that light; in other words, the West is, as well as a real example, in a number of ways also an *illustrative* example owing to its recent dominance and the global scope of its influence. In this regard, it also has to be kept in mind that other local powers may behave in corresponding ways towards those under their influence, even when under an umbrella of a greater power. Underlying all this is the fact that these 500 years of Western domination have marked an (at the very least arguably) unparalleled history of conquest, subjugation and genocide never before seen in the world in its scope and scale (see e.g. Levene 2005b; Stannard 1992; Prior 1997; Brett 2008; cf. Josephy 1995). The Western colonial powers, while certainly not the only ones committing such actions in world history, in many ways erased Native Americans and Australians from history and redrew the world map according to their own interests and understanding of the world. As pointed out time and again by colonial studies, these powers placed their own interests and the welfare of their own society above those of others. They were able to advance their agenda (this agenda was not always explicit, but with similar results to having been explicit) through superior power, itself undoubtedly resulting from their advanced state of technology, reinforced by the development of science and the Industrial Revolution in the modern era. In other words, the 'glory' of Western 'advancement' and 'civilization' brought genocide in its train. At the same time, these powers spoke much about spreading 'civilization' to the world as part of 'legitimizing' their activities.

Even today, the conquest continues. While the era of explicit colonialism is now over, much of the current world map is a result of colonialism. The nation states that formed around the world are at the very least arguably a product of Western ideas. In the two-thirds world in particular, including in Africa and Latin America, such nation states incorporate a number of indigenous groups, largely owing to the way the national borders formed, which itself was mostly a result of colonialism. Such states claim jurisdiction over these indigenous peoples (which are often divided by the national borders), and until now there seems to have been little real redress if the indigenous peoples did not want to cede sovereignty over their traditional lands. The UN Declaration on the Rights of Indigenous Peoples in 2007 (approved by a majority vote of 144 states in favour, 4 votes against [Australia, Canada, New Zealand and the United States] and 11 abstentions [Azerbaijan, Bangladesh, Bhutan, Burundi, Colombia, Georgia, Kenya, Nigeria, the Russian Federation, Samoa and Ukraine]) is a step towards recognizing the rights of these peoples, but it is not a binding resolution and is likely to take many years to implement, at the very least. Also, it has to be emphasized that the declaration is based on the system of nation states, ultimately a Western concept. The UN itself is a product of the Second World War, again an organization profoundly influenced by the West, and, for example, no decisions can ultimately be made today in the Security Council without the agreement of all five permanent members, of which three are explicitly Western nations, and neither of the remaining two is from Africa or Latin America.

I also add that the current world economic system has been profoundly shaped by the West and Western ideologies, including Western economic theory. Capitalism itself presumes private ownership, and much of this is concentrated in the West; and Western companies have been using raw materials and labour markets in the two-thirds world to their advantage, using their collective bargaining mechanisms for best possible prices, even when this means virtual economic slavery for at least some in the two-thirds world. The great powers have also been able to implement changes of government when it has suited their political and economic interests, whether explicitly, as with an invasion (cf. the recent invasion of Iraq by the United States; note also the different value ascribed to the lives of American and Iraqi soldiers), or implicitly (e.g. supporting guerrillas in South America in the past). Even at the time of writing, countries that do not wish to follow rules set by the great powers will be subject to diplomatic and economic sanctions, perhaps even to a threat of war, in order to force them to comply. Such sanctions may cause the death of millions of innocent people, as for example happened in Iraq in the 1990s. The rise of the Far East and the recent global economic crisis have caused the overall balances of power to be in a slight flux at least in economic terms, and time will tell how things will develop, and yet the Far East itself is arguably developing in broadly Western ways, competing with the West on largely Western terms.

Also the current world legal system is in essence a Western creation. The implication of this is that disputes are often resolved on the basis of Western ways of thinking. Plus there are the often less considered implications of the fact that the English language is the lingua franca of the contemporary world. As language always comes together with a culture, this means that the Anglo-Saxon way of thinking is spreading throughout the globe as people and people groups rush to learn English as a second language.

How then should we react to this, and, in particular, in which way should humankind move in the future? In the view of this writer (cf. Tinker 2004), Western civilization is carrying potential seeds of destruction within itself. Setting aside the possibility of a future nuclear conflict, as we all know, the world currently seems to be experiencing climate change, which may ultimately be the result of technological development and the subjugation of nature, and with the current growth rates of both consumption and world population (even if there are signs that world population growth may now be abating), one might ask whether it will be possible to sustain us all on the planet.

In this situation, in the view of this author, humankind should throw away its tendency to egocentrism and ethnocentrism. The implicit and explicit models of conquest, as attested by much of human history, most notably that of the West in the past half-millennium, should be jettisoned in favour of much more inclusive ideas of human life and development. We must understand the past in order to see more clearly where we are at present, and how we can best move into the future. In particular, in the view of this author, the negative aspects of the history of today's ruling powers, including the Anglo-Saxon (which incorporates American) and European peoples in particular, need to be acknowledged collectively. Also, such acknowledgment should take place with considerations of appropriate restoration to the victims in consultation with the victims who (or whose descendants) in many cases still exist in today's world (cf. Tinker 2008; cf. also e.g. the Truth and Reconciliation Commission in South Africa after the fall of apartheid). We must overcome a 'collective amnesia' about the past of the West (cf. Tinker 2008), moving the discussion of conquests by today's ruling powers from the purview of the few in academia (where it is generally well known and analysed) to the consciousness of the public. Undoubtedly, Western technology and culture have much to offer the world in the future, but the West needs to be freed from any of its trappings of power and assumptions of superiority in favour of a more inclusive view of the world (such a comment would also apply to any other group that might wish to claim dominance in the future). In this respect, for example, Tinker's suggestions for reclaiming the concepts of what it means to be a community and communities for the benefit of the whole rather than for individual gain are very stimulating (Tinker 2004, 2008). Also, the world needs to be liberated from searching for solutions in Western terms alone and, in general, it must reorient itself towards giving equal value to those who do not belong to one's particular group or culture. In certain aspects, the concept of multiculturalism in a number of contemporary societies is a step in the right direction as it allows for, and even celebrates, difference (such difference should include the freedom to choose one's religion), and the UN Declaration on the Rights of Indigenous Peoples mentioned above also seems helpful for achieving a better world, even granted its limitations.

The world institutions will also need reforming to reflect a more inclusive setting. Perhaps a global, representative government would also help. In this, one would for example have to be sure that an overall organization allowed for the rights of the smaller constituents based on the desires of such constituents. It is of course true that the United Nations does serve in this way in a number of respects and does a fair bit of very useful work; however, and as already implied above, for example, it has generally been powerless to act when some of its powerful members have decided to act on their own in respect of wars. Overall, ultimately, as we see for example in Deuteronomy and Joshua, ideology guides one's thinking, so it would be important that the global community make it a priority to work towards formulating and propagating a suitable ideology (and ethic) that respects the rights of everyone, both individually and collectively. As power is often the final arbiter, and one cannot in many cases prevent the powerful from breaking even agreed and respected ethical codes (if they exist), it is unlikely that the human community can ever achieve even close to perfect results, but it is worth a try.

As for Christians, they must also realize that the advancement of Christianity often took place under the aegis of colonialism, contributing to the destruction of indigenous cultures and communities (relevant examples are given by Tinker 1993; cf. Josephy 1995, incl. p. 283). In essence, Christianity was often equated with thinking and behaving like a Westerner (see e.g. Tinker 1993). And Christians in expanding societies hardly ever voiced concern about the colonial genocidal advance, choosing instead (even if only tacitly and maybe inadvertently) to enjoy the spoils of such advances, and members of these societies were enriched by taking the lands of the indigenes or by enslaving them. Even today, for example, Christians in Northern America and Australia still enjoy the use of the land of the natives that was forcibly taken away from them, with the indigenous communities still living in traumatic and reduced circumstances (cf. Tinker 2004, incl. p. 5 as regards the US). In this regard, the situation has not essentially changed thus far. As part of the situation, the dominant societies still carry the legacy of the mindset of the conquest, and this would seem to explain why the essentials of the status quo that was achieved by conquest are maintained. In this vein, for example, and as experience has shown, any land claims by indigenes are very hard to achieve even when these might sometimes be discussed, and even on occasions agreed in principle. (It may be kept in mind here, too, that history shows that rarely has any nation voluntarily relinquished territory that it has conquered by war from another nation, and this seems to reflect a recurring human mindset.) All this said, Christians, and for that matter people in general, still have the option of trying to contribute towards alleviating and changing these situations around the world.

With regard to theology, Christians involved in mission should certainly contextualize Christianity to the target cultures, preferably in collaboration with such cultures and with the help of indigenous thinking (it is true that modern missionary theory has moved in this direction). Indeed, it is also true that Christianity always challenges cultures and transforms them, but this must be by way of voluntary transformation, not by imposition. While it seems very likely that Christianity as a whole cannot and will not return to its days of being an illegal religion in the Roman empire (this is not to deny that there are still societies today where Christians are persecuted just for being Christian), Christians can try to jettison ideas of conquest in favour of a peaceful transformation of the world, including when they may be in top positions in the current world hierarchy. Of course, the use of power in world affairs is inevitable, but let it be for the cause of justice that truly serves the global community, and not for example just one interest group within it. In relation to this, as long as we expand the exclusive ideals that Deuteronomy and Joshua hold into an inclusive setting, we can arguably be on the right track. Considering that the book of Joshua advocates a vision in which an important part of achieving an ideal society was to destroy anyone or anything not compatible with its central tenet of Yahwism, and bearing in mind that many of the known genocides that have taken place across the globe have stemmed from the desire of one people group to take forceful measures against another group that may be different from it and may have different ideals, the book of Joshua reminds us of our common humanity and our propensity as humans to exclusivity and to pushing through our views and visions forcefully against those who may not be compatible with them (similarly Mansford 2006).

In fact, such a contemporary reading of Deuteronomy and Joshua is at the very least arguably in line with the thinking of the New Testament documents. While Jesus' programme of reversal of fortunes (e.g. Luke 1:50–53; 4:16–19) could still in many ways be seen as an ethnocentric one, Paul's vision certainly encompasses a Christianity that incorporates peoples from all nations and languages within it (e.g. the letter to the Ephesians, incl. 3:6). In the view of this author, this is the vision that Christianity should strive towards. In this connection, even if the New Testament may make a distinction between various religious allegiances, it does not, at least in sum, seem to advocate denying justice and dignity in life based on such distinctions (the book of Revelation may present some problems with regard to violence, but, and also considering the genre of the writing, does not in the view of this author at least ultimately negate the points made above). In other words, Christians should demonstrate respect and solidarity towards others as they are (cf. Brett 2008: 204). Bearing in mind that humans, whether individually or collectively, can easily have a propensity to force themselves on others, the Christian church should, as Mark Brett has aptly expressed it, 'act as leaven' in the world by 'clasping hands against the mutating arrogances of power' (Brett 2008: 204; see the work as a whole for further related biblical insights).

5.3. Joshua, Israel and the Palestinians

It might at first seem odd to some that a section on the contemporary Israelis and Palestinians should be included in a commentary on Joshua. However, a closer look at the dynamics of the current situation reveals a number of clear similarities with the ancient book of Joshua and my preceding discussions, even if there may be some differences, too. In addition to comments made, readers are invited to make their own connections. However, the author would like to ask readers to think of three issues in particular that have sprung from my considerations of Joshua, that is, how ideology can drive territorial appropriation, the basis from which the concept of justice and fairness should be evaluated, and the role of power in all this. The discussion particularly draws on the work of two modern Israeli historians, Avi Shlaim and Ilan Pappe, and also makes some special reference to comments made by an Israeli Palestinian Christian, Naim Ateek.

As is known, modern Zionism arose at the end of the nineteenth century (see e.g. Shlaim 2000: 1–27; Pappe 2004: 35–56). In its early stages primarily a secular movement, its ideal was to reclaim a homeland for the Israelites (or, rather, Jews) who had been dispersed from the land of Palestine for millennia. Soon a movement was born which encouraged many Jews to emigrate to Palestine. This included buying land from the Palestinians through legitimate transactions (see below on the extent of this), and little by little the Jewish presence grew stronger. Palestine itself had been a province (or three sub-provinces; see Pappe 2004: 14) of the Ottomans in the nineteenth century, and was then taken over by the British in 1917–1919 (see Pappe 2004: 62–72). The Zionists managed to obtain support from Britain in the form of the Balfour Declaration (basically a letter from the then Foreign Secretary Arthur J. Balfour to Lord Rothschild on 2 November 1917), according to which (quoted in Shlaim 2000: 7; note Ateek's [1989: 211] comment that 'Britain was promising a country that was not its own to a people whose country was not theirs. It is as ridiculous as if I were to promise to give another person your home'):

> His Majesty's Government view with favour the establishment in Palestine of a national home for the Jewish people, and will use their best endeavours to facilitate the achievement of this object, it being clearly understood that nothing shall be done which may prejudice the civil and religious rights of existing non-Jewish communities of Palestine, or the rights and political status enjoyed by the Jews in any other country.

This promise by and large ensured a favourable attitude towards the aspirations of the new Jewish immigrants to the area. The war of independence between 1947 and 1949 resulted in the establishment of the state of Israel. The United Nations made a proposal for the partition of Palestine in 1947 (the plan was rejected by the Arabs at large as 'absurd, impracticable and unjust'; see Shlaim 2000: 27), which basically divided the land of Palestine into two roughly equal portions for Jews and Palestinians respectively, with Jerusalem designated as an internationally administered area (see Pappe 2004: 123–129, and the map from Pappe 2004: 127, reproduced in figure 2). In this connection, it should be kept in mind that while the 1947 UN partition plan granted the Jews 57% of the land, they had obtained less than 7% of the total ownership of Palestine by then (as pointed out by Prior 1997).

However, in the course of the fighting, the Jews prevailed and established independence. The division of the area resulted in the borders of the state of Israel that pretty much exist today, with a much larger area for the Jews and a smaller area for the indigenous Palestinians than envisaged in the UN partition plan (see Pappe 2004: 129–141, and the map from Pappe 2004: 140, reproduced in figure 3).

Also in the course of the fighting, whether unintentionally or systematically, some three-quarters of a million Palestinians were forced to flee, with a number of Palestinians massacred and their villages destroyed and land taken from them in the area occupied by Israel (see Pappe 2004: 129–141; Shlaim 2000: 31 claims that the relevant Plan D by the Israelis 'was not a political blueprint for the expulsion of Palestine's Arabs: it was a military plan with military and territorial objectives', however also commenting

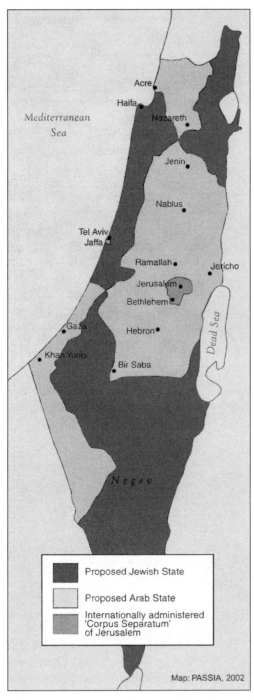

Figure 2: The UNGA partition plan, 1947 (from Pappe 2004: 127)

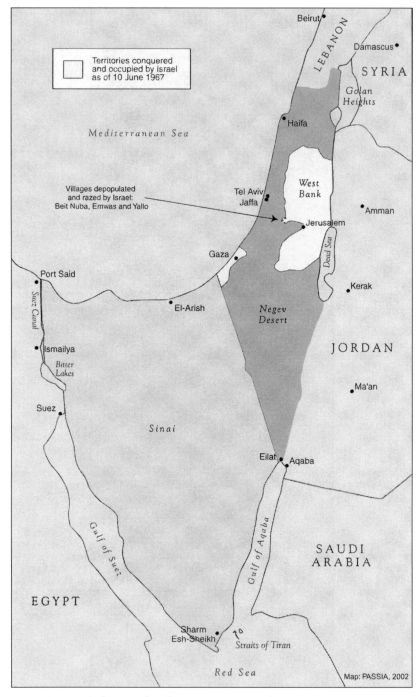

Figure 3: Palestine after the June 1967 War (from Pappe 2004: 140)

that by 'ordering the capture of Arab cities and the destruction of villages, it both permitted and justified the forcible expulsion of Arab civilians'). Accordingly, it is estimated that some 700,000 Palestinian Arabs were displaced in the war (see e.g. Prior 1997: 137), many of whom (or whose descendants) still hope to return. Thus, what the Israelis call the 'War of Independence', the Palestinians designate as the Nakbah, the 'catastrophe'. It should however be noted that, in November 1947, the Israelis made a secret pact with King Abdullah of Jordan that allowed Jordan to annex the West Bank to the kingdom of Jordan, which also then took place (see Shlaim 2000: 29–30, 31–47). This secret pact between Israel and Jordan in many ways helped to seal the fate of Palestinian national aspirations and the UN plan for an independent Palestinian state. As Shlaim notes, 'the Palestinians were left out in the cold' (Shlaim 2000: 47). Gaza was administered by the Egyptians as a result of the war (see Shlaim 2000: 42).

The next important events in regard to territory came in the 1960s. After some escalation with Syria in particular in the mid-1960s, and in connection with Palestinian guerilla attacks against Israel, Egypt, then allied with Syria by a defence pact, closed the Straights of Tiran in east Sinai to Israeli shipping on 22 May 1967 (see Shlaim 2000: 237). The result was the so-called Six-Day War, in which Israel, in many ways also fortuitously, captured Gaza, Sinai, the West Bank and the Golan Heights. Israel had asked Jordan to stay out of the hostilities, but Jordan did not heed the warning and thus lost the West Bank (see Shlaim 2000: 244; as for the Golan Heights, Shlaim [247–249] notes how the Israelites captured them in the latter stages of the war, when Syria had requested a ceasefire, more in order to gain farmland than for security purposes).

Since the Six-Day War, Israeli policy has been to build settlements in the occupied territories, on the West Bank in particular. While not all Israelis or Israeli parties or governments have subscribed to the idea of a 'Greater Israel' involving territory up to the Jordan River, by and large Israel has not stopped building settlements in the occupied territories, at great expense to the Palestinians in particular (see Shlaim 2000: 250ff., *passim*; see also the comments on Gaza below). It is true that peace was made with Egypt in 1979, with a withdrawal from Sinai (see Shlaim 2000: 352–383). Also, there was the peace movement of the 1990s under the premiership of Rabin, which held much promise for the Palestinians and resulted in some agreements in principle on Palestinian autonomy, and even statehood, and a peace treaty with Jordan in 1994 (see Shlaim 2000: 502–545). However, these agreements have not yet in practice stopped Israeli settlement and military rule and associated repression in the occupied territories, and the assassination of Rabin on 4 November 1995 resulted in the end of the peace process, which proved to have been very dependent on him (see Shlaim 2000: 546–563). The policies of the government of Netanyahu in the late 1990s in particular contributed to, if not directly caused, the resurgence of much bad blood between Israel and the Arabs, of course including the

Palestinians (see Shlaim 2000: 564–609). The second Intifada of 2000 (the first having taken place in 1987) lasted till about 2005 (some consider it to be still continuing in some ways), and the subsequent recent problems between the Fatah and Hamas parties have added to the misery of Israeli military and economic retaliation. Recently, even though having withdrawn from and taken out the always ultimately small number of settlements in Gaza, Israel has sealed off Gaza in retaliation against Palestinian resistance, and attacked it in late 2008 (ostensibly owing to rockets being fired by Hamas before the attack), killing more than 1,000 Palestinians. The recent building of walls around the West Bank should also be mentioned as a policy that has at least to some extent resulted in the de facto cutting-off of further territory from the Palestinians.

In all this, while it is fair to say that there has been a diversity of views inside Israeli society, much Israeli policy has in essence been driven by the concept of the 'Iron Wall' advocated by Ze'ev Jabotinsky, one of the early Zionists, in the 1920s (regardless of how representative he was in his time of Jewish views at large; cf. note on this by Prior 1997: 193). According to this idea, Israel's negotiation with the Arabs was to proceed from a position of military strength and irresistible presence in the land (Shlaim 2000: 12–13). According to Jabotinsky (writing in 1923; quoted in Shlaim 2000: 13):

> Every indigenous people will resist alien settlers as long as they see any hope of ridding themselves of the danger of foreign settlement. This is how the Arabs will behave and go on behaving so long as they possess a gleam of hope that they can prevent 'Palestine' from becoming the Land of Israel.

Jabotinsky adds (quoted in Shlaim 2000: 13):

> We cannot promise any reward either to the Arabs of Palestine or to the Arabs outside Palestine. A voluntary agreement is unattainable. And so those who regard an accord with the Arabs as an indispensable condition of Zionism must admit to themselves today that this condition cannot be attained and hence that we must give up Zionism. We must either suspend our settlement efforts or continue them without paying attention to the mood of the natives. Settlement can thus develop under the protection of a force that is not dependent on the local population, behind an iron wall which they will be powerless to break down.

And, further (quoted in Shlaim 2000: 14):

> I do not mean to assert that no agreement whatever is possible with the Arabs of the land of Israel. But a voluntary agreement

is just not possible. As long as the Arabs preserve a gleam of hope that they will succeed in getting rid of us, nothing in the world can cause them to relinquish this hope, precisely because they are not a rabble but a living people. And a living people will be ready to yield on such fateful issues only when they have given up all hope of getting rid of the alien settlers. Only then will extremist groups with their slogans 'No, never' lose their influence, and only then will their influence be transferred to more moderate groups. And only then will the moderates offer suggestions for compromise. Then only will they begin bargaining with us on practical matters, such as guarantees against pushing them out, and equality of civil and national rights.

From here, we can ask the question of who actually has a legitimate claim to the land (as noted just above, Jabotinsky himself did see the possibility of some future peaceful coexistence, but only on the basis of the Iron Wall). It is the view of this author that the Jews do have some good reasons for a claim to the land (the reality of the Holocaust in Nazi Germany in the 1940s and its associated suffering and trauma should undoubtedly also be kept in mind in this connection). But this claim should be balanced with the rights of the indigenous Palestinians. In this regard, especially since the events of 1947–1949, the situation has turned into something that is grossly unfair to and unjust for the Palestinians. While the Israeli encroachment has been the root cause of the problem and the source of most practical misery, the problem has been exacerbated by the fact that the nationalistic aspirations of the Palestinians were also spurned by the Jordanians, and the Arabs at large until quite recently (see Shlaim 2000, *passim*). Owing to the success of the Israelis in establishing facts on the ground by capturing territory, dispelling Palestinians and encroaching onto the land occupied by Palestinians by force, the framework for the basic negotiations has been shifting ever since the War of Independence/the Nakbah. Just as outlined by the ideology of the Iron Wall, the Palestinian negotiation is based on a position of desperation, and, with the passing of time, there is a threat that there will be increasingly less for them to negotiate for. In this respect, Pappe's (2004: 263) comments should be noted:

> Land is still the most valuable resource for survival in Palestine, and the process that began with the first wave of Zionist immigration, the expropriation by purchase or eviction of Palestinian land, is continuing. Since 1882, while many new Jewish villages, settlements and towns have been erected, not one new Palestinian town or village has been built. The obsession with land acquisition continues to threaten the livelihood of Palestinians, who increasingly respond with violence. Villagers in Galilee lose their

land to Judaization programmes, Bedouins in the Negev are
driven out of their traditional territories, and the settlement
project in the West Bank has not ceased since 1967.

On the issue of force, mention should also be made that, from the
beginning, the Jews sought powerful allies, starting with the British at
the time of the Balfour Declaration. Later on, in the late 1950s, the Jews
courted America, with increasingly friendly relations as a whole being
formed between the two countries with the passage of time and through
related political events and crises that took place (see Shlaim 2000, *passim*).
From an ideological perspective, besides American Jewry, Christian
popular eschatology has caused many Christians to support Israel. In
particular, those who take a so-called dispensationalist pre-millennial view
of the Scriptures (see e.g. Clouse 1977 for a basic exposition; see also Court
2008: 123–124 for its origins in nineteenth-century America) argue that
Israel as a literal concept still counts, the return of the Israelites to Palestine
is foretold in the Bible, and even that the temple will be rebuilt in Israel,
if only to administer sacrifices that serve as memorials for Jesus. However,
the dispensationalist view is by no means the only one available. The
so-called historical pre-millenialists, and amillenialists, and probably post-
millennialists, would, in the light of the New Testament, see the promises
to Israel as now applying to the Church (Rom. 9), even if the 'literal' Israel
still has some kind of role (for the basic positions, see e.g. Clouse 1977;
for a historical dimension to millennial movements, see e.g. Court 2008).
In this light, there is no need to interpret biblical material as foretelling
a literal return of the Jews to Israel. Rather, in the view of this writer,
prophecies about Israel's return to the land should be taken metaphorically, not literally (see also comments by Chapman 2005).

In this connection, even if slightly speculative, it is generally not noted
that the descendants of the northern tribes disappeared after their conquest
by the Assyrians in the seventh century into the general Near Eastern
canvas of populations, and it can be thought likely that many of the
present Near Eastern people have more than a drop of their blood in their
veins. They should thus, at least arguably, also be counted as Israelites
(Prior [1997: 197] notes the possibility of Palestinian Arabs themselves
being descendants of the ancients there). In this respect, the fact that only
the modern Jews are in essence at present counted as physical descendants
of (and therefore as recipients of the promises made to) ancient Israel by
certain (Zionist) groups (cf. Prior 1997: 197) highlights the issue that, with
ethnicity, appeals to common ancestry often involve mythical rather than
factual derivations (see Hutchinson and Smith 1996: 5–6, who in fact state
that, with ethnicity, common ancestry is 'a myth rather than a fact').
Besides, there is a sizeable minority of Christians among the current four
million or so Palestinians in the occupied territories (about 8% of the
population of the West Bank, even if marginal in Gaza), and this should

in the view of this author certainly be taken into account by those who try to interpret biblical promises to Israel from a Christian perspective, regardless of their eschatological framework (note that, according to Pappe [2004: 73], the Christian population of Palestine in 1917 when the Zionist immigration was still much in its infancy was about 10% of a total of 800,000).

In sum, the present author sees the Church as the new Israel, and thinks that there should be a just solution to the 'Palestinian problem'. For this writer, such a solution would involve acknowledging the right of a homeland for the Jews as an ethno-religious group, at the same time acknowledging the full rights of the Palestinians as the current indigenous people (including independence). However, because of the current balances of power, it appears that there will be less and less room for a just solution for the Palestinians – ideally, this would at the very least involve the return of all land occupied by force since the Jewish settlement started. Unfortunately, as history has shown (for example in the case of the conquest and ethnic cleansing of North America), from a human standpoint, power politics are the ultimate decider in human affairs, and fait accompli often rules. There are very few at the present time who would acknowledge the still-continuing claim to the North American lands by its indigenous inhabitants. According to Tinker (2008: 81), 'in the United States alone, it is estimated that Indian nations still have a legitimate claim to some two thirds of the U.S. land mass'. (This of course relates to nations that have survived, not those that have been *completely* exterminated; note also that, at the time of writing this commentary, after the election of Barack Obama as the first black US president, which in itself is undoubtedly of significant historical import-ance, there also seems to have been some movement towards recognition of the claims of Native Americans [cf. e.g. http://news.bbc.co.uk/1/hi/world/americas/8344449.stm, 5 November 2009 (accessed 5 November 2009); however, it remains to be seen whether this will make any real practical difference.) Similarly, or at the very least comparably, indigenous peoples around the world have land claims, including in this writer's native Finland (the Saami people). Such claims are often not recognized by states, as indigenous peoples tend to pose a challenge to the legitimacy of states (cf. Tinker 2004, 2008). This is because they have often been forced by states into arrangements not desired by them, including losing their territorial integrity, independence and self-determination, and such forcing has of course often involved violence and conquest, even genocide. Inter-estingly, the situation in Palestine is arguably similar to that in early nineteenth-century America, where a significant part of the land was still held by its native inhabitants. However, equally, as regards the area of the present United States, by about the 1880s, except for in effect minuscule reservation areas, all land had been taken from the indigenous inhabitants, leaving a reduced and in many ways demoralized existence for these inhabit-ants, which has continued to the present day (cf. Tinker 2004, 2008). One may only wonder if the result will be similar for present-day Palestinians, also considering the history of the conflict and the current balances of power.

We should, however, also note in this connection the comment by Naim Ateek, a Palestinian Christian, that 'the elimination of Israel would mean a greater injustice to millions of innocent people who know no home except Israel' (Ateek 1989: 164). Undoubtedly, this mitigates arguments against fait accompli in Palestine, and in other areas in the world where conquests have taken place. At the same time, this should not serve as legitimation of efforts towards establishing a fait accompli by conquerors, including in a historical dimension. And considerations of at least partial restoration should not be sidestepped either.

The situation for Christians is further complicated in that, as we find from Deuteronomy 2:20–23, quoted at the beginning of this Introduction, and of course from the book of Joshua itself (see also esp. Amos 9:7), the Bible claims that God is behind history, and behind conquests and people movements, at least during Old Testament times. If this is the case, we must all the more ask the question of theodicy, the justification of God's actions. That is, why would God work in such a way in history? (In this respect, it seems that technological advantage has generally enabled superior military [and, where applicable, economic] capability, so this involves a question of why God has enabled some societies and people groups to advance in this way, and not others.)

At the same time, while present history has not yet unfolded and we do not yet have relevant historical hindsight, we should not assume any inevitability for the course of history, but should work together to respond to what we see as injustice in our world. In the present, the Palestinians have been suffering and are suffering a great injustice, and any action to alleviate it would surely be welcomed (this also applies to other indigenous people groups around the world that have had to suffer conquests, genocide and subjugation). It is the sincere hope of this author that a just solution can somehow be obtained. While the present writer does not wish to claim that these relatively brief comments are in any way comprehensive as a response to a complex and tragic problem, for example, one's theology *does* matter. In this respect, to start with, relinquishing a dispensational framework could go a long way towards reversing the practically blind support that many American Christians, who collectively have a strong voice in American politics, and other like-minded Christians in other places in the world offer in support of Israel's policies that include continuing oppression, conquest and at the very least ethnocide of the Palestinians. But, beyond that, whether for the Christian, the Jew or anyone else, let justice and mutual respect prevail. Even if, unfortunately, the history and the present state of the matter do not appear to give room for much optimism as things stand at the time of the writing of this commentary, the present writer would be extremely happy to see a positive solution to the situation in present-day Palestine, the land where, according to the Christian canonical documents, the events in the book of Joshua took place and where Jesus Christ, the founder of Christianity, lived, breathed and died for the future of humankind.

NOTE ON TEXT AND TRANSLATIONS, AND ON GEOGRAPHICAL REFERENCES

A few comments on the text and translations and on geographical references are in order here for clarity, even if some of them may sound fairly elementary to certain readers. As far as the text of Joshua is concerned, comments have been made only on matters that have been deemed particularly important. For a full list of textual features, the reader is referred to the standard editions of Hebrew and Greek texts (presently *BHS* and RAHLFS; note that the Göttingen Septuagint is a post-RAHLFS text-critical project; however, it does not have Joshua available at the time of the writing of this book) and their textual apparati, and the commentaries by Butler (1983) and Nelson (1997) in particular (but cf. the general comments in Van Seters 2006 about the likelihood of the existence of various versions of the biblical texts in general [especially in Persian and Greek periods]; cf. also Millard 1982 for more details on scribal practices in the Ancient Near East, and cf. my comments in the section on textual issues above). I have translated directly from Hebrew (*BHS*) with the help of Greek (noting any textual differences between the Hebrew [MT] and the Greek where significant) and any other relevant translations where appropriate.

As for translating from Hebrew to English, the main problem with all translation work in general is that the source and target languages always differ in their grammar, vocabulary and idiom. Consequently, what is said in one language cannot be said in exactly the same way in another. Any translation has to be more or less an approximation of what the original language wishes to convey. Also, the original language can of course sometimes be ambiguous to start with, even to native speakers, as for example the everyday misunderstandings between people in communication and wranglings over interpretations of contracts demonstrate. This means that any translation at the very least *may* involve interpretation.

With this in mind, I have tried to convert the translation into modern English idiom whenever possible (even though this has sometimes not been successful without in my view becoming too removed from the original, and the reader can recognize an unmistakable 'biblical' expression in the translation). In particular, I have often left waw consecutives untranslated. In a few cases I have written out in an accompanying note what a literal translation (as much as it can be fully literal anyway!) might look like, and the reader can see that it often does not make for particularly good English. As for translating perfect and imperfect and other tenses, they do not have exact equivalents in English and context often determines how they should be translated, even though the perfect generally tends to refer to past tense, and imperfect to the future. Also, the narrative structure of Hebrew is different. For example, repetition of words and themes is normal, whereas English shuns repetition, and where English and most Western languages and cultures like a straightforward logical progression of narrative, Hebrew sometimes likes to progress through repetition, and in such cases one can at times discern a pattern where each repetition expands the theme (see e.g. 18:4–10). Textual corruption is of course also always possible. In cases of extensive repetition, I have sometimes simplified the flow of the narrative by leaving a redundant sentence out.

In the same vein, the reader should also note that, as with any language translations, some of the Hebrew words do not have exact equivalents in English. These include such terms as *ḥērem* (~ban), *naḥălah* (~inheritance), *nakah* (~slay), *mišpaḥah* (~family). Rather than using a single word consistently to translate these into English, I have tried to put in something for each occurrence that is suitable for the context. It should also be added that, in any case, the meanings of words in any language vary depending on the context. I believe that this is perfectly adequate for many practical purposes, but, for those readers who desire more exactness, I suggest that they read the original. While it is a fair bit of work to learn Hebrew, it must be said that it is a requirement for a fuller and more careful understanding, and there are no short cuts. In any case, readers are also invited and encouraged to compare my translation with other translations, and are in particular encouraged to refer to NRSV, ESV or NASB when they want to see a literal translation.

A note should also be made about transliteration. When attempting to represent spellings of one script with another completely different script, as is the case with Hebrew, one can only approximate the pronunciation of the source script (as much as this is fully known for classical Hebrew anyway) in the target script and language. Accordingly, there are often several ways one might transliterate. To use one system is mainly a matter of convention. The publisher has its own transliteration guidelines for Hebrew words for the commentary series, and these have normally been followed. In some cases where the corresponding Hebrew word is very well known, an alternative transliteration without diacritics has been used. As for place names, which generally are not transliterated with diacritics, I have mainly followed the transliterations of the ESV, although not necessarily always, in particular where an alternative transliteration may be more commonly used. Of course, ultimately, readers are referred to the text in Hebrew script for closer scrutiny.

It should also be kept in mind that a fair few of the comments in the commentary relate to geography, and it is often helpful to look at them with the aid of a relevant map. Rather than providing maps, I have assumed that readers have access to a good Bible atlas.

TEXT AND COMMENTARY

EXCURSUS 1: GENERAL OBSERVATIONS ON THE LITERARY FORM AND SETTING OF THE BOOK

I have already discussed a number of aspects that relate to the literary composition of Joshua in the Introduction. In this excursus I will make a few further comments, while also drawing in and summarizing some of the issues I have already covered in the Introduction. I start by s ummarizing Noth's seminal views about the literary composition of Joshua. Before Noth, it was generally thought that the book was part of a so-called Hexateuch, an overall work consisting of Genesis–Joshua. As part of such a hypothesis, scholars such as von Rad in general thought that the book of Joshua was composed of the Pentateuchal sources J, E, P and D (see e.g. Noth 1953a: 8; the classic formulation of the source-critical analysis of the Pentateuch can be found in Wellhausen 1905/1878). However, Noth denied the existence of such sources in Joshua and the connection between the Pentateuch and Joshua (see Noth 1991/1943; see also Noth 1953a: 8, 13, 16). Instead, Noth suggested that the book of Joshua is part of Deuteronomistic History, a single historical work which spans from Deuteronomy to 2 Kings and was written in deuter-onomistic style during the Babylonian exile of the Jews in the sixth century BC. In this hypothesis, Joshua connects literarily back only to Deuteronomy. Any further connections are more or less sporadic and of late origin.

Noth's views were by and large followed by Old Testament scholarship, and his approach still influences much of the discussion even though it has been modified and challenged, and even jettisoned by some. It is of primary importance to recognize this, as any modifications to Noth's theory, such as any double (first edition with a positive outlook on the history of Israel in the time of Josiah, and a second more pessimistic edition in the exile) or triple redaction (a basic form [DtrG] followed by 'nomistic' [concerned with law; DtrN] and prophetic [DtrP] redactions, or even several redactions of this type) theories of the Deuteronomistic History are still very much indebted to Noth (for a summary of these, see e.g. McConville 1997; cf. also Nelson 2005). Also, any double or triple redaction theories do not seem to have much essential impact on one's considerations of Joshua (double redaction theories would see Joshua pretty much as part of the first [and thus also single] deuter-onomistic redaction, and any additional redactional layers postulated by triple redaction theories ultimately seem to converge with Noth, as Noth's Deuteronomistic Historian was also concerned with law, and DtrP is less relevant for Joshua). In other words, if one reads Noth, one can quickly get an idea of the foundations of the scholarship of Joshua (and also of the historical books) even for the present day. At the risk of making an oversimplification, it tends to be those works that challenge Noth that provide us with fresh ideas about the literary setting and provenance of the book of Joshua (however, this is not to say that those works that agree with Noth cannot contain valuable insights).

For Noth, the formation of the book of Joshua had three main stages. First, there was a pre-deuteronomistic stage, relating to chapters 1 – 12, 13 – 21 and 24. Each of these blocks of material had a separate prehistory. As regards chapters 1 – 12, these are based on a number of separate (pre-deuteronomistic) stories that were collected together by someone whom Noth called *Sammler* (lit. 'collector') about 900 BC (see Noth 1953a: 12). As for chapters 13 – 21, Noth thought that the boundary lists are based on a document that ultimately dates back to the pre-monarchic period (Noth 1953a: 13). However, the district (and town) list of Judah dates to the time of Josiah and was combined at that time with the boundary list document and with town lists for other tribes by someone whom Noth called *Bearbeiter* (lit. 'arranger'). All this was independent from the material that relates to chapters 1 – 12 (see Noth 1953a: 14). A basic list of Levitical towns which also dates to about the time of Josiah was added to the document next (Noth 1953a: 15). Finally, the document was made to link to the person Joshua (Noth 1953a: 15; it is good to note that Noth in general thinks that the person Joshua was linked/grafted into the traditions only secondarily). The third block, portions of Joshua 24, dates in Noth's opinion to the pre-deuteronomistic time and may have had a connection with material pertaining to chapters 1 – 12, even though one cannot be sure (Noth 1953a: 15–16).

The second stage in the formation of the book was the incorporation of the material pertaining to the first stage as noted above by the Deuteronomistic Historian as part of his overarching work, which spans from Deuteronomy to 2 Kings. Important bits added by the Deuteronomist include Joshua 1:1–18; 21:43 – 22:6; 23:1–16; 8:30–35 and additions to the material otherwise here and there (see Noth 1953a: 9 for further details). There was also a second deuteronomistic stage for the book: an addition of some comments to the town lists (such as Josh. 13:1; 19:1; 21:42) to improve the integration of chapters 13 – 21 into the whole, even if this includes some duplication of verses that would not have been likely to have been undertaken by the original deuteronomistic editor. Similarly, chapter 24 was integrated and edited into the material at this stage, as the book had naturally finished with chapter 23 from the first Deuteronomist (see Noth 1953a: 10 for details).

The final stage in the formation of the book of Joshua was a set of isolated post-deuteronomistic additions (these date to the post-exilic time in line with the then current thinking about the dating of the priestly material). Except for additions to verses, such as 14:1–2; 18:8–10; 19:51, these include Joshua 21:1–2 and 22:9–34 (see Noth 1953a: 10–11). It is important to stress that, for Noth, the priestly additions do not stem from a coherent narrative. The main point here is that if they did, this would speak for a connection with the book of Numbers, which can be argued to contain a lot of priestly material (again, similarly, Noth tried to minimize the extent of priestly material in Numbers; see Noth 1991/1943). This would then undermine Noth's theory about a Deuteronomistic History (one might then for example ask whether the pre-deuteronomistic stage should also be seen to have made a connection with books preceding Deuteronomy in the canon). In addition to the isolated priestly additions, there are also small secondary additions to the book that do not for Noth seem to have any specific ideological provenance that can be traced, such as minor expansion to some of the boundary lists (Noth 1953a: 11).

As one might expect, and as already noted, later scholarship has expanded on Noth and developed his theories further. For example, in addition to the theories about the double and triple redaction of the Deuteronomistic History mentioned above, there have been many discussions about the dating of the boundary and city lists. Suggested dates for the lists generally range from the time of the united monarchy to the time of Josiah, and the interested reader can for example refer to such works as Kallai 1986, Ottosson 1991, Svensson 1994, Lissovski and Na'aman 2003, the appropriate sections of the commentaries of Boling and Wright 1982, Butler 1983, Fritz 1994 and Hess 1996, and the many monographs and articles mentioned in the bibliographies of these works for more details.

Even if there has been some modification of Noth's views, it is important to note here that lines of enquiry and solutions sought for the

date and composition of the book have by and large assumed a pre-
deuteronomistic stage, one or more deuteronomistic redactions, and then
one or more priestly redactions. Such approaches have also assumed
the Wellhausenian idea that pre-deuteronomistic (with Pentateuch, this
means J and E) materials are followed by deuteronomistic and then
priestly redactions and incorporation of material expressing such ideologies and literary style. Much of this is based on the Wellhausenian
assumption of a development of the Israelite cult and related materials
from simple to complex. However, the Wellhausenian premise of such
development can no longer be easily sustained. For example, first of all,
in the light of recent Ancient Near Eastern discoveries, there is no need
to date priestly material to a late period in Israel. Temples and priesthood
were already an established part of Ancient Near Eastern heritage at the
time when the first written records from Egypt and Mesopotamia emerge
at the end of the fourth millennium BC. In addition, one can see some
specific parallels with Israelite priestly thinking from Hittite material that
dates to the second millennium BC (see Weinfeld 2004, esp. pp. 34–63),
and when we know that there was movement of people and ideas across
the Middle East that can in general be attested from a very early time
(cf. the Amarna letters, which are part of a diplomatic correspondence
between Egypt and roughly speaking the whole of the Middle East in the
second millennium, as one [but by no means the only] example), it is
practically impossible to think that the area of ancient Israel would not
have been affected by such ideas (as already indicated in the Introduction,
we also note that dozens of texts in cuneiform have been found from
Israel, with some fifty items dating to the Middle and Late Bronze periods;
see Horowitz, Oshima and Sanders 2006 for the finds thus far, including
pp. 5–6 for a summary; see also Na'aman 1994a and 1994b, and van Soldt
2003 for evidence of apparently considerable Hurrian and northern
influence [including through some considerable migration] in Palestine
and Ugarit – the Hurrians themselves seem to have had close links to
the Hittites, and also to the Assyrians). In addition to this, the Ugaritic
alphabetic cuneiform texts dating from the Late Bronze Age of course
make their own contribution to cultic issues around the area (see e.g.
de Tarragon 1980; Pardee 2002 for further details).

Secondly, although since the time of de Wette in the early nineteenth
century (see de Wette 1830; Wellhausen 1905/1878), Deuteronomy has
been thought by many to have its provenance in the seventh century BC
and the reform of Josiah (or even later than this, as some have recently
assumed; see e.g. Ahlström 1993 etc.) it is not necessary to assume this.
For example, the present author has argued that it is not necessary to date
the book to the seventh century BC based on the history and theology of
centralization of worship, a main reason for such dating (see Pitkänen
2004a). While other reasons for dating Deuteronomy late have been
proposed by scholars, and while it is beyond the scope of this book to get

into a detailed investigation, counter-arguments with regard to centralization and development of cult are reason enough to at the very least start seriously questioning the necessity of a late dating.

Finally, we note that there is also no need to hold on to Martin Noth's theory of the Deuteronomistic History. I have indicated above that Noth started from the premise that the conquest tradition was a set of independent units in the beginning and that the book of Joshua was built around these traditions. As already indicated, importantly, Noth also argued that there was originally no P account of the conquest, but P concluded his account with the death of Moses (see Noth 1987/1943: 135). Noth based this argument on claiming as far as possible that those features that exist in Numbers and relate to the conquest are not priestly. Noth succeeded in eliminating so much material that has commonly been attributed to P that he could argue that those parts that are indisputably priestly are the result of secondary additions and do not stem from a P narrative (cf. Noth 1987/1943: 121–134). However, at the same time, Noth argued that the older literary sources J and E 'culminated in the theme of the conquest' (Noth 1987/1943: 141). According to Noth, 'when they were fitted into the framework provided by the P narrative it was the Pentateuch which emerged, with the theme of the conquest of the land to the west of the Jordan dropping away completely. The conquest narrative in the book of Joshua, on the other hand, was part of the work of Dtr. from the start, and this developed completely independently of the Pentateuch' (Noth 1987/1943: 141). Finally, during the post-exilic period, the Pentateuch and the Deuteronomistic History were joined together, and more connecting links were added between Numbers and Deuteronomy on the one hand, and Numbers and Joshua on the other, and these connections were, as Noth seems to indicate, made in priestly style (Noth 1987/1943: 143–148).

However, as we will see in Excursus 12, Joshua 22:9–34 forms a particularly important counter-example against Noth's theory. It proves to be that there are some very good reasons to think that Joshua 22:9–34 is an integral part of the book of Joshua, and is also explicitly connected to the priestly parts of Numbers 32.

We also note here that Ottosson has analysed the relationship of Joshua to Numbers. The following table indicates links, or at the very least similarities, between Joshua and Numbers (from Ottosson 1991: 31). We can see from the table that it requires some work to deny inherent connections between the two respective corpora.

Numbers	Joshua
31:8, 16	13:21
32	1; 22; cf. 13:15–33
33, list of campsites	12, list of kings
34:1–2	11:16–23; 13:2–5

Numbers (*cont.*)	Joshua (*cont.*)
34:13	13:7
34:14ff.	13:8
34:19, 23–24	14:1–6
35:1–8	21
35:9–34	20
36	17:3

In other words, it is difficult to believe Noth's theory of the Deuter-onomistic History in its present form, especially when Noth has already been criticized for eliminating priestly material from Numbers and Joshua in a way that has a stamp of dubiousness about it (see Weinfeld 1972: 182n1, according to whom Noth's 'attempts to disprove the priestly origin of Num. 32 – 36 and Josh. 14 – 22' are 'unconvincing'). Moreover, Noth's theory, and for that matter a number of the current theories about the Deuteronomistic History, is simply too complicated. Too many redactions, combinations and accretions are postulated, and Noth often treats literary works in a piecemeal and mechanical way (but, as we will see in Excursus 12, nevertheless has great difficulty with dividing Joshua 22:9–34 into sources). Also, it is hard to think that P would have concluded his account with the death of Moses without any regard to the wider context to which that death relates, that is, entering into the promised land. The idea of cutting off the conquest tradition of the older Pentateuchal sources, especially when their accounts 'culminated in the theme of the con-quest', is also problematic. In other words, the Deuteronomistic History hypothesis brings some very serious problems with it, and when we keep in mind that Westermann (see Westermann 1994 and Excursus 12) has added a number of further problems to the equation, which have been left unanswered by other scholars, we can conclude that it is quite unlikely that the book of Joshua is part of a Deuteronomistic History, and there is thus considerably less need to date the book to the seventh century, the exilic period or later by default.

We also note that if the relative dating of Deuteronomy and priestly material were to be reversed (or even equated), one could think that Joshua draws on priestly sources and style as part of its literary formation, however these sources were drawn in. This in fact would be a very logical and natural way of looking at the book, regardless of its (perceived) date and provenance, be it early or late.

Overall, as the book of Joshua in any case most naturally divides into chapters 1 – 12, 13 – 21 and 22 – 24, regardless of whether one follows Noth's ideas or their derivatives about the prehistory of the book, I will follow this division in my considerations and will devote a separate excursus to summary considerations of the form and structure of each of these parts. But note an interesting division of the book by Koorevaar into four main sections (Koorevaar 1990: 283):

1:1 – 5:12	5:13 – 12:24	13:1 – 21:45	22:1 – 24:33
cross	take	divide	serve
'br	*lqḥ*	*ḥlq*	*'bd*

According to Koorevaar, the 'structural-theological purpose' of the book 'is found in the third main section: cross+take=divide' (Koorevaar 1990: 283). It is good to keep this in mind when thinking of the book and its theological message.

EXCURSUS 2: FORM AND STRUCTURE OF JOSHUA 1 – 12

In this section, I relate some of the issues that are particularly relevant to the form and structure of Joshua 1 – 12, partly summarizing points made in the Introduction and elsewhere in this commentary. Readers who wish to look at a detailed history of research are advised to refer to relevant sections in Noort 1998 to start with. As seen in the previous section, Noth thought that these chapters in Joshua stem mostly from early material collected together by someone (Gm. *Sammler*) around 900 BC and then later taken into the overall work of the Deuteronomistic Historian. More specifically, an important aspect for Noth in the prehistory of the text(s) was the concept of so-called aetiologies (and war stories [*Kriegserzählungen*] in chapters 10 – 11:9). As I have already indicated in the Introduction, aetiologies are stories that surround certain places or phenomena and give an explanation for their existence and/or prominence. In particular, for Noth, such stories can be centred on important sanctuaries, and Noth saw the sanctuary at Gilgal as the point of origin for the stories in Joshua 2 – 9. In this vein, Noth also thought that the sanctuary in Gilgal served as a central (at least centrally important) sanctuary during the time of Saul (see Noth 1953a: 12). Noth also considers that Amos' references to Gilgal in Amos 4:4 and 5:5 (Noth 1953a: 12) indicate that it was a cult place that was also visited later in the history of Israel. The important point here is that Noth basically thought that the stories of the distant past were created for the purpose of legitimizing a presently observable phenomenon. However, this need not be the case. For example, a later treatment of the subject of aetiologies can be found in Childs 1963. Childs examines a number of occurrences of the formula *ad hayyom hazzeh* (until this day) across the Old Testament as a whole and notes that the formula is normally tied to the writer's personal witness rather than explaining a phenomenon (see Childs 1963, esp. p. 292). Childs notes in particular that a literary examination of the cases where the formula is used reveals that it has usually been added to the story as a secondary element (Childs 1963: 289–290; for full details, see the whole article).

In other words, as the formula 'until this day', which is supposed to be the distinguishing feature of an aetiology, is not part of the original tradition or story, it is not all that likely that the story arose as an aetiology (similarly Westermann 1994: 51).

We also noted the example of Joshua 9, which has generally been seen as a relatively late aetiology that explains the presence of the Gibeonites (see Younger 1990: 201). In response, Younger gives examples from Assyrian, Hittite and Egyptian sources of attempts to gain favour without fight from conquerors. Especially, the account from the Ten Year Annals of Muršili indicates how Manapa-Datta, the ruler of the Seha River land, sent forth his mother, old men and old women to meet Muršili in order to gain his favour. Muršili indicates that when the women bowed down at his feet, he treated them as they wished (ibid.: 202; incidentally, cf. also Gen. 32 – 33). These Ancient Near Eastern sources were generally pretty much contemporaneous to the events they portray, and thus there is no need to assume a long prehistory for a biblical text that depicts similar events.

Also, as already indicated in the Introduction, the present author has further examined the 'until this day' formula and so-called aetiological stories in the book of Joshua (see above, Introduction, and Pitkänen 2007). Throughout the book, the author of Joshua ties phenomena existing in his day to the time of the conquest. This does not appear to be coincidental. Rather, the author carefully crafts into the book various events that have left a trace that can be observed at present. The present phenomena then serve for the author as reminders of the events behind them, even as proof of the veracity of the tradition (similarly van Dyk 1990: 22–23). It is tempting to say that the writer used such a method at a time when there were few footnotes and cross-references in the literature that was produced. In other words, and even if the book of Joshua were a collection of aetiological stories, in their present arrangement in the book such stories can be seen to serve as a powerful testimony about the Israelite conquest for its readers. And, in this context, the writer tied events to localities, not haphazardly, but as a powerful testimony about the saving acts of Yahweh for the Israelites. For the writer, reading and hearing about these events was to remind the Israelites about who Yahweh is and what he has done for them, so that the Israelites would keep the laws and statutes of Yahweh. This then is history writing with a purpose. It is ancient Israelite history writing intended to persuade its readers to follow the God Yahweh and to keep away from those who might compromise such loyalty, and no room is given to anything or anyone that might compromise it. The later generation is to know the great and veritable deeds of Yahweh so that they can follow his laws and statutes. The narratives of Joshua 2 – 9 function in this context. The stones at Gilgal (Josh. 4, incl. v. 20), the name 'Gibeath Haaraloth' ('hill of foreskins'; Josh. 5:3), the existence of Rahab among the Israelites (Josh. 6:25), the stones at the Valley of Achor (Josh. 7:24–26), the Gibeonites (Josh. 9:27), the record in the book of Yashar (Josh. 10:13), and the rocks in front of the cave of Makkedah (Josh. 10:27) bear witness to the veracity of the conquest in chapters 1 – 12 for the first audience of the book.

Another important observation to make is that the events portrayed in chapters 1 – 10 (or at least the early chapters) happen pretty much at the start of the conquest, possibly even in the space of just a few months. If we then look at chapters 11 – 12, they are a set of summaries of military activity, and chapters 13 – 21 are largely a set of tribal allotments, largely depicted as taking place long after the initial conquest (e.g. Josh. 13:1). Chapters 22 – 24 also relate to events long after the conquest.

In other words, importantly, all of the events in Joshua 1 – 12, and chapters 1 – 10 in particular, are very much initial occurrences and undertakings in Israel's entry into the so-called promised land, in essence in contrast to the rest of the book. The circumcision after crossing and the first Passover celebrations with the manna ceasing (Josh. 5) are important first events in the newly entered land (i.e. west of the Jordan). Also, if we look at the narrative about Jericho, it is equally about a first actual conquest action in the land. The narrative about Ai is itself linked with Jericho, at least in its current form, so is in many ways part of it. The ceremony at Mount Ebal is also a special ceremony (cf. Deut. 27), and while no clear indication is given of its function, it may well have been about establishing the covenant in the promised land, at least confirming the covenant in the new setting (cf. Deut. 27). While the function of the narrative about the Gibeonites (and its follow-up in chapter 10) is less clear in this sense (but see comments on that section), it nevertheless pertains to the early days of the conquest. Thus we may say that the prominence of the material in chapters 1 – 10 is above all a *literary* prominence. If we think of the problems with the archaeology of Jericho and the apparently meagre remains that have been found at the site, the point is that the reason for including the story of Jericho in the narrative is not necessarily because the site was a *prominent* one (even though it is also possible that the site was at least somewhat prominent after all; see Excursus 5 about the archaeology of Jericho for details), but because it was the *first* one conquered. The same goes for Ai: the narrative is again prominent because of its link with the violation of *herem* (ban) and link to the Jericho narrative, not because the site was particularly prominent as such. In other words, one may think that the sites are in many ways like any other sites mentioned in the lists of Joshua (incl. Josh. 12), but become particularly important in association with their literary prominence in the narrative (which itself reflects the importance that the author of Joshua attributed to them in respect of the history of the Israelite conquest).

Another issue worth pointing out is that much of the material in the early chapters of Joshua has a literary connection to preceding material in canonical order. While this is not unique to chapters 1 – 12 and while we will look at full details under each chapter, a few related comments are worth making here. We first note here in passing that the crossing of the river Jordan (Josh. 3 – 4) is reminiscent of the crossing of the Sea of Reeds in Exodus 14 – 15 (and is thus explicitly named in Josh. 4:23). And the ceasing of manna links back to the wilderness period, as does circumcision at Gilgal (it also links back to the exodus). Also, interestingly, Ottosson has suggested direct literary parallels between Exodus 12 – 17 and Joshua 3 – 8, as follows (Ottosson 1991: 79):

Exodus 12 – 17	Joshua 3 – 8
Chs 12 – 14 Passover celebrations, Crossing of Sea of Reeds	Chs 3 – 6 Crossing of Jordan, Passover celebrations
Exod. 14:26 Obliteration of Egyptians	Destruction of Jericho
Chs 15 – 17 Waters of Marah, Elim and Chs 7 – 8 [sic]	Defeat at Ai
(apostasy) with Massah-Meribah	Break of covenant
Loss and victory at Rephidim	Victory at Ai
Moses' staff of God (hands)	Joshua's spear
Building of an altar	Building of an altar at Ebal

I also mention that the removal of shoes in both the account of the burning bush in Exodus 3 (v. 5) and the appearance of the commander of Yahweh's army in Joshua 5:13–15 (v. 15) can be seen to provide a further connection between Joshua and Exodus. Both accounts are of course also theophanies. Such links back to the preceding canonical material seem to emphasize that the events happening in the early chapters of Joshua are a continuation of what has been depicted in the earlier material. From a literary perspective, the idea is that connections are made with material in Exodus–Numbers, therefore rather speaking for an idea of a Hexateuch, and really quite strongly against an idea of a Deuteronomistic History.

JOSHUA 1

Translation

[1]After Moses, the servant of Yahweh had died, Yahweh spoke to Joshua the son of Nun, the attendant of Moses as follows: [2]'My servant Moses is dead, you, go and cross the Jordan together with all the people to the land which I am giving to the Israelites. [3]Every place where you go is yours, in accordance with my promise to Moses. [4]Your borders will range from the desert and from the Lebanese

mountain range to the great river Euphrates, the whole land of the Hittites and to the Mediterranean Sea towards the west. [5]No one will be able to resist you during your whole lifetime. I will be with you as I was with Moses. I will not abandon you. [6]Be strong and courageous, for you will allocate to this people the land of which I swore to their forefathers. [7]Just be very strong and courageous to do carefully according to all the law that Moses my servant commanded you. Do not detract from it so that you will succeed in everything that you do. [8]Let this book of the law not be removed from your thoughts but meditate on it all the time so that you will be able to observe everything that is written in it. In this way you will be wise and successful. [9]Have I not told you to be strong and courageous. Do not be afraid and do not be worried, because Yahweh your God will be with you wherever you go.'

[10]Then Joshua instructed the representatives of the people as follows. [11]'Go through the camp and tell the people: "Prepare supplies for yourselves because you will cross the river Jordan within the next three days in order to take possession of the land that Yahweh your God is giving to you to possess."'

[12]And Joshua said to the Reubenites, the Gadites and those from the eastern half of the Manassites: [13]'Remember the injunction that Moses the servant of Yahweh gave you, saying, "Yahweh your God is giving you rest and has given you this land." [14]Let your women, your children and your livestock stay in the land that Moses gave you from the other side of the Jordan, but you are to go across armed together with your brothers, all the valiant warriors, and help them, [15]until Yahweh gives rest to your brothers as to yourselves and they also take possession of the land that Yahweh your God is giving to them, and then you can return to your allotted land and can take hold of that land which Moses the servant of Yahweh gave you from the east side of Jordan.'

[16]And they answered Joshua and said: 'We will do everything you have commanded us and will go wherever you send us. [17]As we listened to Moses, so will we also listen to you. Let Yahweh your God be with you just as he was with Moses. [18]Let anyone who does not listen to you and disobeys you be but to death. Do remain strong and courageous.'

Notes on the text

1. Servant: Hebr. *'ebed* (from *'ābad*). Attendant: Hebr. *měšārēt* (from *šārat*).

2. Go: lit. *qûm*, 'rise'. Am giving: Hebr. *nōtēn*, part. of *nātan*, to give, which does not entirely translate to any English tense here.

3. Go: lit. 'set foot on'. Is yours: lit. 'I have given it'.

4. Mediterranean Sea: *hayyām haggādôl*. Towards the west: lit. 'entering of the sun' (presumably originally an idiom about the sun entering the netherworld; see Pardee 2002: 133).

5. Abandon you: lit. 'leave (from Hebr. *rāpāh*) you or forsake (from Hebr. *'azāb*) you'.

6. Allocate: hiph. of *nāḥal*.

7. Just: *raq*. **Carefully do:** *tišmor la'aśôt*. Do not detract from it: *'al-tāsûr mimmennû yāmîn ûśĕmōr*. **Law (*tôrāh*):** not included in Greek.

8. Not be removed from your thoughts: lit. not depart from your mouth. **Meditate:** Hebr. *hāḡāh*, also to mutter, speak. **All the time:** lit. 'day and night'.

10. Representatives: *šoṭrîm*.

12. Eastern half of the Manassites: lit. 'the half-tribe of Manasseh', and similarly throughout Joshua.

14. It is not certain whether 'all the valiant warriors' refers to the Transjordanians or the Cisjordanians here. **Armed:** Hebr. *ḥămušîm*, possibly links with five/fifty (so Nelson 1997: 28, who also refers to 2 Kgs 1:9; Isa. 3:3).

15. From the east side of Jordan: lit. 'from the other side of Jordan, the rising/breaking out of the sun'.

17. Listen: also 'obey'. In Hebrew, the sentence 'let' begins with *raq*.

18. Do remain strong and courageous: *raq ḥăzaq wĕ'emāṣ*.

Form and structure

Nelson (Nelson 1997a: 28) helpfully notes how Joshua 1 is constructed around a series of four speeches (vv. 2–9 [Yahweh to Joshua], 10–11 [Joshua to officers], 12–15 [Joshua to the Transjordanians], 16–18 [Transjordanians to Joshua]).

All commentators agree that the chapter has been written in a deuteronomistic style. For Noth, the chapter as a whole should be seen in the context of the wider Deuteronomistic History (see Noth 1953a: 27). Following along the lines of Noth, Nelson (1997a: 29) notes:

> Yahweh's address to Joshua (vv. 1–9) functions as one of the editorial speeches that structure and unify the whole work (Deut. 1 – 3; Josh. 23; 1 Sam. 12; 2 Sam. 7; 1 Kgs 8). These speeches look backward and forward to reflect on the significance of events reported by DH. From a literary standpoint such speeches give an author the chance to address readers directly in order to provide motivations for the characters and to frame the issues at stake. By fading behind the speeches of authoritative characters, an author gains the appearance of greater objectivity. DH used this technique to guide readers into adopting a particular theological interpretation of Israel's history in the land.

The presence of speeches in Deuteronomy–Kings certainly is a strong argument for the concept of a Deuteronomistic History. However, if one thinks that such a framing of speeches in important narratives was characteristic of much Israelite history writing, much of which has taken the form we see as 'deuteronomistic', the argument for their being part of a unified historical work seems less conclusive. Such literary means could have been used at different times according to accepted literary conventions. We certainly know that stock phrases could demonstrably be employed across centuries in Assyria:

> In Assyria one can now see a literary tradition which used the same stock phrasing from the time of Shamshi-Adad I to that of Ashurbanipal, a span of some 1200 years which included some 1100 years during which Akkadian had not been supplanted as a living language. Some of the stock phrasing was employed even several centuries earlier than Shamshi-Adad I, as has been shown. Moreover, it is fair to say that the Assyrian royal literary tradition got a start with the inscriptions of this king. It achieved a more complete crystallization with the annals of Tiglath-Pileser I, in which a style was established and a precedent set for Assyrian annals from that time on, to the end of the Assyrian empire. Every indication is that that style would have continued for many centuries more had the empire itself not collapsed, since many of the stock phrases continued in use in Babylonian and Persian inscriptions of later date. (Niehaus 1985: 413)

Niehaus further shows how subsequent kings used and modified the phraseology of their predecessors (see Niehaus 1985: 28–29). Also, campaign reports of the Assyrian kings are stylistically similar from Tiglath-Pileser I (c. 1115–1077 BC) till the seventh century BC (see Niehaus 1985, *passim*; Younger 1990: 79–115).

Another issue here relates to verses 5–6. Noth saw these verses as being in a deuteronomistic style (Noth 1953a: 28). However, if we look at the Ancient Near East, these verses are not unique. The Zakkur stele (lines 11–16 esp.) from ancient Syria from about 800 BC, in Aramaic, provides a close parallel (restorations in brackets):

> (1) The [st]ela that Zakkur, king of [Ha]ma[th] and Luash, set up for Iluwer, [his god]. (2) I am Zakkur, king of Hama[th] and Luash. I am a humble man, but (3) Baalshamayn [gave] me [victory] and stood with me. Baalsham[ayn] made me king [over] (4) [Ha]zrak. Then Bir-Hadad the son of Hazael, the king of Aram, formed an alliance against me of (5) sev[en]teen king[s]: Bir-Hadad and his army, Bir-Gush and his army, (6) [the king] of Kue and his army, the king of Umq and his army, the king of Gurg[um (7) and] his [arm]y, the king of Sam'al and his army, the king of Miliz [and his army, the king of] (8) (*sic* with square brackets) [. . . and his army, the king of . . . and his army – that

is, seve[nteen] (9) of them with their armies. All these kings set up a siege against Hazr[ak]. (10) They raised a wall higher than the wall of Hazr[ak]. They dug a moat deeper than [its] moa[t]. (11) But I lifted my hands to Baalshamayn, and Baalshamay[n] answered me, [and] (12) Baalshamayn [spoke] to me [thr]ough seers and through visionaries, [and] (13) Baalshamayn [said], 'F[e]ar not, for I have made [you] king, [and I who will (14) st] and with [you], and I will deliver you from all [these kings who] (15) have forced a siege against you!' Then Baalsmayn said to m[e . . . ' (16) [a]ll these kings who have forced [a siege against you . . .] (17) [ ] and this wall whi[ch]. (Translation of front of the inscription, from NISSINEN: 204–206)

Such oracles of salvation and protection are common in the Ancient Near East (see esp. the oracles relating to Esarhaddon in NISSINEN; while these are from the first millennium, this is probably due to accidents of survival), and the motif of divine presence with leaders is well attested in the Ancient Near East (e.g. see Mann 1977).

This brings us to Joshua's relation to kingship: 'there is a definite royal flavour to this chapter [i.e. chapter 1], probably the result of a desire on the part of DH to create parallels between the figures of Joshua and Josiah' (Nelson 1997a: 29, referring back to Nelson 1981). In the words of Nelson (1997a: 29):

Yahweh's charge in vv. 1–9 is paralleled by 1 Kings 2:2–4 and seems to have been composed along the general lines of an enthronement or royal installation. To meditate on the book of the law epitomizes the deuteronomistic royal ideal (v. 8; Deut. 17:8–19). Another royal-sounding element is the pledge of uncompromising obedience by the eastern tribes (vv. 16–18). Yahweh's promise to the entire community is concentrated so that it rests on the military success of a single individual (the second person singular of v. 5), producing another parallel between Joshua and the office of a king (compare David in 2 Sam. 7:9–10). Like Josiah (2 Kgs 22:2) and the ideal king of Deuteronomy 17:20, Joshua is not to deviate from obedience to the right or left (v. 7). Unlike Saul (1 Sam. 16:14), but like David (1 Sam. 16:18) and Hezekiah (2 Kgs 18:7), Joshua's leadership and authority will be legitimated by Yahweh's presence (vv. 9, 17).

In this context, it is also worth noting that the name 'Joshua' sounds similar to the Judean seventh-century King Josiah. And yet none of this is conclusive. With Joshua being a leader of Israel, it would not be at all unlikely to use language in connection with him that would echo language used of kings, the ultimate kings of Israel during the time of kingship.

Above all, it would be natural for Deuteronomy, knowing that kings were the normal leaders in the contemporary ancient world (which would hold true even if Deuteronomy were written before the Israelite monarchy), to seek to regulate the role of king according to deuteronomic ideals. As for differences between Joshua and the Israelite (in the sense of Israel as a whole) kings, the fact that there was no dynastic succession with Joshua is significant and sufficient to distinguish him from them, and Joshua's office can be compared with the office of judges in the book of Judges. The similarity of the names 'Josiah' and 'Joshua' could also simply be coincidental ('Josiah' is based on a different Hebrew root from 'Joshua' ['šh {as it seems}, apparently meaning 'support', vs. yš', 'save'; in any case aleph is used in the former, ayin in the latter]). And it is also possible that Josiah could have been modelled after Joshua or, simply, Deuteronomy in general, in the narrative of 2 Kings.

Comment

1. In the narrative order, Moses' death signals the end of an era. His life belongs to the exodus and wilderness wanderings. In Numbers 13 – 14, he sends men to spy out the land of Canaan. But they bring back a bad report. The original inhabitants of the land seem too strong, and the spies instil fear and pessimism in the Israelites. So the Israelites complain and express regret for having left Egypt. Consequently, Yahweh does not allow the exodus generation to enter the land. Only two of the spies, Joshua and Caleb (see the commentary), are allowed to enter the land with the next generation. Even Moses, while not judged with the murmuring people, is denied entrance to the land owing to a separate offence (Num. 20). In the manner of great bittersweet sagas, he may only view the land from an adjacent mountain before his death (Deut. 34). It is the job of his assistant, Joshua, a faithful spy, to lead the people into the promised land. The narrative at the end of Deuteronomy conveys a great deal of sadness, and, conversely, it is easy to imagine the comments at the beginning of Joshua as a sign of a new beginning and new energy, which is then channelled into the conquest. The end of Joshua itself signals further sadness as Joshua and the leaders of his generation die.

2. Yahweh thus speaks to Joshua and tells him it is time to move on. The Israelites camped on the plains of Moab must cross the bordering river and enter the promised land, their final destination. As Nelson says, 'Yahweh's first directive begins a pattern that is repeated several times in Joshua. Divine command (vv. 2–9) is followed by Joshua's own corresponding directives (vv. 10–15) and then by Israel's subsequent obedience' (Nelson 1997a: 32). Nelson points out that variations of this threefold pattern can be found in chapters 3, 4, 6 and 8 (Nelson 1997a: 32).

3. Yahweh reaffirms his promise of land made through Moses. All the Israelites need to do is take it – it is legally theirs. It is human nature to want to think that one is right. Here divine promise provides the legitimation for Israel's claim to the land. Yahweh, the god of Israel himself, has given them the land. Compare this verse and verses 4–5 with Deuteronomy 11:24–25 (as pointed out by Nelson 1997a: 33).

4. This verse reiterates the extent of Israel's land, an area enclosed by the desert in the south, the mountains in the east and, towards the northeast, the northern border delimited by the river Euphrates and the land of the Hittites (note that it is somewhat further south than Anatolia proper), and finally the western border of the Mediterranean Sea. In the Old Testament, 'the Hittites' can refer either to a group of native inhabitants or to the people of ancient Anatolia (cf. *ABD* 3: 231–234). The origins of the former may at least partially be connected with the latter, too. The Hittite kingdom flourished especially between 1650 and 1200 BC. A peace treaty between Hattusili III and Ramses II of Egypt from c. 1290 BC (treaty originally in Akkadian, the diplomatic language of the day in the Near East; for a translated text of the treaty, see BECKMAN 1996: 90–95. See also an Egyptian version of the treaty in *ANET*: 199–201, based on an Egyptian text) shows that at the time, Egypt and the Hittite kingdom were adjacent powers (empires). The description of the land of the Hittites thus fits well with the situation of the thirteenth century BC (and earlier), even if a later Neo-Hittite state in north Syria could also be referred to. As Nelson comments, this verse reflects the 'most expansive form of Israel's land claim' (Nelson 1997a: 33). See also Deuteronomy 11:24 (as pointed out by Butler 1983: 3–4).

5. Yahweh encourages Joshua with an assurance of his help and presence. Divine promise of presence, especially to kings (note however that many such records are from the court etc.), is a normal feature in the Ancient Near East (see the 'Form and structure' section for this chapter). Yahweh's promise of presence is emphasized in the David narratives in particular, and with Abraham, Jacob and Joseph.

6. A war of conquest is to follow. As with all war and fighting, results will normally only be achieved by forcing the issue. For this, one has to be strong and courageous. Deuteronomy likes to use this type of language (see Deut. 29 – 31; 31:1–6). The link to Abraham and the patriarchs is emphasized. It is important that the land has been given to the Israelites by Yahweh; the divine decree is the ultimate legitimation for the conquest and possession.

7. Here a link is made to Moses, and to the giving of the law through him. The law is to be the basis of the Israelites' life. Just as, with Ancient Near Eastern treaties, blessings are invoked as a result of obeying the terms of the treaty, blessings to the Israelites follow from obeying the law. Curses follow from disobeying it, as can be seen throughout Joshua (e.g. 8:34; 23:16; 24:19–20) and especially in Deuteronomy (see esp. Deut. 28; note also the curses in Deut. 27, the counterpart to Josh. 8:30–35), which has been seen to have similarities with Ancient Near Eastern treaties that also contain blessings and curses (cf. above, v. 4). The Lipit-Ishtar law code from the nineteenth century BC, for example, also contains blessings and curses in relation to treating the stele on which the code was written (see *ANET*: 161). As Nelson points out, the particle *raq* (see textual note on the verse) serves to introduce the qualification or contingency (Nelson 1997a: 34).

8. This suggestion seems to be hyperbole. However, it is important to note that a key point is to keep the law (or instruction, the alternative translation of the word *torah*) in one's mind (or, lit. 'mouth') as the principle that guides one's actions (note that the Hebrew *hāgāh* also means to mutter, speak; cf. also Psalm 1:2). In this way, the follower of *torah* will have success, in line with the blessings of the covenant.

9. The command to be strong and courageous is repeated for the third and (through a negative implying the same) fourth time in the verse. Yahweh's presence is the key (cf. my comments about divine presence in Excursus 3 and elsewhere in this commentary).

10–11. Here a standard leadership form is exercised: Joshua instructs his subordinates who then are to tell the people (cf. comments on v. 2). Also, the narrative describes rather standard preparations for the important step of crossing the Jordan that is to come next. Three days is a time frame often used in the Bible (cf. my comments on 3:2 below; cf. also Jesus' resurrection).

12–18. Here a section on the Transjordanians is inserted. In line with one of the main themes of the book of Joshua, the unity of Israel, it is very important that the Transjordanians who have already received their share of land on the east side of the Jordan (see Num. 32) are fulfilling their obligation to take part in the conquest of the land west of the Jordan, together with the rest of the Israelites. This unity is particularly emphasized in chapter 22. The book of Joshua certainly gives a vision of Israel that includes the full complement of twelve tribes, and encompasses areas both west and east of the Jordan. As stated in the Introduction, this vision fits an early rather than a later period in Israel's history.

16–17. The behaviour of the Transjordanians is portrayed as exemplary. They do as expected of them, indicating an absolute willingness, and back up their consent with a reference to their past record (as pointed out by Nelson 1997a: 35). However, this may be an exaggeration in the light of the preceding Pentateuchal narrative. While Numbers 32 certainly indicates obedience on the part of the Transjordanians, such texts as Numbers 14 do not – in line with the behaviour of most of Israel during its time in the wilderness. The qualifier *raq* (cf. v. 7) in verse 17 calls for Yahweh's help, and its further occurrence in the next verse directly reminds us of verse 7 (see Nelson 1997a: 36).

18. In a military context in times of war, it is normal that those who do not follow the leadership are put to death. This is a simple and effective way of controlling other people. Leadership is sometimes simply based on power and on forcing people to do what is expected, even though losing the respect of the people can prove very problematic (cf. 1 Kgs 12, even if Yahweh is here portrayed as the ultimate force on which everything depends). As for the later Israelites, this verse reminds them of the high authority that Joshua had as Yahweh's representative and as the leader of the Israelites. Again, the comments by the Transjordanians sound perfect (if not too perfect!). They are part of the rhetoric of the book of Joshua in persuading its readers to follow Yahweh, and Joshua's portrayed high authority serves to impress these lessons on the reader. As Nelson points out, the death penalty that the Transjordanians call for for disobedience finds its fulfilment with Achan (Josh. 7:25; 22:20; see Nelson 1997a: 35).

Explanation

Joshua 1 marks the beginning of a new era in Israel's history in the context of the canonical story of the nation. Moses, the leader of the Israelites during the exodus and the period of the wilderness wanderings, has died, and the focus of Israel is now turning to the actual entry into the promised land. In addition to reiterating his promise about the land to be entered and its boundaries, Yahweh reassures Joshua that he is now the leader of Israel and that he should be strong and courageous and follow the law (*torah*) of Yahweh. The authority of Joshua is absolute at this crucial time in order to achieve the stated objective of acquiring the land. Everything in the conquest has as its ultimate source the promises of Yahweh who is giving Israel the land. This state of affairs depicted serves to impress the lessons of the book on its readers. In the same way, they are to follow Yahweh wholeheartedly and courageously. In the narrative framework, verses 10–12 stress the immediacy and urgency of the crossing that is about to take place.

The idea of following the instruction of God has direct resonance with a Christian. While there are no more blessings and curses in the sense of the deuteronomic covenant, a Christian is nevertheless encouraged to remember God's sacrifice through Jesus and do his or her best in following God's commands, as interpreted through the message of the New Testament. Broadly speaking, the ritual aspects of the law, such as animal sacrifices, are no longer applicable, but the ethical demands are, even though the exact nature of these ethical demands is sometimes a matter of debate among theologians and ordinary Christians!

In all human life there are leadership changes. For example, companies change their executives and universities their deans and vice-chancellors, and parents die. In the church, pastors and elders and PCC members change. Such situations are often a time of uncertainty, sometimes even great uncertainty. But they can also be a time of new beginnings. At these times, and otherwise when 'the only constant is change', Christians can think of the words of Yahweh to 'be strong and courageous' (vv. 6–7, 9), especially when they are taking a leadership position, but, equally, one can think that Christians can also trust that there can be a future even under new leaders. Trust in God and in his presence is an important consolation and comfort even in the toughest of situations.

Verses 13–18 turn the focus onto the unity of Israel in the task ahead. All Israel together is to take part in the conquest, including the Transjordanians. In the recent past the Transjordanians have already decided to settle east of the Jordan, and chapter 22 in particular also implies that there may be a question over whether they really are part of Israel. This may have been an issue especially for the first readers of the book. However, the narrative here speaks about Transjordanian unity with Israel in the affirmative, with the Transjordanians readily participating in the relevant conquest activities west of the Jordan.

Certainly, unity is one of the great themes that is also emphasized for Christians in the New Testament (e.g. John 17:20–23), even if this does not mean lack of debate about what is right and wrong (1 Cor. 11:19). Also, in Christian thinking, people from all nations are now partakers of the promises in Christ (e.g. the letter to the Ephesians).

Verse 18 raises an interesting dilemma in a wider context. In a time of war, there may sometimes be only two options: either be killed by the enemy or be killed by one's own side if one does not want to fight. Often, if the latter is stated clearly, it is better to fight and have a chance, and this is the balance of probabilities that is used to coerce people into fighting. Of course, the rhetoric of glory, of fighting for a good cause and for one's loved ones, is also used to motivate people by the societal elite that make decisions about war and peace. In many cases one can of course feel that the reasons given are justified (e.g. when clearly under an invasive attack by another state), but how should a Christian react in a time of war that he or she does not approve of? Also, a Christian is often part of a state (or some other group, e.g. tribe, even though these are mostly controlled by states in the modern world) and relies on the state and its structures for his or her life and survival. In such situations, the resulting ethical dilemma can be a vexing one. Refusing national service for reasons of pacifism can in itself bring a great stigma in societies that have a general draft (not in the UK or the US during peaceful times).

Another theme that is perhaps worth mentioning here is the emphasis on the loyalty of the Transjordanians and on their keeping their promises. This in itself speaks to the modern reader concerning the idea of faithfulness to others and to agreements made in the past.

JOSHUA 2

Translation

¹Then Joshua the son of Nun sent two men from Shittim secretly as spies, instructing them as follows: 'Go and survey the land and Jericho.' So they went and arrived at the house of a woman, a harlot called Rahab. And they lodged there.

²But the king of Jericho was told: 'Look, some Israelite men came here during the night to spy out the land.' ³So the king of Jericho sent a message to Rahab and said, 'Bring out the men who came to you and entered your house, because they have come to spy out the whole land.'

⁴But the woman took the two men and concealed them. She then said as follows: 'The men came to me but I did not know where they were from. ⁵The men departed when the gate was about to be shut by nightfall. I do not know where they went. Quickly, go after them, and you will catch them.' ⁶She had taken the men up to the roof and hidden them among the stalks of flax arranged for her on the roof. ⁷Men from the town then went in pursuit on the way to the Jordan, as far as the fords. The gate was shut as soon as they had gone on the expedition.

⁸Meanwhile, the woman went to the men on the roof before they had fallen asleep. ⁹She said to them, 'I know that Yahweh has given you the land. Terror of you has also fallen upon us, and all inhabitants of the land have melted away before you, ¹⁰because we heard how Yahweh dried the waters of the Sea of Reeds for you when you left Egypt and what you did to Sihon and Og, the two kings of the Amorites on the east side of Jordan, utterly destroying them.' ¹¹As we heard about these things, our hearts sank, and there was no strength left in any man to oppose you. This is because Yahweh your God is a God of the whole universe. ¹²And now, please swear to me by Yahweh that as I have been good to you, so you will be good to my family and will give me a sign of security. ¹³Spare my father and mother and my brothers and sisters and all that they have and let us live.'

¹⁴The men replied to her, 'Our lives against yours as long as you do not reveal anything about our mission. When Yahweh gives us the land we will deal kindly with you.' ¹⁵She then let them through the window by a rope as the house where she lived was part of the town wall. ¹⁶She instructed them, 'Go to the mountains so that the pursuers do not meet with you and hide there for three days until your pursuers return. You can then move on.'

¹⁷The men replied to her, 'We will be free from this oath which you have made us swear ¹⁸unless when we are coming to the land there will be this crimson cord in the window from which you let us out. And you must gather your father, your mother, your brothers and all your family to your house. ¹⁹Anyone who goes out past the doors of your house bears their own responsibility and we will not be held to account. On the other hand, we are responsible for all who are with you inside the house if any harm befalls them. ²⁰Also, if you let anyone

know about our business we will be free from this oath which you have made us swear.'

²¹She replied, 'Let it be as you have said.' Then she sent them off and they left. She moreover tied a crimson cord in the window.

²²The men went to the mountains and stayed there for three days until their pursuers returned. The pursuers sought them along the whole way but did not find them. ²³The two men then left the mountains and returned to Joshua son of Nun and related to him everything that had happened. ²⁴They said to Joshua, 'Surely Yahweh will give the whole land to us! All inhabitants of the land will melt away in front of us!'

Notes on the text

5. Catch: hiph. of *nāśag*.

6. Stalks of flax: *pištê hā'ēṣ*.

7. 'from the town' is not in the Hebrew text, but clearly implied.

9. And all inhabitants of the land have melted away before you: this clause is not included in the Greek.

10. Utterly destroying them: *'ăšer heḥĕramtem'ôtām*.

11. Sunk: lit. 'melted' (niph. impf. of *māsas*). Strength: lit. 'spirit' (*ruăḥ*). A God of the whole universe: lit. 'a God both in heaven above and on earth below'.

12. I have been good to you: *'āśîtî 'immākem ḥāsed*.

13. Let us live: lit. 'deliver our lives from death'.

14. We will deal kindly with you: *wĕ'āśînû 'immāk ḥesed wĕ'emet*.

15. Part of the town wall: lit. '*in* the town wall', and the narrative suggests that the house was part of the town wall (casemate); see comment on the verse.

19. Bears their own responsibility: lit. 'his blood will be on his head' (*dāmô bĕro'šô*).

24. To us: lit. 'in our hands' (*beyyādēnû*).

Form and structure

Nelson describes the basic narrative structure of chapter 2 very well (Nelson 1997a: 40):

> The commissioning and setting out of the two spies, along with their return and report (vv. 1, 23–24), frame three dialogues staged in three different settings. In vv. 3–5, Rahab converses with the king's delegation, while the spies are in hiding. In vv. 8–14, Rahab negotiates with the spies in her roof. In vv. 16–21, her concluding dialogue with them takes place.

In addition (Nelson 1997a: 40) says:

> In between and around these three conversations a tense adventure
> is played out. The spies fall into danger (vv. 1–2), are hidden and
> become trapped at the same time (vv. 6–7), escape the city (v. 15)
> and their pursuers (v. 22), and finally return in safety (v. 24).

Previous academic discussion of the narrative has mainly centred on its
provenance, purpose and literary prehistory, including sources (Noort
1998: 131, 135–143). Noth did however consider the passage in Joshua 2
as essentially a unity that derives from the *Sammler* (see Noth 1953a: 29).
Obviously, in the present narrative form of the book of Joshua, the chapter
ties in to the Jericho narrative of chapter 6, and the story of Rahab itself
has its conclusion in Joshua 6:22–25. However, commentators have
generally thought in essence that the story of Rahab was originally free-
standing and was picked up by the author and tied to its present context
of the conquest of Jericho only later, albeit Noth thought that this was
done by the *Sammler* (collector of tradition) and thus at an early stage
(see Noort 1998: 131–132; cf. Noth 1953a: 29; Nelson 1997a: 41). In this
connection, it has been noted that there are other stories in the Bible that
have a similar motif of betraying a town to an attacking enemy (e.g. Judg.
1:23–26) and being saved from destruction by showing hospitality to
strangers (Gen. 19:1–23; see Nelson 1997a: 41–43). Such parallels extend
beyond the Bible (see Noort 1998: 132). The story as a whole has generally
been seen as aetiological, giving a rationale for the existence of the family
of Rahab in the midst of Israel (Noort 1998: 131). In this, it can be
compared with the story of the Gibeonites (see Nelson 1997a: 44). The
spying motif can also be compared with other accounts of spying in
the Israelite conquest tradition (see Nelson 1997a: 45). Hawk notes
how the inclusion of the outsider Rahab through faith and obedience in
relation to Yahweh contrasts with the exclusion of the insider Achan
through disobedience in Joshua 7 (Hawk 2000: 20).

Be that as it may, we should keep in mind that the narrative of chapter
2 describes preparations for the conquest of Jericho which itself is described
in chapter 6. The emphasis on events surrounding the conquest of Jericho
should be seen as a narrative feature that stresses both the transition of
Israel from wilderness to promised land and the first events in the new
land. It may well be that the story of Rahab was always seen as inseparable
from the conquest of Jericho.

We should also note that it is feasible that a prostitute's house existed
in a town and that it was used by people, including travellers. Prostitution
is of course pretty much universal in human societies. As for travellers,
they would probably by and large be males on a mission that could last
for a considerable time, considering the speed of travel in the ancient
world, and it would be perfectly conceivable that they might use prostitutes

(cf. Gen. 38). Hess notes that there is some evidence for 'overnight places of accommodation and their use by travelling caravans and royal messengers in Canaan of the fourteenth to twelfth centuries BC', although Hess sees these as not related to prostitution (see Hess 1996: 83–84). In other words, overall, the setting is completely plausible.

Also, that the story of Rahab is similar to other stories in the Bible and beyond is not a hindrance to thinking of it as a plausible one at least in its basic contours. For example, betrayal of a town to an enemy could mean a new life with the conquerors for a person who was not likely to have been one of the most appreciated members of society before the conquest.

Comment

1. Spies are sent to Jericho. Entering the house of a prostitute would seem natural, as many people would come and go through such a place, and, judging from modern parallels, most people would not want others to know that they have visited a brothel. One could thus remain as anonymous as possible in such a place. The Hebrew name Rahab means 'spacious, wide', and does not seem to have a particular meaning here in relation to the story. Note that the Hebrew spelling is different from that of the Rahab of Job 9:13; 26:12; Psalms 87:4; 89:10; Isaiah 51:9. As Nelson points out, verses 1 and 23b–24 serve to connect the narrative to the overall context of Joshua (Nelson 1997a: 47). Note that spies were also sent out in Numbers 13.

2–3. The narrative describes how, despite the efforts of the Israelite men to stay incognito, the king somehow gets to hear about the matter. The inhabitants of Jericho correctly suspect that spying is the objective of the Israelites (cf. Gen. 42:30; 2 Sam. 10:3), and, as would be expected, the king sends for Rahab to bring the men out. The plot is thickening, and ancient readers or hearers of the story might have been holding their breath at this time. It seems impossible to ascertain whether the men's stay at Rahab's house had a sexual aspect. A pious reader would of course like to think that this was not the case.

4–7. Rahab hides the men on the roof among stalks of flax, either quickly in response to the search party, or in anticipation before they reach her house. It is important for Western readers to note that roofs were flat in ancient Israel and were used as an extra storey. From a narrative perspective, the tension and excitement of the prospect of capture already starts to be released. Overall, at this stage, the men are at the mercy of Rahab.

8–11. A little interlude where Rahab negotiates her future follows (note that the texts says that she went to the roof before the men had fallen asleep/slept – but who would expect that the men would be able to sleep in a situation like that?). As such, Rahab's confession sounds like a summary of what an Israelite would like to hear. The narrative presents her as saying all the right things, suggesting at least partially a retelling and even rephrasing of the conversation from an Israelite perspective (cf. comments about ancient history writing in the Introduction). Note the similarity of the latter part of verse 9 (cf. v. 11) to Exodus 15:15b (as pointed out by Moran, 'The End of the Unholy War and the Anti-Exodus', in Christensen 1993: 147–155 [p. 155]), and, of course, verse 10 then refers directly back to the miracle at the sea in Exodus 14 – 15. The conquest of Sihon and Og is mentioned as well. Compare these verses also with Joshua 24:6–10. However, interestingly, as Nelson points out, Yahweh is still the God of the Israelites at this point, and not that of Rahab (v. 11; Nelson 1997a: 50), and yet the confession seems to be moving Rahab towards adopting Yahweh as her God. For the Amorites, see comments on 9:1–2 and 13:10. For Sihon and Og, see comments on 13:2, 4.

12–13. Here's the trade: Rahab saves the messengers while the men of Jericho are in control, and the messengers are to save Rahab later once the Israelites are in control. Of course, a discerning reader or hearer would already have sensed a foretelling of things to come here.

14. The Israelites agree to the suggestion and the deal is closed. The important point is that Rahab is not to tell the people of Jericho what has happened. Secrecy is the key here, perhaps at least partly to make sure that any of the inhabitants of Jericho cannot use the oath to their advantage or to Rahab's detriment in some way, for example by arresting Rahab and in effect taking her hostage. Of course, the men could be in danger yet on their return journey if secrecy were broken, too (so Nelson 1997a: 51). The statement 'Our lives against yours' really sounds like an oath and is named as such in verse 17.

15–16. The narrative next indicates a potentially dangerous course of action, serving as a mini-climax. The Israelites are let out by a rope through a window. The narrative seems to state that the house was by the town wall, or even part of the town wall. That the Israelites could be let down by rope through the window would be in line with the house being part of the wall. In other words, it may be that the town was delimited by houses in a casemate-type structure, rather than a wall proper, as in the Middle Bronze Age. This would fit with the idea of a more meagre extent and status of the town during the Late Bronze Age (see Excursus 5 on Jericho below). Also, it would seem that if it were not a known practice to have one's house or dwellings as part of a city wall, the story would not make good sense to its first hearers and they would be likely to question it.

Rahab then suggests a fair ruse: the Israelites are to go to the hills rather than back towards the river. Three days of hiding will be enough to frustrate the efforts of the pursuers.

17–21. A sign of the oath (šĕbûʿāh), even a covenant (the word bĕrît is not used, however), is to be hung in the window through which the men were let down. The crimson cord to be tied in the window does not seem, and neither does it need, to be the same as the rope by which the spies were let out (note also that the Hebrew words are not the same). Rather, the cord is to be a symbolic sign acting as a reminder of the event of the visit of the spies. Rahab's house will then act as a kind of sacred space. Anything in it is outside destruction (*herem*), but anything outside it is under destruction. As Nelson points out, interestingly, the word used for 'cord' in verse 21 also has the meaning 'hope' in Hebrew (Nelson 1997a: 52).

22–24. A final test follows, serving as another mini-climax in the narrative, but things go as planned and the narrative reaches its denouement with the men returning safely to Joshua. They report that their enemies are afraid of them, a good sign for the forthcoming activities.

Explanation

This chapter describes how the Israelites spy on the first town to be conquered in the land of Canaan. The inhabitants have already heard of the incoming Israelites and are fearful of them, according to the Israelite tradition. The idea of Joshua 2 is that the Israelites plan to look at the city and how things stand there before the actual assault. As in any comparable situation, it will be expected that the inhabitants of Jericho will try to capture the spies if found. However, according to the narrative, the Israelites find an ally in a local prostitute who protects them from being discovered even when their presence has become known. A covenant is then established between the Israelites and Rahab and her family. This covenant is then fulfilled in chapter 6 when the conquest becomes reality. For the later Israelites, the narrative serves as an explanation for why Rahab and/or her descendants exist in the midst of Israel, and also as a reference to the time of the conquest and the events at Jericho.

Overall, Rahab was spared from death because she allied herself with the Israelites. In many ways, in the context of the ancient world, this was a religio-political matter. To be Israelite was to be Yahwistic in the thinking of the canonical documents. There could not be one without the other. Yahweh was Israel's national God, just as other nations may have had their set of gods (generally there seems to have been little monotheism in the ancient world at this time, even though the Egyptian pharaoh Akhenaten comes close to this). We may compare Rahab with Ruth 1:16–17; 2:11–12. From the standpoint of ethnicity, which itself importantly links to identity, we can say that Yahwism was an Israelite boundary marker according to the canonical documents. Thus, even if we might ask whether Rahab simply wanted to ally herself with the likely winners, the Israelites (with this involving becoming an Israelite, religion included), the role of religion should nevertheless be seen as inseparable from any other issues. The later canonical documents of course (Hebr. 11:31; Jas 2:25) like to emphasize Rahab's decision as a religious choice. From the standpoint of the narrative, one might also think that a prostitute would not have much to lose by allying herself with invaders, as they could perhaps give her a better life (most societies do not seem to attach much value to a prostitute under normal conditions). In the same way, in the case of conquests, there are usually elements of society that are willing to collaborate with the invaders and achieve better circumstances through such collaboration (cf. Sennacherib's campaigns where puppet kings were installed, and the modern conquest of Iraq by the United States, where surely anyone supporting the deposed dictator would not have been allowed to stand in an election). In the manner of the ancient world and its emphasis on family, Rahab's family is given an opportunity to benefit from the Israelite promises (cf. the punishment on Achan, which includes his whole family [Josh. 7:24–25; cf. also Dan. 6:24; Esth. 9:25] in a style rather typical of the Ancient Near East; cf. however the later Jer. 31:29–30; Ezek. 18:2; cf. also my comments on 7:1 and on the form and structure of 22:9–34).

From a Christian theological perspective, the main application here is probably that Rahab is saved from destruction and is granted a new life (with the conquerors) by means of her (explicit) switch to allegiance to Yahweh and the Israelites. In the same way, typologically, in Christian belief, faith in Jesus Christ saves and moves the person into a new life. Salvation can also often extend to the whole family one way or another (cf. Acts 16:31–34). That Rahab is a prostitute can be seen to emphasize that a new life can dawn under Yahweh's care even for someone for whom one might not naturally expect such things. Rahab herself is of course directly mentioned as an example of faith in Hebrews 11:31 and James 2:25, and may be mentioned in Matthew 1:5, even though another Rahab could also be intended.

JOSHUA 3 – 4

Translation

Joshua 3

[1]Subsequently, Joshua arose early in the morning and he and all the Israelites departed from Shittim and came to the Jordan. They camped there before crossing. [2]At the end of a period of three days the leaders of the people went through the camp. [3]They commanded the people as follows: 'When you see the ark of Yahweh your God and the Levitical priests carrying it, depart from where you are and follow them ([4]only let there be a distance of about a thousand yards between you and them. Do not go nearer to them) so that you will know which way to go. You have not been here before.'

[5]Joshua then instructed the people, 'Consecrate yourselves. Yahweh will do miracles among you from now on.'

⁶To the priests Joshua said, 'Lift the ark of the covenant and set out in the sight of the people.' Accordingly, the priests lifted the ark and walked in front of the people.

⁷And God said to Joshua, 'From this day on I will start making you great in the sight of all the Israelites. They will know that as I was with Moses so I will be with you. ⁸As for you, command the priests who carry the ark of the covenant as follows, "When you come to the edge of the waters of Jordan, wait by the river."'

⁹Joshua then said to the Israelites, 'Come here and listen to the words of Yahweh your God.' ¹⁰Joshua further said, 'From this you will know that a living God is among you and that he will certainly drive out the Canaanites, the Hittites, the Hivites, the Perizzites, the Girgashites, the Amorites and the Jebusites from before you. ¹¹See, the ark of the covenant of the Lord of the whole world will be entering the Jordan ahead of you. ¹²Select now twelve men from the tribes of Israel, one from each tribe. ¹³When the priests who carry the ark of Yahweh the Lord of the whole world step into the waters of the Jordan, the river will be cut off and the waters that are at the upper stream will gather in a heap.'

¹⁴Accordingly, the people set out from their tents for the crossing with the priests who carried the ark of the covenant of Yahweh in front of them. ¹⁵When the priests came to the Jordan and when their feet dipped into the waters at the edge of the river (now the Jordan overflows its banks during harvest time), ¹⁶the waters that flowed from above stopped and gathered in a heap far away by Adam which is by Zarethan. Thus the waters that went towards the Dead Sea were completely cut off, and the people were able to cross over in front of Jericho. ¹⁷The priests who carried the ark of the covenant of Yahweh stood in the middle of the Jordan while all Israel crossed over on dry ground.

Joshua 4

¹Once the whole nation had finished crossing the Jordan, Yahweh said to Joshua, ²'Take for yourself twelve men, one from each tribe. ³Command them, "Take twelve stones from the place where the feet of the priests stood and carry the stones with you. Then set them down at the campsite where you stay for the night."'

⁴Accordingly, Joshua chose twelve men from among the Israelites, one from each tribe, and addressed them. ⁵He said to them, 'Go to the middle of the river where the ark of Yahweh your God is and carry away one stone each to represent all the tribes of Israel. ⁶This will be a sign for you so that when your children ask from you in the future, "What do these stones signify?", ⁷you may reply, "The waters of the Jordan were cut off in front of the ark of the covenant of Yahweh. When the ark was crossing the Jordan, its waters were cut off. These stones serve as a memorial of the event for the Israelites for ever."'

⁸The Israelites did as Joshua told them. They took twelve stones from the middle of the Jordan to represent all the tribes of Israel, just as Yahweh had said to Joshua. They took the stones with them to the place where they stayed the night and set them there. ⁹Joshua set up the twelve stones that were taken from the middle of

the Jordan, from the place where the priests who carried the ark of the covenant stood. The stones are there even now.

¹⁰The priests who were carrying the ark stood in the middle of the Jordan until everything that Yahweh had commanded the people through Joshua, itself in line with Moses' injunctions to Joshua, had been completed. The people hurried through, ¹¹and when all of them had crossed the river, the ark of Yahweh and the priests came through in their sight. ¹²The Reubenites, the Gadites and the eastern half of the Manassites crossed in front of the people, ready for war, just as Moses had commanded them.

¹³An army of about 40,000 crossed over in the presence of Yahweh for war to the plains of Jericho.

¹⁴On that day Yahweh made Joshua highly regarded by the Israelites, and they respected him just as they had respected Moses, all through his life.

¹⁵Yahweh then said to Joshua, ¹⁶'Tell the priests who carry the ark of the testimony to come out of the Jordan.'

¹⁷Joshua therefore commanded the priests, 'Step out of the Jordan.'

¹⁸When the priests who carried the ark of the covenant of Yahweh had stepped out of the Jordan, the waters of the river returned to normal. It overflowed its banks, just as before.

¹⁹The people came out from the Jordan on the tenth of the first month. And they camped at Gilgal at the eastern edge of Jericho. ²⁰As for the twelve stones that they brought out from the Jordan, Joshua set them up at Gilgal. ²¹Joshua said to the people, 'When your children ask their parents in the future, "What are these stones?", ²²tell your children, "Israel crossed the Jordan on dry ground." ²³For Yahweh your God dried the waters of Jordan in front of you when you crossed over, just as he did to the Sea of Reeds when we crossed it, ²⁴so that all people of the world would get to know the might of Yahweh, in order that you would always respect him.'

Notes on the text

Joshua 3

3. Follow them: lit. 'walk after it'.

4. Thousand yards: lit. 'about two thousand cubits (*'ammāh*) using a measure'. Between you and them: Alternatively, 'between you and it'; see textual note in *BHS*.

8. Wait by the river: lit. 'stand (using the verb *'āmad*) by the Jordan'.

10. Certainly drive out: Note that Hebr. uses infinitive absolute here, designating emphasis.

11. The whole world: Hebr. *kol-hā'āreṣ*.

13. The whole world: see note on verse 11. When the priests have stepped into the waters of the Jordan: lit. 'When the soles of the feet of the priests . . . rest in the waters of the Jordan.'

15. The priests: lit. those who were carrying the ark.

16. By Adam which is by Zarethan: Gr. 'as far as the region of Kiriath Jearim'. The Dead Sea: lit. the desert sea, the salt sea. Were able to cross over: lit. 'crossed over'.

Joshua 4

3. From the place: lit. 'from here from the middle of Jordan, from the place'.

7. 'Of the event' in the translation is not explicit in the original Hebrew, but is definitely implied by the context.

9. First part of the verse lit. 'And Joshua set up twelve stones in the middle of Jordan, under the place where the feet of the priests who were carrying the ark of the covenant stood.' For the translation and meaning of this verse, see commentary. Even now: Hebr. *'ad hayyôm hazzeh*.

11. Gr. in essence omits 'priests', and adds at the end of the sentence: 'and the stones before them'.

12. Ready for war: Hebr. *ḥămûšîm*.

14. Highly regarded: lit. 'great in the eyes of'. Respected: lit. 'feared' (*yārē'*). 'All through his life' (lit. 'all the days of his life') could grammatically refer to either Joshua or Moses.

18. When the priests who carried the ark of the covenant of Yahweh had stepped out of the Jordan: lit. 'And when the priests who were carrying the ark of the covenant of Yahweh had come up out of Jordan, when the soles of the feet of the feet of the priests were removed to the plain.' To normal: lit. 'to their place'.

21. Parents: lit. 'fathers'.

24. The world: Hebr. *hā'āreṣ*. Would get to know the might of Yahweh: lit. 'would know the hand of Yahweh, because/that it is strong'. Respect: lit. 'fear' (*yārē'*).

Form and structure

These two chapters logically belong together, and will be treated together for this section. The literary form of this passage has been a subject of much discussion. Above all, there appears to be unevenness in the narrative, and the text seems to present a number of inconsistencies, even contradictions. The main issues raised include the following (from Nelson 1997a: 55, 65):

> an apparent chronological discrepancy between vv. 1, 5 ('overnight, tomorrow') and vv. 2–4 ('three days')
> the awkward placement of the first part of 3:4
> no reported execution of the command of 3:5

the awkward placement of 3:13 and its delayed follow-up (not
    until 4:2)
the ark carriers stand at the edge of the river (3:8, 13, 15) but also
    in the middle (3:17)
the waters are 'cut off', but also 'stand still'
the complex, overfull sentence in 3:14–16
memorial stones interrupt the primary story of crossing and
    compete with it for narrative attention
two groups of stones, one on shore (4:3–5, 8) and one set in the
    river bed (4:9)
the men 'deposit' the stones in an unnamed camp in v. 8, but in
    v. 20 Joshua 'erects' them in Gilgal
two scenes of catechesis, one focusing on 'cutting off' (4:5–7) and
    the other on 'drying up' (4:21–24)
4:1 and 4:10–11 report the completion of the crossing pre-
    maturely (cf. 4:12–13, 16–18)
Various uses of *lipne* create confusion over the order of the pro-
    cession (4:5, 11, 12, 13; cf. 3:6)
An unexpected appearance of the eastern tribes (v. 12) and the
    isolated placement of 4:13 and 4:14
4:11 reports that the ark crossed out of the middle of the Jordan,
    but it is still there in 4:18
Inconsistent nomenclature for the ark.

According to Nelson, 'the logical digressions and persistent reiterations
in chapters 3 and 4 are undoubtedly the result of a complicated history
of composition and redaction' (Nelson 1997a: 55). For attempted solutions
to the redactional history of the narrative, see Noort 1998: 147–164. These
include various source-critical approaches.

In order to respond to the 'charges' of unevenness and inconsistency,
let us first analyse the basic narrative structure of the passage. It can be
described as follows, with a number of the letters signifying motifs, and
corresponding letters with apostrophes signifying action developed from
them (this approach in certain ways resembles approaches that try to
form a chiasm, and this holds partially for the passage here, but a full
chiasm cannot be arrived at):

A   Moving out from Shittim and arrival at Jordan (3:1)
B   Three days' break (3:2)
C   Orders to people by officers about how to march (3:3–4)
C   Order by Joshua to people to consecrate themselves (3:5)
C   Order by Joshua to priests to carry the ark in front of
     people (3:6)
D   Yahweh instructing Joshua about entering the water
     (3:7–8)

D   Joshua instructing people about entering the water
        (3:9–13)
E   The priests entering Jordan with waters stopping
        (3:14–16)
F   The priests standing in the middle of Jordan with people
        crossing (3:17)
G   People pass over the Jordan (3:17)
G'   People finish passing over the Jordan (4:1)
H   Yahweh instructing Joshua about stones to be taken from
        Jordan (4:2–3)
H   Joshua instructing twelve men to take stones from Jordan
        according to Yahweh's command; children's questions
        (4:4–7)
H'   People executing Joshua's command about the stones;
        comment about quick crossing (4:8–10)

E'/C'   Prolepsis about the ark and the priests coming out from
        Jordan after people finish passing (4:11)
G   Comment about the passing of the Transjordanians and
        exaltation of Joshua (4:12–14)
E'   Yahweh commanding Joshua to ask the priests to come
        out of Jordan (4:15–16)
E'   Joshua commanding priests to come out of Jordan (4:17)
E'   Priests coming out of Jordan with waters returning (4:18)
A'   Encamping at Gilgal (4:19)
H'   Setting up stones at Gilgal; children's questions (4:20–24)

With the aid of the above analysis, we can say that there is clear development in the story, with the middle of the Jordan acting as a centre point, with as-if mirrored actions occurring on both sides of this centre line. Certainly, not everything is progressing as one would expect in a modern Western literary product; rather, the narrative progresses in a 'to and fro' style. Having said that, while possibly even annoying to the modern reader, this 'to and fro' style is in fact quite effective, offering recapitulation, prolepsis and fulfilment of intended or ordered action, at the same time moving the story forward. It would probably have been quite useful in storytelling, helping to keep the audience with the story, if the material had an oral existence or was read to audiences. In this light, and when one reads 4:11 as recapitulating that stones are to be taken from the Jordan (see comment section on the verse) and sees the chronology at the beginning of chapter 3 as indicating a move from Shittim to Jordan with a three-day wait before the crossing, little if any inconsistency remains. This then of course casts doubt on the necessity of complicated redactional and source-critical approaches to the narrative. Some textual corruption is of course as such possible in these chapters, as elsewhere in Joshua.

There are further issues to consider, however. The material has been seen as stemming from a cult centre at Gilgal (see Noth 1953a: 11–12). Noth in particular implied that the story, and other stories relating to the area around Gilgal, originally enhanced the legitimation and importance of the sanctuary at Gilgal (Noth 1953a: 11–12). Noth even thought that Gilgal served as a central sanctuary at the time of Saul (Noth 1953a: 12; cf. p. 33). Beyond this, it has at times been suggested that the narrative reflects a cultic procession in the vicinity of the sanctuary, although Noth had already spoken against this view (see Noth 1953a: 33). Whatever the case, certainly, it seems correct to think that Gilgal had an important role in Israelite history. However, in the book of Joshua, the stones set up at Gilgal serve as a memorial and as a sign for future generations. In that sense it then is a holy place, but this does not necessarily imply that the book of Joshua thinks that it was a sanctuary for cultic action. Any such connotations would have to be deduced from other considerations.

It is important to note the similarity of the crossing of the Jordan to the crossing of the Sea of Reeds in the book of Exodus (see Ottosson 1991: 79 for the larger context; reproduced in Excursus 2 above). With regard to the overall story of Israel, the crossing of the Sea of Reeds starts the period of wilderness wanderings, and the crossing of the Jordan ends it. Both stories also involve a miraculous dividing of the waters. A direct link between the two is drawn in Joshua 4:23 (cf. 2:10; for some further detailed connections, see Ottosson 1991: 56). The connection to Exodus and also to the wilderness wanderings especially in the book of Numbers explains many of the stories in Joshua 1 – 12. The connection with the crossing of the Sea of Reeds also helps explain the relatively large amount of space devoted to the narrative of crossing the Jordan in the book of Joshua.

It is also worth noticing that the idea of children's questions in the chapter (4:6–8, 21–24; cf. Josh. 22:24–28) are paralleled with Deuteronomy 6:20–25. This emphasizes the deuteronomic character of the literary unit. At the same time, we note that the cultic procession of the ark is reminiscent of material in Numbers and thus implies priestly appropriation (so also Ottosson 1991: 54; cf. comments on pp. 55–56). We may keep in mind here that, according to the classic Wellhausenian theory, the expression 'Levitical priests' is typical for Deuteronomy, and a full division of priests and Levites came only with the later priestly material (see Wellhausen 1905/1878). However, we may also keep in mind that it is well known that priesthood existed in the Ancient Near East even in the late third millennium, and, as one case in point, Weinfeld has recently given other reasons for dating priestly material early in Israelite history (originating from the time before the monarchy; see Weinfeld 2004 and above, Introduction). From all this it follows that one may think that the Deuteronomist generally appears to use relatively non-technical language about cultic matters, and the exact distinctions within the Levites (and priests) were not a focus of his writing.

Comment

Chapter 3

1. The story now moves forward from Shittim (cf. 2:1). In a sense, the expression 'early in the morning' strikes the modern reader as redundant. Perhaps it intended to convey the idea that the troops were eager and ready to go, as opposed to getting up late and being a bit sluggish etc. (so also Nelson 1997a: 60, also referring to 6:12, 7:16 and 8:10). The troops then depart from Shittim and camp at the river. Note how Numbers 22:1, 25:1 and 33:49 describe the way the Israelites camp on the plains of Moab, and Shittim is explicitly mentioned in Numbers 25:1; 33:49 (assuming that Abel Shittim is the same as Shittim). Tell el-Kefrein and Tell el-Hammam have been suggested as possible sites for Shittim. Both attest remains from Iron I and Iron II, with the former in the form of potsherds, and the latter in the form of remains of a fortress (see *ABD* 5: 1222).

2. Three days are taken for further preparation for the crossing. Note also the usage of three days in 1:11; 2:16, 22; 9:16. Three and seven are numbers that may on occasions have special significance in the Bible (but also in the Ancient Near East). We note here, too, that Christ's death and resurrection of course involved three days, but it would probably be unwise to try to make any further connections here, even in a canonical context, even though, if one were into typological interpretation, one could for example say that the three days of preparation point to three days of preparation between completing the previous life in the wilderness and starting a new life in the promised land. Joshua could then become Jesus who leads the people into new life. In this, we may bear in mind that typological interpretation was of course in vogue in the early history of the church in particular, e.g. in the works of Origen.

3–4. The ark of the covenant is to go first, and the Levitical priests are to carry it. As pointed out in Excursus 3 (which see for a detailed discussion of the ark and Yahweh's presence), the ark itself was an Israelite equivalent of Ancient Near Eastern god images. In other words, Yahweh himself through his presence is travelling in front of the people for war. The Levitical priests carry the ark (with poles as if carrying a king on a sedan chair, as might be done for a king in the Ancient Near East) and the ordinary people are to keep a healthy distance.

For further comments on the Tent of Meeting (although not mentioned in this verse), see commentary on 18:1.

5. The people are to consecrate themselves; the parting of the waters of the Jordan and other spectacular things are to take place soon. Washing may have been understood to be part of such consecration. It was usual for both priests and ordinary people to purify themselves by washing according to cultic legislation (see e.g. Lev. 14 – 15; 16:23–24). But, similarly, washing was normal in other Ancient Near Eastern contexts pertaining to the cult (see e.g. Instructions for Temple Officials, in the Hittite realm in *ANET*: 209, item 14). But, on other occasions, consecration might be related to abstaining from sexual intercourse (see 1 Sam. 21:4).

6. This verse in essence recapitulates and develops the events of verses 3 and 4.

7. An important aspect of leadership is emphasized here: Yahweh's favour. Similar themes recur in Ancient Near Eastern literature. For example, in the Apology of Hattusili, a text from second-millennium Anatolia, the new king Hattusili justifies his accession and taking away of kingship from his brother Muwatalli, repeatedly speaking of the favour of Ishtar his lady; e.g. 1.20–21 (text from STURTEVANT-BECHTEL, translation mine):

> *nuzakan ANA ŠU ᴰIŠTAR GAŠAN-YA lulu uhhun numu ᴰIŠTAR GAŠAN-YA ŠU-za IṢBAT našmukan para hantantešta.*
> And me, I saw prosperity through the hand of Ishtar my lady, and Ishtar my lady grabbed my hand and led me by the way.

The Apology of Hattusili (4.7) also mentions that Ishtar had promised Hattusili kingship (text from STURTEVANT-BECHTEL, translation mine):

> *ammukma LUGAL-UTTA ᴰIŠTAR GAŠAN-YA annišanbe kuit memiskit.*
> And to me Ishtar my Lady had spoken kingship from previously.

Continuity with Moses is emphasized (again). The authority of Joshua is to be in essence the same as that of Moses. This also emphasizes the importance of Joshua from a canonical perspective, even though most readers of the canonical books would undoubtedly see Moses as the greater of the two.

8. Here Joshua tells the priests to carry the ark of the covenant in front of the people into the river (v. 15), but they are first to stop at the edge of the river while Joshua gives some special instructions to the people. The priests were the ministers of Yahweh just as priests in the Ancient Near East were ministers of the relevant gods, and the priests of Yahweh were to carry the ark, the symbol or locus of Yahweh's presence, which here was going with them for both travel and war. The ark, the Israelite equivalent of an Ancient Near Eastern god image (see Excursus 3 for further details about the ark), and the Tent of Meeting, the early Israelite equivalent of a temple, were portable and allowed the deity and his people to move around, fitting the state of the nation as it emerged from Egypt and moved on through Sinai into Canaan according to the canonical documents of the Old Testament. The situation changed with David and Solomon and the building of the temple, but not without careful consideration of the significance of such a change (see 2 Sam. 7).

9–13. Joshua now tells the people what is to happen. The ark of the covenant, and thus by implication Yahweh himself, enters the river first in the sight of the people. A rather spectacular miracle will then shortly follow. The waters will stop and heap up (v. 13), and the subsequent narrative describes how the Israelites cross the river miraculously on dry ground. Yahweh's majesty is also emphasized by the title 'Lord of all the earth' which would translate as 'Lord of the universe' in contemporary garb. Note however that the Jordan is not like the Nile and other big rivers of the modern world, and looks almost like a brook by modern standards if one visits present-day Israel. However, the river was bigger in ancient times when there were no dams upstream. The narrative (v. 15) notes that the river was in an overflowing state at the time of the crossing, and Humphreys notes that a British expedition in the nineteenth century estimated that the river in flood was half a mile (0.8 km) wide (see Humphreys 2003: 25–26). We must also remember the more limited means of crossing rivers available to ancients (note the first-millennium Assyrian military technique of crossing difficult rivers by using wineskin-like sacks of individual soldiers, which were inflated and then used as floats (for an adapted picture, see e.g. http://www.gutenberg.org/files/17326/17326-h/v6b.htm#image-0039, accessed 16 February 2009), even though boats of course were also used, for example in Egypt, as part of normal life from early times.

As described in Excursus 2, which see for details, the narrative has affinities with the crossing of the Sea of Reeds in Exodus 14 – 15. The Sea of Reeds was the border between Egypt and the wilderness wanderings, whereas the Jordan was the border between the wilderness wanderings and the promised land. Both are crossed miraculously. It can also be noted that the pillar of fire serves as the place of the presence of Yahweh in the Exodus narrative and as a guide for directions for the Israelites in the Exodus account, whereas the ark is central in the narrative of the crossing of the Jordan in the Joshua account. At times both the cloud and the ark are implied to operate simultaneously (e.g. Exod. 40; Num. 9; also cf. 1 Kgs 8:10–11). However, in common with the standard thinking of other Ancient Near Eastern peoples, it would not be difficult for the Israelites to imagine Yahweh to be (and to be able to be) present simultaneously in a number of places on earth in addition to his presence in heaven, depending on the situation.

The anticipated miracle serves as a testimony to the Israelites of Yahweh's power and care of Israel, and as a sign of reassurance that Yahweh's promise of helping Israel to take possession of the land is real (v. 10). As Nelson points out, what people can 'know' from Yahweh's actions (cf. v. 7 and 4:22–24) also occurs in Deuteronomy (Deut. 7:9; 9:3; Nelson 1997a: 61), although the comments made in Deuteronomy are more of a proleptic type. Obviously, in its literary context, the miracle serves as a constant reminder to later generations and readers of the book of Yahweh's great deeds for Israel. The stones will serve as a memorial to the event (see below on 4:20 for more details).

As soon as the soles of the priests carrying the ark touch the river, it will be cut off (v. 13). Some have suggested a landslide (or mudslide) upstream as a possible natural cause of the event, pointing out that such landslides have taken place in the past (see e.g. Humphreys 2003: 20–22 and below, commentary on vv. 14–17, for details). Such commentators are all quick to point out that, even if this is the case, the timing is nevertheless providential (see e.g. Humphreys 2003: 22–23). In this connection, it must also be emphasized that, if one looks at a cross-section of Ancient Near Eastern material, one can see that people believed in miracles as part of a widespread and institutionalized belief in the divine.

It is not clear exactly what is meant by the designation 'Canaanite' in conjunction with the other groups listed, but, of course, the land Israel entered is referred to as 'Canaan' (see *ABD* 1: 828–831 for further details). The term 'Canaanite' does occur in Ancient Near Eastern literary documents from the Bronze Ages (see Junkkaala 2006: 315, referring to Rainey). For the Hittites, see comments on 1:4 and 9:1–2. For the Hivites, see comments on 9:1–2. The exact designation and localization of the Perizzites is unclear (see *ABD* 5: 231 for a discussion; but cf. Josh. 11:3 and 17:15, which indicate localization to the hill country); see also comments on 9:1–2. The exact designation and localization of the Girgashites is unclear, albeit a similar name (*grgš* and *bn grgš* [son of *grgš*]) has been found in the Ugaritic texts (see *ABD* 2: 1029). Na'aman suggests that they originate from Karkisha in Western Anatolia (Na'aman 1994b: 240). For the Amorites, see comments on 9:1–2 and 13:10. For the Jebusites, see comments on 9:1–2.

14–17. The narrative then reports how the priests actually enter the Jordan first. The repetitions in the narrative seem to fit very well with Hebrew narrative style. First it tells what is to happen, and then what happens is actually described in almost identical terms, with a bit of extra detail added (cf. Exod. 25 – 31 vs Exod. 35 – 40). Here the location of where the waters stopped and piled up is related, a town called Adam in the vicinity of Zarethan, together with the comment that no water at all could flow to the Dead Sea. Also, the verses relate the crossing of the Jordan (v. 17). The priests, together with the ark, stand in the river while the people cross over opposite Jericho. One might ask the question of whether, according to the narrative, people could get closer to the ark than usual while crossing (cf. 3:4 and comments there). Adam is generally located at Tell ed-Damiyeh (see *ABD* 1: 64; Junkkaala 2006: 208–209).

There is survey evidence of occupation from Late Bronze Age II and the Iron Age (see Junkkaala 2006: 209). According to Humphreys, landslides that cut the river typically for a day or two are recorded to have happened in 1160 (earliest record found), 1267, 1534, 1546, 1834, 1906 and 1927 (Humphreys 2003: 20–21). The 1927 landslide occurred at Damiyeh (Humphreys 2003: 20–21). The location of Zarethan does not seem to be clear (see *ABD* 6: 1041–1043).

Chapter 4

1–7. Twelve men are selected to take twelve stones from the middle of the Jordan as memorials of the crossing. As Nelson points out, 'the last words of 3:17 are repeated in order to introduce a concurrent side plot' describing this (Nelson 1997a: 68). The 'until' of verse 17 becomes the 'once' of the ancillary plot (Nelson 1997a: 68). That everyone is to take a stone on his shoulder implies that these were not understood to be very large stones, such as those famously found at Gezer (see below on 4:20), otherwise it would have been impossible to carry them. It is likely that they would have been deposited in some kind of structure which then became a holy place, possibly even a sanctuary at some point. Naturally, Alt and Noth would state that stories formed and became associated with local sanctuaries, and one of those was a sanctuary at Gilgal. One might think that having a story like that would tie a sanctuary to venerable events and thus legitimate it and increase its prestige. Having no substantial archaeological remains from Gilgal, assuming that one has even identified the site properly (only pre-pottery Neolithic or late Natufian remains have been found from sites that have thus far been seen as possible candidates, even if only a site called Gilgal I has been systematically excavated; see *NEAEHL*: 517–518; note also comments in relation to Khirbet el-Mafjar in *NEAEHL*: 922; note also that Deut. 11:29–30 *may* locate it close to Mount Ebal and Mount Gerizim [cf. Hawking 2007: 180]), we of course cannot in any way prove anything about any possible veracity of this story or the manner in which it originated, whether based on some real events or on folklore. In this, the narrative links with the crossing of the Sea of Reeds tradition in Exodus certainly at least partly point towards a stylized way of expressing the material from a literary standpoint. And yet we must also remember here that Gilgal serves as an important reference point in both early and later Israelite history (Josh. 4 – 5 etc.; 1 Sam. etc.; Hos., Amos), and this would suggest that the site must have existed, even if its location is unknown.

Whatever the case, in the context of the narrative, the stones are to serve as memorials of the conquest for future generations (vv. 6–7; cf. vv. 21–24). Children's questions occur also in Joshua 22:24–28 (the Transjordanian altar), Exodus 12:26 (the origin of the Passover rite), 13:14 (dedication of the firstborn in remembrance of the exodus) and Deuteronomy 6:20 (keeping the law based on remembering the exodus). The questions reflect deuteronomic thinking, emphasizing as a whole that the Israelites should remember the great deeds of Yahweh and keep his law throughout the generations (see Pitkänen 2004a: 207–208 for a fuller analysis).

8. The narrative now notes that the men did as commanded. This is a bit tautologous for the modern reader, but, apart from serving to move the narrative forward in the style of Joshua 3 – 4 as a whole, perhaps the idea is also to emphasize how Israel did as Joshua, the leader of Israel sanctioned by Yahweh, commanded them. The place of lodging is explicitly stated as Gilgal in verse 19. In other words, the people have come from Shittim (3:1) to Gilgal, crossing the river in the process.

9. Here the narrative seems to indicate that the stones are now set up in the middle of the Jordan, if read literally. This is certainly possible, and would suggest that a second memorial was set up in the place where the priests stood. However, while again possible, it sounds odd that the narrator would then say that the stones are there even now, as the stones would be in the middle of the river, unseen and susceptible to being moved by the currents. It is more likely that there has been some kind of confusion, and the verse should refer to the stones that had been taken out of the Jordan (basically replace *bĕtôk* with *mitôk*, and perhaps *taḥat* with *mitaḥat* in the verse). This would make perfect sense in the context of the narrative, and there are others who have taken this view (e.g. NIV; Hess 1996: 109). Admittedly, there is however no actual textual evidence in support of the differing reading.

10–12. The priests stand in the middle of the river with the ark and the people hurry over, with the Reubenites, Gadites and the eastern half of the tribe of Manasseh at the front. The mention of the Transjordanian tribes here emphasizes the unity of Israel and ties back to the narrative in Numbers (Num. 32) and to the beginning of Joshua (1:12–18; see also Deut. 3). Nelson points out how verses 10–11a resemble 3:16b–17, and how this *Wiederaufnahme* (Gm. 'resumption') helps to continue the overall progression of the crossing part of the narrative after the side plot that had started in verse 1 (Nelson 1997a: 69).

13. The number 40,000 seems to refer to all Israelite warriors, even though in this context it could refer only to the Transjordanians. Whatever the case, this implies a number of Israelite males much smaller than the 600,000, or even the 110,000 Transjordanians that are indicated in the book of Numbers (see Num. 1:45–46; 2:10–11, 14–15, 20–21 [counting eastern Manasseh as half of 32,200 in Num. 2:21]). As a whole, based on our present state of knowledge, the numbers given in the Old Testament conquest tradition seem too large. Current authors estimate the Early Iron Age population of Canaan to have been about a maximum of 50,000 in the thirteenth century (see Dever 2003: 97–100, esp. p. 98). If this is roughly in the correct magnitude, the Israelite number must be further scaled down if a resident population existed that in practice was not driven out, at least to a large extent. Thus the immigrating Israelite population should be in the magnitude of a maximum of some tens of thousands at the most. In fact, even the Joshua narrative attests to a smaller number. For example, according to the book of Joshua, Hebron was given to Caleb (Josh. 14:6–15). It is unlikely that the people belonging to Caleb's group were great in number; rather, they would probably number in tens of individuals at most, if even that many.

It would seem that the large numbers are either an exaggeration to emphasize the blessing of Yahweh on Israel so that Israel has become a great nation, or are a later artificial construct (perhaps a reworking of the numbers in an earlier version of the text), or involve some kind of error (for treatments of large numbers in the book of Numbers, see e.g. standard commentaries on the book of Numbers, Humphreys 2003 and the comments in Provan, Long and Longman 2003, including works referred to). But, if so, this does not really depart from the theological message of the narrative. It may even be that the inflated numbers were simply a part of the ancient Israelite way of telling things, naturally recognized as hyperbolic exaggeration by the first readers of the book.

Compare the use of the word *ḥălûṣ* (armed) in this verse with Numbers 32:20–32, Deuteronomy 3:18, and cf. Joshua 6:7, 9, 13, and also compare Joshua 1:14 where *ḥămušîm* is used (as pointed out by Nelson 1997a: 70).

14. Joshua's authority is now made comparable to that of Moses. The narrative here emphasizes that it is Yahweh who exalts Joshua as part of his choice of him as the leader of Israel. But the passage also shows that the leader Joshua derives his authority from actual intervention by Yahweh to demonstrate his choice and favour. People like to see their leaders as strong and capable; conversely, a strong and capable person often becomes a leader and stays one. Whatever Joshua's natural qualities, the events at the river show that the leader Joshua is backed up by Yahweh, the God of Israel who effects great miracles for his people.

15–18. After the people have crossed, the priests come out of the Jordan. The ark, and thus Yahweh, no longer stands in the Jordan and the river resumes its normal flow. As Nelson points out, this verse picks up on verses 10–11, verses 15–17 are a command phase and verse 18 is the action phase (Nelson 1997a: 70).

19. The people camp at Gilgal. As the first month was the start of the new year and was associated with Israel's liberation from Egypt (see Exod. 12:2), in the same way, the Israelites cross the river Jordan to the promised land in the first month, and, in this case, just when the Passover season starts (cf. Exod. 12:3, naming the tenth day as the time to select the sacrificial lambs), and the conquest starts only after the Passover has been celebrated. So here (again) the conquest is strongly tied to the exodus. For the archaeology of Gilgal, see comments on verses 1–7. The date in verse 19 connects the narrative of chapters 3 – 4 to the wider context of Joshua (cf. 5:10; as pointed out by Nelson 1997a:70). Also, of course, Israel has now moved from Shittim (2:1) to Gilgal, having crossed the Jordan in the process. Gilgal itself features as a camp (5:9–10; 9:6; 10:6–9, 15, 43; 14:6) until the Israelites set up the Tent of Meeting at Shiloh (18:1).

20. The point that Joshua set up the stones is repeated here. The comment that these were set up specifically at Gilgal brings in some new information and ties verse 20 to verse 19. One may keep in mind here the prominence of memorials in the book of Joshua (see Introduction). Many of these are stones that are set up. As already mentioned in Excursus 3, in the ancient world, stones were often used also as aniconic (i.e. not picture-like) cult objects. According to ancient belief, the stones would in essence be indwelt by a divinity just as cult objects would, and would similarly be placed in a *cella* (the holy of holies) of a sanctuary for worship. Such a sanctuary then would not involve an image of Yahweh, in violation of the commandment against making a God image (Exod. 20:4). However, Deuteronomy clearly seems to speak against such stones (Deut. 7:5; 12:3; 16:22). Here, however, the function of the stones is purely memorial, with twelve stones corresponding to the twelve tribes of Israel. Whether the monument actually existed at some point in Israel's history cannot be proved (note the comment about their size and about the archaeology of Gilgal in the section on 4:1–7 above), but a big, apparently open stone structure has been found at Gezer from the Middle–Late Bronze Period (see *NEAEHL*: 501), and, while a cultic interpretation is generally favoured, at least a partially memorial function is also a possibility. Hawk also makes a connection with Exodus 24:4 (Hawk 2000: 69–70). Joshua 24:26 should also be mentioned in this context (as pointed out by Nelson 1997a: 71).

21–24. The children's questions from verses 6–7 are repeated here. The verses also explicitly tie the crossing of the Jordan to the crossing of the Sea of Reeds (v. 23). Verse 24 notes that the deeds are a witness to others about the might of Yahweh, and equally to Israel so that Israel would always respect (the Hebrew word *yārē'* implies awe, fear and respect) Yahweh (cf. Exod. 14:31, and also Deut. 5:29; 6:2, as pointed out by Nelson 1997a: 71). If one respects another person, one takes that person seriously. Similarly, by implication, Israel is to take Yahweh seriously and follow his law. Compare also verse 23 with Joshua 2:10 (as pointed out by Nelson 1997a: 71). Interestingly, the focus is on the people ('you') in the crossing of the Jordan, whereas the previous generation ('we') clearly seems to be implied in the crossing of the Sea of Reeds (Nelson 1997a: 71). The crossing of the Jordan and the Sea of Reeds achieves 'not only typological, but mythic' dimensions in later (or, other, if one dates materials differently) Israelite literature (Ps. 66:6; 114:3; see Nelson 1997a: 71).

Explanation

The nation prepares to cross over the river Jordan. This is psychologically important as the Jordan marks a very significant border, even when the Transjordanian tribes of Reuben, Gad and half of Manasseh have already received their allotments on the east side of the Jordan, where Israel has already arrived by the time that the events of Joshua begin (cf. also Josh. 22). The narrator of Joshua draws links and parallels with the crossing of the Sea of Reeds as part of the exodus from Egypt. In many ways, this then delimits the events in Exodus–Joshua into three periods: Egypt, the wilderness, and the promised land. In the narrative frame, it is now time for Israel to leave the wilderness period behind and enter the promised land. Preparations for the crossing are instituted. The Transjordanians are mentioned explicitly in order to stress that all Israel takes part in the crossing. Yahweh through his presence at the ark, carried and accompanied by the priests, crosses with the people. He opens the waters of the Jordan, stays in the river while the people cross, and then closes them once the people have crossed. The event of the crossing is to be commemorated by setting up a memorial made from stones from the river on the side of the promised land. It is to remind future generations about the great deeds of Yahweh for Israel. The events remind the Israelites that Yahweh is with them and that all success eventually comes from him. The wait in the wilderness was long, and the delay was due to the disobedience of the people. But Yahweh is faithful and brings his word to pass for the next generation.

Christians also sometimes have to wait for the promises of God to be fulfilled. It is part of their faith that God will bring them to pass. Sometimes, it is time to move on to new things and to trust that God is on one's side. Of course, it is often difficult to discern when it is actually time to move on to new things. Just as crossing the river Jordan was a defining moment for the Israelites, so, even if somewhat allegorically, Christians sometimes have to cross their own river Jordan, leaving old things behind and trusting in God's help and providence in a new situation. In doing this, Christians may even need a kind of miracle to help them move forward. And there are many people who believe that they have encountered such divine encouragement and help. But, at the same time, let us remember that these kinds of things can also happen to people who do not have a Christian commitment. When the Roman emperor Julius Caesar crossed the river Rubicon he knew it was a point of no return, and is famously said to have declared *Alea iacta est* (The die is cast) in acknowledgment of this. While Caesar may well have prayed to his god, for Christians the main point is that they are trusting the God who revealed himself first to the people of Israel and then through Jesus in the New Testament. Such words can resonate in a pluralistic or multi-religious society. At the same time, in places and societies where there can be widespread agnosticism and even atheism, belief in God is a belief and trust in the divine and a belief in God's companionship and protection in an otherwise sceptical and often lonely world. And, finally, at the end of their lives, Christians may look forward to crossing the river into the promised land, from this life to the next.

The ark features prominently in the narrative as the locus of Yahweh's presence. In contrast, for Christians, an ark or a temple (cf. the tabernacle in Josh. 18:1; cf. also 22:9–34) is no longer necessary as a place of God's presence. Their bodies are now the temple of God (1 Cor. 3:16; 2 Cor. 6:16). Of course, assembling as the church with other people is partaking in the body of Christ, and this has a special significance. But the concepts of holy objects and holy places are now less important in themselves. While most people would feel there is something special about a building that has been dedicated to God, fundamentally the place of worship is no longer crucial from the standpoint of Christianity. It would seem that the statement 'where two or three gather in my name, there am I in their midst' of Matthew 18:20 would also speak for this view, even though the context is not about worship proper. All this said, a church does conjure up an image of Christianity, too, and can even be seen as a memorial in its own way. Thus, when church buildings have to be sold and converted to other purposes in contemporary Britain, this is reason enough for Christians to feel a slight unease. In other words, there are pros and cons for retaining church buildings, but none of the reasons for retaining them is compelling.

One of the emphases of chapters 3 – 4, besides the actual description of the crossing of the river Jordan, is the remembrance of the event throughout the generations, and, at least on this reading, the remembrance of the event is then of course ultimately the central reason for including the story in the book of Joshua. As for Christians, except for churches as just mentioned, what items do they have for remembering God? Many people have crucifixes, for example hung on the wall in their home, or they wear them as pendants. Catholic and Orthodox believers have traditionally used icons, or images of Christ and the saints. Some Protestants in particular have objected to pictorial representations, with the worry that they might become objects of worship in themselves. The issues are surprisingly similar to Joshua 3 – 4 and the use of standing stones. Here the stones are to serve as memorials, but, as indicated above, in the ancient world people might also make stones objects of worship. Thus it seems that an object may in itself be rather neutral: what counts is how it is used. Perhaps we can say that Christians can also be encouraged to use memorials, as long as they do not elevate them to the status of objects of worship. In this connection, Christians may also travel to holy places, but really only so that seeing such places might help them remember the great deeds of God.

Joshua 4:14 indicates that it would be desirable, even necessary, for a leader to have the respect of the people he leads. The verse also indicates that, in an ancient Israelite context, this reverence is effected by God. However, to be helped by God, the leader must keep God's law and respect his holiness (Josh. 1:8). Similar issues relate to ordinary people. If people acted against, or sinned against, Yahweh, bad things could happen, as already attested in Joshua with the incident concerning Achan (Josh. 7). Other notable occasions in the Old Testament on which sin caused problems include the conduct of Phinehas' sons in 1 Samuel 2, Solomon's foreign wives and idolatry in 1 Kings 11, and David and Bathsheba in 2 Samuel 11 – 12. There are also related examples from the Ancient Near East. The plague prayers of Muršili (a late-thirteenth-century Hittite king) relate to a plague that was ravaging the land, seen by Muršili as taking place because of divine displeasure due to sin. Or an extant prayer from the late second millennium BC confesses the sinfulness of all (Foster 2005: 724–725). In the New Testament, matters are easier, as sins against God are forgiven through the sacrifice of Jesus. Yet there are also occasions when the New Testament describes severe punishments, such as that of Ananias and Sapphira in Acts 5 (note that a parallel with the Achan incident in Josh. 7 has been suggested, see Bruce 1990: 162), the communicants in 1 Corinthians 11:22, 30, and apparently the recalcitrant sinner in 1 Corinthians 5. This then raises the question of the nature of such judgments. Without going into a detailed discussion, it would seem to this author that if Christians are the children of God, then God the Father can discipline his children in a manner analogous to how an earthly father might (1 Cor. 11:32). Yet the sins of Christians are forgiven through the work of Christ, and the focus is not on fear but on free grace (John 1:16).

The aspect of human retribution may remain, however. Such popular sayings as 'You reap what you sow' (already in Gal. 6:7, even though Paul was drawing from a known proverbial saying; see Bruce 1982: 264–265) suggest that people often have problems with others as a matter of course if they do not treat them well. Coming back to the Old Testament, Rehoboam lost his leadership because he could not win the respect of the people (1 Kgs 12), even though according to the narrative this was also the working of God in punishment of Solomon's sins (1 Kgs 12:15), whatever the importance of such political considerations as the facts that Solomon's tax burdens had weakened the respect people had towards the united monarchy, and that already existing regional differences also played their part. But, overall, governments have noticed time and again that it is very difficult to rule people solely by force, especially in the longer term. The fall of communism and the non-violent movement led by Gandhi for the independence of India are pertinent recent examples in world history. Even in the workplace, a superior who uses methods of bullying and intimidation often cannot but lose, since people will quietly resist him or her and either leave for another job or refuse to cooperate beyond what is absolutely required.

EXCURSUS 3: THE ARK AND YAHWEH'S PRESENCE

The ark of the covenant features in Joshua 3 – 4, and also in Joshua 7 (7:6) and 8:30–35 (8:33). In this excursus, I will highlight its meaning and significance by placing it in the context of the ancient world. We will also look at issues relating to the presence of Yahweh, which is closely associated with the ark.

On the whole, the ark was an Israelite equivalent of Ancient Near Eastern god images. In the Ancient Near East, god images were objects made as representations of gods. During or after a ritual to initialize, or 'open the mouth' of, a cult image, the god would take up residence in an image, and people would view such an image in many ways as a manifestation of that god. It was typical in an Ancient Near Eastern context that the cult images were kept 'hidden' in a holy of holies, and only the priests would have access to them. The idea was that a temple was an earthly house of a god where the god lived in the midst of the people, often through his or her image. Sometimes gods could also be considered to be present through an aniconic object, such as a cult stele. Such cult stelae have been found in the area of ancient Israel, as it seems, notably from Iron Age IA Arad (see *NEAEHL*: 83) and Late Bronze Hazor (see *NEAEHL*: 596). A special class of people, the priests, generally served the gods (e.g. by making offerings to them, and by feeding and clothing them), and also served as intermediaries between gods and people. When a god lived with the people, it was a sign of good times, but a god could also show his or her displeasure by leaving through being captured by enemies. Gods could also go on journeys, and they could go about in a procession etc. (some have suggested that Ps. 132:2 was sung in a procession of the ark; comparable processions are known from Egypt, Assyria and Ugarit). Divine standards would be used to make gods travel for war with the troops; here again, the god would be present with the troops. The presence of the gods in battle was believed to guarantee victory. In the case of defeat, it was considered that the god had not allowed it or was even angry with the troops (cf. 1 Sam. 4, where Yahweh shows his displeasure by letting Israel be defeated and on top of that by leaving the land to reside in the country of the Philistines).

One aspect that is interesting here is that while god images were normally kept in shrines and inaccessible to common people, during processions, for example in Egypt and Mesopotamia, the people could actually see, and even touch, the god concerned (see e.g. van der Toorn 1997: 233 for Babylonia), and divine standards would be carried by the troops (at least in Assyria; see Uehlinger 1997: 125), with not much distance between the divine and the profane during those times. However, in Israel, it seems that a healthy distance was to be kept from the ark (Josh. 3:4). In this connection, someone who was not appointed to the service of the ark should not touch it, or even look at it, otherwise death might result, as happened to the men of Beth Shemesh (1 Sam. 6:19–20) and to Uzzah (2 Sam. 6:6–7).

While an Ancient Near Eastern cult image was generally a representation of the god concerned, the ark was not a representation of what Yahweh looked like. The Ten Commandments explicitly forbid any representation of Yahweh (Exod. 20:4; Deut. 5:8). Instead, the ark was more like a litter for Yahweh at which Yahweh was somehow present (Exod. 25:22; note that, in general, Kitchen [1993: 125; cf. 2003b: 280] has pointed out Egyptian parallels to the ark from the standpoint of overall construction). Also, Yahweh took up residence in his dwellings, both in the Tent of Meeting (Exod. 40:34–35) and (from the standpoint of the narrative) in the later temple (1 Kgs 8:8–11) after these had been built and the ark brought in. It was typical in the Ancient Near East to have a ritual when a newly built temple was consecrated, and an important moment in this was when the cult image entered the temple. This was also the case in Israel (see Exod. 40; Num. 7; 1 Kgs 8:1–21). As for the form of Yahweh, while the Israelites were not supposed to represent him with an image, the biblical materials contain hints that he was nevertheless at least in some way thought of in human terms. In Exodus 31:18, the tablets of law had been written by the finger of God. In Genesis 3:8, Yahweh walks in the garden with Adam, and God was on the mountain in Deuteronomy 4:11–12 and spoke from the midst of the fire, albeit unseen as dark clouds were covering him.

The ark also contained the tablets of law (Exod. 25:21; Deut. 10:3–5). Based on the fact that the ark is mentioned merely as a receptacle of the law tablets in the latter passage, many scholars have thought that the ark was not a seat of Yahweh in Deuteronomy (see e.g. von Rad 1953/1948; Weinfeld 1972). However, the law tablets attested a covenant between Yahweh and Israel. This covenant on the other hand was modelled after Ancient Near Eastern treaties (see e.g. BECKMAN for Hittite treaties from the second millennium and PARPOLA for Assyrian treaties from the first millennium), and it was normal in the Ancient Near East to place treaties in the divine presence in sanctuaries (see e.g. BECKMAN: 105 (§5), 125 (§§ 6–7)). With this in mind, it would be most natural to have the tablets in the divine presence by putting them in the ark (similarly Millard 2007). Just because divine presence is not mentioned in the passage does not mean that Deuteronomy would not think that the ark was a seat of Yahweh's presence; on the contrary, it is more likely that the matter was self-evident for the writer. Also, in the Ancient Near East, even if gods were dwelling in sanctuaries, they would also always be present in heaven at the same time (e.g. Shamash was the sun and in the sun even if he was also present at his sanctuaries); therefore, that Deuteronomy is emphasizing the heavenly dwelling of Yahweh does not by implication deny that he might dwell on earth at the same time. Rather, again, it is the opinion of this writer that the writer of Deuteronomy would consider these issues self-evident and would probably even be rather surprised by the modern discussions. The book by Ian Wilson (Wilson 1995), which approaches the question of divine presence in Deuteronomy from a slightly different angle and argues for divine presence in Deuteronomy, should also be mentioned here. And Sandra Richter's examination of parallels to the deuteronomic centralization formula in the Ancient Near East shows that 'setting the name' is more about Yahweh conquering the territory for Israel and claiming it for himself, and less about divine presence as such (see Richter 2002). In this, while Richter seems to deny the association of the name with divine presence, there are reasons to see that the name formula may also refer to Yahweh himself, i.e. hypostatizing the name. In fact, a passage in Deuteronomy (Deut. 28:58) associates Yahweh with his name (*haššēm hannikbād wĕhannôrā'hazzeh 'ēt yhwh 'ĕlōhêkā*; see Pitkänen 2004a: 50). Also, 2 Samuel 7:13 in particular indicates how David's descendant is to build a house for Yahweh's name (*yibneh-bayit lišmî*), and in 1 Kings 8:16 Yahweh's name will be in the temple (*lihyôt šĕmî šām*). At the very least, the dwelling of the name and the divine presence of Yahweh are not contradictory in the context of these two passages (see Pitkänen 2004a: 45 and *passim* for the context of 1 Kgs 8 in particular; cf. also the comments by Mettinger 2003: 754–755). From the Ancient Near East, one can see an example of treating Enlil's name in essence as Enlil himself (Pitkänen 2004a: 49). Possible further parallels, as noted by Mettinger, are 1 Samuel 25:25, Isaiah 30:27, the examples of Eshem-Bethel in Elephantine, Astarte as *šm b'l* (referring to *KTU* 1.2.1.8; 1.16.6.56; *KAI* 14:18), and *sumu/samu* in Amorite personal names (Mettinger 2003: 754).

JOSHUA 5

Translation

[1]When all kings of the Amorites who were situated west of the Jordan and all kings of the Canaanites who were by the sea heard that Yahweh had dried the waters of the Jordan for the Israelites, their hearts sank and they did not have any strength left against the Israelites.

[2]At that time Yahweh spoke to Joshua, 'Make flint knives and circumcise the Israelites for the second time.' [3]Joshua then made flint knives and circumcised the Israelites by Gibeath Haaraloth.

[4]The reason that Joshua circumcised them was that all the people who left Egypt, that is, all males fit for war, had died on the way in the desert after they had left Egypt. [5]All people who had left Egypt were circumcised, but none of those born on the way was circumcised. [6]The Israelites spent forty years in the desert until all men of war who had left Egypt had died. They did not

take Yahweh's oath to them seriously and would thus not see the land that Yahweh swore to their fathers to give us, a land flowing with milk and honey. [7]Joshua circumcised their children who were born after them. As they had not been circumcised on the way, they were uncircumcised. [8]Once the people had been circumcised, they rested in the camp until they had recovered.

[9]And Yahweh said to Joshua, 'Today I have taken away the reproach of Egypt from you.' Therefore the name of the place is called Gilgal even now.

[10]The Israelites camped at Gilgal and observed Passover on the evening of the fourteenth day of the month at the plains of Jericho. [11]They ate unleavened bread and roasted grain from the products of the land on the very next day. [12]Manna ceased a day after they had eaten from the produce of the land, and there was no more manna for the Israelites. They ate from the produce of the land of Canaan that year.

[13]When Joshua was at Jericho, the following happened. When he lifted his gaze, he saw a man standing in front of him with a drawn sword in his hand. Joshua went to him and said, 'Are you for us or for our enemies?'

[14]He replied, 'Neither. I am the commander of the army of Yahweh. I have come now.' Joshua then bowed down on the ground and said, 'What does my Lord want to say to his servant?' [15]The commander of the army of Yahweh replied to Joshua, 'Take off your shoes! The place where you stand is holy.' And Joshua did so.

Notes on the text

1. West of the Jordan: Gr. 'beyond the Jordan'. Sank: lit. 'melted' (from Hebr. *māsas*). Strength: Hebr. *rûaḥ*.

2. Note that verses 2–9 in Greek differ slightly from MT, but the thrust is the same (cf. also comments in Butler 1983: 54–55; Nelson 1997a: 72–73).

3. Gibeath Haaraloth: Engl. 'The hill of foreskins'.

4. 'That is' is not in the original, but is helpful for English expression.

5. On the way: lit. 'in the wilderness on the way in them coming out of Egypt'.

6. Did not take Yahweh's oath to them seriously: lit. 'did not hear the word of Yahweh which Yahweh swore to them'. Us: some manuscripts, 'them'.

8. Rested: lit. 'remained in their place'.

9. Taken away: lit. 'rolled away' (*gālal*). Gilgal: pil. from *gālal* (see *HAL* 186; cf. Jer. 51:25; note that the prose of v. 9 here does not use the pil. form). Even now: Hebr. *'ad hayyôm hazzeh* (cf. 4:9).

11. On the very next day: lit. 'on the day following the Passover, that very day'. Gr. omits this expression.

12. Gr. 'on this day' as the temporal reference at the start of this verse.

14. Bowed: traditionally considered to be hith. from *šāḥāh*, but more recently seen as hish. from *ḥāwăh* (cf. *HAL*: 283–284, 1351–1352).

Form and structure

This chapter continues the transition from Egypt and the wilderness into the promised land. Verse 1 is a summary statement about the fear the native inhabitants have of Israel. Verses 2–9 describe the circumcision of the Israelites for the first time after entering the promised land. Verses 10–12 describe the first Passover in Canaan, and verses 13–15 describe Joshua's encounter with the commander of Yahweh's army.

As with chapters 3–4, the link to what has happened before Joshua's time is strong. Verse 1 certainly links back to Deuteronomy's promises about a fear that will fall upon Israel's opponents (Deut. 2:25; 11:25). This fear is emphasized in the opening sections of the book of Joshua (see 2:9, 24; 9:24). Verses 2–9 explicitly link back to Egypt and the wilderness. The reference to manna in 10–12 of course refers to the wilderness, and the story of manna, even though it is also mentioned in Deuteronomy, belongs most properly to the book of Exodus. It is worth noting that the material in Exodus 16, which describes the first occurrence of manna, has generally been seen to consist mostly of P material according to classical source criticism (for source-critical details, see Childs 1974: 275; Durham 1987: 224). If it is correct to assume that P is referred to, this would reinforce the idea that the writer of Joshua was familiar with priestly materials. It would also be rather natural especially in view of the early existence of priestly cultus in the Ancient Near East (cf. comments on the form and structure of chapters 3 – 4 above). In any case, there is much focus on cultic matters in this chapter as a whole. The story about the commander of Yahweh's army reminds one of Exodus 3:1–5 (cf. esp. Josh. 5:15 vs Exod. 3:5), a text generally assigned to JE in classical source criticism (for source-critical details, see Childs 1974: 52).

It is also worth noting that the MT and Greek versions of verses 2–9 differ. This suggests that the text was malleable in its transmission. Nevertheless, there are no major differences between the two versions in this case, which itself speaks for the basic reliability of the transmission process (cf. my comments in the Introduction: p. 62). The main issue is that the clarification that unleavened bread was eaten on the day following the start of Passover is included only in the MT. This brings it in line with Leviticus 23:4–8, whereas the Greek suggests eating unleavened bread on the eve of the Passover, more in line with Deuteronomy 16:1–8 (see Nelson 1997a: 72–73, 78–80). However, that circumcision is described before celebrating Passover, in line with Exodus 12 (see comments on vv. 3, 10–12 for further details), speaks against a straightforward application of the idea that the MT reflects a later stage of the development of the text.

The chapter contains two aetiological comments, on Gilgal (v. 9), and, even if not stated completely explicitly, on the hill of foreskins (v. 3). For comments on the so-called aetiologies, see the Introduction to this commentary.

Comment

1. The narrative here mentions how the opposition become afraid when they hear what is happening, including the miracle. The narrative implies that they are so afraid that they no longer have any courage to face the Israelites. This is hyperbole in typical Ancient Near Eastern fashion, but, presumably, the idea is to emphasize that the crossing of the Jordan nevertheless is part of psychological warfare to terrorize the opposition. Compare this verse with Exodus 15:15; Joshua 2: 9, 11, 24; also Joshua 7:5; 14:8. As Nelson points out, here the Canaanites are located to the area by the Mediterranean Sea and the Amorites to the highlands (Nelson 1997a: 75). It appears that the book of Joshua is not always consistent on the matter, using terms loosely (cf. e.g. 2:8–11; 9:1–2; 13:10 and comments there).

2. Circumcision was not exclusive to ancient Israelites. For example, the Egyptians practised it, and the same seems to be true of a number of other Ancient Near Eastern peoples (cf. Faust 2006: 86). However, for the Israelites it was the sign of the covenant (cf. Gen. 17), and this ritual meaning makes the act important.

3. Here the 'aetiological' focus continues. The circumcision of the Israelites is said to have happened at a place called Gibeath Haaraloth (hill of foreskins). This ties events to a place and thus the place called Gibeath Haaraloth to Israelite memory about the important events of early Israelite history. According to Exodus 12 (vv. 44, 48–49; usually assigned to P [see Childs 1974:184]), one should be circumcised in order to partake of Passover; hence the preparations (for v. 10), even if the expression $b\bar{a}$'$\hat{e}t$ $h\bar{a}h\hat{i}$' (at that time) in verse 2 itself could be interpreted more loosely (cf. 8:30, where '$\bar{a}z$ is used. From a literary perspective, this then seems to reinforce the links with the priestly material of the Pentateuch. Some three to four days seems a short time to heal (4:19 vs 5:10).

4–8. The reason for the circumcision is given: the Israelites who came out of Egypt had been circumcised, but not those born in the wilderness. The forty years in the wilderness seem most naturally to be taken as a round number, signifying a generation. In the ancient world, the average life expectancy was much lower than in today's industrialized societies with their modern housing and medicine. See also comments on 4:21–24 about generational distinction in 4:23.

The words 'a land flowing with milk and honey' (v. 6) are a stock expression about the land of Canaan (see e.g. Exod. 33:3; Num. 14:8; 16:13–14;

Deut. 6:3; 11:9 etc.), in keeping with the hope of the Israelites to enter there from a narrative perspective. One should note here the recent discovery of an apiary, or beehive colony, at Tel Rehov, dated to the tenth to early ninth centuries and containing more than thirty hives, which suggests that the stock expression is likely to have had some factual basis too, in particular referring to bees' honey (see http://www.rehov.org). The find at Tel Rehov is the earliest apiary found to date anywhere in the Ancient Near East. Note the direct mention of bees and/or honey in Judges 14:5–9 with Samson and the dead lion, and in 1 Samuel 14:24–27 with Jonathan and the oath of Saul (as pointed out on http://www.rehov.org). Bees and honey also featured in Egypt from earliest times (see http://www.reshafim.org.il/ad/egypt/timelines/topics/beekeeping.htm, accessed 17 July 2008, which also reminds us that the hieroglyphic symbol for Upper and Lower Egypt features a combination of sedge and a bee). Milk was mostly extracted from goats (rather than from cattle), and goats were certainly not uncommon in the land of Canaan (cf. *ABD* 6: 1127–1130).

9. The reason is given for the name 'Gilgal'. It relates to the taking (rolling) away of the reproach of Egypt from the Israelites (cf. textual note on the verse). Reputation was as much an issue for ancient people as it is for the people of today. Overall, the verse also seems to highlight that the past life in Egypt is becoming more and more distant for the Israelites. For the archaeology of Gilgal, see comments on 4:1–7.

10–12. The Passover is now celebrated (cf. Exod. 12), and, significantly, the Israelites eat some produce of the land (cf. this with Lev. 23:4–8, 9–14). The reference to the produce of the land in effect seems to refer to firstfruits (by virtue of being the first things eaten in the new land), and may have a link with Leviticus 23:9–14 (cf. Nelson 1997a: 78–80). Certainly, the execution of circumcision in verses 2–8 seems to make a clear link with priestly material (cf. comments on v. 3). The manna (Exod. 16) ceases as it is no longer necessary (cf. Exod. 16:35 as pointed out by Nelson 1997a: 79). These events serve to signify that the transition from the wilderness to a new life in the new land is complete.

13–15. In a manner reminiscent of the burning bush narrative (Exod. 3), Joshua encounters the commander of the army of Yahweh from the supernatural realm. In both cases, Moses and Joshua are to take off their shoes, as the ground where they are standing is holy (v. 15; Exod. 3:5). Note that while Joshua asks for the message, the commander of Yahweh asks him to take off his shoes in reverence for the holiness of the place. The question then is, why is the place holy? Is it because of some inherent quality of the place or because Yahweh's messenger has now appeared? Also, is the commander of Yahweh here to be taken as the ultimate commander of the Israelite troops or of the heavenly hosts, perhaps fighting in the supernatural realm (cf. e.g. 1 Kgs 22:19; Ps. 103:21; also Job 1; and, as pointed out by Nelson 1997a: 81, Judg. 5:20; 2 Sam. 5:24), or both? In general terms, however, divine presence in war was seen by Ancient Near Eastern peoples as necessary for success. And gods were seen to be fighting with the troops as a divine vanguard in the Ancient Near East. The Tukulti-Ninurta Epic (late thirteenth century BC) describes how Tukulti-Ninurta followed the gods in the divine vanguard (Niehaus 1995: 133, quoting Mann 1977: 40–41, which also contains the Akkadian in transliteration; on line 26, I have taken *išarrum* to mean possibly 'strike blows' rather than 'dance', as suggested by Mann; note that the arrangement of the battle formation in Josh. 6 seems slightly different, but this does not take away the overall point):

> (23) The fighting line was spread out on the field of battle; fighting commenced.
> (24) A great commotion set in among them; the servants trembled.
> (25) Assur led in the vanguard; he kindled a biting flame against the foes.
> (26) Enlil struck blows (?) in the midst of the enemy; he fanned the burning flame.
> (27) Anu sent a relentless weapon against the evil ones.
> (28) Nannar Sin forced against them the pressure of battle.
> (29) Adad the hero sent down a flood-wind against their fighting line.
> (30) Šamaš, lord of judgment, dimmed the eyes of the forces of Sumer and Akkad.
> (31) Ninurta, the warrior, leader of the gods, shattered their weapons.
> (32) And Ishtar beat her skipping rope which drove their warriors mad.
> (33) Behind the gods, his helpers, the king in the vanguard of the army began the fight.

Explanation

The transition from the wilderness into the promised land continues in this chapter. Yahweh's power and presence with the Israelites is noticed by the indigenous inhabitants with fear. Israel itself pauses in its travel and conquest activities to reinstitute circumcision, one of the important signs of the covenant. The new generation born in the wilderness had not been circumcised, but it was now time to rectify the situation. This also made the time in Egypt a more distant memory, and one could say that the reproach of Egypt had been rolled away. The places where the events take place are also renamed to commemorate what has happened. A first Passover in the land is then celebrated. Manna ceases with the eating of the produce of the promised land, again to indicate and reflect that the time in the wilderness has passed. Finally, Yahweh appears to Joshua through his messenger in preparation for the future battles. The setting is similar to that of Moses' encounter with Yahweh in the burning bush, and serves to draw a link with the exodus, and at the same time serves to present Joshua on par with Moses, or at least close to the level of Moses, thus emphasizing Joshua's authority.

In a narrative sense, the chapter looks back to the past (vv. 4–7), at the present and into the future (v. 12, but also vv. 13–15). Even if it is a truism, apart from looking into the future, transition from old to new usually involves looking back at the old and also seeing the changes that take place with the transition. For Christians, this may involve meditating on the great deeds of God for them, and remembering in faith God's guiding hand and presence in preparation for things to come. Also, just as Yahweh fought for Israel, Christians can trust that God will be on their side, even if this does not involve physical violence.

JOSHUA 6

Translation

[1]Jericho was completely sealed off because of the Israelites. Nobody entered or left the town.

[2]Yahweh said to Joshua, 'Take note, I have given Jericho and its king, mighty warriors, to you. [3]Let the troops encircle the town. Go around it once a day for six days. [4]Seven priests are to carry seven ram's horns in front of the ark. You shall circle the town seven times on the seventh day, and the priests shall blow the horns. [5]When the priests make a long blast with the ram's horns and you hear the horns' sound, all the people shall make a great shout. The wall of the city will collapse, and every man shall then go up straight on.'

[6]Joshua then called the priests and said to them, 'Carry the ark of the covenant and let seven priests carry seven rams' horns in front of the ark of Yahweh.' [7]And he said to the people, 'Depart and circle the town, and let the fighters go in front of the ark.'

[8]It was done as Joshua told the people. Seven priests carried seven ram's horns in the presence of Yahweh. They proceeded and blew the horns, and the ark of the covenant of Yahweh went after them. [9]The fighters went in front of the priests who were blowing the horns. The rest went behind the ark, and the company kept on blowing the horns. [10]Joshua commanded the people, 'Do not make a shout, do not let your voices be heard and do not even say a word until the day I tell you. Then shout!' [11]He made the ark of Yahweh go around the town and circle it once. After that, the company returned to the camp and lodged there for the night.

[12]Joshua then rose in the morning, and the priests took the ark. [13]The seven priests who carried the seven ram's horns in front of the ark went about and blew

the horns. The fighters walked in front of them and the rest walked behind the ark of Yahweh, and the company kept blowing the horns. [14]They went around the town once on the second day and returned to the camp. Thus they did for six days.

[15]On the seventh day they rose early at daybreak. They went around the town seven times in the same manner. Only on that day did they go around the town seven times. [16]On the seventh round, when the priests blew the horns, Joshua told the people, 'Shout! Yahweh has given you the town. [17]The town and everything in it is to be dedicated to Yahweh. Let only Rahab the harlot and everyone in her house be spared. This is because she hid the messengers we sent. [18]Be careful to observe the dedication. Otherwise you yourselves will be under it if you take any of the dedicated objects, and you will also make the camp of Israel dedicated and will cause trouble to yourselves. [19]All silver and gold, and all objects of bronze and iron will be holy to Yahweh. They will be taken to the treasury of Yahweh.'

[20]The people shouted and the priests blew the horns. That is, when the people heard the sound of the horns, they raised a great shout. Then the wall collapsed and all the people went straight up to the town and took it. [21]They killed everything that was in the town, men and women, young and old, cattle and sheep.

[22]To the two men who had spied out the land Joshua said, 'Go to the house of the woman, the harlot, and bring her out from there together with everything that belongs to her, in accordance with the oath you swore to her!' [23]The young men who had been spies then brought out Rahab, her father, her mother, her brothers and everything that belonged to her. They took her whole family and put them outside the camp of Israel.

[24]They burned the town and everything in it. However, they gave silver, gold and any vessels of bronze and iron to the treasury of Yahweh. [25]Also, Joshua left alive the harlot Rahab and her family and everything that belonged to her because she hid the envoys whom he sent to spy out Jericho. She still lives among the Israelites.

[26]Joshua then swore, 'Let the man who re-establishes and builds Jericho be cursed by Yahweh. Let him lose his firstborn when he lays its foundations, and his youngest when he sets up its gates!' [27]So Yahweh was with Joshua and his fame spread over the land.

Notes on the text

1. Note that there are some differences between the LXX and the MT in verses 1–15. The LXX is shorter. However, the thrust of the narrative is the same in both versions. The main essential differences between Hebr. and Gr. in these verses are indicated below. Completely sealed off: lit. 'completely shut'; Hebr. *sōgeret ûměsugeret*.

2. To you: lit. 'in your hand'.

3. 'Go around it once a day for six days' is missing from Gr.

4. Ram's horns: Hebr. *šôprôt hayyôblîm*; cf. *KB*: 381, 1344. Gr. pretty much omits this verse, except for the mention of the trumpet (instead of ram's horns; Gr. *salpinx*; the priests are not mentioned).

5. Make a long blast: Hebr. *māšak*; see KB: 610. Again, Gr. does not mention the priests here.

9. Gr. seems to indicate that the priests are at the very rear, or at least behind the ark, and there seems to be at least a minor contradiction with verses 6–8 in the Greek. There is also no mention of the main company of people in Gr. in verse 9.

12. Gr. mentions, 'on the second day'.

15. 'In the same manner' is not included in Gr.

17. Dedicated: Hebr. *ḥērem*. It is difficult to translate this word. I have mainly translated it as 'dedication'. The term 'ban' is often used. Even the word 'taboo' conveys some of the meaning of the word. See also Excursus 4 on *herem*. Hid: the Hebrew verbal form (hiph. of *ḥābā'*) is written in a slightly odd way (*heḥbe'atāh*), but the meaning is clear. *BHS* suggests a correction (to *heḥbî'āh*, as in v. 25).

18. Gr. translates the verse, 'But you be very careful about the anathema lest you think about it and take from the anathema and make the camp of the children of Israel anathema and destroy yourselves.' The Gr. implies *tāḥmědu* (desire) instead of *tāḥărimu* (to be under the ban).

20. 'The people shouted' is not included in Gr. 'And took it' is not included in Gr.

21. Lit. 'And they devoted everything, men and sheep to/by the edge of the sword' (*wayyaḥărîmû 'et-kāl . . . lěpî-ḥāreb*).

25. She still lives: Hebr. *watēšeb . . . 'ad hayyôm hazzeh*.

26. By Yahweh: lit. 'in the presence of (*lipnê*) Yahweh', not included in Gr. Sets up: hiph. from *nṣb*. Gr. adds at the end of the verse, 'And Ozan of Bethel did so; he laid the foundations with Abiron his firstborn, and set up the gates with his youngest remaining son.'

Form and structure

As already discussed in relation to chapter 2 above, chapters 2 and 6 have a close connection with each other in the present narrative, even if scholars have often liked to see the Rahab materials as originally separate. We however note that verses 22–25 (and the note about Rahab in v. 17) make an obvious connection with chapter 2, and that the overall theme of chapters 2 and 6 (obviously) centres on the conquest of Jericho in the present form of the narrative.

Whatever one thinks of the unity of narrative between chapters 2 and 6, the literary structure of chapter 6 can be described as follows (cf. Nelson 1997a: 83–85):

A. Preliminaries:
1   Note about Jericho being shut
2–5   Yahweh's instructions to Joshua
6–7   Joshua's instructions to the people

B. First day:
8–9   Priests and people marching
10   Joshua's instruction about making a shout
11   Summary of circling during the first day and return to
        camp

C. Days 2–6:
12–14 Priests and people marching

D. Day 7:
15   Priests and people marching
16–19 Joshua's instructions about shouting, and taking the
        city, plus fate of Rahab
20–21 Taking of the town after shouting and blowing of
        trumpets

E. Aftermath:
22   Joshua's instructions to bring out Rahab
23   Rahab brought out of the town
24   Burning of the town and implementation of the ban
        (ḥērem) by putting non-perishables into the treasury of
        Yahweh
25   Rahab's destiny with Israel
26   Curse on Jericho
27   Joshua's fame

One should also note that the MT and LXX differ in verses 1–15, with the LXX clearly shorter than MT (cf. Nelson 1997a: 83–87). It may not be easy to say which may have influenced the other, or if each is based on a separate text tradition. However, while Nelson suggests that the MT reflects a later stage of the materials than Greek, this does not seem likely in the light of what is known about transmission of materials in the Ancient Near East (cf. above, Introduction: p. 62), and one should also note that both versions include a sufficient amount of priestly features to consider the passage as a whole (vv. 1–21) as having clear priestly features and the two versions as essentially compatible.

A number of commentators think that there are some errors and inconsistencies in the presentation of the chapter (Butler 1983: 66–67; Nelson 1997a: 88–89, which see for a list of suggested discrepancies and tensions). However, in this case the problems do not seem to be particularly serious.

While it is difficult to glean some details comfortably from the narrative, a reconstruction of the events to fit the description seems plausible.

Noort (1998: 164–172) gives a summary of some source-critical analyses. These possibly divide the material into pre-deuteronomistic, deuteronomistic and post-deuteronomistic materials, even though, as Noort (1998: 172) notes, there is no comprehensive agreement on the source divisions. Noort however notes that the chapter has a cultic character, pointing out that the procession around the city with the ark and the blowing of the trumpets cannot really be explained otherwise (Noort 1998: 172). This itself reminds one of the marching order of the book of Numbers and also makes one think of a connection with the priestly materials of the Pentateuch, whether directly or indirectly.

In the context of chapters 2 and 6, we should ask why such a large amount of material has been devoted to the conquest of Jericho. As already indicated in Excursus 2, it seems that the first chapters are devoted to the first steps in the conquest. Much attention is given to the crossing, to the manna ceasing and to circumcision as ending the wilderness period and paralleling the exodus. In this context, Jericho is portrayed as the first town that the Israelites conquered west of the Jordan. This seems to explain why so much space and detail are devoted to the conquest. Jericho's importance is above all literary. If the town was much smaller than appears to be depicted in the narrative, this might be partly because the narrative gives a false impression. If so, this shows the significance of selectivity and portrayal in historical writing. Describing something in detail and something else summarily can change the apparent relative priority.

The overall narrative can be compared with 2 Chronicles 20:1–34. While there are many differences, the role of the priests and cultic action as part of the battle is similar in both. This further reinforces the idea that the narrative of Joshua was written by an author with strong priestly concerns. Based on this, one might of course ask whether this similarity would rather imply that this part of the book of Joshua was written around the same time as Chronicles, but this is not necessary. Priestly ideology could have remained in the possession of an (apparently relatively isolated) segment of the society for centuries, finding its manifestation in only a few documents far removed from each other temporally. Such an idea is supported by Ancient Near Eastern evidence. As a pertinent parallel example, Cooper (1983: 11–12; quoting Krecher; my translation from German; see also Pitkänen 2004a: 118–122) notes:

> The discovery of Abu Salabikh versions of compositions otherwise attested only in manuscripts written 700 years later, in the Old Babylonian period, has shaken the confidence of scholars in the common-sense approach to Sumerian literary history that for so long dominated Assyriological studies: 'The archaic style . . . shows moreover that specifically a passage that

above all seems to offer a *terminus post quem* for dating, is itself either a modernization and thus insignificant for dating, or that an expression that is first seen attested and clearly liked in a domain of tradition of a period X, can have existed already before period X, even in another span of tradition.'

(In other words, in a like manner, the priestly style could have originated early, then largely fallen out of use for some time, but be taken into use again later, together with a modernisation of its style.) The priestly and cultic character of Joshua 6 links directly to chapter 7. Chapter 6 details a specific, carefully choreographed cultic act, together with a cultic appropriation of the booty of the town according to regulations pertaining to the ban (*herem*). This cultic emphasis is continued in chapters 7 and 8 where it is revealed how Achan violates the ban and how he then has to bear the ultimate punishment, and how Israel cannot succeed until the perpetrator has been punished and purged from the midst of the community. All of this emphasis that revolves around careful observation of cultic matters then serves the book of Joshua's overall emphasis on following Yahweh carefully and wholeheartedly. In this context, Achan's punishment serves as a warning to Israel of what will happen if the later Israelite generations turn away from following Yahweh.

The comment about the rebuilding of Jericho in verse 26 is generally seen as stemming from the Deuteronomistic Historian, tying up with 1 Kings 16:34 which records the fulfilment of what Joshua says here (see Noth 1953a: 41). However, if the books Deuteronomy–2 Kings are separate, the author of the books of Kings could also have made the comment based on the book of Joshua, of which he was aware.

Comment

1. The narrative now moves to the conquest of Jericho. Verse 1 states that the town is completely sealed off. It is not clear whether it means that the inhabitants of Jericho themselves sealed things off, or whether it was that the town was effectively under siege. Probably the latter is meant, as it fits with sieges known from elsewhere (cf. famously the siege of Jerusalem by Sennacherib [biblical version in 2 Kgs 18 – 19], with Sennacherib himself describing Hezekiah as being 'like a bird in a cage').

2–5. Yahweh's favour towards the Israelites is stated in verse 2 in a typical Ancient Near Eastern manner in which a god's presence and favour guarantees victory. At first sight, the action of circling the town that the Israelites are to take sounds odd, even bizarre. However, if we regard it as ritualistic and symbolic it makes much better sense, regardless of how much we think the narrative may bear relation to actual history (see Excursus 5 below about the archaeology of Jericho, and also issues relating to the historicity of the Israelite conquest in general, as mentioned in the Introduction and throughout this book). The Israelites are to circle the town every day, and seven times on the seventh day. Later verses (e.g. 6–7) note the role of the ark in this. What is happening here is that Yahweh himself is circling the town, as he is present at the ark according to the Old Testament (see Excursus 3; and cf. comments on 5:13–15). The priests naturally carry the ark (cf. 3:3–4). The trumpets have a role in some of the festivals and holy days described in Leviticus (see Lev. 23:23–24; Lev. 25:9 [Day of Atonement in the Sabbath year]). Interestingly, when Yahweh descends on Sinai, a trumpet sound is heard (Exod. 19:16–19; 20:18), suggesting that the trumpet sound is connected with Yahweh's presence on that occasion (cf. also Judg. 7:17–22). Numbers 10:9 suggests a direct link with Yahweh's remembrance of the Israelites in battle (cf. also Num. 10:10). Trumpets were also used to signal actions for the Israelites in the wilderness (Num. 10:1–8; 31:6). Further examples of the use of trumpets abound in the later books in the canonical collection of the Old Testament and can be looked up using a concordance. Kitchen (1993: 124; 2003b: 280) provides examples of comparable use of trumpets in Egypt during the second millennium BC in particular.

We also seem to have a parallel from Ugarit where the king and people circle seven times as part of an entry ritual (i.e. gods entering a temple or palace), the text stating as follows (Pardee 2002: 71–72):

> The king will go to take the gods.
> Everyone will follow the gods on foot;
> the king himself [will g]o on foot,
> seven times for all of them.
> *mlk.ylk.lqḥ.ilm.*
> *átr.ilm.ylk.p'nm.*
> *mlk.p'nm.yl[k].*
> *šb' pámt.l klhm.*

Circling the town in the context of the events portrayed would also perhaps cause terror in the minds of the inhabitants of the besieged town. An interesting point here is that the circling takes place over seven days, and thus the seventh day when the town is circled seven times is a Sabbath. It is not usual to think that a battle would be fought on a Sabbath, but this seems to be the intended meaning of the narrative. This, together with the role of the ark, the priests and the trumpets, apparently emphasizes the holiness of the event of conquering Jericho. The ban (*herem*; see v. 17 below) further emphasizes this holiness and special character of the event of the first conquest in Canaan, and perhaps the analogy of the devotion of firstfruits to Yahweh can also be called to mind (see e.g. Exod. 23:19; Lev. 23:9–22; Num. 18:12–13). Such holiness may also shed light on the severe punishment of Achan for violating the ban (see below, chapter 7). There is lots of symbolism of seven here: seven priests, seven rams' horns, seven days, and seven circumambulations on the seventh day.

The conquest will then be enabled by a miracle from Yahweh: the wall of Jericho will collapse so that the Israelites can enter the town (v. 5).

6–7. As noted above, the ark is to go with the procession: Yahweh himself marches with the people. Fighters, or at least a number of them, march before the ark. The rest are to go behind (v. 8).

8. In the usual manner, the instructions of the preceding verses are carried out, with a bit of expansion on what has already been said.

9–11. The circling during the first day is described. The Israelites keep blowing the trumpets, but do not raise a shout. In a rather mundane way of description, people then return to the camp to sleep!

12. The theme of rising up early in the morning is repeated here (cf. 3:1).

13–14. A repeat of day one is carried out for the next five days.

15–21. Now the description moves to the seventh day. Everything goes as expected, the town is circled seven times, the trumpets are sounded, and then the Israelites raise a great shout. Subsequently, the wall collapses and the Israelites conquer the town. The Israelites are instructed to spare Rahab, and everyone in her house is to be spared, according to the pact made in chapter 2. Everything else is devoted (*herem*) to Yahweh (see also Excursus 4 below for *herem*).

16. A war cry is intended to elicit terror in the enemies, and also give a kind of courageous delirium to the attacker. Those who have done modern team sports will know that the latter is true (at least to some extent). Compare Judges 7:18–20, 1 Samuel 4:5, but cf. also 2 Samuel 6:15, 1 Kings 1:34, 39, 2 Kings 9:13 for a slightly different function of blowing trumpets and shouting.

18. From a narrative perspective, this comment can be taken to give a hint of what will happen because of Achan in the next chapter.

20. Note that towns in ancient Israel were usually (if not always) on a mound, so the people would literally 'go up' (*'ālāh*).

22–25. Rahab and her companions are then brought out by the spies who know her. It is worth noting here that her belongings stay with her. Rahab and her family are then taken outside the camp (v. 23). This may mean that she is not considered Israelite at this time and it is still somewhat a matter of question what exactly should be done with her, but verse 25 suggests that she is probably seen as having become an Israelite (sojourner [*ger*] status might also be implied especially at first; see the many pieces of legislation in the Pentateuch about the *ger*; e.g. Lev. 24:22). Another interesting point to note here is that even though Rahab's father and mother are mentioned, Rahab, a woman and a prostitute, is not counted as part of her father's house, as would be usual for an Israelite (cf. Achan and his family in 7:24). Presumably, this heightens the significance of Rahab's actions, and from now on she is unusually seen as a kind of head of the family, or at least this seems to be true from the literary standpoint of the book of Joshua. The final note about her living among the Israelites 'until now' or 'until this day' would be somewhat surprising if the writer of at least an early version of the narrative, or even the whole book, were not able to substantiate such a claim to his audience. One can of course ask whether the note refers to Rahab or her descendants. The latter is a possibility, even though the Hebrew has a personal prefix which refers to Rahab directly. The reason for Rahab's survival is that she hid the spies. According to the narrative, a new life dawns among the Israelites for a former prostitute (cf. comment on 2:1, and 'Explanation' section of chapter 2).

26. Now a curse is pronounced on Jericho. Putting curses on things one did not wish to be disturbed or altered was normal in the Ancient Near East (see e.g. in Foster 2005: 58 Sargon's curse on anyone doing away with his inscription, and the famous curse of Tutankhamun's tomb against anyone who would disturb it). And we may of course, even if moving to a slightly different sphere, add the curses against those who do not follow Yahweh's law (see e.g. Deut. 27:26; cf. Deut. 12:32). Presumably, Jericho was to stay as a desolate place. It is interesting here that the narrative suggests that Ai will be a ruin for ever, but anticipates that Jericho will be rebuilt. This may point towards a date for the narrative later than the rebuilding of Jericho in Iron Age II, but not conclusively. If the narrative is earlier, it is not clear why a different treatment is given to Jericho from Ai, even though it can also be said that the rebuilding of the bigger of the two according to Joshua (see 7:3) might more easily be anticipated. Whatever the case, the mention in 1 Kings 16:34 of the rebuilding of Jericho and the fulfilment of Joshua's curse is seen by most as stemming from the Deuteronomistic Historian together with the mention here in Joshua 6:26 (see Noth 1991/1943: 63; Noth 1953a: 41). However, the writer of Kings may simply have had the book of Joshua before him and may have found it convenient to refer back to that. Some cross-editing (cf. LXX on the verse) might have been possible too, even without granting the theory of the Deuteronomistic History proper. We should also note here that the work by Weippert and Weippert (1976) indicates that there was already (re-)settlement at Tel es-Sultan from about the eleventh, perhaps even twelfth, century BC. Judges 1:16 (apparently) and 2 Samuel 10:5 (cf. 1 Chr. 19:5) also speak for such early occupation at or around Jericho (cf. Weippert and Weippert 1976: 147). However, the later Iron Age settlement was much larger in scale, and perhaps this is what the writer of 1 Kings 16:34 based his comment on (cf. also below, Excursus 5 on Jericho).

27. Joshua now becomes famous. The events cannot fail to be noticed by others in the area. (Cf. Josh. 9:9; 1 Kgs 4:31; 10:1; 1 Chr. 14:17; 2 Chr. 26:8.)

Explanation

This chapter emphasizes the decisive action of Yahweh in war, perhaps even more than an average Ancient Near Eastern account, which would involve similar motifs. The ark, and thus Yahweh himself, circles the town in a kind of entry ritual through the medium of the priests carrying the ark. Once the priests blow the trumpets, Yahweh himself makes the defences fall, and the Israelites then need only to move into the town and take it. Everything is devoted to Yahweh, in line with the Israelite *herem* theology. The only exception is Rahab, who is saved owing to her allying herself with the Israelites and with Yahweh, the god of Israel.

As for Christian application of this chapter, a lot of the comments about being strong and courageous and following Yahweh's law and Yahweh's will apply here, but seem a bit trivial upon closer inspection. The narrative is rather genocidal in character, and it is therefore a bit difficult for modern tastes. But the material is part of the conquest of Canaan and, more specifically, the beginning and firstfruits of it, and that would explain the emphasis placed on the narrative. Perhaps, if one believes in God's judgment, one can say that belief in him saves one from it. And yet even this is a bit simplistic. Also, putting it crudely, it might be easy for some Christians to think that all who are not Christian are evil and deserve to die. However, this would again seem simplistic and is of course not true according to the New Testament documents. Rather, we come to questions of theodicy, or justifying God's actions. To solve the problem of theodicy, it would in certain ways be easier to take the narrative as a reflection of Israelite ideology, whereby the proponents of that ideology behave just as all other ethnic groups do, even though with reference to one particular god, Yahweh, a god they believe in, and reflect on things based on this belief in a rather typical Ancient Near Eastern and human fashion. Here lies the dilemma of choosing between a secular viewpoint and a Yahwistic and Christian viewpoint. It relates to the question of whether Yahweh really was a true god, as the Israelite documents claim. If we believe that he was, we are left with many questions. If we think that he was not, we are on our way towards losing the possibility of a relationship with a living god. This question cannot be answered rationally, but really only through faith.

EXCURSUS 4: *HEREM*

There has been a lot of discussion about *herem* (translated variously as 'dedication', 'ban' etc.). Historically, *herem* has been linked to an idea of a holy war in Israel, and whole books have been written on the topic (see e.g. von Rad 1991/1951 and Niditch 1993 among many). It is often argued,

broadly speaking in a Wellhausenian manner of believing in an evolutionary development of Israelite religion, that there was an evolutionary
development of *herem*. However, this is not necessary, especially when one
considers Ancient Near Eastern parallels such as those brought forward
by Younger (1990). For our purposes here, it would be quite normal to
consider that certain things would be devoted to a god in an early period,
as most of the ancient conquest ideologies are already clearly attested in
the second millennium and there do not seem to be any developments
in the first millennium in Ancient Near Eastern texts that would parallel
an evolutionary development often postulated for Israel. In connection
with this, it should be noted that *herem* features in the Mesha stele from
the ninth century BC (the stele is written in Moabite, a language similar
to Hebrew; for an English translation, see COS 2: 137–138; *ANET*:
320–321; see also http://en.wikipedia.org/wiki/Mesha_Stele [accessed
27 November 2009] for a translation). Also, whether *herem* is a sacrifice,
a judgment, a discipline etc. (these options are summarized in Cobb 2002),
or, in general, as Nelson (1997b: 54) very plausibly suggests, an instinctive
'part of the natural order of things, part of Israel's culture map', the point
is that the things under *herem* are dedicated to Yahweh. Here they become
the property of Yahweh's treasury, presumably run by the priests or equivalent (cf. Lev. 27:21; Num. 18:14). In other words, it does not mean that
everything under *herem* is necessarily destroyed, but simply becomes the
property of Yahweh and his cultic system. Fitting with this connection,
Manohar has helpfully noted that *herem* is another side of the coin of
qodesh (holy), as both involve dedication to Yahweh (D. Manohar, personal
communication, March 2008). A further issue worth pointing out here is
that it seems that the extent of *herem* was not constant, but could vary
depending on the occasion. In some cases not everything falls under *herem*
(e.g. in Josh. 8:1–2 the people may take the booty and animals from Ai;
cf. Josh. 11:12–14; Num. 31); however, in the case of Jericho *herem* is to
be total, except for Rahab and whatever is inside her house. As discussed
above (vv. 2–5), this may relate to the fact that the first conquest is similar
in a symbolic way to firstfruits that are to be given to Yahweh, even though
it is also true that not everything from firstfruits is given in their usual
context.

EXCURSUS 5: THE ARCHAEOLOGY OF JERICHO

The identification of Jericho with Tell es-Sultan is generally accepted (see
NEAEHL: 674). The mound is an impressive one, rising to a height of
21.5 metres, and covers an area of approximately one acre (0.405 hectares)
(*NEAEHL*: 674). There are also other sites in the vicinity, but these do not
attest occupation from the period concerned (see *NEAEHL*: 681–697).

The site was first sounded in 1868 by C. Warren. The first large-scale excavations were made by E. Sellin and C. Watzinger from 1907 to 1909 (see *NEAEHL*: 674). They dug out fairly extensive areas of the tell (see Kenyon and Holland 1981: *Text*, Figure 1). Unfortunately, there was no accepted chronology at the time, and therefore the usefulness of this work was limited (see *NEAEHL*: 674).

The next excavations were undertaken by J. Garstang of the University of Liverpool from 1930 to 1936 (*NEAEHL*: 674). Most importantly, Garstang suggested that there was evidence from the time attributable to Joshua of occupation in Jericho, including large city walls (see Bienkowski 1986: 2–4). Jericho was again excavated by Kathleen Kenyon from 1952 to 1958, and full excavation reports in five volumes were published subsequently between 1960 and 1982 (see Kenyon 1960 and Kenyon and Holland 1981, 1982, 1983). Kenyon's reports still serve as the main data on which any conclusions about the site should be based. Overall, Kenyon showed that Garstang had made many conclusions that should be modified in accordance with the newer excavation techniques. For example, the wall attributed by Garstang to the Late Bronze Age should in fact be dated to the Early Bronze Age (see Bienkowski 1986: 3). I will next summarize the results of Kenyon's excavations, in parts interpreted further by Bienkowski (1986) and Weippert and Weippert (1976).

As already indicated above, Tell es-Sultan is a comparatively huge site, about 300 by 200 metres at its largest extent. The earliest remains date to about 9000 BC (see *NEAEHL*: 675). The latest occupation dates to the Iron Age II period, and there is some evidence of possible occupation in the Persian period, even though there are no stratigraphic remains (see *NEAEHL*: 680–681).

Even though the site is huge, it has nevertheless suffered massive erosion. Most of the remains in the central and core sections of the tell relate to the Neolithic period, with massive accumulation under them from previous periods (see Kenyon and Holland 1981: *Plates*). It is mainly only at the edges of the tell that the later periods are attested, albeit the central section is in many places overlaid with Byzantine rubble pits. Kenyon dug three trenches at the edge of the tell, and dug further in about four distinct places around the central area of the tell (see Kenyon and Holland 1981: *Text*, Figure 1)

Within this context, there are only meagre remains attested from the Late Bronze Age, although there are also remains of large city walls that have been dated to the Middle Bronze Age. These are in particular attested by a collapsed set of brickwork in trench 1, layer lxiv at the foot of about a 10-metre-high Middle Bronze rampart (see Kenyon and Holland 1981: *Text*, 110; *Plates*, Plate 236; see Figure 4 below). Above this is a layer of gravelly wash which according to Kenyon 'presumably represents gradual erosion after the main collapse' (Kenyon and Holland 1981: *Text*, 110). Partially above it, and overall further away from the centre of the tell, are two thin layers of 'very fine silt (phase lxv a) separated by gravely silt'. Above this layer is an approximately 50-centimetre-thick layer which basically extends from about three-quarters up the tell all the way outwards to the end of the excavation trench (at least according to the accompanying picture) at the foot of the tell (see Kenyon and Holland 1981: *Plates*, Plate 236; also Figure 4 below). According to Kenyon, this 'phase lxvi deposit represents a prolonged period of wash and silt. On the slope of the mound this is pinkish and rather stony. It gradually becomes browner and more silty, and in the level area at the west end it is a very fine compact silt with horizontal striations. It is clearly an entirely natural accumulation produced by gentle erosion from rain wash of the surface of the mound' (Kenyon and Holland 1981: *Text*, 110–111). Pottery remains indicate four items from the Middle Bronze Age, possibly one Late Bronze bowl, a Late Bronze Age jar shoulder fragment, and one bowl from the Iron Age in the layer (see Kenyon and Holland 1983: 58); however, according to Bienkowski (1986: 123), the layer contained twenty-three Middle Bronze, two possible Late Bronze and sixteen Iron Age, or later, items. The exact find spots within the layer do not seem to be available.

On top of the erosion layer, extensive remains from the Iron Age were found in Trench 1. However, it should immediately be noted that the only Iron Age remains in this trench are located away from the top of the tell, beyond the Middle Bronze rampart if one looks away from the centre of the tell (see Kenyon and Holland 1981: *Plates*, Plate 236).

We will next look at Bienkowski's study of Jericho and his conclusions regarding Late Bronze occupation. This will tie back in to our examination of the layers on the tell just mentioned. In general, Bienkowski notes how the pottery from the Late Bronze Age is of poorer quality than that from the preceding periods (Bienkowski 1986: 10–111; conclusion on pp. 110–111). Bienkowski then makes an analysis of the extant Late Bronze remains. According to him, the so-called 'Palace' and the Middle Building (these are closer to the top of the tell) 'are the only major constructions excavated that could conceivably date to the Late Bronze Age' (Bienkowski 1986: 112). Bienkowski then notes that it is difficult to make any conclusions about the 'Palace' (Bienkowski 1986: 112). The Middle Building 'overlay a deep layer of black burnt debris', called 'Streak' by Garstang (Bienkowski 1986: 113). There was apparently even some of the debris on the building, according to Garstang who first noted it (see Bienkowski 1986: 113). Originally there appeared to be associated pottery, but this was denied by Kenyon, and it was concluded that the Middle Building was 'a later intrusive structure lacking datable evidence', except for the burnt debris associated with it (Bienkowski 1986: 114). Later, however, Kenyon changed her mind and dated the building to Late Bronze II, apparently giving no firm explanation, even though the fact that the pottery is mostly Middle Bronze with some Late Bronze may explain this (Bienkowski 1986: 114–115). A picture of the stratigraphical remains can be found in Kenyon

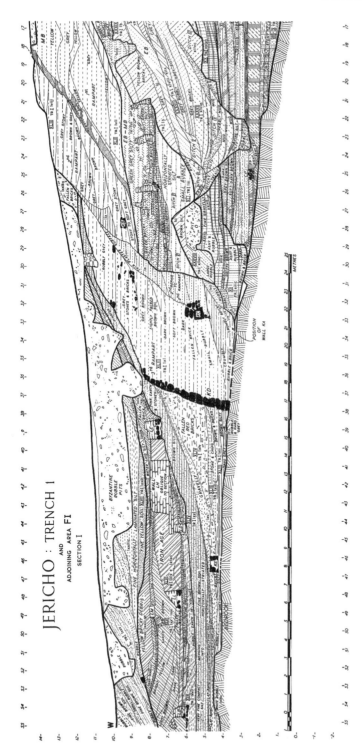

Figure 4: Jericho, Trench 1, west side (from Kenyon and Holland 1981: *Plates*, Plate 236);
note that the section some 25 metres towards the east (towards the right of the picture above;
also towards the top of the mound) shown on Plate 236 has not been reproduced here

and Holland 1981: *Plates*, Plate 339. Bienkowski notes that the building was not isolated 'because of adjacent domestic remains excavated by Kenyon' (Bienkowski 1986: 117). Bienkowski also notes that the closest parallel to the building can be found from Late Bronze Ib.

According to Bienkowski (1986: 120; I have not included Bienkowski's references to other scholars and his cross-references to his own work in the quotation):

> It has been suggested that LBA Jericho was limited in area to the region of the Middle Building. There was evidence of LBII occupation (the Middle Building) beneath the Iron Age 'Hilani' but not underneath a neighbouring Iron Age building which immediately overlay MBA levels. Kenyon similarly noted that while there was evidence for a LBII house in Square HIII, in a neighbouring square the Iron Age filling went right down into the deep gullies cutting into the MBA levels. However, she concluded that this lack of LBA levels was evidence not necessarily of their absence, but of the eroded state of the tell at the time the Iron Age settlement was established.

Bienkowski continues (Bienkowski 1986: 120; here I have not included Bienkowski's references to other scholars, except for Kenyon):

> As support for this conclusion, Kenyon pointed out that the major part of the large MBA town had also eroded. Traces of this erosion have been found in the 'Streak', which is one metre thick in places, extending down the sides of the tell, especially on the east side. On the west side of the tell, Phase XLIV Tr. I lxiv represents the erosion of the MBII rampart and is four metres thick at its deepest. Trenches II and III, on the north and south sides of the tell, did not extend beyond the MBII revetment, so there is no record of any wash at the foot of the tell. However, the East Section of Trench II reveals that a large part of the second and third ramparts has disappeared through erosion (Kenyon 1981, pl. 259) and the West Section of Trench III indicates severe erosion of the MB, IA and Roman levels – only a small area of the plaster of the MBII glacis has survived. If the LBA levels had eroded, traces of this erosion would also have existed as a wash layer down the sides or at the foot of the tell. No such traces have been found.

In addition, Bienkowski notes a possible, but unlikely, dating of a town wall to the Late Bronze Age (Bienkowski 1986: 122–124). Bienkowski concludes (124–125; I have not included a reference by Bienkowski to another scholar in the quotation):

It appears extremely unlikely that there are any town walls at Jericho which could date to the Late Bronze Age. The actual area of occupation in this period seems to have been limited to the area around the Middle Building. Would LB Jericho be unusual in being so small and apparently unfortified? Study of the settlement pattern of the LBA in Canaan shows that in the 14th century B.C., 37% of known settlements were less than one hectare in size. Furthermore, only 8 out of 76 known LBA settlements in the whole of Canaan were fortified, and all but one of these were larger than one hectare. The vast majority of settlements were not fortified. It would seem, therefore, that a tiny unwalled Jericho fits the pattern in LB Canaan extremely well.

To assess Bienkowski's argument, which at first appears persuasive and well thought out, we must note that, as indicated above, the tell has suffered huge amounts of erosion. In fact, the erosion has almost completely wiped out all Iron and Middle and Early Bronze Age layers in a number of places on the tell: with Kenyon's Trench 1, this can be seen at the east side of the trench as it slopes up towards the top (on the other hand, the structures Bienkowski speaks about lie close to the top of one of the mounds of the tell). Bienkowski notes that no Late Bronze erosion layer has been found. However, it might be possible to think (based on the stratigraphy of Trench 1) that, after the collapse of the Middle Bronze wall, after a short period of abandonment, attested by the erosion layer lxv, a town was built which stood in the Late Bronze period. After this, the site lay abandoned, or otherwise exposed to the elements, for hundreds of years, eroding, except for some exceptions, all the way through the Late Bronze layer well into the Middle Bronze remains. The work by Weippert and Weippert (Weippert and Weippert 1976) indicates that there was already (re-)settlement at Tell es-Sultan from about the eleventh, even the twelfth, century BC, even though this evidence is (in essence) confined to only a part of the tell, in fact to about the same place where the Late Bronze remains were found. With this in mind, layer lxvi could have formed through erosion over some 100–150 years or so, taking place before the building of any early Iron Age structures on the tell, and then becoming contaminated with Iron Age pottery.

However, in addition, there is the likelihood of a second period of erosion after Iron Age II when the site (apparently) lay (at least mostly) abandoned for almost a millennium (see Weippert and Weippert 1976: 145–146 for evidence of apparently very limited occupation at the fringes of the tell during parts of that time). This erosion could have again cut through to Middle Bronze levels, and even further in places. That this is possible is shown by the fact that Late Bronze pottery shards have been found close to the edges of the tell, above the Iron Age II remains of the larger town which extended beyond the Middle Bronze and (any possible) Late Bronze and earlier Iron Age towns (see Bienkowski 1986: 120–122). This is in addition to extensive Iron Age pottery found above the later Iron Age layers in Trench 1 (see the plate in Kenyon 1957: 269), suggesting (and being compatible with) erosion from the top of the tell after the town's demise after Iron Age II. Also in this connection clearly at least some of the Early Bronze remains have been eroded (especially towards the centre of the tell). There are traces of such erosion from before the Middle Bronze period on the mound (e.g. Trench 1 layers liii and lvi). However, one cannot be sure that everything had eroded from the top of the mound before the following period, especially as the later layers have been built on top of earlier layers when one goes down the slope away from the centre of the tell (see the stratigraphy of Trench 1). If so, such layers would have had to erode later (similarly with any Middle Bronze levels that might have eroded after Iron Age II). But no evidence of such erosion seems traceable from the mound or its outskirts, whenever this erosion took place (if, say, some Early Bronze material was reused for the later periods, the same could have been done during some other later period, e.g. with Late Bronze Age material). All this said, it is somewhat difficult to make firm conclusions based on traces of erosion. In other words, based on these considerations, it is entirely possible that most of an entire town from the Late Bronze Age has been washed away. In this connection, we should also note that objects from the Late Bronze Age have been found in tombs in the vicinity of the tell (see Kenyon 1957: 233, 260–261), and some of the Late Bronze Age pottery from the tombs may date as late as to the early thirteenth century BC at least (see Bienkowski 1986: 10–110 for the pottery analysis).

As for the question of a possible wall, it should be noted that Joshua 2:15 seems to indicate that Rahab's house was part of the wall (see comments on 2:15). Perhaps this suggests that there was no substantial wall, as there was during the Middle Bronze Age, but houses primarily formed a perimeter around the town and acted as a wall by being connected together, with any gaps between houses perhaps patched up as a kind of wall.

As well as the suggested lack of evidence of erosion (Bienkowski 1986: 122; Weippert and Weippert 1976: 146) discussed above, the fact that no structures have been found immediately adjacent to the Late Bronze Middle Building could speak against a wider extent of the Late Bronze town (see Bienkowski 1986, incl. p. 120; Weippert and Weippert 1976, incl. p. 146). However, the building lies close to the spring, which means that it would be in one of the best locations in the town for accessing water. And again if so, we might at least tentatively suggest that any such area might be occupied by the upper strata of society. And in fact, and whatever the case, as it seems (see Bienkowski 1986: 232, Figure 55), the Middle Bronze palatial area and the Iron Age 'hilani' are located in just about the same place. Richer people might just have a bit of land around their estate, even inside a town.

Thus we might picture the history of the town (during Late Bronze Age to Iron Age) as including the possibility of reasonable occupation during the Late Bronze Age, even if to a much lesser extent than during the Middle Bronze Age. A short occupation gap seems to have taken place after the Late Bronze Age, with reoccupation in the twelfth–eleventh century BC. After this, whether with or without breaks, the town was occupied until the end of the Iron Age. In this regard, whereas in other places in the lowlands the Late Bronze culture continued past the twelfth century (cf. e.g. Junkkaala 2006 in general), at Jericho the transition to Iron Age culture seems to have taken place at around that time, suggesting the possibility of occupation of the Israelite type. Whatever the case, Judges 1:16 (apparently) and 2 Samuel 10:5 (cf. 1 Chr. 19:5) textually indicate early occupation at, or at least around, Jericho early on (cf. Weippert and Weippert 1976: 147). In this context, perhaps one can think it a possibility that Joshua's curse in Joshua 6:26 would have been seen by the writer of the book of Kings (1 Kgs 16:34) to apply to the enlargement of the town during Iron Age II. (Some cross-editing might also have been possible between 1 Kgs 16:34 and Josh. 6:26, even without accepting the theory of the Deuteronomistic History proper.)

All in all, even if in the context of the generally relatively meagre material culture of the Late Bronze Age, we may conclude that it seems entirely possible that a town (albeit most likely a modest one) stood in Jericho at the time when Joshua and the Israelites conquered it, but any traces of such a conquest, and most remains of the town itself, have been lost in the mists of history.

JOSHUA 7 – 8:29

Translation

Joshua 7

[1]However, the Israelites violated the dedication. Achan, the great-grandson of Zerah through Zabdi and Carmi from the tribe of Judah, took some of the devoted things. The Israelites therefore became subject to Yahweh's anger.

[2]Joshua himself sent men from Jericho to Ai, which is by Beth Aven, east of Bethel. He instructed them, 'Go and spy out the land.' So the men went and spied out Ai.

[3]When they returned to Joshua, they said, 'There is no need for everyone to go there. Some 2,000 or 3,000 men may go and take the town. Do not send all the people there, as it is a small place.' [4]About three thousand men went up to Ai, but they had to flee from the men of the town. [5]The men of Ai inflicted damage

on about thirty-six men. They chased the Israelites from the town gate all the way to Shebarim and caused further damage on them on the way down, and the people completely lost their courage.

⁶Subsequently, Joshua tore his clothes and fell on his face on the ground in front of the ark of Yahweh until the evening, together with the elders of Israel. And they put dust on their heads. ⁷Joshua lamented, 'Alas, my Lord Yahweh, why did you bring us over the Jordan to give us into the hands of the Amorites to destroy us? If only we had just stayed on the other side of the Jordan! ⁸My Lord, what can I say now that Israel has turned into flight from their enemies? ⁹The Canaanites and all inhabitants of the land will hear it and turn on us and will erase every trace of us from the land. How will this fit in with your greatness?'

¹⁰But Yahweh replied to Joshua, 'Get up! What are you doing there lying, your face on the ground? ¹¹Israel has sinned. They have violated my covenant by taking some of the dedicated objects. They have stolen them by deceit and have put them among their belongings. ¹²Therefore, the Israelites cannot manage against their enemies but have to turn to flight. They have now themselves become dedicated. I will not be with you any more unless you destroy what has been devoted from among you.

¹³'Arise, and prepare the people. Tell them, "Prepare yourselves for tomorrow. This is what Yahweh the God of Israel says: 'Israel, there is something among you that was devoted. You will not be able to manage against your enemies until you put it away from you.'"

¹⁴"In the morning you are to approach tribe by tribe. The tribe that is chosen by Yahweh shall then approach family by family. The family chosen shall come forward household by household. The household chosen shall approach individual by individual. ¹⁵The individual chosen will be under dedication. He and everything that belongs to him will be burnt in fire because he was foolish and violated the covenant of Yahweh.'

¹⁶Accordingly, Joshua made the Israelites to come forward tribe by tribe in the morning. Then, the tribe of Judah was chosen. ¹⁷When he made the tribe of Judah come forward the family of Zerah was chosen. Then he made each individual head of the family of Zerah come forward, and Zabdi was chosen. ¹⁸When he made Zabdi's house come forward individual by individual, Achan, the great-grandson of Zerah through Zabdi and Carmi, was chosen.

¹⁹Joshua said to Achan, 'My son, honour now Yahweh, the God of Israel. Give him a confession. Tell me what you did, without concealing anything.'

²⁰Achan replied to Joshua, 'It is correct that I have sinned against Yahweh the God of Israel. This is what I did: ²¹I saw a nice Babylonian robe, two hundred shekels of silver and a gold bar of fifty shekels among the booty. I wanted them and took them. They are hidden in the ground in my tent, with the silver underneath.'

²²Joshua then sent men and they ran to the tent. And, indeed, the items were hidden in his tent, with the silver underneath. ²³They took them from the tent and brought them to Joshua and all the Israelites. And they set them in front of Yahweh.

²⁴Joshua then, together with all Israel, took Achan the son of Zerah, the silver, the piece of clothing, the gold bar, his sons, his daughters, his oxen, his donkeys, his sheep, his tent and all that belonged to him. And they brought him to the Valley of Achor. ²⁵Joshua said, 'Why have you troubled us? Yahweh is now bringing trouble on you.'

And all Israel stoned them, burnt them in fire, and covered them with stones. ²⁶They also raised a great heap of stones over him. They are there even now. Yahweh then relented from his great anger. Consequently, the place has been called the Valley of Achor since then.

Joshua 8

¹After this, Yahweh said to Joshua, 'Do not fear or be worried. Take all the warriors with you and go up to Ai. I will now give the king of Ai, his people, his town and his land to you. ²Do to Ai and its king as you did to Jericho and its king. However, you may take its booty and animals for yourselves. Set an ambush behind the town.'

³Accordingly, Joshua and all warriors proceeded to go up to Ai. Joshua chose 30,000 top-class warriors and sent them in the night. ⁴He commanded them, 'Set an ambush behind the town and stay close to it, ready for action. ⁵I will approach the town with the rest of the people. When the inhabitants come to fight us as before, we will feign fleeing from them. ⁶They will come after us away from the town. They will say, "They are fleeing from us as before," and we will feign doing so. ⁷You will then come out from the ambush and capture the town. Yahweh your God will give you success. ⁸When you capture the town, set it on fire. Do as Yahweh has said. See, I am commanding you.'

⁹Joshua then sent them and they went to the place of ambush, staying west of Ai towards Bethel. Joshua himself rested that night together with the people.

¹⁰Next morning Joshua mustered the people, and he and the elders of Israel led them to Ai. ¹¹All warriors who were with him went as well. They drew themselves in front of the town on the north side. A valley was between them and Ai. ¹²(He had also taken about 5,000 men and set them in an ambush on the west side of the town towards Bethel. ¹³Thus they had positioned the people, the whole camp north of the town and the rear guard west of the town. Joshua himself had gone to the valley that night.)

¹⁴When the king of Ai saw this, he and all the men of the town quickly rose up and went out to fight the Israelites on the plain. But he did not know that there was an ambush behind the town. ¹⁵Joshua and the Israelites feigned being struck by them and fled towards the wilderness. ¹⁶All the people in the town got together to chase them. They chased after Joshua and were drawn off the town. ¹⁷Not a man was left in Ai or Bethel who did not go after the Israelites. They left the town open and pursued the Israelites.

¹⁸Then Yahweh told Joshua, 'Point the spear that is in your hand towards Ai. I will give the town to you.' Accordingly, Joshua stretched the spear in his hand

towards the town. ¹⁹When he extended his hand, the ambush came out quickly from their place in the mountains. They ran to the town and took it. And they immediately set the town on fire.

²⁰The men of Ai turned and looked behind them and saw the smoke from the town that was rising high into the sky. Then they had no strength left even to flee anywhere. And the Israelites who were going towards the desert turned back on their pursuers. ²¹When Joshua and all the Israelites saw that the ambush had taken the town and that smoke rose from the town, they turned back and struck down the men of Ai. ²²The men belonging to the ambush also came out from the town towards them. The men of Ai were caught between the Israelites. And the Israelites struck them until none were left. Not even one escaped. ²³But they captured the king of Ai alive and brought him to Joshua.

²⁴When the Israelites had finished killing all inhabitants of Ai who were out in the field or in the desert and whom they were chasing there for the kill, they all returned to Ai and put it to the sword. ²⁵All inhabitants of Ai were killed on that day, numbering 12,000 men and women. ²⁶Joshua did not pull back his extended hand that was holding the spear until they had devoted all inhabitants of Ai to destruction. ²⁷However, they looted the animals and the spoil from the town in line with the command of Yahweh to Joshua.

²⁸Then Joshua burnt Ai and made it a mound of ruins for ever. And it has remained a desolate place to this day. ²⁹As for the king of Ai, they hanged him on a tree until evening, but when the sun set Joshua commanded to take his body down from the tree. They threw him at the entrance of the town and raised a great heap of stones over him. This heap is there even now.

Notes on the text

Chapter 7

1. The Israelites violated the dedication: lit. 'Israelites acted faithlessly (*ma'al*) against the ban (*ḥērem*)'.

2. Gr. omits the mention 'from Jericho'. Gr. simply states that Ai is by Bethel (*kata Baithēl*).

3. 2,000 or 3,000 men: alternatively, 'two or three units of men'. Hebr. *'elep* usually means 'thousand', but it may also mean 'unit' in some cases.

5. The people completely lost their courage: lit. 'the hearts of the people melted and became water'. Shebarim: whether this is a geographical term or otherwise is not clear (see e.g. Butler 1983: 77; Nelson 1997a: 97). Hebr. *šābar*, 'to break into pieces'.

6. The ark is missing in Gr.

8. Turned into flight: lit. 'turned their neck back'.

9. Erase every trace: lit. 'cut our name'. How will this fit in with your greatness?: lit. 'What will then happen to your great name?'

12. Have to turn into flight: cf. note on verse 8. Dedicated: *ḥērem*.

13. Prepare (×2): lit. 'sanctify' (from *qādaš*). Devoted: *ḥērem*.

17. Second part of the verse: lit. 'Then he made the family of Zerah come forward individual by individual'; but in my view the context clearly implies that the heads of the families are meant.

21. Babylonia: Hebr. *šinʿār*.

26. Even now: Hebr. *ʿad hayyôm hazzeh*; not included in Gr. Since then: lit. 'until this day' (*ʿad hayyôm hazzeh*).

Chapter 8

1. Warriors: Hebr. *ʿam hammilḥāmāh*. I will now give: lit. 'See, I have given'.

3. Warriors: cf. note on verse 1. 30,000: Alternatively, '30 units' (Hebr. *šĕlošîm ʾelep*). Hebr. *ʾelep* usually means 'thousand', but it may also mean 'unit' in some cases. Top-class warriors: Hebr. *gibbôrê haḥayil*.

7. Will give you success: lit. 'has given it to your hands'.

11. The geographical reference is to the east side in Gr.

13. Joshua himself had gone to the valley that night: not included in Gr.

17. Gr. does not include mention of Bethel here.

24. For the kill: lit. 'and putting them to the edge of the sword until they were completely finished'.

25. 12,000: Cf. note on verse 3.

26. This verse is not included in Gr.

29. The entrance of the town: Greek reads 'into a pit' (*eis ton bothron*) here. The Hebrew word *ptḥ* ('entrance'; no vowels shown here) has apparently turned into *pḥt* ('pit'; again written here without vowels), keeping in mind that the original Hebrew text of the Old Testament did not have vowels (plus, one may of course surmise that 'the town' dropped out of the text on which the Greek seems to be based). There even now: lit. 'over him to this day'.

Form and structure

Chapters 7 – 8:29 belong together from the standpoint of the narrative of Joshua. Both relate to the conquest of Ai. They also link back to the preceding chapter(s) on Jericho, in that most of chapter 7 describes the results of Achan's taking for himself of the items that had been dedicated (*herem*) to Yahweh at Jericho. Most commentators think that the Achan episode and the narrative that describes the conquest of Ai were originally separate entities that have been woven together to make the Joshua narrative (see Noth 1953a: 43; Nelson 1997a: 98–99; Butler 1983: 81). Both are also seen as aetiological in character, with the Achan story as purely aetiological, and the Ai story having aetiological elements in it (see Noth 1953a: 43, 47; cf. Nelson 1997a: 99, 111, who follows Noth in this for all practical purposes).

Be that as it may, the Achan and Ai narratives have been slotted together nicely in their present form (even if some counter-arguments could be attempted against such interweaving), and the conquest of Ai is tied to that of Jericho through *herem*. The connection to the Jericho narrative explains the prominence of the narrative(s) about Achan and Ai in the book of Joshua. In its current literary setting, Joshua 7 – 8:29 is still part of the larger Jericho narrative. In fact, the cultic emphasis of chapter 6 (and before) continues here (note in particular, in addition to the continued mention of *herem*, the use of the word *ma'al* [act faithlessly] in 7:1, which is associated with priestly terminology [see more on this, and on collective guilt which is involved in this chapter, in comments on 7:1 and in the 'Form and structure' section on chapter 22]) and further explains why the Ai narrative has been included. As noted above (see 'Form and structure' of chapter 6), all this emphasis that revolves around careful observation of cultic matters serves the book of Joshua's overall emphasis on following Yahweh carefully and wholeheartedly. In this context, Achan's punishment serves as a warning to Israel of what will happen if the later Israelite generations turn away from following Yahweh (cf. also Josh. 24).

The structure of 7:1 – 8:29 can be described as follows:

7:1	Note about Achan's crime
7:2–3	Spying-out of Ai
7:4–5	Defeat at Ai
7:6–9	Joshua's lament
7:10–15	Yahweh's response and instructions about uncovering the guilty party
7:16–19	Casting lots to find the culprit
7:20–21	Achan's confession
7:22–26	Achan's punishment
8:1–2	Yahweh's instructions to attack Ai again
8:3	Joshua's march to Ai
8:4–8	Joshua's instructions about ambush
8:9	Spending the night
8:10–11	Encamping before Ai
8:12–13	Summary about how the troops had been set the previous day
8:14–17	Initial feigned flight by the Israelites, with the men of Ai pursuing them
8:18–29	Counter-attack and use of the ambushing troops, conquest and destruction of Ai, and the killing of the king of Ai

Commentators have pointed out some inconsistencies in the narrative (see e.g. Nelson 1997a: 110), but these do not seem to be insurmountable, allowing for the Hebrew narrative style of recapping (see esp. 8:12–13) and simultaneous action, and developing the plot by repeating in a slightly expanded way what has been said previously. One can also note that the attribution of the burning of Ai to Joshua in 8:28 (in comparison to e.g. 8:8, 19) should be seen in the light of Joshua being the commander of the Israelite forces, with the forces carrying out his commands. As a whole, the narrative (chapter 8 in particular) can be seen as a skilful creation (so also Nelson 1997a: 112–113, which see for further details, his comments about apparent inconsistencies notwithstanding), and there are no main obstacles to seeing each of chapters 7 and 8 as essentially unified compositions. That there are some differences between the Greek and Hebrew texts especially in chapter 8 (see Nelson 1997a: 110 for one view on this) does not alter this conclusion.

Commentators have suggested similarities between Joshua 8 and Judges 20 and 1 Samuel 14 – 15. While there are no full correspondences, a number of similar motifs are involved (the reader is encouraged to compare the narratives, and, for example, to note that *herem* is involved in both narratives, and that the punishments of both Saul and Achan are severe, even though Saul's punishment, while bad enough, clearly appears to be less severe than that of Achan), and this reinforces the idea that the narratives, each of which portrays early Israel, attest a similar thought-world. This then rather speaks for a relative antiquity of the tradition that pertains to chapter 8 in Joshua, especially as the books of Samuel have in general been seen as relatively early narratives from a chronological point of view.

Similarity with Numbers 14 has also been suggested, and Joshua's spear (8:18, 26) has been compared with Moses' raising of hands in Exodus 17:8–16 (cf. above: referring to Ottosson 1991: 79).

Hess notes that the items Achan stole fit well in the second millennium. Hess (1996: 152) comments:

> Texts listing textiles, silver and gold are not uncommon in the Ancient Near East. Items such as these can be found in inventory lists from many places, including the West Semitic cities fourteenth- and thirteenth-century Emar, Ugarit and Alalakh. Such items are found in Amarna inventory lists of the fourteenth century which record gifts exchanged between Egypt's Pharaoh and the Mitannian and Babylonian sovereigns. Whether by trade or theft, it is easy to imagine such materials appearing in a Palestinian town.

Hess further notes, in reference to Lawson Younger, that 'these items are also found on booty lists such as are attested from campaigns by

Egyptian and Assyrian kings in the thirteenth and twelfth centuries BC'
(Hess 1996: 152).

That Achan is from Judah may well be significant. That a Judahite is
criticized (cf. 15:63) makes it less likely that the narrative, and, similarly,
the book of Joshua as a whole, is an imaginative creation from monarchic
Judah. However, it could also suggest that even Judahites will not escape
judgment if they break the covenant.

Commentators have also noted how one can contrast the destinies of
Achan and Rahab in their respective narrative settings. Rahab is a non-
Israelite outsider who becomes an insider through her obedience and
confession of Yahweh, while Achan, who is an insider, becomes an outsider
and thus dies through his disobedience towards Yahweh. In other words,
there are some great reversals involved (for more on such motifs, see
especially Hawk 1991; also Nelson 1997a: 102–103). The narratives show
that even a non-Israelite prostitute can have a good fate if she follows
Yahweh, while even a Judahite, a representative of one of the main tribes,
cannot escape his destiny if he is disobedient. In this sense, the contrasting
plots about Rahab and Achan serve further to drive home the importance
of following Yahweh: a, if not *the*, major theme of the book of Joshua.

Comment

Chapter 7

1. The narrative now moves to darker overtones from the Israelite perspective. While conquering Jericho, the Israelites have broken the ban (*herem*).
It is enough that one person violates the *herem*. As the following narrative
indicates, a single person's transgression is enough to jeopardize the whole
Israelite undertaking. It was usual in the ancient world for a family to be
be punished collectively for a crime by one person. Apart from biblical
examples (see 'Explanation', chapter 2), we can otherwise read about collective punishment from a set of Hittite instructions for temple officials
(*ANET*: 208; cf. also Singer 2002: 10 for further comments and examples,
and cf. also 'Form and structure' of 22:9–34):

> If then, on the other hand, anyone arouses the anger of a god,
> does the god take revenge on him alone? Does he not take revenge
> on his wife, his children, his descendants, his kin, his slaves, his
> slave-girls, his cattle (and) sheep together with his crop and will
> utterly destroy him? Be very reverent indeed to the word of a god!

However, here the collective punishment extends to the whole of Israel.
The idea seems to be that Israel is a collective entity and must be pure
as such. As an analogy, it is like a balloon; one prick deflates the whole

balloon (i.e. the *herem* encompasses the whole of Jericho [excluding Rahab and her house/household], and taking one item is like a pinprick in a whole balloon of *herem*). In order to purge the community, the transgressor has to be purged from its midst.

2. Joshua next sends for some reconnaissance of Ai in preparation for an attack on the town. The narrative states that Ai is near Beth Aven, east of Bethel. The location of Beth Aven is unclear, even though Tell Maryam (from which a survey has found Iron Age remains) is a possibility (see *ABD* 1: 682). According to Joshua 18:12, Beth Aven is located between Jericho and Bethel, but exactly where is unclear. In this, according to MT, as both Bethel and Beth Aven are mentioned, it is unlikely that these two should be equated. However, this is complicated by the facts that the LXX simply states that Ai is by Bethel (see textual note to the verse; and cf. Hosea [esp. 4:15], where Beth Aven may mean Bethel), and that it is implied that Ai and Bethel are fairly close to each other in Joshua 7 – 8 (see e.g. Josh. 8:9, 16–17). For further comments on the location of Ai and on the relevant archaeology, see Excursus 6 on Ai at the end of this chapter.

The sending of spies reminds one of Joshua 2:1, even though the spies are not described as visiting or trying to visit Ai in this case.

3. The spies return and report that Ai is small and does not need a big contingent to conquer it. From a narrative standpoint, the reader's knowing what is about to happen heightens the fact that the Israelites are over-confident and that they trust in their own abilities rather than relying on Yahweh's favour. The presentation of the narrative might have also aroused frustration in the mind of the reader or hearer.

4–5. Three thousand men go up and are, from the standpoint of the narrative, predictably routed. Every one then loses their courage. In a short time, and in a couple of verses in the narrative, the tables of Israelite confidence are completely turned. For Shebarim, refer to the textual note on the verse.

6. Joshua and the elders now fall on the ground in front of the ark, i.e. in front of Yahweh, until the evening, and put dust on their heads. This is a sign of contrition and humility, and an expression of extreme shock (cf. 1 Sam. 4:12; 2 Sam. 1:2; 15:32; Job 2:12), and the custom seems to have been attested outside Israel as well in the ancient world.

7–9. Joshua then complains about the matter and accuses Yahweh of bringing the people over the Jordan so that they would die. Joshua regrets that the Israelites have crossed over, and at the same time appeals to Yahweh's own honour (name). One of Joshua's worries is that the Israelites will not now be feared as they were before and will thus have to face more aggressive counters from the enemy. The rhetoric seems to be similar to that of the people's complaints in Exodus and Numbers (e.g. Exod. 14:10–12; Num. 14:1–3 etc.).

10–12. Yahweh responds by pointing out the real reason for the defeat. Interestingly, no rebuke is directed towards Joshua for complaining as such, unlike with the murmuring traditions in Exodus and Numbers. The reason for the defeat is simply revealed.

13. The people are (as it seems) to place themselves in Yahweh's presence, and are to consecrate (*qiddēš*) themselves in preparation for that. Yahweh also notes that until what has been devoted (*herem*) is removed, there can be no further success for Israel. Divine favour has been lost, the worst that could happen to an Ancient Near Eastern people. Fortunately for the community, there is a way to restore that favour.

14–18. A process of casting lots is then used to find the culprit. As before, the action takes place in the early morning (cf. 3:1; 6:12). Casting lots is a kind of divinatory practice. While divination is mostly forbidden in Yahwism, this type is firmly established within it (see Josh. 14:2 etc. on the distribution of the land of Canaan; Lev. 16:9–10; Judg. 20; 1 Sam. 14; 1 Chr. 24 – 26). One may here make comparison with Akkadian liver divination (of which there are numerous examples in Akkadian literature, including catalogues of liver patterns and their interpretations; cf. Ezek. 21:19–23 for a reference to this in the Bible), but the Israelite lot is (apparently) not used for determining the future, but only to give a decision between different alternatives. Another means of divination in Israel seems to have been the breastpiece and the *urim* and *thummim* (Exod. 28:15–30). It is not clear what these mean (see Van Dam 1997), but they may have been somewhat comparable to liver divination in Assyria in that their usage allowed for a variety of answers, even if there is no evidence of, for example, an elaborate library of possible answers as in Assyria (note that liver models themselves have been found in Ugarit and in Canaan; see Pardee 2002; Horowitz, Oshima and Sanders 2006). It would seem that the *urim* and *thummim* and lots were the only acceptable means of divination in a canonical Yahwistic context. In sum, here the Israelites believed that Yahweh's will can be determined by casting lots, or even that, when one casts lots, the decision comes from Yahweh (Prov. 16:33). Cf. also comments on 14:2–3.

19–20. A confession is then sought and obtained from Achan, whom the lot has exposed. As it seems, Joshua appeals to Achan's honesty before Yahweh. Interestingly, being honest here does not help Achan in any way.

21–23. Achan moreover itemizes his takings, and the hiding place, confessing to his succumbing to their appeal. Subsequently, the items are retrieved. Hess notes that the items are best at home in the second millennium BC (see Hess 1996: 152–153). The items are spread before Yahweh, perhaps before the ark, as that particularly was Yahweh's seat of presence (see comments in Excursus 3).

24–25. A punishment by stoning and burning is then meted out. The whole family and the relevant possessions are included (for collective punishment, see also Explanation of chapter 2 and comments on 7:1 above). The violation of the ban (*herem*) is a serious matter, but, from the perspective of the narrative, Achan's transgression has made Israel lose in battle *and* caused loss of life (7:5). Consequently, Achan has to suffer the ultimate punishment.

26. A heap of stones is then raised over the remains of Achan and his family. The place is named a 'valley of trouble' ('*ākôr*), a play on words (Achan vs Achor), also in reference to verse 25. Hess notes the existence of cairns throughout the Ancient Near East, and that many of these were used as tombs (see Hess 1996: 155–156). Yahweh is then placated, and the Israelite campaign can continue, as the next chapter describes. The Valley of Achor has been located at present-day El Buq'eah, even though this identification is not certain (see *ABD* 1: 56). The place also features in the Judean northern boundary description in the book of Joshua (Josh. 15:7).

Chapter 8

1–2. Now that the transgressor of *herem* has been purged from the midst of Israel, the taking of Ai is guaranteed by Yahweh. From the perspective of the narrative, the Israelites are likely to be hesitant after the defeat, but Yahweh's promise is clear. As for the dedication (*herem*), in this case its application is that the Israelites are to kill everyone in Ai but may take booty and animals for themselves.

'To go up' ('*ālāh*; v. 1; also e.g. 6:20) is a stock expression in Hebrew and usually simply means 'to go'. However, as towns usually were on a mound in ancient Israel, and as Ai would also have been up in the hills from Gilgal, which was by the river Jordan, the expression does also have a literal meaning here.

The narrative states that Yahweh also gives Joshua some strategic instruction here. Joshua is to set an ambush behind the town.

3. This time Joshua takes a much larger contingent, 30,000 instead of 3,000 (these may refer to units also: see the translation section and comments on 4:13). The company proceeds by night, which would be normal when one does not want the enemy to see the movements of the troops. It has to be kept in mind that no artificial lighting was available in the ancient world outside the towns. When night came, things pretty well went pitch black. The stars would of course be visible, and the moon might give light if above the horizon and in the visible part of its cycle. Except for in the winter season, clouds would not have been that usual in ancient Israel.

4–8. Here the details of the ambush are given by Joshua. Again, the narrative expands from verse 2. A ruse is set up. One party will lure the defending forces out of the town, and the other will then attack the town and set it on fire. It is a fairly simple but, as it proves, effective strategy. The instructions are said to come from Yahweh (v. 8), and this is standard in ancient Israelite writing. Good instructions, including the Mosaic law, come from Yahweh. Note also 2 Samuel 5:22–25, where Yahweh gives tactical instructions to David and where Yahweh himself goes in front to strike the Philistine army, as one example (also cf. comments on 5:13–15 above). Note also the bad instructions in 1 Kings 22:19–23, which come from a lying spirit, albeit sanctioned by Yahweh.

9. The narrative again progresses with repetition and development. Joshua is described as having spent the night with the people, whatever the exact meaning of this – that is, if this was, say, simply about sleeping or about strategic planning. Note that Joshua is said to have gone to the valley the following night (v. 13).

10–13. The details of the troop movements are now given. Five thousand (or five units) are in the ambush, and therefore 25,000 are in the visible contingent, as the total number is 30,000.

14–17. The king of Ai goes out to meet the main contingent, but without knowing or suspecting a ruse. The Israelites feign weakness and move away from the town as if fleeing. The people of Ai follow in pursuit (a description of following in pursuit is usual in the Israelite battle narratives; presumably this was to kill more and get spoils; see e.g. Judg. 7:25; 1 Sam. 7:11; 17:51–53). Here, however, the men of Ai are apparently overconfident and definitely careless, and all (or too many, if all is an exaggeration) of them follow the Israelites.

18. Joshua now, as the narrative describes, on the instruction of Yahweh, raises a spear which is in his hand. This serves as a sign to the ambush group, but also as a symbolic, if not even 'magical', action for the battle (cf. v. 26). The action is similar to that of Moses in Exodus 17:8–16 (note also the lifting of hands in the Ugaritic text of King Keret, *ANET*: 143, line 76 in relation to a sacrifice, and King Zakkur's lifting of hands in prayer, quoted in the 'Form and structure' section for chapter 1), and, from a narrative standpoint, we here see another example of the book of Joshua referring back to the exodus tradition. In Egypt, the Narmer palette from the late fourth millennium BC already shows an image of the pharaoh with a club in a hand held high, striking an enemy.

19. With all or most of the defenders gone, the ambush group have an easy task. Having entered the town, they capture it and set it on fire. The description follows a fairly logical battle strategy that anyone could have used.

20–23. The tables are now turned, even though this is in appearance only, as the Israelites were never in any real trouble. But the men of Ai are in real trouble. They have nowhere to go, with Israelites in front of them and also behind them, as the ambush comes from the town to attack their rear. (The narrative must here of course imply that the men of Ai have no sideways direction of exit, perhaps considering the location of hills around.) Also, seeing the smoke rising from their town must by implication be demoralizing. Accordingly, everyone is killed except for the king of Ai, who is captured and brought to Joshua. Now the result is beginning to look like that at Jericho.

24. Once the people outside Ai have been killed, the slaughter continues in the town to finish things off.

25. Twelve thousand people are killed – all the people of Ai – including men and women. This sounds a rather large number, considering the archaeological evidence about the size of the settlements in the area, and, again, units may be meant, or it may be intentional exaggeration, even understood as such by the first readers.

26. See comment on verse 18.

27. See comments on verse 2.

28. Joshua destroys the place completely, and the writer of the narrative comments that the situation prevails in his day. The word 'Ai' is conveniently similar to the word '*i*, 'ruin'. To some, this might seem too good to be true, and they might think that either the story was created on the basis of a ruined mound along the line where the Israelites were perceived to have entered the land, according to the Israelite tradition, or, if the narrative has a historical basis, the name of the town might not originally have been Ai, and may even have had that name only in the Joshua narrative (see also Excursus 6 on Ai).

29. The king of Ai is killed and hanged on a tree. As Nelson points out, displaying the body of an enemy leader seems to have been a manifest insult (Nelson 1997a: 115, drawing parallels with 1 Sam. 31:10; cf. also 2 Sam. 4:12). However, the body is taken down in the evening, apparently in compliance with Deuteronomy 21:22–23, at least from the standpoint of the narrative. At the same time, if there is a historical basis to the narrative, the law of Deuteronomy could easily be in line with an ancient custom of the Israelites, if not shaping it. The Israelites throw the body at the entrance to the town and raise a heap of stones over it. The heap is described as being available to be seen at the time of the writer. Cf. comments on 10:26–27.

Explanation

The conquest of Jericho is followed by the conquest of Ai. This is supposed to be a simple matter, considering the success at Jericho and the insignificance of Ai. However, little do the Israelites know that one among them has violated Yahweh's instructions and taken from Jericho something that should have been given to Yahweh. The sin of Achan, whom the culprit turns out to be, has polluted the whole of Israel. Because of this, Yahweh withdraws his support and Israel ends up losing a battle they were expecting to win easily. The only way to correct the situation is to purge the evildoer from the midst of Israel. Yahweh himself reveals the culprit through the casting of lots, the stolen goods are recovered and Achan and his family are punished. Achan and everything that belongs to him is killed. A big heap is raised over Achan's body to remind future Israelites of the events so that they will not repeat the mistake. Yahweh must be followed completely, and there is no room for coveting what belongs to him.

Once the congregation has been purified, Israel's future is back on track. Subsequently, a new plan to conquer the town is made and executed successfully. The men of Ai fall victim to a ruse, the town is captured and its inhabitants are killed. The town becomes a heap of ruins, to remind future generations of what has happened. Again, Joshua's actions with the spear remind one of those of Moses during the time of the exodus and the wilderness wanderings (Exod. 17:8–16).

In these chapters a main point is that one must follow Yahweh's instructions, and it is particularly emphasized that one should not violate what has been devoted to him. It is somewhat difficult to know how to apply this in Christian terms, but perhaps we may note that there may be some parallels to the concept of sin and its punishment. However, whereas Achan had to die, Christians do not need to, as Jesus has borne their transgressions. In this respect, it is true that Ananias and Sapphira died because of their attempted deception against God (Acts 5:1–11), but this seems to be somewhat of an extraordinary exception. It is perhaps true that God also chastises his children, but this should be understood to be for developmental purposes, and the nuance is different from that in Joshua. Christians do not have a spirit of fear, but of sonship (Rom. 8:15). See also comments in the 'Explanation' of chapter 4.

In contrast to disobedience leading to problems, we may draw analogies to Christian life in that following God's will brings success. However, success in society or the like is not something that the Christian gospel is essentially about, even if it might be tempting to think so (cf. 1 Tim. 6:5–6; cf. also modern-day proponents of the 'prosperity gospel'). In fact, many Christians live in difficult situations and it is not immediately obvious that they have done anything particularly wrong to deserve that. However, inner contentment is the main issue (1 Tim. 6:6). Thus this chapter shows that the situation of ancient Israel was different from that of modern-day Christians, and also gives some pointers towards the idea that many of the Old Testament's concerns with the physical are transformed into a spiritual dimension in the New Testament.

EXCURSUS 6: THE ARCHAEOLOGY OF AI

Biblical Ai is generally identified with Et-Tell (which means 'ruin'). Albright in particular argued for this identification, and it has by and large been accepted ever since (see Albright 1924; *NEAEHL*: 39). The site was excavated twice, first by Garstang in 1928 and then by Marquet-Krause from 1933 to 1935 (see *NEAEHL*: 39; Marquet-Krause 1949). The results indicate that there existed an Early Bronze Age town on the tell, from about 3310 BC till about 2400 BC, and then the site was not occupied until the Iron Age, when, around 1220 BC, a town was built on the ruins of the Early Bronze Age town, with no intervening occupation strata (*NEAEHL*: 39). The town was occupied until about 1050 BC and then abandoned, and was never settled again (*NEAEHL*: 39). Some nearby sites have been suggested as a possible location for Ai, such as Khirbet Khaiyan and Khirbet Khudriya, but nothing earlier than Byzantine remains have been found from these in excavations in the 1960s (see *NEAEHL*: 39–40).

With these details in mind, it is difficult to think of Et-Tell or any of the above nearby sites as an Ai that would fit with the conquest as described by the biblical sources. For this reason, those who wish to preserve the possibility that the biblical story has a basis in actual history (for a summary of other views presented, including the obvious aetiological one, see Hess 1996: 157–159) would have to consider other options. One possibility is that the site is located elsewhere. Recently, Bryant Wood suggested that Ai might be located at nearby Khirbet el-Maqatir. Wood has excavated the site, which is located 1 kilometre west of Et-Tell and 1.5 kilometres south-east of Beitin, the proposed site of ancient Bethel (Wood 2000a, 2000b, 2001). The publications by Wood indicate occupation at the site in the Early Bronze, Middle Bronze, Late Bronze I, Iron I, Late Hellenistic/Early Roman and Byzantine periods (Wood 2000a: 125). According to Wood, 'remnants of a small fortress, provisionally dated to the late Bronze Age I pending a detailed study of the pottery, have been found' (Wood 2000a: 125). According to Wood, pottery suggests a twelfth to eleventh-century date for the Iron Age I occupation phase (Wood 2001: 249–250). There is also evidence of a destruction of the Late Bronze Age fortress by fire (Wood 2001: 249). However, it has to be emphasized that Wood himself states that the conclusions made so far about the site are preliminary, and should thus be treated with caution.

Comparing Et-Tell and Khirbet el-Maqatir, and also Bethel (see comments on Bethel in 12:16), we may note that there is evidence of occupation in the overall area in both Late Bronze and Early Iron Ages. Also, the Maqatir site could in theory be associated with Joshua if the final results of dating the fortress were to fall within a reasonable range of possibilities. In this respect, one could speculate that if the narrative were created soon after the conquest, there had not yet been time to rebuild the site, even though it was rebuilt by Iron Age I. At the same time, if one wishes to think of an aetiological explanation, as such, as Maqatir was apparently destroyed at the end of Iron Age I and rebuilt only in Hellenistic times, it could just as well have served as a source for an aetiological story. In other words, we cannot think that an aetiological explanation might have been pertinent to Et-Tell only, which then brings us to the conclusion that Et-Tell does not have to be the only possible candidate for the location of Ai. Clearly, there is at least a possibility that the site is simply unknown, or might even be linked with Khirbet el-Maqatir. Or could it even be located on the outskirts of modern Beitin (cf. comments on 12:16 on

Beitin)? Or, as Beth Aven, whose location is not known, is mentioned in 7:2, could Ai then even be much further away from Bethel than Et-Tell (but cf. comments on 7:2)? And, in general, it seems possible that a place with another name was destroyed, and was named as a 'ruin' (*ʿî*) for the purposes of the Joshua narrative. The name Et-Tell could even have been assigned to the site based on the Joshua narrative at a time later than the conquest, even if fairly early as such in its Hebrew equivalent *ʿî*, with the actual site lying elsewhere. We should also note here that the site of Gilgal is not known (see comments on Josh. 4:1–7), even though it serves as an important reference point in both early and later Israelite history (Josh. 4 – 5 etc.; 1 Sam. etc.; Hos.; Amos). We should further note that, as Faust (2006: 113–119, with a table of sites on pp. 114–115) points out, Et-Tell and Khirbet el-Maqatir are two of a number of sites that were abandoned at about the end of Iron Age I, and one could then ask the question why either of these two in particular would have been chosen as targets of an aetiology that we have in Joshua 7 – 8. Finally, it is conceivable that the identification of Bethel with Beitin is not correct, but it must also be stressed that this identification is generally strongly held (see *NEAEHL*: 192; cf. comments on Bethel/Beitin in 12:16).

On the whole, when thinking of the question of the historicity of the narrative, we must also keep in mind the literary setting of the Ai narrative. The role of the incident in the book of Joshua is very much to emphasize that Israel should not have violated the ban, at the beginning of the conquest in particular, and the incident therefore suggests that the importance of Ai is in itself as much literary as it may have been historical for the writer. Therefore, we may not need to think that Ai was a prominent site as such, but just a small site (cf. Josh. 7:3) that would have sufficed for the writer to fulfil his purposes of stressing the relevant moral of the story in the context of the book of Joshua.

In sum, even though in a number of ways appealing to negative rather than positive evidence, we may conclude that it is not possible to establish/prove conclusively that the events recounted in Joshua in relation to Ai could not have taken place, and, in this connection, it is not clear where the site referred to by the biblical narrative should be located.

JOSHUA 8:30–35

Translation

[30]At that time Joshua built an altar to Yahweh, the God of Israel, on Mount Ebal [31]as Moses, the servant of Yahweh had commanded the Israelites, and according to what is written in the book of the law of Moses, an altar of unhewn stones. The Israelites then offered burnt offerings and peace offerings to Yahweh on it. [32]And he wrote a copy of the law of Moses on the stones, the law which Moses

had written in the presence of the Israelites. [33]And all Israel, both native and sojourner, with its elders, officers and judges, stood around the ark of the covenant of Yahweh in sight of the Levitical priests who were carrying it, half of them towards Mount Gerizim and half towards Mount Ebal, just as Moses the servant of Yahweh had commanded previously, in order to bless the people.

[34]After that, he read all the words of the law, both the blessing and the curse, according to everything written in the book of the law. [35]There was not a word commanded by Moses that Joshua did not read in the presence of all the congregation of Israel, including women and children, and sojourners who dwelt among them.

Notes on the text

30. Gr. has 8:30–35 after 9:2, and a Dead Sea Scroll fragment (4QJosh[a]) places the text before 5:2 (see Hess 1996: 19–20, 176; Nelson 1997a: 73, 116–117).

31. Unhewn stones: lit. 'unhewn stones on which an iron tool has not been worked (swung)'. Gr. omits the mention of 'book'.

32. Alternatively, 'And he wrote a copy of the law of Moses on the stones in the presence of the Israelites, the law he had written.'

Form and structure

The cultic emphasis continues in Joshua 8:30–35. The passage records the fulfilment by the Israelites under the leadership of Joshua of a command of Moses to the Israelites in Deuteronomy 27 (cf. Deut. 11:26–32) to build an altar on Mount Ebal and to offer *oloth* and *shelamim* on it. As regards the literary setting of the passages, in general it has been thought that Joshua 8:30–35 and Deuteronomy 27 do not fit well in their respective books. Leaving aside Deuteronomy 27 here (see Pitkänen 2004a: 158–166 for details on Deut. 27), as Anbar states regarding Joshua 8:30–35, 'The victory over Ai is followed abruptly with '*āz* "at that time" (8,30) by the account of the building of an altar on Mount Ebal and the ceremony of the blessing and curse between Mount Gerizim and Mount Ebal in the presence of "the whole congregation of Israel" (8,35). However, further on, in the account of the covenant with the Gibeonites, we learn that, in effect, the Israelites are still at Gilgal (9,6)' (Anbar 1985: 304). Moreover, a Dead Sea Scroll fragment places the text of Joshua 8:30–35 before 5:2 (see e.g. Hess 1996: 171, 19–20; Nelson 1997a: 116–117), and LXX places Joshua 8:30–35 after 9:2 (cf. Woudstra 1981: 146). Finally, whereas according to the Wellhausenian consensus Deuteronomy was written to centralize all worship at Jerusalem, the Ebal narratives explicitly command the building of a sacrificial altar elsewhere than in Jerusalem. Thus the conclusion is often drawn that Deuteronomy 27 and Joshua 8:30–35 are intrusions in their respective books. Specifically, many scholars have seen the passages as either pre-deuteronomic or post-deuteronomic additions, with the majority adopting the idea of post-deuteronomic additions. Those seeing the passages (or one of them – a number of the following commentators treat only one of the passages) as pre-deuteronomic additions include von Rad (1966/1964: 165; Deut. 27). Those seeing the passages as post-deuteronomic additions include Driver (1901/1895: 294–295; Deut. 27); Mayes (1979: 337; Deut. 27) and P. D. Miller (1990: 190; Deut. 27). According to Anbar (1985: 309n27), 'Josh. 8,30–35 was composed in a late period, when striving for the centralization of the cult was already superfluous, and the central issue in community life was the demand to fulfil *all* the words of the Torah.' According to Eissfeldt (1970: 95), Deuteronomy 27 and Joshua 8:30–35 were put in their places by a post-deuteronomic editor who wanted to 'link the originally independent Deuteronomy with the older Hexateuch'.

It has been noted that 'there is uncertainty about whether the stones of the altar are the same as the stones on which the law was to be inscribed. Joshua 8:30–32 seems to imply they are, though most interpreters of Deuteronomy 27 argue otherwise' (Barker 1998: 278). In the light of Deuteronomy 27 and supposing that the two accounts are consistent, one might point out that Joshua 8:32 allows for the possibility that the stones were not the altar stones. If the writer of Joshua 8:30–35 assumed that the reader was familiar with Deuteronomy 27, he could have changed the topic from the altar in Joshua 8:31 to the stones of Deuteronomy 27 in Joshua 8:32. (One should also note here that writing on plaster is regarded as an Egyptian custom rather than Palestinian or Mesopotamian [Driver 1901/1895: 296; Craigie 1976: 328], and, of course, if the Israelites or at least some of them came from Egypt, there is nothing peculiar about the matter.)

Also, there is reason to think that Joshua 8:30–35 belongs to its literary context, even if its exact place may be slightly unclear. The passage generally fits very well with the early days and events of the conquest, even though the chapter may not record the events in a strict chronological order. That all manuscripts, even though they do not place the passage in exactly the same place, nevertheless place it within the early chapters of Joshua is perfectly compatible with this idea. Moreover, the expression *'az* in Joshua 8:30 can be taken loosely, and not as claiming that Joshua 8:30–35 follows strict chronology (so Anbar 1985: 304), and Joshua 8:30–35 can be taken to form a flashback to what happened during the days of the early conquest after Joshua and the Israelites had crossed the Jordan, especially when there is evidence of comparable literary devices elsewhere in the Ancient Near East. As Younger (1990: 211) comments on Joshua 10:12–15, a comment which is directly applicable to Joshua 8:30–35 as well:

The text of Joshua 10:12–14/15 is very often seen by biblical scholars as a type of separate alternate tradition to the narrative of 10:1–11. However, the use of *'az* and the preterite (*ydbr*) should be understood as a type of flashback – simply introducing a section of the text which narrates material which chronologically belongs between verse 9 and 10. *'az* functions very much like its Assyrian semantic counterpart *ina ūmīšuma* in the Assyrian royal annalistic inscriptions where it lacks strict chronological significance. Hence, the biblical writer relates the principal incident which is connected to the battle (namely, the hailstones) first, before he then proceeds to the special point to be cited from the book of Yashar.

In other words, from a narrative viewpoint, there is no need to regard Joshua 8:30–35 as an addition, but the passage can be seen as an integral part of the design of the book of Joshua as a whole. One may also argue for Joshua 8:30–35 belonging to its present place in the narrative by comparing Joshua 3 – 8 with Exodus 12 – 17, as pointed out above on p. 110 (based on a table in Ottosson 1991: 79).

Moreover, as Sprinkle observes, a 'double insertion' of Deuteronomy 27 and Joshua 8 in the context of Deuteronomy and the book of Joshua, which is clearly deuteronomic, 'shows careful, deliberate editing' (Sprinkle 1994: 43). In the context of a centralization requirement of Deuteronomy 12, according to Sprinkle (1994: 43):

> If such editing occurred, the person adding this material could be expected to delete the contradictory material in Deuteronomy 12 if he considered it contradictory. Furthermore, subsequent editors, if they wanted to stress the Jerusalem sanctuary, would be expected to eliminate these embarrassing additions. The fact that it was not deleted implies either that the person adding this material (along with any editor who followed him) was so incompetent that he did not notice or correct the contradictions between the texts, or else that the contradiction is in our minds rather than in the minds of the transmitters of the tradition.

We may also point out here that it is clear that the Ebal ceremony should be understood as a covenant renewal ceremony (so Barker 1998: 277; Craigie 1976: 326–329; Hill 1988: 405–406; Tigay 1996: 246; Soggin 1972: 240; cf. Driver 1901/1895: 294; Anbar 1985: 306; Butler 1983: 95). It seems natural to think that the purpose of the covenant ceremony on Mount Ebal is to renew and ratify in the promised land the covenantal relationship which had been made between Yahweh and the people of Israel before crossing the Jordan to the promised land (cf. Barker 1998: 301). In this respect, since sacrifices were involved, Weinfeld's assertion that 'In the deuteronomic covenant . . . the sacrificial element is *completely* absent' (Weinfeld 1972: 103; italics mine) is rather odd. One may also note the interesting comment by Levine (1974: 52) that the Deuteronomist associated the Ebal ceremony with the initiation of Yahwistic worship in Canaan. Of course, we do already have the circumcision and the first Passover mentioned in Joshua 5.

That the Ebal ceremony is to be taken as a covenant is confirmed by a number of similarities between it and the Sinai covenant ceremony as described in Exodus 24:4–8 (see Tigay 1996: 247; note that, according to Childs [1974: 500–501], Exod. 24:4–8 has generally been assigned to E [in spite of the divine name 'Yahweh' in the verses]. In both cases, stones were set up (Exod. 24:4 vs Deut. 27:2–4; cf. Tigay 1996: 487), and an altar built and *oloth* and *shelamim* offered (Exod. 24:5 vs Deut. 27:5–7; Josh. 8:30–31; cf. Anbar 1985: 306; Tigay 1996: 247). Also, in the Exodus account Moses reads the book of the covenant to the people (Exod. 24:7), and in Deuteronomy 27 blessings and curses are announced, which according to Joshua 8:34 come from the book of the law (cf. Tigay 1996: 247). Another matter that ties Joshua 8:30–35 and Deuteronomy 27 to the book of Exodus is that, according to Deuteronomy 27:5–6 and Joshua 8:31, the Israelites are to build the altar from unhewn stones, which is perfectly in line with the altar law of Exodus 20:24–26 (see Anbar 1985: 306 for a detailed verse comparison of Deut. 27:5–7 and Exod. 20:24–25). One may note here that the word *brzl*, 'iron', is used in Deuteronomy 27:5 and Joshua 8:31 in regard to the prohibited tool, whereas Exodus 20:25 uses *ḥrb*. (See also Millard 1988 for the use of iron before the Iron Age proper, including finds of artefacts that contain iron and many literary examples that mention iron, the oldest of which come from the Middle Bronze Age.) Overall, the connections with Exodus serve to argue against the concept of Joshua's being part of a Deuteronomistic History.

Then the similarity of the Mount Ebal tradition to the tradition in the book of Exodus speaks rather for the earliness than the lateness of the Mount Ebal tradition. That Deuteronomy 27 refers to the Exodus altar law is analogous to the rest of the book of Deuteronomy, as scholars often think that the book of Deuteronomy used the Covenant Code, including the altar law of Exodus 20, as a basis for its legislation (see Levinson 1997; Otto 1994; Lohfink 1991: 175). Seen this way, the connection of Deuteronomy 27 with the book of Exodus is fully in accord with the idea that the chapter belongs to the book of Deuteronomy as much as the rest of the material, and this of course also strengthens the idea that Joshua 8:30–35 should be seen as a part of the book of Joshua as well.

That Joshua 8:30–35 fits in the deuteronomic book of Joshua (cf. Wenham 1971b for the deuteronomic character of Joshua; cf. also below,

p. 376), and also that Deuteronomy 27 can be considered an integral part of the book of Deuteronomy, implies that the events described by the chapter were seen as fully legitimate from the standpoint of centralization by the writer of Joshua (and the writer of Deuteronomy). I make some comments on this topic here, as the concept of centralization of worship has been a major issue in the dating of Deuteronomy (see Pitkänen 2004a). A most natural explanation for the events from the standpoint of centralization is that *neither the author of Deuteronomy nor the author of Joshua thought that the centralization requirement was in force in the early days of Joshua, to which the events portrayed by Deuteronomy 27 and Joshua 8:30–35 belong.* (Note that, according to Noth [1930: 149], Deut. 27:5–7 was not seen as contradictory to the rest of Deuteronomy by its incorporator, as the Ebal tradition refers to a time before the Jerusalemite central sanctuary, and similarly Tigay [1996: 249], who suggests that the sacrifices described in Deut. 27 and Josh. 8:30–35 are part of a one-time ceremony.) The time after the crossing of the Jordan was a time of a war of conquest. The Israelites were not yet in possession of the land. It would have been out of the question to talk about peace and security, the requirement for Deuteronomy's centralization law (Deut. 12:10). First, the land would have to be conquered and the people would have to settle, and only after that would it be possible to speak about conditions that would allow pilgrimage to a central sanctuary (for further details, see Pitkänen 2004a: chapter 3.3). That the writer of Joshua thought that the chosen place would be established only in the future may also be suggested by Joshua 9:27. No place is mentioned as the place where the Gibeonites would serve, and the imperfect form *ybḥr* in Joshua 9:27 implies that the choice of the place is to happen in the future. (Greek versions add *kyrios* to *ybḥr*, which, if not indicating an underlying text variant that contained the word *ybḥr*, at least indicates that the Greek translator of the verse thought that the expression refers to the chosen place.) It is however also possible that the choice spoken of in Joshua 9:27 means choice from the perspective of the narrator rather than from the perspective of the narrated events. In that case, the narrator of Joshua 9:27 would be speaking at a time when the chosen place was not established. However, I will not explore that possibility and its implications further here, partly for the reason that I make detailed considerations of the date of the book of Joshua elsewhere in this commentary based on more comprehensive criteria.

Also, according to the book of Joshua, the events at the end of the book are temporally distinct from those at the beginning. Whereas the first chapters describe events right after the crossing of the Jordan, the last chapters at least essentially depict a later time when Joshua is 'old and advanced in years' (Josh. 13:1; 23:1–2). Consequently, we may suspect that the situation as regards centralization might be different for the later days of the conquest as described by the latter part of the book of Joshua. This in fact proves to be the case with Joshua 22:9–34 (see 'Form and structure' for 22:9–34 for details). We also note that the wilderness paradigm had passed after the crossing of the river Jordan (e.g. ceasing of the manna in Josh. 5:10–12), and one would not need to follow the requirements of priestly material (Lev. 17) about centralization, at least not directly (for further details on this, see Pitkänen 2004a: chapter 3.2 in particular). Based on the text, the altar at Ebal could have been used only once, or it could have remained in use until Shiloh became the central sanctuary. The archaeological remains from Mount Ebal, if associated with Joshua's altar, would suggest the latter option. It would seem that the altar at Ebal can be seen as a place where Yahweh had caused his name to be remembered (*hammāqôm 'ăšer 'azkîr 'ēt-šĕmî* [Exod. 20:24]; contra Richter's [Richter 2007] suggestion that Mount Ebal was a central sanctuary where Yahweh had caused his name to dwell, and in line with the idea that local altars are places where Yahweh descends for occasions of worship [only], and the central sanctuary is a place of Yahweh's dwelling [see Pitkänen 2004a: 25–67] – albeit, during the Ebal ceremony, Yahweh was already present by virtue of the ark's being at the location anyway).

Comment

30. In fulfilment of the command in Deuteronomy 27, Joshua builds an altar on Mount Ebal. The wording of this verse slightly echoes the building of altars by the patriarchs in Genesis (e.g. Gen. 12:8).

As discussed in the 'Form and structure' section, the passage is somewhat loosely connected to its surrounding text, as the word '*āz* (then, at that time) suggests (v. 30). However, as discussed, it does equally fit the narrative context overall. Burnt offerings (*šrp*) and peace offerings (*šlmm*) are attested in Ugarit, and are often spoken of together there, see e.g. Pardee (2002: 29–35; e.g. *dqt l ṣpn . šrp . w šlmm kmm* – a ewe for Ṣapunu as a burnt offering). And as a peace offering: the same [Pardee 2002: 29, 31, lines 10–11]). Cf. also comments on Joshua 22:23.

31. It is not entirely clear why unhewn stones were used, even though, according to the altar law of Exodus 20:22–26, the use of a tool on the stones would defile the altar.

32. A copy of the law is written on stone, separately from the altar (Deut. 27:2; cf. 'Form and structure' section above). It was typical in the Ancient Near East to make stone monuments when a lasting effect was desired. There are too many examples of this from Egypt to mention, especially in relation to funerary monuments, but we nevertheless mention the Merneptah stele and the walls at Karnak here (for the Merneptah stele, see pp. 43, 48–49 in the Introduction to this commentary). Also, such well-known artefacts as the Babylonian *kudurrus* (boundary markers; one may e.g. search the Internet by the word *kudurru* for pictures and explanation) were also made from stone, as was the law code of Hammurabi from the eighteenth century BC. (As a whole, for monumental inscriptions from the Ancient Near East, see e.g. COS 2, which is devoted to the matter.) No writing has however been found at Mount Ebal, even though remains of plaster were found by Zertal's excavations (see Excursus 7 on Mount Ebal).

33. All Israel is included in the ceremony, including those who were foreigners (*gerim*) living among Israel. The reference to the native (*ezrah*) and the foreigner (*ger*) echoes Pentateuchal language and legislation about natives and foreigners which itself by and large refers to life in the land (see e.g. Lev. 19:33–34). While the reference at first sight seems out of place immediately after the conquest and as the word 'foreigner' (*ger*) is not used in association with the mixed multitude that followed the Israelites in the exodus (Exod. 12: 37–38), it may simply be loose use of language and is possibly intended to remind one of the status of aliens according to the Mosaic legislation. Hess (1996: 172) notes pertinently that verse 35 specifically mentions groups that are weak in respect of power (women, children and sojourners).

The verse does not seem to be completely clear about the exact positioning and location of the people, but it definitely states that they were divided into two groups around the ark and that one was associated with Mount Ebal and the other with Mount Gerizim. At the same time, Deuteronomy 27:11–12 at first sight suggests that half of the people should have stood on Mount Ebal and half on Mount Gerizim. However, the preposition '*al* allows for the meaning 'towards'. Perhaps the idea is that the ark was in the narrow valley between the two mountains. The people might even have climbed just a little way up each mountain, even if, admittedly, this is rather speculative. As Yahweh is present at the ark (see Excursus 3), the Israelites in effect conduct their ceremony in front of their God.

34. Joshua reads the law to the people. This would be very logical, in particular as it has been estimated that only a small percentage of people were literate in ancient Israel, even during the time of the monarchy (see e.g. Dever 2005: 28).

35. That everything from the law is read out and everyone is included in the ceremony of blessings and curses (cf. the note on 1:7 about blessings and curses) is emphasized. As mentioned in my comments on verse 33, groups that are relatively powerless (women, children and sojourners) are specifically mentioned. This stresses the importance of making fair provision for everyone within Israelite society. This is a very deuteronomic theme (see e.g. Deut. 14:27–29), and is also played out in the provision for the Levites in the book of Joshua (esp. Josh. 21), and also in the institution of the cities of refuge (Josh. 20). Also, as Nelson notes, including the women, children and sojourners in the ceremony and its description highlights the fact that keeping the law is everyone's responsibility (Nelson 1997a: 120).

Explanation

The injunction of Deuteronomy 27 is fulfilled in Joshua 8:30–35. Joshua and the Israelites build an altar on Mount Ebal and offer sacrifices on it. All Israel share in a ceremony of blessings and curses around the ark. While it is not exactly clear what the building of the altar signifies here, it may be a sign of the start of Yahwistic worship in the promised land and act as a ceremony that renews and implements the covenant between Yahweh and Israel in the land. The altar and the associated stones also serve as a memorial to Yahweh and his law. It seems clear that the blessings and curses specifically remind one of the injunctions of Deuteronomy and the importance of following Yahweh.

It might be tempting to draw the conclusion based on Joshua 8:30–35 that worship should come first for a Christian, at least at a certain level. However, in the Ancient Near East, if people did not worship their gods properly, this provoked the anger of the gods and could lead to disaster (cf. 1 Sam. 2 – 4). The god(s) concerned could even leave their temples and abandon their people. Thus, the relationship with the gods was tied up with the performance of the people, even if it is also true that the covenant at Sinai was an act of Yahweh's grace (as was the covenant with Abraham). For Christians, performance is not the main issue in their relationship with God, which is based on grace. In particular, there are no covenant curses which follow from disobedience, even though God may chastise his children; and retribution from others, often through society, may not be avoidable. It seems fair to say that grace is more abundant in the Christian covenant, even though it is by no means lacking in the older covenant.

EXCURSUS 7: THE ARCHAEOLOGY OF MOUNT EBAL

In April 1980, an Iron Age site was discovered on Mount Ebal, the only known site from that period on the mountain (Zertal 1986–1987: 105). According to Zertal (105), 'Of the 12 sites discovered, one belonged to Middle Bronze Age IIB and the rest dated to much later periods, beginning with the Persian period.' Excavations were then carried out between 1982 and 1987 under the direction of Zertal (Zertal 1986–1987: 108). A preliminary report of these excavations was published in *Tel Aviv* 1986–1987, and this is the basis for the following discussion. Excavations continued after 1987 but were discontinued in 1989, and part of the site has not been excavated (A. Zertal, personal communication, December 1999). A final report has been due for some time (A. Zertal, personal communication, December 1999). The intriguing site illustrates problems met when trying to correlate archaeological and textual evidence. We therefore look at the site in detail (discussion adapted from Pitkänen 2004a: 167–185, with kind permission of Gorgias Press).

The excavations uncovered a site with two strata, with Stratum I subdivided into Phase B (the main phase) and Phase A (post-occupational phase) (Zertal 1986–1987: 109). Says Zertal, 'Both strata belong to the beginning of Iron Age I, reflecting the material culture of the Israelite settlement period in the central hill country. Both strata were short-lived, and the entire lifespan of the site did not exceed 100–200 years. No signs of destruction or fire were discerned in the transition between the strata nor at the time of abandoning the site' (Zertal 1986–1987: 109). And, 'According to the two Egyptianized scarabs unearthed, the seal and the pottery, Stratum II was founded in the middle of the 13th century B.C.E. or slightly later (c. 1240) and ended around 1200 B.C.E. Stratum IB followed immediately and was abandoned in the middle of the 12th century (c. 1130), and the site was never resettled' (Zertal 1986–1987: 109).

In Stratum II (see overleaf, Figure 5), Area A, an installation (called Installation 94) 2 metres in diameter, located in the exact centre of the overlying building, was found, covered with stones, beneath which was a 10-centimetre layer of clean ash containing many animal bones, some burnt (Zertal 1986–1987: 110–111). The stones of Installation 94 are unhewn, and the structure was hollow (A. Zertal, personal communication, December 1999). According to Zertal, 'a similar round structure, 1.45 m in diameter, discovered in Courtyard 103 of Stratum XI in the Philistine temple at Tell Qasile, was interpreted by the excavator as a sacrificial altar' (Zertal 1986–1987: 111).

In Area A, 'Sizeable quantities of ash, coals, burnt wood and animal bones were found on the bedrock. There were also some dispersed hearth-stones' (Zertal 1986–1987: 111). According to Zertal, 'The picture, as suggested by the burnt bones, is one of cooking, roasting and/or sacrificing, which apparently took place on bedrock in the open' (Zertal 1986–1987: 111). Stratum IB was divided into three main areas, A, B and C. According to Zertal, 'In stratum IB the character of Area B underwent a radical change. In Stratum II it was a domestic quarter, whereas now the architecture took on monumental dimensions, creating a large courtyard, a kind of platform in front of the main complex (Wall 32) and a broad staircase entrance to the enclosure' (Zertal 1986–1987: 119; Zertal says that the staircase had three steps [121]). According to Zertal, the Stratum II structure 'was filled up with stones and earth containing pottery sherds of the Stratum II horizon. All the 1.5 m-high space above the Stratum II floor was thus raised to the height of the upper terrace level. The new levelled unit was paved with stones' (Zertal 1986–1987: 119). Also, 'On this stony pavement some hearths and installations were unearthed together with a large quantity of Stratum IB potsherds stuck between the stones, and many animal bones' (Zertal 1986–1987: 119). As regards

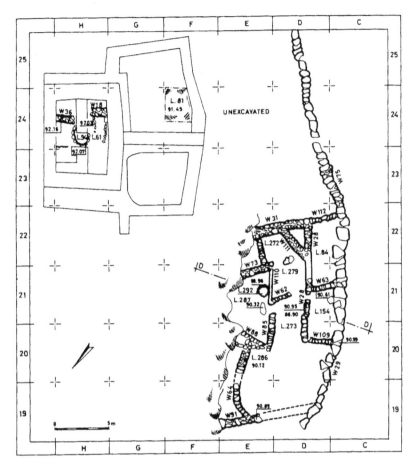

Figure 5: Mt Ebal Stratum II; upper left: Area A
(with main structure of Stratum IB superimposed);
lower right: Area B (from Zertal 1986–1987: 110)

the entrance, according to Zertal, 'The Iron Age I–II entrances known so far are generally fortified and as narrow as possible. The entrance to the site at Mount Ebal has a different concept. Its unusual width and lack of surrounding defensive walls suggests a ceremonial function' (Zertal 1986–1987: 121). According to Zertal, Area C of Stratum IB, 'consists of the northern open ground surrounded by outer enclosure walls 78 and 99 and inner enclosure Wall 77' (Zertal 1986–1987: 121; see also 122 Figure 10). Zertal has interpreted these walls 'as enclosure walls rather than defensive walls because of the unusual entrance structure, the limited height of the walls and the fact that the weakest wall was built on the weakest line' (Zertal 1986–1987: 123). Also, 'The Area C excavations showed that the enclosure walls belong to the main phase of the site, Stratum IB, and that no regular structures were built inside. In all other Iron Age I sites (with the exception of the 'Bull Site'), domestic structures are either part of the wall or located inside it' (Zertal 1986–1987: 123).

Zertal explains about the main structure, part of the so-called central complex of Stratum IB,

> Built of large unhewn stones, this rectangular structure is located on a rocky spine of the ridge in Area A. Erected on bedrock, it rises 3.27 m above it. Its corners are oriented towards the four points of the compass, the south and north corners with an error of less than 1 degree (Zertal 1986–1987: 123; see also ibid.: 114 Fig. 5 for a drawing of the structure, reproduced below, Figure 6). The outer measurements of the main structure are 9 m by 7 m.

Zertal further explains, 'The structure was found to be artificially filled with layers containing various combinations of earth, stones, ashes, animal bones and potsherds' (Zertal 1986–1987: 123). Moreover, 'In the middle of the northern part of the fill [Layer C] some 20 pieces of white plaster about 3 cm thick were neatly arranged in layers. These plaster chunks must have originated in Stratum II, and similar traces of plaster were found in Area B in both strata' (Zertal 1986–1987: 123). Says Zertal, 'To the best of my knowledge, no plaster of any sort has been recovered from any other Iron Age I site' (Zertal 1986–1987: 113–114).

According to Zertal:

> In our opinion, this structure was never used as an ordinary building. It has no entrance and no floor. The Stratum II surface could not be used as a floor either, because its western side is partitioned into cells and the eastern part of the structure stands on irregular bedrock, 50 cm lower than surface 61. Finally, installation 94 of Stratum II juts up in the direct centre of the gap between inner Walls 13 and 16, creating an insurmountable obstacle for any movement inside the structure. We therefore assume that it was constructed as a high platform, filled with Stratum II deposits from elsewhere on the site, such as the bone and ash material found among the hearths of Locus 81. (Zertal 1986–1987: 115)

Furthermore, according to Zertal:

> Two parallel and adjacent walls (Walls 2 and 7) rise from the southwest to the top of the main structure (Figs 5, 6). Wall 2 is 7 m long and 1.2 m wide like a triangular wedge, with its base adjoining Wall 9 of the main structure and its apex on ground

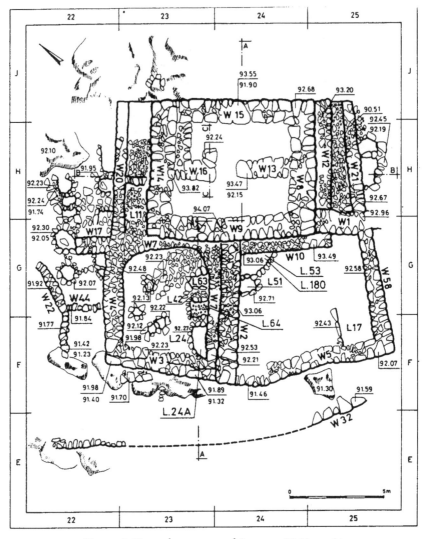

Figure 6: Central structure of Stratum IB (Area A)
(from Zertal 1986–1987: 114)

level perpendicular to Walls 3 and 5 of the courtyards (Fig. 6). Its gradient has been calculated as 22 degrees. At its highest preserved point (not far from the spot where it joins Wall 9), it is one course higher than the main structure, from which we assume that the structure is missing about one course of its stones. Since Wall 2 is an integral part of Walls 3 and 5, which in turn are part of the surrounding wall complex, it appears that all these elements were built in the same phase. . . . We have interpreted Wall 2 as a ramp rather than as an ordinary dividing wall on the following grounds: (1) It is the only means of ascent to the top of the main structure; (2) were it an ordinary wall, its outer end would have joined walls of approximately the same height as the main structure, whereas Walls 3 and 5 are low 'framewalls', whose function was to retain the floors of the open courtyards. If the courtyards had been walled and roofed, their walls would have left some evidence, at least at the points where they joined the main structure. Not only is such evidence lacking, but the entrance into the northern courtyard (and possibly the southern one as well) was by three steps, built along the width of the courtyard. Thus Wall 3 is the top step of a broad stairway on the same level as the paving of the northern courtyard. (Zertal 1986–1987: 117)

Finally, 'The purpose of Wall 7 described above is unclear, since it did not serve any constructional purpose. It may have served as a secondary ramp leading up to the ledges of the main structure' (Zertal 1986–1987: 117).

Zertal further notes, 'About 70 to 80 installations were uncovered to the north, south and east of the central complex. These consisted of crudely arranged stone-bordered circles, squares, or rectangles (and many irregular shapes) with an average diameter or width of 30 cm to 70 cm. They are intermixed and built one upon the other in some cases. They probably represent at least two stages of use (Strata II and IB), but their stratigraphic relation to each other is not always clear. The upper layer was in turn covered by the stone mantle of Stratum IA' (Zertal 1986–1987: 117–118). According to Zertal, 'In view of their great number, their concentration around the main structure and the presence of votive vessels, we interpret these installations as places for visitors to a sacred site to leave their offering vessels' (Zertal 1986–1987: 118, referring on p. 119 also to 1 Sam. 1:24, 10:3 for the attestation of the custom of bringing vessels to a sacred site. Note also that about half of the installations contained vessels or parts of vessels [Zertal 1986–1987: 118]).

Finally, Zertal describes Stratum IA. According to Zertal, as regards Area A, 'When excavating the main structure, parts of it were found covered with stones' (Zertal 1986–1987: 123). In Zertal's judgment, 'These may have been an accumulation due to field cleaning in later periods, but we think it is more likely that they were deliberately placed there' (Zertal 1986–1987: 123). Further, 'If these rocks were indeed intended to cover the structure, then what we may have here is an artificial "burial" of the place, presumably at the time of its abandonment. However, it should be noted that the courtyards were apparently not covered by stones but left exposed to the erosional elements that carried away their beaten earth floors' (Zertal 1986–1987: 124). In Area B, according to Zertal, covering the courtyard paving of Stratum IB and 80 centimetres higher there was another layer of well-arranged medium-sized stones 'whose purpose was apparently to cover the courtyard or to raise its level' (Zertal 1986–1987: 124). Furthermore, 'The external part of the western courtyard, mainly above Walls 29 and 28, was found to be in its covered state, showing the post-occupational phase at the site. In the inner part however, it seems that some of this cover was removed by later cultivation' (Zertal 1986–1987: 124). Overall, Zertal makes the conclusion that, 'before the final abandonment the site was deliberately 'buried' by a layer of stones' (Zertal 1986–1987: 124, which see for still more details).

Zertal has made a careful pottery analysis of the site (Zertal 1986–1987: 124–147): 'The ceramic inventory at Mount Ebal is a homogeneous, well dated and short-lived assemblage' (Zertal 1986–1987: 140).

Regarding stone and metal artefacts, 'Conspicuous by their absence are flint sickle blades, so typical of the agricultural Iron Age I sites. . . . On the other hand, a number of flint knives, which are very rare in Iron Age I sites, were recovered' (Zertal 1986–1987: 148). And, 'The site of Mount Ebal is rich in metal objects. Nearly 50 bronze, iron, silver and gold items were unearthed and registered in seven seasons' (Zertal 1986–1987: 150). These are typical of the Late Bronze–Early Iron Ages (Zertal 1986–1987: 150).

Moreover, Zertal thinks that the Stratum II structure in Area A is cultic. Installation 94 and Surface 61 'point to ritual activities, related to burning and animal sacrifice' (Zertal 1986–1987: 151). Zertal interprets the four-roomed house in Area B to be of domestic nature. 'It may have served as a residence for the people who were in charge of the cultic place on the ridge above' (Zertal 1986–1987: 151).

Regarding Stratum IB, Zertal points out that 'The most difficult obstacle in interpreting the finds of the main stage at Mount Ebal is the lack of any known parallels in Iron Age I' (Zertal 1986–1987: 151). Also, 'Architecturally, four possible interpretations can be given to the main complex in Area A of this stratum: a domestic building (farmhouse), a storehouse, a tower, a cultic structure or a combination of the above' (Zertal 1986–1987: 151). Zertal then notes that the main complex is completely different architecturally from that of any known domestic building from the same time (Zertal 1986–1987: 151–152). Also, the following speak against an interpretation of the structure as a farmhouse: (1) Silos or storage bins are missing. (2) No dog or ass bones are included, in contrast to most Iron Age sites. (3) Sickle blades, used to harvest winter crops, are missing. (4) There is no evidence for the processing of other food products, such as olive presses or winepresses (Zertal 1986–1987: 152). As far as the possibility of a storehouse is concerned, Zertal notes that the storehouse at Shiloh was full of large storage jars and pithoi, whereas the Mount Ebal structure was not (Zertal 1986–1987: 153).

According to Zertal, there are also good reasons for not taking the structure as a tower. First of all, 'no tower dating to the Israelite settlement period is known so far' (Zertal 1986–1987: 153). Secondly, according to Zertal, watchtowers to guard crops appeared only during Iron Age II, when the small Iron Age I settlement sites became bigger and fields expanded further away from the village centres (Zertal 1986–1987: 153). Thirdly, 'Mount Ebal has always been an obstacle to transportation and there is no road there for a watchtower to observe' (Zertal 1986–1987: 153). Fourthly, no security considerations were taken into account in choosing its location, and the site is not surrounded by a defensive wall (Zertal 1986–1987: 153). Finally, the possibility of a tower in a religious context is precluded, since, according to Zertal, known (seeming) examples at Megiddo and Shechem (from the Late Bronze Age) are architecturally 'entirely different' (Zertal 1986–1987: 153). Also, according to Zertal, no evidence for any superstructure exists, the stone debris is insufficient for a second storey, and no evidence of bricks or brick material exists. In addition, 'The fill of the main structure was poured in layers and is not the usual hodgepodge of destruction debris from an upper storey' (Zertal 1986–1987: 153). Thus, according to Zertal, 'By the process of elimination, we are therefore left with the concept of Mount Ebal as a cultic site' (Zertal 1986–1987: 154). Then, according to Zertal, 'The absence of any building in the ordinary sense of the word in Stratum IB at Mount Ebal excludes its definition as a temple' (Zertal 1986–1987: 153). Zertal also notes that the covering of the site with stones in Stratum IA could have taken place because the site was still considered sacred after it was abandoned (Zertal 1986–1987: 156, referring to scholars who have interpreted certain other finds as cultic burials of sacred monuments or sites).

Also, according to Zertal, 'The limited range of the faunal remains, all conforming to Mosaic dietary laws, and all except the fallow deer mentioned in the Bible as suitable for burnt offerings, is probably significant, since the assemblage differs from that found in Bronze Age and Iron Age domestic sites and in Canaanite cultic sites' (Zertal 1986–1987: 157; cf. Horwitz 1986–1987, esp. p. 185 Table 8 and p. 187). Moreover, the structure in Stratum IB 'seems to be designed for a large crowd' (Zertal 1986–1987: 157). According to Zertal, one has to note, though, that despite a large number of pottery offerings, 'except for a few votive vessels, and perhaps the chalices, no cultic vessels were found, unless the unique jar-jug, which has a parallel in the Philistine temple at Tell Qasile, is indeed a cultic vessel. The stone basins, which are not found at any other site, may also have had some unknown cultic function' (Zertal 1986–1987: 157).

Finally, Zertal concludes, 'The question must be raised as to whether there is a connection between the biblical tradition and the finds from the site. No conclusive answer can be given, but it should be noted that this is the only transitional Late Bronze Age/Iron Age site existing on the mountain. It correlates with the biblical tradition by the date of the events, the location and general character of the site' (Zertal 1986–1987: 158).

Archaeologists have generally been either cautious (see Mazar 1990: 350; Finkelstein 1988: 82–85; Hess 1993a: 135–137; Gilmour 1995: 108–120) or negative (Kempinski 1986; Fritz 1993: 185; Ahlström 1993: 366; Ottosson 1991: 241) about a cultic interpretation of the site, let alone about connecting it with Joshua. However, there has been no satisfactory answer to the problem of what the function of the structure is if it is a settlement building, as parallels are lacking (note however that Gilmour [1995: 116–117] suggests that the installations around the main structure should be interpreted as small silos; but cf. Zertal [1986–1987: 152], according to whom, 'The installations surrounding the main structure were definitely not used for grain storage since neither their size nor construction is suitable for such a function').

Also, as already noted above, if the structure is a watchtower, there is the problem of why there is no destruction debris, especially around the sloping 'ramp' which is supposed to have been formed by the collapse of the tower (cf. esp. Kempinski 1986: 45 vs Zertal 1986: 50–51 concerning destruction debris). It has to be pointed out here, however, that an Iron I watchtower has been found at Giloh since Zertal's report on Mount Ebal, and, moreover, this tower was evidently not located inside a defensive wall, even though evidence of a defensive wall exists elsewhere at the site (see Mazar 1990, incl. p. 78, Figure 1; p. 92). It is also worth noting that, as with Mount Ebal, the Iron I tower at Giloh was *not* located on the highest point of the hill (see Mazar 1990, incl. p. 78, Figure 1; pp. 83–84). Finally, the measurements of the tower, (roughly 11 m square; see ibid.: 79) are fairly similar to the main structure at Mount Ebal (7 m by 9 m). That said, the Giloh structure has a solid foundation (the foundation of an Iron Age II tower is similar to the main structure at Mount Ebal; see Mazar 1990: 97, Figure 10), and nothing comparable to Installation 94, the fill of the main structure, and the surrounding wall complex exists at Giloh.

One should moreover add that when scholars object to the possibility of interpreting the site as Joshua's altar based on a reading of the book of Joshua, they are not proceeding on an archaeological basis, but replacing one literary reading of the biblical text with another (see esp. Kempinski 1986: 48–49, criticized by Zertal 1986: 52–53).

Even if the cultic nature of the site is acknowledged, it is by no means certain that the site belonged to the Israelites at the time concerned (cf. Hess 1993a: 136). However, it is true that, if one were to assume a thirteenth-century exodus/early settlement, as most scholars do, the impression given in the biblical sources is that the Shechem area was at least under the strong influence of the Israelites at the time. But, here again, one comes back to the literary sources.

Finkelstein has challenged the dating of Mount Ebal remains based on pottery analysis. According to Finkelstein, there are two specimens at

Shiloh and one at Tell Qasile Stratum X (eleventh century) that are similar to the six storage jars with three handles found at Mount Ebal (Bunimovitz and Finkelstein 1993c: 158; Finkelstein 1988: 85). Owing to the parallels, Finkelstein suggests a later date for Mount Ebal than Zertal (Bunimovitz and Finkelstein 1993c: 158). However, if Late Bronze vessels were still attested at Mount Ebal, it is conceivable that the combination jar-jug in question had a reasonably long period of use even though it is rare among finds.

A clear difficulty in connecting the site with Joshua's covenant ceremony is that deer bones were found among the animal remains, as fallow deer comprised 10% of the total diagnostic bone sample (Horwitz 1986–1987: 174). Also, fallow deer forms 21% of the diagnostic material in the main structure, whereas it forms 5% of the diagnostic material in all the other areas combined (Horwitz 1986–1987: 174; note also that deer bones were found even inside Installation 94 of Stratum II [A. Zertal, personal communication, December 1999]). As deer evidently are not one of the sacrificial animals in the Bible, this makes it more difficult to associate the site with the biblical testimony (Exod. 20:22–26; Josh. 8:30–35; cf. Horwitz 1986–1987: 183, 186). To harmonize, one might for example try to show that the deer remains could originate from outside the main structure itself (i.e. the deer remains should be seen as part of an artificial fill which was inserted when the monumental structure of Stratum IB was constructed), and perhaps think that they are the remains of ceremonial eating (cf. also Deut. 12:7, 17–18; 27:7 concerning ceremonial eating, and note that Deuteronomy explicitly allows the eating of deer [Deut. 14:5]; also cf. Hawking 2007: 265–266). Also, as another alternative, according to Zertal, Mazar thought that deer were still accepted as sacrificial animals at the time of the Ebal ritual, and were only in the process of being removed from that role at the time (A. Zertal, personal communication, December 1999). And one might perhaps also try to think of whether Exodus 20:22–26, Leviticus 17, Deuteronomy 27 and Joshua 8:30–35 exclude the possibility that deer could be offered on a local altar (i.e. outside the central sanctuary regulated by the priestly offering rules), at least in some cases.

In addition, if one were to suppose that the site might be connected with Joshua, a number of detailed questions would remain. A major problem is the relation of Strata II and I. The first issue to point out is that there is clear evidence that both Strata may have involved cultic activity. In fact, Stratum II gives very strong evidence of burning, as the stones of Installation 94 were charred, and ash containing animal bones was found directly by it (Zertal 1986–1987: 109) and inside it (so A. Zertal, personal communication, December 1999), and moreover, the fill of the main structure which contains ash originates from Stratum II (Zertal 1986–1987: 113, and A. Zertal, personal communication, December 1999). Also, as there were hearths and installations on the stony pavement of the courtyard in Area B in Stratum IB together with 'a large quantity of Stratum IB potsherds stuck between the stones' and 'many animal bones' (Zertal 1986–1987: 119), and burnt bones belonging to Stratum IB seem to have been found around the main structure (see Horwitz 1986–1987: 177 Figure 3), there seems to have been cultic activity associated with Stratum IB as well. Also, it is interesting in this regard that the 'ramp' leading to the top of the main structure of Stratum IB was only 1.2 metres wide (Zertal 1986–1987: 117), and it would thus be difficult to bring animals up to the top of the main structure, as Kempinski observes (Kempinski 1986: 45). Yet, even if the structure was an altar, it is by no means certain that the killing of animals would have occurred on the top of the structure (cf. Lev. 1:3–9 etc.).

Another important issue in regard to the relation of Strata II and I is that the main structure of Stratum IB has been built so that Installation 94 of Stratum II is at the exact centre of it (see Figure 5 above). This very strongly suggests that the two belong together. If we were to take at least at face value the biblical tradition of a conquest that included a programme to eliminate Canaanite cultic practices, it would be hard to think that Joshua, the ardent Yahwist, would have built the altar on a Canaanite cultic structure so that the altar was left partly standing neatly in the centre (cf. also Deut. 12:3). We would not expect either that he would fill the new structure with debris from the previous structure, or leave the situation as it was until he could produce debris with which to fill the structure. Rather, even if the structure were not a cultic one, we would expect that he would carefully destroy all the structures of the previous place or build on a previously unused place. (Note also the installations around the main structure, which seem to have been used in both strata [Zertal 1986–1987: 117–119; cf. above, p. 197].) And the biblical tradition naturally indicates that it was the first time that the Israelites had been at the site, since they had just crossed the Jordan. Thus both strata should be seen as Israelite. In connection with this, as indicated above, there is very good reason to think that Installation 94 in Stratum II was an altar (cf. again Zertal 1986–1987: 110–111). Then, if we think that the exodus/early settlement happened in the thirteenth century, it should rather be this altar that should be associated with Joshua, if anything. Zertal himself thinks that the older altar was part of a foundation ceremony before the building of the actual altar (A. Zertal, personal communication, December 1999). Also, except for the living quarters (for which see Zertal 1986–1987: 111–112), it is not certain how long Stratum II lasted. According to Zertal, Stratum II could even have been very short-lived (A. Zertal, personal communication, December 1999). We should also note that there was evidence of layering in Stratum IB, which indicates a longer period of use (A. Zertal, personal communication, December 1999).

Why then would the second structure have been built? The most natural possibility is that Stratum IB was an improved version of the altar, and was built on top of Stratum II. If so, one could think it possible that the new construction was also used as a monument (cf. Zertal 1986–1987: 160). In this regard, we know that, according to Joshua 4, stones were to be set up at Gilgal as a monument for future generations. We also know that, according to Joshua 22:9–34, the Transjordanian altar was a big monument (Josh. 22:10; see the commentary on the passage for more details). That the altar was a monument could be corroborated by the fact that no living quarters have been found for Stratum IB so far (cf. Zertal 1986–1987: 123). Rather, an entrance and a courtyard were built on top of the Stratum II living quarters of Area B (cf. Zertal 1986–1987: 119–121; yet one has to remember that the whole site has not been excavated [A. Zertal, personal communication, December 1999]). This said, that animal bones were found in Stratum IB may suggest cultic activity in association with Stratum IB as well.

One also has to remember that the site as a whole was soon abandoned. Was the site buried intentionally? The matter is not certain, especially as the whole of Stratum IA was not covered with stones. But if the site was buried intentionally, it is possible that this was done in order to prevent it from being abused. One might even think that the site was abandoned in favour of Shiloh (thus also A. Zertal, personal communication, December 1999; for considerations of the role of Shiloh during the last days of Joshua, see commentary on Josh. 22:9–34). This could have taken place when Shiloh was asserting its role as the central sanctuary, which according to the book of Joshua in any case happened only some time after the initial entry into Canaan. Certainly, other instances of burial of monuments and sacred sites are attested in the Ancient Near East (see Hawking 2007: 68–70).

What about the plastered stones? First of all, no writing was found on them (A. Zertal, personal communication, December 1999). Yet Zertal thinks that there could have been writing on them originally (personal communication, December 1999). Also, one has to stress the fact that finding plaster at the site is extraordinary. On this, as already mentioned above, as Zertal (1986–1987: 113–114) notes, 'To the best of my knowledge, no plaster of any sort has been recovered from any other Iron Age I site.' Also, Zertal points out that only two other examples of plastered finds are known otherwise: Tell Deir 'Alla and Kuntillet Ajrud in Sinai (A. Zertal, personal communication, December 1999; cf. Tigay 1996: 248; Boling and Wright 1982: 248). As the pieces of plaster seem to have been arranged neatly (A. Zertal 1986–1987: 113), this suggests that they could have been placed there ceremonially. One might even imagine that the pieces are plaster from the first structure, which had fallen off due to weathering; this said, one should note that traces of plaster were also found in Area B in both Strata II and IB.

In this regard, thinking of the possibility of linking the structure with Joshua, one might ask the question of where the apparently associated standing stones should be. No trace of such stones has been found. Yet, as only part of the site has been excavated, one might think it possible that they lie buried elsewhere nearby (so A. Zertal, personal communication, December 1999; in fact, Zertal notes that about 50 m west there is a big pile of rocks [30 m long and 5 m high], and that a cut was made into the pile, revealing the beginning of walls underneath). One might also think that the stones were carried off or otherwise eliminated when the site was abandoned.

Finally, Zertal suggests the possibility that the current location of Mount Gerizim is not the same as in Joshua's time. According to Zertal, it has been suggested that one of the mountains that faces the altar could be the Mount Gerizim of Joshua (personal communication, December 1999). However, if the location of Mount Gerizim is what is currently thought, even though the structure excavated by Zertal is not visible from there, it would not necessarily preclude the possibility of a connection of the site at Mount Ebal with Joshua. The curses ceremony need not have taken place at the site of the altar.

We may conclude that Zertal has given good reasons to suggest that the Mount Ebal site as a whole could be of cultic nature (see also Hawking 2007), even though the matter is not certain. It is also possible that the site could relate to the Israelites, and even the covenant ceremony of Joshua, although it has to be emphasized that this is by no means certain. All in all, we may conclude that, based on the available evidence, it is possible that the site was connected with Joshua, even though the matter cannot be proved (this is a slightly more positive appropriation than that given in Pitkänen 2004a: 184–185). Whatever the case, the uniqueness of the main structure with its surrounding wall complex and its possible connections with Joshua make the question of the nature of the site at Mount Ebal nothing less than intriguing. Also, the fact that no structure has been found at Mount Ebal from Iron Age II rather speaks for the antiquity of the Joshua tradition, as there is no evidence of a cultic centre at Mount Ebal during the time of the monarchy from which to draw the tradition. (However, based on Deut. 27 and Josh. 8:30–35, one could also argue that the altar was intended to be used only for the one-off event of covenant renewal [cf. Tigay 1996: 249; Levine 1974: 40], and consequently it might be possible that no remains of the altar, which basically could have been located anywhere on the mountain, would have survived in any case. Yet the erecting of stones [Deut. 27:1–4] would suggest monumental usage, and thus an appropriation beyond a one-off ceremony.) Moreover, it is doubtful that a late writer would have created a story about an important ceremony outside Jerusalem in the territory of Joseph if he were promoting the centrality of Jerusalem, even if the story refers to a time before the building of Solomon's temple (cf. Zertal 1986–1987: 158; Soggin 1972: 241, 243–244; Anbar 1985: 309; Gray 1986: 94–95).

JOSHUA 9

Translation

¹When all the kings who dwelt on the west side of the Jordan, in the mountains, on the Shephelah and all along the Mediterranean coast up to Lebanon, the Hittites, the Amorites, the Canaanites, the Perizzites, the Hivites and the Jebusites heard what had happened, ²they gathered together for a united war against Joshua and the Israelites.

³The Gibeonites also heard what Joshua had done to Jericho and Ai. ⁴They acted craftily and pretended to be messengers. They put old sackcloth on their donkeys and worn-out, torn and mended wine bags, ⁵with worn-out and patched sandals on their feet and worn-out garments on themselves. Also, all of their bread was dry and crumbled. ⁶And they came to Joshua to the camp at Gilgal. They said to him and to the Israelites, 'We come from a faraway land. Now, make a covenant with us.'

⁷The Israelites said to the Hivites, 'Perhaps you live among us; how would we make a covenant with you?'

⁸They replied to Joshua, 'We are your servants.' Joshua asked them, 'Who are you and where do you come from?'

⁹They said, 'Your servants have come from a very faraway land on account of the name of Yahweh your God. We heard about his fame and about everything that he did in Egypt ¹⁰and what he did to the two kings of the Amorites which were on the east side of Jordan, to Sihon king of Heshbon and Og king of Bashan who reigned in Ashtaroth. ¹¹Our elders and all the people of our land said to us, "Take provisions with you for the road and travel to meet them, and say to them, 'We are your servants, make a covenant with us.'" ¹²This is our bread; it was warm when we took it from our homes on the day we departed to travel to you. But, see, now it is dry and crumbled! ¹³And these are the wineskins that we filled anew, and, see, now they have been burst! And, these are our clothes and sandals; they have been worn ever so much because of the long way!'

¹⁴Subsequently, the Israelite men partook from their supplies, without however consulting Yahweh. ¹⁵Joshua himself made peace with the Gibeonites. He made a covenant with them, granting them the right to live. Also, the leaders of the assembly swore them an oath.

¹⁶However, three days after making a covenant with the Gibeonites, the Israelites learned that the Gibeonites were living in close proximity to them. ¹⁷The Israelites then travelled to the towns of the Gibeonites, arriving at Gibeon, Kefirah, Beeroth and Kiriath Jearim after three days' travel. ¹⁸But the Israelites did not attack them because the leaders of the assembly had made an oath to them by Yahweh the God of Israel.

The whole assembly grumbled against the leaders, ¹⁹but the leaders answered, 'We made an oath to them by Yahweh the God of Israel. We cannot touch them now. ²⁰We will let them live. Thus we will not incur wrath on ourselves on account of the oath that we swore to them.' ²¹The leaders added, 'They will live and will be woodcutters and water-drawers for the whole assembly.'

[22]Joshua then called for the Gibeonites and said to them, 'Why did you deceive us, saying, "We are very far from you," even though you live among us? [23]Be cursed now! However, none of you will be killed. You will be woodcutters and water-drawers for God's house.'

[24]They replied to Joshua, 'Your servants heard definitively that Yahweh commanded Moses his servant to give you the whole land and destroy all its inhabitants from before you. We really feared for our lives, and that is why we did this trick. [25]We are at your mercy! Do with us what seems best to you.'

[26]Joshua did to them as he promised. He rescued them from the Israelites and left them alive. [27]There he set them as woodcutters and water-drawers for the assembly and for Yahweh's altar for the place that he would choose. And that is how they are till the present day.

Notes on the text

1. All the kings: Gr. adds 'of the Amorites'. West side of the Jordan: lit. 'the other side of the Jordan'. Shephelah: see comment on 15:33. The Mediterranean coast: lit. 'the coast of the great sea'.

5. Pretended to be messengers: a rare form, hith. of *ṣîr*.

6. The Israelites: *BHS* reads 'man of Israel', but the intended meaning seems obvious. Gr. reads 'Israel'. Make: the Hebr. word is *kārat*, 'to cut'. See more on this in the 'Explanation' section.

7. The Israelites: *BHS* reads 'man of Israel'. Gr. reads 'sons of Israel'.

10. The east side: lit. 'the other side'.

12. Took: hith. from *ṣîd*.

16. Were living in close proximity to them: lit. 'were close to them and lived among them'.

17. After three days' travel: lit. 'on the third day'.

18. Attack: lit. 'strike'.

23. None of you will be killed: lit. 'And not (even) a slave will be cut off from you.' For God's house: lit. 'For the house of my God'; Gr. 'for me and my God'.

27. There: lit. 'on that day'. For the place: Gr. 'and for the place'. He: Gr. *kyrios* (Lord).

Form and structure

The literary structure of the chapter can be summarized as follows (expanded from Nelson 1997a: 128):

> First movement – the deception (vv. 1–15)
>   Action (vv. 1–5)
>   Kings gather for war (vv. 1–2)

Gibeonites go to the Israelites (vv. 3–6a)
Dialogue
    The Gibeonite story (v. 6b)
    Question expressing doubt by the Israelites (v. 7)
    Gibeonite commitment (v. 8a)
    Question of whereabouts by the Israelites (v. 8b)
    Expanded story by the Gibeonites (vv. 9–12)
Decision
    Israelites take from Gibeonite provision (v. 13)
    Covenant with the Gibeonites (v. 14)
Second movement – the result of the deception (vv. 16–27)
    Action (vv. 16–18a)
        Israelites hear the Gibeonites are local (v. 16)
        Israelites go to Gibeonite towns without attacking them
            (vv. 17–18a)
    Ancillary movement (dispute) (vv. 18b–21)
        Dialogue (vv. 18b–19)
            People murmur against the leaders (v. 18b)
            Leaders' reply, part A (v. 19)
        Decision (vv. 20–21)
            Leaders' reply, part B (vv. 20–21a)
        Action (v. 21b) – Gibeonites become servants
    Dialogue (vv. 22–25)
        Joshua rebukes the Gibeonites (vv. 22–23)
        The Gibeonites reply (vv. 24–25)
    Decision (v. 26) – Gibeonites spared
    Action (v. 27) – Gibeonites become servants of Yahweh's
        altar

The cultic emphasis continues in this chapter, even though from a slightly different angle from that of previous chapters. By the end of the chapter, it has been established how the Gibeonites become woodcutters and water-drawers for Yahweh's sanctuary. The use of the priestly words *něśî'îm* (elders) and *'ēdāh* (congregation), and possibly *lwn* (murmur [v. 18]; cf. Nelson 1997a: 124) reinforces the cultic interest of the chapter. Thus, while it may be said that the chapter explains, and even legitimates, the existence of the Gibeonites in the midst of Israel, such an explanation is tied to the Israelite cult, even as part and parcel of it (similarly Blenkinsopp 1972: 35–36). In this context, it would be natural to think that any priestly features are integral to the narrative and part of it even in its earliest stages, rather than later additions to it, as one would be likely to be obliged to think if one followed the Wellhausenian dating of priestly material as late and post-exilic (cf. Ottosson 1991: 83). But certainly, the narrative also has deuteronomic features. As Nelson (1997a: 124; cf. Blenkinsopp 1972: 33–34) notes:

For example Israel's problem with the Gibeonite alliance is set forth in terms of the principles of Deut. 20:10–18: 'peace' (v. 15; Deut. 20:10–11) for towns very distant, annihilation for the peoples of the land of inheritance. The claim to be from a '(very) distant country' (variations on *raḥôq*; vv. 6, 9, similarly v. 22) reflects the language of Deut. 20:15. The mere question of a 'covenant' would also recall Deut. 7:1–4 for readers sensitive to Deuteronomy. The language of vv. 9–10 is mostly deuteronomistic (see 2:10 and 1 Kings 8:41), as is that of v. 24 and the last words of v. 27 (centralization). Although the story in its basic form does not require the presuppositions of Deut. 20:10–18 to work, the dilemma faced by Israel has been sharpened by the inclusion of allusions to Deuteronomy in its present shape.

This then reinforces the idea that, in the context of the deuteronomic book of Joshua, the priestly material was worked in by the deuteronomic writer.

In this context, we may also note that there is no need to doubt the essential unity of the chapter and postulate two or more sources for it, in contrast for example to what Noth has suggested (see Noth 1953a: 55). Any unevenness in the narrative, such as the variation between Joshua, Israel and the leaders of the congregation (see Blenkinsopp 1972: 32–33), does not seem serious if one allows for each of the parties to be representative of the whole and thinks that the ancient Hebrew narrative may simply have liked the variation. The expression 'man of Israel' (vv. 6–7) may be shorthand or corrupted for 'men of Israel'.

The historicity of the Gibeonites warrants some discussion here. There are various angles from which one may approach the question. First of all, one may look at the archaeology of the Gibeonite towns. We note (cf. comments on 9:3, 17) that the main problem in this respect lies with Gibeon, as there is occupation at the possible location of Chephirah, uncertainty about the location of Beeroth, and apparently little excavation at the possible location of Kiriath Jearim (cf. 15:60). As for Gibeon, no clear stratigraphical remains have been found from the Late Bronze Age at el-Jib, the most likely site of Gibeon. However, Late Bronze remains have been found from tombs in the vicinity. Also, as Blenkinsopp (1972: 6) notes, only a small portion of the tell has been excavated. Excursus 8 below looks at these issues in detail.

The Gibeonites also feature elsewhere in the Old Testament. In particular, the mention of the Gibeonites in relation to an oath in 2 Samuel 21:1–14 strengthens the claim of historicity of the treaty with the Gibeonites and of the Joshua account (Blenkinsopp 1972, *passim*). In fact, Blenkinsopp's study in the early 1970s took a positive view of the possibility of the existence of the Gibeonites and the importance of the town of Gibeon (el-Jib), even the basic historicity of Joshua 9 – 10:27, including the treaty between Israel and the Gibeonites (see Blenkinsopp 1972: 36,

39–40). Blenkinsopp saw the treaty as a vassal treaty whereby the Gibeonites as servants corresponded to vassals and Israel to an overlord. In relation to this, Blenkinsopp noted that vassals usually called themselves 'servants' in the Amarna letters. Blenkinsopp, partly on the evidence of the Amarna letters, further noted how Canaan's population had a diverse ethnic composition at the time implied by the biblical narrative. In the context of the contemporary diverse ethnic composition of Canaan, Blenkinsopp argued that the Gibeonites may have had some kinds of links to the Hurrians (see Blenkinsopp 1972 for details), and noted that a covenant meal was usual in Hurrianized Alalakh (Blenkinsopp 1972: 118n43). The famine during David's time mentioned in 2 Samuel 21 could be taken as a treaty curse, with possible parallels with the plague prayers of Muršili (Blenkinsopp 1972: 36–37: 119n47).

Blenkinsopp also notes that the social organization of the Gibeonites was similar to that in the Shechem narrative of Genesis 34 in regard to ethnic tension and a possible treaty (Blenkinsopp 1972: 37–38). Blenkinsopp also notes that a reason for the attack by the king of Jerusalem (Josh. 10:1ff.) may have been that the Gibeonites renounced an alliance with Jerusalem (Blenkinsopp 1972: 28–29). Connected with this, the existence of small states in Canaan, Gibeon being one of them, rather speaks for the antiquity of the Joshua narrative, as it fits better with a political organization that precedes the monarchy (cf. Blenkinsopp 1972: 31–32). And the existence of elders among the Gibeonites would seem to fit the Late Bronze Age to Iron Age I time (Blenkinsopp 1972: 31–32). The Israelites are of course also depicted as having had a similar social organization at this time.

That there was a great high place (*bamah*) in Gibeon according to 1 Kings (1 Kgs 3:4) fits with the overall cultic appropriation of the Gibeonites in Joshua 9:27. The post-exilic books of Chronicles (see 1 Chr. 16:39; 21:29 etc.) even state that the Tent of Meeting was at Gibeon at the time of Solomon, before the temple had been completed. It should be noted in this connection that priests could officiate in towns other than those where their property might be located (as with Abiathar who, according to 1 Kgs 2:26, had an estate in Anathoth but officiated in Jerusalem; pointed out by Barmash 2005: 85), and thus it can be inferred that the existence of the Gibeonites in Gibeon would not preclude the idea of their having been active in Shiloh or in Jerusalem. The same goes with the priests and Levites in general (cf. their locations in Josh. 21).

The historicity of the Gibeonite ruse has been doubted (see Blenkinsopp 1972: 34–35). Others have wondered whether the Israelites succumbed willingly (see Nelson 1997a: 126; Hawk 2000: 143, referring to J. Liver). However, Younger has pointed to similar events in the Hittite texts in particular (see Younger 1990: 201–203).

Blenkinsopp (1972: 38–39) notes that the names of the kings in the biblical narrative do not coincide with Amarna names. Blenkinsopp himself (1972: 39) sees that the most likely explanation is that the events took place towards the end of or shortly after the Amarna period.

Blenkinsopp (1972: 39–40) also saw a problem with Israel as the stronger party swearing to the Gibeonites, whereas it (apparently) was the other way around in vassal treaties. However, one may ask whether we have enough examples of Ancient Near Eastern treaties to preclude the possibility of the stronger swearing to the weaker. Also, certainly, Yahweh swears to the Israelites on a number of occasions (see e.g. Gen. 26:3; Exod. 6:8; Josh. 14:10; 1 Sam. 3:14; Ps. 132:11).

In sum it seems plausible, even logical, to think that the narrative(s) about the Gibeonites were included in the book of Joshua because of their subsequent and later cultic importance, and their existence among the Israelites at the time of the writer. This would make sense if the writer belonged to priestly or equivalent circles, including during the time before the monarchy, even if other settings are also possible. While arguing strongly for Yahwism, the writer would like to explain why the Gibeonites were not killed and were in fact taken to be servants of Yahweh's house. That said, we may ask why the (possible) assimilation of the Hepherites, for example (see Josh. 17:2–6 and comments on these verses), was not expressed with similar emphasis. We can only conjecture that other such assimilations perhaps took place outside the direct sphere of influence of the writer and were less related to the cult, and thus, while they were happening, would be less of an issue for the writer to comment on. In any case, all history writing is selective.

Comment

1–2. The narrative now describes how a coalition is formed by local kings to address the threat posed by the incoming Israelites. The Girgashites are missing here from the usual list of seven nations/peoples (see e.g. Deut. 7:1; Josh. 3:10; 24:11; cf. also Gen. 10:15–20, 15:18–21 and Exod. 3:8 as pointed out by David Manohar, private communication March 2008; also note that the Girgashites are included in 24:11). The formulaic nature of the list of seven nations seems clear. While this might lead one to question the historicity of the portrayed peoples, one may also think that the list is intended as representative, and does not need to be an exhaustive or exact list of the actual nations in question. On another level, the list in 9:1–2 may well also be hyperbolic and does not need to be read to mean *all* kings of Canaan (cf. Younger 1990: 251). As for the exact location of each of these people groups, this is unclear, except for the Jebusites, who are clearly located in Jerusalem (e.g. 15:8, 63), even though such localization may not need to be seen as exclusive. As for the other groups, for example, 11:3 and 11:19 may give some hints about their location, and yet these two verses locate the Hivites in two very different places (however, perhaps both are correct after all). Also, 12:2 states that Sihon was a king of the Amorites, and yet 11:1–3 does not quite seem to localize the Amorites in a similar manner (cf. comments on 13:10 about the origin of the Amorites). It thus appears that the peoples in question are not necessarily to be located in one place alone. Numbers 13:29 provides some further information. In addition, Na'aman (1994b) provides some very interesting suggestions about the possible origin of these peoples. He suggests that the designation 'Hittites' actually suggests origins of these peoples in ancient Anatolia (Na'aman 1994b: 239–240). Na'aman also suggests that the Jebusites and Perizzites came, or at least may have come, from the area of the (for Na'aman former) Hittite empire, and the Girgashites 'came from Karkisha in Western Anatolia' (Na'aman 1994b: 240–241). The Hivites 'most probably' arrived from Que (Cilicia) (Na'aman 1994b: 240). For Shephelah, see comment on 15:33.

3–6. The narrative now moves to Gibeon. For the archaeology of the site, see Excursus 8. The Gibeonites act craftily and make a ruse, disguising themselves as weary travellers from a faraway land. According to Deuteronomy (20:10–15), the Israelites can leave such people alive, assigning them to forced labour. The way Joshua 9 progresses fits with this deuteronomic law. It is interesting that the story implies that the Gibeonites knew the deuteronomic injunction. However, if they knew that Israel had a primary interest in the land of Canaan, they might have surmised that attitudes towards foreigners as outsiders to the situation might be more lenient (cf. their portrayed knowledge about past events in the areas east of the Jordan in vv. 9–10). Importantly, the Gibeonites seek a covenant (treaty) with Israel, as pointed out by Nelson (1997a: 130).

7. The narrative describes the initial suspicion of the Israelites. Interestingly, the Israelites do not really seem to know the details of the peoples of the area.

8. The men are then brought to Joshua for questioning at first hand by Israel's leader. Joshua does directly ask the Gibeonites where they come from. The Gibeonites envisage themselves as servants for the future, and, in the light of verse 6, are aiming to obtain a vassal treaty with Israel (as suggested by Nelson 1997a: 129).

9–13. The Gibeonites appeal to Yahweh's reputation and the things Yahweh has done for Israel in Egypt and in the wilderness. The comments in their present form sound textbook-like, as if spoken by an Israelite himself (cf. Rahab's comments in Josh. 2:10). Yet it has to be noted that the narrative implies that the Gibeonites have respect for Yahweh, and this saves them, in a manner comparable to Rahab, even if the particulars of their case are somewhat different. The Gibeonites then offer (fake) evidence of the veracity of their claim to having come from a distant land. They show the bread, wineskins, garments and sandals which they have made to look old for the occasion. For Heshbon, see comments on 12:2. For Bashan and Ashtaroth, see comments on 12:4.

14–16. The point is made that the Israelites believe the story without consulting Yahweh for guidance. Peace is then made with the Gibeonites and an oath sworn to keep them alive. But just a few (three) days later the truth comes out and reality strikes (cf. the occurrence of the expression 'three days' in 1:11; 2:16, 22; 3:2). Verses 14–15 seem to indicate that everyone (men of Israel, Joshua and the leaders) is responsible for the outcome.

17. Having found out the real state of affairs, the Israelites travel to meet the Gibeonites. The mentioning of the towns highlights the fact that the Gibeonites are portrayed as having covered an area larger than the town of Gibeon only. As noted in the 'Form and structure' section, Chephirah is often identified with Khirbet el-Kefireh (see *ABD* 1: 898). Late Bronze shards (see *ABD* 1: 898) and Iron I shards at the site outside a large Iron I lower city wall (see R. D. Miller 2003: 169) have been found at the site. The identification of Beeroth is unclear (see *ABD* 1: 646–647). Kiriath Jearim is generally identified with modern Tell el-Achar (see *ABD* 4: 84–85).

18–20. No attack can be made on the Gibeonites owing to the oath sworn, even though desired by the people. This highlights the seriousness with which oaths (and covenants) were made and treated in the ancient world. As so often, people complain against a bad decision made by their leaders, even when they themselves in this case seem to share in the responsibility (cf. above, v. 14 and comments on vv. 14–16).

21. The Gibeonites are assigned to be 'woodcutters and water-drawers for the whole assembly'. This is apparently a rather menial set of jobs, but better to be a living dog than a dead lion (Eccl. 9:4). Gibeon itself had a (very) good water source, with the pool of Gibeon mentioned in 2 Samuel 2:12–17 and Jeremiah 41:12 (cf. Hess 1996: 183) and attested archaeologically (cf. below, Excursus 8). The usage of a similar expression about woodcutters and water-drawers in Deuteronomy 29:11 suggests that sojourners can be connected with these tasks. However, does the Deuteronomy passage even contain a nod towards the narrative of Joshua 9, suggesting that the Gibeonites should now be considered as sojourners (*gerim*; keeping in mind that *gerim* had a special status in Israelite society)? Verses 23 and 27 however imply that the tasks of cutting wood and drawing water had a prestigious element, as the Gibeonites served the altar of Yahweh, even when a curse was involved (v. 23, and see further comments on v. 27 below).

22–23. Joshua now complains to the Gibeonites about their deception, and, not being able to kill them, has to settle on simply cursing them as the next best alternative. The Gibeonites are to serve the house of God, that is, the Tent of Meeting, and, possibly, later the temple. Cf. also Deuteronomy 20:10–11, as pointed out by Hess (1996: 183). As Nelson points out, the expression 'house of my god' in verse 23 may sound odd (Nelson 1997a: 133; see note on the verse).

24–25. The Gibeonites are simply happy to be alive. The rhetoric of their reply intimates that the Israelites can do whatever they like to them, and yet they know that the Israelites cannot do what they would *really* like. But the narrative in chapter 9 also suggests that they have become Yahwists, or at least clearly moved towards such an understanding. Also cf. verse 24 with 2:11.

26–27. The narrative moves towards its conclusion. The Gibeonites now become in essence temple servants (this includes the Tent of Meeting; cf. comments on vv. 22–23 above). The expression 'the place Yahweh would choose' comes from Deuteronomy, especially chapter 12, and can refer either to Shiloh or to Jerusalem (cf. Pitkänen 2004a). For further comments on Shiloh and on the central sanctuary, see commentary on Joshua 18:1 and 22:10–34.

Explanation

The Gibeonites, upon hearing that the Israelites are sooner or later likely to annihilate them, prepare for a solution different from that found by the indigenous population at large. They seek to make a covenant with the Israelites, and this can to some extent be compared with the narrative about Rahab in Jericho. However, the Gibeonites do not have anything explicit to offer as a trade, and instead pretend that they come from a distant country so that the Israelites can think that they are allowed to make a covenant with them. The Israelites fall into the trap and make the requested covenant. The narrative indicates that if the Israelites had consulted Yahweh, they would have been able to avoid the problem. However, they did not, and they have to honour the covenant, even though made through deception, with the result that the Gibeonites are ostensibly left to live in the midst of Israel, a state of affairs that the writer of Joshua explicitly refers to as current in his time. The Gibeonites are, however, made servants of the Israelites. An apparently lowly status of woodcutters and water-drawers is mitigated by its applying to the cultic service of Yahweh.

We may perhaps enter into some ethical discussion based on this chapter. The Gibeonites lied to save their lives. This suggests that lying is not always detrimental, even if truthfulness is undoubtedly desirable as the main guiding principle. As for the New Testament, Jesus himself told a parable about a shrewd servant who swindled his master in a cunning way, and by and large indicated that the servant's actions were rather to be seen in a positive light (Luke 16:1–9), even when the deception itself is not the main point of the parable. Also, lying in order to save the lives of Jewish people during the Nazi occupation is another oft-quoted example (in relation to Dietrich Bonhoeffer in particular).

Another application can perhaps be seen in the failure of the Israelites to consult Yahweh. Analogously, it would be wise for Christians to pray and to try to seek God's will when making decisions, especially bigger ones. Jesus himself of course was always seeking the will of God and, as the Gospel of Luke in particular demonstrates, prayed regularly. For example, Jesus prayed before choosing his disciples (Luke 6:12–16) and at Gethsemane before his arrest, even if the latter was not strictly speaking primarily about enquiring what the will of God was for him at that moment (Luke 22:39–46).

EXCURSUS 8: THE ARCHAEOLOGY OF GIBEON

Since the time of Robinson in 1838, Gibeon has been identified with the village of el-Jib some 5.5 miles (8.8 kilometres) north of Jerusalem (see *NEAEHL*: 511). The discovery at el-Jib of thirty-one jar handles from Iron Age II inscribed with the name *gbʻn* has now made the identification exceedingly likely (see *NEAEHL*: 511). Based on excavations in the late 1950s, the site was originally occupied in Middle Bronze Age I, and the first permanent settlement dates from Middle Bronze Age II. According to Pritchard, the excavator, evidence from the Late Bronze Age in the form of pottery 'has thus far been found only in tombs, of which eight used in

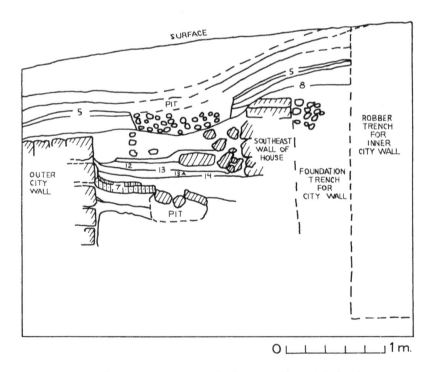

Figure 7: Gibeon section 10–L-5, looking NE (from Pritchard 1964)

this period have been found' (*NEAEHL*: 513). The excavator further describes, 'during the early part of the Iron Age, a massive city wall (3.2 to 3.4 m wide), was built around the scarp of the natural hill, and the great pool was cut into the rock to provide protected access to the hill's water table' (*NEAEHL*: 513). The dating of this town wall (a later one, datable to about the tenth century BC or so has also been found at the site) is based on a plaster floor that connects to it, located just a bit above a foundation trench of the wall, with pottery shards from the twelfth to eleventh centuries 'within the make-up of the plaster floor' (Pritchard 1964: 39, referring to accompanying Figure 21, reproduced in Figure 7).

In this connection, Pritchard notes that this evidence for the dating of the city wall is 'admittedly scant' (Pritchard 1964: 39). He further notes that the building of the pool and an associated stairway is likely to have taken place at the earliest around the same time as the postulated date for the building of the (earlier) city wall, i.e. around the twelfth century BC, even though the conclusion should be seen as tentative (Pritchard 1961: 22). This then suggests that it may not be entirely impossible that the structures could date from a somewhat earlier time.

Pritchard notes the possibility of Late Bronze Age occupation (Pritchard 1962: 157–158):

> It is at the end of the Late Bronze period, late in the thirteenth century, that the earliest biblical reference to Gibeon must be placed. The Gibeonites emerge first on the biblical scene as the wily deceivers of Joshua, the leader of the conquest by which Israel came into control of certain principal cities of Palestine. Since Gibeon is described as a 'great city' at this time, one would expect to find city walls and houses if the tradition preserved in the book of Joshua is historically trustworthy. Yet, traces of this city of the latter part of the Later Bronze period have not come to light in the four seasons of excavations. The two richly furnished tombs of the period discovered on the west side of the mound in 1960 would seem to indicate that somewhere on the mound itself there was a permanent settlement. Tombs filled with articles that had been imported from distant lands are not likely to have been those belonging to nomadic tribes which camped on the site. Perhaps in an area not yet excavated – to date we have dug into but a fraction of the total area – the remains of the 'great city' of Joshua's day are to be found.

Based on this, the possibility of substantial Late Bronze Age occupation at Gibeon does not seem to be ruled out, especially as only a fairly small portion of the tell has been excavated (see *NEAEHL*: 512 for the extent). At the same time, even if there was limited settlement on the tell during the Late Bronze Age, there could have been telescoping of the narrative as well. In other words, say, if the book of Joshua consists of material collected from various sources and then worked into the overall narrative, even as early as sometime towards the end of Iron Age I, this would already be well after the events themselves, and one could imagine that the events at Gibeon could be thought to have taken place at the time when the town was just being, or had been, 'properly' rebuilt at the beginning of Iron Age I, around 1200 BC. Also, while Joshua 10:2 calls Gibeon a 'big town', the description may be part of the book of Joshua's rhetorical strategy to emphasize the fear factor of the opposition. In this respect, there is some difficulty, too, in saying what a 'big town' would mean in the Late Bronze Age context, where material things by and large seemed to be on a much less grand scale than in the preceding Middle Bronze Age (Bienkowski 1986 is one good example of a work that demonstrates this; see esp. Bienkowski 1986: 150–152). On the whole, we may conclude that Gibeon does not have to be seen as posing real major problems for the historicity of the Joshua narrative.

JOSHUA 10

Translation

¹When Adoni-Zedek, the king of Jerusalem, heard that Joshua had conquered Ai and devoted it to destruction, having done to it and its king just as he had done to Jericho and its king, and that the Gibeonites had made peace with Israel and lived among them, ²he was very afraid, because Gibeon was a big town, like one of the major towns, and also because Gibeon was bigger than Ai and its men were valiant. ³Adoni-Zedek the king of Jerusalem then sent for Hoham king of Hebron, Piram king of Jarmuth, Japhia king of Lachish and Debir king of Eglon, saying, ⁴'Come and help me. Let us strike Gibeon because they have made peace with Joshua and the Israelites.'

⁵The five Amorite kings, the king of Jerusalem, king of Hebron, king of Jarmuth, king of Lachish, king of Eglon and their troops gathered together and went to Gibeon to fight against the Gibeonites.

⁶The men of Gibeon sent a message to Joshua at the camp in Gilgal, saying, 'Do not leave your servants alone. Come quickly to help us, and save us. All the kings of the Amorites from the hill country have assembled against us.'

⁷Then Joshua and all the fighting men went out from Gilgal. ⁸Yahweh said to Joshua, 'Do not fear them. I will give you victory over them. They cannot stand against you.'

⁹Joshua came on them quickly, travelling the whole night from Gilgal. ¹⁰Yahweh confounded them before Israel, and the Israelites struck them severely at Gibeon and chased them on the road that ascends to Beth Horon, and kept inflicting losses on them till Azekah and Makkedah. ¹¹When they were fleeing from the Israelites at the descent of Beth Horon to Azekah, Yahweh caused a hailstorm with big

hailstones to fall on them. There were more who died from the hailstorm than those who died by the swords of the Israelites.

¹²At that time, on the day when Yahweh gave the Amorites over to the Israelites, Joshua spoke to Yahweh in the presence of Israel as follows:

'Sun, rest on Gibeon, and moon on the Valley of Aijalon!'
¹³And the sun rested
and the moon stood still
until the people had avenged their enemies.

Is this not written in 'The Book of the Righteous'? The sun stood in its section of the sky without hastening to set for about a whole day. ¹⁴There has not been a day like that previously or afterwards when Yahweh listened to the request of a man in such a way, but this was because Yahweh fought for Israel.

¹⁵Then Joshua and all Israel with him returned to the camp at Gilgal.

¹⁶However, the five kings fled and hid themselves in a cave at Makkedah. ¹⁷Joshua was then told that the five kings who were hiding in the cave at Makkedah had been found. ¹⁸Joshua said, 'Roll big stones on the mouth of the cave and set men to guard it. ¹⁹But you yourselves, do not stand still but chase after your enemies. Destroy them from the rear and do not let them reach their towns since Yahweh has given them into your hands.'

²⁰And when Joshua and the Israelites had completed the great slaughter and any survivors had arrived at the fortified towns, ²¹all the people returned safely to Joshua in the camp at Makkedah. No one would even speak against the Israelites.

²²Joshua then said, 'Open the entrance of the cave and bring the five kings out to me.'

²³They did so. They brought the five kings to him from the cave, that is, the king of Jerusalem, the king of Hebron, the king of Jarmuth, the king of Lachish and the king of Eglon. ²⁴When they had brought these kings to Joshua, he called for all men of Israel, and said to the leaders of the troops, 'Come near and put your feet on the necks of these kings.' And they did so.

²⁵Joshua told them, 'Do not fear and do not be anxious, but be strong and courageous. Yahweh will treat all your enemies whom you will fight in a like manner.' ²⁶After this, Joshua struck them and killed them. Joshua then hanged them on five trees, and they were hanging there until the evening.

²⁷However, when the sun set, Joshua ordered them to be taken down. They then threw them into the cave where they had been hiding and put great stones at the entrance of the cave. The stones are there even now.

²⁸On that day, Joshua also took Makkedah and put it and its king to the sword. He devoted them to destruction, leaving no survivors. He did to the king of Makkedah just as he had done to the king of Jericho.

²⁹Joshua and all Israel with him then travelled from Makkedah to Libnah and made war against it. ³⁰Yahweh gave it and its king into the hands of the Israelites.

The Israelites put them to the sword, leaving no survivors. They did to its king just as they had done to the king of Jericho.

³¹From Libnah, Joshua and the Israelites travelled to Lachish and camped there and fought against it. ³²Yahweh gave Lachish to the Israelites. They captured it on the second day and killed all in it as with Libnah. ³³Horam, the king of Gezer, came to help Lachish, but Joshua destroyed him, together with all his people.

³⁴From Lachish, Joshua and the Israelites went to fight against Eglon. ³⁵And they took it on the first day and put it and all its inhabitants to the sword. They devoted it to destruction like Lachish.

³⁶From Eglon Joshua and all Israelites with him went to Hebron and fought against it. ³⁷They conquered it and put its king, the city and all its people to the sword. They left no survivors, just as with Eglon. They devoted it and all living beings in it to destruction.

³⁸Next Joshua and all Israelites with him returned to Debir and fought against it. ³⁹They conquered its king and all its towns and put them to the sword, devoting all living things in it to destruction. They left no survivors, as with Hebron.

⁴⁰Joshua attacked the whole land, the mountains, the southern desert, the western plain, the valleys and their kings, leaving no survivors. He devoted all living things to destruction, according to the command of Yahweh, the God of Israel. ⁴¹Joshua campaigned from Kadesh Barnea to Gaza, throughout the whole land of Goshen, and up to Gibeon. ⁴²Joshua conquered all these kings and their lands in one swoop because Yahweh was fighting for Israel.

⁴³Then Joshua and all Israel returned to the camp at Gilgal.

Notes on the text

2. Major towns: lit. 'towns of the kingdom'.

9. Quickly: or, 'suddenly' (Hebr. *pit'om*).

11. Hailstorm: lit. only 'hailstones' are mentioned.

15. Gr. omits this verse.

20. The great slaughter: lit. 'the very great slaughter until they were finished'.

21. No one would even speak: lit. 'A man did not sharpen his tongue'.

27. Even now: lit. 'to this selfsame day'.

40. Attacked: lit. 'struck'.

43. Gr. omits this verse.

Form and structure

We can summarize the literary structure of this chapter as follows (expanded from Nelson 1997a: 138):

> Battle at Gibeon against a coalition of five kings (vv. 1–14)
> > Adoni-Zedek's call for help (vv. 1–4)

Formation of a coalition against Gibeon (v. 5):
    Jerusalem, Hebron, Jarmuth, Lachish and Eglon
Gibeonites' call for help (v. 6)
Joshua's intervention (vv. 7–14)
    Joshua's march from Gilgal (v. 7)
    Yahweh's promise (v. 8)
    Israel victorious (vv. 9–14)
        Poetic recollection (vv. 12–14)
Return to Gilgal (v. 15)
Execution of the five kings of the coalition (vv. 16–27)
    Flashback: the kings trapped in cave during fighting
        (vv. 16–21)
      Kings flee to cave at Makkedah (v. 16)
      Joshua told about the hiding place (v. 17)
      Joshua orders them to shut the kings in (v. 18)
      Joshua orders the attack to continue (v. 19)
      Joshua returns to Makkedah after the fight (vv. 20–21)
    Execution of the kings (vv. 22–27)
      Opening of the cave and bringing the kings out
        (vv. 22–23)
      Placing feet on the necks of the kings (vv. 24–25)
      Execution of the kings and hanging bodies on trees (v. 26)
      Burial of the kings (v. 27)
Seven victories in the south (vv. 28–39)
    Makkedah (v. 28)
    Libnah (vv. 29–30)
    Lachish (vv. 31–32)
    King of Gezer (v. 33)
    Eglon (vv. 34–35)
    Hebron (vv. 36–37)
    Debir (vv. 38–39)
Summation of southern conquests (vv. 40–42)
Return to Gilgal (v. 43)

The monograph by Blenkinsopp (1972) remains useful for looking at the Gibeonites in relation to the book of Joshua. I will therefore base much of my analysis here on interacting with Blenkinsopp's book, as chapter 10 ties together with chapter 9.

Noth (1953a: 60) thought that the narrative consists of two originally separate parts, the battle at Gibeon and the execution of five kings at the cave of Makkedah. According to Nelson, verses 28–39 should also be seen as stemming from a separate source (Nelson 1997a: 138; cf. Blenkinsopp 1972: 41, thus dividing into 1–14, 16–27, 28–39). However, Hebron, Eglon, Lachish and Makkedah are found in the preceding narrative, thus linking it at least indirectly. Be that as it may regarding the dual or tripartite division of the chapter (see Noth 1953a: 61–63 and Nelson 1997a: 138 for further possible source analysis within the units, especially with Nelson pointing out the names of the five towns in vv. 5, 23 and the 'poetic fragment with its frame' in vv. 12–14), and noting that there seems to have been a question mark over whether the relationship of chapter 10 to chapter 9 is simply redactional (see Blenkinsopp 1972: 42), everything hangs together in the present arrangement of the narrative.

According to Nelson (1997a: 138), 'Deuteronomic language is visible in v. 25 (Deut. 1:21; 3:28; 31: 6–8, 23), v. 40 ("everything that breathed", Deut. 20:16), and the phrase "left no survivors" throughout vv. 28–40.' Thus the passage fits well in the deuteronomic book of Joshua. At the same time, the language and the narrative style are also compatible with Ancient Near Eastern conquest accounts (see Younger 1990).

It has been suggested that there is apparent inconsistency in the narrative in regard to the place names of Gilgal and Makkedah (see Blenkinsopp 1972: 42–43; 120n7). However, if one allows for slight telescoping of events, these do not seem insurmountable.

We may note that the book of Yashar (Josh. 10:12–14) is mentioned in 2 Samuel 1:18, and possibly in 1 Kings 8:53 LXX (as noted by Blenkinsopp 1972: 45, and related note 20 on p. 121). The occurrences would suggest that the book of Yashar was a poetic collection from early Israel. According to Blenkinsopp, the quotation from the book of Yashar is 'surely of genuine antiquity' (Blenkinsopp 1972: 44). Obviously, that the book is mentioned in 2 Samuel (or 1 Kgs) could easily be seen as a *terminus post quem* for the writing of Joshua as well. However, the book of Yashar might have been a continuously updated collection of notable poetry, in a way resembling annals, or it could simply be that the mention of the book was added to the book of Joshua later on. We cannot be certain, but, if the former, we can think that some of the other poetic collections in the Old Testament itself have been edited in this way. The book of Psalms may also provide a parallel here.

Finally, it has been noted that there is plenty of similarity between Joshua 9 – 10 and Judges 1 (see Blenkinsopp 1972: 43, noting that 'the sphere of operations is identical in both cases [cf. Josh. 9:1; 10:40 with Judg. 1:9]). However, there also appear to be clear discrepancies between the accounts. For example, 'three of the cities which are taken and destroyed by Joshua in Joshua x are captured by Judahites in Judges 1' (see Blenkinsopp 1972: 43). Also, 'e.g. Gezer is taken by Joshua in Joshua 10:33; the Ephraimites attempt unsuccessfully to take it in Judges 1:29' (Blenkinsopp 1972: 44). However, if one allows for hyperbole in the book of Joshua as a whole, in a manner compatible with Ancient Near Eastern conquest accounts, and accepts that conquering an area did not yet necessarily mean subjugation of the peoples, and allows for shifting balances of power, and attribution of conquests for example sometimes to Joshua and sometimes to Judah as meaning the same thing (it is not unusual in history to attribute victories achieved by troops to the leader), many of the problems are solved (for a detailed exposition, see Younger 1990: 242–247). Sometimes, reading the relevant texts carefully may also help. Thus Joshua 10:33 probably refers to the king of Gezer and some of his troops who have arrived in Lachish to help, whereas Judges 1:29 refers to Gezer itself. And Judges 1:8 and 1:21 in themselves could be seen as contradictory. However, the verses (cf. Josh. 15:63) can be read as indicating that Jerusalem was to some extent conquered (this itself may be hyperbolic), but not conclusively and permanently, so that the Jebusites continued to live there.

Comment

1. Hearing about recent events pertaining to the Israelite invasion, Adoni-Zedek, the king of Jerusalem, whose name means 'My Lord is righteousness' in English, now becomes nervous. Note that the priest David appointed was called Zadok (see 2 Sam. 8:17 etc.) and that Abraham dealt with Melchizedek, king of Salem, which may be a reference to Jerusalem (Gen. 14:18–20). It is not exactly clear what the word 'Jerusalem' means. The first part appears to be derived from *yārāh*, perhaps 'establish' (*ABD* 3: 751, but cf. *HAL*: 416–417) and the second part from the root *šlm* which means 'peace', but *šlm* can also be a name of a deity (see *NEAEHL*: 698; *DLU*: 438–440). However, the town is called Urusalim in the Amarna letters (*uru* = 'town' in Akkadian). The same in Hebrew would be something like *'îr šālēm*, and this may then be the ultimate source of the derivation. If so, the name 'Jerusalem' could mean 'town of peace' or 'town of (the god) Salem'.

One could, especially from the name 'Adoni-Zedek', further surmise that (the root) *zdk* (or, transliterated more precisely, *ṣdq*) was the name of a deity related to Jerusalem, even its main deity (cf. comments in Wenham 1987: 316). But the root also means 'righteousness' in Hebrew. It has to be noted here that many have speculated that David took a Canaanite priest, Zadok of Jerusalem, and incorporated him into Israel's worship in association with moving the ark to Jerusalem as part of his programme of choosing the town as Israel's political and religious capital (see e.g. comments in Schley 1989: 142–151). This author has argued (Pitkänen 2004b) that the Israelites assimilated Canaanites and grafted them into the Israelite lineage in the process (cf. Caleb the Kenizzite, who is also part of the tribe of Judah [Num. 13:6; 32:12]), so this line of argument would seem natural in itself. However, David is said already to know Zadok before he becomes king over all Israel and conquers Jerusalem. Thus the connection of the root *zdk* with Jerusalem does not seem to be exclusive. Cf. also Judges 1:4–8, which may or may not bear relation to the topic at hand (cf. Nelson 1997a: 140).

Whatever the case, and whatever the extent of the taking-over, playing-on or demythologizing of ancient Canaanite traditions, Jerusalem was an old and established town with earliest pottery shards and stratigraphic remains found from the latter part of the fourth millennium BC (see *NEAEHL*: 701). The town is also mentioned in Egyptian execration texts (curses against enemies on potsherds) from the twentieth and nineteenth centuries BC (see *NEAEHL*: 698; *ANET*: 428–429). While the extent of settlement in the time attributable to Joshua is not clear from the archaeological record (see *NEAEHL*: 702; Junkkaala 2006: 276–279), there is some evidence of occupation in the city of David section during the Late Bronze and Early Iron Ages (see Junkkaala 2006: 277–278). It should also be noted that the public buildings of Jerusalem are under the Temple Mount, and, in the case of Jerusalem, newer structures were often built on bedrock instead of on top of earlier remains (Junkkaala 2006: 275, quoting Na'aman). Thus it is my view that significant settlement in the town during the period in question is possible, also bearing in mind the importance ascribed to the town by the Amarna letters some 100 years before Joshua (assuming early-thirteenth-century conquest and settlement) in comparison to the meagre contemporary remains found from the site at the time of the Amarna letters (cf. similarly Kitchen 2003b: 151–153).

From a narrative perspective, as Nelson points out, verses 1–14 divide into a description of a threat in verses 1–5 and its repulse in verses 6–14 (Nelson 1997a: 139).

2. The king is greatly alarmed because Gibeon, a large town, has joined forces with the Israelites (for the size, see comment on 9:3). As Nelson points out, 'it would be natural for Jerusalem to be apprehensive about the defection of the four Gibeonite towns to its north and west and to seek alliance with towns farther to the south' (Nelson 1997a: 140). Nelson also says that the apparent folly of Israel's treaty with the Gibeonites now ironically seems to have changed into a strategic advantage (Nelson 1997a: 140).

3–5. Four kings are then called on by Adoni-Zedek, from Hebron, Jarmuth, Lachish and Eglon. These kings respond and join forces with Adoni-Zedek in order to fight against the Gibeonites. The text seems to imply that, in addition to trying to counter a threat caused by the appearance of a new power in the region, the kings want to warn off anyone else who might wish to join forces with the Israelites. For the Amorites, compare comments on 9:1–2 and 13:10.

Hebron is an ancient site, and occupation at Tel Hebron, a prominent mound in the area, dates back to Early Bronze Age I. No stratigraphic remains appear to have been found at Tel Hebron from the Late Bronze Age. However, according to Junkkaala, some archaeological evidence has been found from the Late Bronze period, and even evidence of destruction at the end of this period (Junkkaala 2006: 250–251). Tombs have also yielded some remains from the time in question, suggesting occupation in the area (see *NEAEHL*: 606–609), even if there may not have been a 'large, permanent settlement' then (Junkkaala 2006: 251, referring to Ofer).

Junkkaala notes that the material culture of the Iron Age I settlement was 'similar to the other Iron Age sites in the Hill Country' (Junkkaala 2006: 251). An Akkadian cuneiform tablet from the seventeenth to sixteenth centuries BC with a list of animals has been found at the site (*NEAEHL*: 608). See also comments on 15:13–14. As for Jarmuth, Tel Jarmuth is the closest candidate for being the biblical site. There is evidence of an initial site in the Early Bronze Age, with subsequent abandonment. There is also evidence from the Late Bronze Age onwards (see *NEAEHL*: 665; cf. Junkkaala 2006: 282–283). See further comments on 15:35. Lachish is most likely to be identified with Tel Lachish (Tell ed-Duweir in Arabic). The town is mentioned in an Egyptian document, the so-called Hermitage papyrus, dated to the fifteenth century BC (see *NEAEHL*: 899), and the Amarna letters include messages sent from Lachish (numbers 328 and 329, and probably 330–332; see KNUDTZON: 939–945). Remains from the Late Bronze Age have been found at the site. It appears that the town was unfortified at the time (see *NEAEHL*: 897–905). There is evidence of destruction in the thirteenth century (see Junkkaala 2006: 235). Remains from the twelfth century have been found, even though these still attest Late Bronze Age style, and, after a destruction of c. 1130, there is a gap in occupation until Iron Age II (see *NEAEHL*: 898–905; Junkkaala 2006: 235–237). See also comments on 6:1 and 10:31–32 for Lachish. The identification of Eglon is unclear (see *ABD* 2: 320–321; Junkkaala 2006: 242–245). Even if the passage here (cf. 10:34 and 15:15) should be read 'Eglon king of Debir', we are not faring much better, as Debir's identification is unclear (see *ABD* 2: 112), even though it may be that it can be identified with Khirbet Rabud, which has remains from the Late Bronze and Iron Ages (see *NEAEHL*: 1252).

6–9. The Gibeonites rather predictably call on Joshua for help, and Joshua and the Israelites respond. Victory is promised by Yahweh in typical fashion for the Joshua narrative and the conquest tradition, and also in line with the Ancient Near Eastern tradition of divine assurance (cf. above, 'Form and structure' of chapter 1). Joshua is then described as attacking the opponents quickly. As Nelson suggests, doing a night march from Gilgal in the lowlands to Gibeon in the hill country is an impressive feat (Nelson 1997a: 140).

10. Victory ensues; this is predictable in the light of verse 8. Beth Horon, a twin town (cf. comments on Josh. 16:3), is probably to be located at Beit 'Ur el-Foqa' (Upper Beth Horon) and Beit 'Ur el-Tahta (Lower Beth Horon) (see *ABD* 1: 688). Surveys have found pottery in the area (both Foqa and Tahta) from the Late Bronze and Iron I and II periods (see R. D. Miller 2003: 155). Azekah is usually identified with Tell Zakariya. If so, occupation is attested from the Later Bronze period (see *ABD* 1: 688). The identification of Makkedah is unclear (see *ABD* 4: 478; cf. Junkkaala 2006: 198–199, 257–258).

11. A big hailstorm caused by Yahweh settles the score for the Israelites. Hailstorms are not uncommon in Israel, especially between October and

May. A weather website from 2006 reports, 'A hailstorm on the evening of February 2nd over Jerusalem dumped hail up to 1.5 cm in diameter, with intense lightning activity' (http://israelstorms.netfirms.com, accessed 6 March 2006). Another report states that in October 1997 'A hailstorm with baseball size hail which lasted several hours left three feet of accumulation, scores of injuries and millions of dollars of property damage' (http://www.stormtrack.org/library/archives/stjly98.htm, accessed 6 March 2006). As regards the Joshua narrative, above all, the timing is providential. The storm is sent by Yahweh to help the fighting Israelites. It should also be noted that no Israelites are reportedly harmed, even though the point may simply be that, even if there were Israelite injuries, on the whole, the storm resulted in an advantage to the *Israelites*. That in itself could already be seen as a miracle.

12–14. A bigger miracle is then described. The heavenly bodies stop their travel in the sky until the Israelites are victorious. Taken literally, based on a modern scientific world view, the implication is that the earth's rotation slowed or stopped altogether. This is of course stupendously miraculous to the modern reader, and many commentators have tried to explain the comments in some other way. Blenkinsopp (1972: 44–50) suggests that the references are to local thinking of the sun and the moon as deities, which should be seen to be under Yahweh's control during the battle. Whether or not this was the case, it is true that the sun and moon were considered divine throughout the Ancient Near East at the time. However, it appears that the Israelites were not to think in this way, or at least not to worship these deities (Deut. 4:19). In the context of this poetic quote, then, it cannot be said for sure what (if any) divine implications are intended. Hess (1996: 197–199; cf. Younger 1990: 211–220) has summarized other attempts to solve the meaning of the quote, including an eclipse, and an interpretation of the position of the constellations as an omen, noting however that none of the suggested solutions is 'entirely satisfactory'. Nelson (1997a: 145) suggests that 'these two heavenly bodies were being called upon to stand frozen or fixed, or perhaps silent, in stunned reaction to an awe-inspiring victory', and the (apparently deuteronomic) redactor then directed the speech through the accompanying prose section '*away* from sun and moon and towards Yahweh'. It may be difficult to be certain about how the quote should be read. However, whatever one thinks about the matter, the narrative itself states that what happened was something very special and something that had never happened before, nor since the time of Joshua (v. 14). The occurrence of the miracle is also attested in the 'book of the righteous' (*sefer hayyashar*), and the writer appears to call on the book in support of the authenticity of what he is saying. For comments on the antiquity of the book of Yashar, see 'Form and structure' of Joshua 9. For Gibeon, see comments on 9:3. For Aijalon, see comments on 19:42. For comments on '*az* in verse 12, see 'Form and structure' of Joshua 8:30–35.

15. A short interlude in the narrative notes how the Israelites then return to Gilgal. In the light of what follows in the narrative sequence, this may refer to what happened after the events of the chapter as a whole (cf. v. 43). Note however that this verse is missing from the Greek.

16–18. The kings hide themselves in a cave, but are found. Joshua instructs his people to make sure that the kings do not escape. To achieve this, the cave is blocked by rocks and a guard is put in place. The identification of Makkedah is unclear (cf. v. 10). Nelson aptly describes it thus: 'A new narrative movement begins with the reintroduction of the five kings in v. 16 and ends with their fate in vv. 26–27. Verses 18–20 connect this to what has come before by describing events simultaneous to vv. 10, 11, and 12–13' (Nelson 1997a: 143).

19–20. Joshua instructs the fighters to kill as many of the enemies as possible before they reach their towns. Some are said to escape to fortified towns, however.

21. The camp is at Makkedah here (cf. v. 15). The verse describes how no-one dares to oppose the Israelites, not even by such a relatively feeble means as complaining against them verbally.

22–23. Subsequently, it is time to bring the captive kings out of the cave. As Nelson points out, the towns of these kings are repeated in 12:10–12a (Nelson 1997a: 140; cf. v. 3).

24. Putting one's feet on the neck was a typical Ancient Near Eastern custom of the time (Hess 1996: 201). Note Psalm 110:1 in this context, a verse which otherwise has been used in the New Testament to demonstrate that Christ must be more than David's son (Luke 20:42–43; cf. Acts 2:34–35).

25–27. The narrative also indicates that the placing of their feet on their enemies' necks is intended to instil extra confidence and courage in Israel's leaders. The act serves as assurance that more victories are to come. The kings are then executed and hanged on five trees. However, the bodies are taken down in the evening and thrown into the cave. The hiding place becomes a grave, with the entrance covered by stones. The narrative relates that the stones are still at the location at the time of writing the account; this serves to add authenticity to the account (see detailed comments in the Introduction). The hanging of the bodies, taking them down at sunset and raising a heap of stones at the place where the bodies lie is in essence the same procedure as in 8:29 with the king of Ai (cf. comments on the verse). Note also the comments in 8:29 about similarities with Deuteronomy 21:22–23.

28. Makkedah is then destroyed (cf. comments on v. 10 above). Notice how the verse describes leaders in a *pars pro toto* role. It seems that the king is representative of the town as a whole in the final sentence; certainly, Joshua stands for all Israel in the context. As with Jericho, the dedication (*herem*) is applied, even though it is not clear what happens to the spoils here. It is also possible that, even though a comparison is made with Jericho, the comment about killing everyone is a typical hyperbolic comment in Ancient Near Eastern style and need not be taken literally. It may rather be that only some were killed.

29–43. Verses 29–43 (or, perhaps more accurately, 29–39) are rather formulaic (see Younger 1990: 226–228). While the narrative presents them as a single action, it may well be that they have been collated from a series of battles the Israelites had as part of their settlement process, taking place over a period of many years. The narrative puts the data together to create for its readers the sense of an impressive blitzkrieg campaign in the southern part of the country (note that Lachish and Eglon are described as having been captured in a day or two in vv. 32 and 35). Also, the attribution of the victories to Joshua may be a literary device, as it may well be that Joshua is only to be associated loosely with these battles as the ultimate commander-in-chief of the Israelites. As already indicated (see comment on v. 28), it may further be that not everyone was killed in these towns; the hyperbolic 'all' might be used even if only a (small) minority was killed. It should also be noted that the narrative does not state that any of the buildings or other material things were devoted to destruction in these places, even though verse 37 possibly contains a hint of some material destruction. If, as may well have been the case, material things were not destroyed, the actions should be seen as not really leaving any archaeologically detectable traces behind them. Finally, it is worth noting that verses 29–43 cascade with a reference in each verse to the previous destruction in the list, with the first in the list referring back to Jericho (the last also refers to the first in the list, Libnah). Also, if one includes verse 28 (which [also] refers back to Jericho), the list is composed of seven conquests, with three towns followed by a king and his people (Horam in v. 33), followed by three towns, whatever the meaning of such an arrangement, if any – of course, the number seven is often used in the Old Testament, including in the book of Joshua; e.g. the seven nations of Canaan (cf. comments on 3:2).

29–30. The formulaic southern blitzkrieg starts with Libnah (if not with Makkedah in the previous verse). Libnah is also a Levitical city (Josh. 21:13). Its identification is not clear, with several alternatives put forward in the past (see *ABD* 4: 322–323; Junkkaala 2006: 264–266). The reference to the king of Libnah may cover more than the king himself (cf. comment on v. 28 above).

31–32. Lachish is a well-known site and has been identified fairly securely (see *NEAEHL*: 897). The town is especially famous from the palace reliefs of Sennacherib. One of these reliefs, presently kept in the British Museum, depicts the conquest of the town (which took place in 701 BC; pictures on the Internet e.g. under 'Sennacherib's palace reliefs'; or see e.g. *ANEP*, pictures 371–374). See also comments on 10:3–5. It appears that the town was unfortified during the Late Bronze Age, which would fit with a quick conquest as described in verse 32, and there is evidence of a destruction at the end of the Canaanite period (see *NEAEHL*: 899, 904).

33. Only King Horam of Gezer and his troops which have come out to help Lachish appear to be portrayed as being slain, not the town of Gezer itself (cf. Josh. 11:22). For Gezer, see comments on 12:12. For Lachish, see comments on 10:3–5.

34–39. The identification of Eglon is unclear; cf. also comments on 10:3–5 about Eglon and Debir. For Hebron, see comments on 10:3–5. For Debir, see comments on 10:3–5.

40. This sentence is hyperbolic in a typical ancient Israelite (and Ancient Near Eastern) manner. Despite a statement of total destruction under the Israelite ban (*herem*), the Joshua narrative elsewhere describes how there were quite a few local inhabitants left; see e.g. 11:22; 13:1–7; 15:63, and compare Exodus 9:1–7 with Exodus 9:19–21.

41. This summarizes the fact that Joshua conquered the southern part of the country. Kadesh Barnea is located in (northern) Sinai and is associated with a number of important events in relation to Israel's travels in the wilderness after the exodus (see e.g. Num. 13; 20; Deut. 1:46). It has generally been located at either 'Ain el-Qudeitrat or 'Ain Qadis, both oases in the region, less than 6 miles (10 km) from each other (Hoffmeier 2005: 123; cf. *ABD* 4: 1). An early Iron Age fort has been found at 'Ain Qadis, even though a more exact dating is not clear (Hoffmeier 2005: 123). Nothing from the Later Bronze period has been found at 'Ain Qudeirat, even though there is evidence from earlier periods on site or in the wadi area (Hoffmeier 2005: 124). Hoffmeier (2005: 124) notes that the area as a whole could be intended as the location of Kadesh Barnea, which seems very plausible. We should also keep in mind that the narrative in Numbers (20:2–13) seems to speak about lack of water at Kadesh. Gaza, a town in the western Shephelah (or, perhaps more properly, on the coastal strip; see also comment on 15:33) associated with the Philistines in much of Israelite history (see esp. Judg. 16; 1 Sam. 6:17; 2 Kgs 18:8; Jer. 25:20), has a fairly secure identification. The mound has been partially excavated, but there do not seem to be any securely datable remains from the period we are concerned with (see *NEAEHL*: 464–465), although some evidence exists from the Late Bronze and Early Iron Ages (see Junkkaala 2006: 197). Apart from the Bible, the place is mentioned in the annals of Thutmose III, in a Taanach letter and in the Amarna letters (see *ABD* 2: 912 for a summary; see also Junkkaala 2006: 196–197). The sources indicate that it was the capital of the Egyptian province of Canaan from about 1550 to 1150 BC (*ABD* 2: 912). Goshen here (and apparently 11:16) is different from the Goshen in the Exodus narratives; compare also Joshua 15:51, seemingly yet another place (cf. *ABD* 2: 1076). The exact localization does not seem to be clear (cf. also Boling and Wright 1982: 298). For Gibeon, see comments on 10:3.

According to Nelson, the reference to Gibeon here 'skilfully takes the reader back to the start of the narrative, thus creating a satisfying compositional design', and this seems an apt comment here.

42. Again, the sentence about quick conquest should be taken as hyperbolic (cf. comments on v. 40 above). As one might expect, success was achieved because Yahweh fought for Israel, in line with the Yahwistic Ancient Near Eastern theology of the writer.

43. Once the job has been done, it is time to return to the current base at Gilgal, the place from which the campaign started (vv. 6–7) and where the Israelites are still located as a whole at this stage. It appears that this verse refers to the same return as verse 15, repeated here to achieve narrative symmetry and closure for the parallel and expanded action of verses 16–42 (note however that this verse and v. 15, and thus the two mentions of return to Gilgal, are missing from the Greek; cf. comments on vv. 15 and 16–18 above).

Explanation

The local kings from the southern area of Canaan now form a coalition against the Gibeonites. They apparently want to make an example of the Gibeonites so that others will not ally themselves with the Israelites. However, Joshua and the Israelites, bound in oath to the Gibeonites, help them to thwart the attack. In the process, the coalition is destroyed by the Israelites. Yahweh is explicitly with Israel, and an oracle from him reassures Joshua and predicts success. Yahweh then fights for Israel in an apparently greatly miraculous way in which even the sun and the moon reflect his intervention. Subsequent to the battle, the Israelites capture and execute the kings of the coalition, and then move to various relevant towns and conquer them, destroying their inhabitants.

For Christian application, while it might be tempting to say that Yahweh can work great miracles in order to aid against an enemy, here the thrust is at the very least a bit problematic for a modern reader. Perhaps, however, we can say that Christians can believe that God can help them in their difficulties, even though they do not need to expect a tactic of decimating those who are unfriendly to them or oppose them for some reason. And, in fact, the New Testament asks Christians to love their enemies, instead of hating them and/or cursing them (Matt. 5:43–48; Rom. 12:14). However, one may perhaps draw in some concepts of spiritual warfare here (Eph. 6:10–18). Also, there may be situations in which the use of violence in protecting others may prevent even greater violence, and a Christian may need to consider that, too, even though, and as history demonstrates, it is often all too easy to deceive oneself into thinking that violence, whether physical or psychological, is necessary or unavoidable when in reality it is not.

JOSHUA 11

Translation

[1]When Jabin the king of Hazor heard about these events, he sent for Jobab the king of Madon, for the king of Shimron, for the king of Achsaph, [2]for kings in the northern hill country and in the plains in the south around Kinnereth and in Naphoth Dor in the west, [3]for the Canaanites in the east and in the west, for the Amorites, Hittites, Perizzites and Jebusites in the hill country, and for the Hivites around Hermon in the land of Mizpah. [4]They and all their troops set out, a great multitude like sand on the seashore, including very many horses and chariots. [5]All these kings assembled together and came and camped by the Waters of Merom to fight against Israel.

[6]But Yahweh said to Joshua, 'Do not be afraid of them. Tomorrow at about this time I will give them over to Israel, all slain. You will hamstring their horses and burn their chariots.'

[7]Joshua and all warriors then made a sudden attack on them at the waters of Merom. [8]Yahweh gave them into the hands of Israel. The Israelites defeated them and pursued them all the way to Greater Sidon, Misrephoth Maim and the Valley of Mizpah on the east. They struck them down until no survivors were left. [9]Joshua did to them as Yahweh had told him in advance. He hamstrung their horses and burned their chariots.

[10]Joshua also went on and conquered Hazor and killed its king, as Hazor was the head of all these kingdoms at the time. [11]They also killed all of its people, devoting them to destruction. Nothing was left alive, and they burned Hazor.

[12]Moreover, Joshua conquered all the towns and subordinate kings belonging to the above kings and put them to the sword. He devoted them to destruction as Moses, the servant of Yahweh, had commanded. [13]However, Joshua did not burn any towns that were on a mound, except for Hazor. [14]The Israelites took for themselves all the booty that was in these towns, including their animals. They only killed the people, leaving none of them alive. [15]Joshua did as Yahweh had commanded him through Moses. He did exactly so.

[16]Joshua conquered all the land: the hill country, all the southern desert, the whole land of Goshen, Shephelah, the plain, and the hill country of Israel and its Shephelah, [17]from the Bald Mountain close to Seir to Baal Gad by the Valley of Lebanon under Mount Hermon. He conquered all the kings in these areas and killed them. [18]Joshua fought against these kings for a long time. [19]There were no towns that made a peace with the Israelites except for the Hivites who dwelt in Gibeon. The Israelites took them all by battle. [20]Yahweh made them stubborn so that they would fight against Israel and would then be set for destruction without mercy. Thus they would be annihilated just as Yahweh had commanded Moses.

[21]At that time, Joshua destroyed the Anakites from the hill country, from Hebron, Debir and Anab, and from the whole of the hill country of Israel. Joshua devoted them and their towns to destruction. [22]No Anakites were left in the land of Israel,

except for Gaza, Gath and Ashdod. ²³Joshua conquered all the land, just as Yahweh had promised Moses. He allotted it to Israel based on their tribal system.

And the wars ceased.

Notes on the text

1. Madon: Gr. 'Maron'. Shimron: Gr. 'Shimon'. Achsaph: Gr. 'Azif'.

2. Northern: Gr. Sidon. Plains: Hebr. *'ărābah*. Hebr. Naphoth Dor: lit. 'hills of Dor'. On the West: lit. 'by the sea' (Hebr. *miyyām*).

3. Around: lit. 'under' (Hebr. *tahat*).

5. Merom: Gr. 'Maron', as in verse 1.

7. Merom: cf. notes on verses 1, 5.

8. Misrephoth Maim: Gr. 'Maseron'.

10. Hebrew includes the expression *bā'ēt hahî'*, 'at that time', as a time marker for this verse and forward. At the time: lit. 'formerly'.

11. All of its people: lit. 'every soul which was there'. But, cf. verse 14.

14. Gr. omits mention of the towns and animals.

17. Close to: 'lit. rising (towards) Seir'.

18. For a long time: lit. 'For many days'.

19. Gr. 'There was no city that Israel did not take. They took all in war.'

20. Stubborn: lit. 'Harden the hearts of'.

21. From the whole of the hill country of Israel: Gr. 'and from all the race of Israel, and from all the mountain of Judah, with their towns'.

22. In the land of Israel: Gr. 'by the children of Israel'.

23. And the wars ceased: lit. 'And the land had rest from war.'

Form and structure

As Nelson (1997a: 151) notes, temporal markers (*ba'ēt hahî'*, 'at that time') in verses 10 and 21 divide the chapter conveniently into three sections: 1–9, 10–20 and 21–23. However, verses 16–20 and 23 can be seen to form still separate sections, and we may thus describe the structure of the chapter as follows:

> Battle against a northern coalition headed by Jabin (vv. 1–9)
>> Jabin's call for help (vv. 1–3)
>> Formation of a coalition against Israel at Merom (vv. 4–5):
>>> Hazor, Madon, Shimron, Achsaph et al.
>> Joshua's response (vv. 6–9)
>>> Yahweh's promise to Joshua (v. 6)
>>> Joshua's sudden attack (v. 7)
>>> Israel victorious (v. 8)
>>> Detailed fulfilment of Yahweh's promise (v. 9)

Victories in the north (vv. 10–15)
   Hazor (vv. 10–11)
   Extent and manner of conquests (vv. 12–14)
   Summary statement (v. 15)
Summary of conquests west of Jordan (vv. 16–20)
   Geographical extent of conquests (vv. 16–17)
   Temporal extent of conquests (v. 18)
   The exception of the Gibeonites (v. 19)
   Justification for annihilation (v. 20)
The Anakim (vv. 21–22)
Final summary of conquests (v. 23)

Nelson's (1997a: 151) comments about the structure of the chapter in comparison with chapter 10 are pertinent here:

> [C]hapter 11 is a literary mirror of chapter 10. Now a northern coalition assembles and is destroyed just as handily as the southern alliance was, leading to Israel's control of the rest of the land. The general structure of chapter 10 is repeated. Battle in the field (10:1–14; 11:1–9) is followed by the capture of cities (10:28–39; 11:10–15), followed in turn by a generalizing summary (10:40–42; 11:16–20, 23). The vocabulary also follows the pattern of chapter 10. Compare 10:1 with 11:1, 10:5b with 11:5b, 10:8a with 11:6a, 10:9 with 11:7, and 10:40–41 with 11:16–17.

Verse 18 indicates that Joshua fought against the Canaanites for a long time. In other words, the chapter explicitly claims that it looks back from a time already clearly removed from the events themselves (of course, Joshua's death is narrated in 24:29–30). This means that events are telescoped (the word *ba'ēt hahî'* can be compared with *'az* in 8:30–35), and that the narrative order does not necessarily wholly reflect the (intended) chronological order. In connection with this, it should however be noted that Gilgal is not mentioned in this chapter, whereas it did feature in chapter 10 (vv. 6–7, 9, 15, 43). This on the whole seems to help move the narrative away from the initial events relating to the conquest in the land of Canaan in temporal sequence, even though Gilgal features one more time in 14:6, apparently in a kind of flashback.

It has been noted that Jabin king of Hazor also appears in Judges 4–5, and some have speculated that Joshua 11:1–15 and Judges 4–5 go back to the same tradition (see Nelson 1997a: 151 for further details). However, as Hess (1997: 208) notes, the name 'Jabin' may be a dynastic name and thus repeatable, and, as Nelson (1997a: 151) observes, the two narratives of Joshua 11:1–15 and Judges 4–5 are very different.

As for sources, most of what can be said probably amounts to speculation. However, it appears that a number were used, as the material covers a fair bit of territory and thus must have referred to different campaigns (most notably Hazor in the north vs the Anakites in the south). In its present form, the chapter fits in with the deuteronomic structure of Joshua (e.g. v. 15; cf. also v. 23 vs Deut. 12:10; see also comments in Nelson 1997a: 151) and the Israelite exodus and conquest tradition otherwise (cf. v. 20 with Exod. 7 – 14).

Comment

1–3. The scene now turns to the northern part of Canaan. Like the southern kings in chapter 10 (see vv. 1–5), the northern kings form a coalition (note also that the localities of the kings directly mentioned reappear in 12:19–20). Hazor was a significant urban centre in the Late Bronze Age (for a summary of the remains and excavations, see *NEAEHL*: 594–606; also bearing in mind that the co-writer of the summary, Amnon Ben-Tor, has been excavating at the site from 1990 until the present day; see http://unixware.mscc.huji.ac.il/~hatsor/hazor.html, accessed 20 February 2009). What is particularly interesting is that there is evidence of destruction of the city at the end of the thirteenth century BC. In fact, the remains of the temple of that time indicate a conflagration, and the head of a statue of a seated male figure had been broken, apparently deliberately (see *NEAEHL*: 596, 598). It should also be noted that subsequent Iron Age Hazor differs considerably from Late Bronze Age Hazor, with both the pottery assemblage and the settlement pattern suggesting a culture different from the previous period (see Junkkaala 2006: 234; but cf. Judg. 4, which nevertheless suggests that the Israelites did not hold the town at least during the early part of Iron Age I). While one cannot make any definitive conclusions, because the ruins (as is normally the case) do not tell who destroyed the town, the scene fits very well with what is described in the book of Joshua. In fact, Hazor is perhaps the only site where there is clear reason to accept the testimony of the book of Joshua directly (cf. Junkkaala 2006: 234). Note also that cuneiform material from the second millennium has been found at Hazor (see *NEAEHL*: 598).

The identification of Madon (see *ABD* 4: 463; cf. Junkkaala 2006: 262–263), Shimron (see *ABD* 5: 1218) and Achsaph (see *ABD* 1: 57; note that Achsaph is mentioned in Egyptian second-millennium documents and in the Amarna letters [366:23; 367:1]) is unclear. But note the possibility of an identification of Shimron with Khirbet Sammuniyeh 5 miles (8 km) west of Nazareth (surface surveys indicate Early Bronze to Hellenistic occupation) and the possibility that the place is listed in Egyptian second-millennium documents (*ABD* 5: 1219; cf. Junkkaala 2006: 144–145; see also Hess 1996: 208–209), and the possibility of locating Achsaph at Tell Keisan, from which evidence of occupation has been found from the Late Bronze and Early Iron Ages, with a destruction around

1200 BC (see *ABD* 1: 57; *ABD* 4: 14–16; Junkkaala 2006: 293–294; see also Junkkaala 2006: 118–120). Junkkaala further notes that the material culture suggests occupation by the Sea Peoples during Iron Age I and by the Israelites after 1000 (see Junkkaala 2006: 293–294; Junkkaala also seems to mention a destruction about 1000 BC), which is a possibility. Hess suggests the possibility that 'Madon' should be read as 'Merom', or even that both refer to the same site (see Hess 1996: 208).

Kinnereth refers to the Sea of Galilee, or to the town of Kinnereth, for which see comments on 19:35. Naphoth Dor (apparently the same as Naphat Dor in 12:23) refers to an area around Dor on the coast (see *ABD* 4: 1020–1021). Dor is mentioned in an inscription of Ramses II (thirteenth century BC), and is also mentioned in the well-known Egyptian story of Wenamun, which dates to about 1100 BC (see *NEAEHL*: 357). Dor is identified at Khirbet el-Burj (see *NEAEHL*: 357, and overall 357–372). Remains from the Middle Bronze Age and scarabs and pottery, even though not in situ, from the Late Bronze Age have been found at the site. There is plenty from the Early Iron Age, overall suggesting Philistine occupation (see *NEAEHL*: 358–359; Junkkaala 2006: 285–286; cf. Josh. 17:11; Judg. 1:27). The latest excavations started in 2003 (see http://www.dor.huji.ac.il), and the excavation website suggests that, even though the Late Bronze Age town has not been excavated yet, they know where to locate it (http://www.dor.huji.ac.il). Hermon appears to refer to Mount Hermon in the north.

For comments on the nations that take part in the coalition, see 9:1–2. The exact location of the land of Mizpah is unclear (see *ABD* 4: 880).

4. 'Like the sand on the seashore' seems to be a stock expression in Hebrew. For other examples (including with minor variations), see e.g. Genesis 22:17; 32:12; 41:49; Judges 7:12; 1 Samuel 13:5; 2 Samuel 17:11; 1 Kings 4:20; Isaiah 10:22; 48:19; Hosea 1:10; cf. Psalm 78:27; Job 29:18; Habakkuk 1:9 (for a complete list, see EVEN-SHOSHAN: 350). The point that the writer makes is that the number of opposition troops was great. In addition, again, in true Ancient Near Eastern fashion, the statement may be somewhat hyperbolic, and the question of what a 'great number' signifies in reality can also be relative, especially in the ancient Israelite context of the Joshua narrative. It is also worth noting that horses and chariots are mentioned.

5. The identification of (Waters of) Merom is unclear (see *ABD* 4: 705). That said, it seems to be referred to both in Egyptian second-millennium documents and in Tiglath-Pileser's campaign records, and this would also seem to emphasize the importance of the place at least for this sort of action (see *ABD* 4: 705; cf. Junkkaala 2006: 165–167).

6. A promise from Yahweh is now described, as the God of the warring nation. In particular, Yahweh promises that Israel will destroy the enemy horses and chariots (strictly speaking, he will hamstring the horses, making them unable to run; cf. 2 Sam. 8:4). To help imagine the role of chariots in ancient warfare, a comparable modern example might be a promise of a victory against someone who uses Abrams tanks.

7–9. The Israelites then attack and defeat their enemies, just as promised. Greater Sidon and Misrepoth Maim refer to the north. The coastal town of Sidon is currently being excavated (for details, including comments on site identification, see http://www.sidonexcavation.org/index.html, accessed 12 April 2006). The town is mentioned in the Late Bronze Age in extrabiblical documents (see *ABD* 6: 17) and of course features in biblical narratives relating to later Israelite history (e.g. 1 Kgs 5:6; 16:31; Isa. 23; Ezek. 28:20–24). It tends to be paired with Tyre on a number of occasions in prophetic invectives against foreign nations (or, as they are often called, oracles against nations; see Isa. 23; Ezek. 28). The location of Misrepoth Maim is unclear. The exact location of the Valley of Mizpah is unclear (see *ABD* 4: 880). For Baal Gad and Mount Halak, see comments on verses 16–17.

10–11. The narrative then describes Joshua's conquest of Hazor. As indicated in the comments to 11:1–3, there is evidence of a possible destruction by the Israelites, along the lines suggested by the text here. Again, whether everyone was killed is not clear, owing to possible usage of hyperbole in the expression.

12. As such, it appears that the text says that the people of the towns were killed, in addition to the kings. However, again, the extent of destruction and devastation here is subject to the possible use of hyperbolic language.

13–14. Here comes an important note (v. 13): Joshua did not burn the towns in the north, save for Hazor. Only people are killed, and the possessions of the victims plundered. This would imply that, except for Hazor, the northern conquest really should be seen as pretty undetectable archaeologically.

15. This verse contains a formulaic expression which states that everything was done in a manner ordained by Yahweh through Moses. Both the divine authority behind Joshua's actions and Joshua's obedience to Yahweh's commands are emphasized.

16–17. A summary description follows in verses 16–17: the whole land is said to have been conquered by Joshua. This again should be taken hyperbolically, including in the light of 13:1–7. It appears that the conquest should be seen as establishing a bridgehead and a broad overall control of the land, whatever the exact details of this control. The location of Bald Mountain (Mount Halak) is unclear (see *ABD* 3: 25–26), but the text here states that it is close to Seir, which is of course in the south (cf. 12:7). However, the more exact location of Seir is not clear (see *ABD* 5: 1072–1073 for a summary about Seir). The location of Baal Gad is unclear (cf. Boling and Wright 1982: 314; *ABD* 1: 551), but, again, the text here indicates that it is located in the proximity of Mount Hermon (cf. 12:7). Note that 12:7 also describes Mount Halak and Baal Gad as the southern and northern extremities of the land that Joshua conquered.

18. The narrative here acknowledges that the war of conquest took a long time, even if the narratives, read at face value, appear to describe a quick and easy conquest (10:42). Rather than positing two differing traditions or equivalent, it would seem better to make sense of the narratives on the basis of glowing hyperbolic statements to which there is added some small print about the actual state of affairs.

19. The inhabitants of Gibeon are the only ones who are described as having made peace with the Israelites, and only through a ruse at that (chapter 9). It is interesting that the Gibeonites are described as Hivites, and 11:3 describes Hivites as living around Mount Hermon. This might suggest that at least some of the various people groups of Canaan (cf. 9:1–2 and the comments there) were spread across the country.

20. Now another justification for the destruction of the native inhabitants is offered. Yahweh made them stubborn (hardened their hearts) so that they could only be destroyed. This action by Yahweh reminds one of his hardening of the heart of the Egyptian pharaoh in connection with the exodus (see Exod. 7 – 14). In fact, the comment here may serve to tie the theology of Joshua to the theology of the exodus narratives. This would then be a further reason to see Joshua as part of the so-called Hexateuch rather than as part of a so-called Deuteronomistic History. For at least some modern readers, the justification borders on genocidal and keeps raising the problem of theodicy (cf. Rom. 9:14–18, and see Introduction for a fuller treatment; otherwise, for one searching treatment of theodicy in the Old Testament, see Crenshaw 2005).

21–22. The Anakites are described as particularly tall and strong people in the conquest tradition (Num. 13:22, 28, 32–33; Deut. 1:28; 2:10–11, 21; 9:2). For Hebron and Debir, see comments on 10:3–5. Anab is apparently mentioned in extrabiblical documents (nineteenth-dynasty Egyptian) and can be identified by a modern village bearing the same name (*ABD* 1: 219). It appears that there have been no excavations at the site, even though Finkelstein (1988: 52–53) states that a Late Bronze Age burial ground without corresponding occupation has been found.

Joshua is said to have killed most of the Anakites. It was just that some remained in Gaza, Gath and Ashdod. These towns themselves would soon become three of the five main towns of the Philistines (add Ashkelon and Ekron to make the five), who were the descendants of immigrants from the north-eastern Mediterranean region (for a summary of the Philistines, see e.g. *ABD* 5: 326–333). Gaza has been identified as Tell Harube (see *ABD* 2: 912). Not much has been found from pre-Hellenistic Gaza, even though ceramic wares from the Late Bronze Age and Early Iron Age can be mentioned (see *ABD* 2: 914; see also *NEAEHL*: 464–467). The site was excavated in the late 1990s, but no further finds relating to our period of interest were apparently found. Current political problems in the area have also hampered progress. The town is apparently mentioned in the Amarna letters (Hazatu or Azzatu, 289:17, 33, 40; 296:32).

Ashdod's identification seems clear, apparently based on the overall location and prominence of the mound (see *NEAEHL*: 93). The site has been excavated, and clear remains found from the Late Bronze Age and Early Iron Age (see *NEAEHL*: 93–102 for a summary of all finds). It is worth noting that the Late Bronze Age town was destroyed, as indicated by the remains of an ash layer (see *NEAEHL*: 96), but there is no need at all to think that the Israelites were the cause.

As for Gath, it has been identified as Tell es-Safi (for details, see *ABD* 2: 908–909), and excavations at the site started in 1996, conducted by the Bar Ilan university. The excavations are ongoing (for details, see http://faculty.biu.ac.il/~maeira, accessed 20 February 2009). Both Late Bronze Age and Early Iron Age remains have been found. A very recently found inscription with a name similar to Goliath of 1 Samuel 17 can be both seen to give credence to the biblical framework and confirm the idea that the Philistines came from the Aegean and then adapted to the Semitic cultural environment.

23. The first third of this verse provides a concluding comment to the preceding narrative, even though it is not quite clear how far back in the narrative we should delimit the scope of this comment. Then the narrative starts to look forward to the tribal allotments in chapters 13 – 19. Finally, an important statement is made that the wars ceased (lit. 'the land had rest from war'). The statement also seems to have a connection with the tribal allotments described in chapters 13 – 21, in particular as it is similar in content to Joshua 21:43–45.

Explanation

A coalition broadly similar to the southern coalition in the previous chapter is formed by the northern kings in this chapter. Again, as with the southern coalition, Yahweh reassures Joshua and predicts success, which then takes place. And, again, a set of northern towns is conquered and their inhabitants destroyed. With the southern and northern part conquered, all land has then been taken by Joshua, even if only in broad terms. All of this is Yahweh's plan and doing.

JOSHUA 12

Translation

[1]The following are the kings of the land east of the Jordan whom the Israelites defeated and whose land they took, from the Brook of Arnon to Mount Hermon, and all the eastern plain:

[2]First, Sihon the king of the Amorites who lived in Heshbon and ruled from

Aroer at the edge of the Brook of Arnon, over the area of the brook itself, and half of Gilead to Jabbok, the river which is located at the border of the Ammonites, ³the eastern plain from Lake Gennesaret to the Dead Sea, the road of Beth Jeshimoth, and Teman at the foothills of Pisgah.

⁴Second, the territory of Og, the king of Bashan, one of the remaining Rephaites who lived in Ashtaroth and in Edrei, ⁵who ruled the area of Mount Hermon, Salecah, and all of Bashan to the border of the Geshurites, Maacathites and half Gilead, the territory of Sihon king of Heshbon.

⁶Moses, the servant of Yahweh, and the Israelites defeated them, and Moses gave these areas to the Reubenites, the Gadites and the eastern half of the Manassites.

⁷These are the kings of the land west of Jordan whom Joshua and the Israelites defeated west of Baal Gad in the Valley of Lebanon to the Bald Mountain close to Seir (Joshua gave them to the tribes of Israel as a hereditary possession according to their allotments), ⁸in the hill country, in the Shephelah, in the plains, in the foothills, in the desert and in the Negev, from the Hittites, Amorites, Canaanites, Perizzites, Hivites and Jebusites:

⁹the king of Jericho, one, the king of Ai which is by Bethel, two,
¹⁰the king of Jerusalem, three, the king of Hebron, four,
¹¹the king of Jarmuth, five, the king of Lachish, six,
¹²the king of Eglon, seven, the king of Gezer, eight,
¹³the king of Debir, nine, the king of Geder, ten,
¹⁴the king of Hormah, eleven, the king of Arad, twelve,
¹⁵the king of Libnah, thirteen, the king of Adullam, fourteen,
¹⁶the king of Makkedah, fifteen, the king of Bethel, sixteen,
¹⁷the king of Tappuah, seventeen, the King of Hepher, eighteen,
¹⁸the king of Aphek, nineteen, the king of Lasharon, twenty,
¹⁹the king of Madon, twenty-one, the king of Hazor, twenty-two,
²⁰the king of Shimron Meron, twenty-three, the king of Acshaph, twenty-four,
²¹the king of Taanach, twenty-five, the king of Megiddo, twenty-six,
²²the king of Kedesh, twenty-seven, the king of Jokneam at Carmel, twenty-eight,
²³the king of Dor by Naphath Dor, twenty-nine, the king of Goyim by Gilgal, thirty,
²⁴the king of Tirzah, thirty-one, making a total of thirty-one.

Notes on the text

1. East of the Jordan: lit. 'across the Jordan towards the rising of the sun'. Plain: Hebr. *'ărābāh*, sometimes simply referred to as 'Arabah' in Bible translations.

2. 'First' is not in the original but I have added it for clarity. Over the area of the brook itself: lit. 'in the midst of the brook'.

3. Plain: cf. note on verse 1. Lake Gennesaret: lit. 'lake Kinroth', or Gr. 'Kinneret'; the lake Gennesaret in more modern parlance. Dead Sea: lit. 'the lake/sea of the plain, the Salt Lake/Sea'. Teman: lit. 'and from Teman'. Note that the word *têmān* is also used with the meaning 'south', so one could translate, 'from the south under the foothills of Pisgah'.

4. 'Second' is not in the original but I have added it for clarity. The territory of Og: Gr. 'And Og'. Rephaim: Gr. 'giants'.

5. The area of Mount Hermon: lit. 'at Mount Hermon'. Geshurites: Gr. Girgashites.

7. West of Jordan: lit. 'across Jordan towards the sea'; Gr. reads 'Amorites' instead. Bald Mountain: Hebr. Mount Halak. Close to Seir: lit. 'rising towards Seir'.

9. Two: lit. 'one', and thus for all numbers in the list, except the grand total. Gr. omits the word 'one' throughout the list.

16. Gr. omits Bethel.

18. Greek reads 'king of Aphek of Sharon'.

20. King of Shimron Meron: Gr. 'king of Shimon, king of Marron'. Acshaph: Gr. 'Azif'.

23. Naphath: Some manuscripts, and the Targums, 'Naphoth'. By Gilgal: Gr. 'of Galilee'.

Form and structure

This chapter summarizes conquests both east and west of the Jordan, as follows:

> Summary of conquests east of the Jordan (vv. 1–6)
>> Summary statement about kings east of the Jordan and territory east of the Jordan (v. 1)
>> Sihon and the extent of his land (vv. 2–3)
>> Og and the extent of his land (vv. 4–5)
>> Summary statement about giving the conquered land to the Transjordanian tribes (v. 6)
> Summary of conquests west of the Jordan (vv. 7–24)
>> Summary statement about territory conquered (vv. 7–8)
>> List of thirty-one conquered kings, roughly in order from the Israelite entry point in Jericho to south to north (vv. 9–24)

These chapters are summaries, and it is very possible that verses 7–24 in particular telescope some events that happened somewhat later, citing Joshua and the Israelites of the initial conquest and settlement as their ultimate cause. In fact, the mention of 'the Israelites' in verse 7 in particular seems to allow for the inclusion of Israelites after the time of Joshua.

It should also be noted that the fact that the kings are described as defeated does not necessarily mean that their land was taken, or held conclusively by the Israelites. The list may also reflect hyperbolic features and the claims of Israel to the land. Therefore, there is no need to date the list to the time of the monarchy (as e.g. Junkkaala 2006 has done – Junkkaala [2006: 292] himself acknowledges the possibility of conquest without settling in the case of Aphek), even though such a later dating is of course possible. One could also think of an initial list which was expanded over time. In this respect, it should be noted that the Greek versions of this chapter are slightly different from the MT in a few places.

Younger (1990: 230–232; cf. *passim*) notes that lists of conquered towns similar to this list in Joshua are known from the Ancient Near East. In any case, the Egyptian topographical lists from Thutmose III and Shishak in particular list a large number of localities in Canaan (see Junkkaala 2006). The whole idea of listing one's conquests is logical anyway.

It is suggested that the chapter is deuteronomistic (see Noth 1953a: 71; Nelson 1997a: 159). It is certainly true that Joshua 12 refers back to Deuteronomy 2:26 – 3:22. However, on this occasion, there do not seem to be any distinctive linguistic features that link to Deuteronomy as such (*nkh* and *yrš* seem not to be particularly distinctive here, even though suggested by Nelson 1997a: 159), and the material could just as well link back to Numbers 21:21–35. One could perhaps argue that, as the unity of Israel is a very deuteronomic feature, the listing of territory in both Transjordan and Cisjordan serves to reinforce this unity. Be that as it may, this chapter roughly mirrors the order of conquests in the book as a whole, and also has some similarity with chapters 13 – 21 in that the Transjordanian territories are listed first in those chapters.

Comment

1. Verses 1–6 describe conquests in Transjordan and the modern Golan. The river Arnon is on the eastern side of the Dead Sea, about halfway between the northern and southern ends (see e.g. MacDonald 2000: 102 for a map). For Mount Hermon, see comment on 11:1–3. The eastern plain is likely to cover the relevant section of the highlands at the eastern rim of the Wadi Arabah–Jordan graben, as MacDonald calls the area from a geo-morphological perspective (see MacDonald 2000: 21–29, including the map on p. 24). These highlands are about 30 miles (50 km) wide and the area east of them is in essence desert. It is perhaps also worth mentioning that the highlands slope gently towards the east, but very steeply towards the west into the Dead Sea Rift (see MacDonald 2000: 26). In the north, the Golan area extends to the mountains of Lebanon, which then also extend further to the east.

2. The conquests of Transjordan are described in more detail in Numbers 21:21–35 (cf. Num. 32; Deut. 3:12–22) and recalled in Deuteronomy 2:26 – 3:22. Sihon's defeat is described in Numbers 21:21–30 (and Deut. 2:26–37). In fact, the texts from Numbers and Deuteronomy relate that the Israelites asked only to pass through Sihon's territory peacefully but that Sihon refused the request and was subsequently conquered. The location of Heshbon is not certain, even though most scholars identify it with Tell Hesban, which has been excavated (MacDonald 2000: 91–93). Late Bronze Age shards and remains of what is likely to have been a small unfortified village at the site in the Early Iron Age have been found (MacDonald 2000: 92; *NEAEHL*: 626–630). Hess (1996: 225) notes the possibility of shifting place names and that two sites close by (Tell Jalul, Tell el-Umeiri [West]) were of 'significant size with occupational evidence for the Late Bronze Age and the Iron Age I'. Aroer is generally identified with Arair (MacDonald 2000: 97). Excavations at the site show that it was occupied in the Late Bronze Age and Early Iron Age (MacDonald 2000: 97; *NEAEHL*: 92–93). The river Jabbok is on the east side of the Jordan about halfway between the Lake of Gennesaret and the Dead Sea. The Ammonites are of course mentioned in Genesis 19:30–38. Their origin is traced by the biblical text to Lot's incestuous relationship with his daughters after the destruction of Sodom and Gomorrah, together with the Moabites, another people of the area east of the Jordan. Many think that the ancestors are eponymic and were meant to imply that these peoples were related to Israel, albeit clearly inferior to Israel (cf. MacDonald 2000: 49). Gilead is a somewhat flexible description. As MacDonald (2000: 195) notes, areas south or north of the river Jabbok can be meant, or both, depending on the context. Here it is the last of these options.

3. The plain from Lake Gennesaret to the Dead Sea is fairly explanatory, also in the light of comments in verse 1. The location of Beth Jeshimoth is unclear (see *ABD* 1: 689). The location of Teman here is also unclear (see MacDonald 2000: 192–193).

4. Next the territory of Og, the other defeated Transjordanian king, is described (see Num. 21:31–35 and Deut. 3:1–11). As MacDonald (2000: 130; see pp. 128–131 for further details) describes, Bashan seems to refer to the territory located north of the Jabbok, up to (and including) Mount Sirion (Hermon; for Hermon, see comments on 11:1–3). The place name 'Ashtaroth' is mentioned in Egyptian second-millennium documents, including the Amarna letters (MacDonald 2000: 152–153). Ashtaroth is generally located at either Tall Ashtarah or Tall al-Ashari. Surveys have found Late Bronze and Early Iron Age shards at both sites (MacDonald 2000: 152–153). The location of Edrei is uncertain, even though Deraa, located on a tributary of the Yarmuk, has been suggested by many (MacDonald 2000: 108). Soundings have found both Early Bronze Age and Early Iron Age shards at the site (MacDonald 2000: 108).

The Rephaim are described as big (tall) people (Deut. 2:10–11) and as a people which was destroyed by the Ammonites (Deut. 2:20–21). In the Ugaritic texts (see e.g. *UT*: 485) and in the Old Testament (e.g. Prov. 2:18; 9:18; 21:16; Isa. 14:9; 26:14, 19; Ps. 88:11; Job 26:5), the word *rĕpā'îm* can also be associated with the dead (which may or may not be understood as deified, depending on the context). At the same time, the root *rp'* means 'to heal' in Hebrew.

5. The location of Salecah is uncertain (MacDonald 2000: 152). The exact location of the lands of the Geshurites (and Maacathites; cf. 13:11) does not seem to be clear, even though MacDonald (2000: 154), based on earlier works, suggests they are located in the southern (and northern) segment(s) of the Golan, respectively.

6. A concluding note records the basis for the occupation of this land east of the Jordan: Moses gave it to the Transjordanian tribes. It is good to keep in mind that the decision is not recorded as having come directly from Yahweh, but simply from Moses (cf. Num. 32).

7. Next follows a list of kings defeated by Joshua and the Israelites on the western side of the Jordan, with a summary of the area concerned to begin with. Baal Gad and the Bald Mountain (Mount Halak) are the northern and southern extremities of the land (see comments on 11:16–17). The word 'divisions, allotments' (*maḥlĕqōtām*) appears to refer to the divisions of the land, as it comes from the root *ḥālaq* (to divide). As Nelson (1997a: 161) suggests, this, and the use of the word 'hereditary possession' (*yĕruššâh*), seems to start pointing towards the allotments in chapters 13 – 19 in the narrative presentation. It would seem likely that the list is a telescoping of all conquests that took place in the scope of the Israelite settlement, whether during or after Joshua, especially if the attribution in verse 7 of the victories to Joshua and the Israelites is read in a broad sense. Such a telescoping of past events to their ultimate source would also fit with the concerns of a later writer wanting to sum up the conquest and settlement. As regards the use of the word king (*mlk*), it is likely that it simply means 'leader' in its ancient context and should not be confused with kings of medieval European political entities, for example. In other words, it is likely that it was a designation used even of such rulers who might seem rather insignificant by modern standards.

8. The Arabah (plain) refers to the Jordan to Dead Sea rift valley (see *ABD* 1: 321–324 for details; see also e.g. Deut. 3:17). The Negev is the southern part, and, the further south one goes, the more arid and desert-like the landscape becomes. For the nations/peoples listed, see comment on 9:1–2. As in 9:1–2, the Girgashites are missing here from the list.

9. Jericho and Ai have already been discussed in chapters 2, 6 – 8.

10. For Jerusalem, see comments on 10:1. For Hebron, see comments on 10:3–5.

11. For Jarmuth and Lachish, see comments on 10:3–5.

12. For Eglon, see comments on 10:3–5. Gezer has been identified with Tell Jezer (see *NEAEHL*: 496). The place is mentioned in an inscription of Thutmose III from the early part of the fifteenth century BC and in an inscription by Thutmose IV from the latter part of the same century. It is also worth mentioning that its siege by the Assyrians seems to feature in a palace relief of Tiglath-Pileser III from the eighth century BC (*NEAEHL*: 497). Excavations have uncovered clear evidence of occupation from both the Late Bronze Age and the Early Iron Age (see *NEAEHL*: 501–503; see also Junkkaala 2006: 137–139, 279–281). Evidence of destruction has been found at the end of the Late Bronze Age (see Junkkaala 2006: 279–280). See also comments at the beginning of chapter 4, and on 4:20 for the Gezer calendar and standing stones that were found at the site. And there is evidence of destruction at around the time when the Egyptian pharaoh is supposed to have conquered it according to 1 Kings 9:16 (see Junkkaala 2006: 280).

13. For Debir, see comments on 10:3–5. The location of Geder is unclear (*ABD* 2: 924–925; Junkkaala 2006: 267–268).

14. The identification of Hormah (cf. Num. 14:45; Deut. 1:44) is unclear (see *ABD* 3: 288–289). Junkkaala suggests Tel Halif, which attests occupation in the Late Bronze and Early Iron Ages, and attests destruction at the end of the Late Bronze Age (Junkkaala 2006: 247–250; Finkelstein 1988: 300 also suggests Tel Halif). However, Aharoni has suggested Tel Masos (see *NEAEHL*: 986; and cf. below, Excursus 9). An interesting point noted by Junkkaala is that there is a large number of pig bones at Tel Halif in the Late Bronze Age, but these are absent in the Iron Age (Junkkaala 2006: 250).

It has to be noted that there is a connection with Hormah and Arad (Num. 21:1–3; cf. *ABD* 3: 289; and cf. also Judg. 1:17, as noted in Junkkaala 2006: 246), but here the two are of course distinct. For Arad, see below, Excursus 9.

15. For Libnah, see comments on 10:29–30. Adullam, which also features in the narratives about David (1 Sam. 22:1; 2 Sam. 23:13; 1 Chr. 11:15) and in the story of Judah and Tamar (Gen. 38), has been identified with modern Tel esh-Sheikh Madhkur (*ABD* 1: 81; Junkkaala 2006: 268). Junkkaala notes that the area was surveyed by Amihai Mazar in 1977–1978, but no report is available (Junkkaala 2006: 268–269).

16. For Makkedah, see comment on 10:10. Bethel is generally identified with modern Beitin, based on geographical references in the Bible and in Eusebius (*Onomasticon* 40:20–21 [see http://www.ccel.org]) and as the Arabic name 'Beitin' is similar to Bethel (see *NEAEHL*: 192). Excavations have revealed occupation in both the Late Bronze Age and Iron Age I (see *NEAEHL*: 192–194 for a summary; see also R. D. Miller 2003: 155–157). According to Junkkaala, there is evidence of destruction by fire at the end of the Late Bronze Age, and the first Iron Age occupation attests a totally different pattern (see Junkkaala 2006: 238–239). It should be noted that much of the site is covered by the modern village, the south-eastern corner in particular (see *ABD* 1: 651; *NEAEHL*: 192).

17. The location of Tappuah is unclear (*ABD* 6: 319), although Sheikh Abu Zarad has been considered a possibility (see *ABD* 6: 320), and Tappuah here may be the same as Tappuah in Joshua 16:8 (so also Junkkaala 2006: 259). Late Bronze, Iron I and II remains have been found at the site (see R. D. Miller 2003: 186). The identification of Hepher does not seem to be clear, even though it could perhaps be Tell el-Muhaffar (one of the identifications suggested; Junkkaala 2006: 260 suggests this identification as the best possible candidate: Zertal 2004 also suggests the identification), which appears to have been occupied during the Late Bronze (even if scarcely) and Iron I and II periods (see Zertal 2004: 116–120; *ABD* 3: 138–139 and Junkkaala 2006: 261 for details; cf. R. D. Miller 2003: 175).

18. Aphek (see *NEAEHL*: 62–72) is identified with Tel Aphek, some 7.5 miles (12 km) east of modern Tel Aviv. It was inhabited in the Late Bronze and Iron I periods. There are several references to Aphek in second-millennium Egyptian documents. Also, written documents in Egyptian, Ugaritic and Sumero-Akkadian have been found at the site from the Late Bronze Age strata (in the destruction debris of what seems to have been the residence of the Egyptian governor; apparently the destruction dates to the thirteenth century [*NEAEHL*: 68]). Junkkaala suggests on the basis of material culture that for most of Iron Age I the site was Philistine, and then Israelite from the early tenth century (see Junkkaala 2006: 291), which is a possibility. In addition, it is worth highlighting that one of the documents was a trilingual lexicon in Akkadian, Sumerian and Canaanite. This demonstrates the use of writing in the area, including in Canaanite, at least for administrative and diplomatic purposes at the time when the events described in the book of Joshua are purported to have taken place (assuming the lower date for a possible exodus and conquest). We also note that Aphek is located fairly close to the highlands. From this, we can say that it would be surprising if writing was unknown at the time in the highlands, even if one grants differences between highlands and lowlands. Note also the role of Aphek in 1 Samuel 4.

The location of Lasharon is not known (*ABD* 4: 234). The name Lasharon could however perhaps be read together with Aphek, suggesting Aphek of Sharon (see textual note to this verse), where Sharon is the often-used name for the coastal plain (*ABD* 4: 234; cf. Junkkaala 2006: 292). Of course, the text itself suggests that Aphek and Sharon are distinct.

19. For Madon, see comments on 11:1–3. For Hazor, see comments on 11:1–3.

20. The location of Shimron Meron is unclear (see *ABD* 5: 1219; cf. Junkkaala 2006: 266–267). However, it may be a conflation of Shimron and Meron, which then begs the question of whether Meron is one of the similar-sounding place names mentioned elsewhere (see *ABD* 5: 1219 for detailed comments). The location of Shimron (i.e. the word on its

own) is unclear (see comments on 11:1–3). For Achsaph, see comments on 11:1–3.

21. Taanach is identified with Tell Ta'annek (*NEAEHL*: 1428–1433). There is evidence of occupation for both Late Bronze Age and Iron Age I (also Iron II), even though it is scanty for the period from the mid-fifteenth to the late thirteenth century BC (*NEAEHL*: 1432; see also Junkkaala 2006: 123–124), and there is only evidence of slight occupation in the eleventh century BC. A number of cuneiform tablets (in Akkadian and Ugaritic) have been found at the site from the Late Bronze Age (see *NEAEHL*: 1431). Megiddo is identified with el-Lejjun, just a little south of Tel Megiddo. It was a major site in both the Late Bronze and Early Iron periods (also Iron II; see *NEAEHL*: 1003–1024 for the site). A fragment of a tablet containing a passage from the Gilgamesh epic in cuneiform has been found at the site, dating to the fifteenth century BC (see *NEAEHL*: 1011). For a summary and comments about the redating of the stratigraphy by Finkelstein, with responses from those taking traditional views, see Junkkaala 2006: 129–134, 175–183, 270–274. Junkkaala also notes that the Iron Age culture starts at the site from about the late eleventh to early tenth century, after which it was destroyed, and followed by Iron Age culture, in line with relevant biblical descriptions (see Junkkaala 2006: 273–274; cf. Josh. 17:11–12; Judg. 1:27; 1 Kgs 4:12).

22. Boling and Wright (1982: 329) suggest that Kedesh is to be identified with Tel Kedesh (Tel Abu Kudeis) in the Jezreel valley (so also Junkkaala 2006: 297, as Kedesh is listed together with Taanach, Megiddo and Jokneam here). There is evidence of occupation from the fourteenth century BC on (see Junkkaala 2006: 296). Junkkaala also notes that material culture suggests that Late Bronze Age culture continued until the tenth century at the site (Junkkaala 2006: 296–297). It should be noted that there is another Tel Kedesh about 6 miles (9.7 km) north-west of Hazor in upper Galilee. Trial excavations suggest occupation in the Late Bronze and Early Iron periods (see *NEAEHL*: 855–856). Currently, the Universities of Michigan and Minnesota are excavating at the site, focusing on the Hellenistic and Roman remains. Jokneam is identified with Tel Yoqne'am. There is evidence of occupation from both the Late Bronze and the Early Iron Age (*NEAEHL*: 805–811). Jokneam is mentioned in the town list of Thutmose III in the fifteenth century BC (*NEAEHL*: 809–810). There appears to be evidence of destruction at the site from the mid-thirteenth century BC, with an occupational gap and a reoccupation towards the end of the twelfth or start of the eleventh century, and a destruction by the end of the eleventh century (see Junkkaala 2006: 140). Mount Carmel features prominently in 1 Kings 18, and Jokneam by all accounts appears to be located close by (see *NEAEHL*: 805 for details).

23. For Dor and Naphath Dor, see comments on 11:1–3. The location of Goyim is unclear (see Junkkaala 2006: 269; Butler 1983: 139).

24. The location of Tirzah is uncertain (see *ABD* 6: 573–574). If it is to be identified with Tell el-Far'ah, there is evidence of occupation for the Late Bronze (albeit fragmentary) and Early Iron Age periods (also Iron II; see *NEAEHL*: 439–440; see also *OEANE*: 303–304). According to Junkkaala, there is evidence of destruction at the end of the Late Bronze Age (Junkkaala 2006: 242).

This then brings the list to a close, a total of thirty-one kings. For general considerations about the list, see comments on verse 7. Keeping in mind that there is likely to have been telescoping of events in verses 7–24 (and before), they provide a transition point to chapters 13 onwards, which explicitly describe a time that is clearly later than the initial conquest.

Explanation

This chapter is really a list of conquests around the Israelite territory, including both Transjordan and Cisjordan. The chapter also states that Transjordan was conquered by Moses (i.e. under his command) and Cisjordan by Joshua.

From a theological standpoint, one can think that the list speaks for the faithfulness of Yahweh in giving the Israelites success in taking the land. It gives an impression that Yahweh is true to his promises. In the same way, a Christian can trust that God, who through Jesus Christ is the same yesterday, today and for ever (Heb. 13:8), will be true to his promises.

At the same time, a modern reader cannot but keep wondering about the cost of Yahweh's promises to the original inhabitants of the land. These questions keep bringing us to the problem of theodicy.

EXCURSUS 9: THE ARCHAEOLOGY OF ARAD

Arad is usually identified with Tel Arad. Excavations have revealed occupation in the Chalcolithic and Early Bronze periods, but nothing thereafter up to and including the Late Bronze Age; then again from Iron Age I or Iron Age II on (*NEAEHL*: 76, 82–83 suggests the late twelfth to early eleventh century; others, such as Finkelstein [1988: 39] date it to the eleventh century, and some even later [Finkelstein 1988: 39 mentions Zimhoni, who appears to date it to the tenth century]). However, and assuming that the site identification is correct for the time before the Iron Age, even though just about all of the kings listed in Joshua 12:9–24 are kings of a single town, based on Numbers 21:1–3, which (apparently) speaks about the towns of the king of Arad, it may well be that Arad here refers to an area in the Negev, and not only to the tell (similarly Kitchen 2003b: 192–193, who suggests that the name 'Arad' may have been established from a very early age when it was first occupied and maintained as representative of the area as a whole, with reference to the ancient mound, also noting how the kingdom of Ashur was originally named after its founding capital Ashur but had other capitals later on). With regard to mobility, we may also bear in mind here the possibility of a nomadic population in this area of the land, which is rather arid (while one cannot ascertain the existence of any nomadic population in the area, Herzog for one thinks that this is a possibility, including during periods of lack of permanent settlement [see Herzog 1994: 122], and, if there was a nomadic presence, perhaps some of the possible 'towns' in ancient parlance may have been more like campsites in modern terms). Alternatively, in this respect, assuming the book of Joshua was written during Iron I (or II), one might imagine that it would be convenient for the writer to mention the then already rebuilt/resettled town for convenience as the reference point for his hearers and readers about the earlier events. In this line of thinking, if one were to argue for a break of occupation between Early Bronze and Iron Age Arad (and especially for lack of sufficient nomadic presence as well), one would not even be able to be certain of the name of the town in the earlier period, and in such a case it is even possible to conceive that the area was originally called Arad without reference to the ancient mound and that the name was subsequently transposed to the newly (re)built town. We should also note here that the conquest list of Shishak (from the tenth century BC) mentions two Arads, Arad *rbt* (Great Arad) and Arad *nbt* (see Junkkaala 2006: 182; cf. *NEAEHL*: 86 and references therein), which suggests the possibility that more than one specific place in the area was called Arad even at an earlier time. If so, we could even conjecture for example that Tel Masos was called Arad in the thirteenth century and Tel Halif was Hormah, with the name Arad then given to Tel Malhata when Tel Masos was abandoned (see *NEAEHL*: 988 about the likely move to Tel Malhata, and e.g. *NEAEHL*: 86 for the proposed identification of Tel Malhata with Arad *nbt*).

While there is little evidence of occupation in the overall area during the specific time period that could be associated with the events portrayed in the book of Joshua, there is evidence of thirteenth to twelfth-century settled occupation at the above-mentioned Tel Masos, which is fairly close by (see Herzog 1994: 128–130; Finkelstein 1988: 37–47; cf. also above [comments on 12:14] for the suggestion that Tel Masos might be Hormah), and at Tel Halif (see comments above, and on 12:14), and this would seem to indicate at least some kind of activity in the overall area at the time in question, keeping in mind the possibility of nomadic presence as mentioned above.

We may conclude that there are sufficient reasons to think that evidence from Arad is not conclusive enough to deny the possibility that the events portrayed in Joshua actually took place, even if no positive evidence of them exists.

EXCURSUS 10: FORM AND STRUCTURE OF JOSHUA 13 – 21

While chapters 13 – 21 describe the allotment of land to the tribes of Israel, 13 – 19 pertain to the 'ordinary' tribes, and 20 – 21 describe special provision given to an accidental manslayer (chapter 20) and to the Levites (chapter 21). As a whole, this makes provision for everyone in the land of Canaan.

As Nelson (1997a: 164) notes, 'A major turning point in the book is signalled by a renewed command of Yahweh. Just as the command of 1:2–9 initiated chapters 2 – 12, so the direction of 13:1–7 launches chapters 14 – 21.' In that sense, and in their subject matter, chapters 13 – 21 surely form a distinctive section of Joshua. At the same time, there is no reason not to see this as an integral part of the book, even if it must have been compiled with various geographical materials serving as its basis.

The overall structure of the chapters can be viewed as follows:

    Prologue: land still to be conquered (13:1–7)
    Inheritance east of Jordan (13:8–32)
       Summary prologue with territorial notes (13:8–14)
       Reuben (13:15–23)
       Gad (13:24–28)
       Eastern Manasseh (13:29–31)
    Inheritance west of the Jordan (14:1 – 19:51)
       Summary prologue (14:1–5)
       Caleb (14:6–15)
       Judah (15)
       Ephraim and western Manasseh (16 – 17)
         Prologue about the territory of the Josephites (16:1–4)
         Ephraim (16:5–10)
         Western Manasseh (17:1–13)
         Epilogue about the conquests of the Josephites (17:14–18)
       Tent of Meeting set up at Shiloh (18:1)
       Remaining seven tribes (18:2 – 19:48)
         Mapping the remaining land (18:2–10)
         Benjamin (18:11–28)
         Simeon (19:1–9)
         Zebulun (19:10–16)
         Issachar (19:17–23)
         Asher (19:24–31)
         Naphtali (19:32–39)
         Dan (19:40–48)
       Joshua (19:49–50)
       Summary statement (19:51)

We will next look in detail at some issues that largely relate to the historical background and dating of chapters 13 – 21, with implications for the book of Joshua as a whole (most of the discussion has been adapted from Pitkänen 2004a: 218–240, with the kind permission of Gorgias Press).

If we look at the structure of chapters 14:6 – 19:51 in particular, as Koorevaar (1990: 289) has pointed out, chapters 14:6 – 19:51 can be seen as a concentric-chiastic structure, as follows (in fact, I have taken only the inner part of Koorevaar's larger chiasm, which would cover 13:8 – 21:42. Chapter 13 relating to the Transjordanian tribes can probably be matched with the cities of refuge and the Levitical towns as pertaining to groups that have in some way a special status in Israel, but the link is perhaps somewhat more tenuous than with Joshua 14:6 – 19:51):

1. 14:6–15   Beginning: Caleb's inheritance
2. 15:1 – 17:18   The lot for Judah and Joseph
3. 18:1–10   The Tent of Meeting taken to Shiloh and the
                   apportioning of the land
4. 18:11 – 19:48 The lot for seven remaining tribes
5. 19:49–51   Ending: Joshua's inheritance

Koorevaar (1990: 289) explains the connection between Joshua 14:6–15 and 19:49–51:

> The profane division by the lot is sandwiched between Caleb's inheritance and Joshua's inheritance. . . . These two men were the only ones from that (military) generation that entered the land of Canaan. Through their faithfulness the division of the land was made possible in every respect.

Moreover, Koorevaar (1990: 289–290) explains the linkage of Joshua 15:1 – 17:18 and 18:11 – 19:48:

> 'The lot for Judah and Joseph' stands in contrast to 'The lot for the seven remaining tribes'. The profane designation by means of the lot took place in two phases and in two different places. Between those two portions one finds the portion 'The Tent of Meeting taken to Shiloh and the apportioning of the land'. In this way the two 'head' tribes are separated from the other seven.

Koorevaar (1990: 290) explains about the central section, Joshua 18:1–10:

> The portion 'The Tent of Meeting taken to Shiloh and the apportioning of the land' is placed in the center. In 18:2–9 the rest of the land of Canaan is not only apportioned, but all the preceding divisions and regulations are authorized at Shiloh. This portion is introduced by 18:1. 'The whole assembly of the Israelites gathered at Shiloh and set up the Tent of Meeting there. The country was brought under their control'. Therefore the Tent of Meeting at Shiloh is situated in the center of the third main section and expresses the structural purpose of the whole book of Joshua. The erection of the Tent of Meeting at Shiloh is the fulfillment of an important promise in the Pentateuch. 'I will put my dwelling place among you, and I will not abhor you. I will walk among you and be your God, and you will be my people', Lev 26:11–12.

Whether or not one fully agrees with Koorevaar's analysis of Joshua 14:6 – 19:51, one may nevertheless take note of Koorevaar's (1990: 292) conclusion:

> The editor [of the book of Joshua] knows nothing of the destruction and rejection of Shiloh. Quite contrary; Shiloh is the goal that must be accentuated. This is a deciding bit of evidence for dating the final theological structure of the book of Joshua. It must be placed before the rejection and destruction of the sanctuary in Shiloh.

According to Koorevaar (1990: 292):

> It is difficult to imagine that an editor would bring such a theological structure to the book [of Joshua] if Shiloh had already been rejected and laid waste and another city had come in her place: Zion-Jerusalem.

Koorevaar also gives the following reasons why it is difficult to think that the glorification of Shiloh in Joshua is actually veiled argumentation for the importance of Jerusalem:

1. The author is in no way indicating that Shiloh has been rejected and superseded. Rather, 'Shiloh is not rejected, but is even glorified in a structural-theological manner' (Koorevaar 1990: 292).
2. From a rhetorical standpoint, 'the editor would have a structural-theological message [for his contemporaries] that would not only have been superseded at the moment of writing, but it would also have been reprehensible' (Koorevaar 1990: 292).
3. 'The problem is wanting to see Jerusalem at all! For example, the Jerusalem of the time of the Judean king Josiah in 622 BC is the city that has been chosen by JHWH for the promises of the royal house of David. In the view of the book of Joshua Jerusalem is the city of the Canaanite king Adoni-Zedek that had established a southern coalition with four other kings against Israel in Joshua 10. Although he is defeated there is no mention in that chapter concerning the possession of Jerusalem by Israel. On the contrary, one reads in 15:63, "Judah could not dislodge the Jebusites, who were living in Jerusalem; to this day the Jebusites live there with the people of Judah". Jerusalem is the city where Israel (Judah) had failed! But the city received no special meaning in this way. Previously just such a failure can be seen with the tribes east of the Jordan in 13:13 and thereafter one sees the same thing with Manasseh in 17:12–13. Jerusalem is a foreign place for Israel and Judah. There is absolutely no evidence that Jerusalem possessed a special theological position or that Israel had a special theological task in regard to Jerusalem. The editor has neither openly nor in veiled terms placed such a message in the book of Joshua. The Jerusalem of the time of Josiah with its theological purpose is actually a completely different Jerusalem and bears no resemblance to the Jerusalem of the book of Joshua' (Koorevaar 1990: 292–293; cf. Kaufmann 1985/1955: 44–45). Further, 'How strange it is to want to see the Jerusalem of Josiah *behind* the Shiloh of Joshua, while there is the Jerusalem of Joshua *alongside* the Shiloh of Joshua!' (Koorevaar 1990: 293).

In other words, Koorevaar's analysis of the territorial lists strongly suggests a date before the monarchy for the book of Joshua, in line with the position taken in this commentary about the dating.

In general we should also note, in addition to the importance of Shiloh as the location of the Tent of Meeting, that the Levites are emphasized throughout chapters 13 – 21 (see 13:14, 33; 14:3, 4; 18:7; 21) again shows the cultic interests of the writer of Joshua, in addition to emphasis on the unity of Israel and provision for all in Israel. This itself further suggests that the priestly features are integral to the book, and I have argued that they have been incorporated by the deuteronomic writer of Joshua.

All this said, there are also features which may suggest a Judahite emphasis in the book of Joshua (note that Nelson [1997a: 209] interprets the prominence of Shiloh in the narratives as being due to its having been seen as the forerunner of Jerusalem by the Judahite author of Joshua! This illustrates how one can make differing conclusions based on the same data [whether, and speaking in general terms, legitimately or not]). First of all, even though Judah is listed after the Transjordanians in Joshua 13 – 19, it nevertheless is listed first among the Cisjordanian tribes. Moreover, Judah clearly has the biggest number of towns which have even been divided into 'districts' and its border is described most comprehensively. Another tribe whose allotment is described comprehensively is Benjamin, which also has a detailed boundary description, plus a town list divided into two 'districts', whereas one sees less detail in the description of the allotments the further one goes from Judah and Benjamin (cf. Hawk 1991: 111–113). Especially, there are practically no towns listed for Ephraim and Manasseh and their borders are described less carefully, even though there is every reason to think that they were the most dominant political force in the period of the Judges, based on both archaeological and textual grounds (cf. below, and in the Introduction to this commentary). Moreover, some tribes lack a boundary description (e.g. Simeon and Dan), and the boundary and town lists are seemingly garbled for the Galilean tribes (Josh. 19:10–39). Furthermore, the emphasis on Judean towns contrasts with the present state of archaeological knowledge from the hill country of Judea, which suggests that there was much less settlement there than in the northern hill country during Iron Age I; at the same time, settlement in the south increased strongly from about the time of the beginning of kingship. In fact, what makes the matter even more intriguing is that the large number of towns in Judah even contrasts with Joshua 15 itself, which records only Caleb's success at Hebron (Josh. 15:13–15), the giving of land by Caleb to his daughter (Josh. 15:16–19) and the failure of the Judahites to conquer Jerusalem (Josh. 15:63; Judah's failure with Jerusalem casts some doubt on Hawk's [1991: 109–110] suggestion that Caleb's priority in the narrative order, and success in taking his allotment, contrasts with the failure of the Josephites in Josh. 17:14–18 in their progress, and thus emphasizes the role of Judah). In other words, it is as if the large town list had been tagged in independently of the narrative about Caleb and his family. And, interestingly, if we think that settlement first took place in the central hill country, this is precisely where the Josephites (Ephraim and Manasseh) and the Benjaminites, the descendants of Rachel, the beloved wife of Jacob in Genesis (Gen. 29–30; 35), are portrayed to have dwelt according to the biblical tradition, with Judah being a Leahite tribe. We should however also note here that, nevertheless, a surprising number of the towns listed for Judah attest occupation in the early Iron Age (see 'Comment' section on the towns of Judah).

If one looks at the history of research, the major driving force behind the modern study of the boundary and town lists of Joshua 13 – 19 was Albrecht Alt (see esp. Alt 1927, 1953a/1925, 1953b/1927), whose views were followed in principle by Noth, who also connected Transjordan to the scheme suggested by Alt (see Noth 1935, 1953a). Alt distinguished a list of boundaries and two different lists of towns in Joshua 13 – 19, all of them official documents. The list of boundaries divides the whole western territory from the River of Egypt to the Ladder of Tyre between seven tribes: Judah, Benjamin, Ephraim, Manasseh, Zebulun, Asher, Naphtali, excluding Simeon, Dan and Issachar (as summarized by Kaufmann 1985/1955: 23; see Alt 1953b/1927). One of the town lists includes Judah (and Simeon), Benjamin and Dan, and the other includes the Galilean tribes as given in Joshua 19:10–39 (see Alt 1953a/1925, 1927). According to Alt, the boundary list comes from the pre-monarchic period, independent of the twelve-tribe system (see Alt 1953b/1927, including pp. 197, 199), and the town lists derive from the time of Josiah, reflecting the socio-political and geographical conditions of the kingdom of Josiah (see Alt 1953a/1925, esp. pp. 279–284).

The theories of Alt and Noth were criticized by Mowinckel, who rejected their documentary analysis of Joshua 13 – 19 (see Mowinckel 1946; cf. Kaufmann 1985/1955: 26–29). According to Mowinckel, there existed no list of either Judean or Galilean towns (Mowinckel 1946: 7–11). Also, Mowinckel rejected the view that the boundary list originated in the period of the Judges (Mowinckel 1946: 11–20). Overall, Mowinckel suggested that the town and boundary lists of Joshua 13 – 19 are a post-exilic creation by a priestly writer, albeit drawing on older tradition stemming from different times between Solomon and the post-exilic period (Mowinckel 1946, esp. pp. 7–11, 27–36). One point where Mowinckel essentially agreed with Alt and Noth was that, for him, the list of the towns of Judah, Simeon, Benjamin and Dan is based upon tradition that reflects the conditions of Josiah's kingdom (Mowinckel 1946: 7).

Kaufmann has pointed out some basic problems involved with the recon-structions of Alt, Noth and Mowinckel (see Kaufmann 1985/1955: 30–64 for details; these include some of the points already made, including on p. 57 above). Moreover, when one looks at research after Alt, Noth and Mowinckel, there have been many attempts at a solution, with suggested dates for the lists generally ranging from the time of the united monarchy to the time of Josiah. (For more details, see esp. Kallai 1986, Ottosson

1991, Svensson 1994, the appropriate sections of the commentaries of Boling and Wright 1982, Butler 1983, Fritz 1994 and Hess 1996, and the many monographs and articles mentioned in the bibliographies of these works. See also Noort 1998: 181–197 for a further useful summary of the history of research.) But none of the proposed solutions is without a problem, and none has been able to create a scholarly consensus. In fact, it may even be impossible to solve these problems in a definitive way. Thus, and as a detailed examination is beyond the scope of this study, we will limit ourselves to a few observations.

Let us start by looking at Joshua 13 – 19 from the context of the order of the tribes in the genealogical/tribal lists in the Old Testament, as follows (cf. Noth 1930: 7–28; Weippert 1973: 76–78; Kallai 1991, esp. p. 90):

Gen. 29–30; 35:16–20:	$R_{L1} S_{L2} L_{L3} JU_{L4} D_{B1} N_{B2} G_{Z1} A_{Z2} I_{L5} Z_{L6} J_{R1} B_{R2}$
Gen. 35:23–26:	$R_{L1} S_{L2} L_{L3} JU_{L4} I_{L5} Z_{L6} J_{R1} B_{R2} D_{B1} N_{B2} G_{Z1} A_{Z2}$
Gen. 46:	$R_{L1} S_{L2} L_{L3} JU_{L4} I_{L5} Z_{L6} G_{Z1} A_{Z2} J_{R1} B_{R2} D_{B1} N_{B2}$
Gen. 49:	$R_{L1} S_{L2} L_{L3} JU_{L4} Z_{L6} I_{L5} D_{B1} G_{Z1} A_{Z2} N_{B2} J_{R1} B_{R2}$
Exod. 1:1–6:	$R_{L1} S_{L2} L_{L3} JU_{L4} I_{L5} Z_{L6} B_{R2} D_{B1} N_{B2} G_{Z1} A_{Z2} J_{R1}$

Num. 1:5–16:	$R_{L1} S_{L2} JU_{L4} I_{L5} Z_{L6} J_{R1}(E_{R11} M_{R12}) B_{R2} D_{B1} A_{Z2} G_{Z1} N_{B2}$
Num. 1:17–54:	$R_{L1} S_{L2} G_{Z1} JU_{L4} I_{L5} Z_{L6} J_{R1}(E_{R11} M_{R12}) B_{R2} D_{B1} A_{Z2} N_{B2} L_{L3}$
Num. 2:1–31:	$JU_{L4} I_{L5} Z_{L6} R_{L1} S_{L2} G_{Z1} L_{L3} E_{R11} M_{R12} B_{R2} D_{B1} A_{Z2} N_{B2}$
Num. 7:	$JU_{L4} I_{L5} Z_{L6} R_{L1} S_{L2} G_{Z1} E_{R11} M_{R12} B_{R2} D_{B1} A_{Z2} N_{B2}$
Num. 10:	$JU_{L4} I_{L5} Z_{L6} R_{L1} S_{L2} G_{Z1} E_{R11} M_{R12} B_{R2} D_{B1} A_{Z2} N_{B2}$
Num. 13:	$R_{L1} S_{L2} JU_{L4} I_{L5} E_{R11} B_{R2} Z_{L6} M_{R12} D_{B1} A_{Z2} N_{B2} G_{Z1}$
Num. 26:	$R_{L1} S_{L2} G_{Z1} JU_{L4} I_{L5} Z_{L6} J_{R1}(M_{R12} E_{R11}) B_{R2} D_{B1} A_{Z2} N_{B2}$

Num. 34:	$R_{L1} G_{Z1} M_{R12T} JU_{L4} S_{L2} B_{R2} D_{B1} J_{R1}(M_{R12C} E_{R11}) Z_{L6} I_{L5} A_{Z2} N_{B2}$
Deut. 4:43:	$R_{L1} G_{Z1} M_{R12T}$
Deut. 27:12–13:	$S_{L2} L_{L3} JU_{L4} I_{L5} J_{R1} B_{R2}$ (bless) $R_{L1} G_{Z1} A_{Z2} Z_{L6} D_{B1} N_{B2}$ (curse)
Deut. 33:	$R_{L1} JU_{L4} L_{L3} B_{R2} J_{R1}(E_{R11} M_{R12}) Z_{L6} I_{L5} G_{Z1} D_{B1} N_{B2} A_{Z2} -S_{L2}$
Josh. 13 – 19:	$R_{L1} G_{Z1} M_{R12T} L_{L3} JU_{L4} J_{R1}(E_{R11} M_{R12C}) B_{R2} S_{L2} Z_{L6} I_{L5} A_{Z2} N_{B2} D_{B1}$
Josh. 20:7–8:	$N_{B2} E_{R11} JU_{L4} R_{L1} G_{Z1} M_{R12T}$
Josh. 21:4–7:	$JU_{L4} S_{L2} B_{R2} E_{R11} D_{B1} M_{R12C} I_{L5} A_{Z2} N_{B2} M_{R12T} R_{L1} G_{Z1} Z_{L6}$
Josh. 21:9–40:	$JU_{L4} S_{L2} B_{R2} E_{R11} D_{B1} M_{R12C} M_{R12T} I_{L5} A_{Z2} N_{B2} Z_{L6} R_{L1} G_{Z1}$

Judg. 1:	$JU_{L4} S_{L2} B_{R2} J_{R1} M_{R12C} E_{R11} Z_{L6} A_{Z2} N_{B2} D_{B1} -R_{L1} -G_{Z1} -M_{R12T} -I_{L5}$
Judges deliverers:	$JU_{L4} B_{R2} N_{B2} M_{R12} I_{L5}$ Gilead Gilead $Z_{L6}?/JU_{L4}? Z_{L6} E_{R11} D_{B1}$
Judg. 5:	$E_{R11} B_{R2}$ Makir $Z_{L6} I_{L5} R_{L1}$ Gilead $D_{B1} A_{Z2} Z_{L6} N_{B2} -JU_{L4} -S_{L2} -G_{Z1}$
2 Sam. 2:8–9:	Gilead A_{Z2} Jezreel $E_{R11} B_{R2}$

Ezek. 48:1–28:	$D_{B1} A_{Z2} N_{B2} M_{R12} E_{R11} R_{L1} JU_{L4} L_{L3} B_{R2} S_{L2} I_{L5} Z_{L6} G_{Z1}$
Ezek. 48:31–34:	$R_{L1} JU_{L4} L_{L3} J_{R1} B_{R2} D_{B1} S_{L2} I_{L5} Z_{L6} G_{Z1} A_{Z2} N_{B2}$
1 Chr. 2:1–2:	$R_{L1} S_{L2} L_{L3} JU_{L4} I_{L5} Z_{L6} D_{B1} J_{R1} B_{R2} N_{B2} G_{Z1} A_{Z2}$
1 Chr. 2 – 9:	$JU_{L4} S_{L2} R_{L1} G_{Z1} M_{R12T} L_{L3} I_{L5} B_{R2} N_{B2} M_{R12C} E_{R11} A_{Z2} -D_{B1} -Z_{L6}$

1 Chr. 6:39–48:	JU_{L4} B_{R2} E_{R11} D_{B1} M_{R12C} I_{L5} A_{Z2} N_{B2} M_{R12T} R_{L1} G_{Z1} Z_{L6} $-S_{L2}$
1 Chr. 6:49–66:	JU_{L4} S_{L2} B_{R2} E_{R11} M_{R12C} M_{R12T} I_{L5} A_{Z2} N_{B2} Z_{L6} R_{L1} G_{Z1} $-D_{B1}$
1 Chr. 12:24–38:	JU_{L4} S_{L2} L_{L3} B_{R2} E_{R11} M_{R12C} I_{L5} Z_{L6} N_{B2} D_{B1} A_{Z2} R_{L1} G_{Z1} M_{R12T}
1 Chr. 27:16–22:	R_{L1} S_{L2} L_{L3} JU_{L4} Z_{L6} E_{R11} M_{R12C} M_{R12T} D_{B1} $-G_{Z1}$ $-A_{Z2}$ $-I_{L5}$ $-N_{B2}$ $-B_{R2}$
2 Chr. 31:1:	JU_{L4} B_{R2} E_{R11} M_{R12}

Legend:

* (in subscript:) L=Leah; R=Rachel; B=Bilhah; Z=Zilpah
* (in subscript:) L1= Leah's firstborn; L2=Leah's second etc.
* (in subscript:) R_{L1}=Reuben, S_{L2}=Simeon, L_{L3}=Levi; JU_{L4}=Judah; D_{B1}=Dan; N_{B2}=Naphtali; G_{Z1}=Gad; A_{Z2}=Asher; I_{L5}=Issachar; Z_{L6}=Zebulun; J_{R1}=Joseph; E_{R11}=Ephraim; M_{R12}=Manasseh; B_{R2}=Benjamin; M_{R12T}=Transjordanian Manasseh; M_{R12C}=Cisjordanian Manasseh
* non-mention of tribe is indicated by a minus sign (e.g. $-S_{L2}$ means that Simeon is not mentioned), except in the case of Levi)

(Note that in Num. 34 Joshua the Ephraimite and Eleazar the priest are mentioned after Reuben, Gad and Transjordanian Manasseh. However, I have not mentioned them, as they are spoken of as overseers of the land assignment. Reuben, Gad and Transjordanian Manasseh belong to the context, as they are mentioned first as tribes who already have received their share, even though they do not belong to the sublist which contains the men who would divide Cisjordan. Also, in regard to 1 Chr. 2 – 9, note that 1 Chr. 8 picks Benjamin again and introduces the family of Saul, and chapter 9 lists the inhabitants of Jerusalem, with Judah listed first, then Benjamin, Ephraim, Manasseh [v. 3], then priests [vv. 10–13], then Levites [vv. 14–44].)

Only in Joshua 20:7–8, the list of the six cities of refuge, is Ephraim mentioned before Judah. Ezekiel 48 is arranged chiastically, with Judah and the sanctuary in the centre. Also, Judah is not mentioned in Judges 5 (the Song of Deborah and Barak). 2 Samuel 2:8–9 is a list of tribes that supported Ish-Bosheth, and naturally Judah does not belong to the group. In all other places Judah always comes before Ephraim. This is also consistent with the presentations of the lists in Genesis–Exodus, where the Leah tribes are always listed first and thus Judah always comes before Ephraim. (Note also that even though the sons of the slave maids are generally listed last in Genesis–Exodus, sometimes Joseph and Benjamin are also listed last.) The listing of the Leah tribes comes first also in Numbers 1, 13 and 26, and in the same order as in Genesis–Exodus, with minor exceptions, and with Levi missing or last in the lists due to the subject matter. The Leah tribes come first also in Numbers 2:1–31; 7 and 10, though in a different order. Judah leads the way in the wilderness (Num. 10), and is also listed first in the camp order in Numbers 2:1–31 (cf. Jobling 1980: 199). The dedicatory gifts of the princes in Numbers 7 follow the order of Numbers 2:1–31 and Numbers 10. Issachar and Zebulun have been listed together with Judah in these passages. Leah tribes are also listed first in Deuteronomy 27:12–13, except that Reuben heads the list of tribes who are to curse on Mount Ebal, and Zebulun is quite far towards the back. Dan, Asher and Naphtali, the sons of the slave maids, always come last in Numbers 1 – 26 and in Deuteronomy 27 and 33. Gad, the remaining son of a slave maid, sometimes comes somewhat early and sometimes together with the three other sons of slave maids. In Deuteronomy 33, Benjamin, Ephraim and Manasseh have moved towards the start of the list, yet Reuben, Judah and Levi head the list, with Simeon missing.

In the conquest and settlement tradition of Numbers 34 and Joshua 13 – 19, the Transjordanian tribes stand at the head of the list. Judah comes next. After that, in Numbers 34, Simeon, Benjamin and Dan stand before Ephraim and Manasseh, whereas in Joshua 13 – 19 Ephraim and Manasseh come before Benjamin and Simeon. The Galilean tribes Zebulun, Issachar, Asher and Naphtali come last in both cases, except that Dan comes even after them in Joshua 13 – 19.

Thus one should not be too surprised that Judah is mentioned before Ephraim in Joshua 15 – 17. In this regard, one may also keep in mind that Noth thought that the list in Numbers 26 reflects a situation before the time of David (Noth 1930: 129; similarly Milgrom 1989: 224). The main reason why Noth and Milgrom suggest such an early date for the list is that, according to them, it lists localities in the hill country of Manasseh as belonging to Israel, but not in the plain, thus suggesting that it originates from a time when the hill country but not yet the plain was already conquered/assimilated into Israel (see Noth 1930: 122–132 and Milgrom 1989: 224 for details). Another reason for an early dating for Noth is the extraordinary fact that Gad comes between Simeon and Judah in the list, and that there is the order Manasseh–Ephraim instead of Ephraim–Manasseh, whereas later lists are more standardized (Noth 1930: 17). Then, if one accepts Noth's (and Milgrom's) view, it means that the original order of the list of Numbers 26 has not been changed, and thus Judah comes before Ephraim in a list that originates from before the time of David.

On the other hand, seen from the standpoint of comparison with the order of presentation of the tribes elsewhere in Genesis–Joshua, the fact that Ephraim stands closer to the head in Joshua 13 – 19 may be taken as an additional confirmation of a heightened importance for Ephraim in the conquest/settlement tradition of Joshua. One also has to remember that the inheritance of the Cisjordanian tribes is framed by the inheritance of Caleb (Josh. 14) and the inheritance of Joshua (Josh. 19:49–50), the faithful spies (Num. 14), and that this accords well with the fact that the shares of Judah and Joseph are listed together separately from the rest of the tribes (Josh. 15 – 17; for a detailed treatment of a 'twofold' apportionment of the land, see Assis 2003). In this respect, Caleb comes before Joshua in Numbers 13:2–16, 14:30, 32:12, Deuteronomy 1:36–38 (cf. Num. 13:30–33, which mentions only Caleb as actively trying to pacify the people, and Num. 14:24, Deut. 1:36–38, which explicitly mention only

Caleb's faithfulness), even though this is balanced by the fact that Joshua is mentioned before Caleb in Numbers 14:6, 38 and that Eleazar and Joshua lead the allotment process in Numbers and Joshua (Num. 34:17; Josh. 14:1; 19:51; 21:1; cf. also Josh. 14:6, 13, where Judah and Caleb are explicitly subordinate to Joshua). Thus both Judah and Ephraim are prominent in the conquest tradition, with Joshua the Ephraimite the overall leader (together with the priest Eleazar), but Judah is listed first before Ephraim in accord with the general practice of tribal lists. Moreover, one must keep in mind that the order of the tribes in Joshua 13 – 19 is compatible with the order of the all-Israelite conquest in the book of Joshua, that is, Transjordan – south – north (Josh. 1:15; Josh. 10 – 11; cf. Ottosson 1991: 27; Kallai 1991).

The situation is quite different in 1 Chronicles 2 – 9. Judah comes first (cf. Jobling 1980: 199), including David and his descendants, then Simeon followed by the Transjordanians, but *Ephraim and Cisjordanian Manasseh stand almost at the end of the list*. Thus, if one compares 1 Chronicles 2 – 9 with Joshua 13 – 19, it seems that the influence of the Judean post-exilic setting is clear: Judah is first and Ephraim and Cisjordanian Manasseh are not important. The situation is somewhat different with the other lists of the Chronicles, but 1 Chronicles 2:1–2 is based on the system attested in Genesis–Exodus, 1 Chronicles 12 and 27:16–22 are most naturally understood to derive from pre-exilic lists, and the lists of Levitical towns in 1 Chronicles 6 may be based on the book of Joshua (see 'Form and structure' of Josh. 21 below concerning Levitical towns in particular), whereas 1 Chronicles 2 – 9 is most naturally taken as a freer composition. A comparison with Chronicles thus implies that it is difficult to square Joshua 13 – 19 with post-exilic conditions from a rhetorical standpoint.

As regards Judges 1, Judah and Simeon come first in the chapter, followed by Benjamin, Manasseh and Ephraim and three Galilean tribes, Zebulun, Asher and Naphtali. That the Transjordanian tribes have been omitted (Issachar is also missing, but this may simply be an oversight) and that Judah and Ephraim are not connected together as they are in Joshua 13 – 19 (Simeon and Benjamin are brought to the fore in Judg. 1) suggests a different rhetorical setting in Judges 1 from that in Joshua 13 – 19 and the conquest tradition. Moreover, a Judahite perspective is evident in Judges 1, as Judah is listed first, and half of Judges 1 (vv. 3–20 vs 21–36) is devoted to the activities of Judah, even though, on the other hand, the tribes are in an almost perfect south–north order. We may also add at this point that in the book of Judges as a whole, Judah is first in conquest (Judg. 1:2), has the first judge (Judg. 3:7–11) and leads the way in an (according to the narrative itself) early intertribal conflict (Judg. 20:18; cf. O'Connell 1996: 270). Moreover, not only does Judges 1 give much more room for the description of Judah than for the other tribes, and records Judah's successes, but it more or less criticizes all the other tribes that it lists (see O'Connell 1996: 58–72; Amit 1999: 146–152. Judges 1:19 records a failure by Judah, but nevertheless remains on the positive side in its estimation of Judah [cf. O'Connell 1996: 64; Amit 1999: 147]). In this connection, it is true that, for most of the Judges period, Ephraim and the northern and Transjordanian tribes feature most prominently. However, this prominence, and a relative silence concerning Judah, may also be partly due to the editorial strategy of the book of Judges, which sees the period of judges as confused and apostate. Whereas the activities of Judah are emphasized during the early settlement when people still followed Yahweh (Judg. 1:1 – 2:5), the activities of the northern tribes are emphasized during the time when the people were apostate (cf. Amit 1999: 147–150). One also should note that, in any case, the area occupied by or assigned to Judah is quite large, and thus it would be surprising that Judah would not be considered of any importance during the settlement and judges period, especially as Judah's territory also occupies almost all the area southward from the entrance point of the tribes into Cisjordan (Gilgal and Jericho), according to the conquest tradition. Moreover, one should note that, according to the biblical material, Judah stood separate from the rest of the tribes right before and after the monarchy of David and Solomon (2 Sam. 2 – 3; 1 Kgs 12). The separation of Judah from the north is also attested geographically and climatically (see Finkelstein and Silberman 2001: 131–132, 153–158; Finkelstein 1988, incl. p. 326). It is even possible that the terminology 'Judah vs Israel' in reference to south vs north may date from at least a relatively early period (cf. Josh. 11:16, 21 vs Ottosson 1991: 266; 2 Sam. 2:4; 5:5; 24:1).

Then again, the clear emphasis on Judah in the book of Judges as a whole contrasts with the concerns of the book of Joshua, which is based on the overall leadership of Ephraim, the importance of the Transjordanians and the unity of Israel, even though Judah is listed first in the Cisjordanian allotments (Josh. 13 – 19).

One might also point out that an area where population density is lower might be easier to wage war against successfully than an area where population density is high. Similarly, one might expect more assimilation into the indigenous population and consequently more religious syncretism in areas where the indigenous population is stronger. Therefore, it would perhaps be easier to speak about conquest in the context of relatively more activity and accompanying success in the south than in the north (see esp. Josh. 10 – 12; cf. Ottosson 1991: 100–104 for southern prominence in the list of Josh. 12:9–24).

However, we still need to consider that, if we look at the allotment of Levitical towns in Joshua 21, they have been assigned in a south–north order, with priestly towns having been assigned from the south (Judah, Simeon and Benjamin). Even though this would fit with the idea that priestly towns be assigned from an area that was easier to take control of, it is nevertheless rather intriguing especially as the Tent of Meeting itself was set up at Shiloh according to the book of Joshua, and thus one would expect that it would rather be convenient to assign the priestly towns around Shiloh in the north.

As far as scholarship is concerned, even though most scholars have dated the Levitical towns to the time of the monarchy or later (see e.g. Peterson 1977: 1–18 for an overview of the history of scholarship on the Levitical towns, and see 'Form and structure' of Josh. 21 for further discussion about Levitical towns), Kaufmann interprets the list of Levitical towns as an 'ancient utopia' and dates it to the pre-monarchical period (Kaufmann 1985/1955: 65–71). Kaufmann suggests that the division of the country into two, where one part is reserved for priests and the other for Levites only, and that the system was never implemented in practice reflect the utopian character of the list. Also, according to Kaufmann (1985/1955: 68–69), that the Levitical towns of Dan were assigned from the south, but not from the north whither the Danites later migrated, attests the early date of the list of the Levitical towns. If an early date is accepted, the utopian character is supported by Haran's comments (1978: 84–85, 128 incl. n27), according to which there would hardly have been enough Aaronites to populate thirteen towns right after the settlement, as Aaron's family could not have multiplied much in one or two generations from only Eleazar and Ithamar.

In any case, even those who date the list late (the post-exilic time, and conceivably at least to the time after the Assyrian deportation during the divided monarchy) must take the list as programmatic (so Wellhausen 1905/1878: 153–158; cf. e.g. Svensson 1994: 89). Moreover, an early date is conceivable based on Ancient Near Eastern parallels. As Hess has pointed out, the list has a parallel with land grants and the sale of properties found in texts from Alalakh (Hess 1996: 281; 2002; see Wiseman 1953: texts 1, 76–80, 86–88; cf. Milgrom 1989: 504, who points out that the Akkadian word *tawwertum/tamertu* means extramural land; see also *AHw*: 1341, which also lists the second millennium as a period of use for the word). Further, Milgrom points out that the word *maṭṭeh* in the list of Levitical towns is a term that is attested with the meaning 'tribe' in early, but not in late, biblical documents. According to Milgrom (1983a: 12–15), the word *maṭṭeh* is not attested after the ninth century with the meaning 'tribe', and the occurrence of the term in Chronicles (including the Levitical town list in Chronicles) always comes in material that the Chronicler took directly from early sources available to him. As far as archaeology is concerned, only a half-dozen or so of the Levitical towns have been excavated to date, and all of these attest occupation from the Late Bronze Age or earlier (for further details, see the verse-by-verse commentary section on each of the Levitical towns in chapter 21). Also, surveys have found pottery remains from almost all possible sites for Levitical towns at least from Iron Age I on, and when one combines these finds with the problems of identification of the sites, which are at times considerable (for further details, see the verse-by-verse commentary section on each of the Levitical town in chapter 21), and the fact that, for example, no pottery shards from earlier than the eighth century have been found at suggested sites for Geba and Jattir (see Peterson 1977: 405–408, 496–499), even though Geba and Jattir are mentioned in the books of Samuel (1 Sam. 13 – 14; 2 Sam. 5:25 [cf. Judg. 20:33]; 1 Sam. 30:27; see Peterson 1977: 398–399, 491), which traditionally have been thought to give a reliable picture of the time they depict (see e.g. the comments in Hertzberg 1964: 17–20), one may conclude that, based on archaeological evidence, the Levitical towns could be dated to any period from the settlement on. One should also note here that if the list is programmatic, a number of sites may have been selected even though Israelite occupation and/or settlement followed only later. In this respect, as Millard points out, even uninhabited places may have names (A. R. Millard, personal communication, May 2000).

Moreover, assigning the priestly towns to the south is compatible with the priestly tradition that Judah led in the wilderness (Num. 2; 7), the south–north order of the Cisjordanian conquest and with Numbers 34 (assigned to P), which lists the representatives of the tribes who would allot Cisjordan. (As Transjordan was possibly a somewhat 'dubious' part of Israel [cf. also commentary on Josh. 22:9–34], it would be listed last and one would not expect priests to settle there.) One might also even speculate that the assignment of the priestly towns to the south would contrast with the setting of the tent of meeting at Shiloh and thus create a balance of religious power between north and south, serving to emphasize the all-Israelite character of the book of Joshua. In addition, according to the current identification, the southern Levitical towns are concentrated around Hebron, the most important Judahite town during the pre-monarchical period according to the biblical documents (see Josh. 15:13–14; 2 Sam. 2:1–4). All this said, one must however also remember that Joshua 21 emphasizes that the Levitical towns were divided by lot (vv. 4–8, 10; cf. also Josh. 14:1–2; 19:51; Num. 26:55–56; 33:54).

Thus we may suggest that the conquest tradition saw matters in a south–north order, but this is not necessarily an indication of an overall Judahite perspective. An earlier date than the monarchy is entirely possible for chapters 13 – 21. Also, as can be seen from the verse-by-verse commentary section, many if not most identifiable places have occupation during either the Late Bronze or the Iron I Age, suggesting the plausibility of an early origin of the lists.

This said, it is entirely possible that the town and boundary lists of Judah and Benjamin are extensive, because their town lists were updated or expanded and the boundary lists sharpened during the period of the monarchy, including the divided monarchy. In fact, this is very logical, as it is clearly most natural to think that the text of Joshua was transmitted in the southern kingdom after the split with the north, and, on the other hand, the knowledge of areas outside Judah and Benjamin would evidently have been more difficult to update after the split, and even more so after the Assyrian conquest. It is even possible that whereas the town and boundary lists of Judah and Benjamin were updated, expanded and sharpened, lists outside these became corrupted. In particular, the fact that the boundary and town lists of the Galilean tribes (Josh. 19:10–39) which are far from Judah and Benjamin are garbled suggests that the text has been corrupted. In this respect, it is also possible that an original list of towns of Ephraim and Manasseh was left out, as Kaufmann suggests (Kaufmann 1985/1955: 57–59). In fact, Kaufmann suggests that 'scars' remain, especially in Joshua 16:9 and 17:11. Kaufmann also suggests that portions of the Galilean lists were intentionally abridged (Kaufmann 1985/1955: 59). Whether these updates, corruptions and possible excisions were intentional or not, and, if intentional, whatever their motive, the result would emphasize the role of Judah and Benjamin and naturally strengthen the impression of their relative importance in the final form of the book of Joshua (cf. Hawk 1991: 111–113). In fact, curiously, the stated sum total of the towns of Judah in the MT is 112, equalling the number that one obtains by adding together the stated totals for the other tribes (see Assis 2003: 22). Equally, there are districts only for Judah, Benjamin and Simeon, the tribes falling into the territory of the kingdom of Judah. And yet, at the same time, for example, the towns of Dan are not counted in these totals (there is no stated total in the text after the Danite town list in Josh. 19:41–46), and the same is the case for the towns of the Josephite tribes of Ephraim and Manasseh (Josh. 16 – 17). We should also note that the Greek versions of the town and boundary lists differ somewhat from the MT, and there is no correspondence between the stated tallies of Judah and the rest of the tribes in the Greek.

All this said, if there was updating or expansion in Judah during the monarchy, it must nevertheless have been conservative overall, as the order of the tribes in Joshua 13 – 19 has not been changed to reflect the composition of the southern kingdom of Judah and Benjamin. Moreover, whereas Judah is lauded in various ways in Judges 1 and spoken of much more than the other tribes, all that is really noted of Judah in Joshua 15 besides the town lists is the Caleb tradition in verses 13 – 19 and the mention of Jerusalem in verse 63. In this respect, that Joshua 15:63 records the failure of Judah to conquer Jerusalem further suggests that there is no strong intentional pro-Judahite redaction in the book of Joshua, not even at the time of the monarchy if Joshua 15:63 originates from that time. This becomes especially clear when one contrasts Joshua 15:63 with the facts that, according to the book of Joshua itself, Jerusalem is at the border of Judah and Benjamin but the town proper belongs just to Benjamin (Josh. 15:8; 18:16, 28; cf. Hawk 1991: 104–105), that according to Judges 1:21 it was *Benjamin* who failed to conquer Jerusalem, and that the book of Judges (Judg. 1:8) adds that *Judah* actually conquered Jerusalem during the early period of the conquest.

In support of a plausible overall Late Bronze setting for the boundary and town lists, one may consider the following comment by Hess (1996: 40):

> The form of the boundary descriptions and town lists reflects both the ideal of the early settlement and their usage as legal and administrative documents in later periods. The early origin that the text assigns to these documents is supported by their topographical similarity with Late Bronze Age city states of Palestine, by the need for some sort of boundaries – given the sociological dynamics present in the settlement of the land, and by archaeological evidence of settlement in the hill country of Palestine from 1200 BC.

In fact, a reasonably close parallel from a Hittite treaty from the second millennium, between Tudhaliya IV of Hatti (c. 1240–1210) and Kurunta of Tarhuntassa, is worth quoting at length here in this connection (BECKMAN: 109–111; other Hittite treaties also include descriptions of boundaries and towns; see BECKMAN, *passim*; cf. Lissovsky and Na'aman 2003: 297–298 and Kitchen 2003b: 181–182 for further comparisons and contrasts):

> §3 (i 14–21) When my father deposed Urhi-Teshshup from kingship, my father took Kurunta and installed him in kingship in the land of Tarhuntassa. The treaty which my father made with him, and how he established the frontiers for him – concerning this my father made a written treaty with him, and it is in Kurunta's possession. His frontiers were established as follows: In the direction of the land of Pitassa, his(!) frontier is Mount Hawa, the *kantanna* of the city of Zarniya, and the city of Sanantarwa, but the *kantanna* of Zarniya belongs to the land of the Hulaya River, while Sanantarwa belongs to the land of Pitassa.
>
> §4 (i 22–28) Previously, in the direction of the land of Pitassa, his frontier was the city of Nahhanta. My father pushed back his frontier, and on my father's treaty tablet the sinkholes of the city of Arimmatta are made the frontier. Now I, My Majesty, have re-established the earlier frontier for him. In the direction of the land of Pitassa, in the direction of the border district of the city of Arimmatta, his frontier is the cities of Nahhanta and Hauttassa, but Nahhanta and Hautassa belong to the land of the Hulaya River.
>
> §5 (i 29–42) In the direction of Mount Huwatnuwanta, his frontier is the *hallapuwanza*, but the *hallapuwanza* belongs to the land of the Hulaya River. Up behind the city of Kusawanta, his frontier is the Stone Monument of the Dog. In the direction

of the city of Ussa, his frontier is the city of Zarata, but Zarata belongs to the land of the Hulaya River. In the direction of the city of Wanzataruwa, his frontier is the city of Harazuwa, but Harazuwa belongs to the land of Ussa. In the direction of Mount Kuwakuwaliyatta, the city of Suttasna was made his frontier on my father's first treaty tablets, but it happened that later my father himself made the city Santimma the frontier. But Santimma belongs to the land of the Hulaya River. In the direction of the cities of Wanzataruwa and Kunzinasa, his frontier is Mount Arlanta and the city of Alana. Alana belongs to the land of the Hulaya River, but the water which is upon Mount Arlanta belongs jointly to the land of the Hulaya River and Hatti.

§6 (i 43–47) In the direction of the city of Sinnuwanta, his frontier is Mount Lula and the Sphinx Mountains, but the city of Ninainta belongs to the land of the Hulaya River. However, the service estate of the golden charioteer, which is behind (the city), belongs to My Majesty. In the direction of the city of Zarnusassa, his frontier was the *harmima*, but I, My Majesty, have made the city of Uppassana his frontier. Uppassana belongs to the land of the Hulaya River.

§7 (i 48–52) In the direction of the city of Zarwisa, his frontier is Mount Sarlaimmi and the sinkhole of water . . . In the direction of the mountain heights, his frontier is the cities of Hassuwanta, Mila, Palmata, Hashasa, Sura, and Simmuwanta, but these cities belong to the land of the Hulaya River.

§8 (i 53–67) In the direction of the border district of the city of Hawaliya, his frontier is the cities of Walwara, Harhasuwanta, Tarapa, Sarnanta, Tupisa, Paraiyassa, and the dependency(?) of the city of Nata, but these cities and the dependency(?) of Nata belong to the land of the Hulaya River. In the direction of the sea, his frontier is the cities of Mata, Sanhata, Surimma, Saranduwa, Istapanna, the dependency(?) of the city of Sallusa, and the cities of Tatta and Dasa, but these cities belong to the land of the Hulaya River. In the direction of the border district of the city of Saranduwa, his frontier is the sea. In the direction of the border district of the city of Parha, his frontier is the Kastaraya River. And if the King of Hatti goes on campaign above it (the Kastaraya River) and seizes the land of Parha by force of arms, then this too will belong to the King of Tarhuntassa.

In the direction of the border district of the city of Walma, his frontier is the cities of Huwahhuwarwa, Alluprata, Kaparuwa, Hassuwanta, Walippa, and Wala, but these cities belong to the land of the Hulaya River.

§9 (i 68–90) The cities and population groups within the land of Tarhuntassa which belonged to the King of Hatti were: Anta and its deserted settlements, the cities of Lahhwiyassi, Wastissa, Hadduwassa, Handawa, Daganza, Simmuwa, Sahita, the men of Kammama under service obligation, the golden charioteers of Walistassa, the cities of Inurta, Wattanna, Malhuwaliyata, Kasuriya, Sawiya, Pariyassa, Annauliliya, Puhanta, Gurtanassa, the pomegranate-growers (?) of the town of Aralla, the people of the city of Araunna, the city of Uppassana, and the bird breeders. Those who are in the border districts of the land are also given to him. Also the nomadic populations of the cities of Mattarwanta and Para, the depot administrators of the cities of Dagannunta and Munanta, the caretakers of young animals of the city of Ayara, the spearmen of the city of Tarapa, and the two service estates of the cities of Wattassa and Talwisuwanta. The potters are excluded, and the cupbearers are also excluded. They are turned over to the deities of Tarhuntassa. The *duddushialla*-men of the city of Iyasanta, the city of Azzuwassi, and the watch-men(?) of the city of Washaniya are included. The *warpatala*-men and the cupbearers of the city of Adara are included. Whatever *sarikuwa*-squads, craftsmen, and men under service obligation are in the land of Tarhuntassa and the land of the Hulaya River – my father gave him these cities with their bare walls. He did not give them to him together with their inhabitants. But I myself, Tudhaliya, Great King, interceded already in the reign of my father, so that he gave them to him together with their inhabitants. This is not set down, however, on my father's treaty tablet.

§10 (i 91–ii 3) Concerning the matter of the Eternal Rock Sanctuary, Marassanta made an oral appeal to my father, result-ing in the ruling: 'Kurunta shall not be found near the Eternal Rock Sanctuary.' My father had a tablet made for Marassanta, and Marassanta has it in his possession. My father did not know this, however – how the text concerning the Eternal Rock Sanctuary is inscribed within the *kuntarra*-shrine of the Storm-god, and how for all time it should not be permitted for Kurunta to forfeit the Eternal Rock Sanctuary. But when it happened that my father heard the text, then my father himself reversed the decision. And when I, Tudhaliya, Great King, became King, I sent a man, and he saw how the text concerning the Eternal Rock Sanctuary is inscribed within the *kuntarra*-shrine of the Storm-god: 'For all time it shall not be permitted for Kurunta to forfeit the Eternal Rock Sanctuary.' If it happens that Marassanta brings the tablet which he holds, it shall not be accepted.

§11 (ii 4–20) That which is the border district of the land of Tarhuntassa – it is the land of the Hulaya River – even a goatherd shall not enter. And if they drive their animals from the land of the Hulaya River to the great salt lick rock, they shall not take away his salt lick rights. They are given to the king of the land of Tarhuntassa, and he shall always take the salt. My father, Hattusili, gave to Kurunta, king of the land of Tarhuntassa, the cities of Sarmana, Pantarwanta, and Mahrimma, together with fields, meadow, sheep pasturage, all the salt lick, and I, My Majesty, Tudhaliya, Great King, have also given it to him. No other person shall encroach upon the salt of Sarmana. In the city of Dunna a single *kuwappala* is dedicated to the Storm-god of Lightning, and it belongs to the king of the land of Tarhuntassa. If Kurunta, king of the land of Tarhuntassa, later makes another *kuwappala*, my father, Hattusili, Great King, allowed him that. I, My Majesty, Tudhaliya, Great King, have also allowed him that, and it shall indeed be allowed him.

Having said all this, we should note here that borders were not always regarded in quite the same way in ancient times as they are today. While we do have such examples as the Great Wall of China, in many cases borders were rather porous, and perhaps not always rigidly determined either. If it is correct to assert such ambiguity, this could at least partly account for the differing versions that for example the Old Testament documents attest.

Finally, we note that it has often been thought that the lists, as Na'aman notes, can be seen to contain 'phrases and themes associated with what scholars call "the Priestly School", and there has been an extensive debate on the question whether the system of tribal allotments was composed by an author belonging to the Priestly School, or was based on an ancient composition that an editor of that school redacted and added to, giving it its consistency and ideological character' (Lissovsky and Na'aman 2003: 291, with references, including to Mowinckel 1946 and Cortese 1990; Noth and those who follow his views would of course rather like to see the material as deuteronomistic, as priestly features in the material would by and large work against the concept of a Deuteronomistic History; see Noth 1991/1943: 66–67; Noth 1953a: 9–15, and see below, 'Form and structure' of Josh. 22). Be that as it may, priestly characteristics in Joshua 13 – 19 would fit with my overall view that a deuteronomic author utilized priestly material when composing the book of Joshua.

JOSHUA 13

Translation

[1]When Joshua had become old, Yahweh spoke to him, 'You have become old, but there is still very much land left that has not yet been conquered.

²'This is the land that remains: all the areas of the Philistines and the Geshurites ³from Shihor which is by Egypt to the territory of Ekron in the north (it is counted as Canaanite), the territory of the five princes of the Philistines in Gaza, Ashdod, Ashkelon, Gath and Ekron, and of the Avvim ⁴in the south, all the land of the Canaanites, and the area from Arah which belongs to the Sidonites to Aphek and to the territory of the Amorites, ⁵and the land of the Gebalites and all of Lebanon in the east, from Baal Gad at the foot of Mount Hermon till Lebo Hamath, ⁶all inhabitants of the hill country from Lebanon to Misrepoth Maim, the Sidonians. I will drive them away so that the land can be allotted as a hereditary possession for Israel as I have commanded. ⁷Now divide this land as a hereditary possession to the remaining nine tribes and the western half of the Manassites.'

⁸The Reubenites and the Gadites had already received their share which Moses the servant of Yahweh gave to them on the eastern side of the Jordan, ⁹from Aroer which is by the river Arnon and the town which is in the midst of the gorge, and all the plateau of Medeba to Dibon, ¹⁰all the towns of Sihon the king of the Amorites who ruled in Heshbon, all the way to the territory of the Ammonites. ¹¹Gilead and the territory of the Geshurites and the Maacathites, the whole of Mount Hermon and all Bashan till Salecah, ¹²the kingdom of Og in Bashan who ruled in Ashtaroth and Edrei (he was one of the remaining Rephaites; Moses defeated him and took his lands). ¹³However, the Israelites did not manage to destroy the Geshurites and the Maacathites, but they live among the Israelites even now.

¹⁴Levi was the only tribe to whom Joshua did not give a hereditary possession. Yahweh, the God of Israel, had told them that his sacrifices were their inheritance.

¹⁵Moses allotted land to the Reubenites according to their clans ¹⁶as follows:

the territory from Aroer which is at the edge of River Arnon and the town which is in the midst of the gorge and all the plain of Medeba, ¹⁷Heshbon and all towns belonging to it on the tableland, Dibon, Bamoth Baal, Beth Baal Meon, ¹⁸Jahaz, Kedemoth, Mephaath ¹⁹Kiriathaim, Sibmah, Zereth Shahar on the hill of the valley, ²⁰Beth Peor, Ashdoth Pisgah, Beth Jeshimoth, ²¹all towns of the tableland, the whole kingdom of Sihon the king of the Amorites who ruled in Heshbon and whom Moses defeated, together with the nobles of Midian, Evi, Rekem, Zur, Hur and Reba, the deputies of Sihon who lived in the land. ²²The Israelites also killed Balaam son of Beor the diviner among others. ²³Jordan was the border of the Reubenites. This territory was the inheritance of the Reubenites according to their clans, towns and villages.

²⁴Moses allotted land to the Gadites according to their clans ²⁵as follows:

the territory Jazer, all towns of Gilead, half of the land of the Ammonites till Aroer which is by Rabbah, ²⁶from Heshbon to Ramath Mizpah and Betonim, from Mahanaim to the territory of Li-debir, ²⁷and in the Valley of Beth Haram, Beth Nimrah, Sukkoth and Zaphon, the remainder of the kingdom of Sihon the king of Heshbon, the Jordan, and the territory to the edge of Lake Gennesaret on the east side of the Jordan. ²⁸This was the allotted territory of the Gadites according to their clans, towns and villages.

²⁹Moses allotted land to the eastern half of the Manassites according to their clans ³⁰as follows:

The territory from Mahanaim, all Bashan, the whole kingdom of Og king of Bashan and all of Havvoth Jair which is in Bashan, sixty towns, ³¹half of Gilead, Ashtaroth, Edrei. The towns of the kingdom of Og in Bashan were for the sons of Makir the son of Manasseh, more specifically, for one half of the sons of Makir according to their clans.

³²This was what Moses allotted at the plains of Moab on the other side of the Jordan, east of Jericho. ³³However, Moses did not give any hereditary possession to the tribe of Levi. Yahweh, the God of Israel had told them that he himself was their inheritance.

Notes on the text

2. The Geshurites: Gr. reads 'Gerissites and Canaanites'.

3. Shihor: Gr. 'uninhabited area'. Ekron: Gr. 'Akkaron'.

4. From Arah: or 'and Mearah', as most works seem to read the word, not seeing the *mĕ* as deriving from the preposition *min* (so *ABD* 4: 665; it is also correct that *me* would rather be expected if *min* was intended). To Aphek and: 'and' is not in the original, but I have inserted the word to reflect a very possible intended meaning.

5. And the land of the Gebalites: Gr. reads 'And all the land of Galiath of the Philistines'. Lebo: Engl. 'entrance'.

7. Gr. adds 'from Jordan to the Great Sea towards the setting of the sun you will give them, the great sea will be boundary'.

9. Gorge: lit. 'river' (*nahal*; presumably refers to a wadi). Dibon is not included in Gr.

11. The Geshurites and the Maacathites: Gr. adds 'and the Canaanites'.

12. Defeated him and took his lands: lit. 'struck them and dispossessed them'.

13. The Geshurites and the Maacathites: Gr. adds 'and the Canaanites' (cf. v. 11). Even now: lit. 'to this day'.

14. Gr. omits 'the sacrifices', thus Yahweh was their inheritance. I've omitted the clause 'just as he had told them' at the end of the verse in the translation as essentially redundant. Gr. adds at the end of the verse 'and this is the allotment that Moses allotted for the sons of Israel in Araboth Moab on the other side of the Jordan opposite Jericho'.

15. Clans: or 'families'.

16. Gorge: cf. v. 9. Gr. omits Medeba.

18. Jahaz: Actually spelled as 'Jahzah', but read as 'Jahaz' in the literature; cf. Joshua 21:36.

19. Zereth Shahar on the hill of the valley: or 'Zereth Zahar at Har Emeq' (Har Emeq = 'hill of the valley').

20. Who ruled in Heshbon: omitted in Gr. Ashdoth Pisgah: or 'slopes of Pisgah'.

21. Deputies: lit. 'princes, rulers'.

23. Clans: cf. note on verse 15 above.

25. By: lit. 'in front of'. Till Aroer which is by Rabbah: Gr. 'to Araba which is over against Arad'.

26. Heshbon: LXX[B] diverges from Hebr. for the rest of the verse, following with 'to Araboth by Massepha, and Botanim, and Maan to the borders of Daibon'.

27. And in the Valley of Beth Haram, Beth Nimrah: LXX[B] reads 'and Enadom and Othargai and Bainthanabra'. Lake Gennesaret: lit. 'Sea of Kinneret'.

30. Here it is somewhat difficult to say whether the sixty towns refer to Havvoth Jair or to all the places mentioned in the verse, even though it seems to me that the former is more likely; cf. Numbers 32:41.

33. This verse is not included in Gr. I've omitted the clause 'just as he had told them' at the end of the verse in the translation as essentially redundant (cf. v. 14).

Form and structure

The literary structure of the chapter can be described as follows:

> Land to be divided and parts still to be conquered (vv. 1–7)
> > Yahweh's note to the aged Joshua about land still to be conquered (vv. 1–6a)
> > Yahweh's command to allot the land (vv. 6b–7)
> Land allotment east of the Jordan (vv. 8–33)
> > Land east of the Jordan (vv. 8–13)
> > The territory of Reuben (vv. 10–23)
> > The territory of Gad (vv. 24–28)
> > The territory of eastern Manasseh (vv. 29–32)
> > Summary statement about territory east of the Jordan (v. 32)
> > Note about Levi (v. 33)

The extent of the territory listed in verses 2–6 includes only areas west of the Jordan. It should be taken as loose language about the areas that are still to be conquered, excluding Transjordan and the eastern tribal allotments, which are treated from verse 8 onwards. The overall boundary description of Canaan fits with Egyptian New Kingdom sources (see Hess 1996: 26, 230–231; cf. *ABD* 1: 829).

There is some uncertainty about the respective locations of Reuben and Gad (vv. 8–33). Numbers 32:34–39 seems to locate Gad to the south of Reuben, even though it also appears that some of the Gadite towns, such as Jogbehah, are located north of Reuben (see *ABD* 2: 864–865; MacDonald 2000: 103–125). However, in the deuteronomic tradition, including the book of Joshua, the Gadites are located north of Reuben (see MacDonald 2000: 125–146; cf. *ABD* 2: 865). The presence of Gad in the north is confirmed by the enumeration of the cities of refuge in Transjordan (Deut. 4:41–43; Josh. 20) and the use of a concordance for Judges–Samuel. For this reason, commentators have generally thought that the lists derive from different times. It is also curious that Reuben is not mentioned in the Mesha stele (c. 835 BC) which relates to these areas (for an English translation, see COS 2: 137–138; *ANET*: 320–321; see also http://en.wikipedia.org/wiki/ Mesha_Stele [accessed 27 November 2009] for a translation). At the same time, Reuben is mentioned in the Song of Deborah, but not Gad. Some have suggested that Reuben came to be incorporated into Gad as time passed (see MacDonald 2000: 134).

It should however be noted that the overall area of settlement of the eastern tribes is more in the south in Numbers than in subsequent books in the canonical order (see MacDonald 2000: 123–125). This seems to include eastern Manasseh, which is also located slightly further south than in subsequent books (see MacDonald 2000: 123–125). At the same time, it should be kept in mind that the book of Numbers indicates that the Israelites approached the land of Canaan from the south (and east). In this light, one may suggest a plausible scenario. The list in Numbers is meant to indicate a situation at the beginning of the settlement; and the lists thereafter, the situation later on. At that time, according to the canonical description, the Gadites and the eastern half of Manasseh moved northwards, with the territorial lists reflecting the situation. Any Gadites originally living south of Reuben could then also be counted with Reuben in the lists that are canonically later. It would seem that, roughly speaking, if the development of the lists at least in some way refers to historical events, all of this could have taken place even before the time of the monarchy. Within such a context, it is of course also possible that some of the lists have suffered corruption, and might also have been updated to some extent as the book of Joshua was transmitted through the centuries thereafter.

The note about Balaam in 13:22 (cf. 24:9–10) reminds one of Numbers 22 – 24 and 31:8, 16. It is not quite clear why so much attention is given to Balaam, but it is known that he was a well-known figure in the area. Plaster inscriptions found from Deir 'Alla, Jordan, in 1967 (see MacDonald 2000: 148–149 for details of the site) from about 800 BC reveal a story about Balaam (for overall notes about the two reconstructed texts and for a translation, see COS 2: 140–145; see also http://www.livius.org/de-dh/ deir_alla/deir_alla_inscr.html [accessed 27 November 2009] for a trans-lation). That the Balaam inscription dates to about 800 BC could be seen as confirmation that the biblical text is late (early for some, though). This is a possibility. However, it is well known that traditions can be transmitted over long periods in the Ancient Near East, and thus one could for example think that the Balaam tradition was already in existence much earlier than 800 BC, from which time a relevant inscription has been found. The biblical texts and the Deir 'Alla inscription then simply reflect two differing versions of the tradition, one Yahwistic and the other non-Yahwistic. It should also be kept in mind that the Deir 'Alla inscription differs from the biblical text in a number of important respects.

Comment

1. Here the scene shifts explicitly to a time clearly later than the initial conquest. Joshua is now an old man. Yet much land remains to be conquered. In fact, the verse provides a more realistic statement about the conquest than some of the earlier chapters have, at least at first sight. And yet, if one reads the previous chapters carefully bearing in mind the tendency of Ancient Near Eastern rhetoric to exaggeration and considering possible telescoping, the discrepancy is less than it may at first appear. The verse can also be seen as providing an introduction to the tribal allotments in chapters 13 – 21.

2. The unconquered areas of the land are then described. The Philistines were a people of Aegean origin who settled in the coastal area in the western part of Canaan (see above, comments on 11:21–22). Less is known of the Geshurites, except that they appear in 1 Samuel 27:8–9 as longstanding inhabitants of the land. This area is not to be confused with Geshur in Bashan (see comment on 12:5; cf. 13:11, 13; 1 Chr. 2:23; 3:2; Deut. 3:14). Absalom seems to have come from Geshur in the south (cf. 1 Sam. 27:8 with 2 Sam. 3:3; 13 – 15), also considering that David apparently took a wife at Hebron (2 Sam. 3:3) and crossed the Jordan towards the east to escape Absalom (2 Sam. 17:21–22). As Nelson (1997a: 166) points out, the description moves from south to north in verses 2–5.

3. The exact location of Shihor is unclear, even though it refers to a river near the border of Egypt (see *ABD* 5: 1212, including for the various identifications that have been suggested). Ekron is one of the five prominent towns of the Philistines (see above, comments on 11:21–22. Apparently the Hebrew text is to be read here to mean that the Geshurite areas are counted as Canaanite. Ekron is identified with Tel Miqne and is one of the largest Iron Age sites in Israel (*NEAEHL*: 1051). It had continuous occupation during the Late Bronze Age and Iron Age I, with more in the Late Bronze era than Iron Age I (see *NEAEHL*: 1051–1059, and a summary of recent excavations and bibliography at http://www.aiar.org/docs/EkronSummary.pdf [accessed 23 February 2009] for details). For Gaza, Gath and Ashdod, see comments on 11:21–22. Ashkelon is mentioned in second-millennium Egyptian documents, including the Merneptah stele and Amarna letters (see *NEAEHL*: 103 for a list). A large site, it is identified on the coast about 39 miles (63 km) south of Tel Aviv on the Mediterranean coast (see *NEAEHL*: 103). There was occupation at the site in both Late Bronze and Iron I periods (see *NEAEHL*: 107). There have been recent excavations at Ashkelon by Harvard University (see http:// www.fas.harvard.edu/~semitic/ashkelon_dig.html, accessed 23 February 2009).

Based on Deuteronomy 2:23 (and the opening words of the next verse here), the Avvim seem to have lived around the southern part of the area of the Philistines before being taken over by them and destroyed (see *ABD* 1: 531–532 for more details about a possible identification of this people; cf. also comments on Josh. 18:23).

4. The location of Arah (or Mearah; see notes on the translation) is unknown. For Sidon, see comment on 11:7–9. For Aphek, see comments on 12:18. For the Amorites, see comments on 9:1–2 and 13:10.

5–7. Gebal is the famous Byblos, as the Greeks called it, located some 20 miles (32 km) north of modern Beirut. It is an ancient Phoenician seaport, already featuring in the third millennium BC (see *ABD* 2: 922–923). In the second millennium, a large number of the Amarna letters were written by Rib-Addi from Byblos (see KNUDTZON for these), and the famous sarcophagus of Ahiram from the eleventh century BC was found at Byblos (see *ABD* 2: 922). The famous Egyptian story of Wenamun (c. 1100 BC) takes place chiefly at Byblos (see *ANET*: 25–29).

Lebanon (see also *ABD* 4: 268–270) here refers to the highlands north of Canaan proper, pretty much within modern Lebanon. The area received some good rainfall, and its trees were famous in Old Testament times. Also, the mountains did see snow at the higher elevations, hence presumably the name 'Lebanon' for the area (the Semitic root *lbn* means 'white'). See also comments on 12:1.

For Baal Gad, see comments on 11:16–17. For Mount Hermon, see comments on 11:1–3. The location of Lebo Hamath is uncertain (see *ABD* 3: 36–37), but Hamath itself was a well-known ancient city in Syria (see *ABD* 3: 33–36 for details). The place may be mentioned in the conquest lists of Thutmose III (see Junkkaala 2006: 153–154). For Sidon and Misrepoth Maim, see comments on 11:7–9.

Yahweh himself will dispossess the nations mentioned. All that Israel needs to do is to trust in Yahweh's promises. And Israel is to allot the land based on this trust.

7. Next follows a very straightforward statement: Joshua is to divide the land for the nine and a half tribes. The land here refers to the west side of the Jordan. The Reubenites, the Gadites and half of the tribe of Manasseh have already received their share east of the Jordan.

8. In effect, what follows next until the end of chapter 21 is a complete description of the allotment of the land. Border descriptions were normal in the ancient world in the second millennium BC. As we noted in Excursus 10, for example, one can see a number of border descriptions in the Hittite treaties (see e.g. BECKMAN: 20–21, 31, 41), and the second-millennium Babylonian *kudurrus*, or boundary stones, were related to land grants (for examples, search the Internet by the word *kudurru*). Beyond this, when we keep in mind, as e.g. BECKMAN, KNUDTZON attest, that diplomatic activity in the Near East in the Late Bronze Age was broadly speaking comparable to any such activity at any later time, it is inconceivable to think that such aspects as borders would not at least in broad terms be considered in the same way as they have been at any later time. Thus any of the Israelite border depictions could easily originate from the second millennium BC.

Verses 8–31 of chapter 13 describe the Transjordanian allotments/territories as a whole. Here as elsewhere the division is said to be based on Moses' command, as the territories were allotted in Moses' time (cf. Num. 32 etc.), in contrast to the Cisjordanian allotments, which derive from Joshua and his time. As Nelson (1997a: 170) points out, verses 9–12 are a general description, and verses 15–31 provide a more detailed description by each tribe.

9. For Aroer and Arnon, see comments on 12:1–2. Medeba is generally located at the modern town of Madaba, 20 miles (32 km) south-west of Amman (see MacDonald 2000: 109). Surface shards have been found from the Early Bronze Age on, and two tombs have been found from around the ancient tell, dating to the thirteenth–tenth centuries BC (MacDonald 2000: 110; see also *NEAEHL*: 992–993). Medeba is also mentioned on the Mesha stele (line 30). Dibon is identified by most with modern Dhiban, some 5 miles (8 km) north of the Arnon (MacDonald 2000: 84). It is also mentioned on the Mesha stele (lines 22, 28), and the stele itself was found at Dhiban (MacDonald 2000: 85). Evidence of occupation has been found from the Early Bronze Age, but none from the Middle or Late Bronze Ages, although some pottery has been found from the Early Iron Age (MacDonald 2000: 85; see also *NEAEHL*: 350–352).

10. For Heshbon and for Sihon and for the Ammonites, see comments on 12:1–2. The Amorites may well be related to the Amorites who are attested in and around north-west Mesopotamia in the fourth–second millennia (from Akkadian *amurru*, meaning west; for further details, see *ABD* 1: 199–202).

11. Gilead in its widest sense refers to the area east of the Jordan from the river Arnon in the south to about the latitude of the lake Gennesaret, from which the area of Bashan starts (*ABD* 2: 1020; see also comments on 12:2, 4). For Mount Hermon, see comments on 11:1–3. For Salecah, and for the lands of the Geshurites and Maacathites, see comments on 12:5.

12. See comments on 12:4.

13. Here the writer of the book of Joshua notes that the Geshurites and Maacathites live among the people of Israel in his day. The comment refers to these peoples as existing during the writer's lifetime and also traces them to the time of the conquest and beyond for the reader of the first 'edition' of the book. In a sense (even if not exclusively), it can be thought that, for the author of Joshua, the existence of these peoples in his day serves as proof of the conquest for the first readers.

14. The tribe of Levi get no land, even though they get some towns and pasturelands as per chapter 21. By and large, tithes and portions of offerings are to be their livelihood (see Lev. 6:24 – 7:36; Num. 18:21–28). The sacrifices are emphasized here, but they are likely to include anything related, as described elsewhere in Exodus–Joshua (synecdoche).

15–16. Next comes a detailed description of the Reubenite territories (vv. 16–23).

16. For the territories stated in this verse, see comments on verse 9.

17. For Heshbon, see comments on 12:1–2. For Dibon, see comments on verse 9. The location of Bamoth Baal is uncertain (see MacDonald 2000: 77–78). The location of Beth Baal Meon is also uncertain (see MacDonald 2000: 117–118).

18. The location of Jahaz is uncertain (see MacDonald 2000: 103–106). The same goes for Kedemoth (see MacDonald 2000: 93–95) and Mephaath (see MacDonald 2000: 135–137).

19. The location of Kiriathaim is unclear (see MacDonald 2000: 122–123). The same goes for Sibmah (see MacDonald 2000: 116–117) and Zereth Shahar on the hill of the valley (Har Emeq), even though it is worth mentioning that pottery from Iron I and II and shards from the Late Bronze Age have been found from Boz al-Mushelle, which has been suggested as a candidate (see MacDonald 2000: 137).

20. The location of Beth Peor is uncertain (see MacDonald 2000: 138–139). Pisgah may be the hill/mountain at Ras al-Siyagha (see MacDonald 2000: 79). For Beth Jeshimoth, see comments on 12:3.

21. The tableland (*mîšōr*) here is frequently seen to refer to 'the plain area between Heshbon in the north, the Arnon in the south, the Dead Sea escarpment in the west, and the desert in the east' (see MacDonald 2000: 108). For Heshbon and Sihon, see comments on 12:1–2. The five nobles are listed in Numbers 31:8, named as kings (it is good to keep in mind here, however, that, as already mentioned, in this area and time period kingship should not really be seen as the same as kingship in a modern or pre-modern state, but on a much smaller scale).

22. Balaam, among others, is here noted to have been killed by the Israelites. We read of Balaam extensively in the book of Numbers (Num. 22 – 24, 31; cf. Num. 25).

23. The description finishes with the note that the Jordan formed the border of the Reubenites (in the west, of course). Finally, a summary note is given that closes the boundary description of the Reubenites.

24. The narrative next moves to describe the inheritance of Gad.

25. The location of Jazer is uncertain (see the discussion in MacDonald 2000: 106–108). For Gilead, the see comments on 12:2, 4, 13:11 and MacDonald 2000: 195–199. For the Ammonites, see the comments in

12:2, 4. The land of the Ammonites is not delimited exactly in the Bible (save possibly Judg. 11:13) and is likely to have been fluid over time anyway (see MacDonald 2000: 157–170 for a detailed discussion). For Aroer, see first comments on 12:2. However, the Aroer here may not be the same Aroer as in 12:2; 13:9 (see MacDonald 2000: 166). If so, the location is unknown (see MacDonald 2000: 166–167). The location of Rabbah, which also features elsewhere in the biblical narrative (see esp. 2 Sam. 11 – 12), is held to equate to the location of the modern city of Amman in Jordan. Excavations show occupation from Neolithic times through to Iron II, and in Roman times (see *NEAEHL*: 1243–1249; cf. Junkkaala 2006: 150–151). Most notably for the Late Bronze Age, a temple from the period has been found (see *NEAEHL*: 1246 for further details). Rabbah appears to be mentioned in the conquest list of Thutmose III (see Junkkaala 2006: 150–151).

26. For Heshbon, see comments on 12:2. The location of Ramath Mizpah is unknown (see MacDonald 2000: 139). The location of Betonim is likewise unknown, although it is often identified with Khirbat Batneh, from where some Iron Age shards have been found (see MacDonald 2000: 140). The location of Mahanaim, a name that otherwise appears from time to time in the biblical narrative, is unknown (see MacDonald 2000: 140–142). For the territory of Li-debir, see first comments on Debir in 10:3–5. Li-debir refers to a different area, however, and the exact details are uncertain (see MacDonald 2000: 142–143).

27. Beth Haram may be the same site as Beth Haran in Numbers 32:36 (see MacDonald 2000: 120). Certainly, both are listed as belonging to the territory of Gad in their respective textual settings, together with Beth Nimrah (albeit the word 'Beth' is missing in the Greek of Num. 32:36 with Beth Nimrah). The location of Beth Haran is unclear, although either Tall Iktanu or Tall ar-Rama is most often suggested. Evidence of Iron I and II occupation (at least pottery shards) has been found at Tall Iktanu, and evidence of Iron II occupation at Tall ar-Rama (see MacDonald 2000: 120–122). Beth Nimrah may be rather Tall Nimrin or Tall Bleibel. Both show evidence of occupation in the Iron I and II periods. Tall Bleibel may also have evidence of Late Bronze occupation (see MacDonald 2000: 114–115).

The location of Succoth, which features elsewhere in the Old Testament narrative, is unclear, although at one of the candidates, Tall al-Khisas, shards have been found from the Late Bronze II and Iron I–II periods (see MacDonald 2000: 143–144). The location of Zaphon (which itself has the meaning 'north', an often-used word) is uncertain, albeit Tall as-Sa'idiyya, which has often been suggested, has yielded shards from the Late Bronze II and Iron I and II periods, and extensive remains from the Iron Age (MacDonald 2000: 144–145).

For Sihon and Heshbon, see comments on 12:1–2. Lake Gennesaret, or the Sea of Galilee, the big lake in northern Israel, features in the New Testament as one of the places of Jesus' activity. It serves as a conspicuous northern boundary. The river Jordan then is the western boundary, another conspicuous landmark.

28. A summary statement concludes the border description of the Gadites.

29. Last in the list of Transjordanian allotments, the inheritance of the (eastern) half-tribe of Manasseh is described. As Nelson points out, the description is rather vague (Nelson 1997a: 174). Also, Nelson suggests that 'after mention of Og's capital cities, attention abruptly narrows to the clans of Machir east of the Jordan. This transition is awkward . . . ' (Nelson 1997a: 174). It is even possible to imagine that something could have dropped out from an originally more detailed list.

30–31. For Mahanaim, see comments on 13:26. For Og and Bashan, see comments on 12:4. The more specific location of the various Havvoth Jair (which means 'the villages of Jair') is not clear (cf. Num. 32:41 etc. and the discussion in MacDonald 2000: 123). For Gilead, see comments on 12:2, 4; 13:11. For Ashtaroth and Edrei, see comments on 12:4.

Makir (or Machir) is the son of Manasseh, according to tradition. He has descendants and holdings both east and west of the Jordan. The eastern holdings are mentioned here, with a quick reference to the existence of the relevant clans. The western ones, involving the interesting case of the daughters of Zelophehad, are mentioned in Joshua 17:1–6 (see also Num. 27:1–11; 36:1–12). I have argued that the names of the Manassites, including Gilead, Tirzah etc. may reflect the place/district names and assimilation of the corresponding peoples to the Israelites (see Pitkänen 2004b; see also comments on 17:2–3 below). Thus place names may have been named after the Israelites, or some of the Israelite names in genealogies may have been taken from the names of places where the various Israelites settled. Overall, the issue of genealogies and their origin is somewhat complex and a full discussion is beyond the scope of this commentary. For some further views of related matters and a more detailed discussion about Makir, see *ABD* 4: 458–460.

32. The text reiterates that these particular inheritances were given by Moses prior to entry to the promised land (cf. Num. 32 etc.). See also comments on verse 8.

33. The text then reiterates the situation with Levi (cf. v. 14 and comments on the verse). Here, slightly differently, Yahweh is the inheritance of Levi, whereas it is Yahweh's offerings that are said to be the inheritance in verse 14 in a similar summary statement. In essence, the two are the same, as Yahweh is associated with his cult, and Yahweh's offerings provide a practical means of livelihood for the Levites.

Explanation

This chapter starts the process of land allotment that encompasses chapters 13 – 21. In chapter 13, Joshua is exhorted to divide and allot the land even though not all of it has yet been conquered. The Transjordanians who have already received their inheritance come first in the lists, reflecting the fact that they were allotted their territory first. After a summary statement about the land on the western side of the river Jordan, the chapter includes a delimitation of the borders of the Transjordanians and summaries of some of the conquests made. Failures to conquer certain areas are also mentioned.

Overall, perhaps we can think of the situation that the Israelites are seen to be in as taking a step in faith with the hope of success even if everything that one desires has not yet taken place. God's people, and, undoubtedly, people as a whole, should not be timid but should plan for goals they wish to achieve, and, if convinced that the aim is a worthy one, move forward even if there are obstacles to clear and work to be done before a vision can be fulfilled.

At the same time, one cannot but remember that the plan is to be fulfilled at the cost of the indigenous inhabitants, at least as it is being visualized by the author of the book of Joshua. In the modern world, the land of Israel/Palestine is again being contested, by the Israelis and the Palestinians. The radical Jewish settlers still refer to Israel's ancient occupation of the land in justification of their acts of appropriating territory to themselves. Also, indigenous people all around the world have suffered and are still suffering conquests, dispossession and other forced measures by people groups stronger than they are. Whether in ancient or modern settings, theology and ideology are important driving forces for the actions of people. From this, perhaps we can say that, for Christians, among any other thoughts this raises, it should serve as a reminder that they should try to pay considerable attention to forming their theology 'correctly' before they take action based on it. And Christians could lobby respective political entities so that justice might prevail in these respects. Of course, the actions of Christians may sometimes involve legitimately taking away the opportunities of some, as was the case with Demetrius, a man who sold idols but whose trade was threatened by the increasing popularity of Christianity (Acts 19:23–41). However, the process was peaceful in that case, even when Demetrius tried to use violence to counter the Christians.

JOSHUA 14

Translation

[1]This is the land which the Israelites received in Canaan and which Eleazar the priest, Joshua the son of Nun and the heads of the tribes allotted to them. [2]They allotted them by lot for the nine and a half tribes, just as Yahweh had commanded through Moses. [3]Moses had already given an allotted portion to two and a half tribes from the east side of Jordan, and no allotted portion was given to the

Levites among the tribes. ⁴The descendants of Joseph consisted of two tribes, Manasseh and Ephraim, and, again, no land was given to the Levites, except for selected towns and their surroundings for them and their cattle and other possessions. ⁵The Israelites distributed the land according to Yahweh's instructions to Moses.

⁶Now the Judahites approached Joshua in Gilgal, and Caleb the son of Jephunneh the Kenizzite said, 'Remember what Yahweh said to Moses the man of God about you and me in Kadesh Barnea. ⁷I was forty years old when Moses the servant of Yahweh sent me from Kadesh Barnea to spy out the land, and I brought back my report to him according to what was in my heart. ⁸My fellow companions who went with me made the people discouraged, but I was happy to follow Yahweh. ⁹Moses swore on that day, "Surely the land on which you have trodden will be a permanent hereditary possession for you and your descendants because you have followed Yahweh faithfully."

¹⁰'And now, see, Yahweh has kept me alive for these forty-five years as he said, all the way from the time he gave this promise to Moses when Israel wandered in the wilderness. See, I am now eighty-five years old. ¹¹I am still as strong now as I was when Moses sent me. I am now as capable of fighting and of other activities as I was then. ¹²Now, give me this hill country about which Yahweh spoke at the time. You heard at that time that the Anakites lived there and that the towns were big and inaccessible. Perhaps Yahweh will be with us and I can drive them out from there as he promised.'

¹³Joshua then blessed Caleb the son of Jephunneh and gave him Hebron as a hereditary possession. ¹⁴Thus Hebron became a hereditary possession of Caleb the son of Jephunneh the Kenizzite and has been so till this day because he had followed Yahweh the God of Israel faithfully. ¹⁵(Hebron was previously called Kiriath Arba on account of a prominent man among the Anakites.) And there was now peace in the land.

Notes on the text

1. Received: lit. 'inherited' (Hebr. *nāḥal*).

2. From the east side of Jordan: lit. 'from beyond Jordan'. Moses: Gr. Joshua.

6. Remember: lit. 'You know'.

8. Made the people discouraged: lit. 'made the heart of the people melt'.

9. You have followed Yahweh faithfully: lit. 'You have been satisfied to follow Yahweh our God'.

14. Had followed Yahweh the God of Israel faithfully: 'was satisfied to follow Yahweh the God of Israel' (cf. v. 9).

15. On account of a prominent man among the Anakites: Gr. 'it was a mother town (*mētropolis*) of the Enakim'. There was now peace in the land: lit. 'And the land had rest from war.'

Form and structure

The structure of this chapter can be described as follows:

> Introduction to land division west of the Jordan (vv. 1–7)
> Caleb's inheritance (vv. 8–15)
>> Caleb's request (vv. 6–12)
>> The giving of Hebron to Caleb (vv. 13–15)

As Nelson (1997a: 177) helpfully notes, a pattern similar to verses 6–15 (generally consisting of a number or all of the following elements: confrontation, statement of case and request, flashback to Moses, grant, reference to Yahweh's command, summary) can be observed in Joshua 15:18–19 (Achsah), 17:3–6 (the daughters of Zelophehad), 17:14–18 (Joseph), and 21:1–3 (Levi). All these relate to the giving of land upon request. In some cases the land had already been promised earlier in the canonical context (e.g. Num. 27, 36 with the daughters of Zelophehad) and the request serves as a reminder, and in others (e.g. Achsah), it is about a fresh request.

Comment

1. Having considered Transjordan in chapter 13, the narrative moves to the Cisjordanian allotments. It states that the leaders carry out the allotments. Except for Joshua and the tribal leaders, note in particular that Eleazar the priest is among the allotters. He is undoubtedly, among other things, the representative of priests and Levites. This reinforces the importance of priests and Levites in the book of Joshua. However, at the same time, one should keep in mind the all-Israelite emphasis of the book. Joshua 19:51 expressly indicates that the allotment takes place at Shiloh. This is the case at least for the seven tribes that remain after Judah and Ephraim have received their share, with a slight possibility that the allotment for Judah and Joseph took place at Gilgal (see, however, comments on vv. 6a, 10 below).

2–3. The narrative states that the Cisjordanian land will be divided for the remaining nine and a half tribes by lot (*gôrāl*). The lot is used in various places in the Old Testament where a divine decision is sought (see e.g. Prov. 16:33). The ephod (presumably including *urim* and *thummim*; cf. below and comments on 7:14–18) is also sometimes used (see e.g. 1 Sam. 23:6–12; 30:7–8). Other methods of obtaining divine counsel are dreams (e.g. for Joseph in Gen. 37:5–11 and for Solomon in 1 Kgs 3:5–15), the *urim* and *thummim* (lit. prob. 'lights and perfection'; Exod. 28:30), and through the prophets (e.g. 1 Kgs 22:1–28), nicely summarized in 1 Samuel 28:6. It is sometimes thought that the Old Testament prohibits divination

(Deut. 18:9–14), but it is clear from these examples that the situation is not as clear-cut as is sometimes thought. While working out exact details is beyond the scope of this book, the main point is that divination is not completely forbidden but is regulated to include only certain forms that are compatible with Yahwism. A number of common Near Eastern forms such as liver divination, which was practised extensively in Assyro-Babylonia (where it was in a sense almost an art form), or shamanism or being a medium or seeking one (cf. 1 Sam. 28:7–25) is forbidden (for an extensive analysis of the various practices listed in Deut. 18:9–14, see Taylor 2006). Cf. also *ABD* 4: 464–471.

It is not clear exactly how the lot is used here, in the sense of what exactly is decided by it. Clearly Judah is given a large chunk of land in the south, and the Josephites (Ephraim and [half] Manasseh) a large area in the central hill country. The remaining seven tribes are then allocated land around these. In fact, it may be that it should be understood that the lot was used only for the seven tribes (Josh. 18, incl. v. 10).

Judah and Joseph (through Joshua) are also the two tribes whose representatives were faithful when the Israelites spied out the land (see Num. 13 – 14, esp. 13:30 and 14:6–9, 30). In other words, the allotments link back to the events of the book of Numbers (cf. also vv. 6–15 below). But they also link back to the book of Genesis, where the prominence of Judah and Joseph is already established (e.g. Gen. 37:5–11 and forward; Gen. 48; 49). It would of course be possible to think, as many do, that these stories reflect a later situation in which existing tribal territories and the power of the respective tribes are portrayed in the narrative and even told from the perspective of one particular tribe. It is certainly clear that the books of Judges–Kings are told from a Judahite perspective. However, here, as in Genesis, in addition to giving some substantial prominence to Judah, the role of Ephraim is emphasized strongly, and the book of Joshua otherwise has an all-Israelite perspective. One should also keep in mind that the southern part of the land received less rainfall and was thus less fertile than the central highlands, reflected in the fact that there was much less settlement in the south than in the central highlands in the Early Iron Age (see e.g. Finkelstein 1988). Overall, it is not clear that the book reflects the concerns of Judah so much that one can say that its original provenance is in Judah. This has bearing on the dating and setting of the book, as already discussed elsewhere in this commentary (see Introduction and Excursus 10).

The narrative reminds the reader that the authorization for the division of the land stems from Moses. This links back to the book of Numbers (e.g. Num. 34:13) which itself states that Moses' command stems from Yahweh (e.g. Num. 26:52–56). Similarly, and linking back to the book of Numbers, the allotment of the Transjordanian tribes is recapitulated, as is the status of the Levites.

4. The narrative reminds the reader/hearer that the Josephites consisted of two tribes, Manasseh and Ephraim, and again that no land was given to the Levites, except that now it is explicitly summarized that they would receive selected towns and their pasturelands (see Josh. 21). Considering that there were twelve tribes including Levi and Joseph, counting Levi out but then counting Joseph as two tribes via Ephraim and Manasseh keeps the total at twelve. Subtracting the two and a half tribes who have already received their inheritance in Transjordan gives a total of nine and a half Cisjordanian tribes to whom territory needs to be allotted. The comment about the Josephites dividing into two could be thought to be a later remark, but could also have been made from the start as a reminder.

5. A summary statement notes that all went as planned earlier. The plan itself stems from Yahweh's command. As ever, this is the ultimate divine legitimation for the tribal territories of Israel.

6a. The narrative next moves to describe Caleb's inheritance (vv. 6–15). As described above (see comments on vv. 2–3), Caleb and Joshua were the two faithful spies. With this narrative about Caleb and comments about him in 15:13–19, Caleb's prominence is emphasized. In fact, the Cisjordanian allotments are framed by the narrative about Caleb and Joshua's inheritances (14:6–15 vs 19:49–50). Caleb the Judahite gets more space in the allotments, but Joshua the Ephraimite is the overall leader in the book. In fact, here Caleb and the people of Judah are said to come to Joshua, with Caleb requesting his allotment from Joshua. In other words, Caleb and the Judahites are subservient to Joshua. It is also interesting that the request is said to take place at Gilgal, whereas Joshua 19:51 implies that the allotment took place at Shiloh, unless this pertains only to the seven remaining tribes, with the possibility of Judah and Joseph having been allotted at Gilgal. In the former case, considering that the events of the early chapters of Joshua are said to have taken place at Gilgal, one might think that the events of 14:6–15 took place earlier than the tribal allotments proper and are placed here for thematic and narrative reasons. In the latter case, there is more chronological ordering. Also in the former case, the relevant chronological understanding would reinforce the idea that lots were used only after Judah, Ephraim and Manasseh had received their inheritance (see comments on vv. 2–3 above), as one would expect that Caleb's inheritance should be in the territory of Judah. However, Caleb's stated age at the time of the request (see comments on v. 10 below) implies placing the request early in the overall narrative chronology.

6b–9. Caleb reminds Joshua about the events pertaining to Numbers 13 – 14, adding the detail about his age and about Moses' oath to him. As Nelson points out, Caleb's loyalty is mentioned twice here, and repeated once more in verse 15 (Nelson 1997a: 178).

10. Caleb notes that forty-five years have passed since the events at Kadesh Barnea. From a narrative perspective, bearing in mind that the Israelites spent forty years in the wilderness, this places the request about five years after the start of the conquest. This would seem rather early in the course of the conquest, as Joshua is portrayed as 'old and advanced in years' at the time of the allotments (Josh. 13:1). In other words, the implication clearly seems to be that Caleb, and probably Judah and Joseph, should be understood to have received their inheritance before the allotments proper as described in Joshua 13 – 21. This itself then attests to the relative prominence of Judah and Joseph in comparison to the other tribes of Israel in the narrative. But also, in general, the idea of Joshua's being 'old and advanced in years' may be a narrative device used for chapters 13 – 21 overall in order to telescope a window of time from before the time when Joshua was 'old and advanced in years' to a time after Joshua, even till the time of the writer of the first edition of the book.

11. Having noted that Yahweh has kept him alive, undoubtedly hinting at the fact that the rest of the wilderness generation died because of their rebellion (Num. 14), Caleb notes that his strength is still intact as it was when the events at Kadesh Barnea took place. This is obviously remarkable for a man of eighty-five, but perhaps the numbers here are not to be taken literally. The expression may also be a (proverbial) stock phrase that indicates that the person in question is still in good health (cf. Deut. 34:7).

12. Caleb has his eye on the hill country, apparently around Hebron (for the place, see comments on 10:3–5). He reminds Joshua that he saw the area at the time of the spying expedition from Kadesh Barnea (cf. Num. 13:22; 14:28). He is confident, or at least hopeful, that, with the help of Yahweh and his promises, he can drive the Anakites out, and, according to Joshua 15:14, succeeds in this (cf. the contrast with the fear of the Israelites in Num. 13, as pointed out by Nelson 1997a: 178). Note how Judges 1:10 attributes the success in the conquest of Hebron to the Judahites, which is looking at the same thing from a slightly different angle (cf. Younger's comments on such attribution of success to various people who are part of a collective effort; e.g. a general vs his troops [Younger 1990: 226]).

13–14. The request is granted. Joshua gives Hebron to Caleb. It is interesting to note that Caleb is said to be a Kenizzite in the book of Joshua (see also 14:6; Num. 32:12). At the same time, he is said to be a Judahite (Num. 13:6). Here it clearly seems that we have the assimilation of a non-Israelite into the tribe of Judah. In the context of the narrative, it appears that Caleb has a kind of 'dual citizenship'. While Caleb is portrayed as having been assimilated into Israel early, this nevertheless suggests that such assimilation was understood to have been possible. There may even have been many more examples (cf. e.g. Rahab in Josh. 6 etc.; cf. e.g. Judg. 3:5–6). This means that the distinction between Israel and others was in practice likely to have been less than what the book of Joshua (and Deut. etc.) advocates (see Pitkänen 2004b for a comprehensive treatment), with entry into Israel easier than some of the rhetoric of Joshua (and Deuteronomy) indicates.

The mention of Caleb's faithfulness in verse 14 seems to have a didactic flavour about it for the readers of the book of Joshua. Also, the formula 'until this day' gives a reason why Hebron belonged to the descendants of Caleb at the time of the writer of the episode, or the writer of the book as a whole. Interestingly, as Nelson points out, there seems to be movement of focus through the expressions of 'the land where Caleb has trodden' (v. 9; cf. Deut. 1:36), 'this hill country' (v. 12) and Hebron (vv. 13–14). Perhaps an originally grander claim is here limited in stages to a realistic actual holding (Nelson 1997a: 179). While the holding seems to include both the town and its environs, it seems to diminish just a bit more when Hebron is designated as a Levitical town (Josh. 21:11–12).

Joshua also blesses Caleb. As Nelson points out, blessings in the Old Testament have a special purpose and efficacy associated with them (Nelson 1997a: 179; cf. e.g. Gen. 27; 48 – 49). Covenants, including Deuteronomy, of course have blessings and curses included (cf. e.g. comments on 1:7 and 8:30–35).

15. The former name for Hebron is given, with a comment that it was based on one of the illustrious previous occupants of the city ('town of Arba', note that *'arba'* also means 'four' in Hebrew). It is often the case that new people who settle in a place give it a new name. A good example of this is North America, where European settlers have given new names to many of the places, occasionally retaining an original place name based on Native American nomenclature. For the Anakites in general, see comments on 11:21–22.

A note that the land had rest from war is given after the description of the allotment and conquest of Hebron. This should probably be taken as a general statement in the context of Joshua 11:23 and 21:43–45, and the tribal allotments as a whole (see comments on 11:23 above; cf. 21:43–45).

Explanation

Chapter 14 notes how the Israelites divided the land just as Yahweh had instructed them. A note about the lack of inheritance of the Levites is made in anticipation of the special provision given to them in chapter 21.

The narrative about Caleb shows how Yahweh has rewarded Caleb for his faithfulness to him, and kept his promises. He has let Caleb live when other Israelites of his generation (except for Joshua) died because of their faithlessness. Caleb was then given Hebron, and chapter 15 (esp. v. 14) shows how he actually succeeds in capturing the town. In a comparable way, Christians can trust in the faithfulness of Yahweh. And yet, in the context of the whole, the question of theodicy keeps coming to the fore.

JOSHUA 15

Translation

[1]The area of the tribe of Judah according to their families reached to the boundary of Edom, the wilderness of Zin at the far south.

[2]Their southern border started at the southernmost end of the Dead Sea. [3]It then went out south of the ascent of Akrabim, crossed over to Zin, went on from the south of Kadesh Barnea, crossed over Hezron, went on to Addar and then turned to Karka, [4]next crossed to Azmon, went on to the brook of Egypt and ended in the sea. This was their southern border.

[5]The eastern border was the Dead Sea to the mouth of the river Jordan.

The northern border started from the northern end of the sea at the mouth of the Jordan. [6]And the border went to Beth Hoglah and went on from the north to Beth Arabah. Then the border went to the stone of Bohan the son of Reuben. [7]And the border continued to Debir from the Valley of Achor and towards the north, turning to Gilgal which is over against the ascent of Adummim which itself is south of the valley. Then the border went on to the waters of En Shemesh and ended at En Rogel. [8]The border went on to the Valley of the Son of Hinnom at the southern flank of the Jebusites in Jerusalem. Then the border continued to the top of the mountain which faces the Valley of Hinnom westward, which itself is at the northern end of the Valley of the Rephaites. [9]The border then turned from the top of the mountain to the spring of the waters of Nephtoah and went out to the towns of Mount Ephron. The border then bent to Baalah, that is, Kiriath Jearim. [10]After this, the border turned westward from Baalah to Mount Seir and went on to the flank of Mount Jearim, that is, Kesalon, from the north. It then went down to Beth Shemesh and crossed over to Timnah. [11]And the border went out towards the north to the side of Ekron, then bent towards Shikkeron, crossed over Mount Baalah and went out to Jabneel. Finally, the border ended in the sea.

[12]The western border was the Mediterranean Sea. This was the area of the Judahites as a whole for their families.

[13]And Joshua gave an allotted portion to Caleb in the midst of the Judahites as Yahweh had command him: Kiriath Arba, that is, Hebron (Arba was the father of Anak). [14]And Caleb drove out the three sons of Anak from there, Sheshai, Ahiman and Talmai. [15]From there he went against the inhabitants of Debir. The former name of Debir was Kiriath Sepher. [16]Caleb said, 'For the one who strikes Kiriath Sepher and conquers it I will give Achsah my daughter as a wife.' [17]Othniel the son of Kenaz, Caleb's brother, conquered it, and Caleb gave him Achsah as a wife.

[18]When she arrived, she urged him to ask for a field from her father. When she got off her donkey, Caleb asked, 'What is the matter with you?'

[19]She replied, 'Give me something more because you have only given me a barren land. Give me some springs that have water!' And he gave her the upper and lower springs.

²⁰The following was the hereditary possession of the Judahites.

²¹The towns of the tribe of Judah were:

at the border with Edom in the far south, Kabzeel, Eder, Jagur, ²²Kinah, Dimonah, Adadah, ²³Kedesh, Hazor, Ithnan, ²⁴Ziph, Telem, Bealoth, ²⁵Hazor Hadattah, Kerioth Hezron (that is, Hazor), ²⁶Amam, Shema, Moladah, ²⁷Hazar Gaddah, Heshmon, Beth Palet, ²⁸Hazar Shual, Beersheba, Biziothiah, ²⁹Baalah, Iim, Ezem, ³⁰Eltolad, Kesil, Hormah, ³¹Ziklag, Madmannah, Sansannah ³²Lebaoth, Shilhim, Ain and Rimmon, a total of twenty-nine towns with their villages.

³³On the Shephelah, Eshtaol, Zorah, Ashnah, ³⁴Zanoah, En Gannim, Tappuah, Enam, ³⁵Jarmuth, Adullam, Socoh, Azekah, ³⁶Shaaraim, Adithaim, Gederah and Gederothaim, fourteen towns and their villages. ³⁷Zenan, Hadashah, Migdal Gad, ³⁸Dilean, Mizpah, Joktheel, ³⁹Lachish, Bozkath, Eglon, ⁴⁰Cabbon, Lahmas, Chitlish, ⁴¹Gederoth, Beth Dagon, Naamah and Makkedah, sixteen towns with their villages. ⁴²Libnah, Ether, Ashan, ⁴³Iphtah, Ashnah, Nezib, ⁴⁴Keilah, Akzib and Mareshah, nine towns with their villages. ⁴⁵Ekron with its towns and villages, ⁴⁶from Ekron towards the sea, everything that was by Ashdod and its villages, ⁴⁷Ashdod with its towns and villages, Gaza with its towns and villages, to the Brook of Egypt and the Mediterranean Sea.

⁴⁸In the hill country, Shamir, Jattir, Sokah, ⁴⁹Dannah, Kiriath Sannah which is Debir, ⁵⁰Anab, Eshtemoh, Anim, ⁵¹Goshen, Holon and Giloh, eleven towns and their villages. ⁵²Arab, Dumah, Eshan, ⁵³Janim, Beth Tappuah, Aphekah, ⁵⁴Humtah, Kiriath Arba, which is Hebron, and Zior, nine towns and their villages. ⁵⁵Maon, Carmel, Ziph, Juttah, ⁵⁶Jizreel, Jokdeam, Zanoah, ⁵⁷Kain, Gibeah and Timnah, ten towns with their villages. ⁵⁸Halhul, Beth Zur, Gedor, ⁵⁹Maarath, Beth Anoth and Eltekon, six towns with their villages. ⁶⁰Kiriath Baal, which is Kiriath Jearim, and Rabbah, two towns with their villages.

⁶¹In the wilderness, Beth Arabah, Middin, Secacah, ⁶²Nibshan, the Town of Salt and En Gedi, six towns with their villages.

⁶³The Judahites could not dislodge the Jebusites who were living in Jerusalem, and thus the Jebusites live among the Judahites in Jerusalem even now.

Notes on the text

1. Area: lit. 'lot' (*gôrāl*), Gr. 'border (*orion*)'. At the far south: or, 'towards the south from the border of Teman', but Teman may either mean an Edomite district or simply 'south'. Most translations take it as 'south', and I have followed them here.

2. Started at the southernmost end of the Dead Sea: lit. 'was from the end of the Salt Sea from the bay of the corner towards south'.

3. South of the ascent of Akrabim: Gr. 'opposite the ascent of Akrabim'. Akrabim: Engl. 'scorpions'.

4. Their: lit. 'your', but the Greek also reads 'their'.

5. Dead Sea: lit. 'Salt Sea'.

8. Jebusites in Jerusalem: lit. 'Jebusites (that is Jerusalem)'.

12. The Mediterranean Sea: lit. 'the great sea'.

13. Father: or 'forefather'. Kiriath Arba, that is, Hebron (Arba was the father of Anak): Gr. 'the town Arbok, the mother town (*mētropolis*) of Enak' (cf. 14:15).

14. The verse ends lit. 'Talmai sons of Anak'; i.e. Hebr. adds the 'sons of Anak' for a second time (using *yeled* rather than *ben* for 'son', however), even though this second addition of 'sons of Anak' is missing from Gr.

19. Lit. 'Give me a blessing because you have given me a desert. Give me springs of water!'

21. Verses 21–62 differ so much between Codex Vaticanus and Codex Alexandrinus that RAHLFS lists the two separately. I will comment only on selected differences between these versions and the MT here. Note that south is *neḡeb* in Hebrew, and the word 'Negeb' (or 'Negev') is often used about the desert area in southern Israel.

28. Biziothiah: Greek reads *komai autōn*, 'its villages', referring to Beersheba.

36. Gederah and Gederothaim: Greek reads 'Gederah and its dwellings' instead of 'Gederah and Gederothaim'.

40. Lahmas: or 'Lahmam', as many manuscripts read.

45. Towns: lit. 'daughters'.

46. Or, with a slightly different nuance, 'everything that was by Ashdod, and its villages'.

47. Towns: cf. note on verse 45. The Mediterranean Sea: lit. 'and the great sea and the border'. Note that there is a *qere* (i.e. Masoretic scribal note) with the reading of the word 'great' (*gāḏôl*), as it was (fairly clearly) written incorrectly (*gāḇôl*) in the text.

49. Gr. reads the verse, 'And Rennah, the town of writing (which is Debir)'.

59. Note that Gr. adds a number of other towns here: Tekoa, Ephratah which is Beth Lehem, Phagor (probably Peor), Etam, Koulon, Tatami, Sores (or Eobis), Kerem, Gallim (or Galem), Baithir (or Thether), Manocho, 'eleven towns and their villages'.

62. Town of Salt: LXX[B] reads 'towns (*poleis*) of Sodom'.

63. Even now: 'until this day'.

Form and structure

The structure of chapter 15 can be described as follows:

> Judah's allotment (vv. 1–63)
>> Judah's borders (vv. 1–12)
>>> Southern limits of Judah (v. 1)
>>> Southern boundary, east to west (vv. 2–4)
>>> Eastern boundary, south to north (v. 5a)

Northern boundary, east to west (vv. 5b–11)
Western boundary (v. 12)
The inheritance of Caleb and his daughter (vv. 13–19)
Caleb's inheritance at Hebron (vv. 13–14)
Caleb's daughter's inheritance
Conquest of Debir (vv. 15–17)
Giving of springs of water to Achsah, Caleb's daughter
(vv. 18–19)
Judah's towns (vv. 20–63)
Introductory statement (v. 20)
District 1: South, bordering Edom (vv. 21–32)
District 2: Shephelah 1 (vv. 33–36)
District 3: Shephelah 2 (vv. 37–41)
District 4: Shephelah 3 (vv. 42–44)
District 5: Shephelah 4 (vv. 45–47)
District 6: Hill country 1 (vv. 48–51)
District 7: Hill country 2 (vv. 52–54)
District 8: Hill country 3 (vv. 55–57)
District 9: Hill country 4 (vv. 58–59)
District 10: Hill country 5 (v. 60)
District 11: Wilderness (vv. 61–62)
Note about Jerusalem (v. 63)

The towns of Judah can be seen to divide into eleven districts. The Greek adds a further district at the end of verse 59, which would make a total of twelve districts (for details, see RAHLFS; Boling and Wright 1982: 380, 390–391; Noth 1953a: 99).

The narrative about Caleb is practically a direct continuation of Joshua 14:6–15 (as pointed out in Butler 1983: 185–186). Basically, the narrative has been slotted in between the boundary and town lists of Judah.

It can be noted that Joshua 15:28–32 has similarities to the list of the towns of Simeon in 19:1–9, and that, for example, Zorah and Eshtaol in 15:33 is repeated in Dan's town list in 19:41. The town list of Judah also has some similarity with the lists in 1 Chronicles 4:24–43 and Nehemiah 12. I will not try to speculate about the relationships between these lists here. Note however that, for the sake of the presentation of the lists, 19:1–9 could perhaps be thought to have repeated towns in Judah's list to emphasize the fact that Simeon's territory was allotted from that of Judah.

Finally, we note that, although it would be easy to date the town list of Judah to the period of the monarchy, surprisingly many sites, where they can be identified, have an earlier occupational history (see 'Comment' section below). And, whether or not the towns always fall exactly within the stated boundaries of Judah (cf. Nelson 1997a: 185–186) may not be all that important as, for example, a boundary list may reflect an idealized division, whereas the actual situation on the ground may have been slightly different, with the town lists reflecting that. Of course, the idea that the town and boundary lists date from different times is also one potential explanation. I will not attempt to be more specific here.

Comment

1. The allotment of Judah is described. It has by far the largest number of towns, indicating an emphasis on Judah in the lists. This would seem to fit with the idea that the town lists for Judah essentially derive from the period of the monarchy.

The border description starts from the southern part of the territory of Judah. It first notes the overall southern limit of Judah. Judah borders on the territory of Edom. Edom of course is related to Esau, the brother of Jacob in the narrative of Genesis, who loses his birthright to Jacob through deception (Gen. 27). The early Israelite tradition then places Esau in the area of Edom (Gen. 36; cf. Num. 20:14–21). From an archaeological perspective, until recently not much had been found in the area from before the seventh century BC that indicated a settled kingdom (see Edelman 1995). However, recently there has been some debate on the matter based on an article about the chronology of a copper-smelting site in the area, with this possibly serving as evidence of a state of Edom from the twelfth to tenth centuries on (see Levy, Adams, Najjar, Hauptmann, Anderson, Brandl, Robinson and Higham 2004, and the further discussion about the matter on http://www.wadiarabahproject.man.ac.uk, accessed 13 March 2007; updated 2009; cf. also Levy 2009). While it is hard to draw any conclusions about Edomite statehood in this sense, we can look at the matter in a slightly different way. We know that there were (Egyptian) copper mines at Timna in the Late Bronze Age (see Rothenberg 1972). In addition, Egyptian sources refer to the Shasu tribes in the area of southern Sinai during the Late Bronze Age, and during the nineteenth dynasty even to 'Shasu tribes of Edom' (see *ABD* 5: 1165–1167; Levy, Adams and Muniz 2004, including pp. 66–67; Levy 2009: 157). In other words, there were people groups inhabiting or interacting with the area of Edom. Speaking of the Shasu in particular, even if they were largely nomadic, one would expect them to have had their own political organization, and the leader of such a society might have been called a king (*melek*), and any Edomite kingship should be taken in this sense, not in a, say, medieval European or modern sense of kingship (and associated statehood) (cf. the comments in Kitchen 2003b: 196–197). It is also worth keeping in mind that nomadic peoples often leave behind little trace of themselves (see e.g. Levy, Adams and Muniz 2004: 68–71).

The wilderness of Zin is located around Kadesh (Kadesh Barnea), one of the main theatres of activity in the book of Numbers (e.g. Num. 20:1). It is one of the six or seven wildernesses (Shur, Etham, Sin, Sinai, Paran,

Zin and possibly Kadesh) crossed by Moses and the Israelites after the exodus (as noted in *ABD* 6: 1095). See also comments on 10:41.

2. The southern end of the Dead Sea is a clear landmark for the southern border in the east. Whether it was the extreme end of the Dead Sea or somewhat north(-west) of its southern tip is not quite clear from the Hebrew.

3. The ascent of Akrabim may be mentioned in Egyptian documents from the Late Bronze Age (see *ABD* 1: 141). Its exact location does not seem to be clear, even though it is usually identified with Naqb ets-Tsfar (see *ABD* 1: 141). For Zin, see comments on verse 1, assuming that the same place is referred to, although it may be about a specific place in the region here. For Kadesh Barnea, see comments on verse 1 above, and on 10:41. The location of Hezron is unclear (see *ABD* 3: 194). The location of Addar is unclear (see *ABD* 1: 70). The location of Karka is also unclear (see *ABD* 4: 6).

4. The location of Azmon is not known, although one candidate, Ain Muweilih, has revealed a station on the ancient road to southern Sinai that dates to the Iron I period (see *ABD* 1: 540). The Brook of Egypt, which at times features in biblical border descriptions (see e.g. 1 Kgs 8:65; 2 Kgs 24:7), is often identified with Wadi el Arish (some 50 miles (80 km) south-west of Gaza; see *ABD* 2: 321). Another candidate that has been given is Nahal Bezor (located near Gaza), and the location of the Brook of Egypt is (thus) not entirely certain (cf. *ABD* 2: 321). Finally, the southern border ends in the Mediterranean Sea.

5. The Dead Sea constitutes the eastern border. The northernmost part of the eastern border is the place where the river Jordan joins the Dead Sea. From this point, the northern boundary is then described, east to west.

6. The location of Beth Hoglah is unclear (see *ABD* 1: 687–688), although the name is apparently preserved in modern-day Deir Hajlah. But no remains from before the Byzantine period have been found there (see *ABD* 1: 687; cf. *ABD* 2: 496; Boling and Wright 1982: 366). The location of Beth Arabah is unclear, albeit that 'Ain El Gharbeh is often suggested (see *ABD* 1: 681). An interesting point here is that the place is listed as belonging to both Judah (15:61) and Benjamin (18:22). This has created speculation that the border between Judah and Benjamin was changeable and that the two listings reflect two different time periods (see *ABD* 1: 681). Be that as it may, the Hebrew in this verse (Josh. 15:6) can be translated to indicate that the border ran through Beth Arabah. The other possible verse that relates to the topic, Joshua 18:18, is somewhat ambiguous about the matter, as only the Greek text makes reference to Beth Arabah in the verse (see textual notes on the verse). If the border went through the town, it could have been counted as belonging to both Judah and Benjamin. And it would seem that the town would in any case have been very close to the border. Bohan is mentioned only here and in Joshua 18:17. His stone is likely to have been a reasonably prominent landmark, of which nothing more is known (see *ABD* 1: 772).

7. For Debir, see comments on 10:3–5. For the Valley of Achor, see comments on Joshua 7:26. For Gilgal, see comments on 4:1–7. The location of Adummim is unclear (see *ABD* 1: 86). Adummim is mentioned in Egyptian documents from the second millennium BC (list by Thutmose III, and Papyrus Anastasi, also a list of Pharaoh Sheshonk I from the tenth century BC), although they may refer to a different Adummim (see *ABD* 1: 86). En Shemesh (*en* = 'spring') is usually identified with Ein Haud (see *ABD* 2: 504; Boling and Wright 1982: 368). Already close to Jerusalem (see v. 8), En Rogel is generally located at Bir Ayyub ('Jacob's well'), near the junction of the Hinnom and Kidron valleys (see *ABD* 2: 503–504; Boling and Wright 1982: 368).

8. The Valley of Hinnom/the Son of Hinnom is located on the west and south sides of Jerusalem (see *ABD* 3: 202). For Jerusalem, see comments on 10:1. The Valley of Rephaim is located towards the south-west of Jerusalem (see *ABD* 5: 676). For the word *rĕpā'îm*, see comments on 12:4. For the Jebusites, see also comments on 9:1–2.

9. The location of the spring of the waters of Nephtoah has been suggested at present-day Lifta, some 3 miles (5 km) north-west of Jerusalem (see *ABD* 4: 1073). The 'waters of Nephtoah' (*mê neptôah*), if written as one word in Hebrew, approximates to Merneptah; in other words, the place name could be 'spring of Merneptah', the Egyptian pharaoh from whose preserved victory stele from about 1200 BC we famously know that he attacked the area of Palestine and claimed to have prevailed over a people called Israel (see Introduction).

The location of the towns of Mount Ephron is uncertain (see *ABD* 2: 558). For Baalah/Kiriath Jearim/Kiriath Baal, see comments on 9:17 and 15:60. Baalah appears to have been the older name (see *ABD* 1: 555; 4: 85). Note also the role of Kiriath Jearim in 1 Samuel 6:21 – 7:2 as the place where the ark was kept after its return from the land of the Philistines.

10. The location of Mount Seir is uncertain (*ABD* 5: 1072–1073). See also comments on 11:16–17. The location of Mount Jearim/Chesalon is uncertain, although it may be Kesla, some 12 miles (19 km) west of Jerusalem (see *ABD* 1: 900; 3: 652). Beth Shemesh has been identified with Rumeileh, just west of the Arab village of 'Ain Shems (see *NEAEHL*: 249). Occupation has been found from both the Late Bronze Age and Iron Age I, with evidence of Philistine pottery in the Iron Age I period (see *NEAEHL*: 249–250), highlighting the proximity of the town to the Philistine areas. Beth Shemesh features prominently in 1 Samuel 6:10–21 as the place where the ark was first returned after its stay in the land of the Philistines. There have also been recent excavations at Beth Shemesh; information about these can be accessed, e.g., via the Internet; see e.g. http://www.indiana.edu/~relstud/betshem/index.shtml (accessed

25 February 2009) and http://www.tau.ac.il/humanities/archaeology/ projects/proj_bethshemesh.html (accessed 25 February 2009), and through the *IEJ*. Timnah (different from Timna where there were Egyptian copper mines; cf. comments on 15:1) is generally identified with Tel Batash (see *NEAEHL*: 152). Tel Batash was occupied in the Late Bronze and Iron I Ages, with evidence of Philistine occupation in Iron I (see *NEAEHL*: 152–153). Timnah features elsewhere in the Old Testament, including the Samson narratives (Judg. 14).

11–12. For Ekron, see comments on 13:3. The location of Shikkeron is uncertain (see *ABD* 5: 1213). The location of Mount Baalah is uncertain, albeit it has been identified with the ridge of Mughar, north-west of Ekron (see *ABD* 1: 555). The location of Jabneel is uncertain (see *ABD* 3: 596). Finally, we meet the Mediterranean Sea as the end point of the northern border of Judah. The Mediterranean Sea also serves as the western border of Judah.

13–14. Verses 13–19 continue the story given in 14:6–15, having a parallel in Judges 1:10–15 (Judg. 1:10 attributes the conquest of Hebron more generally to the men of Judah, even though Caleb himself is directly mentioned in verses 11ff.; cf. comments in 'Form and structure' of Josh. 10). Verses 13–14 here are almost the same as 14:14–15, and, in addition to what I have commented on 14:14–15, we note that Arba is here said to be the father (or forefather) of Anak. The three sons of Anak are mentioned here, as in Numbers 13:22 and Judges 1:10. For the Anakites in general, see comments on 11:21–22. According to Na'aman, 'Ahiman, Sheshai and Talmai – whose names are non-Semitic, may have been members of a northern migrating group that settled at Hebron' (Na'aman 1994b: 240).

15. Debir is then conquered by Othniel, increasing the land holdings of the Calebites (cf. Nelson 1997a: 188). For Debir itself, see comments on 10:3–5. The text notes that the former name of the town was Kiriath Sepher. On the change of place names, see comments on 14:15.

16. The motif of a ruler giving his daughter to a valiant warrior is well known in folk tales, though this does not say anything about the historicity of the story here. But, if any of the candidates had wanted to marry the daughter of Caleb to start with, this would certainly have motivated them to do the job.

17. The text at first sight implies that Achsah was almost a commodity for her father, and literally speaking a trophy wife for Othniel. However, one must bear in mind that family relationships were very important in ancient Israel, and by giving his daughter to the conqueror of the city Caleb in reality made that person a close member of his family. Thus Caleb might have said, 'Whoever conquers Hebron will be part of my family.' Perhaps in giving his daughter to an able man he would also be looking for security for her. It should be noted that Achsah and Othniel were (apparently) cousins, and, in another sense, may already have been friendly before the 'transaction' mentioned.

18–19. Apparently, Caleb had given some land as a dowry for his daughter. However, this is not enough. Achsah wants more, a place where there is water available from the ground. This is especially relevant in an area that is desert or semi-desert (cf. Boling and Wright 1982: 375). Hence the request. There is a possible pair of wells near Khirbet Rabud, one candidate for the location of Debir (Boling and Wright 1982: 376; for Debir in general, see comments on 10:3–5). As Nelson points out, the word 'give' is repeated three times by Achsah, linking with a blessing of water (Nelson 1997a: 189). Also, as Nelson suggests, Achsah's dismounting from her donkey appears to be a sign of respect (cf. Gen. 24:64; 1 Sam. 25:23; Nelson 1997a: 189).

20. The scene now moves to a description of the towns of Judah. It can be seen to divide into eleven or twelve 'districts' (cf. Boling and Wright 1982: 377–379). I will refrain from detailed comments about the literary arrangement and historical background to the list; however, see related comments made in the 'Form and structure' section of this chapter, and in Excursus 10.

21. The first 'district' listed is located in the south, bordering the territory of Edom. For Edom, see comments on 15:1. The location of Kabzeel is unclear, albeit Tell Gharreh midway between Beersheba and Arad has been suggested (see *ABD* 4: 1). The location of Eder does not seem to be clear, even though it has been suggested that Eder may be a copyist's error for Arad (see *ABD* 2: 284; one LXX manuscript attests this reading, and it should be kept in mind that only consonants were written in Hebrew originally). The location of Jagur is unknown (see *ABD* 3: 611).

22. The location of Kinah is uncertain (see *ABD* 4: 39). The location of Dimonah is also uncertain (see *ABD* 2: 199–200). The same is true for Adadah (*ABD* 1: 60).

23. 'Kedesh' may be a variant form of Kadesh Barnea (see *ABD* 4: 11; Boling and Wright 1982: 382). This is very possible, as Kadesh Barnea is referred to as 'Kadesh' in a number of places (e.g. Num. 32:8 vs Deut. 1:46 in their context[s], and the consonants for 'Kedesh' are the same as those for 'Kadesh', bearing in mind that the Hebrew text of the Old Testament was originally consonantal). For comments on Kadesh Barnea itself, see commentary on verse 1 above, and on 10:41. If the reference is not to Kadesh Barnea, it seems that the location is unclear. The location of Hazor, which is not the famous Hazor in the north (e.g. Josh. 11:1), is unknown (see *ABD* 3: 88). The location of Ithnan is unclear (see *ABD* 3: 582).

24. The location of Ziph is unknown (see *ABD* 6: 1104). Ziph here does not seem to be associated with the wilderness of Ziph, which itself is associated with David (cf. *ABD* 6: 1104; see 1 Sam. 23:14ff.; 1 Sam. 26). See also comments on the Ziph of verse 55. The location of Telem is unknown (see *ABD* 6: 345). It may be the same as Telaim in 1 Samuel 15:4 (*ABD* 6: 345); however, the Hebrew consonantal spelling of each is different, with an additional aleph in Telaim. The location of Bealoth is unknown (see *ABD* 1: 628–629).

25. The location of Hazor Hadattah is unknown (see *ABD* 3: 88). The location of Kerioth Hezron, that is (another) Hazor (in this context; cf. also v. 23), is unknown (see also *ABD* 3: 88).

26. The location of Amam is unclear (see *ABD* 1: 171–172). The location of Shema is unknown (see *ABD* 5: 1197). The location of Moladah is unclear, even though it could be Khirbet el-Waten, north-east of Beersheba (see *ABD* 4: 895; Boling and Wright 1982: 382). The identification is made on the basis of both Moladah (Hebrew) and el-Waten (Arabic), referring to kinship and childbearing (*ABD* 4: 895).

27. The location of Hazar Gaddah is unknown (see *ABD* 3: 84). The location of Heshmon is unknown (see *ABD* 3: 184). The location of Beth Palet is unknown (see *ABD* 1: 691).

28. The location of Hazar Shual is unclear (see *ABD* 3: 84). Beersheba is generally located at Tell Beersheba, even though some have challenged this (*NEAEHL*: 168). Tell Beersheba was occupied in the Iron Age I and II periods, with Iron II the principal period with extensive settlement (see *NEAEHL*: 167–173). The location of Biziothiah is unclear, and, based on a similar list in Nehemiah 11:27 and the Greek text of Joshua 15:28, it has been suggested that it may be an error for *běnôtěyāh* (dependent villages [lit. 'daughters']) (see *ABD* 1: 753).

29. The location of Baalah here (not the same Baalah as in v. 9) is unclear, albeit Tulul el-Medbah has been suggested (see *ABD* 1: 555). The location of Iim is unknown (see *ABD* 3: 387). The location of Ezem is unclear (see *ABD* 2: 722).

30. The location of Eltolad is unclear (see *ABD* 2: 484). The location of Chesil is unclear (*ABD* 1: 900). For Hormah, see comments on 12:14.

31. Ziklag features in the narratives about David (see 1 Sam. 27:6; 30 etc.). Its identification is uncertain, but it is often thought to be located at Tell esh-Sharia, which was occupied from the Middle Bronze Age on (see *ABD* 6: 1090–1093). The location of Madmannah is unclear (see *ABD* 4: 462). Sansannah has been identified with Kirbet esh-Shamsaniyat (see *ABD* 5: 980), albeit this is probably again fairly uncertain.

32. The location of Lebaoth is not known (see *ABD* 1: 689–690). The location of Shilhim is unclear (see *ABD* 5: 1213). The location of Ain is unclear (see *ABD* 1: 131–132). The location of Rimmon is unclear, even though it may be Tel Halif from where remains from Iron I–II and also the Late Bronze Age have been found (see *ABD* 5: 773; see also Junkkaala 2006: 247–250, who however suggests that the site be identified with Hormah – see comments on 12:14). Some have suggested that Ain and Rimmon should be read together as En Rimmon (so *ABD* 5: 773; cf. Neh. 11:29; Ain and En have the same Hebrew consonants).

Finally, a total number of towns in the southern 'district' is given. The number does not tally completely with the number of towns suggested by the MT. This, among other things (see 'Form and structure' of Josh. 15), suggests that the town lists may well have been subject to corruption (and/or editing) during transmission.

33. Towns on the Judean Shephelah (Shephelah essentially refers to the areas on the lower slopes of the mountains/highlands if one descends from the east towards the Mediterranean Sea; see *ABD* 5: 1204 for detailed comments) are then listed. The location of Eshtaol, which features in the biblical narratives portraying early Israel (see Judg. 13:25; 18), is not clear, but it may be Khirbet Deir Shubeib (see *ABD* 2: 617). Note that Eshtaol is listed as belonging to the territory of Dan in Joshua 19:41. The (well-known) point is that this area was originally conceived as belonging to Dan, but owing to their migration (see Josh. 19:47; Judg. 18) was then granted to Judah. Zorah, which often features together with Eshtaol in the biblical narrative (see Judg. 13:25; 18), is often identified with Sar'a/Tel Zor'a (see *ABD* 6: 1168). The town appears to feature in the Amarna letters (*alu*ṣarḫa; EA 273, line 21) as a target of the attack of the *habiru* (cf. *ABD* 6: 1168; for the *habiru*, see Introduction). The location of Ashnah is uncertain (see *ABD* 1: 490). Note that there is another town with the same name in Joshua 15:43 (cf. Boling and Wright 1982: 384).

34. The location of Zanoah is uncertain, but it may be Khirbet Zanu, two miles (3 km) south-east of Beth Shemesh (see *ABD* 6: 1039). Iron Age pottery has been found on the surface of the site (see *ABD* 6: 1039). There is another town with the same name in Joshua 15:56. The location of En Gannim is not known (see *ABD* 2: 501–502). The location of Tappuah is unclear (see *ABD* 6: 319). Note that another Tappuah is mentioned in Joshua 16:8 (see *ABD* 6: 319–320). The location of Enam is not known (see *ABD* 2: 505).

35. Jarmuth is generally identified with Tel Jarmuth, even if the matter is not considered certain (see *NEAEHL*: 661). Remains have been found at the site from the Early Bronze Age in particular (see *NEAEHL*: 661–665), but soundings and surveys have also 'revealed traces of more or less continuous occupation from the Late Bronze Age II to the Early Byzantine period, including three Iron Age I strata' (*NEAEHL*: 665; Junkkaala 2006: 282–283 adds some detail based on the later publications of the excavator [de Miroschedji]). The excavator also suggests that the site was destroyed in the mid-eleventh century (*NEAEHL*: 665; *ABD* 3: 646; cf. Junkkaala 2006: 283). See also comments on 10:3–5. For Adullam, see comments on 12:15. Socoh could be located at Khirbet 'Abbad (see *ABD* 6: 99; cf. Junkkaala 2006: 209–210, who suggests Khirbet Shuweika erRas). Note that there are other places with the same name (cf. *ABD* 6: 99). For Azekah, see comments on 10:10. It may be mentioned in the conquest list of Thutmose III (see Junkkaala 2006: 148–149).

36. The location of Shaaraim is unknown (see *ABD* 5: 1148). The location of Adithaim is unknown (see *ABD* 1: 73). The location of Gederah is unclear (see *ABD* 2: 925). The location of Gederothaim is unclear, but, basically having a meaning of 'two enclosures', it may refer to Gederah, meaning 'Gederah and its two enclosures' rather than Gederah and Gederothaim. Or, if we follow the Greek, we get Gederah and its villages. If the two towns were to be read as one, we would also get the correct total of fourteen towns for the Shephelah district of verses 33–36. But there could also be another reason for the actual number of towns not equalling the total.

37. A second district in the Shephelah (cf. comments on v. 33 above) is now listed. The location of Zenan is not known (see *ABD* 6: 1074). The location of Hadashah is not known (see *ABD* 3: 13). The location of Migdal Gad is unclear, although Khirbet el Mejdeleh (which however has no evidence of occupation in the Iron Age) 4 miles (6.5 km) south-east of Lachish has been suggested (see *ABD* 4: 822).

38. The location of Dilean is not known (see *ABD* 2: 199). There are several locations called Mizpah (or Mizpeh) in the Old Testament (see *ABD* 4: 879–881 for a list with comments). The location of the Mizpah given here is unclear (see *ABD* 4: 880). The location of Joktheel is not known (see *ABD* 3: 935).

39. For Lachish, see comments on 10:3–5. The location of Bozkath is unknown (see *ABD* 1: 774). For Eglon, see comments on 10:3–5.

40. The location of Cabbon is unknown (see *ABD* 1: 797). The location of Lahmas (or Lahmam; see translation and textual notes section) is unclear (see *ABD* 4: 129–130), albeit Khirbet el-Lahm has been suggested by Boling and Wright as a possibility (see Boling and Wright 1982: 382). The location of Chitlish is unknown (see *ABD* 1: 911).

41. The location of Gederoth is unclear (see *ABD* 2: 925). The location of Beth Dagon is unclear (see *ABD* 1: 683). Note that there is a town with the same name in Joshua 19:27. The location of Naamah is unclear (see *ABD* 4: 967). For Makkedah, see comments on Joshua 10:10. The total number of towns given agrees with the actual number of towns listed.

42. Next we have a third district in the Shephelah (cf. comments on v. 33 above). For Libnah, see comments on 10:29–30. Ether is often identified with Khirbet el-Ater (see *ABD* 2: 645). Note that there is a town with the same name in Joshua 19:7. The location of Ashan is unclear (see *ABD* 1: 476). It is perhaps worth noting at this point that, as the parallel to Ain in the Levitical town list of 1 Chronicles 6:59 seems to be Ashan, and some Greek manuscripts read Asa for Joshua 21:16, some have suggested that the town in Joshua 21:16 should be Ashan rather than Ain (see *ABD* 1: 476–477). In addition, some have suggested that, mindful of possible confusion between Ashan and Ain in Joshua 21:16, Ashan should really be placed in 15:32 in the Judahite list, as this might fit better with its probable location based on the Simeonite lists in 19:7 and in 1 Chronicles 4:32 (see *ABD* 1: 476).

43. The location of Iphtah is unclear, even though modern Terqumiyeh has been suggested (see *ABD* 3: 445). The location of Ashnah is unclear, even though modern Idna, located some 6 miles (9.7 km) east of Lachish, has been suggested (see *ABD* 1: 490). Note that there is another town with the same name in Joshua 15:33. Nezib is identified with Khirbet Beit Nesib, albeit there is no evidence of occupation during a relevant time period (see *ABD* 4: 1104; Boling and Wright 1982: 387).

44. Keilah features in the David narratives (1 Sam. 23:1–14). It is generally identified with Khirbet Qila (see *ABD* 4: 13), and it has been suggested that it features in the Amarna letters (289, 290; see *ABD* 4: 13–14), although this does not seem to be all that clear if one compares the names of the towns in the respective documents. The identification of Achzib is unclear; Tell el-Beida is a good possibility (see *ABD* 1: 57). Note that there is another town with the same name in Joshua 19:29. Mareshah is generally identified with Tell Sandahanna (see *NEAEHL*: 948). Some remains have been found dating to Iron Age II (eighth century onwards), but most material relates to the Persian and especially Hellenistic periods (see *NEAEHL*: 948–957). The total number of towns given for the district equals the actual number of towns listed.

45–47. A list on the coast follows. For Ekron, see comments on 13:3. For Ashdod, see comments on 11:21–22. For Gaza, see comments on 10:41. All these towns are relatively close to the sea, as the verses imply. For the Brook of Egypt, see comments on 15:4. The list ends with a mention of the Mediterranean Sea. No totals of towns are given.

48. The list now moves to the Judean (southern) hill country. The location of Shamir is unclear. Khirbet es-Sumara has been suggested, but the site lacks evidence from the expected periods (see *ABD* 5: 1157). Jattir has generally been identified with Khirbet 'Attir (see *ABD* 3: 649–650). However, and even though the site is mentioned in association with David (1 Sam. 30:28), surveys have found evidence of occupation only from the eighth century on (see *ABD* 3: 650). If the identification is correct, this discrepancy may easily be due to the site's not having been excavated. Socoh is generally located at Khirbet Shuweikeh, an unexcavated site some 10 miles (16 km) south-west of Hebron (see *ABD* 6: 99), although it is not clear how certain this identification is. Note that there are other places with the name 'Socoh' in the Old Testament (see *ABD* 6: 99 for details).

49. The location of Dannah is unknown (see *ABD* 2: 37). For Debir, see comments on 10:3–5.

50. For Anab, see comments on 11:21–22. As regards Eshtemoh, as Boling and Wright (1982) note, 'the name survives at es-Semu'' (Boling and Wright 1982: 388). Should the identification be correct, it should be noted that the modern village of Eshtemoa' covers the ancient occupation, and there have been no real excavations, albeit a couple of vessels dated to the ninth–eighth century have been found there (see *ABD* 2: 617–618 for further details). The location of Anim is unclear (see *ABD* 1: 256).

51. As regards Goshen (note the similarity of name to the Egyptian land of Goshen, which features in the book of Exodus), Boling and Wright suggest that it could be located at ed-Dahariyeh (Boling and Wright 1982: 388). The location of Holon is unclear, although Khirbet 'Alin has been suggested by some (see *ABD* 3: 257; cf. Boling and Wright 1982: 388). The location of Giloh is unclear (see *ABD* 2: 1027). Note that there is a rather famous archaeological site near Jerusalem with the same name (see *ABD* 2: 1027–1028 for details). The total number of towns stated equals the number of towns listed.

52. Arab is generally located at Khirbet er-Rabiyeh, some 8 miles (13 km) south-west of Hebron, but it is not known whether there was occupation at the site in biblical times (see *ABD* 1: 321). Dumah may be located at the village of ed-Daumeh (see *ABD* 2: 240). The LXX (also) reads Rumah (cf. 2 Kgs 23:36), the location of which is unknown (see *ABD* 5: 82). The location of Eshan is unclear (see *ABD* 2: 615).

53. The location of Janim is unclear (see *ABD* 3: 638). Beth Tappuah is apparently mentioned in an inscription by Shishak (see *ABD* 1: 699; Junkkaala 2006: 219). The name appears to have been preserved in Taffuh, a modern village about 3 miles (5 km) west of Hebron (see *ABD* 1: 699), even though the identification is not by any means certain (see Junkkaala 2006: 219–220 for a discussion). The location of Aphekah is unclear, even though Khirbet el Hadah, from which Iron Age shards have been found, is a possibility (see *ABD* 1: 276).

54. The location of Humtah is not known (see *ABD* 3: 333). For Hebron, see comments on 10:3–5 and 15:13–14. The location of Zior is unclear (see *ABD* 6: 1103–1104). The total number of towns stated tallies with the actual number of towns listed.

55. Maon is generally identified with Tell Ma'in (see *ABD* 4: 512), some 8 miles (13 km) south of Hebron (see Boling and Wright 1982: 389). It also features in 1 Samuel 23:24–35 and 25:2. Carmel is identified with Khirbet el-Kirmil, some 7 miles (11 km) south of Hebron (see Boling and Wright 1982: 389). It features in narratives about David (see e.g. 1 Sam. 15:12; 25:2, 5, 7 etc.). The location of Ziph here (cf. v. 24) is not completely clear, but there are two places that attest the word Ziph some 4–5 miles (6.5–8 km) east of Hebron, Tell Zif and Khirbet Zif. No systematic excavations have been made at Tell Zif, which is generally thought to be the biblical site (see *ABD* 6: 1104). Ziph here may be connected with the wilderness of Ziph, which is associated with David (cf. *ABD* 6: 1104; see 1 Sam. 23:14ff.; 26). Juttah is often identified with Yatta, a modern village close to Hebron. No excavations, and very few surveys, have been done at the site (see *ABD* 3: 1135).

56. The location of Jezreel is unclear (see *ABD* 3: 850). Note that there is a town with the same name in Joshua 19:18, one that is more famously known in the Old Testament narrative. The location of Jokdeam is unclear (see *ABD* 3: 932–933). The location of Zanoah is unclear, albeit Khirbet Zanuta some 6 miles (9.7 km) south-west of Hebron has been suggested by some (see *ABD* 6: 1039). But there is no evidence of pre-Roman occupation from Khirbet Zanuta (see *ABD* 6: 1039). There is another town with the same name (Zanoah) in Joshua 15:34.

57. The location of Kain is unclear, although Khirbet Yaqin is suggested by Boling and Wright (1982: 389). The location of Gibeah is unknown (see *ABD* 2: 1007). Note that there are other towns called Gibeah in the Old Testament, including in Joshua 24:33, and Judges 19 – 20 (these two may be the same; see comments on Josh. 24:32–33). The location of Timnah is unclear (see *ABD* 6: 557). Note that there is another town called Timnah in Joshua 15:10. The total number of towns stated matches the actual number of towns listed.

58. The location of Halhul is unclear, albeit the name is preserved at modern Halhul, about 4 miles (6.5 km) north of Hebron (see *ABD* 3: 27). Beth Zur is generally located at Khirbet et-Tubeiqa, adjacent to Khirbet Burj es-Sur, which seems to have preserved the ancient name (see *NEAEHL*: 259). The evidence at Khirbet et-Tubeiqa suggests that the site was occupied during the Early Bronze Age at the earliest, but was unoccupied during the Late Bronze Age, then occupied during Iron Age I (eleventh century BC), and then relatively unoccupied until later in Iron Age II (see *NEAEHL*: 259–261). Gedor is generally located at Khirbet Jedur, which was inhabited after the Late Bronze period (see *ABD* 2: 925).

59. The location of Maarath is unclear, though some have suggested Khirbet Qufin, about 7 miles (11 km) north of Hebron (see *ABD* 4: 431). It has been suggested that Beth Anoth should be identified with modern Khirbet Beit 'Anun (see *ABD* 1: 681; Boling and Wright 1982: 390). The location of Eltekon is unclear, although Khirbet ed-Deir, some 5 miles (8 km) west of Bethlehem, has been suggested, with little archaeological evidence to show, however (see *ABD* 2: 484). Finally, a total of the number of towns in this group, or district, is stated, with the total of six agreeing with the actual number of towns given. Gr. adds a number of towns here; see textual notes on the verse.

60. Kiriath Jearim is generally identified with modern Tell el-Achar (see *ABD* 4: 84–85). There appear to have been no excavations. See also comments on 9:17 and 15:9. The location of Rabbah, which is not to be confused with Rabbah of the Ammonites, is unknown (see *ABD* 5: 600). A total of two towns is then given, as per the number of towns actually listed.

61–62. The final district is located in the wilderness, in the east, close to the Dead Sea (cf. Boling and Wright 1982: 392). For Beth Arabah, see comments on 15:6. The location of Middin is unclear, although Khirbet Abu Tabaq is one possibility (see *ABD* 4: 815). The location of Secacah is unclear, even though Khirbet es-Samrah is one possibility (see *ABD* 5: 1065). The location of Nibshan is also unclear, though Khirbet el-Maqari is a possibility (see *ABD* 4: 1104). Khirbet Abu Tabaq, Khirbet es-Samrah and Khirbet el-Maqari are Iron Age fortress farms that have been found in the Buqeiah Valley, and there is evidence of occupation from about the eighth century onwards at these sites (see Boling and Wright 1982: 392; *NEAEHL*: 267–269). The identification of the Town of Salt is unclear, but Khirbet Qumran, associated with the later famous Dead Sea Scrolls, is one possibility (see *ABD* 1: 1053; Boling and Wright 1982: 392). En Gedi is associated with a well-known oasis on the Dead Sea shore (see *ABD* 2: 502–503). En Gedi also features in the narratives about David (1 Sam. 23 – 24). Nearby Tell el-Jurn has yielded evidence of buildings from about 600 BC (see *ABD* 2: 502–503). The total number of towns is then stated, matching the number of towns listed.

63. This verse notes that the people of Judah could not conquer Jerusalem. While one can of course argue that a later author wanted to create an impression of antiquity by shaping the verse in this way, this statement seems to imply that it, and similarly, in essence, the surrounding narrative, was written before David conquered Jerusalem as attested by 2 Samuel 5:6–9 (cf. Judg. 19:10–12) The alternative tradition in Judges 1:5–9 suggests that the Judahites did conquer Jerusalem during the time of the conquest, although Judges 1:21 itself suggests that this did not result in a lasting grip on the town. It should be noted that Jerusalem was a border town (Josh. 15:8), and thus more properly part of the Benjaminite territory (Josh. 18:28). Therefore, it may be significant that Judah is blamed for the inability to conquer Jerusalem here, whereas Benjamin is blamed for it in Judges 1:21. As seems fairly clear (see Pitkänen 2004a; cf. Introduction and Excursus 10), the book of Judges was written from a strong Judahite perspective. However, as suggested in the Introduction to this commentary, the book of Joshua was in contrast written from an all-Israelite perspective, and the mention of Judah as not being able to conquer Jerusalem fits with the idea of no exclusive prominence for Judah (cf. e.g. 13:13, 16:10, 17:11–13 for criticism across the board in relation to the 'leading' tribes; cf. also 19:47). It is also interesting to note in this context that, if the book of Joshua originates from the time before the monarchy, the blame was not shifted away from Judah when the book was transmitted through Judah, as would seem likely to have happened at some point.

It appears that the name 'Jebus' was an alternative name for Jerusalem, as the name 'Jerusalem' is also attested from a much earlier time than the Israelite period (see comments on 10:1 for further details about Jerusalem).

Explanation

Chapter 15 describes the allotment of Judah in great detail in the present form of the book. Both a boundary list and a town list divided into districts are given. Judah's prominence here also reflects his prominence in a number of places in Genesis (including Gen. 49:8–12). It is also notable that Caleb, one of the faithful spies in the book of Numbers (Num. 14) comes from Judah, and he is in fact mentioned again in this chapter. It is however equally notable that even Judah does not succeed in everything, as the tribe are unable to conquer Jerusalem (Josh. 15:63). Certainly, Judah might already have had special significance at the beginning of the allotment process, even before they became particularly prominent and obtained kingship in the time of David.

JOSHUA 16

Translation

[1]The boundary of the Josephites went out from Jericho at the Jordan, east of the waters of Jericho to the wilderness. It went up from Jericho to the hill country of Bethel. [2]From Bethel it went to Luz and crossed over to Ataroth to the territory of the Arkites. [3]Then it went down towards the sea to the territory of the Japhletites and to the territory of Lower Beth Horon and to Gezer, and then ended in the sea.

[4]The tribes of Manasseh and Ephraim, the sons of Joseph, received their inheritance.

[5]The territory of the Ephraimites was divided according to their families. Their territory on the east was Ataroth Addar to upper Beth Horon. [6]The boundary then went out towards the west. Michmethath was in the north. And the border turned towards the east to Taanath Shiloh and crossed over it from the east side to Janoah. [7]The border then went down from Janoah to Ataroth and Naarah, reached Jericho and ended in Jordan. [8]From Tappuah the border went towards the sea to the brook of Kanah and ended in the sea. This was the allotted portion of the Ephraimites, [9]and all the towns and villages that went to the Ephraimites in the midst of the allotted territory of the Manassites.

[10]The Ephraimites could not drive out the Canaanites who lived in Gezer. These Canaanites live in the midst of Ephraim even now. However, they were put to forced labour.

Notes on the text

1. Note that the Gr. text has a fair bit of variation in the place names that relate to this chapter. We will not look into all of the details here, but the reader should be aware of the variation. Boundary: lit. 'the lot'. Gr. reads 'boundary' (*orion*), which corresponds to Hebr. *gĕbul* which is similar to 'lot' (*gôrāl*). 'The waters of Jericho' is missing in the Greek text.

2. LXX in essence equates Bethel and Luz.

5. Territory: lit. 'area of inheritance'.

6. Hebr. *hayyāmmāh hammikmĕtāt miṣṣāpôn* is difficult to translate. It could be translated either as above (towards the west. Michmethath was in the north), or as 'to the sea with Micmetah in the north' as some other translations do. See the commentary on the text for further comments.

10. Even now: lit. 'until this day'. However, they were put to forced labour: Gr. lacks this sentence. Instead, Gr. states (in continuation to 'even now'), 'until Pharaoh, the king of Egypt came up and took it and burnt it in fire, and massacred those Canaanites and Philistines who lived in Gaza, and gave it as a dowry for his daughter.'

Form and structure

This chapter can be structured as follows:

> The allotment of the Josephites (vv. 1–4)
> > The southern border of the Josephites, east to west (vv. 1–3)
> > Note about Ephraim and Manasseh (v. 4)
> The allotment of the Ephraimites
> > The southern border of Ephraim, east to west (vv. 5–6a)
> > The northern border of Ephraim, part 1, west to east
> > (vv. 6b–7)
> > The northern border of Ephraim, part 2, east to west (v. 8a)
> > Ephraimite towns (v. 9)
> > Note about Gezer (v. 10)

We must keep in mind that the amount of information is less than in the preceding chapter. There is no town list, yet the way verses 8 and 9 link may suggest that something has dropped out between them (Kaufmann 1985/1955: 57–59). Kaufmann even suggests that portions of the Galilean lists were intentionally abridged (Kaufmann 1985/1955: 59). Kaufmann's suggestion is supported by the fact that the Greek text has a fair bit of variation in the place names that relate to this chapter. That is, as two different textual traditions had their own version of the list, this suggests the possibility that the list was flexible and changed over time when the text was transmitted. The note about the inability of the Josephites to drive out Canaanites from Gezer in verse 10 is repeated in Judges 1:29.

Comment

1. The allotment of the people of Joseph is listed next. The southern boundary description starts from the Jordan at Jericho. It appears unclear exactly what the 'waters of Jericho' refers to (note that 'waters of Jericho' is missing in the Greek), albeit there are a couple of springs around modern Tel el-Jisr about 3.5 miles (5.5 km) north-west of Jericho that could be meant (see *ABD* 4: 969). The boundary then goes up to the mountains around Bethel, and to Bethel itself as the next verse indicates.

2. For Bethel, see comments on 12:16. Luz is here distinguished from Bethel in MT, whereas in other places (see Gen. 28:19; 35:6; Judg. 1:23; Josh. 18:13) it is equated with Bethel, with Luz being the former name. It is not clear why there is a difference here; in any case, if two towns are intended here, the implication is that they are adjacent to each other (cf. *ABD* 4: 420). The location of Ataroth is unclear, even though Khirbet ʿAtarah may be a possibility (see *ABD* 1: 510 and Boling and Wright 1982: 397–398). Iron I shards have been found at the site (see R. D. Miller 2003: 153). Note that there is another Ataroth in 16:7, and Ataroth Addar in 16:5 could possibly be the same as Ataroth here, although this is by no means clear (see *ABD* 1: 510; Boling and Wright 1982: 402–403; cf. Josh. 18:13). The Arkites feature most prominently in the narrative about Absalom's rebellion against David in 2 Sam. 15 – 17. Not much is known about them otherwise (cf. comments in *ABD* 1: 369). They may have been one of the ethnic groups that constituted the mosaic of the peoples of ancient Canaan.

3. The Japhletites are a further (possibly ethnic) group in the area (cf. comments on v. 2 above). Not much more is known about them (but cf. 1 Chr. 7:32–33, even though these seem to be unrelated). Beth Horon (see also Josh. 21:22, and cf. 2 Chr. 8:5–6) appears to be divided into Upper Beth Horon and Lower Beth Horon (see *ABD* 1: 688), and we are of course dealing with the latter here. For identification and finds, see comments on Joshua 10:10. For Gezer, see comments at the beginning of chapter 4, on Joshua 4:20 and on Joshua 12:12. Finally, the southern boundary ends at the Mediterranean Sea.

4. The description then moves on to delineate each of the territories of Ephraim and Manasseh, the two sons of Joseph (cf. Gen. 41:50–52; Gen. 48).

5. The location of Ataroth Addar is unclear (cf. comments on v. 2 above). For Beth Horon and Upper Beth Horon, see comments on Joshua 16:3 and 10:10. The border description could, roughly speaking, be an abbreviation of the border description in 16:1–3, especially if Ataroth Addar is the same as Ataroth (see comments on v. 2 above).

6. At first sight, the border behaves somewhat strangely here, and the text may well have been corrupted (cf. Boling and Wright 1982: 402). The expression *hāyamah hămĭkmetat mĭṣapon* is unclear in this context. Albeit the location of Michmethath is not clear (see *ABD* 4: 815), it is otherwise said to be close to Shechem in Joshua 17:7, and there thus seems to be a big jump geographically from Upper Beth Horon to Michmethath in the boundary description. Taanath Shiloh may be located at Khirbet Taʿna et-Tahta or Khirbet Taʿna el-Foqa, from both of which material relating to the pre-monarchic and monarchic periods has been found (see *ABD* 6: 290–291; R. D. Miller 2003: 190). Janoah may be located at Yanun or Khirbet Yanun nearby (see *ABD* 3: 640). Iron I and II material has been found at both sites, and there was an Iron Ia citadel at Khirbet Yanun, 'abandoned before the end of the twelfth century' (see R. D. Miller 2003: 195). Note that there is another town with the same name in 2 Kings 15:29.

7. The location of Ataroth here is unclear (cf. comments in *ABD* 1: 510 and Boling and Wright 1982: 397–398, 404; see also comments on v. 2 above). The location of Naarah is unclear (see *ABD* 4: 969). For Jericho, see comments on Joshua 2 and 6. The boundary then ends at the river Jordan.

8–9. Next follows a short boundary description westward from Tappuah on the northern side of the territory of Ephraim. For Tappuah itself, see comments on Joshua 12:17, assuming that the two towns are the same, which is very possible (cf. *ABD* 6: 320–321; Junkkaala 2006: 259). Note also that there is a further Tappuah in Joshua 15:34. Kanah is usually identified with Wadi Qanah, although this is not certain (see *ABD* 4: 5). The border section described in this verse then ends at the Mediterranean Sea. Verse 8 finishes off with a concluding summary about the territory of Ephraim. The text then (v. 9) refers to Ephraimite towns in the territory of Manasseh. However, no actual towns are listed, which makes one suspect that the text may have been corrupted and even that a town list has dropped out, albeit one cannot be certain.

10. The description of Ephraimite territory ends with the comment that they could not drive out the Canaanites who lived in Gezer. However, the Israelites were powerful enough to reduce them to forced labour. The text suggests that it was written before the Egyptian pharaoh captured Gezer in the time of Solomon and before Solomon himself rebuilt the town (1 Kgs 9:15–16). For further information about Gezer, see comments at the beginning of chapter 4 (vv. 1–7), on Joshua 4:20 and on Joshua 12:12. As Miller summarizes, lowland sites were typically much larger than those in the highlands, and had a material culture that was 'totally unlike that of the highlands' (R. D. Miller 2003: 143), and this provides some explanation for the difficulties that the Israelites had in conquering (or subjugating and/or integrating) sites that belonged to the lowland sphere.

Explanation

This chapter, together with chapter 17, describes the allotment of Joseph. The Josephites were divided into Ephraim and Manasseh, and the allotment for the former is described here. The lists are much less detailed than with Judah; nevertheless, the Josephites follow Judah in the order of presentation, and the allotment of Joshua the Ephraimite, the other faithful spy (Num. 14), later closes the allotments of the tribes (Josh. 19:49–50), even if this is still followed by the allotments of the Levitical towns in Joshua 21, which are, however, slightly different conceptually. In the Israelite tradition, Joseph himself was of course the man who led the ancestors of Israel to Egypt (Gen. 37ff.), and was spoken of favourably in Jacob's blessing (Gen. 49:22–26). However, a note of the failure of the Ephraimites to conquer Gezer is included, just as the failure of the Judahites to conquer Jerusalem is mentioned in Joshua 15:63.

JOSHUA 17

Translation

¹And the lot fell for the tribe of Manasseh, the firstborn of Joseph. To Makir, the firstborn of Manasseh and Gilead's father, was given Gilead and Bashan because he was a soldier. ²As for the rest of the Manassites and their clans, they were the descendants of Abiezer, Heleq, Azriel, Shechem, Hepher and Shemida, the other sons of Manasseh.

³Shelophadad the son of Hepher, the grandson of Gilead, the great-grandson of Makir, the great-great-grandson of Manasseh, did not have sons, but only daughters. His daughters were Mahlah, Noah, Hoglah, Milcah and Tirzah. ⁴They approached Eleazar the priest, Joshua the son of Nun, and the leaders and said, 'Yahweh told Moses to give us a hereditary possession among our brothers.' And he gave them a hereditary possession among their father's brothers according to the command of Yahweh. ⁵Ten districts were allocated to Manasseh, in addition to the lands of Gilead and Bashan which are on the east side of the Jordan. ⁶This is because the daughters of Manasseh received hereditary land from among their brothers, and the land of Gilead was for the rest of the descendants of Manasseh.

⁷The border of Manasseh spanned from Asher to Micmethath, which is by Shechem. And the border went south towards the inhabitants of En Tappuah. ⁸The land of Tappuah belonged to Manasseh, but Tappuah itself by the border of Manasseh belonged to Ephraim. ⁹And the border went to the brook Kanah. These towns belonged to Ephraim, south of the brook in the midst of the towns of Manasseh. Then the border of Manasseh went from the north of the brook and ended in the sea. ¹⁰Ephraim was in the south and Manasseh in the north. The sea was one of the borders that reached Asher in the north and Issachar in the east.

¹¹In Issachar and Asher, Beth Shan and its towns, Jibleam and its towns, the inhabitants of Dor and its towns, the inhabitants of En Dor and its towns, the inhabitants of Taanach and its towns, and the inhabitants of Megiddo and its towns, the third of which is Naphath, belonged to Manasseh.

¹²However, the Manassites were not able to possess these towns, but the Canaanites persisted in living in the area. ¹³Once the Israelites got stronger, they put the Canaanites to forced labour, but did not completely dispossess them.

¹⁴The Josephites said to Joshua, 'Why have you given us only one allotted portion even though we are a numerous people because Yahweh has blessed us thus far?'

¹⁵Joshua replied them, 'If you are a numerous people and the hill country of Ephraim is too small for you, go to the woodlands and clear land for yourselves there in the territory of the Perizzites and the Rephaites.'

¹⁶The Josephites then said, 'The hill country is not enough for us; and all the Canaanites who live in the lowlands, those in Beth Shan and its towns, and those in the Valley of Jezreel, have iron chariots.'

¹⁷But Joshua said to the people of Joseph, to Ephraim and to Manasseh, 'If you are numerous and your power is strong, you will not have only one allotment. ¹⁸The hill country will be yours, and you will clear its forests to their farthest ends, and you will drive out the Canaanites even though they have iron chariots and are strong.'

Notes on the text

1. Lot: Gr. reads 'boundary' (*orion*), which corresponds to Hebr. *gĕbul* which is similar to 'lot' (*gôrāl*; cf. 16:1). Fell: lit. 'was' in MT, but the reading 'fell' is also attested by another set of Hebrew manuscripts. The firstborn of Joseph: lit. 'because he was the firstborn of Joseph'.

2. The Hebrew for verses 1–2 reads slightly differently, but I have taken the essential meaning to be as translated.

4. Leader: lit. 'chief, prince' (*nasî*). He: presumably refers to Joshua. Them: masc., but presumably the daughters are meant.

5. Gr. reads 'And their lot fell from Anassa, and the plain of Labek from the land of Gilead, which is beyond the Jordan.'

6. Among their brothers: lit. 'among his sons', presumably referring to Manasseh.

7. Gr. reads 'And the borders of the sons of Manasseh were Delanath, which is before the sons of Anath, and it proceeds to borders, to Iamin and Iassib to the fountain of Thaphthoth.'

9. It seems that there is corruption here (following Kaufmann 1985/1955), and something, such as a list of towns, may be missing. Gr. reads for the first two translated sentences in the verse, 'And the border shall go to the brook Karana by Liba at the opposite of the brook of Iariel; the terebinth of Ephraim is in the midst of the town of Manasseh.'

13. Completely dispossess: infinitive absolute is used in Hebrew here (*wĕhôrēš lo' hôrîšô*).

14. Thus far: not included in Greek.

15. Hill country of Ephraim: Hebr. *har-'eprāyim*. The territory of the Perizzites and the Rephaites: not included in Greek. Have iron chariots and are strong: Gr. 'have choice horses and iron'.

16. Is not enough: Hebr. *lo'-yimmāṣē'*.

17. People: lit. 'house'.

18. To their farthest ends: lit. 'and its farthest ends will be yours'. Gr. reads for the verse 'Because you shall have wood, for there is wood, and you shall clear it, and it will be yours, whenever you shall have completely destroyed the Canaanites, for he has choice horses and iron; you however are stronger than they.'

Form and structure

This chapter can be divided as follows:

> The allotment of western Manasseh (vv. 1–13)
>> Note about the allotment of Makir in eastern Manasseh (v. 1)
>> Allotment of other (western) Manassite clans (vv. 2–6)
>>> Allotment of 'male' clans (v. 2)
>>> Allotment of Zelophehad, a 'female clan' (vv. 3–4)
>>> Summary (vv. 5–6)
>> The partial southern border of western Manasseh on the west side, east to west (vv. 7–8)
>> Note about Ephraim in the south and Asher and Issachar in the north and east (v. 10)
>> Western Manassite towns (v. 11)
>> Difficulties with conquering allotted western Manassite towns (vv. 12–13)
> The remaining task of the Josephites in conquering and utilizing their allotted land (vv. 14–18)

A main point to bear in mind regarding this chapter is that the amount of information is clearly less than for Judah in chapter 15. There is no real town list, yet the way verses 9–11 link may suggest that something has dropped out of the text around there (Kaufmann 1985/1955: 57–59). Kaufmann even suggests that this was done by a late Judahite editor (Kaufmann 1985/1955: 59). The note about Manasseh's inability to drive out the Canaanites in Beth Shan (cf. v. 16), Ibleam, Dor, En Dor, Taanach and Megiddo (including Naphath) in verses 11–13 is repeated in Judges 1:27.

The story of the daughters of Zelophehad also features in Numbers 26:33; 27:1–10; 36:1–12, where their case is introduced. The book of Joshua describes how what was agreed in the book of Numbers is carried out. It is interesting to note that most of the names of the daughters appear in the Samaria ostraca dated to the early eighth century BC (see Kaufman 1982). The ostraca consist of sixty-six pen-and-ink inscriptions on potsherds, recording delivery of wine and oil to the town of Samaria (see ABD 5: 921–925). Certainly, the occurrence of the names suggests that the tradition in Joshua 17 has a historical basis. Otherwise, while it is somewhat difficult to draw exact conclusions about the relationship of the list in Joshua with the Samaria ostraca, one might for example think that the names of the daughters are eponymic, i.e. have been created based on the towns or districts in question. If so, as women are mentioned, one might think that this could suggest a lower social status of the towns or districts in some respect. However, the towns or districts could also have been named (or renamed) based on the people settling in them, or, even if in some sense eponymic, the names of the towns or districts might have been left on record instead of the daughters who settled in the area in question. One should also note that Gilead (v. 1) could similarly be seen as eponymic, though in this case the reference is to a male. In other words, it seems that there are some intriguing possibilities about the relationship between the names of the daughters and the towns or districts bearing the same names in Samaria, but firm conclusions cannot easily be made. As for theological purposes, Budd notes that the regulations concerning the daughters can actually be seen to be about the inheritance of daughters and have a link to the levirate marriage (see Budd 1984: 301). The fact that both Numbers 27:1–10 and 36:1–12 are traditionally ascribed to P (see Budd 1984: 299–300, 388) again makes it very natural to think that the book of Joshua (here Josh. 17, of course) utilized priestly material in the composition of the book, fitting it to deuteronomic purposes. Noth thought that the material pertaining to the daughters of Zelophehad was part of a (later) priestly redaction (see Noth 1953a: 103), but such an explanation, while conceivable, seems much less elegant.

Comment

1. The allotted territory of the Manassites is then described. It does not seem clear why the fact of his being the firstborn is emphasized here. Otherwise, however, he is described as coming after Ephraim, as in Genesis 48 and in the order of allotted territory here. Makir, the firstborn of Manasseh, is said to be given Gilead, which is also the name of Makir's son. For Gilead as a territory, see comments on 12:2, 4; 13:11. For Bashan, see comments on 12:4. The geographical name 'Gilead' here is the same as the name of Manasseh's son Gilead. Either the territory was named after the son, or the son after the existing name of the territory (see comments on vv. 2–3 below), at least for the purposes of Israelite historiography. Otherwise, it is stated that the reason for allotting Gilead and Bashan to Makir was Makir's prowess in war.

2–3. Other clans of Manasseh are now named. The names are the same as in Numbers 26:29–32, except that Iezer is not mentioned here. It is intriguing that clans are only really mentioned for Manasseh. The case for Zelophehad is then rehearsed, having already been introduced in Numbers 27 and 36 (at least from a canonical perspective; cf. comments on v. 4 below). These women are told that they can possess the inheritance of their father in the absence of male heirs, but are to marry men from their own tribe so that the inheritance stays within that tribe. As discussed in the 'Form and structure' section, the intriguing point with this story is that a number of the names of the sons of Manasseh and daughters of Zelophehad are (apparently) the same as districts in the area of Manasseh mentioned in the Samaria ostraca. Tirzah is also mentioned in the book of Joshua as a city state conquered by Israel (see Josh. 12:24 and comments there; see also Milgrom 1989: 224). In addition, Shechem, a name which coincides with the well-known already-existing Canaanite town, is listed as a son of Gilead, which itself coincides with the name of a geographical area in Transjordan. For comments on the archaeology of Shechem, see commentary on verses 7–8 below. Similarly, Hepher, the grandfather of the daughters of Zelophehad, is listed as a town in Joshua 12:17 (see comments there) and Numbers 26:32. For the identification of Abiezer, Helek, Asriel, Shechem, Hepher and Shemida as districts, and for the identification of other towns mentioned in the Samaria ostraca, see Campbell 1991: 109–112 (cf. also *KAI* 1: 34 and *KAI* 2: 183–186). It is unlikely that this is all coincidence. While it is possible to consider these names as eponyms (see e.g. Milgrom 1989: 224), it might also be that the names reflect the early settlement of these areas, with the areas themselves becoming part of Israel, but the original names of the individuals and clans being lost from the tradition and replaced by the names of the localities where they existed beforehand; otherwise they could have been named by the settling individuals and their associated clans (it would seem less likely that any of the individuals and clans should be named after the already-existing names of the localities after moving there). Whatever the case, it would seem that one family received a fairly large area to settle, which in itself would raise the question of how it could populate and take care of such an area by itself. Bearing in mind that most of the localities that are described as conquered in the book of Joshua are not said to have been destroyed, it would seem possible that the Israelites simply took overall control of them and their inhabitants, who themselves attested to a highland culture (and probably language, even a number of customs) similar to that of the Israelites, and the relevant peoples would in this case eventually become part of Israel through incorporation and assimilation. In this connection, we may note that, for example, Caleb is said to have been a Kenizzite (see Num. 32:12), and yet he became an Israelite (e.g. Num. 13:6). In a wider sense, with the assumption that the conquest described in the book of Joshua took place, it is likely that, contrary to the ideology and injunctions of the book of Joshua (and Numbers and Deuteronomy), the Israelites incorporated and assimilated local peoples after entering the land of Canaan and establishing a foothold there (cf. also Judg. 3:5–6). Not all these peoples would have been incorporated into Israel early, of course, as the case of Jerusalem shows (cf. Josh. 15:63 and comments on the verse; see also Pitkänen 2004b for further details on issues relating to assimilation).

4. The comments in this verse most naturally refer to Numbers 27 and 36 as they present themselves as recording the implementation of previous promises.

5–6. The number ten here is (apparently) the result of adding five daughters of Zelophehad in verse 3 to five sons (descendants) of Manasseh in verse 2, excluding Hepher, who is counted as five through his grand-daughters (see also Boling and Wright 1982: 412). The total number excludes Gilead and Bashan, which are located east of the river Jordan.

7–8. A part of the southern boundary of Manasseh is described next. It is a reflection of the northern border of Ephraim in 16:6–8. The location of Asher is unclear (cf. Boling and Wright 1982: 409, who emend the text to refer to something other than a place name). For Michmethath, see comments on 16:6. Shechem, a famous place in the biblical narratives (including Josh. 24), is identified with Tell Balatah (see *NEAEHL*: 1345–1346). The site was occupied in the Chalcolithic and Early Bronze Ages at the earliest, and was occupied during the Late Bronze and Early Iron (also Iron II) Ages (see *NEAEHL*: 1347–1353). For En Tappuah in verse 7, which may be the same as Tappuah in verse 8 and in 16:8, see comments on 16:8 and 12:17. Verse 8 notes that the land of Tappuah belonged to Manasseh, while the town itself belonged to Ephraim.

9. For the brook of Kanah, see comments on 16:8. Next follows an apparently slightly cryptic reference to towns around the brook that belong to Ephraim in the Manassite territory, and it may be that something has been corrupted here in the original text (see also textual note on the verse about the Greek text). The boundary then goes north of the brook and ends at the Mediterranean Sea.

10–11. After a further note about the sea, reference is also made to Asher and Issachar in the north and east. This serves as a connector to towns in the territory of Asher and Issachar. No further details are given about the northern border of Manasseh, albeit both Asher and Issachar have boundary descriptions listed separately (see Josh. 19:17–31 and comments on these verses for details). There then follows, however, a list of towns that the Manassites owned in the midst of Issachar and Asher but could not conquer (see below, vv. 12–13; cf. Judg. 1:27 for the list). Beth Shan is located at Tel Beth Shean fairly close to the river Jordan in the lowlands. A large tell occupied from a very early period, it was a Canaanite centre controlled by the Egyptians in the Late Bronze Age and retained its Canaanite character well into the Iron Age (see *NEAEHL*: 214–223 for details; see also Junkkaala 2006: 126–129, 187–190). The biblical data also acknowledge the Canaanite character of the place (see v. 16; Judg. 1:27). According to the biblical material, Beth Shan had entered the Israelite sphere by the time of Saul and David (see 1 Sam. 31:10, 12; 2 Sam. 21:12), and is listed as a centre of one of the administrative districts of Solomon (see 1 Kgs 4:12). Ibleam is generally identified with Khirbet Bel'ameh (see *ABD* 3: 355), a highland site located some distance south-east of Taanach, and has apparently not been excavated. It is mentioned as a royal town in Egyptian archives and is also included in the conquest lists of Thutmose III (fifteenth century BC; see *ABD* 3: 355; cf. Junkkaala 2006: 148). For Dor, see comments on 11:1–3. The location of En Dor is unclear (see *ABD* 2: 499–501), albeit the town is famously mentioned in 1 Samuel 28 as the site where Saul consulted a medium before his death. For Taanach, see comments on 12:21. For Megiddo, see comments on 12:21.

12–13. The text notes that the Israelites could not conquer the towns listed in verse 11, but could control them and their inhabitants when they grew stronger. This would seem to fit with the archaeology of Beth Shan (see comments on vv. 10–11 above).

14–18. The comment here reflects the fact that by far the largest number of new settlements was in the central and northern hill country in Iron Age I (see e.g. Finkelstein 1988). Ultimately, any forests were cleared over the course of many centuries, even if the extent of forests at the time of the settlement may not have been quite as large as has sometimes been thought, but was rather concentrated more towards the western slopes and foothills (cf. Finkelstein 1988: 200; note that Finkelstein thinks that Josh. 17:14–18 reflects not the initial but a later phase of the Israelite settlement when these forests started to be cleared, from a later stage of Iron I on). Iron was already in use before the start of the Iron Age proper; at the same time, it was not used extensively even in Iron Age I (cf. comments in Dever 2003: 117–118). The comment on the lowlands having iron chariots would seem entirely possible as the lowlands quite clearly seem to have been more connected internationally than the highlands, including being in the Egyptian sphere during the Late Bronze Age and until about 1150 BC. A technological advantage in warfare in the hands of the opposition would obviously make conquest and subjugation more difficult. For the Perizzites, see comments on 3:9–13. For the Rephaim, see comments on 12:4. As Nelson points out, in these verses, Joshua turns the complaint of the Josephites about the large number of people on a small patch of land on its head. Their large numbers are actually a strength, and can make it possible for them to clear the forests and even conquer the Canaanites in the lowlands (Nelson 1997a: 204).

Explanation

This chapter, together with chapter 16, describes the allotment of Joseph. The Josephites were divided into Ephraim and Manasseh, and the allotment for the latter is described here (Cisjordanian part). As with chapter 16, the lists are much less detailed than for Judah; nevertheless, the Josephites follow Judah in the order of presentation, and the allotment of Joshua the Ephraimite, the other faithful spy (Num. 14), later closes the allotments of the tribes (Josh. 19:49–50; even if this is still followed by the allotments of the Levitical towns in Josh. 21, which are, however, slightly different conceptually). In the Israelite tradition, Joseph himself was of course the man who brought the ancestors of Israel to Egypt (Gen. 37ff.), and was spoken of favourably in Jacob's blessing (Gen. 49:22–26). Interestingly, the Manassites include clans whose names seem to link with geographical entities. The daughters of Zelophehad are the case in point in this chapter, which describes western Manasseh. In the context of the chapter, the daughters of Zelophehad are receiving a share of land under a special order from Yahweh through Moses.

The chapter concludes with a mention of the difficulties that the Josephites encountered with the conquest. This reflects Israel's overall ability to dominate the hill country and their difficulties with the lowlands. Nevertheless, there is optimism from Joshua that the lowlands can also be conquered, in addition to settling the hill country, which offers fewer problems, even if there are still some.

JOSHUA 18

Translation

[1]The whole assembly of the Israelites gathered at Shiloh. They set up the Tent of Meeting there, and the land was subdued before them. [2]However, there were still seven tribes within Israel who had not received their allotted portion.

[3]And Joshua said to the Israelites, 'Till when will you delay taking possession of the land which Yahweh, the God of your fathers, has given you? [4]Select now three men from each tribe. I will send them to traverse the land and to record it for the allotments before returning to me. [5]Divide it into seven portions, with Judah staying in its territory in the south and the house of Joseph in its territory in the north. [6]And you, divide the land into seven portions and then return to me here. I will then cast lots for you all here in the presence of Yahweh. [7]No hereditary portion will be assigned to the Levites from among you because Yahweh's priesthood is their share, and Gad, Reuben and half of Manasseh have already received their share from the east side of the Jordan, given to them by Moses.'

[8]Accordingly, the men departed, with Joshua having instructed them, 'Go through the land and record it and return to me. I will then cast lots for you in the presence of Yahweh at Shiloh.' [9]The men went and traversed the land. They recorded its towns in a book based on seven divisions of the land. They then returned to Joshua at the encampment of Shiloh. [10]And Joshua cast lots in the presence of Yahweh at Shiloh and divided the land for the Israelites there, to each one their share.

[11]The lot came up for the Benjaminites according to their clans. Their territory was between the Judahites and the Josephites. [12]The northern side of the territory started at Jordan. The border went past Jericho from the north side and then westward towards the hills, ending in the wilderness of Beth Aven. [13]From there the border went towards Luz, to the side of Luz towards the south (that is, Bethel). Then the border went down to Ataroth Addar past the hills that are south of Lower Beth Horon.

[14]Then the border made a change of course towards the western end, south from the hill which is on the south side of Beth Horon. The westernmost end was Kiriath Baal, that is, Kiriath Jearim, the town of the Judahites.

[15]The southern side started from the outskirts of Kiriath Jearim, and the border went westward to the spring of the waters of Nephtoah. [16]Then the border went down to the outskirts of the mountain that faces the Valley of Ben Hinnom which itself is on the north side of the Valley of Rephaim. It went down to the Valley of Hinnom, southward to the shoulder of the Jebusites, and then down to En Rogel. [17]It curved from the north and progressed to En Shemesh, then went on to the territory which is over against the ascent of Adummim, and then went down to the stone of Bohan, Reuben's son. [18]After that, it crossed over to the northern side of Arabah and then went down to Arabah. [19]From there, it crossed to the northern flank of Beth Hoglah, and terminated at the place where the Jordan runs into the northern end of the Dead Sea. This was the southern border. [20]The Jordan was their eastern border. This concludes the border description of the allotted portion of the Benjaminites.

[21]The towns of the Benjaminites were Jericho, Beth Hoglah, Emek Keziz, [22]Beth Arabah, Zemaraim, Bethel, [23]Avvim, Parah, Ophrah, [24]Chephar Ammoni, Ophni and Geba, twelve towns and their villages. [25]Gibeon, Ramah, Beeroth, [26]Mizpah, Chephirah, Mozah, [27]Rekem, Irpeel, Taralah, [28]Zela Haeleph, Jebus which is Jerusalem, and Gibeath Kiriath, fourteen towns and their villages. This was the allotted portion of the Benjaminites.

Notes on the text

6. Divide: lit. 'record' (Hebr. *kātab*), as in verse 4. In Hebr., 'lot' is in singular, also verses 8, 10.

   7. East side of Jordan: lit. 'beyond Jordan towards the east'.

   9. The encampment of Shiloh: not included in Gr.

   10. And divided the land for the Israelites there, to each one their share: Not included in Gr.

   13. Past: lit. 'on' (Hebr. *'al*).

   15. Westward: MT reads 'westward' here as indicated, but this does not seem to fit the context, unless a slight detour from the general eastward direction is somehow described (Gr. reads 'to Gasin'). Kiriath Jearim: Gr. reads Kiriath Baal.

   16. Shoulder: or, 'side'.

   17. En Shemesh: Gr. reads Beth Shemesh.

   18. To the northern side of Arabah: Greek reads 'through the back of Beth Arabah from the north'. Gr. omits Arabah and Beth Hoglah in verses 18–19.

   19. Dead Sea: lit. 'Salt Sea'.

   22. 18:22 – 19:45 differ enough between Codex Vaticanus (LXX[B]) and Codex Alexandrinus (LXX[A]) for RAHLFS to list the two separately. I will make comments only on selected differences from the MT.

   26. Note that LXX[B] in particular considerably diverges from MT in verses 26–27, reading 'Massema, Miron, Amoke, Phira, Kaphan, Nakan, Selekan, Thareela'.

28. Gibeath Kiriath: Some corruption is likely with Gibeath Kiriath (see comments on the verse). LXX^A reads 'Gabaath and towns of Iarim', and LXX^B reads 'Gabaothiarim'. Fourteen: LXX gives a total of thirteen.

Form and structure

The structure of chapter 18 can be described as follows:

> The setting of the Tent of Meeting at Shiloh (v. 1)
> Introduction to the allotment of the seven remaining tribes of
>   Benjamin, Simeon, Zebulun, Issachar, Asher, Naphtali
>   and Dan (vv. 2–10)
> Allotment of Benjamin (vv. 11–27)
>   Introductory statement (v. 11)
>   Northern and north-western border, east to west (vv. 12–14)
>   South-western and southern border, west to east (vv. 15–19)
>   Eastern border (v. 20)
>   Towns of Benjamin (vv. 21–28)
>   District 1 (vv. 21–24)
>   District 2 (vv. 25–28)

Chapter 18 is part of a larger entity of Joshua 18 – 19, which describes the allotments of the remaining seven tribes. The importance of Shiloh is highlighted (see Excursus 10 for details). The order of the allotments is basically from south to north, even though Benjamin comes first here rather than Simeon (which follows Benjamin in Josh. 19:1–9). In general, one may keep in mind that the order of listing tribes is not constant in the tribal lists (see above, Excursus 10 for details).

The allotment of Benjamin is quite detailed, both in terms of its boundary and in terms of towns that are divided into two districts. This fits with the idea that it was updated during the time of the divided monarchy within the southern entity consisting of Judah and Benjamin. And yet, interestingly, Simeon (Josh. 19:1–9), which certainly lay in the southern kingdom, within Judah, does not have a border description.

That the allotment for the rest of the tribes follows the allotment of Judah, Joseph and the Transjordanians may at least generally reflect a somewhat later settlement of those areas by the Israelites, as hinted at by Hawking (2007: 301–302). In other words, this would at least broadly speaking fit with the idea that Israel was at first confined to the hill country, which is attested both by the biblical text (e.g. Josh. 17:11–13, 16–18; 19:47) and the archaeological record (see e.g. Introduction).

Comment

1. The Israelites are described as setting up the Tent of Meeting at Shiloh. The Tent of Meeting was the 'house' of Yahweh, where he dwelt in the midst of the people of Israel (Exod. 29:43–45; cf. comments on 3:3–4), and Joshua 22 implies that the writer of Joshua thought that Shiloh was an exclusive place of worship at that time. Deuteronomy, chapter 12 in particular, speaks about an exclusive place for sacrifices. The injunctions about sacrificing only at an exclusive central sanctuary are in force when the people have had rest from their enemies and live safely (Deut. 12:8–12; see Pitkänen 2004a for further details and detailed argumentation). The present verse in its context of the latter part of the book of Joshua implies that the required condition of peace has now been obtained (Josh. 11:23; 14:15), albeit the peaceful state of affairs should undoubtedly be taken as a general and relatively approximate statement. With overall peaceful conditions achieved, the Tent of Meeting now serves as an exclusive central sanctuary for the Israelites in a deuteronomic sense. For the importance of the setting-up of the Tent of Meeting in the context of Joshua from a literary perspective, see Excursus 10.

Shiloh is generally identified with Tell Seilun. According to Finkelstein (1988: 206; cf. Finkelstein 1993a: 1–4), the identification of Tell Seilun with Shiloh is very plausible because of the directions in Judges 21:19, because of a reference to the location in the fourth-century AD *Onomasticon* of Eusebius and because of the name (Seilun) of the village that stood at the site until the sixteenth century AD and of the adjacent spring. Also, according to Finkelstein (1988: 206), 'the excavated remains accord with the history of Shiloh as reflected in the written sources' (see below for further details). One should however note that Richardson (Richardson 1927), based on the variations in spelling of the name Shiloh in the Old Testament, intriguingly suggested that there were originally two Shilohs, Tell Seilun and Beit Sila, and that Beit Sila, which is located in the territory of Benjamin fairly close to Jerusalem, was the location of the Tent of Meeting. Richardson was bluntly rejected by Albright (Albright 1927 in the same issue of PEFQS as Richardson), and the matter has not been raised since (see Schley 1989: 67–68; cf. Finkelstein 1993a: 4).

Archaeological finds at Tell Seilun indicate that Shiloh was an important centre in Iron Age I (See Finkelstein 1986; 1988: 205–234; 1993c). Extensive remains from Iron Age I were found virtually everywhere that was excavated. Buildings, stone-lined silos and other remains were discovered from the period (Finkelstein 1986: 36). As for the regional settlement pattern, the survey by Finkelstein and his companions indicated that population density in the immediate vicinity of Shiloh was two and even three times greater than at other places in the territory of Ephraim. Some 100 sites of Israelite settlement were found in the survey, of which twenty-two were apparently within a radius of about 3–4 miles (5–6.5 km) of Shiloh.

By comparison, in a similar radius around Bethel, only twelve sites from Iron Age I were discovered; moreover, it seems clear that at least half of the settlements near Shiloh began in a later phase of Iron Age I when the site reached its zenith. According to Finkelstein, it is clear that the density of population in the region was influenced by Shiloh as the cultic and economic centre (Finkelstein 1986: 40).

Shiloh was also apparently at least a religious centre in the Late Bronze Age. According to Finkelstein:

> Data from all over the tell indicate that there was no real settlement at Shiloh during the Late Bronze Age. Instead, on the summit of the tell, there was probably an isolated cultic place to which offerings were brought by people from various places in the region. The fact that there were very few permanent Late Bronze sites anywhere in the vicinity of Shiloh may indicate that many of these people lived in pastoral groups, in temporary dwellings. It is probable that these offerings, many of them Late Bronze I (15th century B.C.) in date, were brought to the site of the destroyed Middle Bronze Age sanctuary, which may even have been reconstructed. The steadily declining amount of pottery indicates a decrease in activity at the site, and then a complete cessation, apparently before the end of the Late Bronze Age. (Finkelstein 1986: 35–36)

Iron II remains from Shiloh are less prominent. According to Finkelstein, a small village occupied the site in Iron Age II (tenth–eighth centuries BC), and a few structures were found immediately to the north of the tell from the end of the Iron Age (see Finkelstein 1986: 41 and 1988: 228). In relation to Shiloh, one may further note here the rock-hewn altar that has recently been found in the close vicinity, even though the altar is undated (see Hawking 2007: 200–203).

Since Wellhausen, it has been suggested that the Tent of Meeting is a late priestly fiction, in line with a late development of a priestly cultus (system of worship) in ancient Israel. However, there are reasons to consider that the Tent of Meeting and its associated cult may have a historical basis (see also Introduction for further details). First of all, parallels from the Hittite realm indicate a full-fledged priestly cult in Anatolia in the second millennium BC (see esp. Weinfeld 2004: 34–63). Also, there were clearly links between peoples in the Ancient Near East, even in the second millennium. Such links are attested for example by the Amarna letters, and by cuneiform documents found in Israel from the second millennium BC (see Horowitz, Oshima and Sanders 2006), which indicate links with the Assyro-Babylonian realm. There is also evidence of considerable Hurrian migration towards the south, including Ugarit and Canaan, around the end of the Middle Bronze Age and during the

Late Bronze Age (see van Soldt 2003 and Na'aman 1994a and 1994b), and one should keep in mind here that the Hurrians bordered the Hittites (they also bordered the Assyrians, and seemingly controlled them for a time during the Late Bronze Age; see Kuhrt 1995: 293). All this then suggests that the concept of a full-fledged cult as described in Leviticus–Numbers is nothing special or unexpected for ancient Israel at the time.

In addition, Kitchen (1993; see also Kitchen 2003b: 274–283; Hoffmeier 2005: 193–222) has given a good number of parallels that suggest a Late Bronze context for the Tent of Meeting. Structures, or descriptions of structures comparable to the Tent of Meeting, with beams and curtains, have been found from Egypt from both the third and the second millennium BC, including the time of the New Kingdom during the Late Bronze to Early Iron Ages (Kitchen 1993: 119–121). Kitchen also notes the qĕrāšîm, or 'frames', and the likely sacrificial action of King Keret in a tent in Ugaritic texts from the fourteenth/thirteenth centuries BC and the evident tent sanctuary at Timna during the twelfth century BC (Kitchen 1993: 121; see Rothenberg 1972 for details about Timna, and Weinfeld 2004: 41 for more details about tent sanctuaries; see also Pitkänen 2004a: 141–142). Kitchen further notes that the basically rectangular form of the Hebrew camp in Numbers resembles rectangular Egyptian camps in the thirteenth century BC, and, in fact, there are no known examples of rectangular camps from the first millennium (Kitchen 1993: 123). Kitchen further notes the duality of duties of cultic personnel in Hittite instructions (Kitchen 1993: 124; see also Weinfeld 2004: 58). The rituals also have their parallels in the Ancient Near East (see Kitchen 1993: 125–126; and Weinfeld 2004: 42–57).

For further comments relating to the function of the Tent of Meeting, see Excursus 3. Cf. also comments on 9:21–27.

2–8. With Judah, Ephraim, Manasseh, Reuben and Gad having received their allotments and with the Levites excluded from the count, seven tribes still remain to receive their share. Joshua gives orders to send surveyors across the land in preparation for the allotment. Lots will also be cast as part of the process. It appears to be Joshua himself who casts the lots here (vv. 6, 8, 10; cf. 14:1–2; 19:51).

9–10. Joshua's orders are carried out, and the men return with a description of the land according to its towns. Lots are then cast. It is not clear exactly what the expression 'in the presence of Yahweh' means. It may refer to being in the vicinity of the ark, the sanctuary as a whole, or, even though probably less likely, to a general attitude towards Yahweh. The narrative in verses 9–10 progresses through repetition of what has already been said in verses 2–8, which is typical for the Hebrew literary style, even if it may be less exciting for some modern readers.

11. The inheritance of Benjamin is described first among the seven remaining tribes. The territory is located between Judah and Ephraim as the southern one of the two Josephite tribes. According to the biblical documents, Benjamin, the ancestor of the Benjaminites, was the second son of Rachel, Jacob's favourite wife (Gen. 29; 35:16–20), the first son being Joseph (Gen. 30:22–24; cf. Gen. 35:24).

12. The northern boundary (which corresponds to the southern border of Ephraim) begins at Jordan. For Beth Aven, see comments on 7:2.

13. For Luz/Bethel, see comments on 16:2 and 12:16. For Ataroth Addar, see comments on 16:2. For Lower Beth Horon, see comments on 16:2.

14. For Beth Horon, see comments on 16:3. For Baalah/Kiriath Jearim/Kiriath Baal, the western end of the northern boundary, see comments on 9:17, 15:9 and 15:60. The border description explicitly states that Kiriath Baal belongs to Judah.

15. The southern border (which corresponds to the northern border of Judah) is then described, starting from the western end from where the northern border ends. For the spring of the waters of Nephtoah, see comments on 15:9.

16. For the Valley of Hinnom/the Son of Hinnom, see comments on 15:8. For the Valley of Rephaim, see comments on 15:8. For the Jebusites and for Jerusalem, see comments on 9:1–2, 10:1. Note however that reference to Jebusites here rather points towards an early date for the border description, as the Jebusites (or at least Jerusalem as a Jebusite stronghold) were conquered by David. For En Rogel, see comments on 15:7.

17. For En Shemesh, see comments on 15:7. For Adummim, see comments on 15:7. For the stone of Bohan, see comments on 15:6.

18. For Arabah/Beth Arabah, see comments on 15:6. For Arabah 'proper', see comments on 12:8.

19. For Beth Hoglah, see comments on 15:6. The southern border of Benjamin then ends at the place where the river Jordan meets the Dead Sea.

20. The river Jordan (as far as Jericho) forms a natural eastern border for the Benjaminites. The description is concluded by a summary statement.

21. A town list for the tribe of Benjamin follows, in two parts or 'districts' (vv. 21–24 and 25–28). For Jericho, see comments on chapters 2 and 6, and Excursus 5. For Beth Hoglah, see comments on 15:6. This border town is listed as belonging to Benjamin. The location of Emek Keziz is unclear (see *ABD* 2: 496).

22. For Arabah/Beth Arabah, see comments on 15:6. The location of Zemaraim is unclear, albeit Ras et-Tahuneh is a possibility (see *ABD* 6: 1074). Junkkaala mentions Iron I and Iron II pottery finds from the site (see Junkkaala 2006: 209). For Bethel, see comments on 12:16.

23. As Avvim is used as a designation of a people group elsewhere in Joshua (see 13:3 and comments on the verse), it can be tempting to think of the usage here as gentilic as well (see e.g. Boling and Wright 1982: 430–431; *ABD* 1: 530). One can then speculate that the reference is to some place in the vicinity of Bethel or Parah, as commentators have done (see e.g. Boling and Wright 1982: 430–431; *ABD* 1: 530). However, the location is ultimately not clear, that is, of course, if the reference here is to a location. Also, the localization of the Avvim in Deuteronomy 2:23 and in Joshua 13:3 clearly seems different from here, even though they could perhaps be found in more than one place or area. The location of Parah is uncertain, albeit Tell Fara some 6 miles (9.7 km) north of Jerusalem has generally been suggested (see *ABD* 5: 155). Remains from both Iron I and II have been found at the site (see R. D. Miller 2003: 150). The location of Ophrah (not the same Ophrah as in the Gideon stories of Judg. 6ff.) is uncertain, but et-Taiyibeh has been suggested (see *ABD* 5: 27; see also Junkkaala 2006: 140–141, who suggests 'Afula from which evidence from both Late Bronze I and Iron Age I has been found). Iron I shards have been found at the site, also Iron II (see R. D. Miller 2003: 189).

24. The location of Chephar Ammoni is unclear (see *ABD* 1: 898). The location of Ophni is unclear (see *ABD* 5: 27; cf. Boling and Wright 1982: 431). For Geba, see comments on 24:32–33. A summary count of the number of towns in the first 'district' is given, with the total tallying with the number of towns actually listed.

25. For Gibeon, see comments on 9:3. Ramah appears to have been Samuel's birthplace (1 Sam. 1:19), albeit a different Ramah could also be meant (cf. *ABD* 5: 613). The town is usually identified with er-Ram (see *ABD* 5: 613). Iron I material has been found at the site, also Iron II (see R. D. Miller 2003: 181). For Beeroth, see comments on 9:17. It should be noted that Gibeonite towns are listed as part of Benjamin (cf. 9:17), suggesting the close association of the Gibeonites with the Israelites. It appears that the Gibeonites were assimilated to Israel, even already at an early stage (cf. 1 Kgs 3:4, 2 Chr. 1:3 and of course Josh. 9).

26. There are several places named Mizpah (or Mizpeh) in the Old Testament (see *ABD* 4: 879–881 for a concise summary). Assuming that there is only one Mizpah/Mizpeh in Benjamin, the location features fairly prominently in the Old Testament narrative (esp. Judg. 19 – 21; 1 Sam. 7; Jer. 41). The identification of Mizpah/Mizpeh is uncertain. The most likely candidate that has been suggested is Tell en Nasbeh. The site was originally occupied in the Chalcolithic and Early Bronze I periods as 'a small village', then from Iron I on into the Hellenistic period (see *NEAEHL*: 1098–1102; see also R. D. Miller 2003: 176–177). For Chephirah, see comments on 9:17. The location of Mozah is unclear (see *ABD* 4: 925–926; cf. Boling and Wright 1982: 431).

27. The location of Rekem is unclear (see *ABD* 5: 665). The location of Irpeel is unclear (see *ABD* 3: 462). The location of Taralah is also unclear (see *ABD* 6: 320).

28. The location of Zela Haeleph is not really known (see *ABD* 6: 1072). Sometimes Zela and (Ha)Eleph ('Ha' is the Hebrew definite article) have been seen as separate names, especially as that would help towards obtaining a count of fourteen for the group of towns in verses 25–28. However, it seems more natural to consider them as a compound name as there is no waw (lit. 'and') between Zela and (Ha)Eleph, whereas having the waw would be normal between names in town lists, and the compound 'Zela Haelef' means 'the rib of an ox' (similarly *ABD* 6: 1072). This said, Zela Haelef could be the same place as Zela in 2 Samuel 21:14 (so *ABD* 6: 1072), with the latter name of course an abbreviation of the former. Note that Jebus/Jerusalem is depicted as a border town between Judah and Benjamin (see Josh. 15:8). As Kallai (1958: 146–148; cf. Peterson 1977: 294–295) points out, a town may occupy a territory, even a reasonably considerable one. Thus, even if the border strictly speaking leaves the town of Jerusalem itself to Benjamin, when one considers the possibility of territories outside a town proper, Jerusalem could be a 'true' border town between Judah and Benjamin (v. 16 in Hebr. can be read thus). For more on Jebus/Jerusalem, see comments on 9:1–2; 10:1 and 15:63. What the compound Gibeath Kiriath refers to is not clear. Some corruption is likely (cf. textual notes). However, Gibeah as such means 'hill', and it has been suggested that Gibeath Kiriath could be a reference to the 'hill of Kiriath Jearim', and the LXX supports this possibility (see *ABD* 2: 1007; see also textual notes). However, one cannot be certain. For the various occurrences of the place name 'Gibeah' in the Old Testament, see *ABD* 2: 1007–1009, and see also comments on 24:32–33. For Kiriath Jearim, see comments on 9:17 and 15:60. With the compounds Zela Haelef and Gibeath Kiriath, the total number of towns is twelve rather than the fourteen given in the summary of the total count in this verse. LXX gives a total count of thirteen. Some corruption and/or confusion is likely. As already implied, it has been suggested that someone counted Zela, Haelef, Gibeath and Kiriath as distinct and thus gave a total of fourteen (so *ABD* 6: 1072). This is very possible, but other explanations can also be brought forward; e.g. a couple of towns might have dropped off the list somewhere.

Explanation

The setting-up of the Tent of Meeting at Shiloh was an important milestone for the Israelites. A sufficient foothold had been obtained in the land, and Shiloh could thus be established as a central sanctuary (cf. Deut. 12, esp. v. 10; and see Pitkänen 2004a for a detailed treatment of this motif; cf. also comments on 11:23). The promises of Yahweh had thus been fulfilled in many respects. At the same time, there was still much work to do (cf. also 13:1–7 vs 11:23). The allotment of the land had not yet been completed for all tribes, and this and the following chapter effect that (chapters 20 – 21 can also be included in this). Whichever way the lot was taken, its decision was believed and trusted to come from Yahweh (cf. Prov. 16:33, and cf. comments on 7:14–18).

The allotment of Benjamin is described in the latter part of the chapter, with much detail given to both the border description and the towns, which are divided into two districts. Benjamin himself was seen as the second son of Jacob by Rachel, his favourite wife (Gen. 35:16–20; cf. Gen. 29 – 30; cf. also comments on v. 11), and thus dear and appreciated in the Israelite tradition.

Much of the overall thrust of this chapter may perhaps be taken to assure the Christian that God will fulfil his promises. At the same time, the achievement of promises is not to be construed as a passive process, but is to be pursued actively in line with God's will, in whichever way it is possible to determine what that will is. A modern Christian may perhaps be wary of using lots or corresponding means to make decisions, although it is noteworthy that the method was still utilized in the early church (see e.g. Acts 1:26 in the context of Acts 1:12–26).

JOSHUA 19

Translation

[1]The second lot fell to the tribe of Simeon. Their allotted portion was within the territory of Judah.

[2]The following towns were located within their inheritance: Beersheba, Sheba, Moladah, [3]Hazar Shual, Balah, Ezem, [4]Eltolad, Bethul, Hormah, [5]Ziklag, Beth Marcaboth, Hazar Susah, [6]Beth Lebaoth and Sharuhen, thirteen towns with their villages. [7]Ain Rimmon, Ether and Ashan, four towns with their villages. [8]And all villages which were around these towns up to Baalath Beer and Ramath Negev. This was the allotted portion of the Simeonites. [9]The inheritance of the Simeonites was given from within the inheritance of the Judahites because the portion of the Judahites was larger than necessary.

[10]The third lot fell to Zebulun. Their border reached Sarid. [11]The border then went up westwards to Mareal, reached Dabbesheth, and reached the brook which is by Jokneam. [12]Then it turned eastward from Sarid to the border of Chisloth Tabor, went forward to Daberath and then up to Japhia. [13]From there it went eastward to Gath Hepher and Eth Kazin and continued to Rimmon, curving towards Neah. [14]The border went around it from the north to Hannathon and ended at the Valley of Iphtahel. [15] . . . and Kattath, Nahalal, Shimron, Idalah and Bethlehem, twelve towns and their villages. [16]This is the allotted portion of the Zebulunites, the above towns and villages.

[17]The fourth lot fell for Issachar. [18]Their territory included Jezreel, Chesulloth, Shunem, [19]Hapharaim, Shion, Anaharath, [20]Rabbith, Kishion, Ebez, [21]Remeth, En Gannim, En Haddah and Beth Pazzez. [22]Then the border reached Tabor, Shahazumah and Beth Shemesh. It ended at Jordan, sixteen towns and their villages. [23]This was the allotted portion of the descendants of Issachar by their towns and villages.

[24]The fifth lot fell on the tribe of Asher. [25]Their border included Helkath, Hali, Beten, Achsaph, [26]Allammelech, Amad and Mishal. Then it reached Carmel and

Shihor Libnath in the west [27]and turned at the east side of Beth Dagon and reached Zebulun and the Valley of Iphtahel from the north side of Beth Emek and Neiel and went on to Cabul from the northern side [28]and to Ebron, Rehob, Hammon, Kanah, and as far as Great Sidon. [29]Then the border turned to Ramah and to the fortified town of Tyre, turned to Hosah and ended at the sea. Mahalab, Achzib. [30]Ummah, Aphek and Rehob, twenty-two towns and their villages. [31]This was the inheritance of the Asherites, these towns and their villages.

[32]The sixth lot fell on the tribe of Naphtali. [33]Their border ran from Heleph, from the oak at Zaanannim, to Adami Nekeb and Jabneel and to Lakkum. It then ended at Jordan. [34]The border turned towards the west to Aznoth Tabor, went on from there to Hukkok, and touched Zebulun from the south and Asher from the west. Jordan was part of Judah in the east. [35]The fortified towns were Ziddim, Zer, Hammath, Rakkath, Kinnereth, [36]Adamah, Ramah, Hazor, [37]Kedesh, Edrei, En Hazor, [38]Yiron, Migdal El, Horem, Beth Anath and Beth Shemesh, nineteen towns and their villages. [39]This was the allotted portion of the tribe of Naphtali, their towns and villages.

[40]The seventh lot fell on the tribe of Dan. [41]The territory of their allotted portion included Zorah, Eshtaol, Ir Shemesh, [42]Shaalabbin, Aijalon, Ithlah, [43]Elon, Timnah, Ekron, [44]Eltekeh, Gibbethon, Baalath, [45]Jehud, Bene Berak, Gath Rimmon, [46]Me Jarkon and Rakkon, together with the territory that faces Joppa. [47]However, this territory was lost by the Danites. Subsequently, the Danites went and fought against Leshem and conquered it. They killed its people, took the town for themselves and settled there. They called Leshem Dan according to the name of their forefather. [48]The above was the inheritance of the tribe of Dan, the named towns and villages.

[49]The Israelites also gave an allotted portion to Joshua among them after they had finished allocating the land. [50]Based on the command of Yahweh, they gave him a town which he had requested, Timnath Serah in the hill country of Ephraim. He built up the town and settled there.

[51]The foregoing were the allotted portions that Eleazar the priest, Joshua the son of Nun and the heads of the tribes of Israel assigned by lot at Shiloh in the presence of Yahweh at the entrance of the tent of meeting. And they finished dividing the land.

Notes on the text

1. 18:22 – 19:45 differ so much between Codex Vaticanus (LXX[B]) and Codex Alexandrinus (LXX[A]) that RAHLFS lists the two separately. I will only make comments on selected differences from the MT.

2. Sheba: Gr. 'Sama'. Greek has otherwise either adapted the spellings (as usual) or sometimes used something slightly different in this whole section. Also, some translations take Sheba as an alternate name for Beersheba.

6. Thirteen: the total does actually come to fourteen (cf. the following note).

7. Four: the total comes to three here (cf. previous footnote). At the same time, it should be noted that most translations take Ain and Rimmon as separate towns, which brings the total to four.

8. Baalath Beer and Ramath Negev: the Hebrew reads in essence 'to Baalath Beer Ramath Negev'. It is somewhat difficult to determine what the word divisions are; hence differing translations take the entity in a slightly different manner.

9. Larger than necessary: Hebr. *rab mēhem*. The Hebrew then goes on with, 'And the sons of Simeon inherited from within their (referring to the Judahites) inheritance.' But this is typical Hebrew repetition and I have left it out here as it does not add any new information.

10. Note that, again, Gr. has some different readings for Zebulun's borders.

12. Eastward: 'eastward towards the rising of the sun'.

13. Eastward: cf. note on verse 12.

15. This verse suggests corruption in the Hebr. text. Gr. lists only the five place names of the verse and omits the statement about the total.

18. This may also start off as a border description. Corruption is also possible, so that what starts as a border description turns into a list of towns (and back to the border in v. 22).

22. There seems to be corruption here, as the number of towns does not tally with the list of the border towns. Even so, it matches with the total number of towns listed as a whole for Issachar.

28. The Targum and some Hebr. manuscripts read 'Abdon'.

29. Mahalab: Hebr. reads 'Mehebel', but it is usually transliterated as 'Mahalab'. Mahalab, Achzib: The text is a bit unclear here; it could also be 'from Hebel to Achzib'.

30. Some corruption seems to have taken place in verses 29–30, as the border description is suddenly followed by the names of at least three towns (five towns if one excludes Mehebel and Achzib from the border description in v. 29; see previous note) and then a total count of twenty-two (which does not tally with the total number of towns listed in vv. 25–30).

34. This sentence is odd and suggests corruption (it is also difficult to translate). LXX omits the mention of Judah here.

35. The fortified towns were Ziddim, Zer: Gr. reads 'And the fortified towns of the Tyrians, Tyre'.

41. Territory: could also be translated as 'border'.

46. Me Jarkon: Engl. 'waters of Jarkon'. Rakkon is not included in Gr.

47. Forefather: lit. 'father'. LXX reads for verses 47–48:

> This is the inheritance of the tribe of the children of Dan according to their families; these are their towns and villages. And the children of Dan did not drive out the Amorites who pressed on them in the mountains. And the Amorites would not allow them to come down into the valley, but they forcibly took

from them the border of their portion. And the sons of Dan went and fought against Lachish and took it and struck it with the edge of the sword. And they dwelt in it and called its name Lasen-Dak. And the Amorites continued to dwell in Elom and Salamin, and the hand of Ephraim was heavy on them, and they became tributaries to them.

50. Based on the command of Yahweh: lit. 'According to the mouth of Yahweh' (*'al-pî yĕhwāh*).

Form and structure

The structure of this chapter can be described as follows:

    Allotment of Simeon (vv. 1–9)
       Introductory statement (v. 1)
       District 1 (v. 2–6)
       District 2 (v. 7)
       'Border' towns (v. 8a)
       Concluding comments (vv. 8b–9)
    Allotment of Zebulun (vv. 10–16)
       Southern boundary of Zebulun, west to east from Sarid
          (vv. 10–11)
       Southern boundary of Zebulun, east to west from Sarid
          (vv. 12–14)
       List of Zebulunite towns (v. 15)
    Allotment of Issachar (vv. 17–23)
       List of towns (vv. 18–21)
       Southern boundary of Issachar, west to east (v. 22)
    Allotment of Asher (vv. 24–31)
       Border of Asher, east to west and then north (vv. 25–29)
       Asherite towns (vv. 29c–30)
    Allotment of Naphtali (vv. 32–39)
       Southern border of Naphtali, east side, west to east (v. 33)
       Southern border of Naphtali, west side, east to west (v. 34)
       Towns of Naphtali (vv. 35–38)
    Allotment of Dan (vv. 40–48)
       Original towns of Dan (vv. 41–46)
       Later conquest of Leshem/Dan and removal there (v. 47)
    Joshua's allotment (vv. 49–50)
    Conclusion of allotments west of the Jordan (v. 51)

It can be noted that the list of towns for Simeon in Joshua 19:1–9 has similarities to the list of the towns of Judah in 15:28–32, and that, for example, Zorah and Eshtaol in 19:41 are repeated in Judah's town list in 15:33. Note also that there is no boundary description, only a list of towns divided into two districts. I will not speculate about the relationships of these lists here. We note however that, for example, for the sake of the presentation of the lists, 19:1–9 could be thought to have repeated towns in Judah's list to emphasize the fact that Simeon's territory was allotted from that of Judah, although this is fairly tentative.

It should also be noted that the movement of the Danites (v. 47) is described in greater detail in Judges 17 – 18. Both accounts agree with each other. This, and the fact that the materials state that the Danites had to move away from their original location, suggests an early date for the list of Danite allotments. We should also note that a couple of the towns listed for Dan are also listed as belonging to Judah in Joshua 15.

The order of the allotments in the chapter is basically from south to north; note however that, among the seven remaining tribes in Joshua 18 – 19, Benjamin (18:11–28) comes first rather than Simeon (19:1–9). In general, one may also keep in mind that the order of listing tribes is not constant in the tribal lists (see above, Excursus 10 for details).

Comment

1. The narrative now moves to describe the allotment of Simeon. The text notes that the allotment of Simeon was in the midst of the allotment of Judah. Verse 9 explains that the portion of Judah was particularly large, and thus some territory within it was given to Simeon.

2. For Beersheba, see comments on 15:28. The location of Sheba is unclear (see *ABD* 5: 1170). A possible link with Beersheba just before, or with Shema in 15:26, and possible related corruption of the text or place names has been suggested (see *ABD* 5: 1170). For Moladah, see comments on 15:26.

3. For Hazar Shual, see comments on 15:28. For Balah, see comments on 15:28, assuming this is the same as Baalah – if not, no more seems to be known about the site. For Ezem, see comments on 15:29.

4. For Eltolad, see comments on 15:30. The location of Bethul is not known (see *ABD* 1: 715 under Bethuel). It appears to be the same as Bethuel in 1 Chronicles 4:30. It may also be the same as Chesil in Joshua 15:30, albeit one cannot be certain (the location of Chesil is in any case not clear – see *ABD* 1: 900). For Hormah, see comments on 12:14.

5. For Ziklag, see comments on 15:31. The location of Beth Marcaboth is unclear (see *ABD* 1: 690; Boling and Wright 1982: 437). The location of Hazar Susah is unclear, albeit Boling and Wright suggest Sabalat Abu Susein (Boling and Wright 1982: 437–438).

6. For Beth Lebaoth, see comments on 15:32, assuming, as is generally done, that it is the same as Lebaoth. The location of Sharuhen, a place that features prominently in Egyptian documents from the Late Bronze Age, is unknown (see *ABD* 5: 1163–1165). The text states that the total number of towns in the first district is thirteen, but the actual number is fourteen.

7. The location of Ain Rimmon is unclear, although Tel Halif, from which remains dating to Iron I–II and also the Late Bronze Age have been found, is a possibility (see *ABD* 5: 773; see also Junkkaala 2006: 247–250, who however suggests that the site be identified with Hormah – see comments on 12:14). Some take Ain and Rimmon as separate towns here (e.g. ESV). See also comments on 15:32. The location of Ether is uncertain, even though (Khirbet Attir has been suggested (see *ABD* 2: 645; Boling and Wright 1982: 438). Note that there is a town with the same name in Joshua 15:42. For Ashan, see comments on 15:42. The text states that the total number of towns just listed is four, but the actual number is three, assuming that Ain Rimmon refers to one town, rather than to towns of Ain and Rimmon.

8. The location of Baalath Beer is unclear (see *ABD* 1: 555–556). The location of Ramath Negev is unclear (see *ABD* 5: 614). It may well be the same place as that mentioned in 1 Samuel 30:27, albeit the consonantal spellings are slightly different. A summary statement about the allotted portion of the Simeonites follows.

9. It is interesting that the narrative here acknowledges the large size of the territory of Judah. This raises some interesting thoughts. In particular, it again tempers the idea that Judah is particularly emphasized in the book of Joshua. This then reminds us about the all-Israelite character of the book (see e.g. Introduction).

10. Next comes the allotment of Zebulun. The text contains both a boundary description (vv. 10–14) and a town list (v. 15). Starting with a boundary description, the location of Sarid is uncertain, although Tel Shadud, from which survey evidence of Late Bronze to Iron I occupation has been found, is a good possibility (see *ABD* 5: 985; Boling and Wright 1982: 443).

11. The location of Mareal is unclear (see *ABD* 4: 523), as is that of Dabbesheth (see *ABD* 2: 1). For Jokneam, see comments on 12:22.

12. The location of Chisloth Tabor is uncertain. The village of Iksal some 3 miles (5 km) west of Mount Tabor is generally suggested, albeit no Iron Age shards have been found from the place (see *ABD* 1: 910–911). The location of Daberath is uncertain, although it has been identified with Khirbet Dabbura, on the north-western side of Mount Tabor. The site is 'nearly engulfed' by a modern village, and there is as yet no certainty about its occupational history, albeit there is evidence of pottery from the Bronze and Iron Ages (see *ABD* 2: 1). The location of Japhia is unclear (see *ABD* 3: 642–643). The locality may well appear in the Amarna letters as Iapu (see *ABD* 3: 643; KNUDTZON: 1576 lists 294:20, 296:33, 138:6 and 138:85 in the letters in this context).

13. Gath Hepher (cf. 2 Kgs 14:25, which gives it as the home town of Jonah) is generally identified with Tel Gat-hefer, from which remains have been found from the Late Bronze and Iron I periods (see *ABD* 2: 909–910). The location of Eth Kazin is not known (see *ABD* 2: 644). Rimmon is generally identified with modern Rummanah, some 5 miles (8 km) north of Nazareth (see *ABD* 5: 773). The location of Neah is unknown (see *ABD* 4: 1052).

14. Hannathon features in the Amarna letters (EA 8:17, as Hinnatuni in the land of Kinahhi [which is Canaan]); see KNUDTZON: 86–87). It is generally located at Tell Hannaton, a large site of which surveys have revealed evidence of earliest settlement in the Chalcolithic period, and settlement in both the Late Bronze and Iron I Ages (see *ABD* 3: 52). The exact location of the Valley of Iphtahel is unclear (see *ABD* 3: 445).

15. The description jumps to a town list which itself is deficient, as only five towns are listed, whereas the text states twelve. The location of Kattath is unknown (see *ABD* 4: 7–8). The location of Nahalal is uncertain. The two unlikely candidates of Tell el-Beida and Tell an-Nahl both attest occupation in the Late Bronze and Iron I periods (though see *ABD* 4: 994–995). The town appears to be the same as Nahalol in Judges 1:30 (so *ABD* 4: 994), especially as only the vowel pointing is different between the two. For Shimron, see comments on 11:1–3. The location of Idalah is unclear, although Khirbet el-Hurwarah may be a possibility (see *ABD* 3: 374). Bethlehem (not the same as Bethlehem in Judah) may be associated with the modern Arab village of Beit Lahm (see *ABD* 1: 714; Boling and Wright 1982: 446).

16. A summary note concludes the description of the allotted portion of the Zebulunites.

17. The list for Issachar apparently includes both a town list (vv. 18–21) and a (short) boundary description (v. 22).

18. Jezreel features in a number of places in the biblical narrative (see e.g. 1 Kgs 18:45–46; 21). It is generally identified with (the modern) Zerin/Tel Yizre'el (see *ABD* 3: 850). Evidence from the Late Bronze and Iron I Ages (also Iron II) has been found at the site (see R. D. Miller 2003: 168). Note that there is a town with the same name in Joshua 15:56. Chesulloth is generally thought to be the same as Chisloth Tabor (see v. 12 and comments there); if not, it is difficult to make any further comments, as no particular further suggestions for identification appear to exist. Shunem (cf. 1 Sam. 28:4; 1 Kgs 1:3, 15; 2:17, 21–22; 2 Kgs 4) is generally identified with modern Solem, from where surface surveys have yielded remains from the Late Bronze and Iron I periods (see *ABD* 5: 1228). The town is also apparently mentioned in the conquest list of the Egyptian pharaoh Thutmose III from the Late Bronze Age (see *ABD* 5: 1229; Junkkaala 2006: 146), and in the Amarna letters (EA 250:43; see KNUDTZON: 804–805).

19. The location of Hapharaim is unclear, albeit the village of et-Taibiyeh has often been suggested (see *ABD* 3: 55). However, the earliest pottery that has been found (by surveys) dates to the Hellenistic period, and the identification has thus been questioned (see Junkkaala 2006: 216). The location of Shion is unclear, although Ayun es-Shain 3 miles (5 km) east of Nazareth has been suggested. The location of Anaharath, which seems to appear in the list of Thutmose III from the Late Bronze Age, is unclear, albeit Tell el-Mukharkhask is 'the only true tel in the region with suitable LB finds' (see *ABD* 1: 221–222), and Junkkaala also notes that evidence from Iron Age I (and II) has been found at the site (Junkkaala 2006: 142).

20. The location of Rabbith is unclear, although some have suggested that it may be the same as Daberath, as this is what LXX^B may read for the verse and as Daberath is grouped with Kishion, the next town listed here, in the list of Joshua 21:28 (see *ABD* 5: 604–605; see comments on Josh. 21:28 for Daberath itself). However, this is ultimately somewhat speculative, especially as LXX^B actually reads 'Debba' rather than 'Daberath' for Joshua 21:28. Kishion may be mentioned in the list of Thutmose III, which dates to the Late Bronze Age. The identification of the site is uncertain (see *ABD* 4: 88–89, including for comments about possible candidates; cf. Junkkaala 2006: 151–152). The location of Ebez is not known, although 'Ain el-Hbus has been suggested (see *ABD* 2: 260).

21. The location of Remeth is unclear, although Kokab el-Hawa has been tentatively suggested (see *ABD* 5: 669). The location of En Gannim is unclear, albeit Khirbet Beit Jann would attest occupation in the Late Bronze and Early Iron (and Iron II) periods (see *ABD* 2: 501–502). The location of En-Haddah is unclear, although the former village of el-Hadatheh has generally been suggested (see *ABD* 2: 503). The identification of Beth Pazzez is unknown, albeit Kerm el-Haditeh has been suggested by Abel (see *ABD* 1: 691).

22. Tabor here (cf. 1 Chr. 6:77) apparently refers to some town near Mount Tabor, a well-known landmark in the area, or even to the mountain itself (cf. *ABD* 6: 304–305; Boling and Wright 1982: 450). The location of Shahazumah is uncertain (see *ABD* 5: 1152). The location of Beth Shemesh (not to be confused with Beth Shemesh in 15:10) is unclear, but Khirbet Sheikh esh-Shamsawi has been suggested as it seems to preserve the name (see *ABD* 1: 698). Finally, the border ends at the river Jordan. The stated total of sixteen matches with the actual number of towns listed, counting Tabor as the name of a town, and counting the total over the town list of verses 18–21 and the border description of verse 22. That the total spans the border towns and the separately listed towns seems slightly odd, assuming that verse 22 constitutes a short boundary description.

23. A summary statement concludes the description of Issachar.

24. The allotted portion of Asher comes next (apparently) by way of a border description.

25. Helkath is apparently mentioned in the list of Thutmose III from the Late Bronze Age; and two possible candidates, Tell el-Qassis and Tell el-Harbaj, have attested evidence from the Late Bronze and Iron I (also Iron II) Ages (see *ABD* 3: 125–126; cf. Junkkaala 2006: 154–155). The location of Hali is uncertain, but one of the candidates, Khirbet Ras 'Ali, shows evidence of occupation in the Late Bronze and Early Iron Ages (see *ABD* 3: 27). The location of Beten is unclear, but Tell el-Far is a possibility (see *ABD* 1: 680; 3: 27). For Achsaph, see comments on 11:1–3.

26. The location of Allammelech is unclear, albeit Tell en-Nahal has at times been suggested (see *ABD* 1: 158). It may be mentioned in the conquest list of Thutmose III (see Junkkaala 2006: 148). The location of Amad is not known (see *ABD* 1: 169). The location of Mishal is not known, although it has been suggested that it is mentioned in Egyptian execration texts from the nineteenth century BC and in the list of Thutmose III from the Late Bronze Age (see *ABD* 4: 871; Junkkaala 2006: 146–147). Note that Junkkaala suggests Tel Regev, a site that 'lacks any ancient identification' and attests remains from the Late Bronze Age and Iron Age based on a salvage excavation and surface survey (Junkkaala 2006: 146–147). It is possible that Carmel (not the same as Carmel in Joshua 15:55) here refers to Mount Carmel, which is a prominent landmark by the coast and features prominently in 1 Kings 18. If the reference is to a town, its location would perhaps need to be sought in the area around the mountain. The location of Shihor Libnath is unclear (see *ABD* 5: 1212–1213; Boling and Wright 1982: 454). It may refer to a brook in the area (see *ABD* 5: 1212–1213), but this does not seem certain.

27. The location of Beth Dagon is unclear, although Tell Regev has been suggested by Boling and Wright (see *ABD* 1: 683; Boling and Wright 1982: 454; for Tell Regev, see comments on v. 26 above). Note that there is a town with the same name in Joshua 15:41. Zebulun here apparently refers to the territory of Zebulun. For the Valley of Iphtahel, see comments on 19:14. The location of Beth Emek is unclear, although Tel Mimas, from which evidence from both the Late Bronze and the Iron Age has been found, is a good possibility (see *ABD* 1: 685–686). Neiel is generally identified with Khirbet Ya'nin (see *ABD* 4: 1071). The name Cabul (cf. the play on words in 1 Kgs 9:10–14) seems to have been preserved in the name of the village of Kabul, from which no Iron Age remains have been found, however (see *ABD* 1: 797). In association with this, Khirbet Ras ez-Zeitun from the vicinity has been suggested, with remains from the Early Iron Age (*ABD* 1: 797).

28. Ebron is generally taken to be the same as the Abdon of Joshua 21:30, based on possible confusion between the Hebrew consonants *d* and *r* and on the fact that the reading 'Abdon' occurs in some Hebrew manuscripts (see *ABD* 2: 270; Boling and Wright 1982: 452). If not, the location is unknown. As for Abdon, it has been suggested that it is located at

Khirbet 'Abda, from which indication of occupation from the Late Bronze and Iron I (also Iron II) Ages has been found (see *ABD* 1: 9). The identification of Rehob is not clear (see *ABD* 5: 660–661), albeit Boling and Wright suggest Tell el-Gharbi, which attests Late Bronze and Iron I occupation (see Boling and Wright 1982: 454). In the light of verse 30 it has been suggested that it is even unclear whether there were one or two Rehobs in Asher (*ABD* 5: 661), albeit it is entirely possible that two separate towns with the same name existed there. Rehob is apparently mentioned in second-millennium Egyptian texts, though it is not quite clear which town it refers to, and the reference could in fact also be to a place outside the territory of Asher (*ABD* 5: 660–661; cf. also the discussion about Rehob in the list of Thutmose III in Junkkaala 2006: 160–163; see also Junkkaala 2006: 190–193, including for a summary of debates between Finkelstein and archaeological 'low chronology' and Mazar and the 'high chronology'). Hammon is generally identified with Khirbet Umm el-Awamid (see *ABD* 3: 38–39), although nothing certain can apparently be said about this connection (cf. Boling and Wright 1982: 454). Kanah is generally identified with modern Qana (see *ABD* 4: 5; Boling and Wright 1982: 454). Note that this Kanah is different from Cana of Galilee (cf. esp. John 2:1–11). For Great Sidon, see comments on 11:7–9.

29. The identification of Ramah (not the same Ramah as in Josh. 18:25) is uncertain, albeit modern Ramieh has been suggested (see *ABD* 5: 614). Tyre, which of course features rather prominently in biblical texts as a whole, was 'one of the most ancient towns on the Phoenician coast' (see *ABD* 6: 686). References to it occur in the Ugaritic texts and the Amarna letters in the Late Bronze Age, and subsequently in Egyptian, Assyro-Babylonian, Persian and other texts (see *OEANE*: 247–248). Excavations have confirmed occupation from about 2700 BC, including during the Late Bronze and Early Iron Ages (see *OEANE*: 247–248; note that there is an apparent gap from about 2000 to 1600 BC). The location of Hosah is uncertain. It may be identical to Usu mentioned in extrabiblical texts in connection with Tyre (see *ABD* 3: 299). It is generally suggested that Hosah be located at either Tell Rashidiyeh or Khirbet el-Hos (see *ABD* 3: 291). The name 'Mahalab' (really 'Mehebel' in Hebrew) is not certain; it could also for example be Hebel if the *m* at the beginning of the word is taken as the prefix 'from' (cf. *ABD* 4: 471–472). The location is not clear, though Khirbet el-Mahalib is a possibility (see *ABD* 4: 471–472; cf. Boling and Wright 1982: 455). If the name is Hebel, the location does not seem to be known. The remains of Achzib are considered to be located on a mound south of the Nahan Keziv estuary, 9 miles (14.5 km) north of Acco on the Mediterranean coast (see *NEAEHL*: 32). Remains have been found from Middle Bronze IIB on, including the Late Bronze and Iron Ages (see *NEAEHL*: 32–36). Note that there is another town with the same name in Joshua 19:44. The names here have often been compared with names listed in Judges 1:31 (see *ABD* 4: 471–472; Boling and Wright 1982: 455).

30. The location of Ummah is unclear, albeit some suggest that it should be seen as referring to Acco, with corruption of the Hebrew consonantal text (see *ABD* 6: 728). Acco itself is a well-known town, settled early and with remains from the Late Bronze and Iron I periods, and is mentioned in Egyptian execration texts from the Middle Bronze Age and Egyptian texts from the Late Bronze Age, including the Amarna letters (see *ABD* 1: 50–53). Egyptian remains have been found at the site from the Late Bronze Age (see Junkkaala 2006: 107). The identification of Aphek (not the same Aphek as in 12:18) is uncertain, albeit Tel Kurdana and Tel Kabri are the main candidates that have been suggested (see *ABD* 1: 275–276). Late Bronze remains have been found at Tel Kurdana, and after that from the Roman period (Lehmann 2002: 70). Tel Kabri is a large site, with excavations taking place from the 1950s (see *NEAEHL*: 839–841), and there are excavations going on there (in 2009). There are extensive remains from the Middle Bronze Age, then isolated shards from the Late Bronze Age, and some from the Iron Age, from a fortress constructed in the tenth century (http://www.tau.ac.il, accessed 2 March 2009). For Rehob, see comments on the Rehob of 19:28. The identification of Rehob here is unclear, as with the Rehob of 19:28 (see *ABD* 5: 660–661). The summary count of twenty-two seems just a bit lower than what can be arrived at by adding up the towns listed.

31. A summary statement concludes the description of Asher.

32. Next, the allotted portion of Naphtali is described. Verses 33–34 are a border description, and verses 35–38 a town list.

33. The location of Heleph is unclear, though as the border description (part of the southern border) moves towards the east in this verse and ends at the Jordan, it may be close to Mount Tabor (see *ABD* 3: 120–121; Boling and Wright 1982: 458; cf. v. 34 below). The location of Zaanannim (cf. Judg. 4:11) is not known (see *ABD* 6: 1029). An oak is often a good landmark in places where there are few trees, and it appears that this is likely to have been the case here. It is generally suggested that Adami Nekeb be located at Khirbet Damiyeh, some 7 miles (11 km) north-west of the southern tip of the Sea of Galilee, and evidence of occupation has been found at the site from the Late Bronze and Iron Ages (see *ABD* 1: 69). The location of Jabneel is uncertain, but it is often identified with Tell Yin'am (see *ABD* 3: 596), from which occupation has been found from the Late Bronze and Iron I (also Iron II) periods (see *NEAEHL*: 1515–1516). The location of Lakkum is uncertain, albeit Khirbet el-Mansurah is most often suggested (see *ABD* 4: 131). The border stretch described then ends in the river Jordan.

34. Another stretch of the southern border appears to be described here, again (apparently) starting from around Mount Tabor and now proceeding westward (cf. v. 33), and also northward, keeping in mind that Asher is west and north of Mount Tabor. The location of Aznoth Tabor is unclear, albeit Khirbet Umm-Jubeil has been suggested, from which however surveys have found pottery only from Iron Age II and later (see *ABD* 1: 540). The location of Hukkok is unclear (see *ABD* 3: 320). The border then reaches Zebulun and Asher at the south and west. Why Judah is mentioned here is uncertain; it is not mentioned in the LXX, however.

35. The list then describes individual (fortified) towns. It may be that Ziddim and Zer are not real towns here but part of a corrupted stretch of the Hebrew text that possibly refers to Tyre and the Sidonians (see *ABD* 6: 1080, 1089–1090; cf. Boling and Wright 1982: 457–459). Otherwise, the location of Ziddim and Zer is unknown. For Tyre itself, see comments on 19:29. For Sidon, see comments on 11:7–9. Hammath is generally identified with Hammam Tabariyeh based on rabbinical writings; however, no remains from earlier than the Hellenistic period have been found at the site (see *ABD* 3: 37–39; *NEAEHL*: 573–577). The location of Rakkath is unknown (see *ABD* 5: 613–614, including for suggestions of possible identifications). Kinnereth is generally identified with Tel Kinnereth, a few miles north of Tiberias on the north-western shore of Lake Gennesaret (see *ABD* 1: 909–910). Kinnereth is mentioned in the conquest lists of Thutmose III from the Late Bronze Age, and a fragment of an Egyptian eighteenth-dynasty stele has been found at Tel Kinnereth (see *NEAEHL*: 299). Excavations have found evidence of occupation from the Early Bronze Age on, including the Late Bronze and Iron I (also Iron II) Ages (see *NEAEHL*: 299–301). The latest excavations suggest that the occupation in Iron Age I starts from the eleventh century, and that the 'history of the site during the Middle and Late Bronze Ages (= MB and LB) is complex and still poorly known' (Pakkala, Münger and Zangenberg 2004: 13). At present, occupation between the fourteenth and twelfth century seems not to be attested. However, according to Pakkala, Münger and Zangenberg (2004: 15), 'a scarab bearing the name of queen Teje/Tye – wife of Amenophis III (1390–1353 BCE) and mother of Akhenaten (1353–1336 BCE) – could indicate some activity in first half of the 14th century', even though 'one should not make far-reaching conclusions about individual surface finds'. It is also worth noting that excavations suggest that the town was (strongly) fortified in the eleventh century (Pakkala, Münger and Zangenberg 2004: 17). The town was fortified also in the earlier part of Iron Age II.

36. The location of Adamah is unknown (see *ABD* 1: 69). Ramah is generally identified with modern er-Rameh (see *ABD* 5: 614). Ramah here is not to be confused with the famous Ramah in Benjamin, which may be listed in 18:25 (see comments on 18:25). For Hazor, see comments on 11:1–3.

37. For Kedesh, see comments on 12:22. The location of Edrei (presumably not the same Edrei as in 12:4) is not known, albeit the place may have been mentioned in the campaign list of Thutmose III from the Late Bronze Age (see *ABD* 2: 301; see also Junkkaala 2006: 168). The location of En Hazor is unknown (see *ABD* 2: 503).

38. Yiron is generally identified with Yarun, and surveys have found Iron Age shards from the place (see *ABD* 6: 1024). The location of Migdal El is not known (see *ABD* 4: 822). The location of Horem is unknown (see *ABD* 3: 287–288). The location of Beth Anath (cf. Judg. 1:33) is unknown, even though the town is evidently mentioned in the lists of Thutmose III and Ramses II from the Late Bronze and Early Iron Ages (see *ABD* 1: 680–681). The location of Beth Shemesh (cf. Judg. 1:33; not to be confused with Beth Shemesh in 15:10) is not known (see *ABD* 1: 698). The total number of towns stated does not quite tally with the actual number of towns listed, whether one counts Ziddim and Zer (see comments on v. 35 above) in or not, and whether one adds the boundary towns (vv. 33–34) and separately listed towns (35–38) together or not.

39. A summary statement concludes the list for Naphtali.

40. We next move to the land allotted for Dan. It appears to consist of a town list, with no boundary description.

41. For Zorah, see comments on 15:33. For Eshtaol, see comments on 15:33. Ir Shemesh is generally considered to be the same as Beth Shemesh (see *ABD* 3: 446; Boling and Wright 1982: 464), for which see comments on 15:10. If not, the location is unknown.

42. Shaalabbin (apparent Shaalbim in Judg. 1:35) is generally identified with Selbit, from which excavations have uncovered only remains belonging to the first millennium AD (see *ABD* 5: 1147; *NEAEHL*: 1338). Aijalon (cf. Judg. 1:35) is generally identified with either Yalo or Tell Qoqa, two sites that are fairly close to each other, and evidence of occupation from both the Late Bronze and Iron I (also Iron II) Ages has been found at both sites by surveys (see *ABD* 1: 131). The location of Ithlah is unknown (see *ABD* 3: 582).

43. The location of Elon is not known (see *ABD* 2: 482–483). For Timnah, see comments on 15:10 (if the name should be Timnatah [Hebr. strictly thus], the location does not seem to be known). For Ekron, see comments on 13:3.

44. The location of Eltekeh is unclear, albeit Tell esh-Shalaf might be a possibility, and evidence of occupation from the Late Bronze and Early Iron (also Iron II) Ages has been found at the site (see *ABD* 2: 483–484). The location of Gibbethon, which appears to feature in the campaign list of Thutmose III (see Junkkaala 2006: 149–150), is unclear, although it could be Tell Malat, from which evidence of occupation from the Late Bronze and Early Iron (also Iron II) Ages has been found (see *ABD* 2: 1006–1007; Junkkaala 2006: 149). The location of Baalath is unclear, but el-Maghar, at which shards from the Late Bronze and Iron Ages have been found, has been suggested (see *ABD* 1: 555).

45. Jehud has been identified with modern Yehud, and shards from the Middle Bronze and Iron Ages have been found at the place (see *ABD* 3: 674). The location of Bene Berak is unclear, albeit el-Kheiriyah, where surface surveys have found Iron II pottery, has been suggested (see *ABD* 1: 668). Boling and Wright (interestingly) suggest that the place should be located in the suburbs of modern Tel Aviv (Boling and Wright 1982: 465). The location of Gath Rimmon is unclear, but Tell Abu Zeitun and Tell Jerishe have been suggested, and evidence of occupation during the Late Bronze and Iron I (also Iron II) Ages has been found at both of these sites (see *ABD* 2: 910). The place may be mentioned in the campaign list of Thutmose III and in the Amarna letters from the Late Bronze Age (see *ABD* 2: 910).

46. The location of Me Jarkon, which many have argued to be a water-course rather than a town, is unclear, albeit the river Nahr el-Auja has generally been suggested (see *ABD* 4: 648). As for Rakkon, it has often been seen as partial dittography (i.e. repetition with slight corruption) of Me Jarkon, or, if it is to be seen as an entity of its own, there has not been agreement on whether it is a town or a river (*ABD* 5: 613). If a town is meant, the location is unknown; for the option of river, Nahar el-Barideh has been suggested (see *ABD* 5: 613). Joppa (cf. e.g. Jon. 1:3) is identified with modern Jaffa (*ABD* 3: 946). The town is mentioned in the conquest lists of Thutmose III and in the Amarna letters from the Late Bronze Age (*NEAEHL*: 655). Remains from the Middle Bronze Age on, including from the Late Bronze and Iron I (also Iron II) Ages, have been found in excavations of the tell (*NEAEHL*: 655–659). A fragment from the jamb of the fortress gate, which has been inscribed with the name of Ramses II, is one prominent find from a Late Bronze Age stratum (see *NEAEHL*: 655 for a photograph, and p. 656 for an explanation). No total number of towns is stated at the conclusion of the list of the Danite towns.

47. The Old Testament does not directly tell us why the Danites lost their allocated territory, even though difficulties in settling around the Canaanite/Philistine coastal plain seem a logical explanation. On the other hand, there is a detailed account in the book of Judges (Judg. 17 – 18) of the move of the Danites to the north, to Leshem (Laish in Judg. 18:27, 29). Laish is mentioned in the conquest list of Thutmose III (see *NEAEHL*: 323). Dan/Leshem/Laish is generally identified with Tel Dan, which is in essence located by a large oasis fed by a powerful spring, and remains from the Neolithic period, then from the Early Bronze Age on, including from the Late Bronze and Iron I (also Iron II) Ages, have been found in excavations (see *NEAEHL*: 324–332; *ABD* 2: 12–17). Also, evidence of a destruction by fire has been unearthed from about 1200 BC, with a subsequent change in material culture, well in line with the biblical tradition (see Junkkaala 2006: 298–299). It is worth noting that two Egyptian fragments of statues have been found from the Late Bronze Age (see Junkkaala 2006: 116).

48. A summary statement rounds off the description of the territory of the Danites. It should be noted (again) that no total count of towns is given for Dan.

49–50. The Israelites also give an allotted portion to Joshua. For Timnath Serah, see comments on 24:30. The allotment of Caleb, one of the two faithful spies (Num. 13 – 14; cf. comments on 1:1), begins the Cisjordanian allotments in the literary order (Josh. 14:6–15), and the allotment of Joshua, the other faithful spy, closes them. That said, the cities of refuge and the towns for the Levites are dealt with in chapters 20 – 21.

51. The comment here acts as a closure to what has been said in 14:1 and concludes the Cisjordanian land allotments. The cities of refuge and the towns for the Levites are however dealt with in chapters 20 – 21.

Explanation

This chapter contains the allotments of the six remaining Cisjordanian tribes. They are all descendants of Leah, Jacob's unloved wife, or of the slave maids Bilhah and Zilpah (see Gen. 35:22–26; 29 – 30). Arguably, it is only Judah of the sons of these three women who becomes significant in the history of Israel (cf. 1 Chr. 5:1–2), plus Levi as the priestly tribe. The allotments consist of boundary descriptions and town lists that are less complete than those for Judah and Benjamin. Interestingly, Simeon's allotment in the midst of Judah seems to be reflected in Genesis 49:5–7 (itself apparently referring back to Gen. 34, esp. vv. 25–29), considering that Levi is certainly scattered in the midst of Israel (e.g. Josh. 21). The Danites could not take up their inheritance, apparently largely because of the power of the Canaanites/Philistines, and consequently sought an inheritance elsewhere (see also Judg. 17 – 18).

There is a sense of closure in this chapter, even if the cities of refuge and the Levitical towns are still to be dealt with in chapters 20 – 21. The general feel is that Yahweh has fulfilled his promises, including to Joshua, the leader of Israel himself.

JOSHUA 20

Translation

[1]Then Yahweh spoke to Joshua, [2]'Tell the Israelites to designate cities of refuge of which I spoke to you through Moses, [3]so that a person who has killed someone accidentally can flee there. It will be a place of refuge from the avenger of blood.

[4]'When he flees to one of these towns, let him stand at the entrance of the gate of the town and state his case at the hearing of the elders of the town. Let them then take him into the town and give him a place to live among them. [5]When the avenger of blood pursues him, they are not to give the killer over to him because he killed his fellow man unintentionally, without hating him previously. [6]He is to live in that town until he stands on trial in front of the assembly, until the death

of the high priest of the time. After that, the killer may return to his own home in the town from which he fled.'

⁷And they set apart Kedesh in Galilee in the hill country of Naphtali, Shechem in the hill country of Ephraim and Kiriath Arba (that is, Hebron) in the hill country of Judah. ⁸From the east side of the Jordan they dedicated Bezer in the wilderness on the tableland from the tribe of Reuben, Ramoth Gilead from the tribe of Gad, and Golan in Bashan from the tribe of Manasseh. ⁹These were the cities of refuge for all Israelites and for any sojourners living among them so that anyone who would kill a person accidentally could flee there and would not be killed by an avenger of blood before he stood on trial before the assembly.

Notes on the text

3. Accidentally: lit. 'accidentally and without knowledge'. Avenger of blood: lit. 'redeemer of blood' (Hebr. *gô'ēl hadām*). Gr. phrases it slightly differently and adds to the end of the verse 'until he has stood before the congregation for judgment'.

4. Note that verses 4–6 are missing from LXX^B. See RAHLFS for details.

5. Fellow man: lit. 'neighbour' (Hebr. *rē'a*).

6. The first translated sentence reflects the slight ambiguity of the original.

7. Set apart: Hebr. *qādaš*.

8. From the east side of the Jordan: lit. 'From the other side of the Jordan, east of Jericho'. Gr. omits Jericho. Dedicated: lit. 'gave'.

9. Living: lit. 'sojourning as an alien'.

Form and structure

The structure of this chapter can be described as follows:

> Cities of refuge (vv. 1–9)
>> Rationale for the cities of refuge (vv. 1–6)
>> Appointed cities of refuge (vv. 7–8)
>>> West of the Jordan (v. 7)
>>> East of the Jordan (v. 8)
>> Summary statement (v. 9)

The cities of refuge are first introduced in Numbers 35:6, 9–34. The story is continued in Deuteronomy 4:41–43; 19:1–13. The passage here in the book of Joshua provides a fulfilment of the stipulations. The laws in these texts have some slightly differing emphases and details (treated in Barmash 2006: 79–92). The main possible potentially contradictory divergence is that Deuteronomy 19:8–9 may refer to a total of nine towns, or even only three. However, it can also be seen to refer to six, as suggested by the other passages (for details, see e.g. ben Zvi 1992: 94–95; Barmash 2005: 87–88). The cities of refuge are also cursorily mentioned in the list of Levitical towns in 1 Chronicles 6:54–81 [Hebr. 39–66].

It appears that there are no known direct parallels to the system of cities of refuge from elsewhere in the Ancient Near East (see Barmash 2005: 203–204). Diplomatic asylum as such, however, is well known in the Ancient Near East (see e.g. BECKMAN, *passim*), and of course makes sense, just as diplomatic asylum is known in the modern world (e.g. Soviet defectors during the Cold War era, or North Korean defectors to the South even today). In this connection, it would also make sense that a killer might flee to another country (as did Moses, according to the Bible itself, in Exod. 2:11–15).

The system of blood avenging as such seems to be attested in the Ancient Near East, even in the second millennium. The victim's family generally had a chance to choose between killing the offender and receiving 'blood money' in compensation (see Barmash 2005: 20–70). The vassal treaties of Esarhaddon directly mention that 'just as a stag is overtaken and killed, so may the avenger overtake and kill you, your sons and daughters' (see Barmash 2005: 54). Also, cuneiform legal material stipulated capital punishments in cases of homicide (see e.g. Barmash 2005: 168–170). We may conclude from this that the system of cities of refuge has its grounding in Ancient Near Eastern law and practice, but appears to have a slant that is specifically Israelite. The Ancient Near Eastern parallels also show that the system could have been set up at any time in Israel's history.

In their present form, the towns have been set up roughly evenly across the Israelite territory (comments by ben Zvi 1992: 97–98 notwithstanding). This would grant people equally easy access to any city of refuge throughout the land (as observed by Barmash 2005: 85; see also Boling and Wright 1982 for a rough map).

Traditionally, Wellhausen (1905/1878) thought that the cities of refuge developed from sacrificial altars. In the Wellhausenian system, the earliest sources J and E allowed sacrificing everywhere. Deuteronomy then restricted this to a central sanctuary, and P assumed that sacrifice was centralized. For Wellhausen, the altars were originally asylums (Exod. 21:13–14; 1 Kgs 2:28). In order not to abolish the asylums together with the altars, the deuteronomic legislator desired that certain holy places should continue as places of refuge. There would primarily be three for Judah, and, when the territory of the kingdom extended, three others were to be added afterwards. The priestly code then adopts the arrangement, and specifies three definite cities west of the Jordan and three on the east side of the Jordan (Num. 35; Josh. 20). Subsequent scholars have by and large followed Wellhausen (see Barmash 2005: 72). However, as Barmash conveniently points out, there are problems with the Wellhausenian reconstruction. First of all, it is not at all clear that a system of altar asylum was in place at an early stage. The flights of Joab and Adonijah (1 Kgs 1:50–53; 2:28–34) are based rather on political asylum (see Barmash 2005: 73). The reference to a place (*māqôm*) in Exodus 21:13 does not need to refer to an altar or a sanctuary, and can thus easily be seen to be referring to something different from an altar, which is mentioned in the following verse (Barmash 2005: 77–78). Barmash continues, 'The import of Exod. 21:14 is that intentional, premeditated homicide is so heinous that the one who commits such a transgression could even be arrested at an altar, generally an area with restrictions against interlopers and encroachers who have no ritual business there' (Barmash 2005: 78). In other words, even the perceived sanctity of an altar in itself would not protect the offender. Finally, while not a conclusive argument, Barmash also suggests that there is nothing in the system of cities of refuge that suggests that they are particularly an innovation in radical discontinuity with some older practice (see Barmash 2005: 80). It can also be added that if the cities of refuge are not a development from a system of altar asylum, they do not need to be specifically related to altars.

Barmash suggests that the Joshua 20 account includes elements from both Numbers 35 and Deuteronomy 19. Barmash gives the following comments (Barmash 2005: 91–92; I am quoting selectively, but readers interested in fuller details are encouraged to look at Barmash and *BHS*. Paragraph numbering is mine):

1. Josh. 20:21: The term '*ārê miqlāṭ*, 'cities of refuge' in Joshua 20:2 appears only in Numbers 35 (vv. 11, 14, 25, 26, 27, 28, 32). The verb used for assigning cities here and in Num. 35:13–14 is *n-t-n*.

2. Josh. 20:3: 'to which a slayer who strikes down a person by mistake unintentionally may flee; they shall be a refuge for you from the blood avenger.' – The entire verse is an almost complete parallel to Num. 35:11b–12a, which reads 'to which a slayer who strikes down a person unintentionally may flee; the cities shall be as a refuge from the avenger.' The double characterization of this type of murder, *bišgāgâ biblî-d'at* 'by mistake unintentionally,' is a conflation of the criteria of Numbers and Deuteronomy. Num. 35:11b denotes this category of killing by the term *bišgāga* 'by mistake,' while Deut. 19:4 uses *biblî-d'at* 'unintentionally'.

3. Josh. 20:4a 'He shall flee to one of these cities.' – This clause is similar to Deut. 19:5b, 'that man shall flee to one of these cities and live.'

4. Josh. 20:5aα 'If the blood avenger should pursue him' – This is paralleled in Deut. 19:6, 'lest the blood avenger pursue him.'

5. Josh. 20:5b 'for he struck his neighbour unintentionally and had not been his enemy before.' – This is paralleled in Deut.

19:4b, 'whoever slays his fellow without intent and was not hostile to him in the past.'

6. Josh. 20:6aβ 'until he stands before the assembly for trial.' – A trial before the assembly is stipulated in Num. 35:24.

7. Josh 20:6γ 'until the death of the priest' – The release date of the accidental homicide is the same as in Numbers 35:28.

8. Josh 20:6b 'Then the killer may return to his town and his home from where he fled.' – Num. 35:28 stipulates that the killer may return to his patrimonial estate, naḥălâ. Deut. 19:12 mentions that the killer departed from 'his town', 'îrô.

In addition, Barmash suggests that a new element in Joshua 20, the admission procedure in verse 4, can be compared to Deuteronomy 19:12, and that the language of Joshua 20:5–6 can be compared with Deuteronomy 23:16–17 (Barmash 2005: 92). Based on these and certain other considerations (see Barmash 2005: 92–93 for details), Barmash suggests that 'Joshua 20 is a Deuteronomic reworking of a priestly kernel' (Barmash 2005: 92). Certainly, it would be natural to think that Joshua 20 is based on both Deuteronomy and priestly material, in line with what has been suggested consistently elsewhere in this commentary.

We may note here that the issue of cities of refuge and Levitical towns does make some contribution to the question of whether and how much Ancient Near Eastern legal material was considered theoretical; i.e. whether such material was more of an academic exercise and only paradigmatic in its application, or whether it was intended to be taken as real practical injunctions (cf. e.g. F. R. Kraus 1984, esp. pp. 111–123, for stating this question). As the book of Joshua clearly states that the cities of refuge and Levitical towns were actually set up in response to earlier injunctions, this would speak for shifting the balance towards the latter option. That said, the injunctions about the cities of refuge and Levitical towns only pertain to a relatively small part of the legislation contained in the Pentateuch and are about territory, and could be argued to be fictional if one were to take a less historical approach to the Joshua materials.

Comment

1–2. Hess helpfully notes (Hess 1996: 277) that chapters 20 – 21 make reference to towns that are 'taken back' from the tribal allotments for a specific purpose (cf. also comments by Weinfeld in the 'Form and structure' section of chapter 21). In the narrative sequence, the institution of both cities of refuge (chapter 20) and Levitical towns (chapter 21) is based on Yahweh's command, originally given in Numbers 35 (see Num. 35:1, 9). The instruction to appoint cities of refuge also appears in

Deuteronomy 19:1–13. The Transjordanian towns have already been listed in Deuteronomy 4:41–43.

3–5. The idea of the cities of refuge is to provide a haven for someone who has killed another person unintentionally. The text implies that a specific person, apparently from among the relatives of the victim, would be expected to avenge the death. This would apparently involve killing the offender (see Num. 35:19). The unintentional killer would go to one of the cities of refuge and present his case to the leaders of the town. These, being aware of the special status of their city, would protect the unintentional killer and arrange for the practicalities of his life there.

6. The idea here is that the killer is to be protected so that he can be brought to a (fair) trial. Also, it clearly appears that the death of the high priest, the cultic leader of the nation, nullifies the requirement to avenge. It thus appears to act as atonement for the unintentional manslaughter (cf. Hess 1996: 279). It is not clear from the verse on its own whether the killer could go back to his own home in his own town after either a trial or the death of the high priest, or whether both the trial and the death of the high priest were required. However, Numbers 35:24–25 seem to make it clear that both the trial and the death of the high priest were required. The parallel passages in Numbers 35:9–29 and Deuteronomy 19:1–13 explicitly state that no protection is to be offered to a person who has killed intentionally; i.e. murdered the other person.

7. A list of towns is then given, three from Cisjordan and three from Transjordan. The three Cisjordanian towns are listed first, in a north-to-south order. This makes a fairly balanced coverage of Cisjordan. For Kedesh, listed for Naphtali in 19:37, see comments on 12:22. For Shechem, a town located in southern Manasseh/northern Ephraim, see comments on 17:7. For Hebron, located in Judah, see comments on 10:3–5.

8. The three Transjordanian towns are listed after the Cisjordanian ones, in a south-to-north order. This makes a fairly balanced coverage of Transjordan. The towns have already been listed in Deuteronomy 4:41–43. The location of Bezer, which is not listed in the tribal allotments proper in Joshua 13 – 19 (but is mentioned in Josh. 21:36), is uncertain, albeit Umm al-'Amad and Tall Jalul, from both of which shards from the Early Iron Age (and also evidence from Iron II) have been found, are possible candidates (see MacDonald 2000: 177–178). MacDonald (see MacDonald 2000: 177) also notes that Bezer may be the same as Bozrah in Jer. 48:24). The location of Ramoth in Gilead, which is not listed in the tribal allotments proper in Joshua 13 – 19 (but is mentioned in Josh. 21:38), is unclear, albeit ar-Ramtha, Tall ar-Rumeith and Tall al-Husn have been suggested (see MacDonald 2000: 201–202). Ar-Ramtha and Tall ar-Rumeith have yielded evidence from the Iron I and II Ages, and Iron Age pottery has been found at Tall al Husn (MacDonald 2000: 201–202). The location of the town of Golan, which is not listed in the tribal allotments proper in Joshua 13 – 19 (but is mentioned in Josh. 21:27), is unclear.

Saham al-Jaulan has been suggested as a possible candidate for identification, as it seems to have preserved the ancient name, but no remains have been found at the site from earlier than the Christian period (see MacDonald 2000: 155).

9. A summary statement concludes the description of the cities of refuge.

Explanation

The ancient designation of cities of refuge, an institution that reflects the desire of the book of Joshua to create provision for the people of Israel across the board, was created to minimize the spilling of innocent blood. If a person killed another person unintentionally, no further bloodshed should occur. However, equally, someone who had murdered another person should not be spared and allowed to give the excuse that the killing was unintentional. A trial would help distinguish real claims from fraudulent ones. The killer would be allocated places where he could stay in safety while waiting for the trial. It is interesting that the system of blood avenging (which is still used in some places in the world, at least on a literary level in modern Mafia stories from Sicily, and was used in Corsica at least in the fairly recent past) is not as such at all condemned by the biblical text. Be that as it may, in the context of Joshua 20, it is important that justice is done, and this theme occurs in many places in the Old Testament. From here we can say that, based on this passage and the Old Testament in general, upholding justice serves as a good general principle for modern Christians. But, again, we note that, in Joshua, the rules for those within the society are different from those without (i.e. these concepts of justice do not apply to the Canaanites).

JOSHUA 21

Translation

[1]The heads of the Levites approached Eleazar the priest, Joshua the son of Nun and the heads of the tribes of Israel. [2]They spoke to them at Shiloh in the land of Canaan: 'Yahweh commanded through Moses to give us towns to live in, with their pasturelands for our cattle.' [3]And the Israelites gave the Levites towns and pasturelands from among their land as Yahweh had commanded.

[4]The lot came out for the families of Kohath. Thirteen towns were given for the descendants of Aaron the priest from the tribes of Judah, Simeon and Benjamin. [5]The rest of the descendants of Kohath received ten towns from the tribes of Ephraim, Dan and Manasseh, [6]the descendants of Gershon received thirteen towns from the tribes of Issachar, Asher, Naphtali and the eastern half of Manasseh in

Bashan, [7]and the descendants of Merari received twelve towns from the tribes of Reuben, Gad and Zebulun.

[8]The Israelites gave these towns and their pasturelands to the Levites by lot as Yahweh had commanded them through Moses. [9]They gave them the following named towns from the tribes of Judah and Simeon, [10]and these were for the descendants of Aaron from the family of the Kohathites because the first lot fell to them.

[11]The Israelites gave them Kiriath Arba (Arba was the father of Anak), that is, Hebron, in the hill country of Judah, and the pasturelands around it. [12]However, they gave the fields and villages belonging to the town to Caleb the son of Jephunneh as his possession.

[13]So, to the descendants of Aaron were given Hebron, the city of refuge, and its pasturelands, Libnah and its pasturelands, [14]Jattir and its pasturelands, Eshtemoa and its pasturelands, [15]Holon and pasturelands, Debir and its pasturelands, [16]Ain and its pasturelands, Juttah and its pasturelands, and Beth Shemesh and its pasturelands, nine towns from these two tribes.

[17]From the tribe of Benjamin they were given Gibeon and its pasturelands, Geba and its pasturelands, [18]Anathoth and its pasturelands, and Almon and its pasturelands, four towns. [19]The total number of the towns of the descendants of Aaron together with the pasturelands of these towns was thirteen.

[20]The remaining descendants of Kohath were allocated towns from the tribe of Ephraim. [21]They were given Shechem, the city of refuge, and its pasturelands from the hill country of Ephraim, Gezer and its pasturelands, [22]Kibzaim and its pasturelands, and Beth Horon and its pasturelands, four towns.

[23]From the tribe of Dan they were given Elteke and its pasturelands, Gibbethon and its pasturelands, [24]Aijalon and its pasturelands, and Gath Rimmon and its pasturelands, four towns.

[25]From the western half of Manasseh they were given Taanach and its pasturelands, and Gath Rimmon and its pasturelands, two towns.

[26]The total number of the towns for the rest of the Kohathites together with the pasturelands of these towns was ten.

[27]To the descendants of Gershon were given from the eastern half of Manasseh Golan in Bashan, the city of refuge, and its pasturelands, and Beeshterah and its pasturelands, two towns.

[28]From the tribe of Issachar they were given Kishion and its pasturelands, Daberath and its pasturelands, [29]Jarmuth and its pasturelands, and En Gannim and its pasturelands, four towns.

[30]From the tribe of Asher they were given Mishal and its pasturelands, Abdon and its pasturelands, [31]Helkath and its pasturelands, and Rehob and its pasturelands, four towns.

[32]And from the tribe of Naphtali they were given Kedesh in Galilee, the city of refuge, and its pasturelands, Hammoth Dor and its pasturelands, and Kartan and its pasturelands, three towns.

[33]The total number of the towns of the Gershonites together with the pasturelands of these towns was thirteen.

³⁴To the descendants of Merari, the remaining Levites, were given Jokneam and its pasturelands, Kartah and its pasturelands, ³⁵Dimnah and it pasturelands, and Nahalal and its pasturelands, four towns from the tribe of Zebulun.

³⁶From the tribe of Reuben they were given Bezer and its pasturelands, Jahaz and its pasturelands, ³⁷Kedemoth and its pasturelands and Mephaath and its pasturelands, four towns.

³⁸From the tribe of Gad they were given Ramoth in Gilead, the city of refuge, and its pasturelands, Mahanaim and its pasturelands, ³⁹Heshbon and its pasturelands, Jazer and its pasturelands, a total of four towns.

⁴⁰The total number of the towns of the remaining Merarites by lot was twelve.

⁴¹The total number of the towns of the Levites among the hereditary portion of the Israelites together with the pasturelands of these towns was forty-eight. ⁴²All these towns included their pasturelands around them.

⁴³Yahweh gave Israel all the land he had sworn to give to their fathers. They took possession of it and lived there. ⁴⁴Yahweh also gave them peace throughout, as he had sworn to their fathers. No one could withstand them. He gave all their enemies in their hands. ⁴⁵Not one of the good promises that Yahweh had spoken to Israel failed; all came to pass.

Notes on the text

1. One may compare this chapter with 1 Chronicles 6:54–81. I have not made notes about the differences in the place names here, as it is relatively easy to compare the differences by placing the two texts side by side (including the English translations).

11. Kiriath Arba (Arba was the father of Anak): lit. 'Kiriath Arba, the father of Anak'. The text also reads 'Anok' (*'anôq*) instead of Anak, but I have followed the reading in 15:13, in line with a number of other manuscripts. Kiriath Arba (Arba was the father of Anak): Gr. 'Chariatharboc, the mother town (*mētropolis*) of Enak' (cf. 14:15; 15:13).

12. As: the particle *bĕ* (in) is used here rather than the expected *lĕ* (for).

14. Gr. diverges to some extent from Hebr. from here on for the list; see LXX for (full) details.

16. Ain: RAHLFS reads Asa; LXX^A however has Ain.

29. Jarmuth: Gr. Remmath.

36. Some manuscripts do not include verses 36–37.

42. Gr. adds at the end of this verse: 'And Joshua finished dividing the land according to its borders, and the sons of Israel gave a share to Joshua according to the command of the Lord. They gave him the town which he asked for; they gave him Tamnasachar from the mountain of Ephraim. And Joshua built the town, and lived in it. Joshua also took the knives of stone with which he circumcised the sons of Israel that had been born on the way in the wilderness, and put them in Tamnasachar.'

44. Gave them peace: lit. 'Gave them rest'.

Form and structure

The structure of chapter 21 can be described as follows (see also 'Form and structure' of chapter 22 for more on verses 43–45):

> Levitical towns (vv. 1–42)
>> Introduction and summary of rationale for the Levitical towns (vv. 1–3)
>> Summary of tribes from which Levitical towns were allotted (vv. 4–7)
>>> For Aaronite Kohathites (v. 4)
>>> For non-Aaronite Kohathites (v. 5)
>>> For the Gershonites (v. 6)
>>> For the Merarites (v. 7)
>> Enumeration of Levitical towns (vv. 8–42)
>>> Towns for Aaronite Kohathites, from Judah, Simeon and Benjamin (vv. 9–19)
>>> Towns for non-Aaronite Kohathites, from Ephraim, Dan and Western Manasseh (vv. 20–26)
>>> Towns for the Gershonites, from eastern Manasseh, Issachar and Naphtali (vv. 27–33)
>>> Towns for the Merarites, from Zebulun, Reuben and Gad (vv. 34–40)
>>> Concluding summary (vv. 41–42)
>> Summary of Israel taking the land (vv. 43–45)

Apart from their first mention in Leviticus 25:32–34 as (if) something known, the Levitical towns are first 'properly' introduced in Numbers 35:1–8 in the canonical context (and order), and the passage here in the book of Joshua provides a fulfilment of the stipulations in Numbers. The Levitical towns are not directly mentioned in Deuteronomy proper. The legislation about the towns in Leviticus 25:32–34 is in agreement with the corresponding legislation in Numbers–Joshua. Apart from Joshua 21, another list of the towns is provided in 1 Chronicles 6:54–81 [Hebr. 39–66]. The lists in Joshua and Chronicles differ somewhat, as do the Hebrew and Greek versions of Joshua 21 (for details about some of the Greek divergences, see 'Notes' to the translation of Josh. 21).

Much discussion has surrounded the Levitical towns (see e.g. Kallai 1986: 447–458; 1998: 23–62; ben Zvi 1992; Nelson 1997a: 238; Auld 1998: 25–36). By and large, they have been dated from the early monarchy to the post-exilic period. Much of the discussion has centred on the question of whether the system should be seen as programmatic (or idealistic, even 'utopian'), or as based on some actual historical reality during the history of Israel, and one's view of the matter has affected one's dating of the material. It has also been asked whether the Chronicles list is based on that of Joshua or vice versa, with varying suggestions for a solution. It appears to me that it is difficult to make any definitive conclusions about the matter of textual dependency (including the possibility of a combination of mutual influence). Certainly, it seems plausible that there was some editing of the list in Joshua in particular as it passed through various hands over time, especially if it was composed early.

It should also be noted that there are a large number of towns in the south, with towns from Judah, Simeon and Benjamin allotted to the Aaronites. Also, the number of towns allotted from these three tribes is thirteen, one more than would be expected with an equal distribution of a total of forty-eight towns for twelve tribes (see 'Comment' section for details). In addition, there is a lacuna around the middle of the country, including in areas surrounding Shiloh in Ephraim, the purported location of the Tent of Meeting at around the time of Joshua – the place where actual cultic activity is supposed to have taken place (see Boling and Wright 1982: 477 for a rough map). For this reason, it would be easy to conclude that the list has been created in Judah, with an emphasis on Judah.

However, the idea of Levitical towns as such is compatible with second-millennium Ancient Near Eastern practice. As Weinfeld notes (Weinfeld 2004: 32–33; I have not included Weinfeld's references to other scholars with the quotation):

> As is known from Ugaritic documents, royal servants were granted whole cities for the collection of tithes for the great king. These cities did not actually become the property of the servants; rather, they were given the perpetual right to collect the tithes from the inhabitants and equally had their homes there (cf. the grant in PRU III 16.153: ' . . . he gives the city forever [*ana dāriš*] to his grandchildren . . . his grain, his wine of its tithe'). This indeed explains the long misunderstood fact that large cities such as Shechem, Hebron, Ramoth-Gilead, etc., were 'given away' to the priests and Levites (Josh. 21:11, 21). These cities were the Levites' home, not their property, and it is in this context that they functioned; never is it said that these cities were their inheritance (*nhlh*), only that they were 'cities in which to dwell' (Num. 35:2–3; Josh. 21:2).

Hess has also pointed out that the list has a parallel with land grants and the sale of properties found in texts from Alalakh (Hess 1996: 281 and Hess 2002; see Wiseman 1953, texts 1, 76–80, 86–88; cf. Milgrom 1989: 504, who points out that the Akkadian word *tawwertum/tamertu* means extramural land; see also *AHw*: 1341, which also lists the second millennium as a period of use for the word).

That the towns were given in south–north order and from Judah may not be as surprising as it sounds, even if we were to think of an origin before the monarchy. In the context of the book of Joshua, the man Joshua the Ephraimite is the clear leader of the Israelites, and the Tent of Meeting is set up at Shiloh. At the same time, Caleb is one of the faithful spies (Num. 13 – 14 etc.), and giving priestly towns from the south would serve as a balance to the northern hegemony and emphasize the all-Israelite character of the book of Joshua. And, overall, starting from the south with the allotment would seem a completely legitimate strategy as such. In this connection, it can be noted that there is also a good cluster of Levitical towns in the north of Ephraim and Manasseh, and also in Transjordan. To speculate a bit further, if the list is programmatic, with the Levites intended to help provide dissemination of Yahwism in Israel, the existence of Shiloh in Ephraim may even have reduced the need for Levitical towns in that area (note that the allocated area of Ephraim and Manasseh was large, with only four towns allocated to each, respectively [four for both eastern and western Manasseh together]). In general, if there were a good number of priests in the south, at least this would not have been likely to work against David's claims to kingship. Assigning the priestly towns to the south is also compatible with the priestly tradition that Judah led in the wilderness (Num. 2; Num. 7), with the south–north order of the Cisjordanian conquest, and with Numbers 34 (assigned to P), which lists the representatives of the tribes who would allot Cisjordan. (As Transjordan was a somewhat 'dubious' part of Israel [see section on Josh. 22:9–34], one could perhaps speculate that it would be listed last in this respect, and one would not expect to settle priests there.) Yet one must also remember that Joshua 21 emphasizes that the Levitical towns were divided by lot (vv. 4–8, 10; cf. also Josh. 14:1–2; 19:51; Num. 26:55–56; 33:54).

It should be noted in this connection that priests could officiate in different towns from where their property might be located (as with Abiathar, who has an estate in Anathoth, but officiates in Jerusalem [1 Kgs 2:26]; pointed out by Barmash 2005: 85), and thus it can be inferred that locating the towns of priests and Levites around the country would not preclude the idea of their being active in Shiloh (or in Jerusalem). In this respect, one would not need to think that, for example, all Aaronites should be seen to be active in the duties of the central sanctuary (at least not all the time). Further, Milgrom points out that the word *maṭṭeh* in the list of Levitical towns is a term that is attested with the meaning 'tribe' in early, but not in late, biblical documents. According to Milgrom (1983a: 12–15), the word *maṭṭeh* is not attested after the ninth century as meaning 'tribe', and the occurrence of the term in Chronicles (including the Levitical town list in Chronicles) always comes in material that the Chronicler took directly from early sources available to him.

The books of Chronicles suggest that the Levites were living across the area of Canaan prior to the time of Jeroboam (2 Chr. 11:13–14; as noted by ben Zvi 1992: 80). One may of course question the reliability of this mention in Chronicles and also what the reference exactly means, but it is nevertheless a biblical reference that gives some support to the possible earliness of the system of Levitical towns. The fact that Levitical towns were assigned from the idealized initial location of Dan is also rather a sign of the earliness of the list. The town of Leshem/Dan which was conquered later is not included (even though it would not necessarily have to be included anyway). It should further be noted that Jerusalem is not mentioned in the list of Levitical towns, which rather speaks for an early appropriation/date for the list. One may also note that, according to the current identification, the southern Levitical towns are concentrated around Hebron, the most important Judahite town during the pre-monarchical period according to the biblical documents (see Josh. 15:13–14; 2 Sam. 2:1–4).

It is possible that the list was programmatic. If so, it would clearly seem harder to date it, at least at first. Certainly, the list in Ezekiel 40 – 48, which can be dated much more securely, was utopian. And that towns from the tribe of Dan, who were never able to take hold of their allotment, are listed without listing Leshem/Dan, besides suggesting an early date for the list as mentioned above, might also give further reason to think that the list is programmatic. The fact that a number of Canaanite strongholds are set up as Levitical towns would further support such an idea (albeit these areas were at least pretty much claimed to have been held by the united monarchy, and the list would then be more based on reality in this respect if it derives from that time). If one were to date the list later than the united monarchy, one would also pretty much need to see it as programmatic or utopian. (See also the comments in Nelson 1997a: 240–241 about further features in the list that, according to Nelson, speak for an 'artificial composition' of the list. However, features such as non-adjacency between some of the territories of the Levitical groups, while worth noting, do not seem conclusive for claiming 'artificiality' for the lists.)

Interestingly, there is a tension between Joshua 21 and Numbers 35:8 as the latter passage suggests giving more towns to bigger tribes and fewer to smaller tribes, whereas the distribution in Joshua 21 is basically equal (as noted by ben Zvi 1992: 81). If anything, it would be surprising if the Numbers passage, which is generally seen to belong to P (see Budd 1984: 371), were added later in contradiction to the Joshua one (so Milgrom 1989: 290, as pointed out by ben Zvi 1992: 81). That said, it still remains almost as unclear why things would be fine the other way around (i.e. if Josh. 21 was later than the passage in Numbers). In other words, it seems that no firm conclusions can be made based on this state of affairs.

As far as archaeology is concerned, only a half a dozen or so of the Levitical towns have been excavated to date, and all of these attest occupation from the Late Bronze Age or earlier (for further details, see the verse-by-verse commentary section on each of the Levitical towns). Also, surveys have found pottery remains at almost all possible sites for Levitical towns at least from Iron Age I on (for further details, see the verse-by-verse commentary section on each of the Levitical towns), and when one combines these finds with the problems of identification of the sites, which are at times considerable (for further details, see the verse-by-verse commentary section on each of the Levitical towns), and the fact that, for example, no pottery shards from earlier than the eighth century have been found at suggested sites for Geba and Jattir (see Peterson 1977: 405–408, 496–499), even though Geba and Jattir are mentioned in the books of Samuel (1 Sam. 13 – 14; 2 Sam. 5:25 [cf. Judg. 20:33]; 1 Sam. 30:27; see Peterson 1977: 398–399, 491), which traditionally have been thought to give a reliable picture of the time they portray (see e.g. the comments in Hertzberg 1964: 17–20; one may of course try to break this argument by being sceptical), one may conclude that, based on archaeological evidence, the list of the Levitical towns could be dated to any period from the settlement onwards. One should also note here that if the list is programmatic, a number of sites may have been selected, even though Israelite occupation and/or settlement followed only later. In this respect, as Millard points out, even uninhabited places may have names (A. R. Millard, personal communication, May 2000).

For comments about the theoretical versus the practical in Ancient Near Eastern legislation, see 'Form and structure' of chapter 20.

Comment

1–2. As noted above (on 20:1), Hess helpfully notes (Hess 1996: 277) that chapters 20 – 21 make reference to towns that are 'taken back' from the tribal allotments for a specific purpose (cf. also comments by Weinfeld above in the 'Form and structure' section). Chapter 20 dealt with the so-called cities of refuge. Chapter 21 deals with the Levitical towns. The institution of both cities of refuge and Levitical towns is based on Yahweh's command, originally given in Numbers 35 (see Num. 35:1, 9) in narrative order. A list of Levitical towns also occurs in 1 Chronicles 6:54–81. The list in 1 Chronicles 6 somewhat diverges from the list here (for details about some of the Greek divergences, see 'Notes' to translation of Josh. 21). In the narrative here, it is the Levites who remind Joshua at Shiloh about the earlier promise to allot towns for the Levites.

3–7. The Israelites then fulfil the obligation. They give forty-eight towns, of which six are the cities of refuge, to the Levites according to the tripartite division of the Levites into the clans of the Kohathites, the Gershonites and the Merarites (Num. 3:17–37). The Kohathites are further divided into Aaronite priests and non-Aaronites. Each of the four overall divisions then receives towns from the territory of three tribes, respectively. However, there is an exception in that the territory of Manasseh is divided so that the western half goes to the non-Aaronite Kohathites and the Transjordanian half goes to the Gershonites, so that the non-Aaronite Kohathites receive towns from two and a half tribes (a total of thirteen towns) and the Gershonites receive towns from three and a half tribes. The non-Aaronite Kohathites also receive the smallest number of towns, only ten overall, whereas the Aaronite Kohathites and Gershonites receive thirteen towns each, and the Merarites twelve towns. Thinking in terms of the tripartite division, the Kohathites receive a total of twenty-three towns from five and a half tribes, the Gershonites thirteen towns from three and a half tribes and the Merarites twelve towns from three tribes. The allotment also moves from southern Cisjordan (Aaronite Kohathites from Judah, Simeon and Benjamin) towards the north (non-Aaronite Kohathites from Ephraim, Dan and Manasseh), then further north and towards Transjordan (Gershonites from Issachar, Asher, Naphtali and the Transjordanian half-tribe of Manasseh) and to Transjordan (Merarites from Reuben, Gad and Zebulun). As the Kohathites receive the largest allotment in terms of the number of tribes and towns from the largest and most central tribal areas, it clearly appears that they are considered the most important Levitical division, as if the fact that the Aaronites belong to them were not enough. It should be noted that Dan's allotment portrayed here is the original allotment prior to their move to the north (see comments on Josh. 19:40–48 on this move). That Judah, Simeon and Benjamin feature prominently as the donors of the towns for the Aaronites speaks for the relative importance of these tribes, albeit their prominence may also be coincidental. For example, their choice as the donors of the Aaronite towns could counterbalance the importance of Shiloh in Ephraim as the central sanctuary and the overall leadership of the northern hill country and, as archaeology attests, its supremacy in terms of population at the time (see 'Form and structure' section for further details). Of course, some would see such an allocation as a reflection of later monarchic realities.

8–40. A list of the Levitical towns follows. We will present it in the form of a table. Nine of the towns are not listed elsewhere in Joshua (note however that Beeshterah of v. 27 is generally taken to be the same as Ashtaroth, which occurs in Josh. 12:4; 13:12, 31), and I will comment on them separately after the table. A further five are not listed in Joshua 13 – 21 (not counting the mention of Shechem in Josh. 17:2 as a direct mention of the town Shechem). All the counts in verses 19, 26, 33 and 40 tally with the number of towns actually listed in verses 11–18, 21–25, 27–32 and 34–39, respectively. Note that Judah and Simeon receive a total of nine towns, whereas Naphtali receives three towns, and all other tribes receive four towns.

Verse	Levitical division	Town	Tribe	Previously commented in	Any special comments
11, 13	Aaronite Kohath	Kiriath Arba/ Hebron	Judah and Simeon	10:3–5; 15:13–14	City of refuge. 15:54 in the list of Judah
13	Aaronite Kohath	Libnah	Judah and Simeon	10:29–30	15:42 in the list of Judah
14	Aaronite Kohath	Jattir	Judah and Simeon	15:48	
14	Aaronite Kohath	Eshtemoa	Judah and Simeon	15:50	Note the slightly differing spelling in 15:50, but the towns are apparently the same
15	Aaronite Kohath	Holon	Judah and Simeon	15:51	
15	Aaronite Kohath	Debir	Judah and Simeon	10:3–5	15:7, 49 in the lists of Judah
16	Aaronite Kohath	Ain	Judah and Simeon	15:32	
16	Aaronite Kohath	Juttah	Judah and Simeon	15:55	
16	Aaronite Kohath	Beth Shemesh	Judah and Simeon	15:10	Note that Levites are associated with Beth Shemesh in 1 Sam. 6:15
17	Aaronite Kohath	Gibeon	Benjamin	9:3	18:25 in the list of Benjamin
17	Aaronite Kohath	Geba	Benjamin	24:32–33	18:24 in the list of Benjamin
18	Aaronite Kohath	Anathoth	Benjamin	* not listed in Joshua otherwise	See comments below following the table
18	Aaronite Kohath	Almon	Benjamin	* not listed in Joshua otherwise	See comments below following the table

Verse	Levitical division	Town	Tribe	Previously commented in	Any special comments
21	Non-Aaronite Kohath	Shechem	Ephraim	17:7–8	City of refuge. Note also 17:2. Not listed directly in Joshua 13 – 19 as a town belonging to a tribe, albeit implied to be part of Manasseh in 17:2
21	Non-Aaronite Kohath	Gezer	Ephraim	12:12	16:3 in the list of Ephraim.
22	Non-Aaronite Kohath	Kibzaim	Ephraim	* not listed in Joshua otherwise	See comments below following the table
22	Non-Aaronite Kohath	Beth Horon	Ephraim	16:3	
23	Non-Aaronite Kohath	Elteke	Dan	19:44	Note the slightly different spelling in 19:44
23	Non-Aaronite Kohath	Gibbethon	Dan	19:44	
24	Non-Aaronite Kohath	Aijalon	Dan	19:42	See also 10:12–14
24	Non-Aaronite Kohath	Gath Rimmon	Dan	19:45	
25	Non-Aaronite Kohath	Taanach	Western Manasseh	12:21	17:11 in the list of western Manasseh.
25	Non-Aaronite Kohath	Gath Rimmon	Western Manasseh	* not listed in Joshua otherwise	See comments below following the table
27	Gershon	Golan	Eastern Manasseh	20:8	City of refuge; not listed in Joshua 13 – 19

Verse	Levitical division	Town	Tribe	Previously commented in	Any special comments
27	Gershon	Beeshterah	Eastern Manasseh	* not listed in Joshua otherwise, unless the same as Ashtaroth, in which case see 12:4	See comments below following the table
28	Gershon	Kishion	Issachar	19:20	
28	Gershon	Daberath	Issachar	19:12	
29	Gershon	Jarmuth	Issachar	* not listed in Joshua otherwise	See comments below following the table
29	Gershon	En Gannim	Issachar	19:21	
30	Gershon	Mishal	Asher	19:26	
30	Gershon	Abdon	Asher	19:28	Ebron in 19:28; see comments on the verse
31	Gershon	Helkath	Asher	19:25	
31	Gershon	Rehob	Asher	19:28	
32	Gershon	Kedesh	Naphtali	12:22	City of refuge; 19:37 in the list of Naphtali
32	Gershon	Hammoth Dor	Naphtali	19:35	Hammath in 19:35; if not, the location of Hammoth Dor is unknown
32	Gershon	Kartan	Naphtali	* not listed in Joshua otherwise	See comments below following the table
34	Merari	Jokneam	Zebulun	12:22	Not listed in Joshua 13 – 19
34	Merari	Kartah	Zebulun	* not listed in Joshua otherwise	See comments below following the table

Verse	Levitical division	Town	Tribe	Previously commented in	Any special comments
35	Merari	Dimnah	Zebulun	* not listed in Joshua otherwise	See comments below following the table
35	Merari	Nahalal	Zebulun	19:15	
36	Merari	Bezer	Reuben	20:8	City of refuge; not listed in Joshua 13–19
36	Merari	Jahaz	Reuben	13:18	
37	Merari	Kedemoth	Reuben	13:18	
37	Merari	Mephaath	Reuben	13:18	
38	Merari	Ramoth	Gad	20:8	City of refuge; not listed in Joshua 13–19
38	Merari	Mahanaim	Gad	13:26	
39	Merari	Heshbon	Gad	12:2	13:26 in the list of Gad, but also with Reuben in 13:17
39	Merari	Jazer	Gad	13:25	

9–11. The Aaronites clearly seem to be considered the most important group as the lot falls to them first (though this is rather natural based on Leviticus, of course). Otherwise, cf. table above.

12. The text takes care to note that Hebron had also been given to Caleb. There was thus sharing, apparently with Levites by and large concentrating on the core of the town, and Caleb by and large concentrating on the environs of the town. Cf. also comments on 14:13–14.

13–17. Cf. table above. Note that Beth Shemesh in Judah and Simeon (v. 16) may be the same as Ir Shemesh in 19:41 for Dan (as noted by Nelson 1997a: 239; and see comments on 19:41). But, if so, the mention for Dan could simply be a result of inaccuracy by the compiler, or be part of a town list edited later. Or it could have been considered a border town (cf. 15:10) with varying attributions between Judah and Dan, including possibly during different times if and when the lists were edited and updated.

18. Anathoth (cf. Jer. 1:1 etc.) is not listed in Joshua 13 – 19. It is generally identified with Ras el-Kharrubeh, from which surveys have found pottery evidence from the end of Iron Age I and from Iron Age II (see *ABD* 1:

227–228). Almon is not listed in Joshua 13 – 19. It is generally identified with Khirbet 'Almit, and survey evidence from both Iron Age I and II has been found at the site (see Boling and Wright 1982: 489).

19–21. Cf. table above.

22. Kibzaim is not listed in Joshua 13 – 19. Its location is not really known (see *ABD* 4: 36). Otherwise, cf. table above.

23–24. Cf. table above.

25. Gath Rimmon in western Manasseh is not listed in Joshua 13 – 19. The location is unknown, in fact, e.g. Boling and Wright consider the mention here a scribal error (Boling and Wright 1982: 465). It could be considered to refer to Gath Rimmon in 19:45, perhaps most naturally as a border town with dual attribution, if Gath Rimmon were not already mentioned for Dan in the previous verse (21:24). Otherwise, cf. table above.

26. Cf. table above.

27. Beeshterah is not listed in Joshua 13 – 19. However, most take it to be the same as Ashtaroth (see MacDonald 2000: 155; *ABD* 1: 491, 647–648), for which see comments on 12:4. If this equation with Ashtaroth is not valid, the location of Beeshterah is not known. Otherwise, cf. table above.

28. Cf. table above.

29. The identification of Jarmuth (not the same Jarmuth as in 10:5, 23; 12:11 or 15:35) is unclear (see *ABD* 3: 644–645). Mount Yarmuta is however mentioned in a basalt stele of Seti I from about 1300 BC found at Beth Shan (see *ABD* 3: 645; *NEAEHL*: 217, 219 [photo]). Otherwise, cf. table above.

30–31. Cf. table above.

32. The location of Kartan is unclear, albeit Tel Raqqat from which evidence from the Late Bronze and Iron Ages has been found, and Khirbet el-Qureiyeh, a site with difficult geographical access, have been suggested as possibilities (see *ABD* 4: 7). Otherwise, cf. table above.

33. Cf. table above.

34. The location of Kartah is not known. Some have suggested that it is a repetition for Kartan in verse 32 or a corruption of some other town name (see *ABD* 4: 6–7). Otherwise, cf. table above.

35. The location of Dimnah is not known, albeit some have suggested that, based on 1 Chronicles 6:77, it should be Rimmon as in 19:13 (see *ABD* 2: 199). Otherwise, cf. table above.

36–40. Cf. table above. Note that Heshbon is here listed with Gad, whereas it is listed with Reuben in 13:17. However, 13:26 (if not 13:17) implies that it could be a border town between Reuben and Gad, and perhaps dual attribution can be thought of.

41–42. A summary about the allotment of the Levites concludes the list. The number of towns actually listed in verses 8–40 tallies with the total count of forty-eight given.

43–45. The book of Joshua states that the Israelites took the land and subsequently lived in peace. Apart from being garbed in deuteronomic language (cf. Deut. 12; cf. also 11:23; 14:15 and comments there; cf. further with comments on Josh. 18:1, and 'Form and structure' of Josh. 8:30–35), this is obviously an idealized and exaggerated statement, and perhaps this can be argued to have been couched in fairly typical Ancient Near Eastern fashion (cf. Younger 1990). In reality, even the book of Joshua itself states that the situation was not in fact this rosy, as I have already pointed out. However, the comment here gives the author an opportunity to highlight his conviction that Yahweh had been faithful to his promises. This serves the author's theological purpose of promoting Yahwism as he does by various means throughout the book (cf. Introduction to this commentary etc.).

Explanation

Chapter 21 concludes the tribal allotments. The final stage of the allotments is ensuring that the Aaronite priests and the Levites get their share, so that provision is made for everyone in Israel. The priests are mentioned first among the Levites. Interestingly, Levi's lot clearly seems to be reflected in Genesis 49:5–7 (itself apparently referring back to Gen. 34, esp. vv. 25–29). However, equally, the Levites are extremely important for Israel owing to their taking care of cultic duties. The priests and Levites were already to be recipients of parts of sacrifices and of tithes, as legislated in the Pentateuch (see esp. Num. 18), but did not really have any land of their own. The system of Levitical towns provides a further means of livelihood and stability. In this way, justice and provision for all is ensured, and this is also a good principle for today's Christians to consider. Also, the provision for the Levites can help Christians to bear in mind that it would be helpful if they could provide for Christian ministers. We should note that there is a voluntary aspect to this, and yet it is an important aspect that should not be forgotten or otherwise neglected (cf. Deut. 12:19).

EXCURSUS 11: FORM AND STRUCTURE OF JOSHUA 22 – 24 AND THE END OF GENESIS–JOSHUA

These chapters clearly portray a time after the initial conquest (Josh. 1 – 12) and the allotment of territory for the Israelites (Josh. 13 – 21), constituting the final main section of the book of Joshua. The emphasis here shifts to serving Yahweh in the future. This is somewhat implicit in chapter 22, but completely explicit in chapters 23 and 24. A fair bit of the material here has been considered to be later additions. Noth basically thought that Joshua 21:43–45 together with Joshua 22:1–6 and 23:1–16 formed the deuteronomistic conclusion to the conquest tradition, and that the rest is an addition. I will in particular argue below (Excursus 12) that Joshua 22:9–34 can be seen as an integral part of the book of Joshua, and that, in addition to the point itself, this has implications that relate to the concept of the Deuteronomistic History. The status of Joshua 24 is somewhat more complicated. As we will see, Joshua 24 can in many ways be seen as a conclusion to Genesis–Joshua as a whole. In this manner, a reading of Joshua 24 is in particular tied up with the question of whether there existed a Hexateuch (a work encompassing Genesis–Joshua), over against the idea of Deuteronomy–Kings forming a separate Deuteronomistic History.

In relation to the question of a Hexateuch versus a Deuteronomistic History, we note here that chapter 24 makes reference to the Pentateuch, including patriarchal traditions in relation to Genesis. The visit of Jacob to Shechem in Genesis 35:1–5 is alluded to in verses 23–26, and the mention of the burial of the bones of Joseph in verse 32 refers back to Genesis 50:25 and Exodus 13:19 and serves as a counterpart to them. The fact that the passage takes place in Shechem connects with Genesis 12:6–7; 34; 37:12–13; Deuteronomy 11:29–30; 27:1–26 and Joshua 8:30–35 (cf. Judg. 9). The historical recital in verses 2–13 of course makes reference to the whole sweep of the Pentateuchal history, starting from Genesis 12. We should also bear in mind that much of the material in the initial chapters of the book of Joshua (more specifically, chapters 3 – 8) seem to attest clear literary links back to the book of Exodus (more specifically, Exod. 3; 12 – 17; see Excursus 2). In addition, I have also commented elsewhere in this commentary on other likely links to Exodus–Numbers, in particular in the book of Joshua (e.g. Caleb's and Joshua's faithfulness in Numbers and their share in the tribal allotments, references to Transjordanian allotments listed in Num., and the allotment of cities of refuge and Levitical towns, which was instituted in Num.). And, as discussed in the Introduction, we should not forget that, notably, there is a kind of 'break' in style and approach between Joshua and Judges. All this serves to reinforce the idea that something has been meant to conclude at the end of Joshua, at least in the present form of the book, even if Israel's story as a whole nevertheless continues afterwards in the books of Judges, Samuel and Kings. Of course, Noth in essence argued that no such break between Joshua and Judges originally existed, but, in effect, any impression of a break has come about through later (priestly) additions. I leave it to the reader to decide which explanation of this intriguing problem sounds more convincing, even though my position here is clear. That is, I think that Joshua is a conclusion to a story that has begun in Genesis and continued through Exodus, Leviticus, Numbers and Deuteronomy. As I have suggested a date in the time before the Israelite monarchy for the first version of the book of Joshua, this would imply a date at around that time for the basic form of the books of Genesis, Exodus, Leviticus, Numbers and Deuteronomy as well. However, as discussed in the Introduction, further examination of the books of the Pentateuch would be required in order to see whether such a hypothesis can be substantiated. Be that as it may, as we noted in the Introduction, for example, Faust (2006) has suggested that Israelite ethnicity emerged in the Early Iron Age as a response to the Philistine threat. If this threat indeed contributed towards the emergence of such an identity, then the writing down of relevant ancestral traditions around this time would surely have helped in the process of forming and propagating this identity.

JOSHUA 22

Translation

¹At that time Joshua called for the Reubenites, the Gadites and the eastern half of the Manassites. ²He said to them, 'You have kept everything that Moses the servant of Yahweh commanded you, and you have obeyed me in everything I have told you. ³You have not abandoned your fellow Israelites during this long time but have kept the commandment of Yahweh. ⁴See, Yahweh has now given peace to your brothers as he promised them. Now, return to your homes and to the land of your inheritance which Moses the servant of Yahweh gave you east of Jordan. ⁵Only be very careful to keep the law and the commandments that Moses gave you, to love Yahweh your God, to follow him, to keep his ordinances, to attach yourselves to him and to serve him with all your heart and all your soul.'

⁶Joshua blessed them and sent them away, and they went to their homes. ⁷(Moses had given Bashan to one half of the tribe of Manasseh, and Joshua had given land from the west side of Jordan to the other half.) When Joshua sent them to their homes, he blessed them. ⁸He said to them, 'You are returning to your homes with much wealth: with numerous cattle, with silver, gold, bronze, iron and lots of clothes. Do divide the spoils from your enemies with your brothers.'

⁹Then the Reubenites, Gadites and the eastern half of the Manassites departed from the Israelites from Shiloh in the land of Canaan to go to the land of Gilead, the land allotted to them by Moses in accordance with the word of Yahweh.

¹⁰They arrived at the region of the Jordan in the land of Canaan. Soon after, they built an imposing altar there by the river Jordan. ¹¹The Israelites heard this and said, 'Look, the Reubenites, the Gadites and the eastern Manassites have built an altar opposite the land of Canaan at the circuit of Jordan, opposite the Israelites.' ¹²The Israelites heard this, and the whole assembly of the Israelites gathered at Shiloh in preparation to go to war against them.

¹³The Israelites sent a delegation to the Reubenites, the Gadites and the eastern half of the Manassites in the land of Gilead, consisting of Phinehas the son of Eleazar the priest ¹⁴and ten leaders with them, one leader from each tribe of Israel, a head of their respective families and divisions.

¹⁵They came to the Reubenites, Gadites and the eastern Manassites in the land of Gilead and said to them, ¹⁶'This is what the whole assembly of Yahweh says,

"What is this faithless act that you have now turned away from the God of Israel and have built an altar, disobeying him? [17]Was the sin of Peor from which we have not yet been purified and due to which there was a plague on the people of Yahweh a small matter for us? [18]You have turned away from Yahweh today and have rebelled against him. Soon his anger will be on the whole people of Israel. [19]However, if your land is unclean, cross over to the land of Yahweh where the tabernacle of Yahweh is located. You can then take holdings from among us. However, do not rebel against Yahweh and against us by building an altar other than that of Yahweh our God. [20]Did not Achan the son of Zerah violate the dedication, with wrath falling on the whole people of Israel? And was it him only who died because of his sin?"'

[21]The Reubenites, the Gadites and the eastern Manassites replied to the leaders of Israel, [22]'Yahweh, Yahweh the greatest God knows, and let Israel know that if we have rebelled against Yahweh or betrayed him, you are not to let us go today. [23]If we have built for ourselves an altar to turn away from Yahweh, to offer burnt offerings, grain offerings or peace offerings on it, may Yahweh himself call us to account.

[24]'We did this because we were concerned that your descendants would say to our descendants in the future, "What do you have to do with Yahweh, the God of Israel? [25]Yahweh has set Jordan as a border between us and you, you Reubenites and Gadites. You have no relation to Yahweh." Your descendants may then prevent our descendants from fearing Yahweh.

[26]'Therefore we thought, "Let us make ourselves an altar, but not for burnt offerings or for sacrifices. [27]It will be a witness between you and us throughout our generations of our service of Yahweh at his presence with our burnt offerings, sacrifices and peace offerings. Then your descendants will not be saying to our descendants in the future, 'You have no relation to Yahweh.'" [28]And we said to ourselves, "If they talk to us and to our descendants in this way in the future, we will say, 'See this model of the altar of Yahweh which our fathers made, not for burnt offerings or for sacrifices, but to be a witness between you and us.'"

[29]'Far it be from us that we would rebel against Yahweh and turn away from him by building an altar for burnt offerings, grain offerings or sacrifices, other than the altar that is in front of his tabernacle.'

[30]When the priest Phinehas and the leaders of the assembly, the heads of the Israelites who were with them, heard what the Reubenites, the Gadites and the Manassites had to say, they were pleased. [31]Phinehas then said to the Reubenites, Gadites and the Manassites, 'Today we know that Yahweh is with us since you have not betrayed Yahweh, and Israel is safe from his anger.'

[32]And Phinehas and the leaders departed from the Reubenites and Gadites from the land of Gilead to the Israelites in the land of Canaan and reported these events to them. [33]The Israelites were happy with this report. They blessed God and did not think any more about going to war to destroy the land where the Reubenites and the Gadites lived.

[34]And the Reubenites and the Gadites named the altar, 'because it is a witness between us that Yahweh is God'.

Notes on the text

1. Obeyed me: lit. 'listened to my voice'.

4. Homes: lit. 'tents', thus also in verses 6–8. East of Jordan: lit. 'on the other side of Jordan'.

5. Follow him: lit. 'walk in all his ways'.

8. You are returning: lit. 'Return'. Gr. does not phrase the verse as a command, but as a narrative of the eastern tribes returning and dividing.

10. The region of the Jordan: Hebr. *gelîlôt hayyardēn*.

11. Opposite the land of Canaan: Gr. 'at the boundary of the land of Canaan'. Opposite the Israelites: Hebr. *'el-'ēber běnê yiśrā'ēl*.

12. The Israelites heard this: not included in Gr.

17. People: lit. 'congregation' (Hebr. *'ēdāh*).

18. Soon: lit. 'tomorrow'. People: cf. note on verse 17.

19. Tabernacle: Hebr. *miškan*. Is located: lit. 'dwells' (Hebr. *šākan*). Against us: not included in Gr.

20. The dedication: Hebr. *ḥērem*.

22. Betrayed: Hebr. *mā'al*, cf. note on verse 31. Let us go: lit. 'save'.

23. Grain offerings: Hebr. *minḥāh*; cf. esp. Lev. 2.

24. Descendants: lit. 'sons', so also in verses 25, 27–28.

25. Prevent: lit. 'stop' (Hebr. *šābat*).

26. Thought: lit. 'said'.

28. Model: Hebr. *tabnît*.

30. Leaders: lit. princes (Hebr. *nāśî'*). Note the apparent defectiveness in the mentioning of the Manassites for these last verses of this chapter (i.e. the 'qualifier' half-tribe/eastern is not included). They were pleased: lit. 'it was good in their eyes'.

31. Have not betrayed: lit. 'that you did not forsake (Hebr. *mā'al*) Yahweh with this faithlessness (Hebr. *ma'al*)'. Cf. note on verse 22. His anger: lit. 'hand of Yahweh'.

33. Were happy: lit. 'was good in the eyes'. They blessed God: Gr. 'And they spoke to the sons of Israel, and blessed the God of the sons of Israel.'

34. The name of the altar may also be missing and the text I have put in quotation marks can be an explanation of the name. Gr. 'And Joshua named the altar of Reuben, Gad and the half-tribe of Manasseh and said that it is a witness between them that the Lord is their God.'

Form and structure

The structure of chapter 22 can be described as follows:

> The Transjordanians permitted to return home (vv. 1–8)
> Joshua summons the Transjordanians (v. 1)

Joshua's speech (vv. 2–5)
Joshua blesses the Transjordanians and sends them away
    (v. 6)
Note about the division of Manasseh into eastern and
    western halves (v. 7a)
Joshua's admonition at point of departure of the
    Transjordanians (vv. 7b–8)
The return of the Transjordanians and the altar incident
    (vv. 9–34)
The Transjordanians return home (v. 9)
The altar incident (vv. 10–34; the chiastic structure for the
    story is from Jobling 1980: 191)
  (a) Transjordanians build the altar (v. 10)
    (b) Cisjordanians threaten war (v. 12)
      (c) Cisjordanians send an embassy (vv. 13–15)
        (d) Accusatory speech by the embassy (vv. 15b–20)
          (e) Transjordanians' reply (vv. 21–29)
        (d') Accepting speech by the embassy (vv. 30–31)
      (c') Return of the embassy to Cisjordan (v. 32)
    (b') Withdrawal of the Cisjordanian threat of war (v. 33)
  (a') Transjordanians name the altar (v. 34)

As Nelson (1997a: 247) aptly notes, 'This chapter divides into deuteronom-istic and priestly halves along the hinge of vv. 7 and 8. The language of vv. 1–6 is unquestionably deuteronomistic, whereas vv. 9–34 exhibit characteristics associated with priestly composition.' Nelson also comments how verses 9–34 can function 'perfectly well as a story' without the initial verses 1–8 (Nelson 1997a: 247). Regarding verses 1–6 more specifically, according to Noth, Joshua 21:43–45, 22:1–6 and 23:1–16 basically con-stitute the deuteronomistic conclusion to the settlement tradition. 21:43–45 serves as a summary of the fulfilment of the conquest and settlement. It should be seen as an introduction to 22:1–6, in which statements are anticipated which then are made again in the ceremonious farewell speech of Joshua (Josh. 23). Joshua 22:1–6 looks back to 1:12–18, and both are part of the deuteronomistic redaction (Noth 1953a: 133). The concept of rest in Joshua 22:4 ties back to Deuteronomy 3:20 and Joshua 1:13, 15 (Noth 1953a: 133; Noth also mentions Josh. 21:44 in this connection).

Verses 9–34 are important in relation to the Deuteronomistic History hypothesis that stems from Noth, and also have their implications for the dating of Joshua. A detailed discussion of the matter is provided in Excursus 12 below. To sum up the argument here, originally, when Noth argued for his theory of a Deuteronomistic History, it was thought that the postulated classic Pentateuchal sources J, E, D and P continued into Joshua and beyond, and the books Genesis–Joshua were seen to constitute an entity called a Hexateuch. Noth responded to this by severing the connection between Genesis–Numbers and Deuteronomy–2 Kings. Noth argued that the priestly source (P) did not continue beyond Numbers (he also minimized the amount of priestly material in the conquest tradition of Numbers). Also, while the (narrative) JE sources did originally include accounts about the conquest and settlement, the books of Deuteronomy (D) and Joshua developed separately from the JE tradition, and the JE account of the conquest was dropped when Genesis–Numbers and Deuteronomy–2 Kings were joined. Any priestly material relating to the conquest tradition in Numbers, and in Joshua in particular, is the result of isolated, insignificant additions. However, if one looks at Joshua 22:9–34, a counter-argument can be formed. Joshua 22:9–34 can be seen to attest priestly features that are intertwined in an overall deuteronomistic narrative. In other words, priestly material is integral to the narrative of Joshua 22:9–34 and is not constituted of isolated additions. Moreover, Joshua 22:9–34 has links to the rest of the book of Joshua and can thus be seen as an integral part of the book, rather than an isolated addition. Also, Joshua 22:9–34 links to Numbers 32 through a common plotline from a priestly standpoint. This then suggests that Numbers 32 and Joshua 22:9–34 are closely connected, which itself suggests some deliberate design. On conventional source criticism, this then suggests that a priestly source that includes concerns about the conquest exists. Also considering the overall connections that can easily be made at face value between the conquest traditions of Numbers and Joshua, it is then more difficult to accept that the conquest tradition of the JE sources would have been dropped. This then implies that a theory of a Hexateuch would be more correct, rather than one of a Deuteronomistic History. At the same time, if one thinks that priestly material is earlier than deuteronomic material (contra classic Wellhausenian thinking), one may think that Joshua is simply in all accounts a direct continuation of Numbers (and Deuteronomy).

The literary composition of Joshua also implies that the reason why the books of Judges, Samuel and Kings do not include much priestly material is not that priestly material did not exist at the time these books were written, but that there must have been some other reason. It is possible to conceive that since the priestly material is associated with the Tent of Meeting, which is most at home in Shiloh, the Judahite and Jerusalemite writer of the books of Samuel did not wish to emphasize the role of the old order of Shiloh and Ephraim, which had passed away, and the same would apply to the book of Judges as well, as it also attests Judahite concerns. Moreover, as the priestly material directly concerns the Tent of Meeting and its cult, it cannot have been applied directly to the Jerusalemite temple and cult, but only indirectly. Thus the priestly material does not fit well conceptually in the time of the monarchy. Rather, and as argued throughout the commentary, and as an exilic date seems a bit late for the book of Joshua, it is most logical to think that the priestly material, or at least substantial parts of it, dates not from the time of the monarchy, but from before it. As Shiloh was rejected and its importance taken away after the disaster at Aphek (1 Sam. 4; See Pitkänen 2004a: 127–158), this then naturally suggests a time before the disaster. We may also summarize that, overall, the lack of priestly material in Judges–2 Kings highlights the literary distinctiveness of these books from Genesis–Joshua and a kind of 'break' between the two sets of material, a feature which I have already commented on elsewhere in this commentary, whether directly or indirectly.

For further comments that involve the form and structure of this chapter, see Excursus 12.

Comment

1–4. After the land has been conquered (in a rough overall sense) and allotted, the narrative describes how Joshua sends the Transjordanian tribes home. The comments refer back to Joshua 1:12–18 (cf. 4:12; 13) and, from a canonical perspective, to Numbers 32. Note the use of *'āz* in this verse, which seems to serve as a loose temporal marker (cf. 8:30 and comments there).

5. A standard (albeit slightly lengthy) admonition of keeping the law is inserted in a very deuteronomic style (cf. Deut. 4:6, 9, 15, 23; 5:32; 6:3, 12, 25; 7:12 etc.; cf. also 1:7; 23:6 in Josh. and comments on the verses; but also cf. Lev. 18:4; 25:18; 26:3).

6–8. Then follows a blessing, and an admonition to share acquisitions by war with everyone. On the significance of blessing, cf. comments on 14:14. As it seems, mention of details of plunder taken from the conquered peoples is included in verse 8, and this has now considerably added to the possessions of the Transjordanians.

9. After verses 1–8, which are very much in a deuteronomic style, the narrative moves to more priestly overtones in 9–34 (see 'Form and structure' section). For Gilead, see comments on 12:2, 4; 13:11. The term is probably (or possibly) used loosely here to refer to the whole of Transjordan.

10. The Transjordanians, upon arriving at a certain place in the vicinity of the river Jordan, build an altar of an imposing type, apparently on the Transjordanian side (the location is not entirely clear [see e.g. Nelson 1997a: 251–252; Snaith 1978: 330–335; Kloppenborg 1981: 368–369], but it would in any case seem to make sense for the Transjordanians to be seen to have thought of their own territory as the place for building the altar). Hess notes that it was not unknown in later Israel to establish a sanctuary on the border of the land, pointing out in 1 Kings 12:28–29 Jeroboam's establishing of altars in Bethel and Dan (Hess 1996: 291). Cf. also Isaiah 19:19, which speaks of a standing stone for Yahweh at the border with Egypt, and if this were to be seen as a monument, it would fit with the overall thrust of the narrative of Joshua 22:9–34, where the altar proves to be a monument. As Nelson points out, the reader (or hearer) is held in suspense until verses 27–28, where the exact nature of the construction is revealed (Nelson 1997a: 253). And one might add that the overall tension is really released only in verses 30–33, where the Cisjordanians accept the explanation of the Transjordanians.

11–12. The Israelites are rather angry to hear about the building of the altar, and get together at Shiloh to prepare for war. Note that the comment about gathering suggests that the western Israelites have also already dispersed away from a centralized camp by this time (cf. comments on v. 1 above). The detailed reasons for the crisis are spelled out in the following verses.

13–14. An executive delegation is sent to the Transjordanians, consisting of Phinehas, the son of the most prominent priest, Eleazar, and one leader from each Cisjordanian tribe. Interestingly, neither Joshua nor Eleazar seems to take part; i.e. the interactions do not take place quite at the highest level on the part of the western Israelites.

15–17. The delegation accuses the Transjordanians of a cultic violation. A violation against gods or their cult is a violation of the highest order in the Ancient Near East (cf. 'Explanation' section below, and comments on 7:1 and throughout the commentary). The reference to (Baal) Peor is a reference to the events of Numbers 25 and to the worship of Baal there.

18–20. The point is made here that the sin of the Transjordanians will pollute the whole community. Verse 20 makes an explicit reference to Achan (Josh. 7; see comments there) and similar effects resulting from his sins.

The reason why it is suggested in verse 19 that the land east of the Jordan might be unclean is not entirely clear. However, it may be because, according to a number of descriptions, the original territory of Canaan is to be seen as west of the Jordan and thus land outside such territory, not really being Yahweh's territory, would be unclean (so also Butler 1983: 247, pointing out Amos 7:17 as well; cf. Nelson 1997a: 252). But this still does not show what the uncleanness has to do with the altar in this context, even though we can speculate that the narrative may imply that the Cisjordanians think that establishing an altar on the Transjordanian side might be seen by the Transjordanians to allow for appeasing Yahweh through cultic acts on that altar, thus removing or alleviating the uncleanness of the Transjordanian land. If so, moving to Cisjordan would remove the problem.

21–22. The Transjordanians vehemently deny the charge, noting that they know that if they have done something inappropriate, they will not get away with it. That is, Yahweh himself, the divine judge, will call them to account. The reader might be slightly suspicious of whether the Transjordanians are really telling the truth about their original intentions in what follows, or whether they are now taking a line that they know may be accepted by the Cisjordanians. However, the narrative does not give any confirmation of such suspicions (cf. Nelson 1997a: 253), and the explanation of the Transjordanians is accepted, without hesitation, once it is brought forward, as will be seen.

23. The Transjordanians note the main offerings and say that offering them was not the intention. As we noted in 8:30, burnt offerings and peace offerings are attested in Ugarit, and are often spoken of together there; see e.g. Pardee 2002: 29–35 (e.g. *dqt l ṣpn . šrp . w šlmm kmm* – 'a ewe for *Ṣapunu* as a burnt offering. And as a peace offering: the same' [Pardee 2002: 29, 31, lines 10–11]). Here a grain offering (*minḥāh*) is mentioned in addition. In Ugarit grain was also offered (see Pardee 2002: 67, 68, which seems to mention two grain types together: *dtt.w.ksm*). Overall, offerings in general were a way of giving to the divine, so it would be natural that such entities or materials that were most readily available and considered valuable would be offered. In this, as animals and grain were things that humans consumed, it would seem natural that these would be offered to the divine as well.

24–29. The point is to build the altar as a witness (and a memorial) for the descendants of both Transjordanians and Cisjordanians. Seeing the altar will remind the parties that the Transjordanians are part of Israel and part of Yahweh's worship at the central sanctuary, the tabernacle (cf. 18:1 and comments on the verse). The deuteronomic injunctions about sacrificing only at the central sanctuary are in force as the land has had rest from war (see Deut. 12:8–12; Josh. 11:23; 14:15; 22:4). A non-sacrificial altar might at first sight seem a contradiction in terms (as the Hebrew for 'altar', *mizbēaḥ*, is derived from *zābaḥ*, which means 'to sacrifice'), but it appears that the altar form itself helps to serve as part of the reminder for the Transjordanians about the central sanctuary at Shiloh (but cf. my comments on vv. 21–22 above). For children's questions, see comments on 4:1–7.

30–33. The explanation satisfies the Cisjordanian delegation. They are pleased and relieved. They will not now need to expect such problems as arose with Achan or with the incident of (Baal) Peor (cf. vv. 16–20; note also that the word *māʿal*, 'to act faithlessly', serves as a further connecting link to Josh. 7). The delegation then returns, and the news is greeted with joy by the rest of the Cisjordanians. The crisis is over, and the narrative is drawing to a close, save for a final explanatory comment in verse 34.

34. The Transjordanians give the altar a name. What the name actually is is somewhat unclear (see the textual note on the verse, and see also e.g. Snaith 1978: 330–335; Kloppenborg 1981: 368–369).

Explanation

The idea of the unity of Israel in war (vv. 1–8) and worship (vv. 9–34) underlies this chapter. The Transjordanians have fulfilled their obligations and can now return home. They are exhorted to follow Yahweh just as all the other Israelites should. Upon return, the Transjordanians build a large altar by the Jordan. This is misunderstood as an act of rebellion in building a place of sacrifice in addition to the central sanctuary at Shiloh, but careful diplomacy averts disaster. Above all, any misunderstandings are corrected and unity is restored.

This chapter points out how important the unity of the whole of Israel, and, in general, proper conduct of worship, was for the writer of the book of Joshua. Here we must keep in mind that the deuteronomic idea of a central sanctuary underlies the text (cf. Deut. 12 in particular). In Joshua 22, all Israelites were to take part in Yahweh's worship in one place, his tabernacle, where he was present in the midst of his people, Israel. However, the tabernacle was superseded by the temple (see Pitkänen 2004a and 2004c). According to the biblical documents, Yahweh left his sanctuary in Shiloh, largely because of the sins of the priesthood (1 Sam. 2:15 – 4:22), but also because of the sins of the people (Ps. 78:56–64, 67). Because of Yahweh's anger, the ark, and thus Yahweh himself (cf. Excursus 3), went into exile (1 Sam. 5), but returned again (1 Sam. 6; cf. Ps. 78:65–66), and eventually entered a newly built temple in Jerusalem (1 Kgs 8:1–21; Ps. 78:68–72). All this demonstrates how important the conduct of proper worship was in ancient Israel, in line with the rest of the Ancient Near East.

The legacy of the importance of worship remains for Christians. However, Christian worship differs from that in the Old Testament. There are no more sacrifices, as Christ has abolished the need for further sacrifices through his own sacrifice. Also, for Christians, the temple was superseded by the (role of the) Holy Spirit in New Testament times. Whereas the Israelites needed to travel to find Yahweh's presence at the tabernacle or temple, Christians *are* the temple of God. Accordingly, the concept of unity is different for Christians from that of the ancient Israelites. Also, Christians do not generally need to be afraid that they will receive severe punishment if they somehow neglect worship or conduct it in a way that is not entirely 'appropriate' (whatever 'appropriate' means). However, despite many changes in form and content, the emphasis on God as the object of worship for Christians remains. Unity between Christians is of course also always helpful, whatever the case (see esp. John 17:23). And, of course, Christians are encouraged to worship their God not out of fear but out of gratitude (cf. Rom. 8:15; Gal. 4:6). Of course, bad behaviour in worship should never be encouraged either (see e.g. 1 Cor. 11:27–32), but, at least for this writer, the focus is not on judgment or fear in Christianity. Finally, as in Joshua 22, we might say that Christians can also be exhorted to handle conflict situations skilfully, even though such a comment really applies to anyone.

EXCURSUS 12: JOSHUA 22:9–34 AND THE DEUTERONOMISTIC HISTORY HYPOTHESIS, WITH IMPLICATIONS FOR THE DATE OF JOSHUA

Seen from a canonical perspective, the narratives about the Transjordanians connect directly back to Numbers (chapter 32). This connection of the book of Joshua with Numbers has been an important topic in academic discussion, and its relevance to Joshua 22:9–34 is a crucial matter, and I will therefore discuss it carefully. Martin Noth, the eminent German scholar of the early and mid-twentieth century, in essence needed to break a connection between Numbers and Joshua in order to present his famous theory of the so-called Deuteronomistic History, a continuous narrative comprising Deuteronomy, Joshua, Judges and Kings, separate from Genesis–Numbers. What was particularly important for Noth was that the latest layer of the Pentateuchal sources, the so-called priestly source, did not continue from Numbers to Joshua (otherwise one could say that the two were designed together, in contradiction of the Deuteronomistic History theory). Thus Noth suggested that there were only very isolated priestly additions in Joshua. However, an investigation of the message and literary composition of Joshua 22:9–34 will lead us to take issue with Noth's view on the relationship of the book of Joshua to the Pentateuch and to Judges–2 Kings. It will also help us to think about the question of the date and provenance of the book of Joshua as a whole. (The discussion below has been adapted from Pitkänen 2004a: 185–218, with the kind permission of Gorgias Press.)

As I have already discussed in relation to the passage, Joshua 22:9–34 describes an incident regarding the Transjordanian tribes of Reuben, Gad and Half-Manasseh. When the Transjordanians return from the conquest to their allotted territory, they build a big altar at the side of the Jordan (v. 10; concerning the problems involved in determining the exact location [vv. 10–11] and the name [v. 34] of the altar, see Snaith 1978: 330–335; Kloppenborg 1981: 368–369). Upon hearing this, the rest of the Israelites see the matter as a cultic violation and send a delegation to confront the Transjordanians (vv. 11–20). However, the Transjordanians explain that the altar is not to be for sacrifice, but it is to serve only as a memorial and a reminder for proper worship in front of the altar of Yahweh which is before his tabernacle (*mškn*; vv. 21–29). The Israelite delegation, led by Phinehas *ben* Eleazar, then accepts this explanation and returns home to Cisjordan (vv. 30–34).

According to J. S. Kloppenborg (1981: 347):

> The story of the departure of the two and one-half Transjordanian tribes following the completion of the conquest and the building of their altar remains a puzzle in spite of the attention which it

has received. Viewed in the context of Joshua, chap 22 is anomalous on several counts. It relates action of the confederacy not against the Canaanite inhabitants of the land but against another Israelite group. In this it resembles the attack on Benjamin (and Jabesh-Gilead) in Jgs 19–21. The dispute does not appear to be primarily political or territorial but cultic, and it presupposes (anachronistically) the legitimacy of a single cult-center. Accordingly it is not Joshua, but a priest, Phinehas son of Eleazar who is the central actor. Equally remarkable is the solution to the dispute: the Transjordanian altar is no altar at all, but only a 'witness stone'. It is perhaps these and other problems that explain the general uneasiness felt with this chapter and the reluctance of the standard histories of Israel to treat it in any depth (or even to suggest an appropriate chronological framework for the events narrated).

Considering these comments by Kloppenborg in regard to Joshua 22:9–34, it should come as no surprise that scholarly interpretation of the passage is very diverse. Various opinions exist as to the purpose and setting of the narrative and its traditio-historical formation. Kloppenborg (1981: 347–348) summarizes Noth, Steuernagel, Herzberg and Möhlenbrink as follows:

Noth sees an old aetiological legend explaining the now-missing name in v. 34, although he hesitates to say more in view of the thorough re-editing of the chapter. Steuernagel posits an old story of an altar named 'witness' ('d) at a cultic city with a stone circle (glylwt), perhaps near Gilgal. To this Herzberg adds that behind the deuteronomistic theology of centralization of the cult lies an old story whose purpose it was to attest the unity in worship of the Trans- and Cis-Jordanian tribes. Möhlenbrink goes much beyond these reconstructions: Jos 22:9–34 is a cult-polemic legend from the period of the judges which reveals the conflict of two amphictyonic centers, Gilgal, the cult center for a Reubenite–Gadite–Benjaminite confederacy, and the Israelite (Ephraimite) sanctuary at Shiloh.

Also (Kloppenborg 1981: 348–349):

Perhaps the most radical thesis is that of J. Dus who recognizes both P and Dtr editing but dates both to the period of judges! In his view, during the period of judges the ark was periodically placed upon a wagon pulled by cows and allowed to go wherever the cows took it. It was by this method that the 'place which Yahweh himself shall choose among the tribes' (Deuteronomy

12:5) was determined. Since Jordan formed a barrier to the cows, Reuben and Gad felt it necessary to build their own sanctuary. This provoked hostilities and eventually led to the decision to keep the ark at Shiloh.

Kloppenborg himself thinks that Joshua 22:9–34 is based on an old tradition of a Yahwistic altar which a post-exilic priestly writer has changed into a non-sacrificial altar and added the elements of conflict in the story (Kloppenborg 1981: 365–370). De Vaux (1978/1971: 583) writes that all that he would venture to say is that the story preserves the memory of conflicting cults. According to Eissfeldt (1962–1979b/1973: 14), Joshua 22 presents 'a story about an attack against the cultic monopoly of the Sanctuary of Shiloh and its repulsion'. Moreover, for Eissfeldt (1962–1979b/1973: 14), 'The story of Joshua 22 is, at least in its basic elements, not about the cultic trends of the three centuries from 700 to 400 BC, but about events of the 12th century BC, centering on Shiloh, and have been arranged to address the cultic problems of these three centuries only secondarily.' Butler thinks that the tradition originally restricted sacrificial worship to Shiloh, and was forbidden at Gilgal, the place where the rival altar stood. According to Butler, the original tradition, which comes from the time prior to Samuel, was taken up in the book of Joshua in the post-exilic era to speak to the Babylonian exiles concerning worship outside the land of Israel. However, Butler leaves open the extent of editing of the ancient tradition in the post-exilic period, noting, 'Did the tradition as a whole gain its contours at the time of Shiloh's dominance?' (Butler 1983: 243–244). Finally, according to McConville (1993: 100), 'at least the core of the present narrative belongs to a time before the period of the monarchy, when the centrality of Shiloh in Israel was in fact being asserted (cf. Judges 21:21; 1 Sam. 1–3)'.

All the above scholars think that Joshua 22:9–34 is based on an old tradition which has undergone more or less extensive editing to reach its present form. Yet, in Kloppenborg's words (Kloppenborg 1981: 349):

> While most critics admit either Deuteronomistic or Priestly editing of the passage (or both), some insist that Jos 22 is a retrojection of Priestly and post-exilic concerns into the period of the conquest. No early tradition is present at all. A. Menes, for example, sought to show that the passage is an aetiology for the synagogue ('an altar without sacrifice'). The exiles, for whom worship outside Israel was necessary (Ez 11:14–16), solved their dilemma by regarding the synagogue as a 'copy' (Jos 22:28; cf. Ez 11:16) of the altar in Jerusalem, but they avoided sacrifice in accordance with the post-deuteronomistic understanding of the cult. Jos 22:9–34 was therefore to be regarded as a legitimation of the synagogue and an exilic creation. Likewise rejecting the

presence of ancient tradition in this chapter, J. G. Vink believes that Jos 22 is a late post-exilic aetiology which, far from warning against illegitimate sanctuaries, actually legitimates limited cultic use of altars outside Palestine, such as the one at Yeb mentioned in the Elephantine Papyri (EP 32).

Kloppenborg has argued well against the interpretation of Menes. In Kloppenborg's words (Kloppenborg 1981: 363):

It seems most unlikely that an aetiology for the synagogue would involve an altar, since that was not a usual part of the synagogue furnishings. Had the tribes built a *bet el* not for sacrifice, or a place of assembly (*byt hknst*) or had the account mentioned 'prayer' there would be more justification in seeing an aetiology for the synagogue.

Against Vink, one may say that the priests at Yeb in their letter to Judah (EA 30, lines 24–28; see PORTEN-YARDENI, vol. 1: 68–69 for the text, including a copy of the original manuscript; cf. Cowley 1967/1923: 111–113; the letter dated to 408 BC; see Cowley 1967/1923: 108) say that they would like to get the temple rebuilt as formerly (lines 4–13 tell how the temple was destroyed by Egyptians three years earlier) so that they could offer there on the altar meal offering, incense and sacrifice (note also that lines 20–22 lament that meal offering, incense or sacrifice had not been able to be offered since the temple was destroyed [cf. lines 4–6]). The answer from Judah (EA 32; lines 8–11; see PORTEN-YARDENI, vol. 1: 76–77 for the text, including a copy of the original manuscript; cf. Cowley 1967/1923: 123; letter dated to about 408 BC; see Cowley 1967/1923: 122) authorizes the building of a new temple in place of the former, and offering meal offering and incense on the altar 'as formerly was done' [lines 10–11]). Whatever one thinks of the disposition and knowledge of the Judean writers regarding the legal requirements of the Pentateuch (cf. Cowley 1967/1923: xix–xxii), especially bearing in mind that the correspondence is between the priests of Elephantine and the political establishment of Judah (EA 30 was addressed to Bigvai, [Persian] governor of Judah [EA 30, line 1], and the reply in EA 32 [line 1] is a memorandum from Bigvai, and Delaiah, son of Sanballat governor of Samaria [cf. EA 30, line 29]), the disposition and knowledge are not the same as that indicated by Joshua 22:9–34. Based on Joshua 22:9–34, there should have been no cultic activity on the Elephantine altar whatsoever. In relation to this, Joshua 22:23, 29 specifically exclude meal offerings, which the reply from Judah to Elephantine explicitly authorizes. Thus it is hardly likely that Joshua 22 can be interpreted on the basis of the evidence of the Elephantine papyri as an aetiology which legitimates the Elephantine temple (cf. Kloppenborg 1981: 364).

Another scholar who has argued for a purely post-exilic setting of the narrative is Fritz. According to Fritz (1994: 222; my translation from German), 'The material fits with the disputes of the post-exilic time when the Jerusalem temple had become the central place of the Israelite cult and the question about the belonging of Jews from outside Judea in legitimate Israel had become a pressing issue.'

However, Fritz's interpretation has immediate problems. Simply, why would the Jews outside Judea, either in Samaria or more probably in Babylonia, be addressed via the appellation of Reubenites, Gadites and Manassites? Moreover, for the Judeans of the post-exilic time, the Transjordanians had been deported some 300 years earlier, and had not returned (1 Chr. 5:26). Thus, to speak about the Transjordanians already suggests a historical reminiscence of past days, a matter which Fritz's approach excludes. Further, who would have thought that Babylonia or Egypt, where the Elephantine colony is, is a land which the Israelites inherited (Josh. 22:19)? What meaning would an altar at the side of Jordan have either for the Babylonians, for the people of Elephantine or even for the Samaritans (Josh. 22:10, 23–27)? Moreover, in Joshua 22 it is only the land east of Jordan which may be unclean, not Samaria or Egypt (Josh. 22:19; cf. the importance of the river Jordan in Josh. 22:25). Why would a possible settlement in Judah be mentioned (Josh. 22:19) if it were not in any way necessary for those Jews who lived in Samaria, or even for those who lived in Elephantine? There are simply too many things that do not make sense if one wishes to suggest that Joshua 22 was composed to address Jews outside Judah in the post-exilic era.

Thus it is not easy to find a post-exilic *Sitz im Leben* for the narrative as a whole. As regards the views of those scholars who think that there was an original story which was substantially different from its present form, the fact that practically all of them disagree concerning what the original form of the story was underlines the problem of trying to discover one from the present form of the narrative. The problem is even more underlined especially when none of these scholars, except for Dus, has even ventured to do a source-critical analysis of the text, even if every one of them agrees that the passage has gone through either deuteronomistic or priestly editing, or both (see Kloppenborg 1981: 349 [quoted above]; Eissfeldt 1962–1979b/1973: 10–14; Dus 1964: 539–545; also cf. Noth [1953: 134], according to whom the passage 'cannot be divided into sources'). The problem of separating the passage into sources is also demonstrated by the fact that one can conveniently describe the passage by a palistrophic model (see 'Form and structure' of Josh. 22).

In any case, those scholars who think that the original form of the account was at least reasonably similar to its present form all broadly agree that the passage is about the cultic hegemony of Shiloh in the pre-monarchic period (Eissfeldt [1962–1979b/1973: 14], Butler [1983: 243] and McConville [1993: 100]. Dus and Möhlenbrink can also be included in this group).

Thus it is not at all unnatural or unreasonable to see at least the basic form of Joshua 22:9–34 as concerning the pre-monarchic period, in line with the narrative's self-presentation. Then a major issue is the priestly and deuteronomic features of the narrative and their implications for the dating, provenance and interpretation of the narrative.

D. G. Schley (1989: 205, table 5) has listed the following priestly expressions in Joshua 22:9–34:

'Land of Canaan': vv. 9a, 10a, 11, 32
Shiloh: vv. 9a, 12b
'ḥzzh: vv. 9, 19 (with verb)
'by Moses in accordance to the word of Yahweh': v. 9
'the whole assembly of the Israelites gathered': v. 12
    (cf. Josh 18:2 [*sic*; actually 18:1])
'the whole assembly of Yahweh': v. 15b [*sic*; actually v. 16]
Phinehas the son of Eleazar the priest: vv. 13b, 31a, 32a
'Phinehas the priest': v. 30a
'to serve the service of Yahweh': v. 27
'your land is unclean': v. 19a
'peace offerings': v. 23
mered. v. 22
mārad. vv. 16, 18, 19, 29
ma'al . . . mā'al. vv. 16, 20, 31
ns'ym. vv. 14 (3×), 30a, 32a (cf. Num 17:17, 21; Josh 22:14a;
    Num 4:34; Josh 22:30a)
hṯhrnw. v. 17
mškn [*yhwh*]: vv. 19, 29

It is clear from Schley's list that the passage has many affinities with priestly language and ideas. Deuteronomic features are more difficult to find. However, McConville has pointed out that the unity of Israel, which is one of the great themes of Deuteronomy, is affirmed in Joshua 22:9–34 (McConville 1993: 99–100. Cf. McConville's reference to von Rad on the concept of the unity of Israel as a great concept of Deuteronomy in McConville 1993: 99n84; cf. also Wenham 1971b: 144–145). Clearly, a main thrust of the narrative is to affirm the unity of the Transjordanians with the rest of Israel.

As regards the unity of worship in the passage, all commentators agree that such a concept is advocated by the narrative in its final form. However, even though Wellhausen thought that the passage attests priestly concerns of the unity of worship (see Wellhausen 1905/1878: 37–38), later commentators have not agreed whether a priestly or a deuteronomistic conception of unity of worship underlies the passage. A number of commentators think that the conception of the unity of worship is deuteronomistic (see esp. Snaith 1978: 330; Soggin 1972: 214; de Vaux

1978/1971: 581). Others think that it is priestly (Schley 1989: 125; Weinfeld 1972: 181; Dus 1964: 542; Kloppenborg 1981: 359). Some do not indicate either way or do not at least make the matter clear. Eissfeldt (1962–1979b/1973: 14) thinks that the concept was originally neither priestly nor deuteronomistic, even though the narrative has affinities to P and D. Noth (1953a: 133) seems to indicate a deuteronomistic concept, but one cannot be absolutely certain. Gray (1986: 52) on the other hand seems to lean towards a priestly appropriation. Certainly, the passage contains many priestly features, with Joshua 22:29 explicitly stating, 'Far be it from us that we would rebel against Yahweh and turn away from following Yahweh to build an altar for burnt offering, meal offering, or sacrifice in addition to the altar of Yahweh our God which is in front of his tabernacle'. Also, the passage clearly seems to affirm that all sacrifices should be centralized to the tent of meeting. Then, if one follows the Wellhausenian interpretation of Leviticus 17, according to which the priestly material assumes centralization, one can naturally think that the concept of worship in the passage is priestly. However, at the same time, as the passage as a whole attests the unity of Israel, a great deuteronomic theme, it is also easy to think that the centralization requirement is deuteronomic (according to McConville 1993: 100, 'The "Deuteronomic" character of the issues here are beyond dispute').

In search of a solution, I have argued elsewhere that the centralization requirement of Leviticus 17 was valid only paradigmatically after the wilderness period (see Pitkänen 2004a). In other words, centralization was required only in the wilderness, but, thereafter, the importance of the central sanctuary is emphasized without actually demanding centralization (Pitkänen 2004a). Thus the centralization requirement in Joshua 22:9–34 is not priestly. On the other hand, if we look at the narrative in the book of Joshua which surrounds Joshua 22:9–34, according to Joshua 21:43–45:

> Yahweh gave Israel all of the land he swore to their fathers to give them. They took possession of it and lived there. Yahweh also gave them peace throughout as he had sworn to their fathers. No one could withstand them. He gave all their enemies into their hands. Not one of the good promises that Yahweh had spoken to Israel failed; all came to pass.

This links back to the book of Deuteronomy. Deuteronomy 12:9–11 contains a promise that the Israelites will cross the Jordan and settle in the land, and that Yahweh will also give them rest from all their enemies. Moreover, according to Deuteronomy 26:1, Yahweh will give the land to the Israelites as an inheritance and they will take possession of it and settle in it. The book of Joshua presents this promise as actually fulfilled. According to Joshua 21:43–45, the Israelites have taken possession of the land and have settled in it, and Yahweh has given them rest all around

(v. 44) from all their enemies so that the enemies cannot stand before the Israelites. This rest is also referred to in Joshua 22:4 and Joshua 23:1. Thus Joshua 21:43–45, 22:4, 23:1 refer back to concepts expressed by Deuteronomy 12:10 and 26:1 (cf. also Josh. 21:44 vs Deut. 7:24), and Joshua 21:45 indicates that the settlement, rest and inheritance promised by Yahweh in the book of Deuteronomy has now come to fruition (note also the correspondence of *nḥlh* in Deut. 12:10, 26:1 and the distribution of the land in Josh. 13 – 19 etc., including Josh. 23:4). Moreover, everything in the book of Joshua indicates that Joshua 21:43–45, 22 – 24 occur many days after the events portrayed at the beginning of the book of Joshua (see esp. Josh. 11:18; 13:1; 22:3; 23:1). One may compare this self-presentation of the book of Joshua with Deuteronomy 7:22–23 (cf. Exod. 23:27–30), according to which the conquest would not happen all at once, but gradually.

Then, Joshua 21:43–45, 22:4, 23:1 affirm that the deuteronomic conditions required for the centralization of worship were achieved during the last days of Joshua (cf. Riley 1993: 82, 'The Deuteronomist . . . specifies that the granting of Israel's rest will signify that the central sanctuary must be used exclusively. This rest is actually granted to Israel under Joshua [Josh 21:44; 22:4; 23:1]'; similarly Tigay 1996: 123; cf. Kaufmann 1985/1955: 18). As regards the problem of complete vs incomplete conquest (cf. also Hess 1996: 284–286; Younger 1990: 241–243 on the problem; cf. Kaufmann 1985/1955: 91–95), the main point for us is that the author of Joshua indicates that the conditions required for centralization have been realized. In this respect, nations have been dispossessed, but not necessarily *all* nations in the land (see esp. Josh. 23:9; 24:11–12 vs esp. Josh. 23:5, 13, and compare these with Exod. 23:28; 34:24), and note that Exodus 34:24 does not necessarily need to be taken to indicate that *all* nations must be dispossessed before conditions can be considered peaceful enough for pilgrimage, even though, undoubtedly, the dispossessing of all nations is the ultimate promise and goal.

The idea that the deuteronomic conditions required for the centralization of worship were achieved during the last days of Joshua fits perfectly with the portrayal of the events of Joshua 22:9–34. The Transjordanian altar threatened to be a violation of the injunctions in Deuteronomy to centralize worship to a place which Yahweh would choose. At the same time, as the book of Joshua indicates that the Tent of Meeting was in Shiloh during that time (Josh. 18:1; 19:51; 22:9), it follows that the author of Joshua indicates that, during the last days of Joshua, Shiloh was the place where Yahweh's name dwelt in the way expressed by Deuteronomy 12, and that consequently, all worship should have been centralized to Shiloh (for the relationship of this rest to other periods of Israel's history, see Pitkänen 2004a: 198–199).

Thus we have a passage that attests not only deuteronomic concerns, including a requirement of centralization of worship, but that has strong priestly features as well. Then, if one thinks that the priestly features were simply inserted into the book of Joshua by a deuteronomic editor, it is very natural to imagine how the passage came into being, in line with my considerations throughout the commentary. However, if one thinks that priestly material in general is later than Deuteronomy, one runs into formidable difficulties. As I have indicated above, scholars have found it very difficult to divide the passage into sources. Moreover, the view of worship in the passage is deuteronomic. Thus one would have to postulate a later priestly redaction of the passage, which is difficult to separate from the overall narrative and for which it is difficult to give a good motivation, as the earlier version already basically includes all the information necessary to argue for the centralization of worship and the unity of Israel, the main thrusts of the narrative.

To confirm further the idea that priestly material has been taken in to support a deuteronomic purpose, it is also useful to look at how the passage relates to its literary environment, both in the book of Joshua and outside it. Then, except for the deuteronomic concern of centralization during the last days of Joshua, with which Joshua 22:9–34 fits perfectly, let us start by observing that if one reads Joshua 22 as a whole, verses 9–34 naturally continue the story of verses 1–8, and both narratives fit together very well, even though there are differences between them. Even though Joshua 22:1–8 (to be precise, vv. 1–6 would be enough to be taken as a unit. According to Noth [1953a: 133], Josh. 22:1–6, together with 21:43–45 and 23:1–16, forms the deuteronomistic conclusion of the occupation tradition, and vv. 7–8 are a 'redactional link') is deuteronomic both in language and content (see Noth 1953a: 133; de Vaux 1978/1971: 581; Gray 1986: 169; Soggin 1972: 212; Kloppenborg 1981: 351), and Joshua 22:9–34 includes a number of priestly features, both narratives at least can be thought to be deuteronomic as a whole. Moreover, even though both narratives are intelligible on their own (according to Kloppenborg [1981: 351], 'Vv. 1–8, while in their present state serving as an introduction to 9–34, anticipate none of the hostilities of the latter. On the other hand, 9–34 are completely intelligible without 1–8'), they nevertheless make a perfectly connected and intelligible story together. Finally, even though, as Kloppenborg points out, 'The central character in 1–8 is Joshua but Phinehas and the *nesi'im* in 9–34' (Kloppenborg 1981: 351), this does not mean that the two do not fit together.

Also, Joshua 22:20 refers directly back to Joshua 7, the narrative of the Achan incident in association with the conquest of Ai. It is especially noteworthy that the priestly word *m'l* used to describe Achan in Joshua 7:1 occurs also in Joshua 22:20 (cf. also Josh. 22:31). Moreover, the concept of divine retribution based on *m'l* is similar in Joshua 22 and Joshua 7. In both cases, the whole congregation of the Israelites would suffer because of a sin of an individual or a part of the community. As Joosten points out, this concept of divine retribution is priestly (Joosten 1996: 41–42;

86–87). Then this in fact suggests that both Joshua 22:9–34 and Joshua 7 draw on priestly concepts (cf. Ottosson 1991: 26). One may note in this respect that, according to Noth 1991/1943: 63, Dtr received the Ai story (Josh. 7–8) as such, making only a very minor modification in Joshua 8:1. Noth (1953: 43) even stresses that Joshua 7:1 is not a later addition but belongs to the original Ai story. Also, even though Fritz (1994: 79) thinks that there are a number of minor additions in Joshua 7, such as the priestly and thus post-exilic addition of *m'l* in 7:1, he nevertheless thinks that these additions have not changed the character of the story of Joshua 7, which according to him is the composition of the Deuteronomistic historian, as its structure, style and didactic character show.

It is also interesting to compare this concept of divine retribution in Joshua 22:9–34 and Joshua 7 with 1 Chronicles 5. In 1 Chronicles 5:25 it is said that the Transjordanians 'became faithless (*m'l*) against the God of their fathers and played the harlot after the gods of the nations which God destroyed before them'. However, whereas in Joshua 22:31 it would have been the *Israelites* who would have suffered because of the sin of the Transjordanians, in 1 Chronicles 5:25 it is the *Transjordanians themselves* who suffer because of their sin. Thus the post-exilic Chronicles emphasize a different concept of divine retribution from the book of Joshua (cf. Riley 1993: 42–53, 147–148 for more use of *m'l* in Chronicles), and when one couples this with the impression that around the time of the exile the previously more dominant concept of collective guilt (cf. comments on 7:1 above) moved towards the concept of individual guilt (cf. Jer. 31:29–30; Ezek. 18:2 ff.), this further suggests a pre-exilic setting for Joshua 22:9–34 (cf. Joosten 1996: 121–122, and note that Tigay [1996: 227] suggests that Deut. 24:16 refers to judicial rather than divine punishment; cf. 2 Kgs 14:6; 2 Chr. 25:4). Furthermore, whereas in Joshua 22:31 the Transjordanians are cleared of faithlessness (*m'l*), according to 1 Chronicles 5:25, the Transjordanians were faithless, and went into exile for that reason.

Another passage that may attest the concept of divine retribution on the whole congregation is Joshua 22:17. According to Joshua 22:17, punishment fell on the congregation because of the Peor incident and the people have not yet purified themselves of it. It seems clear that the verse refers back to Numbers 25 (Deut. 4:3 also refers back to Num. 25). On conventional source criticism, Numbers 25:1–5 belongs to JE, and Numbers 25:6–18 belongs to P (see e.g. Wenham 1981: 19 for this), and the passage could thus refer back either to the JE or P version of the events. However, as Joshua 22:9–34 contains many priestly features and Numbers 25:1–5 present nothing particular in themselves in addition to verses 6–18, it is entirely possible to think that the passage refers to Numbers 25 as a whole.

A further feature that ties Joshua 22:9–34 to the rest of Joshua, and to the Pentateuch, is the existence in Joshua 22:24 of a variant of the 'catechetical' formula which recurs several times in the Hexateuch, in Exodus 12:26; 13:14; Deuteronomy 6:20; Joshua 4:6, 21; 22:24. Now,

Exodus 12:26 and 13:14 can be assigned to D (so Childs 1974: 184), and there is no doubt about the deuteronomic character of Joshua 4:6, 21 (cf. Noth 1987/1943: 111). This then suggests that Joshua 22:24 is also a deuteronomic feature, tying Joshua 22:9–34 to the rest of the book of Joshua (note also that, certainly, the usage of the formula in 22:24 serves specifically to emphasize the unity of Israel in Josh. 22:9–34). Furthermore, the existence of this 'catechetical' formula strongly implies that the altar of witness was intended to serve an important role in Israelite tradition, and this underlines the importance of the narrative of Joshua 22:9–34 for the original audience of the book of Joshua. In this context we might also add that the existence of the catechetical formula in Joshua 4:6, 21 makes it extremely unlikely that the Gilgal narratives (Josh. 4 – 5) serve as an aetiology to legitimate a (sacrificial) sanctuary at Gilgal, at least if the author wrote from a Jerusalemite perspective, as the catechetical formula is part of the idea that the stones are to be signs 'for ever' (Josh. 4:7). It is hard to believe that a Jerusalemite deuteronomic author would have promoted a rival sanctuary to be valid 'for ever'. Thus, it is entirely possible, and in fact more logical, that the author of Joshua understood the stones at Gilgal to act purely as signs, and yet as objects of religious pilgrimage.

Joshua 22:9–34 also has similarities to Judges 19 – 21. In both cases the narratives involve an action taken by the Israelite confederacy against another Israelite group (Benjamin, Jabesh-Gilead; so also Kloppenborg 1981: 347, quoted above). In both narratives Phinehas *ben* Eleazar features. In both narratives there is a trip to Transjordan involved (Judg. 21:10–12). Shiloh features in both narratives (Josh. 22:9, 12; Judg. 21:12), as does the expression 'land of Canaan' (Josh. 22:9; Judg. 21:12; in both of these cases the expression is actually 'Shiloh which is in the land of Canaan'; cf. Schley 1989: 132). And both narratives purport to describe the period of conquest or the early period of the judges. Then this speaks against detaching Joshua 22:9–34 from the rest of the book of Joshua.

We have also seen throughout the commentary that, in general, much material in Joshua attests cultic concerns. With this in mind, there is no need to think that Joshua 22:9–34 is out of place in the book; on the contrary, it fits in perfectly fine.

We now move into looking more directly at how the existence of the passage works against Noth's theory of the Deuteronomistic History. If one compares Joshua 22:9–34 with Numbers 32, one can find a number of important similarities in the storylines of these two passages as follows, as pointed out by Jobling (1980: 192):

(a) A Transjordanian initiative sets the story in motion (Num 32:1–5; Jos 22:10).
(b) Moses/the Cisjordanian embassy express anger at the initiative. Each (particularly in the second case) goes to some lengths of implausibility to put the worst possible construction upon it.

And each makes allusions to the past to establish the case (and to help introduce Yahweh).

(c) The Transjordanians make a suggestion/response which is satisfactory, and in fact provides the substance of a bargain (Num 32:16–19; Jos 22:22–29)

(d) Acceptance by Moses / the Cisjordanian embassy (Num 32:20–24, Jos 22:30–31).

Furthermore,

(e) In both accounts there is a hint of a possible settlement of the Transjordanians to the west as part of the argumentation (Num. 32:30; Josh. 22:19; Jobling 1980: 193).

(f) In both accounts the Transjordanians have a concern for their children (Num. 32:16–17, 26; Josh. 22:24–28; cf. Num. 32:11–13; see Jobling 1980: 196).

(g) 'In both stories, the Transjordanians undertake to cross the Jordan for the service of Yahweh' (Jobling 1980: 196).

Moreover, one may arrange the passages that concern the Transjordanians in the Hexateuch in the following way:

> A. Num. 32: intro to the Transjordanian issue with
> conflict-resolution
>> B. Deut. 3:12–16: obligation to the Transjordanians
>> [Deut. 29:6–8: review of Transjordanian issue]
>> B. Josh. 1:12–18: repeat obligation to the Transjordanians
>> [Josh. 4:12: honouring of obligation by the
>> Transjordanians]
>> [Josh. 13:8–31: review of allotment of territory to the
>> Transjordanians]
>> B' Josh. 22:1–8: obligation to the Transjordanians fulfilled
> A' Josh. 22:9–34: final story with conflict-resolution

Even though everything does not fit neatly into a chiasm, it is clear that in the final form of the 'Hexateuch', A is the introduction to the Transjordanian issue and A' is its conclusion. Also, if one ignores AA', which contain priestly material, BB' forms a bracket of a deuteronomic introduction and conclusion.

That Joshua 22:9–34 and Numbers 32 are connected is further confirmed by the following considerations. According to Noth, Numbers 32 can be divided into sources as follows: 32:1–5, 16a, 39–42 belong to older sources (J or E); 32:16–17, 24, 33–38 belong to deuteronomistic redaction; and the rest is priestly redaction (Noth 1987/1943: 128–129; see also Noth 1968: 235–236). Moreover, Noth notes concerning the priestly redaction, 'These are admittedly reminiscent of the language and style of P but they do not represent this language and style in its pure form. Above all, they are so clearly dependent, from a literary point of view, on the older text that they cannot be regarded as elements of a once independent narrative tradition' (Noth 1987/1943: 129). Other commentators, before and after Noth, have held similar, even if not exactly same, opinions (cf. the helpful summary in Budd 1984: 337–342). It is also worth noting that Gray (1903: 426) thought of Numbers 32 that 'a strict analysis of the chapter as between JE and P cannot be satisfactorily carried through'.

Then, according to customary source division, 'conflict-resolution' is missing in both the JE and D versions of Numbers 32. In other words, the conflict-resolution plot is the creation of priestly editing, according to source-critical theory. Then, if the conflict-resolution plot is not the creation of priestly editing in Joshua 22:9–34, it is most likely that Joshua 22:9–34 is primary, and that Numbers 32 is based on it. On the other hand, if the conflict-resolution plot is the creation of priestly editing in Joshua 22:9–34, it would be easy to postulate that both Joshua 22:9–34 and Numbers 32 come from the same hand, or at least that their present arrangement has been carefully thought out. This then implies that the priestly tradition deliberately connects Joshua 22:9–34 and Numbers 32, and, remembering also the connection of Joshua 22:17 to Numbers 25 (see above), rather suggests that Joshua 22:9–34 is aware of the conquest tradition of Numbers.

These issues then naturally bring us to the problem of the literary composition and provenance of the book of Joshua. Especially since Wellhausen it was generally thought that Joshua formed part of the Hexateuch, which meant that the book was to be seen together with the Pentateuch and as having been composed from the Pentateuchal sources. However, since Noth's *Überlieferungsgeschichtliche Studien* (Noth 1991/1943 and Noth 1987/1943), Joshua has generally been seen as a part of the Deuteronomistic History rather than as belonging to the Pentateuch. The major tantalizing issue concerning the theories of the Hexateuch and the Deuteronomistic History is that, on one hand, when one reads Joshua in its final form, it is quite natural to see Joshua as the fulfilment of the exodus/Sinai tradition as depicted in Exodus–Numbers. Especially, it is clear that Numbers 32 links to Joshua 1:12–18, 4:12, 13:8–33, 22:1–8, 9–34, that Numbers 33:50 – 34:29 links to Joshua 13 – 19, and that Numbers 35 links to Joshua 20 – 21 (cf. Ottosson 1991: 11–37, esp. pp. 29–31 for overall literary connections between Joshua and Numbers). Furthermore, Numbers 32 and 33:50–56 are recognized to contain priestly material, and Numbers 34 and 35 have often been assigned to P (see e.g. Wenham 1981: 19. Note also that, according to Wenham [ibid.], 'In chapters 32 and 33 G. B. Gray believes both JE and P are present, but he does not think they can be disentangled convincingly'). What is more, Joshua 13 – 19 contain at least some priestly material, and, as we have seen, Joshua 22:9–34 are clearly influenced by priestly material. There are also other connecting features between Numbers and Joshua. For instance, as Noth points out, in

Numbers 14:24 (assigned to JE), 'there is a reference forward to Caleb's occupation of the land' (Noth 1987/1943: 140). Thus it is easy to think that Joshua is firmly connected with Numbers. Then, if one would see those parts in Joshua that connect to priestly material in Numbers as priestly (esp. Josh. 13 – 19 and 22:9–34), one would naturally lean towards a theory of a Hexateuch, with Joshua being a logical continuation of the conquest tradition(s) in Numbers.

At the same time, the overall theology of Joshua is clearly deuteronomic. As we have noted in the Introduction, the theological concepts of holy war, the land and its distribution, the unity of Israel, the role of Joshua and the covenant and the law of Moses are the main conceptual links between Joshua and Deuteronomy. Moreover, Joshua is the direct continuation of Deuteronomy 31 – 34, and not of Numbers. Seen from this angle, Joshua seems to be firmly connected with Deuteronomy rather than with Numbers. Furthermore, being deuteronomic in its general character, Joshua is similar to the historical books Judges–Kings, which from the narrative standpoint continue from where Joshua leaves off, and also, like Deuteronomy, seem to include little if any priestly material.

Martin Noth, whose views are still often followed at present (cf. Ottosson 1991: 13, according to whom [my translation from Swedish] 'Noth may continuously be considered as the exegetical standard, even though sometimes inclinations are seen to put P earlier)', suggested a solution to this problem by starting from the premise that the conquest tradition was an independent unit in the beginning. The book of Joshua was built around this tradition. Noth also argued that there was originally no P account of the conquest, but P concluded his account with the death of Moses (Noth 1987/1943: 135). In essence, Noth based this argument on claiming as far as possible that those features that exist in Numbers and relate to the conquest are not priestly. Noth succeeded in eliminating so much material that has commonly been attributed to P that he could argue that those parts which are indisputably priestly are the result of secondary additions and do not stem from a P narrative (Noth 1987/1943: 121–134). On the other hand, Noth argued that the older literary sources J and E 'culminated in the theme of the conquest' (Noth 1987/1943: 141). However, according to Noth, 'when they were fitted into the framework provided by the P narrative it was the Pentateuch which emerged, with the theme of the conquest of the land to the west of the Jordan dropping away completely. The conquest narrative in the book of Joshua, on the other hand, was part of the work of Dtr. from the start, and this developed completely independently of the Pentateuch' (Noth 1987/1943: 141). Finally, during the post-exilic period, the Pentateuch and the Deuteronomistic History were joined together, and more connecting links were added between Numbers and Deuteronomy on one hand, and Numbers and Joshua on the other, and these connections were, as Noth seems to indicate, made in priestly style (Noth 1987/1943: 143–148).

Noth did not have a very high regard for Joshua 22:9–34 as a part of the book of Joshua. According to Noth, the language and content of Joshua 22:9–34 'are reminiscent of P', but on the other hand 'there are such clear deviations in language and content from P, that this peculiar passage . . . is no longer ascribed to the "Hexateuchal" source P' (Noth 1987/1943: 118). Joshua 22:9–34 'must obviously be a very late isolated supplement to the book of Joshua' (Noth 1987/1943: 118). It is quite obvious why Noth thought this way. The existence of a priestly account in Joshua, especially if it is well grafted into the book, would indicate that a priestly author was interested in the conquest tradition, which in turn casts doubt on the validity of Noth's denial of priestly material in the books of Numbers and Joshua.

However, we have seen that Joshua 22:9–34 is an integral part of the book of Joshua, and that it is also explicitly connected to the priestly parts of Numbers 32. Thus it is difficult to believe Noth's theory of the Deuteronomistic history in its present form, especially when Noth has already been criticized for eliminating priestly material from Numbers and Joshua in a way that has a stamp of dubiousness about it (see Weinfeld 1972: 182n1, according to whom Noth's 'attempts to disprove the priestly origin of Num 32–6 and Josh 14–22' are 'unconvincing'). Moreover, Noth's theory is simply too complicated. Too many redactions, combinations and accretions are postulated, and it could at least be argued that Noth treats literary works in a piecemeal and mechanical way (but nevertheless finds that he cannot divide Joshua 22:9–34 into sources). Also, it is hard to think that P would have concluded his account with the death of Moses without any regard to the wider context to which that death relates; that is, entering into the promised land. The idea of cutting off the conquest tradition of the older Pentateuchal sources, especially when their accounts 'culminated in the theme of the conquest', is also problematic.

However, and as I have already indicated, if one sees the priestly material of the Pentateuch as earlier than Deuteronomy, and the priestly material in Joshua as material that was taken over and used by the deuteronomic editor of Joshua, all these problems disappear completely (cf. Ottosson 1991, esp. pp. 11–37, for other reasons to see priestly material in Joshua as prior to deuteronomic material). The author of Joshua drew on both priestly and deuteronomic tradition. Moreover, the connections from Joshua back to the priestly tradition of Numbers and to the exodus motif in the Pentateuch imply that there was no 'Deuteronomistic History' in the sense Noth has suggested. In this respect, we should keep in mind that, according to Westermann (1994: 39; my translation from German), 'The exodus motif appears 27 times in the historical books, with summaries in Deuteronomy 30–32 times'. Westermann then lists major occurrences in speeches, including a comment on Joshua 24:2–8 (Westermann 1994: 39; my translation from German),

'Joshua 24:2–8 includes an explicit look back at history, a developing further of the short summaries of Deuteronomy.' After this, Westermann notes (Westermann 1994: 39–40; my translation from German):

> All these passages are considered to come from the Deuteronomistic historian. This however means that the author or the final redactor must have known the exodus motif, as he himself utilizes it often. This being the case, it is very difficult to answer the question of why he did not introduce and start his work with the history of the exodus. I am not aware of a single study on this in the academic literature. An answer to the question is hardly to be found. However, the problem that arises here is solved when one gives up the hypothesis of DtrG [a basic form of deuteronomistic history]. In its place appears a series of historical books starting with Exodus + Numbers which is interrupted in two places by legal collections. In this series the history of Israel begins with the book of Exodus and spans to its end in 2 Kings. The series is held together and becomes unified due to each book treating a section of the history of Israel, even if not so with the inserted legal collections.

Westermann also points out Joshua 2:8–11, 5:1, 9:9, non-Israelite speeches that refer to the exodus motif (Westermann 1994: 40). Finally, there are also connections of the narrative of the Jordan crossing with the crossing of the Sea of Reeds in Exodus (see above, Excursus 2).

Having made the above considerations, I make some comments based on them about the date of Joshua here. As I have already indicated elsewhere, the literary composition of Joshua implies that the reason why the books of Judges, Samuel and Kings do not include much priestly material is not that priestly material did not exist during the time these books were written, but that there must have been some other reason why they did not include much priestly material. It is possible to conceive that, since the priestly material is associated with the Tent of Meeting, which is most at home in Shiloh, the Judahite and Jerusalemite writer of the books of Samuel did not wish to emphasize the role of the old order of Shiloh and Ephraim, which had passed away (see Ps. 78:60–72 and 1 Sam. 4, 2 Sam. 6, 1 Kgs 8, which show how Yahweh's presence in conjunction with the ark, and thus Yahweh himself, rejects Shiloh, and later chooses Jerusalem, expounded in Pitkänen 2004a: 127–158), and the same would apply to the book of Judges as well, as it also attests Judahite concerns (for more details regarding the book of Judges, see Pitkänen 2004a: 241–269. Also, the motif of the covenant, and thus deuteronomic material and style, would in general be fitting for historical recollection in Israelite thinking and historiography). If Jerusalem wanted to emphasize its election over Shiloh, and the role of the temple over that of the Tent of Meeting, as Psalm 78 attests, it is difficult to think that the priestly material would originate from Jerusalem. In this, also, in view of Jeroboam's actions in the north, as described in 1 Kings 12:26–33, it is unlikely that the priestly material has its provenance in the north after the division of the kingdom. Moreover, as the priestly material directly concerns the Tent of Meeting and its cult, it cannot have been applied directly to the Jerusalemite temple and cult, but only indirectly. One may keep in mind here that the books of Chronicles explicitly describe how David rearranged the cult in Jerusalem in priestly terms, which, however, even with a casual look at the details, were more of an adaptation of the priestly injunctions in the Pentateuch (see esp. 1 Chr. 16; 23–26; 28). Even to say that the priestly material is late historical fiction does not take away the incompatibility between the priestly material and the (portrayed) monarchic situation. Overall, the priestly material does not fit well conceptually with the time of the monarchy. Rather, and as argued throughout the commentary, and as an exilic date seems a bit late for the book of Joshua, it is most logical to think that the priestly material, or at least substantial parts of it, dates not from the time of the monarchy but from the pre-monarchical period. As Shiloh was rejected and its importance taken away after the disaster at Aphek (1 Sam. 4; see Pitkänen 2004a: 127–158), this then naturally suggests a time before the disaster. Of course, the comments I have already made above about the date of Joshua 22:9–34 also fit well with this idea.

One may also draw in here the observations of Milgrom (1991: 30–35), who dates the origins of P to the pre-monarchical period during the prominence of Shiloh. Note that, according to Milgrom (1983a), the word *'dh* does not occur in post-exilic texts, and on the other hand is replaced by *qhl* in post-exilic texts (Milgrom 1983a: 2–12; note that 2 Chr. 5:6 is practically the same as 1 Kgs 8:5, suggesting that it was directly copied from there), the word *mth* in the sense of 'tribe' does not occur in post-exilic documents, and not even in Deuteronomy, Jeremiah or Ezekiel (Milgrom 1983a: 12–15; the occurrences in Chronicles are in texts copied from older sources), and that *r'š* in conjunction with *'lpy yśr'l* 'goes back to the time when the clan structure was fully operative' (Milgrom 1983a: 15–17). Milgrom concludes that the temporal distribution of these priestly terms supports 'the view that the priestly account of the wilderness sojourn has accurately preserved a host of institutions that accurately reflect the social and political realities of Israel's pre-monarchic age' (ibid.). It is also worth pointing out that these terms all occur in Joshua 22:9–34 in their early meanings (22:12, 16 ['dh]; 22:14 [mth]; 22:14 [r'š . . . 'lpy yśr'l]), rather suggesting an early date for Joshua 22:9–34.

Overall, one might then think that while the priestly material would not be in vogue during the monarchy and in monarchic historiography, it would be reasonable for the priestly material to come back into vogue with the priest Ezekiel and his vision of the restoration of the temple and its cult, and during the post-exilic period when both the old order of Shiloh and the new order of Jerusalem had failed and the community had to reflect on and reinvent its identity. As far as the exilic book of Kings is concerned, the interest of the author is not in the exact details of the Jerusalemite cult or other related technicalities, but in the failure of the Israelites to worship Yahweh, which goes hand in hand with the deuteronomic concerns about worship at *bāmôt* after the building of Solomon's temple and the resulting exile of the northern and southern kingdoms. It is also conceivable that the author is influenced by a deuteronomic tradition current in Judah before the exile, after finding the book of law during the time of Josiah (2 Kgs 22; cf. the book of Jeremiah which has some deuteronomistic features). The author then interprets his fairly non-technical sources from a deuteronomic viewpoint (note however that some priestly features are nevertheless included in his sources as well; e.g. in 1 Kgs 8:1–11; deuteronomic sources may also be included). In this respect, a new style would then be reflected in Chronicles in the new situation of the community after the exile, including attesting both the priestly and the deuteronomic concerns of history.

And again, when we couple these observations with Shiloh as the place of the Tent of Meeting playing a prominent part at the end of the book of Joshua, from both a priestly and a deuteronomic standpoint, this then suggests that it is logical to think that at least a substantial part of the book of Joshua dates from the pre-monarchic period when Shiloh was the main sanctuary in Israel (cf. also Ottosson 1991: 36 [my translation from Swedish], 'However, it is clear that the local colour in the priestly material [of Joshua] is northern in many cases. Here belong not the least the Shiloh traditions').

JOSHUA 23

Translation

[1]After a long time had passed since Yahweh had given rest to the Israelites from all their enemies around them and when Joshua had become old, [2]Joshua called all the Israelites, their elders, leaders, judges and scribes, and said to them, 'I have become old. [3]You yourselves have seen what Yahweh your God has done to all these peoples for your sake. It was he who fought for you. [4]See, I have given the remaining peoples as an inheritance for your tribes from the Jordan to the Mediterranean Sea in the west. [5]Yahweh your God will expel them from your presence, driving them away. You will take possession of their land as Yahweh promised you.

[6]'Be very disciplined to pay attention to everything that has been written in the book of the law of Moses and to follow it completely. [7]Do not get together with

these remaining peoples. Do not think of their gods, swear by them, serve them or bow to them. [8]But stick to Yahweh your God as you have done thus far. [9]Yahweh has driven away big and powerful peoples for you. No one has been able to withstand you. [10]One of you chases away many because Yahweh fights for you as he promised. [11]Take great care to love Yahweh your God.

[12]'If you change your direction and get together with these remaining peoples and intermarry with them, [13]be aware that Yahweh will not continue dispossessing these peoples for you. They will become a snare and a trap for you, a scourge on your side and a prick in your eye until you perish from this good land which he gave to you.

[14]'I am now about to die. You know well that none of the good promises that Yahweh has given you have failed. They have all happened. [15]However, just as all the good promises of Yahweh have taken place, in the same way he will cause all evil to befall you until he destroys you from this good land that he gave you, [16]if you violate his covenant which he gave you and go and serve other gods and bow to them. Then Yahweh will be furious with you, and you will quickly perish from the good land that he has given you.'

Notes on the text

1. Long time: lit. 'many days'. Old: lit. 'old in days'.

2. Leaders: Hebr. *rāʾšîm*. Scribes: or overseers (Hebr. *šōṭērîm*). Old: cf. note on verse 1.

3. Peoples: or 'nations'.

4. Mediterranean Sea in the west: lit. 'the Great Sea of the setting of the sun'.

5. LXX reads for the verse: 'But the Lord our God will destroy them before us until they perish. And he will send wild animals against them until he will have completely destroyed them and their kings from before you, and you will inherit their land as the Lord your God said to you.'

6. To follow it completely: lit. 'Not turn from it either to the right or to the left'.

8. Thus far: lit. 'until this day' (Hebr. *ʿad hayyôm hazzeh*).

10. Many: lit. 'thousand' or 'unit' (Hebr. *ʾelep*).

13. Be aware: Hebr. emphatic (infinitive absolute). Snare and a trap: lit. 'snare and a hook'. The Hebr. seems to be idiomatic, referring to something relating to trapping animals. Scourge: the Hebr. word *šōṭēṭ* is only attested here in the HB.

14. I am now about to die: lit. 'And see, I am now one walking in the way of all the land.' You know well: 'you know by all your hearts and all your minds'. Good: omitted in Gr.

16. Yahweh will be furious with you: 'Yahweh's anger will burn in you'. The clause 'Then Yahweh will . . . he has given you' is not attested in Gr.

Form and structure

The structure of chapter 23, while slightly difficult to delimit, can be described as follows (partly based on Nelson 1997a: 256):

> Joshua summons Israel in his old age (vv. 1–2a)
> Joshua's speech (vv. 2b–16)
>   Joshua's note about his old age (v. 2b)
>   Review: Yahweh's victory and land allotment (vv. 3–5)
>   Yahweh's faithfulness (v. 3)
>   Overview of conquest and settlement thus far, and
>   promise of driving out remaining nations in the
>   future (vv. 4–5)
>   Exhortation to follow the law of Moses and not to join with
>   the remaining nations and their gods (vv. 6–8)
>   Review: Yahweh's victorious fighting for Israel (vv. 9–10)
>   Exhortation to love Yahweh and conditional threat in regard
>   to alien nations, with special mention against
>   intermarrying (vv. 11–13)
>   Joshua's note about his impending death (v. 14a)
>   Review: fulfilment of all of Yahweh's promises (v. 14b)
>   Conditional threat about covenant violation (vv. 15–16)

As already noted in the 'Form and structure' section on Joshua 22, according to Noth (1953a: 133), Joshua 21:43–45, 22:1–6 and 23:1–16 basically constitute the deuteronomistic conclusion to the settlement tradition. In this, 21:43–45 serve as a summary of the fulfilment of the conquest and settlement. The passage should be seen as an introduction to 22:1–6 (cf. Josh. 1:15), in which statements are anticipated which are then made again in the ceremonious farewell speech of Joshua (cf. 23:9b, 14b against 21:43–45; see Noth 1953a: 133). Noth thought that the book of Joshua originally ended with Joshua 23, 'as edited by a "Deuteronomistic writer"' (see Noth 1991/1943: 24). Noth also suggested that Joshua 23 was one of the recurrent 'retrospective and anticipatory' speeches by the Deuteronomist throughout his historical composition that also prove the existence of such a history (these include 1 Sam. 12 and 1 Kgs 8:14ff.; see Noth 1991/1943: 18–20, cf. p. 24 and *passim*). We may note here that this is one of the stronger arguments for the concept of the Deuteronomistic History. However, as Deuteronomy is in the form of a speech (or series of speeches), it would not be unnatural to think that any other books that are deuteronomic in style could easily use similar rhetorical devices.

Nelson (1997a: 256) helpfully notes how there is increasing severity in the threats made as the chapter progresses (cf. vv. 6–8, 13 and 15–16). The word 'peoples' is used six times (vv. 3, 4, 7, 9, 12, 13), and the expression 'good land' is important at the end of the passage (cf. Nelson 1997a:

256–257). Nelson also points out similarities in language with such passages as Deuteronomy 6:13, 7:16, 10:20, 11:16–17, 22–25, 12:3, 13:4–5 (3–4 in English), and 7:1–5 in particular (Nelson 1997a: 257).

The warning against intermarriage belongs best to the period portrayed, albeit it could also be considered to have been valid for any subsequent period in Israel's history. As a whole, as such, in its tone of warning the coming generation the speech could fit any period from the time portrayed all the way into the exile and the post-exilic period. In a strongly deuteronomistic style, the readers are ultimately asked to choose between good and bad, and life and death (cf. Deut. 11:28–30; 30:15–18; cf. Nelson 1997a: 257). In this, the chapter also broadly reflects standard ancient treaty concepts with its blessings for obedience and curses for disobedience.

Comment

1. The events here are explicitly stated to have taken place when Joshua is old. The reader (or hearer) gets the impression that much time has now passed since the initial events of the book. Otherwise, it seems impossible to establish exactly how this event relates to the chronology of the book as a whole (cf. this verse with 13:1). In its narrative placement, it implies a time shortly before Joshua's death, at which time Joshua would be 110 years old (24:29).

2. Joshua gathers all Israel, even though this seems to be clarified to mean elders, leaders, judges and scribes (or overseers) rather than everyone. This seems practical for obvious reasons of logistics, and the implied idea seems to be that the leaders then instruct the people under their authority based on the address that Joshua gives them. Looking at the matter from a slightly different angle, Nelson suggests that 'in order to emphasize that "all Israel" is responsible for keeping the law, the catalog of leaders who are present is exhaustive' (Nelson 1997a: 260). The location of the event is not mentioned and cannot be inferred from the context, being thus unknown.

3. Joshua looks back at history. He reminds the Israelites how Yahweh has given them success with the settlement. Looking at history is much in line with many speeches recorded in the Old Testament, and, in general, with the idea that memory shapes the identity of peoples, Joshua wishes to reinforce that memory, and also to shape it further. Of course, such a portrayal of Joshua is part of the strategy of the author of the book.

4. However, there are still indigenous peoples that remain in the land west of the Jordan, in line with the book of Joshua as a whole. Nelson points out that the word *gôyîm* is used only in this chapter in Joshua for peoples (or nations), even though its usage is common in Deuteronomy and the Deuteronomistic History (Nelson 1997a: 260; referring to Weinfeld 1972a: 342–343).

5. Joshua assures the Israelites that Yahweh will help them so that they can rid the land of its indigenous inhabitants, and then possess the land for themselves only. He also refers to Yahweh's promise in this respect. In line with the rest of the book, it appears that the issue was still a concern for the writer of Joshua. Such a concern would seem to fit best with the time before David and Solomon, and this would be in line with the dating suggested for the book elsewhere in this commentary.

6. Success in obtaining the land completely will come by following the law of Moses carefully (cf. 1:7, 22:5 and comments there). The passage speaks about the 'book of the law of Moses', implying that such a book existed at the time the passage was written (cf. Deut. 31:24–26).

7–8. Part of following the law of Moses is not to get together with the remaining peoples. This includes not taking part in their non-Yahwistic ways. The idea is to maintain a purely Yahwistic outlook on life. It is good to keep in mind here that we can deduce from ancient sources that religion was an integral part of life for the ancients, affecting everything in it. Worshipping a god meant recognizing that god's power over one's environment. For example, in indigenous religion, Baal was considered among other things to be a storm god, thus affecting rains. Religion was also communal, and it appears that societal entities were typically committed to the worship of one god, or a combination of gods. In the context of Pentateuchal legal material, the idea here is that the community stays committed to Yahweh, both as individuals and as a whole. Following other gods would break the people's relationship with Yahweh.

9. Again, Yahweh's role in giving Israel a foothold in the land is recognized. The driving-out of nations expression/motif (cf. vv. 5, 13, and 3:10, 13:6) occurs throughout the Israelite conquest tradition, and it is Yahweh himself who accomplishes this, either implicitly or explicitly (see Exod. 23:28–31; 33:2; 34:11, 24; Lev. 18:24; 20:23; Num. 32:21; 33:52, 55; Deut. 4:38; 7:1, 22; 9:3–5; 11:23; 12:29; 18:12; 19:1; 33:27; cf. also Deut. 28:7 as pointed out by Nelson 1997a: 261).

10. The Yahwistic rhetoric of persuasion continues. Here the idea is that a victory can be achieved with little effort because it is really Yahweh who does the fighting, not the Israelites. There may also be an implication that the number of Israelites is actually fairly small (cf. the report of the first spies in Num. 13:25–29), at least in comparison to the indigenous inhabitants, and, yet, because of Yahweh, it is possible to attain success in the conquest and settlement in the midst of the indigenous peoples.

11. The Israelites are also exhorted to love (*'āhab*) Yahweh, and be very careful in that. This recalls Deuteronomy 6:5 (which itself relates to the *shema* [*šāma'* = 'to hear'], the famous later Jewish summary affirmation about the nature of God based on Deut. 6:4). It is worth noting that it was typical in Ancient Near Eastern treaties to compel love between the treaty participants. This included love from a vassal towards a suzerain, and it seems very reasonable to conclude that such treaty language is alluded to here (see Moran 1963 for a good treatment on the subject as early as forty years before writing this). Thus love here is connected with binding devotion.

12–13. Again, the Israelites are warned against associating themselves with the indigenous peoples. Marriage is focused on here. Anthropological research indicates that, with familial ties being an important part of belonging to an ethnic group, the ease with which marriage outside the group can take place is one indicator of the strength of the sense of ethnic identity (Horowitz 2000/1985: 61). As Horowitz (2000/1985: 62, with examples) notes, 'rates of exogamy for severely divided societies typically run below 10 percent of all marriages, and probably lower if only unions between the most-conflicted groups are counted'. On the other hand, 'societies with more moderate levels of ethnic conflict generally have somewhat higher rates of exogamy' (Horowitz 2000/1985: 62, with examples). That Joshua (and Deuteronomy) wishes explicitly to deny intermarriage fits perfectly with the desire to keep the Israelite community separate from any surrounding peoples (for some further comments, see Pitkänen 2004b).

If, then, the Israelites do not keep separate but intermarry, they will become involved with the life of these communities, in the manner of 'bad company corrupts good morals' (cf. 1 Cor. 15:33). Once the Israelites get mixed up with these peoples, they will also get involved with their non-Yahwistic practices, and the stage will then be set for a disaster.

14–16. According to the narrative, Joshua now explicitly states that this is a farewell address. He will die soon. This is ultimately a repetition of verses 1–2 in order to enhance the rhetoric, to point out that the people will soon not have a chance to hear him any more (cf. Nelson 1997a: 261). Joshua (again) notes that the people themselves know by experience that Yahweh has been faithful and has fulfilled his promises. However, Joshua emphasizes that the present good state of affairs is not automatic. It requires constant watchful following of Yahweh. Otherwise, death and destruction and the loss of land await, in line with covenant curses (*hadābār hārā‘* in v. 15 undoubtedly refers to these, in the light of the expression *haddābār haṭôb ’ăšer dibber yhwh ’ĕlōhêkem ‘ălêkem* in the same verse). Joshua is concerned about the time after his death, and wants to exhort people to keep doing the right things even after he is no longer on the scene. After stating the curses, the narrative breaks off somewhat abruptly, without for instance saying that Joshua then sent the people away. However, the wordplay between *‘ābad* (serve) and *’ābad* (perish) seems to help spice up the closing comment in the original (see Nelson 1997a: 262).

Explanation

This chapter aptly summarizes a lot of the ideology of Joshua about the conquest and the settlement. In line with Pentateuchal, and especially deuteronomic, thinking, Israel is to follow Yahweh wholeheartedly, without wavering from his injunctions. If they do so, they can count on the continual fulfilment of Yahweh's promises. If they do not, the anger of Yahweh will be kindled against them, and great disasters will result. It is ultimately a simple message that is brought forward with some considerable rhetorical flair.

JOSHUA 24

Translation

[1]Then Joshua gathered all the tribes of Israel to Shechem. He called for the elders, leaders, judges and scribes, and they presented themselves before God. [2]Joshua said to all the people, 'This is what Yahweh, the God of Israel, says, "Your fathers lived in Mesopotamia in the past, Terah, the father of Abraham and Nahor. They served other gods. [3]But I took your father Abraham from Mesopotamia and made him traverse the land of Canaan. I increased his progeny and gave him Isaac. [4]I gave Jacob and Esau to Isaac. I gave Mount Seir to Esau, but Jacob and his sons went down to Egypt.

[5]"Then I sent Moses and Aaron and punished Egypt through what I did in its midst. Subsequently, I brought you out from there. [6]I brought your fathers out from Egypt, and you came to the sea. The Egyptians pursued your fathers with horses and chariots to the Sea of Reeds. [7]Your fathers cried to Yahweh, and he put a darkness between them and the Egyptians. He also brought the sea on the Egyptians and it covered them. You saw what I did to the Egyptians. You then spent a long time in the wilderness.

[8]"I brought you to the land of the Amorites who lived east of Jordan. They fought against you but I gave you victory over them. You took possession of their land while I destroyed them for you. [9]Balak the son of Zippor king of Moab also arose and fought against Israel and sent for Balaam the son of Beor to curse him. [10]But I did not want this to happen and he ended up blessing you instead. Thus I saved you from him.

[11]"You crossed the Jordan and came to Jericho. The inhabitants of Jericho, the Amorites, the Perizzites, the Canaanites, the Hittites, the Girgashites, the Hivites and the Jebusites fought against you but I let you prevail. [12]I sent hornets before you and they drove the two Amorite kings away. You did not do this by your own power. [13]And I gave you a land which you had not worked and towns which you had not built, and you settled in them. You ate from vineyards and olive fields that you had not planted."

[14]"Now, revere Yahweh and serve him sincerely and truly. Remove the gods that your fathers served in Mesopotamia and in Egypt and serve Yahweh. [15]However, if it displeases you to serve Yahweh, then choose now whether you will serve the gods that your fathers served in Mesopotamia or the gods of the Amorites in whose land you are living. As for me and my family, we will serve Yahweh.'

¹⁶The people replied, 'Far be it from us that we would abandon Yahweh for other gods! ¹⁷Yahweh our God is the one who brought us and our fathers out of slavery from Egypt and who did great things in our sight. He kept us safe during our whole journey and among all the peoples whose territory we crossed. ¹⁸Yahweh drove away from us all the peoples who dwelt in the land, including the Amorites. Of course we will serve Yahweh for he is our God.'

¹⁹Joshua then said to the people, 'You will not be able to serve Yahweh for he is a holy and jealous God. He will not bear with your transgressions. ²⁰You will let go of Yahweh and serve foreign gods. He will then change and treat you badly and destroy you just as he has done good to you.'

²¹The people said to Joshua, 'No, we will serve Yahweh!'

²²Joshua then said to the people, 'You yourselves are witnesses that you have chosen Yahweh to serve him.' The people replied, 'We are witnesses!'

²³'Now remove the foreign gods from among you and orient yourselves towards Yahweh the God of Israel.'

²⁴The people said to Joshua, 'We will serve Yahweh our God and listen to his voice.'

²⁵And Joshua made a covenant with the people on that day and set them laws and decrees at Shechem. ²⁶Joshua also wrote these things in the book of the law of God. He then took a big stone and set it up under the oak that is in the sanctuary of Yahweh.

²⁷Joshua said to all the people, 'See, this stone will be a witness between us, because it has heard all the words of Yahweh which he has spoken to us. It will be a witness for you so that you will not deceive your God.' ²⁸After this, Joshua sent everyone to their homes.

²⁹After these events, Joshua the son of Nun, the servant of Yahweh, died at the age of 110. ³⁰The Israelites buried him in his allotted territory, in Timnath Serah in the hill country of Ephraim, north of the mountain of Gaash.

³¹Israel served Yahweh during the time of Joshua and the time of the elders who lived after Joshua and who had experienced all the deeds that Yahweh had done for Israel.

³²The Israelites buried the bones of Joseph which they had brought with them from Egypt in Shechem in the field that Jacob had bought from the sons of Hamor the father of Shechem for 100 kesitahs, and which had become an inheritance of the Josephites.

³³And Eleazar the son of Aaron died, and they buried him in Gibeah, the town of his son Phinehas, which had been given to him in the hill country of Ephraim.

Notes on the text

1. Shechem: Gr. Shiloh, also in verse 25. Leaders: Hebr. *rāʾšîm*. Scribes: or overseers (Hebr. *šoṭērîm*). Cf. 23:2.

   2. Mesopotamia: lit. 'beyond the river', also verses 3, 14–15.

   3. Canaan: not included in Gr. Progeny: lit. 'seed' (Hebr. *zeraʿ*).

4. Gr. adds at the end of this verse 'And they became a great, populous and strong nation there, and the Egyptians afflicted them.'

5. I sent Moses and Aaron: not included in Gr.

6. The Sea of Reeds: Hebr. *yam-sûp*; Gr. has the Red Sea.

7. Darkness: Gr. 'cloud and darkness'. You saw: lit. 'Your eyes saw'. A long time: lit. 'many days'.

8. East of Jordan: lit. 'beyond Jordan'. Gave you victory over them: lit. 'gave them into your hands'.

9. Son of Beor: not in Gr.

10. Did not want this to happen: lit. 'did not want to listen to Balaam'. Ended up blessing you instead: lit. 'continually blessed you', with infinitive absolute. Saved you from him: lit. 'delivered you from his hand'. Gr. reads for the verse 'But the Lord your God would not destroy you. He greatly blessed us and rescued us from their hands, and delivered them over.'

11. Inhabitants: lit. 'lords' (Hebr. *ba'al*); Gr. has 'inhabitants'. Let you prevail: lit. 'gave them into your hands'.

12. Two: Gr. 'twelve'. With your own power: lit. 'by your sword or by your bow'.

13. Settled: lit. 'dwelt'. Olive fields: lit. 'olive trees'.

14. The gods: Gr. 'the foreign (*allotrios*) gods'. Mesopotamia: Cf. verse 2.

15. Displeases you: lit. 'is bad in your eyes'. Gr. has 'If it does not seem good to you'. Family: lit. 'house'. Gr. adds at the end of the verse 'Because he is holy'.

17. Slavery: lit. 'house of slavery'; not included in Gr. Who did great things in our sight: not included in Gr.

19. Transgressions: lit. 'transgressions and sins'.

20. Foreign: Hebr. *nākrî*; Gr. 'other' (*heteros*).

22. The people replied, 'We are witnesses!': not included in Gr.

23. Orient yourselves: lit. 'stretch out your hearts'.

24. Our God: not in Gr.

25. Make a covenant: Hebr. *kārat běrît*. Shechem: Gr. 'Shiloh before the tent of meeting of the God of Israel'; cf. verse 1.

26. Sanctuary: or holy place (Hebr. *miqdāš*). Gr. reads 'before the Lord' instead of 'in the sanctuary of Yahweh'.

27. To us: Gr. 'to it, for he has spoken to you today'. Witness for you: Gr. 'among you for a witness in the last days'. So that you would not deceive your God: Gr. 'Whenever you will deal falsely with the Lord my God'.

28. To their homes: lit. 'to his tent'.

30. Timnath Serah: Arabic has Timnath Heres, tallying with Judges 2:9. Gaash: Gr. Galaad. Gr. adds at the end of this verse (literal translation) 'There they put with him in the tomb, to bury him there, the stone knives with which he circumcised the sons of Israel in Gilgal when he had brought them out of Egypt, according to what the Lord decreed them, and they are there to this day.'

31. Experienced: lit. 'knew'.

32. Kesitahs: Gr. 'lambs'. The sons of Hamor: Gr. 'the Amorites'.

33. To him: Hebr. is ambiguous as to whether 'to him' refers to Eleazar or Phinehas, even though the latter seems much more probable. Gibeah: Gr. Gabaar. Gr. adds at the end of this verse (literal translation) 'On that day the sons of Israel, taking the ark of God, carried it around among them, and Phinehas ministered as a priest instead of Eleazar his father, until he died and was buried in Gabaath of himself. But the sons of Israel departed each to his place and his own town. And the sons of Israel worshipped Astarte and Ashtaroth and the gods of the peoples around them. And the Lord gave them to the hands of Eglon the king of Moab, and he dominated them for eighteen years.'

Form and structure

In its current setting, Joshua 24 in its literary context undoubtedly belongs to the last days of Joshua, judging both from its setting at the end of the book of Joshua and from the statement in Joshua 24:18 that Yahweh has driven out all nations before Israel. Moreover, according to Joshua 24:29, Joshua dies after the events depicted in Joshua 24, or at least after the events related in the latter part of the book.

In general, the chapter and verses 1–28 in particular have been treated exhaustively, especially by Koopmans (1990). We will restrict ourselves to the most pertinent observations here, and the interested reader is referred to Koopmans's book for further study.

The structure of the chapter can be described as follows:

> The covenant renewal at Shechem (vv. 1–28)
> > Joshua assembles Israel at Shechem (v. 1)
> > Joshua's first speech: Yahweh's message (vv. 2–16)
> > > Historical recital (vv. 2–13)
> > > > Call of Abraham (vv. 2–3)
> > > > Isaac, Jacob, Esau, and going down to Egypt (v. 4)
> > > > Moses and Aaron and the exodus (v. 5)
> > > > Miracle at the Sea of Reeds (vv. 6–7a)
> > > > Wilderness wanderings (v. 7b)
> > > > The conquest of Transjordan (v. 8)
> > > > Balaam incident (vv. 9–10)
> > > > Conquest of Canaan with Yahweh's help (vv. 11–13)
> > > Exhortation to serve Yahweh (vv. 14–15)
> > Response by the people (vv. 16–18)
> > > Denial that the people will serve other gods (v. 16)
> > > Acknowledgment of Yahweh's work (vv. 17–18a)
> > > Promise to serve Yahweh (v. 18b)

Joshua's second speech (vv. 19–20)
  People cannot serve Yahweh (v. 19a)
  Threat of punishment (vv. 19b–20)
Response by the people, promising to serve Yahweh (v. 21)
Joshua's response, making people witnesses (v. 22a)
Response by the people, acknowledging that they are
    witnesses (v. 22b)
Joshua's exhortation to put away foreign gods (v. 23)
Response by the people, promising to serve Yahweh (v. 24)
Summary about making a covenant (v. 25)
Joshua writes the words of the covenant in a book of the
    law of God (v. 26a)
The stone of witness (vv. 26b–27)
  Setting up the stone (v. 26b)
  Joshua's summary about the role of the stone (v. 27)
Joshua sends the people back to their homes (v. 28)
Joshua's death and burial, and two other grave traditions
    (vv. 29–33)
Joshua's death and burial (vv. 29–30)
Summary about Israel's following Yahweh for a generation
    after Joshua (v. 31)
Burial of the bones of Joseph (v. 32)
Burial of Eleazar (v. 33)

The chapter naturally divides into verses 1–28 and 29–33. As for the former, according to Noth (1991/1943: 23; the references Noth makes to his earlier book are not included with the quotation):

> Joshua 24:1–28 which stands by itself and has an independent origin shows no knowledge of the traditional version of the conquest in Josh. 2ff., and this passage was apparently unknown to Dtr. It was subsequently revised extensively in the style of Dtr. and incorporated into Dtr.'s long historical composition at a suitable point, because it contributes something important to the history of Joshua. Later the secondary vv. 29–33 were added.

A more detailed source-critical analysis of the passage by Noth can be found in Noth 1953a: 135–139. There have been various subsequent source-critical approaches to it, but these have not produced unanimity about the composition, or even the fundamental purpose of Joshua 24:1–28 (Koopmans 1990: 117; see Koopmans 1990: 97–117 and Noort 1998: 205–222 for a history of interpretation). That said, one may make the obvious, yet not insignificant, conclusion that the passage is in a deuteronomistic style overall. According to Nelson's analysis, 'A moderate list of deuteronomistic language would be the leadership catalog of v. 1; "saw with your own eyes", v. 7; "took possession of their land," v. 8; the nation list of v. 11; v. 13 as a whole; "fear and serve," v. 14; "forsake Yahweh to serve other gods," v. 16 and probably v. 20; "serve and obey," v. 25' (Nelson 1997a: 266). From here, one could just as well think that the passage was incorporated into the book of Joshua by the overall author at the very start. The author could have thought that it was not easy to integrate it directly into the chronological framework, and thus he added it to the end with the loose remark in 24:1. In addition, the overall purpose of the narrative can be seen as serving to strengthen the overall rhetoric of Joshua in exhorting the Israelites to follow Yahweh exclusively. The forming of a covenant (see Koopmans 1990, *passim* for this aspect, including comparisons with Ancient Near Eastern treaty formats; but note also the *misharum* acts in Babylonia, which were basically minor legal edicts addressing specific situations, meant to be understood as additions to existing legal or legal-related practice), examples from history, and various exhortations throughout serve to reinforce this objective. As Nelson notes, repetition serves to 'impel the reader to go along with the assembled Israel and to concur with the text's agenda' (Nelson 1997a: 268).

As for Joshua 24:29–33, according to Noth (Noth 1991/1943: 22; the references Noth makes in the passage to Rudolph, to his earlier book and to his current book are not included with the quotation):

> Rudolph was right to emphasize that Judg. 2.6 is directly and closely linked to Josh. 23. Within the straightforward context of Judg. 2.6–10 the statements on Joshua's age and his burial place should also be attributed to Dtr. Since Dtr. is capable of making similar statements, e.g. about the 'minor judges' in Judges, we are not entitled to attribute Judges 2.8–9 to a 'source' preserved in the Old Testament. On literary-critical grounds we must assume that this information was taken over by a secondary hand from Judg. 2 into Josh. 24.29–31 when the book of Joshua was made into an independent literary unit and thus a concluding remark on the death of Joshua was felt to be necessary. In this process Judg. 2.7 (= Josh. 24.31) was inserted after Judg. 2.8–9 (= Josh. 24.29–30), losing the appropriate order of Judg. 2, in order to give the book a resounding ending. Later the statement in Josh. 24.32, compiled from other Old Testament passages, and finally Josh. 24.33 were added.

Noth's comments illustrate the question of the relationship of the end of the book of Joshua to the beginning of the book of Judges (see also Koopmans 1990: 363–369; and cf. Noort 1998: 198–205). Overall, it seems that, while it is useful to draw parallels, it is difficult to reach definitive conclusions. While many scholars have followed Noth and considered the Judges account as primary and Joshua as secondary, there are no compelling reasons why the matter could not at least in its essential features be the other way around, and such a position has in fact been advocated by a number of scholars (see Koopmans 1990: 363 for a summary). In this regard, it may also be somewhat difficult to make firm conclusions about the LXX addition at the end of the chapter.

Chapter 24 makes reference to Genesis–Exodus and the patriarchal traditions. The visit of Jacob to Shechem in Genesis 35:1–5 is alluded to in verses 23–26, and the mention of the burial of the bones of Joseph in verse 32 refers back to Genesis 50:25 and Exodus 13:19. The fact that the passage takes place in Shechem connects with Genesis 12:6–7, Genesis 34, 37:12–13, Deuteronomy 11:29–30, 27:1–26 and Joshua 8:30–35 (cf. Judg. 9; also cf. 1 Kgs 12:1, 25, as pointed out by Nelson 1997a: 273). The historical recital in verses 2–13 of course makes reference to the whole sweep of the Pentateuchal history, starting from Genesis 12. In that respect, as Nelson (1997a: 268, referring to Brekelmans) suggests, and coupled with verses 29–33, it is fitting to see chapter 24 in its present form as a conclusion to the Hexateuchal narrative (Nelson 1997a: 269 helpfully notes that Shechem features in both Gen. 12 and Josh. 24). Also, the overall structure of Joshua 24:1–28 is similar to Joshua 23. As Nelson notes, both include a survey of the past, imperative and exhortation and the 'Yahweh alone' ideology, albeit there are some differences as well, including that while Joshua 24 extends the considerations to the full sweep of Pentateuchal history, Joshua 23 can be seen to look back at the book to Joshua only (Nelson 1997a: 268–269). For further literary parallels, see Koopmans 1990: 353–400.

As Nelson (1997a: 266) notes, the mention of the worship of other gods beyond the river Euphrates by Abraham and his family in verses 2, 14–15 and of the battle at Jericho in verse 11 are not found outside the narrative. This obviously suggests that Joshua 24:1–28 has utilized some unique tradition, or at least offers some unique viewpoints on past history.

That there are foreign gods (v. 23) seems at first to be in contradiction with e.g. verse 31 (see Nelson 1997a: 267). However, we can also think of passages such as verse 31 as overall relative statements, perhaps roughly in line with considerations of complete and incomplete conquest in Joshua. As for the stone of witness, it can be compared with the memorial stones of Joshua 4. Nelson (1997a: 272) also notes a fairly direct parallel with Genesis 31:48–50.

As for the date of the passage, there seems to be no reason to deny the possibility of an early date. As we have noted, and as can be seen for example in Koopmans 1990, a study of the literary aspects cannot provide any decisive conclusions. That Joshua 24 serves as a conclusion to the Hexateuch is not in itself conclusive as such, even if one were to date some of the materials of, say, Genesis–Deuteronomy late, as the historical recital uses elements from an independent tradition. As covenants date back to the pre-Israelite time in the Ancient Near East, this aspect of the narrative would fit with a provenance of the narrative from an early time. All this said, the literary setting of the chapter in its present form is tied to wider concerns about the dating of Genesis–Joshua, a question that involves issues that are beyond the scope of this book.

Comment

1. The chapter starts by describing how Joshua gathers all the tribes of Israel to Shechem, represented by much the same officials as in 23:1 (as pointed out by Nelson 1997a: 273, who also suggests a link with 8:33). Again, the word 'all tribes of Israel' should be understood as representative here; it is unlikely even from a logistical viewpoint that one would have been able to have mustered everybody (cf. my comments on 23:2). For Shechem itself, see comments on 17:7. The (various) leaders present themselves before Yahweh, the God of Israel. In order to try to understand the meaning of being in the presence of Yahweh, we can make the following observations. In the ancient world, gods would be present in their sanctuaries, or through a cult object. In Israel, the sanctuary would refer to the Tent of Meeting or (later) the temple, and the cult object to the ark (see comments on chapter 3, and Excursus 3). It also seems that, in the Old Testament, Yahweh could be present where a worshipper sacrificed to him (Exod. 20:22–26; see Pitkänen 2004a: 52–67 for details about interpreting this passage). However, in the light of chapter 22:10–34 of Joshua and the accompanying requirement to centralize sacrifices at Shiloh, it may be inferred that it is likely that the writer of Joshua thought that an altar would not have existed at Shechem at this time. Here it could for example have been that the ark had been brought to Shechem for the ceremony (cf. Judg. 20:18–28, esp. vv. 26–28). Or it may even simply have been that Yahweh could have been present with the Israelites of his own volition, without reference to any external cult appurtenances, when they gathered together and presented themselves with an attitude of seeking him (cf. David and Jonathan's covenant in 1 Sam. 23:15–18, which probably did not take place at a sanctuary or by an altar with sacrifices, and probably did not involve any external cult object). However, our knowledge of ancient Israel seems incomplete here and we therefore cannot speak with certainty but only in terms of plausibility.

2–3. Bearing in mind that this chapter is about covenant renewal (see also the 'Form and structure' section), and that the Israelite covenants seem to have been modelled on secular treaties, we note that it was typical that Ancient Near Eastern treaties of the second millennium had a historical introduction (or prologue) before the actual stipulations and other matters recorded (see Kitchen 2003b: 283–294 for a fuller discussion). This related history that was relevant to the making of the treaty. Verses 2–13 provide such an introduction here. Yahweh's great acts of salvation are recalled as a rhetorical device for encouraging obedience. First, the story of Abraham and his family in ancient Babylonia is summarized (vv. 2–3; cf. Gen. 11:24ff.). It is interesting that the narrative here states explicitly that all of the family, including Abraham, served other gods (v. 2). However, it should be understood from the biblical accounts that Abraham was a normal person in a land where Yahweh was not known, and thus it was not possible for him to know about Yahweh and serve him; rather, Abraham would naturally serve the gods of his own country. It should be understood that Abraham got to know Yahweh as he experienced his call and went along in response to it. Nelson helpfully notes that, according to the narrative, Yahweh 'took' Abraham from Mesopotamia to the land of Canaan (Nelson 1997a: 269). The passage emphasizes the fact that Yahweh elected and blessed Abraham, the forefather of Israel. Also, as Nelson points out, the rhetoric serves implicitly to disparage other gods (Nelson 1997a: 274)

4–6. The stories of the other patriarchs and the descent to Egypt and the exodus away from there are narrated in rather familiar terms. The only point is that space is given to mentioning Esau and his possession of Seir (v. 4). Perhaps this emphasizes the fact that the Israelites do not have claim to that area, keeping in mind that large parts of the book of Joshua are about the appropriation of the land of Israel.

7. The narrative makes a specific note that the Israelites were genuine witnesses of the events relating to the exodus, and the miracle(s) at the Sea of Reeds in particular (cf. Exod. 14 – 15). Then a short note is made about the wilderness wanderings (even though, strictly speaking, vv. 9–11 refer to this period too). No mention is made here that the Israelites had to stay in the wilderness for a long time because of their refusal to enter the land in the first instance (cf. Num. 13 – 14).

8. The land of Canaan is here referred to as the land of the Amorites (for the Amorites, see comments on 9:1–2 and 13:10). The destruction of the indigenous peoples is here (as elsewhere) related to Yahweh's action (cf. comments on 23:9).

9–10. The events relating to Balaam and Balak are summarized here. We read of them, especially Balaam in Numbers 22 – 24, 31 (cf. Num. 25). The power of curses and blessings is attested in the Old Testament (e.g. Gen. 27, 48 – 49). It remains however a bit of a mystery why Balaam is such an important person that his blessing or curse makes a big difference. But we must keep in mind that an inscription has been found at Deir 'Alla from about 800 BC in the area east of the Jordan that mentions Balaam as a prominent person and seer (see 'Form and structure' of chapter 13), suggesting that he was a well-known figure in the area. If this is the case, it would make sense that the Israelite tradition included him and mentioned that he submitted to Yahweh's power, as in Numbers 22 – 24. Note that Moab features in thirteenth century BC Egyptian texts (see Kitchen 2003b: 195).

11. Joshua recaps the events relating to the crossing of the river Jordan and aspects of the conquest of Canaan. The statement that the inhabitants of Jericho fought against the Israelites is often seen to be in contradiction

to the portrayal of events in Joshua 2 and 6, where the Israelites seem to conquer the city without any particular effort. However, if one remembers that Joshua 6 is a stylized depiction of victory in battle in accordance with the genre of fervent Yahwistic Ancient Near Eastern history writing, one can think that it purposefully emphasizes Yahweh's role in giving victory and rather minimizes the role of any human agency. (For example, say, when the people went on to the city as in 6:20, it is unlikely that the inhabitants of Jericho would simply have dropped their weapons in panic and waited for the Israelites to slaughter them.)

The rest of the people who fought against Israel are then described. These are the seven nations of Canaan, listed in full here (see comment in 9:1–2).

12. Joshua recounts that Yahweh sent hornets ahead of the Israelites (cf. Exod. 23:28; Deut. 7:20). This is a figurative way of stating that Yahweh caused the inhabitants to flee from the Israelites. Faced with a swarm of hornets (without, say, a bee farmer's protective gear), one cannot but flee. The point is that it was not the weapons and the skill and power of the Israelites that brought success, but Yahweh's (supernatural) action. The reference to the two kings of the Amorites is apparently a reference to certain specific kings, but it is not clear from the book of Joshua which kings are meant. The label 'Amorites' may refer to the Amorites proper, or it may be representative of the land of Canaan as a whole (cf. 24:8, and comments on the verse as above).

13. The point here is that the Israelites take possession of an already established infrastructure of building and cultivation, instead of having to start from scratch in the new land. This is convenient for the Israelites, minimizing the effort they have to make in establishing their life in the land. However, in line with what I have already discussed in this commentary, including in the Introduction, we may here ask the question, what about the Canaanites? And, in a wider sense, the world has seen conquests throughout its history in which conquerors take over the land and property of those conquered. Such events can also happen inside a society, when a dominant people group takes over what has hitherto belonged to another people group. In this vein, for example, a parallel of sorts can be mentioned from Germany in the 1930s and 1940s. When the Jewish people were sent to ghettos and concentration camps, their houses and property were reallocated to the main German population. Of course, one may find such a comparison with ancient Israel shocking. The shock effect in this case is created because many Christian people in essence tend to see the Nazis as evil but may see the ancient Israelites as good and as Yahweh's chosen people. Another parallel, from the Holy Land itself, has been furnished by Naim Ateek, a Palestinian Christian, describing via personal recollection how his family was forcefully evacuated from their family home by the Israelis in 1948 and how they were later denied permission even to see inside by its new occupants (Ateek 1989: 7–13). Or the mother of this author has often related to him how she was evacuated from Vyborg as a one-year-old, together with her family, when the Russians took Karelia from Finland after the Winter War of 1939–1940. In this way, and leaving everything behind, the family became refugees who had to be resettled elsewhere in Finland, being victims of circumstances in which a powerful group of people was imposing its will on a weaker group (cf. my comments in the Introduction, in the section on the modern application of the book of Joshua.

14–15. Joshua pleads with the people to follow Yahweh only. They are to remove any gods that they may have served in the past. Mesopotamia and Egypt refer to this past, and it is good to keep in mind that these countries worshipped a number of gods, some of them as part of the national religion. Joshua also charges the people not to serve the gods of Canaan (the label 'Amorites' again serves as representative of the whole of Canaan; cf. above, vv. 8 and 12, and comments thereon). In a sense, the Old Testament as a whole implies that, for the Israelites, the possession of a land of their own means the freedom to worship a god of their choice. Here, of course, Joshua wants the choice to be Yahweh. After making the choice out to be unusually free for the people, Joshua states that he as the leader of Israel will set an example and serve Yahweh, naturally together with his household, which, in the manner of ancient Israelite thinking, is under his power, and, equally, for whose behaviour he is accountable. The thrust of the rhetoric here is that Joshua wants the people to choose Yahweh out of free will rather than compulsion.

16. The people respond favourably. They even imply that it is unthinkable that they would serve any other god than Yahweh. For the readers (or hearers) of Joshua, this would be likely to impress on them that just as the people of the past were willing, so should they be.

17–18. The people affirm that they remember Yahweh's great deeds for them through the exodus and the conquest. The people affirm that Yahweh is their God. Again, this serves to help persuade the reader or hearer (cf. comments on v. 16).

19–21. Joshua's rhetoric now moves from supplication to charge. He states that the people will actually not be able to serve Yahweh and that Yahweh, as the holy and jealous God, will not tolerate such behaviour. Joshua's charge here should be seen as a rhetorical accusation. With this, he tests the resolve of the people. Even with these threats, do they really want to serve Yahweh and commit themselves to him? Will they accept future punishment for any possible failings? The people respond with an affirmation that they do indeed want to serve Yahweh, even under these terms and conditions.

22. Joshua then states that the people themselves, having affirmed their decision to serve Yahweh, are witnesses of the matter. The people further affirm that they are witnesses. This echoes covenantal language (cf. e.g. Deut. 4:26; 31:19, 26), even though the people themselves serve as witnesses in the rhetoric here, rather than some object (which however will also be introduced in v. 27). But it also seems that making the people themselves witnesses heightens their own responsibility, as Nelson (1997a: 276) suggests.

23–24. Joshua next charges the people to remove all foreign gods and consider Yahweh only. It seems that this should be taken as ceremonial and symbolic rhetoric: no actual action of removal is likely to have taken place on the spot, especially considering that not all the people were present anyway (cf. v. 1). The location of the ceremony of course heightens the symbolic aspect, as this is *the* place (see below, vv. 25–26 and comments there) where Jacob, the grand patriarch of Israel, *in actuality* threw away *his* foreign gods (Gen. 35:1–5). Thus, the whole point of the ceremony in this chapter is to emphasize total commitment to Yahweh, a decisive point of no return in the life of (the new) Israel in the land of their forefathers, to which they have now returned after a long time away. Just as Jacob was to purify himself of foreign gods after his stay in Paddan Aram and Yahweh's gracious granting of return and prosperity to him, so are Israel to do. Of course, the reader (or hearer) of the book of Joshua is expected to take note accordingly.

25–26a. The act of commitment is formally acknowledged and enacted as a covenant. It is difficult to say exactly what the laws and decrees refer to. It is however likely that they should be seen as a renewal and restatement of the laws of Moses. It may be possible that something else was involved, but this would be minor in comparison with the main thrust of the laws of Moses. It does not seem clear whether the passage should be understood to mean that Joshua made a separate document or whether he appended the events and agreements that had just taken place to a/the law book he had received (presumably from Moses). Whatever the case, the *misharum* edicts in Babylonia might provide at least a kind of parallel to the case described here (cf. above, 'Form and structure' section).

In general, we may also note here that the Hebrew expression for cutting a covenant is *kārat běrît*, 'to cut a covenant'. In the Ancient Near East, covenants often included cutting an animal into pieces as part of the ceremony (cf. e.g. Gen. 15; Vassal Treaties of Esarhaddon 69, 70 [see e.g. *ANET*: 539]).

26b–27. Joshua next takes a big stone and sets it up under the oak at the sanctuary (or holy place) of Yahweh. It is hard to say what the sanctuary (or holy place) of Yahweh should be taken to mean, but in the light of chapter 22 and the centralization requirement expressed therein, it is unlikely that the writer of the book of Joshua at least would have seen this as a place of offering. It is better to take this as a memorial, like the stones in Gilgal (Josh. 4; cf. also Judg. 9:6 which may indicate a pillar by a tree, and is likely to refer to the same place as here), and the place at Shechem is already holy due to the (obvious) association of Jacob with it (Gen. 35:1–5; the very trees are implied to be the same). While stones could be treated as cult objects where a deity could then dwell (cf. Excursus 3), it is unlikely to be the case here, but, rather, Joshua is speaking metaphorically as if the stone is a living being that has heard the words of the covenant. The point is that the people know that the oath took place, the stone was set up in the sanctuary (holy place) as a memorial of the occasion, and the events were recorded in a book. Thus what has been agreed should be remembered and upheld.

28. In contrast to the apparently slightly abrupt ending in Joshua 23 (see comments on 23:16), the text here makes mention of Joshua sending the people home. Perhaps this also serves to prepare for the impending ending of the book.

29–30. Finally, the inevitable is recorded and an era comes to a close. Joshua dies at the age of 110, the same age as Joseph (Gen. 50:22). One hundred and ten years was an ideal lifespan for the Egyptians (see *ANET*: 414, Instruction of the Vizier Ptah-Hotep: 'I attained one hundred and ten years of life which the king gave me, with favour foremost among the ancestors, through doing right for the king up to the point of veneration'; note that the chief manuscript of the text comes from the Middle Kingdom [around the early second millennium BC]; see *ANET*: 412; cf. Kitchen 2003b). As Nelson points out, Joshua's lifespan is nevertheless still ten years short of Moses' (Deut. 34:7; Nelson 1997a: 279). Also, after this, there does not seem to be anyone in the history of Israel who had such an extensive lifespan (cf. Nelson 1997a: 279). In other words, and interestingly, long lifespans occur only in Genesis–Joshua, giving a further reason for thinking of these books together (cf. also the Sumerian King List, with earliest extant copies from the early second millennium BC, which gives some very long reigns and thus lifespans for the pre-dynastic kings mentioned in it, and still considerably long reigns for a number of the early dynastic kings).

Joshua the Ephraimite is buried in the land of his inheritance, the hill country of Ephraim, at Timnath Serah (var. Timnath Heres; see Judg. 2:9). Timnath Serah has been identified with Khirbet Tibnah, which was occupied as early as Middle Bronze II, mostly abandoned in the Late Bronze Age, and then a rather large village in Iron I (see *ABD* 6: 557–558). If the site identification is correct, the archaeological evidence seems to fit with what is said in 19:50 and Joshua's (re)building of the town. The burial note (also keeping in mind the number 110) seems further to link Joshua to Joseph and the end of the book of Genesis (assuming that Gen. was originally, or at least in early times, seen as a separate book; cf. also comments on v. 32), albeit one is also reminded of Moses' death and burial note in Deuteronomy 34. The location of the mountain of Gaash is uncertain (see *ABD* 2: 861).

31. The book notes that Israel served Yahweh as long as Joshua lived and as long as there were living witnesses to the events of the exodus and conquest. The term 'elders' may refer to the leaders of Israel, but it has to be remembered that people who lived long in ancient Israel probably also achieved the status of eldership just by virtue of 'sticking around', so the note may also mean that as long as there were people alive who had seen the events, Israel followed Yahweh.

We of course know that the book of Judges describes how things took a bad turn soon afterwards. In fact, if one considers that the events of Judges 17 – 21 were likely to have been understood to have taken place early in the period of judges (see e.g. Judg. 18:1, which indicates that the Danites had not yet settled; 18:30 which may indicate a time of only two generations away from Moses, even though there may have been further unmentioned 'fathers' between Jonathan and Moses), Joshua here represents an idealized break-off point. It should probably be understood that it is more likely that things turned in a non-Yahwistic direction pretty soon after the conquest, if the situation ever was purely Yahwistic. It would seem reasonable to think that the number of 'pure' Yahwists might have been comparatively high after the conquest, but the whole society was never fully Yahwistic. The number of Yahwists could then have declined over the Early Iron Age, with the hold of indigenous religions firmly established, as the book of Judges describes. Verse 31 serves as a premonition of the things to come. In fact, the Septuagint adds a verse to the end of Joshua that directly mentions the apostasy of Israel and the first cycle of oppression during the time of the judges (see note on v. 33 in the translation and textual notes section). In the context of the whole, it is not entirely unreasonable to think that if an outside group manages to get a foothold in a new area with the help of a charismatic leader, after that leader's death it may be that the power of the group diminishes and the power of some other adjacent group increases, at least in a relative sense, with a resulting stronger grip of the adjacent group on the first group. The first group then, often with the help of another charismatic leader, may find a way to be 'independent' again, etc. Certainly, that the vicissitudes of groups and countries ebb and flow is known from history throughout the world. Here of course the Israelite historian of Judges in particular sees such vicissitudes as tied to Yahweh's action in response to Israel's adherence to Yahwistic life and worship. (In Israel's case, as per the books of Samuel and 1 Kings, the vicissitudes eventually move on to the rise of a charismatic leader, and after him his son, who manage to secure the loyalty of a group of loosely scattered tribes tied together by a common ethnic consciousness, and effect institutions that lead to an overall centralization of power and the establishment of a state.)

32–33. A link with Joseph, and thus the end of the book of Genesis, is made explicitly here (cf. above, vv. 29–30, and comments there) through the mention of the burial of Joseph's bones at Shechem, which itself lies in the region allotted to his sons Ephraim and Manasseh. A further link to Jacob and the land he bought from the Shechemites is made as well (cf. Gen. 33:19; cf. comments on vv. 23–24, 26–27 above), albeit Jacob himself is said to have been buried near Mamre (Gen. 50:13). The value (or weight) of a *qĕśîṭāh* seems to be unknown (cf. Boling and Wright 1982: 542; cf. also Job 42:11 in addition to Gen. 33:19).

Finally, we have a note of the death of Eleazar the priest. However, not quite everyone of importance passes away by the end of the book of Joshua. We meet Phinehas the son of Eleazar (who features in Josh. 22) in the book of Judges (see Judg. 20:27–28). That Joseph is buried in the place that his father bought and his sons now possess, and Eleazar is buried in the place allotted to his son, serve to emphasize the importance that was attributed to family in ancient Israel. Of course, Genesis 50:25 implies that Joseph eventually wanted to have his bones buried in Canaan.

The location of Gibeah is unclear (see *ABD* 2: 1007). It may however be possible that Gibeah here should be seen to refer to Geba of Joshua 21:17, as Phinehas was an Aaronite and the (consonantal) spellings of both Gibeah and Geba are similar (cf. the discussions in *ABD* 2: 921–922, 1007–1009; cf. also *NEAEHL*: 445). If so, the Gibeah referred to here is probably the same as Gibeah in Benjamin, which features in a number of Old Testament narratives (e.g. Judg. 19 – 20). The actual location of Gibeah (and Geba) here is not quite clear, but it could be Tell el-Ful, from which material from Iron Age I on has been found (see *NEAEHL*: 445–448; Miller 2003: 164) or (particularly in reference to Geba) modern Jaba, of which only surface surveys have been made, with Iron I (and Iron II) shards uncovered (see *ABD* 2: 921, 1007; R. D. Miller 2003: 167). If Gibeah in Benjamin is meant, even if one is not able to see the burial place as located quite in the Ephraimite area, it could broadly speaking be seen as part of the hill country of Ephraim. It is also possible, although perhaps somewhat questionable in the light of the system of Levitical towns as described in Joshua 21, that the book of Joshua indicates that Phinehas was given a further town separately.

Explanation

In a manner reminiscent of Ancient Near Eastern vassal treaties, chapter 24 summarizes Israel's self-understanding as portrayed in the book of Joshua. The people of Israel are Yahweh's people. That Yahweh has taken an interest in them and is their God is shown by all the good deeds that Yahweh has done for them in the past, with a summary of these included in the chapter. The Israelites are to remember Yahweh's provision for them, and thus commit themselves to serving him. Serving Yahweh is Israel's part; provision for Israel is Yahweh's part. Yahweh guarantees that he will take care of Israel as long as the Israelites serve him and conduct themselves in a prescribed manner. Should the Israelites fail to do this, Yahweh will no longer protect them and provide for them, and will in fact turn against them and cause problems for them (cf. Deut.). The chapter serves as the last testimony of Joshua, and the death of Joshua is described at the end of the chapter. The burying of the bones of Joseph and the death of Eleazar further heighten the sense of an end of an era, an important one in Israel's history. As known from elsewhere, this era is to be followed by the period of judges, an era clearly different in tone from Joshua with its emphasis on the apostasy of Israel and the subsequent raising of judges by Yahweh to deliver Israel.

Christians, when thinking about their covenant ('treaty') with God, can also reflect on their history with him. Such a history consists of Yahweh's acts throughout history as expressed in the Bible (both the Old Testament and the New Testament) and in church history, and a remembrance of Yahweh's acts in their personal lives (and in the lives of others they may know [about] in their communities). Such memory and understanding serve as a vital basis for one's faith. If one wishes, one may also write down one's experiences in a book and arrange for some kind of object (maybe a cross etc.) to commemorate such events and experiences. Christians may also reflect on other aspects of the treaty, which was established through the sacrifice of Christ on the cross. I have already made comments on some of these aspects elsewhere in this commentary, where such considerations naturally arise from a reading of the book of Joshua.

Finally, let us pay close attention to Joshua's call to his hearers to choose between Yahweh and other gods. This call to follow Yahweh is also reflected in Jesus' call: 'Follow me!'

BIBLIOGRAPHY

COMMENTARIES ON JOSHUA

Boling, R. G., and G. E. Wright (1982), *Joshua: A New Translation with Introduction and Commentary*, AB, Garden City, New York: Doubleday.

Butler, T. C. (1983), *Joshua*, WBC, Waco, TX: Word Books.

Fritz, V. (1994), *Das Buch Josua*, HAT 1.7, Tübingen: J. C. B. Mohr.

Gray, J. (1986), *Joshua, Judges, Ruth*, NCBC, Grand Rapids, MI: Eerdmans; Basingstoke: Marshall, Morgan & Scott.

Harstad, A. (2004), *Joshua: A Theological Exposition of Sacred Scripture*, Concordia Commentary Series, Minneapolis: Concordia Publishing House.

Hawk, L. D. (2000), *Joshua*, Berit Olam, Collegeville, MN: Liturgical Press.

Hess, R. S. (1996), *Joshua: An Introduction and Commentary*, TOTC, Leicester: Inter-Varsity Press.

Nelson, R. D. (1997a), *Joshua*, OTL, Philadelphia: Westminster John Knox Press.

Noth, M. (1953a), *Das Buch Josua*, 2nd edn, HAT 7, Tübingen: J. C. B. Mohr (Paul Siebeck).

Soggin, J. A. (1972), *Joshua*, OTL, London: SCM Press. French original: *Le Livre de Josué*, CAT 5.a, Neuchatel: Delachau & Niestle.

Woudstra, M. H. (1981), *The Book of Joshua*, NICOT, Grand Rapids, MI: Eerdmans.

OTHER WORKS

Ahlström, G. W. (1993), *The History of Ancient Palestine*, Minneapolis: Fortress Press.

Albright, W. F. (1924), 'Ai and Beth-Aven', ASOR 4:141–149.

—— (1927), 'The Danish Excavations at Seilun – A Correction', PEFQS 59:157–158.

—— (1966), *The Proto-Sinaitic Inscriptions and Their Decipherment*, HTS 22, Cambridge, MA: Harvard University Press; London: Oxford University Press.

Alt, A. (1927), 'Eine galiläische Ortsliste in Jos. 19', ZAW 45:59–81.

—— (1953a/1925), 'Judas Gaue unter Josia', KS 2, Munich: C. H. Beck, pp. 276–288. Original in *PJB* 21 (1925):100–117.

———— (1953b/1927), 'Das System der Stammesgrenzen im Buche Josua', KS 1, Munich: C. H. Beck, pp. 193–202. Original in Sellin-Festschrift 1927, pp. 13–24.

———— (1953c), 'Israels Gaue unter Salomo', KS 2, Munich: C. H. Beck, pp. 76–89. Original in *Alttestamentliche Studien R. Kittel zum 60. Geburtstag dargebracht*, 1913, pp. 1–19.

———— (1953d), 'Josua', in KS 1, Munich: C. H. Beck 1953, pp. 176–192. Original in BZAW 66 (1936):13–29.

———— (1966a), 'The Settlement of the Israelites in Palestine', in *Essays on Old Testament History and Religion*, Oxford: Basil Blackwell, pp. 133–169. German original: *Die Landnahme der Israeliten in Palästina*, Reformationsprogramm der Universität Leipzig, 1925.

———— (1966b), 'The Formation of the Israelite State in Palestine', in *Essays on Old Testament History and Religion*, Oxford: Basil Blackwell, pp. 171–237. German original: *Die Staatenbildung der Israeliten in Palästina*, Reformationsprogramm der Universität Leipzig, 1930.

Amit, Y. (1999), *The Book of Judges: The Art of Editing*, Biblical Interpretation Series 38, Leiden: E. J. Brill.

Anbar, M. (1985), 'The Story about the Building of an Altar on Mount Ebal', in N. Lohfink (ed.), *Das Deuteronomium: Entstehung, Gestalt und Botschaft (BETL LXVIII)*, Leuven: University Press, pp. 304–309.

Assis, E. (2003), '"How Long Are You Slack to Go to Possess the Land" (Jos. XVIII 3): Ideal and Reality in the Distribution Descriptions in Joshua XIII–XIX', *VT* 53:1.

Ateek, N. S. (1989), *Justice and Only Justice: A Palestinian Theology of Liberation*, New York: Orbis Books.

Auld, A. G. (1980), *Joshua, Moses & the Land: Tetrateuch–Pentateuch–Hexateuch in a Generation since 1938*, Edinburgh: T. & T. Clark.

———— (1998), *Joshua Retold: Synoptic Perspectives*, Edinburgh: T. & T. Clark.

Barker, P. A. (1998), *The Theology of Deuteronomy 27*, TynB 49.2:277–303.

Barmash, P. (2005), *Homicide in the Biblical World*, Cambridge: Cambridge University Press.

Bienkowski, P. (1986), *Jericho in the Late Bronze Age*, Warminster: Aris & Phillips.

Bimson, J. J. (1981), *Redating Exodus and the Conquest*, JSOTSup 5, Sheffield: Almond Press.

Blenkinsopp, J. (1972), *Gibeon and Israel: The Role of Gibeon and the Gibeonites in the Political and Religious History of Early Israel*, Cambridge: Cambridge University Press.

Block, D. (1988), *The Gods of the Nations: Studies in Ancient Near Eastern National Theology*, Evangelical Theological Society Monograph Series 2, Jackson, MS: Evangelical Theological Society.

Brandl, B. (1986–1987), 'Two Scarabs and a Trapezoidal Seal from Mount Ebal', *TA* 13–14:166–172.

Brett, M. G. (2008), *Decolonizing God: The Bible in the Tides of Empire*, Bible in Modern World 16, Sheffield: Sheffield Phoenix Press.

Bruce, F. F. (1982), *Commentary on Galatians*, NIGTC, Grand Rapids, MI: Eerdmans.

—— (1990), *The Acts of the Apostles: Greek Text with Introduction and Commentary*, Grand Rapids, MI: Eerdmans.

Brueggemann, W. (2009), *Divine Presence amid Violence: Contextualising the Book of Joshua*, Carlisle: Paternoster Press.

Budd, P. J. (1984), *Numbers*, WBC, Waco, TX: Word Books.

Bunimovitz, S. (1993), 'Area C: The Iron Age I Pillared Buildings and Other Remains', in I. Finkelstein (ed.), *Shiloh: The Archaeology of a Biblical Site*, Tel Aviv: The Institute of Archaeology of Tel Aviv University, pp. 15–34 (ch. 2).

Bunimovitz, S., and I. Finkelstein (1993), 'Pottery', in I. Finkelstein (ed.), *Shiloh: The Archaeology of a Biblical Site*, Tel Aviv: The Institute of Archaeology of Tel Aviv University, pp. 81–196 (ch. 6).

Callaway, J. A. (1964), *Pottery from the Tombs at 'Ai (et–Tell)*, London: B. Quaritch.

—— (1972), *The Early Bronze Age Sanctuary at Ai (et-Tell)*, London: B. Quaritch.

—— with the assistance of Kermit Schoonover and William W. Ellinger III (1980), *The Early Bronze Age Citadel and Lower City at Ai (et-Tell): A Report of the Joint Archaeological Expedition to Ai (et-Tell), No. 2*, Cambridge, MA: American Schools of Oriental Research.

Calvin, J. (1847–1850/1565), *Commentaries on the Book of Joshua*, translated from the original Latin, and collated with the French edn by Henry Beveridge, ESQ, Edinburgh: Calvin Translation Society. French translation and Latin original 1565.

Campbell, E. F., Jr (1991), *Shechem II: Portrait of a Hill Country Vale*, Atlanta: Scholars Press.

Chapman, C. (2005), 'God's Covenant – God's Land?', in Alistair I. Wilson and Jamie A. Grant (eds), *The God of Covenant*, Leicester: IVP, pp. 221–256.

Childs, B. S. (1963), 'A Study of the Formula "Until This Day"', *JBL* 82:279–292.

—— (1974), *Exodus: A Commentary*, OTL, London: SCM Press.

Christensen, D. L. (ed.) (1993), *A Song of Power and the Power of Song: Essays of the Book of Deuteronomy*, Winona Lake, IN: Eisenbrauns.

Clouse, R. D. (ed.) (1977), *The Meaning of the Millennium: Four Views*, Downers Grove, IL: InterVarsity Press.

Cobb, V. (2002), 'The Ban (Herem) in the Israelite Conquest Tradition with Particular Reference to Deuteronomy 7', BA dissertation, Cheltenham: University of Gloucestershire.

Cooper, J. S. (1983), *The Curse of Agade*, Baltimore and London: Johns Hopkins University Press.

Coote, R. B., and K. W. Whitelam (1987), *The Emergence of Early Israel in Historical Perspective*, Sheffield: Almond Press.

Cortese, E. (1990), *Josua 13 – 21: Ein priesterschriftlicher Abschnitt im deuteronomistischen Geschichtswerk*, Göttingen: Vandenhoeck & Ruprecht.

Court, J. M. (2008), *Approaching the Apocalypse: A Short History of Christian Millenarianism*, London: I. B. Tauris.

Cowley, A. (1967), *Aramaic Papyri of the Fifth Century B.C.*, Osnabrück: Otto Zeller (repr. of 1923 edn).

Craigie, P. C. (1976), *The Book of Deuteronomy*, NICOT, Grand Rapids, MI: Eerdmans.

Crenshaw, J. L. (2005), *Defending God: Biblical Responses to the Problem of Evil*, Oxford: Oxford University Press.

Curtis, A. H. W. (1994), *Joshua*, OTG, Sheffield: Sheffield Academic Press.

Davies, B. (1997), *Egyptian Historical Inscriptions of the Nineteenth Dynasty*, Jonsered: Paul Åströms förlag.

Davies, P. R. (1992), *In Search of 'Ancient Israel'*, JSOTSup 148, Sheffield: JSOT Press.

Day, J. (1979), 'The Destruction of the Shiloh Sanctuary and Jeremiah vii 12, 14', VTSup 30:87–94.

Dever, W. G. (2001), *What Did the Biblical Writers Know and When Did They Know It? What Archaeology Can Tell Us about the Reality of Ancient Israel*, Grand Rapids, MI; Cambridge, UK: Eerdmans.

——— (2003), *Who Were the Early Israelites and Where Did They Come From?* Grand Rapids, MI: Eerdmans.

——— (2005), *Did God Have a Wife? Archaeology and Folk Religion in Ancient Israel*, Grand Rapids, MI: Eerdmans.

Driver, S. R. (1901/1895), *A Critical and Exegetical Commentary on Deuteronomy*, 3rd edn, ICC, Edinburgh: T. & T. Clark (1st edn 1895).

Durham, J. I. (1987), *Exodus*, in WBC, Waco, TX: Word Books.

Dus, J. (1964), 'Die Lösung des Rätsels von Jos 22', AO 32:529–546.

Dyk, P. J. van (1990), 'The Function of So-Called Etiological Elements in Narratives', ZAW 102.1, pp. 19–33.

Edel, E. (1994), *Die ägyptisch-hethitische Korrespondenz aus Boghazköi in babylonischer und hethitischer Sprache* (Band 1: Umschriften und Übersetzung; Band 2: Kommentar), Oplag: Westdeutscher Verlag.

Edelman, D. V. (ed.) (1995), *You Shall not Abhor an Edomite for He Is Your Brother: Edom and Seir in History and Tradition*, SBL and ASOR Archaeology and Biblical Studies 3, Atlanta: Scholars Press.

Eissfeldt, O. (1956), 'Silo und Jerusalem', in *Congress Volume, Strasbourg 1956*, ed. J. A. Emerton et al., VTSup 4, Leiden: E. J. Brill, pp. 138–148.

——— (1962–1979a), 'Kultzelt und Tempel', KS 6, Tübingen: J. C. B. Mohr, pp. 1–7. Original in *Wort und Geschichte. FS Karl Elliger*, Neukirchen-Vluyn, 1973, pp. 51–55.

—— (1962–1979b/1973), 'Monopol-Ansprüche des Heiligtums von Silo', KS 6, Tübingen: J. C. B. Mohr, pp. 8–14. Original in *OLZ* 68 (1973): 327–333.

—— (1970), 'Gilgal or Shechem?', in J. I. Durham and J. R. Porter (eds), *Proclamation and Presence: Old Testament Essays in Honour of Gwynne Henton Davies*, London: SCM Press, pp. 90–101.

Fara, P. (2009), *Science: A Four Thousand Year History*, Oxford: Oxford University Press.

Faust, A. (2006), *Israel's Ethnogenesis: Settlement, Interaction, Expansion and Resistance*, London: Equinox.

Feyerabend, P. (1993), *Against Method*, 3rd edn, London: Verso.

Finkelstein, I. (1986), 'Shiloh Yields Some, But Not All, of Its Secrets', *BAR* 12.1:22–41.

—— (1988), *The Archaeology of the Israelite Settlement*, Jerusalem: Israel Exploration Society.

—— (1993a), 'Introduction', in Finkelstein 1993c: 1–12.

—— (1993b), 'Excavations Results in Areas E, G, J, K, L and M', in Finkelstein 1993c: 65–78.

—— (ed.) (1993c), *Shiloh: The Archaeology of a Biblical Site*, Tel Aviv: Institute of Archaeology of Tel Aviv University.

Finkelstein, I., and N. Na'aman (eds) (1994), *From Nomadism to Monarchy: Archaeological and Historical Aspects of Early Israel*, Jerusalem: Israel Exploration Society.

Finkelstein, I., and N. A. Silberman (2001), *The Bible Unearthed: Archaeology's New Vision of Ancient Israel and the Origin of Its Sacred Texts*, New York: Simon & Schuster.

Foster, B. R. (2005), *Before the Muses: An Anthology of Akkadian Literature*, 3rd edn, Bethesda, MD: CDL Press.

Fowler, M. D. (1987), 'The Meaning of *lipne YHWH* in the Old Testament', *ZAW* 99:384–390.

Freedman, D. N. (1981), 'Temple Without Hands', in A. Biran (ed.), *Temples and High Places in Biblical Times: Proceedings of the Colloquium in Honor of the Centennial of Hebrew Union College – Jewish Institute of Religion*, Jerusalem: Hebrew Union College, pp. 21–30.

Freedman, R. E. (1992), 'Tabernacle', *ABD* 6:292–300.

Fritz, V. (1977), *Tempel und Zelt: Studien zum Tempelbau in Israel und zu dem Zeltheiligtum der Priesterschrift*, Neukirchen: Neukirchener Verlag.

—— (1993), 'Open Cult Places in Israel in the Light of Parallels from Prehistoric Europe and Pre-Classical Greece', in *Biblical Archaeology Today, 1990: Proceedings of the Second International Congress on Biblical Archaeology*, Jerusalem: Israel Exploration Society / Keterpress, pp. 182–187.

George, A. R. (1993), *House Most High: Temples of Ancient Mesopotamia*, Mesopotamian Civilizations 5, Eisenbrauns: Winona Lake, IN.

Gilmour, G. H. (1995), 'The Archaeology of Cult in the Southern Levant in the Early Iron Age: An Analytical and Comparative Approach', PhD thesis, University of Oxford.

Gleis, M. (1997), *Die Bamah*, BZAW 251, Berlin: Walter de Gruyter.

Gottwald, N. (1999/1979), *The Tribes of Yahweh: A Sociology of the Religion of Liberated Israel, 1250*, Sheffield: Sheffield Academic Press.

Gray, G. B., (1903), *A Critical and Exegetical Commentary on Numbers*, ICC, Edinburgh: T. & T. Clark.

Greenberg, R., and A. Keinan (2009), *Israeli Archaeological Activity in the West Bank, 1967–2007: A Sourcebook*, The West Bank and East Jerusalem Archaeological Database Project/Ostracon. Also available at http://digitallibrary.usc.edu/wbarc, accessed 4 August 2010.

Hallo, W. W. (1996a), *Origins: The Ancient Near Eastern Background of Some Modern Western Institutions*, Leiden: E. J. Brill.

—— (1996b), 'Lamentations and Prayers in Sumer and Akkad', in *CANE* 3, pp. 1871–1881.

Haran, M. (1960), 'The OHEL MOED in Pentateuchal Sources', *JSS* 5:50–65.

—— (1962), 'Shiloh and Jerusalem: The Origin of the Priestly Tradition in the Pentateuch', *JBL* 81:14–24.

—— (1965), 'The Priestly Image of the Tabernacle', *HUCA* 36:191–226.

—— (1969a), 'The Divine Presence in the Israelite Cult and the Cultic Institutions', *Bib* 50:251–267.

—— (1969b), 'Zebah Hayyamim', *VT* 19.1:11–22.

—— (1978), *Temples and Temple Service in Ancient Israel: An Inquiry into the Character of Cult Phenomena and the Historical Setting of the Priestly School*, Oxford: Clarendon Press.

—— (1981), 'Temples and Cultic Open Areas as Reflected in the Bible', in A. Biran (ed.), *Temples and High Places in Biblical Times: Proceedings of the Colloquium in Honor of the Centennial of Hebrew Union College – Jewish Institute of Religion*, Jerusalem: Hebrew Union College, pp. 31–37.

Hawk, L. D. (1991), *Every Promise Fulfilled: Contesting Plots in Joshua*, Louisville, KY: Westminster John Knox Press.

—— (1997), 'The Problem with Pagans', in *Reading Bibles, Writing Bodies: Identity and the Book*, ed. T. K. Beal and D. M. Gunn, London: Routledge.

Hawking, R. K. (2007), 'The Iron Age Structure on Mount Ebal: Excavation and Interpretation', PhD thesis, Andrews University. Also forthcoming in rev. form by Winona Lake, IN: Eisenbrauns.

Heinrich, E. (1982), *Die Tempel und Heiligtümer in Alten Mesopotamien: Typologie, Morphologie, Geschichte*, 2 vols, Berlin: Walter de Gruyter.

Henry, M. (2008/1706), *Matthew Henry's Commentary on the Whole Bible: Complete and Unabridged*, Peabody, MA: Hendrickson. Originally published 1706.

Hertzberg, H. W. (1964), *I & II Samuel*, in OTL, London: SCM Press. German original: *Die Samuelbücher*, ATD 10, 2nd rev. edn, Göttingen: Vandenhoeck & Ruprecht, 1960.

Herzog, Z. (1994), 'The Beer-Sheba Valley: From Nomadism to Monarchy', in Finkelstein and Na'aman 1994: 122–149.

Hess, R. S. (1993a), 'Early Israel in Canaan: A Survey of Recent Evidence and Interpretations', *PEQ* 125:125–142.

—— (1993b), *Amarna Personal Names*, ASOR dissertation series 9, Winona Lake, IN: Eisenbrauns.

—— (1994), 'Asking Historical Questions of Joshua 13 – 19: Recent Discussion Concerning the Date of the Boundary Lists', in *Faith, Tradition and History: Old Testament Historiography in Its Near Eastern Context*, Winona Lake, IN: Eisenbrauns, 1994, pp. 191–205.

—— (1997), 'West Semitic Texts and the Book of Joshua', *BBR* 7:63–76. Also available at http://www.ibr-bbr.org/IBRBulletin/BBR_1997/ BBR_1997_05_Hess_Joshua.pdf, accessed 30 November 2009.

—— (2002), 'The Book of Joshua as a Land Grant', *Bib* 83:493–506. Also available at http://www.bsw.org/?l=71831&a=Comm15.html, accessed 5 November 2007.

Hill, A. E. (1988), 'The Ebal Ceremony as Hebrew Land Grant?', *JETS* 31:399–406.

Hoffmann, H. D. (1980), *Reform und Reformen: Untersuchung zu einen Grundthema der Deuteronomistischen Geschichtsschreibung*, ATANT 66, Zürich: Theologischer Verlag.

Hoffmeier, J. K. (1997), *Israel in Egypt: The Evidence for the Authenticity of the Exodus Tradition*, Oxford: Oxford University Press.

—— (2005), *Ancient Israel in Sinai: The Evidence for the Authenticity of the Wilderness Traditions*, Oxford: Oxford University Press.

Hoffmeier, J. K., and A. R. Millard (eds) (2004), *The Future of Biblical Archaeology: Reassessing Methodologies and Assumptions*, Grand Rapids, MI: Eerdmans.

Hoffner, H. A. (1969), 'Some Contributions of Hittitology to Old Testament Study', *TynB* 20:27–55.

Holladay, J. S., Jr (1987), 'Religion in Israel and Judah Under the Monarchy: An Explicitly Archaeological Approach', in *Ancient Israelite Religion: Essays in Honor of Frank Moore Cross*, ed. P. D. Miller, Jr, P. D. Hanson and S. D. McBride, Philadelphia: Fortress Press, pp. 249–299.

Horowitz, D. (2000/1985), *Ethnic Groups in Conflict*, Berkeley: University of California Press; repr of 1985 edn with a new preface.

Horowitz, W., T. Oshima and S. Sanders (2006), *Cuneiform in Canaan: Cuneiform Sources from the Land of Israel in Ancient Times*, Jerusalem: Israel Exploration Society.

Horwitz, L. K. (1986–1987), 'Faunal Remains from the Early Iron Age Site on Mount Ebal', *TA* 13–14:173–189.

Humphreys, C. J. (2003), *The Miracles of Exodus: A Scientist's Discovery of the Extraordinary Natural Causes of the Biblical Stories*, New York: HarperOne.

Hurvitz, A. (1982), *A Linguistic Study of the Relationship Between the Priestly Source and the Book of Ezekiel: A New Approach to an Old Problem*, CahRB 20, Paris: J. Gabalda.

Hutchinson, J., and A. D. Smith (eds) (1996), *Ethnicity*, Oxford Readers, Oxford: Oxford University Press.

Jalalzai, Z. (2004), 'Race and the Puritan Body Politic', *Society for the Study of Multi-Ethnic Literature of the United States (MELUS)* 29.3–4, http://www.findarticles.com.

Jobling, D. (1980), '"The Jordan a Boundary": A Reading of Numbers 32 and Joshua 22', *SBLSP* 19:183–207.

——— (1984), 'Levi-Strauss and the Structural Analysis of the Hebrew Bible', in R. Moore and F. Reynolds (eds), *Anthropology and the Study of Religion*, Chicago: Center for the Scientific Study of Religion, pp. 192–211.

Joosten, J. (1996), *People and Land in the Holiness Code: An Exegetical Study of the Ideational Framework of the Law in Leviticus 17–26*, Leiden: E. J. Brill.

Josephy, A. (1995), *500 Nations: An Illustrated History of North American Indians*, London: Hutchinson/Pimlico.

Junkkaala, E. (2006), *Three Conquests of Canaan: A Comparative Study of Two Egyptian Military Campaigns and Joshua 10–12 in the Light of Recent Archaeological Evidence*, Turku: Åbo Akademi University Press. PDF version available for download from https://oa.doria.fi/handle/10024/4162, accessed 27 April 2007.

Kallai, Z. (1958), 'The Town Lists of Judah, Simeon, Benjamin and Dan', *VT* 8:134–160.

——— (1986), *Historical Geography of the Bible: The Tribal Territories of Israel*, Jerusalem: Magnes Press; Leiden: E. J. Brill.

——— (1991), 'The Twelve-Tribe Systems of Israel', *VT* 47.1:53–90.

——— (1998), *Biblical Historiography and Historical Geography: Collection of Studies*, BZEATAJ 44, Frankfurt am Main: Peter Lang.

Kaufman, I. T. (1982), 'The Samaria Ostraca: An Early Witness to Hebrew Writing', *BA* 45, 4:229–239.

Kaufmann, Y. (1985/1955), *The Biblical Account of the Conquest of Canaan*, 2nd edn, Jerusalem: Magnes Press. Original in Hebrew 1955.

Kempinski, A. (1986), 'Joshua's Altar – An Iron Age Watchtower', *BAR* 12.1:42, 44–49.

Kenyon, K. M. (1957), *Digging Up Jericho*, London: Ernest Benn.

——— (1960), *Excavations at Jericho*, Vols 1 & 2: *The Tombs Excavated in 1952–1958*, London: British School of Archaeology.

Kenyon, K. M., and T. A. Holland (eds), with contributions by R. Burleigh et al. (1981), *Excavations at Jericho*, Vol. 3: *The Architecture and*

Stratigraphy of the Tell (2 vols: Text and Plates), London: British School of Archaeology.

Kenyon, K. M., and T. A. Holland, with contributions by J. R. Bartlett et al. (1982), *Excavations at Jericho*, Vol. 4: *The Pottery Type Series and Other Finds*, London: British School of Archaeology.

Kenyon, K. M., and T. A. Holland, with contributions by R. Burleigh et al. (1983), *Excavations at Jericho*, Vol. 5: *The Pottery Phases of the Tell and Other Finds*, London: British School of Archaeology.

Kitchen, K. A. (1982), *Ramesside Inscriptions: Historical and Biographical*, vol. 4, Oxford: Blackwell.

—— (1993), 'The Tabernacle – A Bronze Age Artefact', in *Eretz-Israel* 24 (Avraham Malamat vol.), pp. 119–129.

—— (2003a), *Ramesside Inscriptions: Translated & Annotated, Translations*, Vol. 4: *Merneptah & the Late Nineteenth Dynasty*, Oxford: Blackwell.

—— (2003b), *On the Reliability of the Old Testament*, Grand Rapids, MI: Eerdmans.

Kloppenborg, J. S. (1981), 'Joshua 22: The Priestly Editing of an Ancient Tradition', *Bib* 62.3:347–371.

Knohl, I. (1995), *The Sanctuary of Silence: The Priestly Torah and the Holiness School*, Minneapolis: Fortress Press.

—— (1997), 'Two Aspects of the "Tent of Meeting"', in M. Cogan, B. L. Eichler and J. H. Tigay (eds), *Tehillah le-Moshe: Biblical and Judaic Studies in Honor of Moshe Greenberg*, Winona Lake, IN: Eisenbrauns, pp. 73–79.

Kofoed, J. B. (2005), *Text and History: Historiography and the Study of the Biblical Text*, Winona Lake, IN: Eisenbrauns.

Koopmans, W. T. (1990), *Joshua 24 as Poetic Narrative*, JSOTSup 93, Sheffield: Sheffield Academic Press.

Koorevaar, H. J. (1990), *De Opbouw van het Boek Jozua*, Heverlee: Centrum voor Bijbelse Vorming Belgie v.z.w. (in Dutch, with an English summary).

Kraus, F. R. (1984), *Königliche Verfügungen in Altbabylonischer Zeit*, Studia et Documenta ad iura orientis antiqui pertinentia, vol. 11, Leiden: E. J. Brill.

Kraus, H. J. (1966), *Worship in Israel: A Cultic History of the Old Testament*, Oxford: Basil Blackwell. German original 1962.

Kuhn, T. S. (1962), *The Structure of Scientific Revolutions*, Chicago: University of Chicago Press.

Kuhrt, A. (1995), *The Ancient Near East: c. 3000–330*, 2 vols, London: Routledge.

Kuschke, A. (1951), 'Die Lagervorstellung der priesterschriftlichen Erzählung', *ZAW* 63:74–105.

Lambert, W. G. (1957–1958) 'Three Unpublished Fragments of the Tukulti-Ninurta Epic', *AfO* 18:38–51.

—— (1967), 'Enmeduranki and Related Matters', *JCS* 21:126–138.

Lamont, M. (2009), *How Professors Think: Inside the Curious World of Academic Judgment*, Cambridge, MA: Harvard University Press.

Lehmann, G. (2002), 'Zur Siedlungsgeschichte des Hinterlandes von Akko (Israel) in der Eisenzeit: Erste Ergebnisse einer archäologischen Landesaufnahme', in R. Eichmann (ed.), *Ausgrabungen und Surveys im Vorderen Orient I*, Rahden/Westf.: Verlag Marie Leidorf, pp. 49–75.

Lemche, N. P. (1998), *The Israelites in History and Tradition*, London: SPCK; Louisville, KY: Westminster John Knox Press.

—— (2008), *The Old Testament Between Theology and History: A Critical Survey*, Louisville, KY: Westminster John Knox Press.

Levene, M. (2005a), *Genocide in the Age of the Nation State*, Vol. 1: *The Meaning of Genocide*, London: I. B. Tauris.

—— (2005b), *Genocide in the Age of the Nation State*, Vol. 2: *The Rise of the West and the Coming of Genocide*, London: I. B. Tauris.

Levine, B. A. (1974), *In the Presence of the Lord: A Study of Cult and Some Cultic Terms in Ancient Israel*, Leiden: E. J. Brill.

—— (1993), 'Lpny YHWH – Phenomenology of the Open-Air-Altar in Biblical Israel', in *Biblical Archaeology Today, 1990: Proceedings of the Second International Congress on Biblical Archaeology*, Jerusalem: Israel Exploration Society / Keterpress, pp. 196–205.

Levinson, B. M. (1997), *Deuteronomy and the Hermeneutics of Legal Innovation*, Oxford: Oxford University Press.

—— (ed.) (1994), *Theory and Method in Biblical and Cuneiform Law: Revision, Interpolation and Development*, JSOTSup 181, Sheffield: Sheffield Academic Press.

Levy, T. E. (2009), 'Pastoral Nomads and Iron Age Metal Production in Ancient Edom', in J. Szuchman (ed.) *Nomads, Tribes and the State in the Ancient Near East: Cross-Disciplinary Perspectives*, pp. 147–162. Also available at http://oi.uchicago.edu/pdf/ois5.pdf, accessed 13 March 2007.

Levy, T. E., R. B. Adams and A. Muniz (2004), 'Archaeology and the Shasu Nomads: Recent Excavations in the Jabal Hamrat Fidan, Jordan', in W. H. Propp and R. E. Friedman (eds), *Festschrift for David Noel Freedman*, UCSD Judaic Studies Program, pp. 63–89. Also available at http://www.anthro.ucsd.edu/.

Levy, T. E., R. B. Adams, M. Najjar, A. Hauptmann, J. D. Anderson, B. Brandl, M. A. Robinson and T. Higham (2004), 'Reassessing the Chronology of Biblical Edom: New Excavations and 14C Dates from Khirbat en-Nahas (Jordan)', *Antiquity* 302:865–879. Also available at http://russellbadams.brinkster.net/publications/Levy%20and%20Adams%20et%20al.%20Antiquity%202004.pdf, accessed 13 March 2007.

Lindblom, J. (1961), 'Theophanies in Holy Places in Hebrew Religion', *HUCA* 32:91–106.

Liphschitz, N. (1986–1987), 'Paleobotanical Remains from Mount Ebal', *TA* 13–14:190–191.

Lissovski, N., and N. Na'aman (2003), 'A New Outlook at the Boundary System of the Twelve Tribes', *UF* 35:291–332.

Lohfink, N. (1986), '*herem*', *TDOT* 5:180–199.

—— (1991), 'Zur deuteronomischen Zentralisationsformel', in N. Lohfink, *Studien zum Deuteronomium und zur deuteronomistischen Literatur II*, Stuttgart: Verlag Katholisches Bibelwerk, pp. 147–177.

Long, V. P. (1994), *The Art of Biblical History*, Grand Rapids, MI: Zondervan.

Long, V. P., D. W. Baker and G. J. Wenham (eds) (2002), *Windows into Old Testament History: Evidence, Argument, and the Crisis of 'Biblical Israel'*, Grand Rapids, MI: Eerdmans.

Lorton, D. (1999), 'The Theology of Cult Statues in Ancient Egypt', in *Born in Heaven, Made on Earth: The Making of the Cult Image in the Ancient Near East*, Winona Lake, IN: Eisenbrauns, pp. 123–210.

McConville, G. (1984), *Law and Theology in Deuteronomy*, JSOTSup 33, Sheffield: JSOT Press.

—— (1993), *Grace in the End – A Study in Deuteronomic Theology*, Grand Rapids, MI: Zondervan; Carlisle: Paternoster Press.

—— (1997), 'The Old Testament Historical Books in Modern Scholarship', *Them* 22.3:3–13.

McCown, C. C. (1950), 'Hebrew High Places and Cult Remains', *JBL* 69:205–219.

MacDonald, B. (2000), *'East of the Jordan': Territories and Sites of the Hebrew Scriptures*, ASOR Books 6, Boston, MA: American Schools of Oriental Research.

Machinist, P. (1976), 'Literature as Politics: The Tukulti-Ninurta Epic and the Bible', *CBQ* 38:455–482.

McNutt, P. (1999), *Reconstructing the Society of Ancient Israel*, Library of Ancient Israel, Louisville, KY: Westminster John Knox Press.

Mann, T. W. (1977), *Divine Presence and Guidance in Israelite Traditions: The Typology of Exaltation*, Baltimore: Johns Hopkins University Press.

Mansford, J. (2006), '"Power" and "the Other" in Joshua: The Brutal Birthing of a Group Identity', *Mission Studies* 23.1:27–43.

Marquet-Krause, J. (1949), *Les fouilles de Áy (Et-Tell) 1933–1935: une résurrection d'une grande cité biblique*, 2 vols (text and atlas), Paris: Paul Geuthner.

Mayes, A. D. H. (1979), *Deuteronomy*, NCBC, Grand Rapids, MI: Eerdmans; London: Marshall, Morgan & Scott.

Mazar, A. (1990), 'Iron Age I and II Towers at Giloh and the Israelite Settlement', *IEJ* 40.2–3:77–101.

—— (1992), *Archaeology and the Land of the Bible 10000–586 BCE*, Anchor Bible Library, New York: Doubleday.

—— (1997), 'Iron Age Chronology: A Reply to I. Finkelstein', *Levant* 29:157–167.

Mendenhall, G. E. (2001), *Ancient Israel's Faith and History: Introduction to the Bible in Context*, Louisville, KY: Westminster John Knox Press.

Meshel, Z. (1981), 'A Religious Center at Kuntillet-Ajrud, Sinai', in A. Biran (ed.), *Temples and High Places in Biblical Times: Proceedings of the*

*Colloquium in Honor of the Centennial of Hebrew Union College –
Jewish Institute of Religion*, Jerusalem: Hebrew Union College, p. 161.

Mettinger, T. N. D. (1982), *The Dethronement of Sabaoth: Studies in the
Shem and Kabod Theologies*, CBOTS 18, Lund: CWK Gleerup.

—— (1995), *No Graven Image? Israelite Aniconism in its Ancient Near
Eastern Context*, CBOTS 42, Stockholm: Almqvist & Wiksell.

—— (2003), Review of Sandra L. Richter, *The Deuteronomistic History
and the Name Theology: lĕšakkēn šĕmô šām in the Bible and the
Ancient Near East, JBL* 122.4:753–755.

Milgrom, J. (1983a), 'Priestly Terminology and the Political and Social
Structure of Pre-Monarchic Israel', in J. Milgrom, *Studies in Cultic
Theology and Terminology*, Leiden: E. J. Brill, pp. 1–17.

—— (1983b), 'The Term '*bdh*', in J. Milgrom, *Studies in Cultic Theology
and Terminology*, Leiden: E. J. Brill, pp. 19–46. Original in J. Milgrom,
Studies in Levitical Terminology, Berkeley: University of California,
1970, pp. 60–87.

—— (1989), *Numbers*, JPS Torah Commentary, Philadelphia: Jewish
Publication Society.

—— (1991), *Leviticus 1 – 16*, AB, New York: Doubleday.

Millard, A. R. (1982), 'In Praise of Ancient Scribes', *Bible and Spade* 2
(spring–summer–autumn 1982):33–46. Also available at http://
faculty.gordon.edu/hu/bi/Ted_Hildebrandt/OTeSources/20–Proverbs/
Text/Articles/Millard-Scribes-B-S.pdf, accessed 3 April 2009.

—— (1988), 'King Og's Bed and Other Ancient Ironmongery', in *Ascribe
to the Lord: Biblical & Other Studies in Memory of Peter C. Craigie*,
JSOTSup 67, Sheffield: Sheffield Academic Press, pp. 481–492.

—— (1995), 'The Knowledge of Writing in Iron Age Palestine', *TynB*
46.2:207–217.

—— (2007), 'The Tablets in the Ark', in J. G. McConville and K. Möller
(eds), *Reading the Law: Studies in Honour of Gordon J. Wenham*,
New York: T. & T. Clark, pp. 254–266.

Miller, J. M., and J. H. Hayes (2006), *A History of Ancient Israel and Judah*,
2nd edn, London: SCM Press.

Miller, P. D. (1990), *Deuteronomy*, Interpretation, Louisville, KY: John Knox
Press.

Miller, P. D., Jr, and J. J. M. Roberts (1977), *The Hand of the Lord:
A Reassessment of the 'Ark Narrative' of 1 Samuel*, Baltimore: Johns
Hopkins University Press.

Miller, R. D. (2003), 'A Gazetteer of Iron I Sites in the North-Central
Highlands of Palestine', in *Preliminary Excavation Reports and
Other Archaeological Investigations: Tell Qarqur, Iron I Sites in the
North-Central Highlands of Palestine*, ed. N. Lapp, AASOR 56 (1999),
Boston, MA: American Schools of Oriental Research, pp. 143–218.

—— (2005), *Chieftains of the Highland Clans: A History of Israel in the
12th and 11th Centuries B.C.*, Grand Rapids, MI: Eerdmans.

Moberly, R. W. L. (1999), 'Toward an Interpretation of the Shema', in C. Seitz and K. Greene-McCreight (eds), *Theological Exegesis: Essays in Honor of Brevard S. Childs*, Grand Rapids, MI: Eerdmans.

Moorey, P. R. S. (1991), *A Century of Biblical Archaeology*, Cambridge: Lutterworth Press.

Moran, W. (1963), 'Ancient Near Eastern Background of the Love of God in Deuteronomy', *CBQ* 25.1:77–87.

——— (1992), *The Amarna Letters*, Baltimore: Johns Hopkins University Press.

Mowinckel, S. (1946), 'Zur Frage nach dokumentarischen Quellen in Josua 13 – 19', in *Avhandlingar utgitt av Det Norske Videnskaps-Akademi i Oslo II*, Hist-Filos. Klasse 1946, No. 1, Oslo: A. W. Broggers Boktryggeri A/S.

——— (1964), *Tetrateuch–Pentateuch–Hexateuch*, BZAW 90, Berlin: Alfred Töpelmann.

Munn-Rankin, J. M. (1956), 'Diplomacy in Western Asia in the Early Second Millennium BC', *Iraq* 18:68–110.

Na'aman, N. (1992), 'Canaanite Jerusalem and its Central Hill Country Neighbours in the Second Millennium B.C.E.', *UF* 24:275–291.

——— (1994a), 'The Hurrians and the End of the Middle Bronze Age in Palestine', *Levant* 26:175–187.

——— (1994b), 'The "Conquest of Canaan" in the Book of Joshua and History', in Finkelstein and Na'aman 1994: 218–281.

Nelson, R. D. (1981), 'Josiah in the Book of Joshua', *JBL* 100.4:531–540.

——— (1997b), 'Herem and the Deuteronomic Social Conscience', in M. Vervenne and J. Lust (eds), *Deuteronomy and Deuteronomic Literature: Festschrift C. H. W. Brekelmans*, Leuven: Leuven University Press, pp. 39–54.

——— (2005), 'The Double Redaction of the Deuteronomistic History: The Case Is Still Compelling', *JSOT* 29.3:319–337.

Niditch, S. (1993), *War in the Hebrew Bible: A Study in the Ethics of Violence*, Oxford: Oxford University Press.

Niehaus, J. J. (1985), 'The Deuteronomic Style: An Examination of the Deuteronomic Style in the Light of Ancient Near Eastern Literature', PhD thesis, University of Liverpool.

——— (1992), 'The Central Sanctuary: Where and When?', *TynB* 43.1:3–30.

——— (1994), 'The Warrior and His God: The Covenant Foundation of History and Historiography', in *Faith, Tradition and History: Old Testament Historiography in Its Near Eastern Context*, Winona Lake, IN: Eisenbrauns, 1994, pp. 299–312.

——— (1995), *God at Sinai: Covenant and Theophany in the Bible and Ancient Near East*, Carlisle: Paternoster Press.

Noort, E. (1998), *Das Buch Josua: Forschungsgeschichte und Problemfelder*, Darmstadt: Wissenschaftliche Buchgesellschaft.

Noth, M. (1930), *Das System der zwölf Stämme Israels*, Stuttgart: W. Kohlhammer.

—— (1935), 'Studien zu den historisch-geographischen Dokumenten des Josuabuches', *ZDPV* 58:185–255.

—— (1953b), *Die Welt des Alten Testaments*, 2nd edn, Berlin (collection Töpelmann Theologische Hilfsbücher 3).

—— (1960), *The History of Israel*, reissue of the 2nd edn in rev. and corrected translation, London: SCM Press.

—— (1963), 'Samuel und Silo', *VT* 13:390–400.

—— (1968), 'The Background of Judges 17–18', in B. W. Anderson and W. Harrelson (eds), *Israel's Prophetic Heritage: Essays in Honor of J. Muilenburg*, New York: Doubleday, pp. 68–85. German original 1962: 'Der Hintergrund von Richter 17–18', repr. in *Archäologische, exegetische und topographische Untersuchungen zur Geschichte Israels, in Aufsätze zur Biblischen Landes und Altertumskunde*, 2 vols, H. W. Wolff (ed.), Neukirchen-Vluyn, 1971, vol.1, pp. 133–147.

—— (1972/1948), *A History of Pentateuchal Traditions*, Englewood Cliffs, NJ: Prentice Hall. German original: *Überlieferungsgeschichte des Pentateuchs*, Stuttgart: W. Kohlhammer, 1948.

—— (1987/1943), *The Chronicler's History*, JSOTSup 50, Sheffield: Sheffield Academic Press. German original: *Überlieferungsgeschichtliche Studien II*, Halle: M. Niemeyer, 1943.

—— (1991/1943), *The Deuteronomistic History*, 2nd edn, JSOTSup 15, Sheffield: Sheffield Academic Press. German original: *Überlieferungsgeschichtliche Studien I*, Halle: M. Niemeyer, 1943.

O'Connell, R. H. (1996), *The Rhetoric of the Book of Judges*, Leiden: E. J. Brill.

Orlinsky, H. (1962), 'The Tribal System of Israel and Related Groups in the Period of the Judges', in M. Ben-Horin et al. (eds), *Studies and Essays in Honor of A. A. Neuman*, Leiden: E. J. Brill, pp. 375–387.

Otto, E. (1976), 'Silo und Jerusalem', *TZ* 32:65–77.

—— (1994), 'Aspects of Legal Reforms and Reformulations in Ancient Cuneiform and Israelite Law', in B. M. Levinson (ed.), *Theory and Method in Biblical and Cuneiform Law*, JSOTSup 181, Sheffield: Sheffield Academic Press, pp. 160–196.

Ottosson, M. (1980), *Temples and Cult Places in Palestine*, Acta Universitatis Uppsaliensis/Boreas 12, Motala: Borgströms Tryckeri.

—— (1991), *Josuaboken: en programskrift för davidisk restauration*, Acta Universitatis Uppsaliensis, Studia Biblica Uppsaliensia 1, Stockholm: Almqvist & Wiksell.

Pakkala, J., S. Münger and J. Zangenberg (2004), *Kinneret Regional Project: Tel Kinrot Excavations. Tel Kinrot – Tell el-'Oreme – Kinneret*, Proceedings of the Finnish Institute in the Middle East, Vantaa, 2004. Available electronically via http://www.kinneret-excavations.org/publications.html, accessed 22 October 2007.

Pappe, I. (2004), *A History of Modern Palestine: One Land, Two Peoples*, Cambridge: Cambridge University Press.

Pardee, D. (2002), *Ritual and Cult at Ugarit*, SBL Writings from the Ancient World 10, Atlanta: Society of Biblical Literature.

Peterson, J. L. (1977), 'A Topographical Surface Survey of the Levitical "Cities" of Joshua 21 and I Chronicles 6: Studies on the Levites in Israelite Life and Religion', ThD thesis, Chicago Institute of Advanced Theological Studies and Seabury-Western Theological Seminary.

Pitkänen, P. (2004a), *Central Sanctuary and Centralization of Worship in Ancient Israel: From the Settlement to the Building of Solomon's Temple*, 2nd Gorgias Press edn, Piscataway, NJ: Gorgias Press (1st edn 2003).

—— (2004b), 'Ethnicity, Assimilation and the Israelite Settlement', *TynB* 55.2:161–182.

—— (2004c), 'From Tent of Meeting to Temple: Presence, Rejection and Renewal of Divine Favour', in D. Alexander (ed.), *Heaven on Earth*, Carlisle: Paternoster Press, pp. 23–34.

—— (2007), 'Memory, Witnesses and Genocide in the Book of Joshua', in J. G. McConville and K. Möller (eds), *Reading the Law: Studies in Honour of Gordon J. Wenham*, New York: T. & T. Clark, pp. 267–282.

—— (2010), 'Dr Jekyll and Mr Hyde? Deuteronomy and the Rights of Indigenous Peoples', *Political Theology* 11.3:399–409.

Polzin, R. (1980), *Moses and the Deuteronomist: A Literary Study of the Deuteronomic History*, Part 1: *Deuteronomy, Joshua, Judges*, New York: Seabury Press.

—— (1989), *Samuel and the Deuteronomist: A Literary Study of the Deuteronomic History*, Part 2: *1 Samuel*, Bloomington: Indiana University Press.

Pongratz-Leisten, B., K. Deller and E. Bleibtreu (1992), 'Götterstreitwagen und Götterstandarten: Götter auf dem Feldzug und ihr Kult im Feldlager', *BM* 23:291–356.

Poo, M. (2005), *Enemies of Civilization: Attitudes toward Foreigners in Ancient Mesopotamia, Egypt and China*, Albany: State University of New York Press.

Postgate, J. N. (1992), *Early Mesopotamia: Society and Economy at the Dawn of History*, London: Routledge.

Prior, M. (1997), *The Bible and Colonialism: A Moral Critique*, Biblical Seminar 48, Sheffield: Sheffield Academic Press.

Pritchard, J. B. (1961), *The Water System of Gibeon*, Philadelphia: University Museum.

—— (1962), *Gibeon, Where the Sun Stood Still: The Discovery of the Biblical City*, Princeton, NJ: Princeton University Press.

—— (1964), *Winery, Defences and Soundings at Gibeon*, Philadelphia: University Museum.

Provan, I., V. P. Long and T. Longman III (2003), *A Biblical History of Israel*, Louisville, KY: Westminster John Knox Press.

Rad, G. von (1953/1948), *Studies in Deuteronomy*, SBT 9, Chicago: Henry Regnery. German original: *Deuteronomium-Studien*, Göttingen: Vandenhoeck & Ruprecht, 1948.

——— (1965/1931), 'The Tent and the Ark', in idem, *The Problem of the Hexateuch and other Essays*, Edinburgh: Oliver & Boyd, pp. 103–124. German original: 'Zelt und Lade', *KZ* 42 (1931):476–498.

——— (1965/1933) 'There Remains Still a Rest for the People of God: An Investigation of a Biblical Conception', in idem, *The Problem of the Hexateuch and other Essays*, Edinburgh: Oliver & Boyd, pp. 94–102. German original in *Zwischen den Zeiten, 11th year*, Munich: Christian Kaiser Verlag, 1933, pp. 104–11.

——— (1965/1938), 'The Form-Critical Problem of the Hexateuch', in idem, *The Problem of the Hexateuch and other Essays*, Edinburgh: Oliver & Boyd, pp. 1–78. German original in BWANT 4.26, Stuttgart: Kohlhammer, 1938.

——— (1965/1944), 'The Beginnings of Historical Writing in Ancient Israel', in idem, *The Problem of the Hexateuch and other Essays*, Edinburgh: Oliver & Boyd, pp. 166–204. German original in *Archiv für Kulturgeschichte* 32 (1944):1–42.

——— (1966/1964), *Deuteronomy*, OTL, London: SCM Press. German original: *Das fünfte Buch Mose: Deuteronomium*, ATD 8, Göttingen: Vandenhoeck & Ruprecht, 1964.

——— (1991/1951/1952/1958), *Holy War in Ancient Israel*, Göttingen: Vandenhoeck & Ruprecht. German original: *Der Heilige Krieg im alten Israel*, ATANT 20, Zurich: Zwingli-Verlag, 1951; 5th edn Göttingen: Vandenhoeck & Ruprecht, 1969.

Rendtorff, R. (1990), *The Problem of the Process of Transmission in the Pentateuch*, JSOTSup 89, Sheffield: JSOT Press. German original: *Das überlieferungsgeschichtliche Problem des Pentateuch*, BZAW 147, Berlin: Walter de Gruyter, 1977.

Reuter, E. (1993), *Kultzentralisation: Entstehung und Theologie von Dtn 12*, BBB 87, Frankfurt am Main: Verlag Anton Hain.

Richardson, A. T. (1927), 'The Site of Shiloh', PEFQS 59:85–88.

Richter, S. L. (2002), 'The Deuteronomistic History and the Name Theology: *lĕšakkēn šĕmô šām* in the Bible and the Ancient Near East', BZAW 318, Berlin: Walter de Gruyter.

——— (2007), 'The Place of the Name in Deuteronomy', *VT* 57:342–366.

Riley, W. (1993), *King and Cultus in Chronicles: Worship and the Reinterpretation of History*, JSOTSup 160, Sheffield: JSOT Press.

Rost, L. (1982/1926), *The Succession to the Throne of David*, Historic Texts and Interpreters in Biblical Scholarship 1, Sheffield: Almond Press. German original: *Die Überlieferung von der Thronnachfolge Davids*, Stuttgart: W. Kohlhammer, 1926.

Rothenberg, B. (1972), *Timna: Valley of the Biblical Copper Mines*, London: Thames & Hudson.

Routledge, B. (2004), *Moab in the Iron Age: Hegemony, Polity, Archaeology*, Philadelphia: University of Pennsylvania Press.

Rowley, H. H. (1967), *Worship in Ancient Israel*, London: SPCK.

Satterthwaite, P. E. (1989), 'Narrative Artistry and the Composition of Judges 17 – 21', PhD thesis, University of Manchester.

Schicklberger, F. (1973), *Die Ladeerzählungen des ersten Samuel-Buches: Eine literaturwissenschaftlicher und theologiegeschichtliche Untersuchung*, FB 7, Würzburg: Echter Verlag.

Schley, D. G. (1989), *Shiloh: A Biblical City in Tradition and History*, JSOTSup 63, Sheffield: Sheffield Academic Press.

Schmitt, R. (1972), *Zelt und Lade als Thema alttestamentlicher Wissenschaft: Eine kritische forschungsgeschichtliche Darstellung*, Gütersloh: Gütersloher Verlagshaus Gerd Mohn.

Schwartz, B. J. (1996), '"Profane" Slaughter and the Integrity of the Priestly Code', *HUCA* 67:15–42.

Schwartz, R. M. (1997), *The Curse of Cain: The Violent Legacy of Monotheism*, Chicago: University of Chicago Press.

Seow, C. L. (1992), 'Ark of the Covenant', *ABD* 1:386–393.

Sheriffs, D. C. T. (1979), 'The Phrases *ina IGI DN* and *lipeney Yhwh* in Treaty and Covenant Contexts', *JNSL* 7:55–68.

Shlaim, A. (2000), *The Iron Wall: Israel and the Arab World*, London: Penguin Books.

Singer, I. (2002), *Hittite Prayers*, SBLWAW 11, Atlanta: Society of Biblical Literature.

Smith, A. D. (2003), *Chosen Peoples: Sacred Sources of National Identity*, Oxford: Oxford University Press.

Smith, M. S. (2002), *The Early History of God: Yahweh and Other Deities in Ancient Israel*, 2nd edn, Grand Rapids, MI: Eerdmans, 2002.

Snaith, N. H. (1978), 'The Altar at Gilgal: Joshua XXII 23–29', *VT* 28:330–335.

Soggin, J. A. (1960), 'Kultätiologische Sagen und Katechese im Hexateuch', *VT* 10.1:341–347.

Soldt, W. van (2003), 'The Use of Hurrian Names at Ugarit', *UF* 35:681–707.

Spaey, J. (1993), 'Emblems in Rituals in the Old Babylonian Period', in J. Quaegebeur (ed.), *Ritual and Sacrifice in the Ancient Near East: Proceedings of the International Conference organized by the Katholieke Universiteit Leuven from the 17th to the 20th of April 1991*, OLA 55, Leuven: Uitgeverij Peeters en Departement Oriëntalistiek, pp. 411–420.

Sprinkle, J. M. (1994), *The Book of the Covenant: A Literary Approach*, JSOTSup 174, Sheffield: Sheffield Academic Press.

Stannard, D. E. (1992), *American Holocaust: Columbus and the Conquest of the New World*, Oxford: Oxford University Press.

Stern, E. (1981), 'Late Bronze Age Sanctuary at Tel Mevorakh', in A. Biran (ed.), *Temples and High Places in Biblical Times: Proceedings of the*

*Colloquium in Honor of the Centennial of Hebrew Union College –
Jewish Institute of Religion*, Jerusalem: Hebrew Union College,
p. 160.

Svensson, J. (1994), *Towns and Toponyms in the Old Testament with Special
Emphasis on Joshua 14 – 21*, CBOTS 38, Stockholm: Almqvist &
Wiksell.

Tarragon, J.-M. de (1980), *Le Culte à Ugarit: d'après les textes de la pratique
en cunéiformes alphabétiques*, Paris: J. Gabalda.

Taylor, G. (2006), 'Supernatural Power, Ritual and Divination in Ancient
Israelite Society: An Examination of Deuteronomy 18', PhD
dissertation, University of Gloucestershire.

Thompson, J. A. (1963), *The Ancient Near Eastern Treaties and the Old
Testament*, London: Tyndale Press.

Thompson, T. L. (1992), *Early History of the Israelite People: From the Written
& Archaeological Sources*, Leiden: E. J. Brill.

——— (1999), *The Bible in History: How Writers Create a Past*, London:
Jonathan Cape.

Tichi, C. (1971), 'The Puritan Historians and their New Jerusalem', *Early
American Literature* 6.2:143–155.

Tigay, J. H. (1996), *Deuteronomy*, in JPS Torah Commentary, Philadelphia:
Jewish Publication Society.

Tinker, G. E. (1993), *Missionary Conquest: The Gospel and Native American
Cultural Genocide*, Minneapolis: Fortress Press.

——— (2004), *Spirit and Resistance: Political Theology and American Indian
Liberation*, Minneapolis: Fortress Press.

——— (2008), *American Indian Liberation: A Theology of Sovereignty*, New
York: Orbis Books.

Toorn, K. van der (1997), 'The Iconic Book: Analogies between the Babylonian
Cult of Images and the Veneration of the Torah', in idem (ed.), *The
Image and the Book: Iconic Cults, Aniconism, and the Rise of Book
Religion in Israel and the Ancient Near East*, CBET 21, Leuven: Peeters,
pp. 229–248.

Uehlinger, C. (1997), 'Anthropomorphic Cult Statuary in Iron Age Palestine
and the Search for Yahweh's Cult Images', in K. van der Toorn (ed.),
*The Image and the Book: Iconic Cults, Aniconism, and the Rise of
Book Religion in Israel and the Ancient Near East*, CBET 21, Leuven:
Peeters, pp. 97–156.

Van Dam, C. (1997), *The Urim and Thummim: A Means of Revelation in
Ancient Israel*, Winona Lake, IN: Eisenbrauns.

Van Seters, J. (1983), *In Search of History*, New Haven, CT: Yale University
Press.

——— (2006), *The Edited Bible: The Curious History of the 'Editor' in Biblical
Criticism*, Winona Lake, IN: Eisenbrauns.

Vaughan, P. H. (1974), *The Meaning of 'Bama' in the Old Testament*,
SOTSMS 3, Cambridge: Cambridge University Press.

Vaux, R. de (1961/1958–1960), *Ancient Israel: Its Life and Institutions*, London: Lutterworth Press. French original: Les Institutions de l'Ancien Testament, Paris: Les Éditions du Cerf, 2 vols, 1958, 1960.

———— (1972/1967), 'Ark of the Covenant and Tent of Reunion', in *The Bible and the Ancient Near East*, London: Darton Longman & Todd, pp. 136–151. French original: *Bible et Orient*, Paris: Les Éditions du Cerf, 1967.

———— (1978/1971), *The Early History of Israel*, London: Darton Longman & Todd. French original: *Histoire Ancienne d'Israël*, Paris: J. Gabalda, 1971.

Veen, P. van der, and U. Zerbst (eds) (2002), *Biblische Archäologie am Scheideweg? Für und Wider einer Neudatierung archäologischer Epochen im alttestamentlichen Palästina*, Holzgerlingen: Hänssler.

Veijola, T. (1977), *Das Königtum in der Beurteilung der deuteronomistischen Historiographie: Eine redaktionsgeschichtliche Untersuchung*, AASF Series B, vol. 198, Helsinki: Suomalainen Tiedeakatemia.

Walker, C., and M. B. Dick (1999), 'The Induction of the Cult Image in Ancient Mesopotamia: The Mesopotamian *mīs pî* Ritual', in *Born in Heaven, Made on Earth: The Making of the Cult Image in the Ancient Near East*, Winona Lake, IN: Eisenbrauns, pp. 55–121.

Warrior, R. A. (2000), 'Canaanites, Cowboys and Indians: Deliverance, Conquest and Liberation Theology Today', in R. T. Albert (ed.), *Voices of the Religious Left: A Contemporary Sourcebook*, Philadelphia: Temple University Press, pp. 51–57.

Weinfeld, M. (1964), 'Cult Centralization in Israel in the Light of a Neo-Babylonian Analogy', *JNES* 23:202–212.

———— (1967), 'The Period of the Conquest and of the Judges as Seen by the Earlier and the Later Sources', *VT* 17:93–113.

———— (1972), *Deuteronomy and the Deuteronomic School*, Oxford: Clarendon Press. Repr. Winona Lake, IN: Eisenbrauns 1992.

———— (1991), *Deuteronomy 1 – 11*, AB 5, New York: Doubleday.

———— (2004), *The Place of Law in the Religion of Ancient Israel*, VTSup 100, Leiden: E. J. Brill.

Weippert, H. (1973), 'Das geographische System der Stämme Israels', *VT* 23:76–89.

———— (1980), 'Der Ort, den Jahwe erwählen wird, um dort seinen Namen wohnen zu lassen: Die Geschichte einer alttestamentlichen Formel', *BZ* 24.1:76–94.

Weippert, H. and M. (1976), 'Jericho in der Eisenzeit', *ZDPV* 92:105–148.

Wellhausen, J. (1905/1878), *Prolegomena zur Geschichte Israel*, 6th edn, Berlin: Druck und Verlag Georg Reimer. An English translation of the *Prolegomena* is available from Project Gutenberg at http://www.gutenberg.org/etext/4732 (as of April 2009).

———— (1963/1876), *Die Composition des Hexateuchs und der historischen Bücher des alten Testaments*, 4th edn, Berlin: Walter de Gruyter.

Wenham, G. J. (1971a), 'Deuteronomy and the Central Sanctuary',
    TB 22:103–118.
—— (1971b), 'The Deuteronomic Theology of the Book of Joshua', JBL
    90:140–148.
—— (1981), Numbers: An Introduction and Commentary, TOTC, Leicester:
    Inter-Varsity Press.
—— (1987), Genesis 1 – 15, WBC, Waco, TX: Word Books.
—— (1999a), 'Pondering the Pentateuch: The Search for a New Paradigm',
    in D. W. Baker and B. T. Arnold (eds), The Face of Old Testament
    Studies: A Survey of Contemporary Approaches, Grand Rapids, MI:
    Baker Books, pp. 116–144.
—— (1999b), 'The Priority of P', VT 49.2:240–258.
Westermann, C. (1994), Die Geschichtsbücher des Alten Testaments: Gab
    es ein deuteronomistisches Geschichtswerk?, Gütersloh: Chr. Kaiser /
    Gütersloher Verlagshaus.
Wette, W. M. L. de (1830), 'Dissertatio critica qua a prioribus Deuteronomium
    Pentateuchi libris diversum, alius cuiusdam recentioris auctoris opus
    esse monstratur', pro venia legendi publice defensa Ienae a. 1805, in
    W. M. L. de Wette, Opuscula Theologica, Berlin: G. Reimerum,
    pp. 149–168.
Whitelam, K. W. (1994), 'The Identity of Early Israel: The Realignment and
    Transformation of Late Bronze–Iron Age Palestine', JSOT 63:57–87.
Whybray, R. N. (1987), The Making of the Pentateuch: A Methodological
    Study, JSOTSup 53, Sheffield: Sheffield Academic Press.
Wilson, I. (1995), Out of the Midst of the Fire: Divine Presence in
    Deuteronomy, SBLDS, Atlanta: Scholars Press.
Wiseman, D. J. (1953), The Alalakh Tablets, Occasional Publications of the
    British Institute of Archaeology at Ankara 2, London: British Institute
    of Archaeology at Ankara.
Wood, B. G. (2000a), 'Khirbet el-Maqatir, 1995–1998', IEJ 50.1–2:123–130.
—— (2000b), 'Khirbet el-Maqatir, 1999', IEJ 50.3–4:249–254.
—— (2001), 'Khirbet el-Maqatir, 2000', IEJ 51.2:246–252.
Woudstra, M. H. (1961), 'The Ark of the Covenant from Conquest to Kingship',
    PhD thesis, Philadelphia: Westminster Theological Seminary.
Wright, C. J. H. (2004), Old Testament Ethics for the People of God, Leicester:
    Inter-Varsity Press.
Younger, K. L. (1990), Ancient Conquest Accounts: A Study in Ancient Near
    Eastern and Biblical History Writing, JSOTSup 98, Sheffield: Sheffield
    Academic Press.
—— (1999), 'Early Israel in Recent Biblical Scholarship', in D. W. Baker and
    B. T. Arnold (eds), The Face of Old Testament Studies: A Survey of
    Contemporary Approaches, Grand Rapids, MI: Baker Books,
    pp. 176–206.
Zerbst, U., and P. van der Veen (eds) (2005), Keine Posaunen vor Jericho? Beiträge
    zur Archäologie der Landnahme, Holzgerlingen: Hänssler-Verlag.

Zertal, A. (1986), 'How Can Kempinski Be So Wrong!', *BAR* 12.1:43, 49–53.

—— (1986–1987) 'Mount Ebal: Excavation Seasons 1982–1987, Preliminary Report', *TA* 13–14:105–165.

—— (2004), *The Manasseh Hill Country Survey*, Vol. 1: *The Shechem Syncline*, Culture and History of the Ancient Near East 21.1, Leiden: E. J. Brill.

Zevit, Z. (2001), *The Religions of Ancient Israel: A Synthesis of Parallactic Approaches*, London: Continuum.

Zobel, H.-J. (1977), '*aron*', *TDOT* 1:363–374.

Zvi, E. ben (1992), 'The List of the Levitical Cities', *JSOT* 54:77–106.

INDEX OF REFERENCES
TO SCRIPTURE AND RELATED
LITERATURE

INDEX OF AUTHORS

INDEX OF SUBJECTS

INDEX OF ARCHAEOLOGICAL SITES AND RELATED PLACES